DEFY THE STARS

DEFY THE STARS

THE LIFE AND TRAGIC DEATH OF TOM HURNDALL

JOCELYN HURNDALL

WITH HAZEL WOOD

BLOOMSBURY

First published 2007

Copyright © 2007 by Jocelyn Hurndall

Map © John Gilkes

Lyrics of 'Hotel California' (Felder/Henley/Frey) courtesy of Warner Chappell Ltd

The moral right of the author has been asserted

Bloomsbury Publishing Plc, 36 Soho Square, London WID 3QY

A CIP catalogue record is available from the British Library

Hardback ISBN 978 0 7475 8944 0
10 9 8 7 6 5 4 3 2 1

Trade Paperback ISBN 978 0 7475 9102 3
10 9 8 7 6 5 4 3 2 1

Typeset by Hewer Text UK Ltd, Edinburgh
Printed in Great Britain by Clays Ltd, St Ives plc

www.bloomsbury.com

The paper this book is printed on is certified by the © 1996 Forest Stewardship
Council A.C. (FSC). It is ancient-forest friendly. The printer holds
FSC chain of custody SGS-COC-2061

FSC
Mixed Sources
Product group from well-managed
forests and other controlled sources
Cert no. SGS-COC-2061
www.fsc.org
© 1996 Forest Stewardship Council

for Sophie, Bill and Fred

We did not travel for adventures, nor for company,
but to see with our eyes and to measure with our hearts.

John Ruskin, *Praeterita*

Abbreviations

IDF   Israeli Defence Force
ISM   International Solidarity Movement

CONTENTS

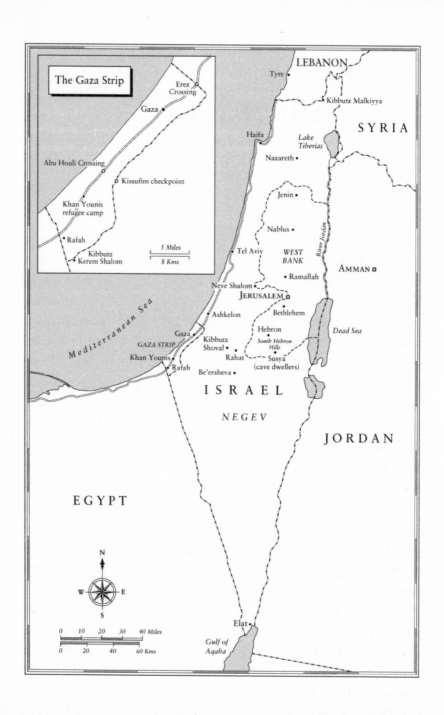

The Gaza Strip

Erez Crossing

Gaza

Abu Houli Crossing

Kissufim checkpoint

Khan Younis refugee camp

Rafah

Kibbutz Kerem Shalom

5 Miles

8 Kms

LEBANON

Tyre

Kibbutz Malkiyya

SYRIA

Haifa

Lake Tiberias

Nazareth

Jenin

Nablus

Tel Aviv

WEST BANK

River Jordan

AMMAN □

Ramallah

Neve Shalom

JERUSALEM □

Ashkelon

Bethlehem

Dead Sea

Gaza

Hebron

Kibbutz Shoval

South Hebron Hills

Khan Younis

GAZA STRIP

Rahat

Susya (cave dwellers)

Rafah

Be'ersheva

Mediterranean Sea

ISRAEL

NEGEV

JORDAN

EGYPT

N

W E

S

0 10 20 30 40 Miles

0 20 40 60 Kms

Elat

Gulf of Aqaba

THE BEGINNING

'Joss, can you come down? There's a phone call for you, Joss.'

It was the last day of term, and I'd been working that afternoon to finish a report for the educational psychologist on a child who had been diagnosed with Asperger's syndrome. I'd just printed it out and was making my way downstairs to the photocopying machine in the main office when I heard the call on the tannoy. Jean, the school's warm and efficient admin officer, always sounded definite, and there was nothing particularly unusual in her tone. As I crossed the hall my mind was still on the report, but I was also aware of a kind of question mark, a wordless anxiety that had hovered behind my conscious thoughts all week, while I considered now who would need to see the report . . . how many copies I should make . . .

Jean held out the phone: 'Joss, it's your daughter. It's Sophie.' I looked at Jean as I took the phone.

'Hi, darling.'

I was aware of continuing to look at Jean as I heard Sophie's voice.

'Mum, I've got to tell you something. Tom's been shot. Can you come home?'

Between the single second of receiving bad news and the next in comprehending it, there is a silent space like the eye of a storm. You know that every cell in your body is going to be shaken, and you freeze to delay the moment of impact. Your whole life is concertinaed into the still space between the blow and the pain. I remember sitting down, and I remember Jean reaching for my hand. Although she had no idea why Sophie was phoning, she must have heard the anxiety in her voice and seen the look on my face.

'Who told you?' I tried to sound calm.

'I think it was a paper. I can't remember. I think it was the *Daily Mirror*. They were asking me all these questions, what I knew about the shooting. That's how I found out. They said it was on Reuters, that he was helping a woman and child across a road. The phone keeps on ringing. Please, Mum, can you come home?'

'Darling, it's OK, I'm coming, straight away,' I said, aware that Jean was still looking at me, still holding my hand. 'Did they tell you anything else?'

'The Foreign Office called and they're going to phone back. They don't know where Tom is. Nobody knows where he is. But I think they said he was shot in a place called Rafah, in the Gaza Strip. There's a number for you to ring.'

Strangely, when I'd put the phone down, like an automaton I photocopied the report, wrote the initials of the recipients at the top of it, systematically distributed copies to the various trays and addressed a copy to the educational psychologist. I suppose I was trying to delay discovering the truth, to convince myself that this was some melodrama stirred up by the media, that Tom's was only a minor injury, though in my heart I knew that it was something really serious. I was aware of Jean beside me in the office, of people leaving, getting their things together for the Easter break. Someone came up to me and said, 'I hear Tom's been shot', and I could only nod and say 'Yes'.

It was the kind of news I had been dreading ever since my twenty-one-year-old son had left for Baghdad two months before with a group who had volunteered themselves as human shields against the threat of Anglo-American attack. He had been relatively conscientious about keeping in touch, e-mailing us from internet cafés and phoning when he could. We knew that he had left Iraq after it had become clear that the authorities intended to use the volunteers to protect power stations and other installations rather than schools and hospitals. Tom wanted to prevent loss of life, but he wasn't prepared to be a sitting target, and there were many other reasons for this journey. The last we had heard he was in a refugee camp in Jordan, helping to put up tents.

But then the e-mails had stopped and for ten days we'd heard nothing. The previous evening Sophie and I had discussed whether we should get in touch with my former husband Anthony, who was away in Russia. It was quite possible, Sophie and I thought, that he would have heard from Tom.

So I'd phoned Anthony that morning soon after our regular 7.40 senior management team meeting. Standing in the school's inspiring, purpose-built learning support unit of which I was manager, looking out of its wide, roof-level windows at the dappled April sky behind the dark London buildings, I had heard Anthony's voice, strangely clear from St Petersburg. No, he'd heard nothing from Tom either, he said. Yes, it was a bit worrying. But he'd be home tomorrow, and we'd decide then what to do.

I picked up the phone again now and dialled the number I had presumed was for the Foreign Office. But it was the *Sunday Times* news desk. As I started asking questions, I could hear a change in the voice of the journalist at the other end as he began to grasp the situation and who it was he was talking to. 'Look,' he said, 'I'm terribly sorry. I'll look on Reuters for you. But just be aware – when things first come through they're not always accurate.'

There was a pause, during which I could hear the click of the computer keys and the sound of my own uneven breathing.

'What's coming up,' he said slowly, 'is that peace activist Tom Hurndall has been shot, and that he's brain dead.' And then, as if to cancel out the brutal words, 'But as I said, you really mustn't believe everything you first hear.'

I

LONDON – BE'ERSHEVA
APRIL–MAY 2003

ONE

Tom had left London for Baghdad on 21 February 2003. I had important meetings at school that day, but even if I'd been able to I wouldn't have gone to the airport to see him off. This journey didn't – couldn't – have my blessing, though I understood why Tom felt he must go.

So our last and final hug was outside Tom's bedroom the night before he left. How often in the past, hearing him moving around in the early hours of the morning, I'd tiptoed into that untidy room to bring him a cup of cocoa and found him sitting on the low chair in front of the window, feet up on the ledge, long legs stretched out, notepad on his knees, pencil in hand. Tom was always writing; he wanted to record every moment, to forget nothing. He wrote slowly because, though he had an exceptionally quick intelligence, he had a minor condition which affected his fine motor control. During his early days at Winchester College, a highly academic school, it had caused no particular problem, and as he grew older it began to work in his favour, the slight physical effort required for writing chiming with his unusual depth of thought and concise use of words. I worried about Tom's insomnia, but he'd always refused to see the doctor. 'There's nothing he can do,' he'd say. 'There's no point.' I understood. Rather than take pills, you might as well do something useful.

Over the previous months, particularly since the huge 'Stop the War' protest in central London on 15 February, we'd all noticed a change in Tom. He'd come down for the march from Manchester

Metropolitan University, where he had recently changed his course from criminology to photography, and though he was clearly ill with flu he'd insisted on going, taking his camera with him – Tom photographed wherever he went. It was on that march, as his girlfriend Kay told me later, that he had been handed a leaflet by the group who were volunteering to go out to Iraq as human shields.

Though Tom did go through the motions of consulting his family and friends – most of whom were, of course, appalled – I think that from the moment he was given that leaflet his mind was made up. Nothing any of us said could change it. A deep chord had been struck. As he was to say in a television interview, he didn't see why, by a mere accident of geography, other twenty-one-year-olds should be living in a state of conflict while he wasn't, and he wanted to show solidarity. He wanted to record the risks they were facing.

Anthony and I went over those risks with him, but he knew what we were going to say before we said it. I realised, as we talked, that even if I had not quite accepted it before, he was no longer a child, but a thoughtful young man who had made it his business to understand the main issues and was determined to try to make a difference. It was clear that while he was away at university he'd done a lot of research into the Middle East – its geography, its political history, even its religions – and now the walls of his room were covered with a series of eerie aerial pictures of the region that I suppose he must have found on the internet. They seemed to have been taken from a great height, almost from space. He had even written in the scale.

Now Tom, adventurous Tom, who even as a toddler was forever wanting to see over walls, down drains and round corners, was going to this unforgiving terrain. I was shocked, yet somehow resigned. We'd been here before – Tom was always challenging, always questioning. As I hugged him that last evening I could feel the nervous tension. I knew he was scared – he was too well informed not to be – and that when he'd had lunch with Kay that day he had still been questioning his real motives for going. Tom wasn't offering himself simply as a human shield, though he was angry about the war in Iraq. The reporter in him wanted to see, to photograph and record for himself what the human shields were doing. As I held him I was almost unable to speak. All I could do was repeat, over and over, 'Take care, Tom. Take care. Keep safe.'

I had driven barely two hundred yards out of the school car park when my mobile rang. I pulled in to the curb outside the headquarters of my own union, the National Union of Teachers, and opposite another, UNISON, two organisations that were to play a supportive role in what was to come, though of course I had no idea of it then. It was the journalist from the *Sunday Times*.

'Are you're all right?' he said. 'Please do drive carefully. How far do you have to go? Look, I live just near you, in Tufnell Park. Please let me know if there's anything I can do to help.' He was no longer wearing his journalist's hat but speaking simply as one human being to another, and I could hear that he was genuinely concerned.

As I put my key in the front door I could hear the phone ringing. It stopped briefly, then started again. I put my bag down on the black and white tiled hall floor – everything so comfortingly familiar, yet an entirely different place now from the one I had left that morning. Sophie came up the stairs from the kitchen and for a long moment we just held one another. 'Where's Billy?' I said.

Apparently after hearing the news, my middle son, eighteen-year-old Billy, had sat for some time at the kitchen table, silently, with his head in his hands, and had then gone out for a walk on his own: thinking things through, working things out quietly, as Billy always does.

As the phone continued ringing – the national newspapers, *London Tonight*, all wanting to come round and interview us – I was thankful that Fred, our youngest, who was just twelve, was out with friends. He and Tom adored one another and Tom's first thought was always for Fred. As soon as Tom came through the front door he'd always yell for him, and Fred would come running. They'd smack hands with a 'Gimme Five!', and Tom would pick his brother up and sling him over his shoulder while Fred laughed and struggled, pretending to hate it, shouting to be put down. Fred looked up to Tom. How could I tell him now?

When finally I heard the car and Fred hopped out, muddy and cheerful from quad-biking, I stood with him at the gate for longer than we needed to, waving our friends goodbye. 'Let him have these last few minutes of happiness,' I kept thinking.

Like all of us, Fred was barely able to absorb the news. 'Shot?' he said, blank, gazing out at the blossom trees. 'Shot? Where was he shot?'

Still we didn't know, despite a call from the Foreign Office. All the duty officer could tell me was that Tom had been flown by helicopter to a hospital in Israel, but they didn't know which one. They would call me when they knew more.

Between interviews and phone calls from the press, and from concerned friends who had now heard the news, I tried desperately to get hold of Anthony, but his phone was switched off. At 11.30 p.m. an acquaintance of Anthony's finally managed to reach him – that very evening his mobile had been stolen – and he rang immediately. It was 3 a.m. Russian time, and he had been woken by the phone call. We had some minutes of desperate conversation: What had Tom been doing in the Gaza Strip? How could we discover what his condition really was, and which hospital he had been taken to? Anthony said he'd be on the earliest flight the next day.

Afterwards I simply stood for a moment holding the phone, shaking my head, unable to believe what was happening. *Brain dead* – I had been pushing the fearful words to the back of my mind ever since my conversation with the journalist at the *Sunday Times*, and I hadn't used them to the children who, by this time, had finally gone upstairs, though I could still hear them moving about. Now I knew without question that I must discover every detail of what had happened to Tom. As his mother, I had an absolute compulsion to know. Around midnight I began phoning Israeli hospitals until finally I got through to the main hospital in Jerusalem.

As with the previous calls, a voice answered in Hebrew, then hearing my question switched quickly to English. No, I was told yet again, he wasn't there.

'So he was in Rafah? Then he would have been taken to the Soroka Hospital in Be'ersheva,' said the voice on the other end of the phone.

'The Soroka Hospital?'

'Yes. That serves the whole of southern Israel, the Negev. This is the number.'

'I'm trying to discover the whereabouts of my son, Tom Hurndall, who was shot today in Rafah, in the Gaza Strip. I'm told he would have been brought to your hospital,' I said when the phone was answered at the Soroka Hospital.

There was a perceptible pause. 'One moment.' Then, 'I'm putting you through to the Director.'

Another voice. 'Hello.' The same question. Another pause. 'Yes, your son is here.'

'Please tell me his condition.'

'It's not good news, I'm afraid. He has a very, very serious head wound.'

'A gunshot wound?'

'Yes.'

'Is he conscious?'

'No. I have to tell you, Mrs Hurndall, the situation is very bad. The bullet entered the left frontal lobe and exited at the back. It has done extensive damage and he has lost a great deal of blood. I'm sorry to have to tell you this when you are so far away, but I'm doubtful Tom is going to make it. He could last until tomorrow, or he could go in half an hour.'

Tom had arrived a few hours before by helicopter, the Director told me, and had been taken immediately to the emergency room next to the helicopter pad, where they had attempted to stop the bleeding and had given him blood transfusions. He was now in the Intensive Care Unit but still bleeding heavily. He was in a critical state.

'I'm coming,' I said. 'I'll be on a plane in the morning.'

'Really,' said the even voice, 'I must emphasise how serious his condition is, Mrs Hurndall. Is it really necessary for you to come? If Tom dies your journey may be for nothing . . . And you know, he can be sent back.'

Sent back? I was conscious that though he hadn't actually said so in as many words, the Director was telling me it wasn't worth my while to fly to Israel. That they could fly Tom's body back to England and spare me the journey. But whether Tom lasted the night or not, there was no doubt whatever that I was going to him. Nothing was going to stop me reaching my son.

'There's absolutely no question, I shall be coming tomorrow,' I said.

An hour later the Director phoned to tell me they had decided to operate, to clear the detritus from around the wound in Tom's head, and to stop the bleeding. It was the smallest ray of hope, but I clung on to it through a sleepless night. As I lay there I was so tense I felt dizzy, almost disembodied, as if my head was no longer mine. There was a humming in my ears, and my mind raced with anxieties about Billy and Sophie and Fred and how they would cope. Pictures of Tom lying injured and alone in a foreign hospital bed were overlaid with other images: Tom as a baby, full of curiosity, his feet running in the air, his arms waving like propellers as I held him up to see, touch or smell something that had caught his attention; skinny six-year-old Tom, tipping out of the car as we arrived from London at his grandmother's cottage in the country, throwing his clothes off to run laughing round the croquet lawn, stark naked in the pouring rain; Tom with blackberry-stained face and chest and hands . . . Tom . . . Tom . . .

At eight o'clock the next morning the Director phoned again to tell me that the operation had been completed. They had removed much of the detritus from around the wound, managed to stop most of the bleeding and given Tom further huge quantities of blood. He had made it through the night.

As I came out of my room into the arid greyness of the morning, I saw two figures on the landing. Sophie and Billy stood hugging one another and quietly weeping. I hesitated for a moment, not wanting to intrude, to break the comfort they were giving each another: Billy, so tall and gentle and thoughtful, Sophie, so strong and extreme yet vulnerable too, and frightened. All of us frightened. I went up to them and gently put my arms round them, but knew there was nothing I could do to help. I think it was then that I began to understand something of the isolation of grief. Also a flickering premonition of the anger that comes with it. How could they know that grieving is lonely, something you have to do on your own?

Anthony arrived back in England that morning, and at about twelve o'clock I saw his familiar figure walking down the road, carrying his briefcase, and I sensed his numbness. I felt the same huge sadness I had felt for Sophie and Billy at the thought at what he would have to face. Anthony had worked hard at his relationship with Tom – we'd both had to at different times. Unlike me, he had been able to be supportive of Tom's decision to go to Iraq, believing that he should be given his head. It was Anthony who had taken him to the airport, discussed with him yet again the dangers of taking photographs, and how careful he must be to respect the local culture and customs. Anthony was the last member of the family to have seen Tom before this terrible thing happened. He told me later how much he regretted not giving him a hug at the airport. Instead he'd given him a Swiss Army knife which Tom had stowed away in his main rucksack, and then waved him goodbye at the barrier, man to man. Now all we could do was hold one another in silence in our hallway. For those moments there was nothing to say.

We sat at the kitchen table, trying to work out the best thing to do, one or other of us reaching out from time to time to answer the ceaselessly ringing phone. Every cell in my body demanded that I should be with Tom, but I also knew that the other children needed me, particularly Fred. I knew, too, that Anthony's analytical mind and lawyer's training, his objectivity and assertiveness, would be vital when it came to gathering information in Israel. I knew we had to be strictly practical. So we agreed that Anthony would fly to Tel Aviv that night. Billy quietly decided that he was going with him. He knew he had to be there. Billy had made up his own mind and I respected him for it.

How can I begin to describe this weekend that changed our lives? Close friends came round, bringing us food and consolation and making practical arrangements, booking the flight to Tel Aviv, taking Anthony and Billy to the airport, doing their best to fill the hours for Fred, who was a lost soul, like the rest of us. By Saturday evening, Sophie and I were left in the echoing house to answer the doorbell and take calls from the media, all eager to have the Hurndall 'take' on the story and to find out about Tom – what had made him volunteer to be a human shield, was he a 'peace activist', why had he been in the Gaza Strip? The interest from the media was overwhelming, and Anthony had already seen that this was an opportunity to draw attention to what was happening in Gaza. Often they asked questions I couldn't answer – we did not know then that Tom had sent Anthony a series of e-mails explaining his decision to go to Gaza, which Anthony was unable to access for a week. But they made me search my heart again about what had impelled Tom to go. Shortly before he left, a remark he had made to a journalist from the *Independent* had been picked up by the paper as one of its 'Quotes of the Week': 'I want to put a real face on the situation, instead of what most people think. That we are tree-hugging hippies.' Even then Tom was creating waves.

Now it came to me that he had always been a kind of human shield. 'Tom was the sort of person,' I overheard Sophie saying to a journalist, 'who used to help schoolchildren at Tufnell Park tube when the older kids were trying to pinch their mobiles. Tom's always stuck up for people who were at a disadvantage.' She was right. The headmaster of his prep school had told us that it was always Tom who protected the younger boys from bullies. Tom's impulse to go to Iraq hadn't been simply a kind of aberration, but an extension of who he was.

Gradually, through Reuters and the other news media, more information was emerging. The first official Israeli version was that a Palestinian gunman wearing fatigues had been shooting a pistol at a watchtower and had been targeted by a member of the Israeli Defence Force. But the story now coming to us from all quarters was that Tom, unarmed and wearing an internationally recognised peaceworker's fluorescent jacket, had been rescuing some Palestinian children from Israeli sniper fire and had been gunned down himself. This was soon endorsed by such responsible foreign correspondents as James Reynolds of the BBC and Chris McGreal of the *Guardian*, both of whom had a deep knowledge of the situation in the area.

Talking to the press was draining, but also a relief. There really seemed nothing else to talk about, and Sophie and I both felt passionately that we wanted to speak out, to tell the world of this terrible wrong that had been committed. I watched Sophie as she answered the phone and dealt with the media in her usual clear and assertive way. Now twenty-three, Sophie, the first of my children, was protective of all her brothers. Tom was the closest to her in age, and even at five she was keeping an anxious eye on him as he wandered off to explore, always wanting to know, to test the boundaries, to see what was going on *out there*. For Tom, Sophie was a very solid presence and they confided in one another. She had tried to dissuade him from going to Iraq, and now under her warm, larger-than-life exterior I sensed she was frozen with grief. Once too often Tom's need to see what was happening had taken him off 'out there', and she hadn't managed to stop him. It was a trait of Tom's we all recognised.

Anthony phoned early on Sunday morning from the hotel in Be'ersheva where he and Billy were staying. His voice was bleak, and what he had to tell me of the situation was bleaker. My impulse was to go, *now*, but how could I leave Sophie and Fred? During the day several good friends who lived nearby and whose children knew ours arrived, and I remember that we all sat in my bedroom, going over and over the situation. I shall be eternally grateful that they understood my need to be with Tom and strongly endorsed my decision to go. When they reassured me that they would watch over Sophie and Fred I knew I could trust them absolutely, and Sophie and Fred bravely convinced me they could cope.

On Monday night I was on a flight to Tel Aviv.

TWO

I dozed uneasily during the long, dark, fearful flight, glad that I had a row of seats to myself, for I don't think I could have spoken to anyone sitting next to me. By now I was so exhausted I felt quite unconnected to what was happening around me. It was as if I was seeing everything through glass. All past life seemed to have been erased. It had ceased to matter. Time and space were mangled into a meaningless mass. Walls closed around me one minute and didn't seem to be there the next. It was possible only to think of the next few seconds, or of what was immediately around me. My head was filled with terrible images of Tom and of the distress of our other children.

A friend had driven me to Heathrow and I'd gone through the formalities in a daze. When the girl behind the check-in desk asked me the usual questions – whether I'd packed my own bag, left it unattended, or been given anything by anyone – I answered automatically. I'd brought very few clothes and hadn't even thought to find out what the temperature would be in Israel. My overwhelming thought was of getting to Tom. It was the beginning of a feeling that was to become familiar, of functioning on many different levels. I wondered, was this normal?

Fortunately the night flight was fairly empty, and I was grateful for somewhere quiet where I could sit and wait. Huddled in an armchair in a corner of the departure lounge I'd phoned a close friend, Vicky, and it was reassuring to hear her voice. I could see her, standing in the kitchen of the warm north London home I knew so well, cradling the phone as she waved to one of her teenage children on his way out, checking when he'd be back. It gave me a glimmer of comfort to think of ordinary life continuing – of blinds being lowered, of people clearing supper tables, homework being done – as I waited for the plane that would fly me eastwards into this grim and uncertain future. Only last week we had been a relatively 'normal' family, but now, it seemed, the whole world was focused in outrage on Tom's shooting. I don't think it was the natural reaction of a protective mother that made me feel this. There was a deep and genuine sense of public shock in Britain.

I think my state must have been obvious, or perhaps the airline staff had been warned, because one of them came up to me and said kindly, 'Why don't you go to sleep? I'll wake you when they call your flight.' I tried to close my eyes but my thoughts took off into the past, to happy family times at the cottage on the Essex/Suffolk border – days of wood chopping and evenings in front of the log fire as a storm blew up across the mud flats from the Harwich Estuary. And always at the centre of these memories, Tom – tall, skinny and strong, a lovely sight as he ran across the grass or down the lane beside the cottage, completely single-minded and full of verve and mischief. It dawned on me that Tom, at twenty-one, was exactly the same age as I had been when I first went to Israel.

I tried to reconcile in my mind this place where he was lying at death's door with the place in which my father had developed a passionate interest and where I had spent a couple of months of carefree work and travel. My father had been a scientist with a mission – the generation of energy from wave power – and had been decorated for his pioneering contribution to engineering projects in the Middle East. Before the Six-Day War in 1967 he had spent time in Jordan as a consultant with what was then the Ministry of Overseas Development. I loved him dearly, although he was a somewhat remote figure in my childhood. But in later life, when we came to know each other better, he often spoke to me of his time there. I remembered his telling me how, one day when he was walking beside the Dead Sea, King Hussein's helicopter had landed not far away. My father, who respected this leader who had shown himself to be a man of vision with a well-known interest in alternative energy, had strolled over and struck up a conversation on this topic of mutual interest. It was to be the first of many meetings during which they shared this concern. I remember the signed photograph of the King in my father's study, alongside some carved camels and other bits of Middle Eastern memorabilia.

Just like Tom, I thought. It was the issue that counted. Not much regard for formalities – just straight to the matter in hand. I knew, too, how painfully my father had struggled to reconcile his passionate interest in engineering with his Christian beliefs. It was something that troubled him. A family friend once told me that he had gone through the entire Bible, New and Old Testaments, highlighting every reference to the sea. Was this his effort to resolve an internal conflict between science and religion? It was a search I had respected. That seemed like Tom, too – the idealism, the questioning, the independence – and the aloneness. Even when Tom was a little boy I had sensed a restless streak in him.

Sometimes, when I saw him sitting at the kitchen table or at the desk in his room, forehead on hand, shoulders hunched, I would come and sit quietly beside him. He didn't always want to talk. He just needed to know I was there. He was never short of friends, who were profoundly important to him, but I sensed there were times when he felt in some way separate, different. People didn't always understand his thinking, and this was certainly true when he made up his mind to go to Iraq with the human shields. But Tom kept his own counsel.

At about five in the morning, as the plane began its descent into Tel Aviv, I looked down at the harsh outlines of the modern city, the arterial roads and roundabouts, the high-rise blocks all touched with gold by the rising sun. Although it was so early I could already sense the heat of the day, bringing with it that feeling of being in a foreign country which I'd found so exciting as a student, arriving all those years ago to work on a kibbutz. As the plane taxied along the runway, I remembered landing at Lod airport, as it was then called, and even more vividly leaving it on my way back to London. I could see myself, wearing sawn-off jeans, a tank top, and carrying a smelly white Afghan coat I'd bargained for in a Jerusalem market, bundled up in a sheet from my sleeping bag.

I was thrilled with this ankle-length Dr Zhivago-style coat that looked as though it had been freshly shorn, and just as pleased with the empty cartridge hipster belt I was wearing, all the rage back in London in the 1970s. Even in those days Lod airport was bristling with young soldiers and within minutes one of them had motioned me over with a blank, impersonal look and, without a word or a glance directly at me, indicated that I should take the belt off. He raised it to eye level to let the daylight shine in and looked slowly and purposefully inside every cartridge case before handing it back. Then, seeing my strangely shaped bundle, he showed me into a cubicle, where a female soldier unwrapped and searched the coat laboriously. Little did I realise then that this was routine, for I had never before witnessed such treatment, let alone experienced it first-hand. Unused to being considered a suspicious character, I found this brush with the military distinctly thought-provoking, and I boarded the plane rather relieved to be on board a British flight home. That had been the summer of 1972.

As the plane juddered to a halt now and I began to unwind my cramped and painful limbs, a stewardess appeared beside me.

'There's an Embassy car waiting for you on the tarmac,' she said. 'As soon as the steps are down, follow me. Just bring your hand luggage, don't worry about anything else. The driver will deal with all that.'

The plane doors opened and a wave of heat hit me as I followed her down the steps to where an official looking car and a driver were waiting. It was a huge relief to sink into the comfortable anonymity of the back seat as we drove off across the airport. I suppose we must have gone through passport control, must have collected my luggage. I don't remember. I felt drained, and glad to be guided through the formalities, glad that everything was being taken care of.

In a car parking space reserved for diplomatic vehicles behind the Arrivals terminal we drew up behind a Range Rover flying a Union Jack. Someone with a friendly face was standing waiting.

'Mrs Hurndall? Tom Fitzalan Howard. I'm the Defence Attaché, British Embassy. Extremely good to meet you, but I'm sorry it's in these circumstances. I hope you had a reasonable flight.'

I heard myself uttering the usual pleasantries as my hand was taken in a firm and reassuring grasp by a rather military looking man with a kind and humorous expression. 'I'm so very sorry about Tom,' he said in the direct way I would come to know. 'Let me tell you what the arrangements are today. We're going to drive straight down to Be'ersheva to the hospital now so that you can see Tom, and we'll collect Anthony from the hotel on the way. Here, let me take your things. Do get into the front.'

I clambered up into the Range Rover but I felt I hadn't a muscle in my body. My legs were leaden and I had the sense of being outside my physical self that comes with extreme shock. Tom Fitzalan Howard took my arm sympathetically, helped me in and got into the driving seat beside me; the heavy door closed with a resounding clunk. Shut away from the loud airport noises, there was an immediate silence. It felt like being in an armoured car – which, of course, I soon realised it was.

As we left Ben Gurion airport through various guard posts and checkpoints, I became aware that they were all manned by uniformed soldiers carrying rifles. I was struck by how small and wiry these soldiers were, and how young – most of them looked no more than eighteen. The way their rifles were slung so casually across their shoulders, swinging around like menacing toys, shocked me. Ordinary to Israeli culture, obviously, but not to a Brit. Further on I saw groups of young soldiers standing at bus stops, hitching lifts, talking on their mobiles, just gathering in groups waiting to move on. What was the point of carrying these guns around? There seemed to be people in military uniform everywhere, men and women. I did not yet fully understand how profoundly militarised Israeli society is, how deeply this runs through the whole cultural fabric, but I knew immediately I was in a country permanently geared for war. And I sensed a challenge in this degree of alertness, almost a provocation.

We drove out through the Tel Aviv suburbs, along streets where the bougainvillea was in flower and past roundabouts filled with great succulent sharp-leaved aloe vera plants. At first I had the impression that the outside of every apartment block, every roof, terrace and balcony, was studded with industrial-sized refrigerators, but soon realised these must be air-conditioning units. Before long we hit the motorway south. On long stretches of it the jacaranda trees were coming into bloom, and suddenly it seemed that everything was enveloped in a cloud of luminescent lilac. I realised then that I could not allow myself to feel the beauty of that exquisite sight. If I did, my heart would break. The consciousness of what Tom might have lost came over me in waves and my eyes filled with tears.

As we drove Colonel Fitzalan Howard, or TFH as we would come to know him, steered the conversation with all the ease of the practised diplomat; we found we had a number of acquaintances in common, including an old friend of mine I had not seen for years, now a general in the Royal Green Jackets who had served in Northern Ireland. It was an odd sensation to find myself able to converse at this polite and social level while my mind was filled with thoughts of how soon we would reach the hospital and dread at what I would find. I heard myself thanking TFH for collecting me from the airport and apologising for the early start he must have had to make.

'Oh, no trouble at all,' he said warmly. 'I'm quite used to it. We've had a number of diplomats arriving recently and this is the flight we usually meet.'

It was a curious split feeling to continue to smile, to exchange ordinary civilities, not to reveal that my body felt as if it had been hurled against a brick wall and my mind had gone missing. But I knew I must not fall apart. Yet even though we were talking at this superficial level I very quickly became aware that I was not talking to a superficial man. Though it was clear that TFH was a practical person and not one for getting bogged down in sentimentality, I sensed that here was someone I could trust absolutely, who understood every aspect of the situation. During the one-and-a-half-hour journey he impressed me as intelligent, knowledgeable and confident – someone who said exactly what he thought but only after he had given it much consideration and had gathered all the information. A straight talker, who brooked no nonsense and was wholly unafraid to challenge immorality and untruth in any given situation. Someone who would want to do the right thing for the greater good and not just for his own country. I also sensed a mischievous wit to which, in different circumstances, I knew I would have been able to respond.

'You realise, don't you,' he said, looking at me very directly, 'that we're not going to get anywhere with the Israelis.'

At first I didn't understand. 'All we want is to get at the truth. Doesn't everyone?'

'It's not quite as simple as that,' said TFH. 'They're a hard-bitten lot. They're not going to admit to anything. A lot of people have tried to call them to account, but I'm afraid they haven't succeeded.'

I was too tired and terrified for Tom to say much, but I tried to take in everything he was telling me, though I found it hard to concentrate. But as TFH talked on, I came to understand that we were going to get no cooperation whatever from the Israeli authorities. Worse, there would probably be obstruction. When the IDF's propaganda about Tom's shooting had appeared in the Israeli press we had certainly been deeply suspicious, but to have the position stated so starkly now by someone so well informed was something of a shock.

'Most people living outside the Middle East have no idea what the Israeli Defence Force is like,' TFH said.

I realised he was trying to brief me, to prepare me for the reality of what I would be seeing and hearing.

'When we travel down into the Gaza Strip later today and pass through UN refugee camps,' he went on, 'you'll see for yourself the destruction that's taken place.'

What did he mean? Destruction of homes? Destruction of land? Thinking back to my last visit to Israel, I remembered how even then, in the early 1970s, it was not advisable to enter Gaza. I now began to wonder why. When I was twenty-one I hadn't been drawn there by political anger, and, therefore, hadn't asked the questions. I recall learning that the Israeli government had declared that theirs was 'the most moral army in the world'. I remember thinking then that it was a strange way to describe your army. What reason could there be for making such a declaration? What Israeli general had come up with such an idea? If you were a moral army, why would you have to say it? Thinking in terms of a scale of military morality, with 'moral' at one end and 'immoral' at the other, I wondered where you would place other world armies? Who was convincing whom?

That statement had left me uneasy. It didn't ring true. I could relate to a motto such as that of the SAS: 'Who dares wins'. Mottos helped to build morale, self-belief, and act as an inspiration. But 'a moral army' – was it an indoctrination of the young or a statement designed to boost public image? A suggestion to the outside world to view it in that way? I did not know much about the young state of Israel. I had put my unease, then, down to my own lack of political awareness and of historical knowledge about the region, and pushed this unresolved feeling on to the back burner.

I focused my thoughts back on what TFH was saying. 'Have I understood you correctly?' I asked. 'I thought the Israeli army was supposed to be a moral army.'

'You know an Israeli soldier is not like a British soldier,' said TFH.

What exactly was he getting at, I wondered.

'The concept of minimum force is central to a British soldier who is trained, absolutely, to be accountable for his actions,' he went on. 'The British rules of engagement are very strict on this, and they are always applied. It's quite different with the IDF. For a start their soldiers are very young – conscripts, mainly, though there are professional soldiers. The soldiers are invariably backed up by their commander and the chain of command. Jocelyn, I have to tell you' – here he spoke slowly as if for emphasis – 'that the investigations are invariably a sham. This will be difficult for you and Anthony to deal with. A soldier is rarely held to account, and whatever he's done he would never face a murder or manslaughter charge – he'd only be on a lesser charge, perhaps failing to carry out the correct drills. I really don't want you to expect too much.'

So we had been warned. Though I had a feeling of blankness, at the same time I knew, with burning certainty, that we were going to use every possible means to get at the truth. I was sure the family would want to keep an open mind until we'd seen for ourselves everything there was to see. It was not that I didn't believe what this experienced military man was saying. It was just that we needed first-hand evidence before coming to any conclusions, and I suspected there would be a long way to go before any of us made up our minds. Anthony, as a lawyer, would be adamant about retaining objectivity and I knew he would not be hurried. His personality and training picked up on every detail, and he would insist on thoroughness. He would not settle for half measures.

The closer we came to the Negev, the more parched the land became. Strings of camels appeared on the skyline – that sure and magical sign of the East. They were cropping the scorched grass in small enclosures beside the motorway, tethered near groups of makeshift corrugated-iron shacks surrounded by a few olive trees. The contrast between the raggedness of the dwellings and the care with which the olive trees were clearly tended was striking. TFH told me these were Bedouin settlements.

'The Bedouin have a hard time of it,' he said. 'From time to time the Israelis simply come along and bulldoze these huts because they claim they're illegal. In the Negev they've herded the Bedouin together in seven shanty towns – you'll see the largest of them, Rahat, when we reach the Negev.'

It was impossible to open the bullet-proof windows, but I could see that the heat outside was intense, shimmering. It seemed too hot for even the olive trees to survive. I tried to imagine the life of these people who had once had the freedom of the desert, now cooped up in crude settlements. Why were they treated like this, how did they survive, what crops were they tending, what facilities did they have? It was as if, in this extreme situation, this unfamiliar territory, my sensibility was somehow heightened and my mind was bristling with questions, my whole being ringing with adrenaline.

TFH was speaking again. 'You also need to know that it's only with political support at the highest level that we've achieved anything with any IDF investigations. Problem is that with media pressure alone they hunker down under the anti-Semitic charge which they level against anyone who dares to criticise.'

This last comment hit home. It touched something in me and I felt my own anger. At times like this you have a strange feeling of striving to look down at yourself, of taking an aerial view in order to get the broad picture. It's an effort, but in the end it's what you have to do.

The colonel's last words reminded me acutely of Tom's Jewish friends with whom I had hardly had time to talk before leaving, and of the many Jewish people we knew in London. The present situation was not about race, religion, or getting sucked into any propaganda or political agenda. We wanted nothing but an objective search for truth, even if it meant believing that my pacifist son, Tom, really had dressed in army fatigues and been foolish enough to shoot at a watchtower, which was what that first absurd broadcast in Israel had stated.

That was the bottom line. We were a family that tried to build on insights and understandings about the reasons why people – in this case a foreign government and its army – did what they did. But there was no question that we wanted the truth. I knew this would be Anthony's view. And Tom's.

The nearer we got to Be'ersheva, the less we spoke. The dark knot in my stomach grew tighter as I went over in my mind what Anthony had told me and tried to imagine precisely what Tom's condition was, what the future really held for him and for all of us. Soon we were driving alongside the palm trees of Be'ersheva's central boulevard. With its buildings of sand-coloured stone the fifth largest city in Israel looked to me as if it had risen straight out of the desert. It was relatively new, built in 1948, TFH told me.

'That's the hospital, there,' he said pointing to a large blue semi-crescent-shaped building on one of the slight hills in the centre of the town. Now we were approaching the hotel where Anthony and Billy were staying and I called Anthony's mobile. He must have been wide awake and waiting for the call, for he answered instantly. The hotel was an ugly skyscraper block and as we entered the drive I was once more aware of security, of the spikes in the tarmac that slashed your tyres if you drove over them the wrong way, of the uniformed guard waiting at the front entrance to search us as we went in. I would soon become accustomed to all this, to the fact that it mattered not who you were – a habitual visitor, a bereaved parent, a near-death stretcher case, the most trustworthy looking person on the planet – there was no differentiation. The routine at every building was the same: you were always searched. Now, though, I was mildly surprised, since we were in a diplomatic vehicle with distinctive white number plates, and our unusual circumstances would have been known.

A sullen girl whose eyes never met mine telephoned Anthony's room, and we took the lift to the seventh floor. As he opened the door to his room Anthony's face told me everything. I had never seen him look so pale and drawn. TFH hung back tactfully as we talked and Anthony assembled a few things. Billy was still asleep and we decided to leave him and drive to the hospital on our own. It was still not yet 8 a.m.

I have no recollection of walking up the stairs of the hospital to the second floor, and along the passages and long corridors. I have a dim memory of benches along a wall on which Arab men in white robes were sitting, smoking, and of stepping over sleeping bodies in what seemed like a waiting room. I did not know then, Tom, that these were people who had come from all over Israel to be with you. The antiseptic smell struck me first as I was shown where to wash, and put on rubber gloves and a green gown. The crucial health and safety ritual added to my sense of the fragility of the lives of those in the Intensive Care Unit.

I don't think I breathed as I walked down the ward, past the semi-enclosed beds of the very sick. There were sounds but no sounds, smells but no smells. I approached your bed and recognised your face in spite of the bandages round your dreadfully swollen head, covering your eyes. Lights, moving wavy or straight lines on a screen with tubes, plugs everywhere, and a wide orange neck brace that came up over your chin. You were still bleeding from your left ear. There were cuts on your nose and hands where you must have fallen. Your hands and feet terribly swollen. I looked down at you surrounded by dials with changing numbers, luminous lines measuring blood pressure and heartbeats with the blip of a machine, searching for meaning for the state you were in.

I seemed to be looking at you from very far away, down a long tunnel. I do not know what the meaning of that tunnel was. Perhaps the shock of seeing you caused me to distance myself for that moment. I was there, gazing down at you, and yet I was not there. This was you, and yet it was not you. Too frightened to touch you for fear of hurting you. Unable to whisper for the choking in my throat. An echo, in the centre of my being, reverberated round my head, banging the drums of my ears. A voice spoke through me. It was you, Tom. Yet I knew I could not reach you, however

many times I called your name. The moment I saw you reality had begun
to creep slowly towards me, invading me like a dark shadow.

Dearest Tom, at that moment, life stopped for a part of me, as it had for
you. My heart reached out to you, and I broke down. I was filled with
terror at your absolute fragility and your uncertain future. I could not even
pray.

I don't know how long I stood gazing down at my son in total
disbelief. It was as if time had stopped, and the past, Tom's past,
our past, had disappeared, to be replaced by a colourless space. A
veil seemed to stretch round him on this bed, blocking out
everything else. This was the centre of our existence now,
nothing else mattered. I felt like two people, one looking at
the other. But as I gradually became aware of my surroundings I
realised that there was someone else standing beside the bed. As I
slowly raised my head I saw a lovely young woman with dark, sad
eyes overflowing with tears. She took me in her arms and, with
both of us in a state of complete distress, she repeated over and
over, 'I am so sorry for my country. I am so sorry.'

Those real, human words coming from an Israeli were like a
kind of explosion in my head. What must it have taken for her to
voice them? What must she have experienced in life to be in a
position to say them? What pain had she been through that she
could relate so intimately to other people's suffering? Two parallel
paths opened up. Her words came from another pain, another
story, which now seemed to be part of my own.

'I am Michal,' she said simply.

We stood there together beside Tom's bed, our arms around
each other, and this moment of sharing, of human compassion,
seemed to me at that moment to represent the epitome of
civilisation, of humanity, of what we are put on earth for.
And I wept even more because it contrasted so starkly with
the extreme inhumanity, the brutality, of what had happened to
Tom.

After a while she gently disengaged herself, laid her hand on my arm, and when I looked round she had slipped away. I had no idea then how close we would become to Michal and her family, or what a significant part they would play in Tom's story. At this moment I was too shocked and bewildered even to ask who she was.

After a while Anthony joined me. He stood looking down at Tom with an expression of infinite pity and sadness, and I could see the strain of the past forty-eight hours on his face. We left the ward and stood talking quietly about the meeting he had had the day before with the medical staff.

'We must be prepared for him to go at any time,' he said. 'It's unbelievable that he's lasted this long.'

We agreed that we must arrange for Sophie and Fred to fly out as soon as possible. I knew how painful it was going to be for both of them to see Tom in this condition. But I knew that it would be even worse if they were unable to say goodbye to him before he died. Even then some part of my brain remembered that Fred's passport was out of date, and that we would somehow have to arrange for him to renew it.

Some of what Anthony was telling me was hard to absorb. At the previous day's meeting, it seemed, one senior doctor had suggested that Tom's wound was 'commensurate with a blow from a baseball bat'. I looked across at the body of my son, swathed in bandages, connected to a battery of machines. I could see now that there was something terrible at the back of his head, where blood was still seeping through the bandage. Blood was seeping from his left ear. His long hands and feet were grotesquely swollen. Could any sane person, possibly – *possibly* – connect these terrible injuries with a blow from a baseball bat? When we looked at the notes at the foot of Tom's bed, the summary of his injury, which appeared at the top of each page, quite clearly stated that Tom had suffered a 'gunshot wound'. A senior hospital official had described the entry and exit wounds to Anthony, but he had seemed to backtrack when Anthony expressed surprise at the 'baseball bat' suggestion. Anthony had somehow gathered, too, that the consultant in charge of Tom's case had asked for a member of the IDF medical team to visit him.

What could all this mean? Uneasy as we already were about the possibility of a cover-up, and remembering the extraordinary reports which had appeared in the Israeli press, soon after Tom was shot, of a gunman in fatigues targeting an Israeli Defence Force watchtower, I began to feel the ground shifting under me – especially when I thought of TFH's uncompromising remarks about the IDF. From what little I had been able to take in, it seemed that Tom was receiving the best and most up-to-date medical care, but when it came to the medical evidence, to the politics of this situation, we both, I know, began to wonder whom could we trust. Yet at that moment I was too exhausted to pursue this train of thought. All I wanted to know was what had really happened to my son, how he had come to be where he was at the time he was shot, and what I, or anyone, could do now to help him.

Eventually we went out through the double doors with their porthole windows into the waiting room. It was still relatively early in the morning, and the scene there was like a campsite, with sleeping bags, rugs, pillows and rucksacks taking up most of the floor. Water bottles, soft drink cans and packets of half-eaten food lay here and there. A group of young people were standing by the window smoking the first cigarette of the day. It was impossible to imagine any of this happening in a London hospital. As we stepped carefully between recumbent bodies, several of the group by the window saw us and came towards us, and Anthony began to introduce me.

'This is Alison,' I remember him saying as a tall, slim, dark-haired girl in slacks held out her hand. 'Joe, Laura, Raph, Michelle, Nathan. Nathan and Michelle were with Tom in Baghdad . . .' A young woman with olive skin and dark eyes came forward and took my hands in both of hers, looking at me sadly and intently.

Apart from those two I had only the vaguest impression of a crowd of serious faces, of tousled heads and T-shirts and baggy trousers, as the group clustered round. Someone put a hand on my shoulder, someone hugged me, someone else took my hand. It was impossible to register names and information, though it did occur to me to wonder who on earth these young people were and why they were there. I think I remember hearing someone talking about the 'ISM', but it meant nothing to me. What I felt strongly was their affection and the warmth of their concern. Like an automaton, I heard myself asking them about themselves – how long they had been at the hospital, where they had come from – but was unable to take in a single answer. It felt important to respond but it took every ounce of energy I had. The tension in my head was so great that I was simply staring without seeing, hearing without registering. Yet at a deeper level I was already aware that these, too, were people who were in shock.

As I heard my voice asking these normal questions I wondered how I could be operating at these two levels. Shouldn't I be showing grief, weeping, collapsing even? Yet I already knew the answer. I was in a place beyond tears.

By this time Billy had arrived. Everyone greeted him by name when he came in and it was obvious that he had already become part of the group. But as I reached out to touch him, I was alarmed by the change I saw. Billy looked tense and drawn, and I could see immediately how much my sensitive, thoughtful second son was suffering – and suffering in silence. Billy is an unselfish person and his main concern, I knew, would be not to make things more difficult for anyone else. He'd always been like that. Almost as soon as he was born he lay on his side in the transparent-sided hospital cot with his eyes wide open, looking out at the world in the most peaceful and trusting way.

Yet I soon became aware that in this new situation something had shaken his trust. I tried to ask him how he was, but, as always, he found it difficult to talk about himself. But when we began talking about Tom I was taken aback to discover how extremely suspicious Billy seemed to be. Though normally so equable, he has a passionate, outspoken streak when roused, and at these times nothing one can say can change his mind. The comment about the baseball bat had poisoned the atmosphere and he had concluded that he must keep a very close watch on his brother and anyone who treated him. Tom and Billy were different personalities, but their unspoken love for one another was absolute. Though it was hard for us to say very much at this point, Billy's few caustic remarks only added to my own uneasiness. What was really going on here, I wondered again. How impartial were the hospital staff, how much pressure were they under from forces as yet unknown to us?

When TFH finally appeared in the waiting room at about 11 a.m. and announced that it was time for us to start for Rafah – an expedition I knew he and Anthony had planned the day before – Billy decided he wouldn't be going with us. I sensed that he wanted to stay near to Tom. Billy was Tom's self-appointed guardian, and he rarely left his brother's bedside during the month he spent in Israel.

THREE

We left Billy sitting, immovable, beside Tom's bed and once again joined TFH for the journey to Rafah. Leading the way was another Range Rover containing Andy Whittaker, the second secretary from the British Consulate in East Jerusalem who covered issues in Gaza. TFH explained that the Embassy and the Consulate worked closely together. The Ambassador in Tel Aviv was accredited to the Israeli government and dealt with all issues in Israel itself. The Consul General in Jerusalem was accredited to the Palestinian Authority and covered everything that happened in the Occupied Territories – that is, East Jerusalem, the West Bank and Gaza. The Embassy was in Tel Aviv because the city was recognised by Britain as the capital of the State of Israel, while Palestine wasn't yet recognised as a state.

'But the fact that we and a lot of other countries have Consulates in East Jerusalem gives an important message to the Israelis,' he said

We were told it was Embassy policy always to go into the Occupied Territories in pairs. It was a safety measure. 'You never quite know what you'll come up against,' TFH said with a laugh. 'And by that I don't mean any threat from the Palestinians. I'm much more worried by the IDF. I'm not saying it's anything deliberate. More to do with lack of accountability and loose rules of engagement. It's easy to be mistaken for someone else – even in an Embassy Range Rover.' As Defence Attaché, he told us, he was the point of contact for all matters involving the IDF, both for the Embassy and the Consulate General.

With his wry humour, his military bearing and authoritative manner, I found TFH deeply reassuring. Later I was to learn how his thinking on the conflict had changed when he first visited the Occupied Territories and what deep anger at injustice was hidden behind his calm rather aristocratic exterior. But now I was too emotionally drained and physically exhausted for discussion of any kind.

We drove southwards along tarmac roads, through lush farm-lands and well-tended fields of lemons and maize. I was astonished by the abundance of this prosperous landscape. We were in the waterless area of the Negev, yet huge shining sprays of water played continuously on the fields. From a distance they looked like hazy fluctuating mirages that glistened occasionally, but as we drew closer I realised the sheer extent of the irrigation. I'd never seen water used so freely.

Half an hour later we were approaching the Erez Crossing, the checkpoint which marks the Israeli-imposed 'border' between Israel and the Gaza Strip and is the only entry into Gaza from the north. We joined a queue of vehicles drawn up outside a low concrete building, with a guard box on either side of the gated checkpoint. TFH explained that over the past days he had been in contact with the Consulate in East Jerusalem about whether it was safe to go into the Occupied Territories – in other words, to discover whether the Israelis were planning another incursion – and had been given the all-clear. The Israeli authorities had been given notice of our impending visit, and had been provided with all our details – our names, our passport numbers, the 'purpose of our visit'. As I would learn, going into Gaza is not something anyone does lightly.

'But don't imagine all that's going to speed things up much,' he said as he got out of the car and disappeared into the office building with our passports and documents.

The minutes ticked heavily by. I think I dozed a little, my half-dreams full of Tom, of Billy, Sophie and Fred, while Anthony sat preoccupied, gazing out of the window. When I opened my eyes

I could glimpse, beyond the checkpoint, concrete stretching into the distance, and I could see people moving about behind the glass and steel windows of the checkpoint building. Eventually TFH came out.

'I'm sorry about this,' he said, 'we're just going to have to wait. This is what they do. They make you wait. It's even worse for the Palestinians. They can be here for days or even weeks. Sometimes they wait and wait and after all that they're still not let through.' Sitting in the luxury of the air-conditioned Range Rover, I tried to imagine what it would be like to be on foot, waiting and waiting in the horrendous heat. There was no comparison.

Some huge grey armoured Chevys with American flags flying drew up beside us. Some uniformed personnel went into the checkpoint building, the rest lounged around the vehicles. TFH explained to us that US Embassy cars always travelled in convoy. 'As you can see,' he said, 'they're not taking any chances. They roar in and roar out. They're not very popular in these parts. They try not to get up too close to the ordinary, local people. They have an overwhelming fear of casualties so they just don't travel in the Occupied Territories.' Ten minutes later the Americans were hopping into their vehicles and the whole ungainly procession lumbered through the checkpoint. It looked menacing, over-bearing, all shiny chrome and darkened windows. I couldn't help comparing the impression the Americans made with that of the English contingent, which was unobtrusive and low-key. TFH, I would discover, carried nothing more menacing than a bag of sweets in the Range Rover's glove compartment.

Thirty minutes . . . forty minutes passed as we waited in the car park. Finally TFH was back, this time with a young man who introduced himself as Inigo Gilmour, a correspondent for the *Daily Telegraph*, who would be coming with us to Rafah. Suddenly I registered who he was. His mother was a friend of Julia, a close friend of mine. In the confusion of arrangements before I left London, I dimly remembered Julia telling me that Inigo would be getting in touch. It felt comforting to have someone along with such close links to the family, who spoke the same language in every sense, and who could easily have been a friend. After a moment or two's conversation the barrier gate was lifted, and we were through into no-man's-land. Inigo followed in a taxi.

My first impression was of a sterile greyness, like an airport, a huge tarmac area with high concrete walls topped with barbed wire rising on either side. TFH pointed out some metal cages, approached by covered alleyways and turnstiles. 'That's where they search the Palestinian workers as they come through,' he said. 'X-rays and everything. They call it "processing". Makes me think of a concentration camp.'

We drove slowly, zigzagging between giant clumps of concrete. It was rather like being in a maze, except that there were no choices. On either side of us, about every fifty yards, were machine-gun posts guarded by tanks and at intervals tall posts with what looked like cameras on them. It was truly no-man's-land, a place with no sign of human occupation. The Israeli military were hidden, watching us through slits in their guard posts, which bristled with masts and antennae for electronic monitoring. It seemed a place devoid of humanity, empty and menacing. It sucked your hope away.

It came to me forcibly that this checkpoint was not just a formality. We were in the midst of a fearful conflict, where life and death hung in the balance. There was threat in the air, a feeling of oppression that weighed me down. It was a feeling I recognised, though at first I couldn't place it. Travelling back to England on leave from Mauritius where we had lived when I was five, we had stopped off briefly in South Africa. I was shocked and bewildered when I understood the meaning of the notice on the park bench that said 'Europeans Only'. It meant that if my much-loved Indian nanny Hannah had been with us, we wouldn't have been allowed to sit together. I can still remember my anger, even then, at the injustice of apartheid, though I did not know its name. The oppression of apartheid was what I felt I was witnessing now. Nobody had told me to look for it, but from the minute I entered the Occupied Territories I was piercingly aware of it. The stench of it hung in the air and went straight to my stomach.

But nothing had prepared me for what was to come next. As we were let through the Palestinian side of the checkpoint – an exchange which seemed to consist simply of a smile and a wave from the border guard – and out the other side, all I could see at first was mud, a brown quagmire stretching into the distance as far as the eye could see. Where the car had sped along tarmac roads on the Israeli side, now it sank into ruts and jolted over potholes, bumped and swerved, its speed slowed almost to walking pace. I'd travelled across the world that day, but one mile on Palestinian roads shook me up more than any other part of the journey. Everything in this desolate landscape seemed to have been dug up, bulldozed or flattened, the land pulped into muddy chaos. Great clumps of upended tree roots lay exposed. It was like some battlefield of the First World War. The terrible inequality bled through the crushed earth.

As we drove TFH pointed out to us the places where there had once been orchards, which had been ripped out of the ground and cleared by the bulldozers of the Israeli Defence Force. He described the countryside as it had once been, a land covered by acres of orange trees and olive groves hundreds of years old, passed from father to son by generations of Palestinian farmers. Yet however bruised and abused this landscape, I felt that a soul lingered in the churned-up earth that had once provided people with a living.

The journey took us through Gaza City, one of the most densely populated cities in the world, where we stopped to pick up an interpreter. The car crept at snail's pace through narrow streets so thick with people that there seemed to be no distinction between the pavement and the road, a heaving, shifting mass of women carrying bags of fruit, men on bicycles, wooden carts pulled by donkeys. Yet though the crowds moved they seemed to be going nowhere. There was a sense of aimlessness and disorientation, though here and there we saw groups of cleanly dressed children on their way home from school. The feeling was even more powerful in the Khan Younis refugee camp. TFH told us that in this destroyed economy there was huge unemployment, and everywhere the poverty was evident. Coming from the steely efficiency of Israel into Gaza, we had moved from the Developed World into the Third.

As we drove towards Rafah, TFH pointed out Israeli settlements off in the distance, clusters of attractive looking, low bungalow-style buildings, some with beautiful views out over the Mediterranean. What on earth were these settlements doing in Palestinian territory, I wondered. It astonishes me now to think how little I knew then about the situation in Gaza. Like so many people in the West, I'd had no need to. TFH explained that these settlements had been part of the stealthy land grab encouraged by Ariel Sharon twenty or thirty years earlier. From time to time he would point to a road saying, 'That's a road Palestinians don't use.' It was all extraordinary and bewildering.

All the settlements were surrounded by dark, ominous-looking watchtowers built of concrete or scaffolding with grey steel cabins perched on top. Bizarrely the cabins were crowned by great lumps of thick camouflage netting made from rope, like giant hair nets, which made them look doubly menacing. What, I wondered, could be the purpose of these? The Palestinians certainly had no possibility of bombing from the air – their only airport had been closed. It seemed simply another detail in the process of intimidation.

As we approached Rafah we passed through the infamous Abu Houli Crossing, one of the many that the Israelis use to control the movements of the Palestinian population in the Gaza Strip and elsewhere in the Occupied Territories, and here we sat again, patiently waiting to be allowed through. A tower on either side controlled the traffic coming in both directions, with only a single line allowed through at any one time. I was surprised to hear the clunk of the vehicle's central locking system and wondered what the danger was.

The dust and the brilliant sunshine drained colour out of everything so that it was almost impossible to read the warning traffic light. Little boys ran along beside the line of waiting cars, peering in through the windows, gesturing to the drivers. Occasionally a door would open and a child would get in. TFH explained that cars with a single person in them weren't allowed through, because the Israelis feared they might be suicide bombers. The children made a little money by hopping into the passenger seat to get the car through the checkpoint. Other small boys moved up and down the line of cars selling chewing gum and sweets.

'Not so bad today,' TFH said as we finally drove through. 'Sometimes you get here to find it's closed for no apparent reason. You could be waiting hours or days, so you have to decide whether to sit it out or turn round – and that includes ambulances and UN vehicles. I try to get down into Gaza once or twice a month, and into the West Bank twice a week, just to check up on what's happening, use my eyes and ears, ask a few difficult questions. It's remarkable what an effect just parking near a checkpoint can sometimes have. When the soldiers on duty realise there's a diplomat watching, the traffic queue often starts flowing again quite quickly. Very satisfying!'

So this was what it meant to be a Palestinian in Gaza – constant humiliation and frustration, your every movement checked and controlled.

The first indication that we had arrived in Rafah was the sight of dense clusters of watchtowers on the skyline. Soon we found ourselves directly beneath their terrifying Big Brother gaze as we drove into the desolation that is Rafah. It must, I suppose, once have been an ordinary town, where people went about their ordinary lives, but it was hard to imagine that now. For every crumbling house left standing, its stucco pockmarked with black bullet holes, there were whole streets that had been demolished.

Here and there a single wall stood up like a broken tooth. In some places only the upper floors of houses had survived, balanced precariously on concrete piers, and in the rubble beneath them children were playing. Balconies hung crazily, windows gaped, mangled steel girders hung silhouetted against the sky like left-over strands of blackened spaghetti.

Sometimes a family had erected a tent beside their demolished house, and these small shelters looked tragic and vulnerable, clinging to the place that had once been home. Rafah seemed to me a ghost town, filled with dispossessed souls who had nowhere else to go. TFH told us that many of the population lived in the open, on the streets, on football pitches, forced from their homes by bulldozers and tanks. In the previous thirty-one months the Israeli Defence Force had demolished 788 homes in Rafah, according to Palestinian sources. 'Why?' I kept thinking. 'How can all this be happening?'

We were heading slowly into the Yibnah district, to the headquarters of an organisation TFH kept referring to as the ISM, where, we were told, we would meet people who would be able to tell us about Tom's last days there; some of them had been with him when he was shot. Anthony was determined to speak to as many witnesses as possible. My overwhelming need was to know, to understand, why Tom had been in this desolate place and what he had been doing here.

Our vehicle wove a tortuous path through the streets, man-oeuvring to left and right as we encountered roadblocks, made from the rubble of bulldozed houses. Here, it seemed, even the fabric of people's own homes was used against them. Whole streets were sealed off. Nothing could enter them, not even ambulances.

We turned the final corner into a central square and there was a large crowd. We could see that we were expected.

The two Range Rovers pulled up on a potholed piece of waste ground between two buildings which, when it rained, must have been a sea of mud. Everything in sight here had a temporary look

– corrugated-iron sheets nailed over damaged doorways, patches of unpainted plaster slapped on to hold disintegrating brickwork together. At the back of the waste ground was a crumbling wall, and across it was written in black and red letters:

> Rachel, Who Came To Rafah
> To Stop The Tanks, We
> Remember her with Love
> And honour as an Inspiration.

I turned towards TFH. I knew that Rachel Corrie was the American girl who had been crushed by an Israeli bulldozer only weeks before, and although I had no inkling then of her significance in Tom's story, I wanted to know more. But TFH was busy directing the driver.

'Park round so we're facing outwards,' I heard him say, waving at the other Range Rover to do the same. As the vehicles reversed, I wondered why this was necessary, though I would soon become familiar with these basic safety precautions.

Our driver, whom TFH now introduced as Sgt Hogan, released the central locking system and we climbed out, picking our way across the potholed patch to the square. My impression was of damaged or half-finished buildings, of breeze-block and cracked stucco, of flat roofs covered in a sharp forest of TV aerials, washing lines and huge water tanks. What seemed like hundreds of people, including a group carrying microphones and hand-held television cameras who were clearly from the press, were waiting patiently, almost blocking the entrance to one of the houses. There was no hint of aggression – in fact the crowd seemed strangely subdued – but I could tell that both TFH and Andy Whittaker were uneasy as they shepherded us quickly through the crowd, past some fruit and vegetable stalls filled with luscious tomatoes and oranges, into an open doorway and up a flight of stone stairs. Inigo Gilmour followed quietly behind.

To describe the room we entered as sparse would be an

understatement. There were a couple of mattresses on the bare floor against the far wall, and a few battered plastic chairs dotted randomly about. The most striking feature was a tattered banner draped against the right-hand wall. For a moment it reminded me strangely of the ancient banners I'd seen in English country churches, transparent with age. There was very little left of this one; it seemed to have been almost torn apart, but it was just possible to read the words: 'We are Internationals – don't shoot'.

There were a number of people in the room and they immediately came towards us, holding out their hands and introducing themselves. Anthony was ashen-faced, but he was immediately focused, asking questions and collecting facts. By this time my terror for Tom, my lack of sleep and the sense of being outside my body had induced a kind of mental paralysis, and I found it impossible to take in people's names, or indeed, initially, very much of what they were saying. After shaking hands I sat down on one of the plastic chairs, and a tall olive-skinned young man with thick curly dark hair and deep-set, intelligent eyes came and sat next to me.

'I am Mohammed. I was with Tom when he was shot,' he said in excellent English. 'I knew him for only a few days, but he had become my friend. He cared about us and about what is going on here. He is a special person. I am very, very sorry for what has happened and I miss him very much.' He put his hand over his eyes and turned away.

I realised with a lurch of my heart that, for the first time, I was with someone who had witnessed what had happened to Tom, who knew, perhaps, his reasons for coming here and what he had been doing in those last hours before the bullet struck.

I put my hand on Mohammed's arm, and we sat in silence for a moment.

'Please,' I said, 'do you know what Tom was doing in Rafah? We had no idea he was here. How did you meet him? Why was he shot? What was he doing to be targeted? I still don't under-stand.'

'I met him first when he came here to the ISM headquarters,' said Mohammed. 'He stayed the first night with the family of Dr Samir, right on the border there, where they are shooting at the houses day and night.'

The depth of my ignorance seemed like a chasm. 'I'm sorry,' I said. 'I know nothing about the ISM. What do the letters stand for? And what did Tom have to do with the ISM?'

'This here,' said Mohammed, sweeping his hand round to take in the rest of the room, 'is the headquarters of the ISM, the International Solidarity Movement. This is a peaceful movement, though the Israeli army and the Israeli press will tell you many lies about us. We try to stop the destruction of Palestinian homes, to monitor and bring attention to what is happening here, the shootings of civilians, the abuses of human rights.' Here Mohammed struck his forehead with his fist and sat for a moment as if in deep gloom. He himself, I felt sure now, was a Palestinian, though there seemed to be young people of many different nationalities in the room.

I had brought a notebook with me and I forced myself to concentrate, writing down Mohammed's replies to my rather incoherent questions, knowing that all this would be of importance later on. When I look at my notes now they seem scrappy and unconnected, but I no longer need them, for I know the story of Tom's last days so well that it has become a part of me, like a continuously running film.

Mohammed told me he had first met Tom a few days before the shooting. Mohammed, Alison and Raph had gone to meet him at the bus stop when he arrived. He had come from a refugee camp in Jordan, where he had been helping to put up tents with the Red Crescent. He had travelled to Gaza from Jerusalem, where he had spent some days in a student hostel on the Nablus Road.

'He had been travelling all day,' said Mohammed, 'and he was thirsty, yes, very thirsty. Tom, he sat on one of those mattresses over there and drank a couple of cans of Coke.'

Yes, that would be Tom, I thought. He drank gallons of Coke, despite my occasional protests. I could just picture him sitting in the corner with his long legs against the wall, tired and dusty, good-humouredly observing the scene around him. Though Tom appeared laid-back, his eyes missed nothing.

Mohammed told me that Tom had come through the Erez Crossing to Rafah under the auspices of the ISM. 'He had heard what happened to Rachel – you know about Rachel Corrie? – she was making peaceful protest here with the ISM, defending Palestinian homes, when the Israeli army ran over her with a bulldozer,' said Mohammed, and there was simmering anger in his voice. 'Tom told me that when he heard about Rachel he wanted to see what was going on here in Gaza, to make a record. He had with him his camera, always his camera, and his little book and pen.' He made the motions of someone writing.

So that was why Tom had come to Rafah. After leaving Iraq, he must have moved on to Jordan, and then come on down here.

For the first two nights in Rafah, Mohammed told me, Tom had stayed with the family of a Dr Samir, whose house was in an area the army were in the process of clearing – that is to say, demolishing – which they called the 'security zone', right on the Egyptian border. The army's way of doing this began, apparently, with intimidation. Each night a tank stationed permanently nearby would position itself at the end of the street and fire warning shots at the houses, terrifying the inhabitants, especially the children, and often injuring and killing civilians. During the day it lurked outside a mosque, making it impossible for local people to go in.

On the day of Tom's shooting, the ISM had decided to stage a peaceful protest by pitching a tent outside the mosque. Tom and Mohammed had met in the morning and gone to a café, where they talked about the proposed demonstration. Mohammed had been feeling very down, very depressed about the whole situation. Tom had asked him what the matter was. 'How are you feeling?' he'd said.

'I told him,' said Mohammed, 'that to me everything was

hopeless. Nothing is ever going to change here for my people. There is no future. But Tom, he put his arm round me and told me I must have hope. That he and the others of the ISM are here to give support, to try to change things for us. He really tried to give me hope.'

When they left the café to go down to the ISM headquarters, Mohammed had felt irritated because, as usual, they were followed by a crowd of inquisitive children and Tom seemed to be encouraging them. 'Already that morning he had been out playing football with some of them,' he said, with some exasperation.

I could easily picture the scene. Tom was at ease with children and was always ready to engage with them, whether it was by showing them his camera or kicking a football around. I could see that particular expression of his which carried a challenge, an invitation to stretch the boundaries, a mischievous look that said, 'Come on then. Have a try!' Whereas Mohammed, depressed as he was, would have seen these youngsters as a nuisance, Tom would have seen them simply as children who needed to have a bit of fun. And my throat suddenly constricted when I thought of Fred.

Now other people began to join us. Anthony, his pen poised over his notebook and now in deep conversation with an older woman I would later discover was called Alison, came over to where we were sitting. A pale, strained-looking young woman with very short hair, whom Mohammed introduced as Alice, appeared with a tray of tea in glass cups. Alice told me that she had been with Tom and Mohammed that day when they had set out from the ISM headquarters, carrying tent poles for the proposed demonstration.

By this time I had given up trying to record what people were saying but Anthony was still asking questions and making detailed notes. Looking at his drawn face I could see how much the experience was costing him. But this, I knew, was his way of dealing with our new and tragic reality. I didn't realise at the time that without it we would have got nowhere. It was the first step of our intense investigation.

It seemed that a couple of other young ISM members, Laura and Amjad, had been sent on ahead to see the lie of the land and had quickly returned to report to the others that there was shooting in the area of the mosque, probably from one of the Israeli Defence Force watchtowers which overlooked the square. By this time the remainder of the party had reached a mound of rubble blocking the street which led to the mosque. They could hear shooting, though they could not see where it was coming from, the tank or the watchtower. A quick discussion ensued, and it was decided to cancel the demonstration – it simply wasn't safe, they decided, and it was the policy of the ISM never to demonstrate in an area where there was shooting.

Meantime the shots continued, and they could see bullets ricocheting off the building beside the mound, on which a group of about twenty or thirty children were playing, apparently accustomed to the danger. But gradually the shots hit lower and lower, flying close over the children's heads, and when they began scuffing up the sand, most of them jumped off the mound and ran away down an alleyway between the houses. Only a boy and two little girls, about six years old, stayed rooted to the spot, terrified and crying for help, not knowing which way to turn.

Apparently Tom had seen a little boy shot in the shoulder after throwing stones at a tank only five days before. Now he saw what was happening, handed back his camera to one of the group and went towards the children. He beckoned to the boy, holding out his arms, lifted him off the mound and carried him down the street out of range of the shooting. Then he went back for the two little girls, bent down and put his arm round one of them.

'They shot him,' said Alice. 'Right there. When he was rescuing those two children. The IDF shot him.'

It was a stark and brutal statement. 'But why?' I said. 'Why would they do that? Surely they could see what he was doing. Couldn't they see he wasn't armed?'

'Oh, sure,' said Alice bitterly. 'He was wearing an orange jacket – we were all wearing orange jackets. Everyone recognises that means you're a non-combatant. Do you think that makes any difference to them? They don't like the ISM. They know we see what they're doing here, and they want us out. Just the way they want the Palestinians out.'

'Do you think it could have been a mistake?' I said. 'The shooting?'

'A mistake?' said Alice. 'You don't make mistakes with telescopic sights like the IDF have got. You could shoot the buttons off someone's coat with those.'

I remembered the reports of the Palestinian gunman targeting an Israeli watchtower.

'But was there any other shooting going on? Was there crossfire?' I said.

'None,' said Alice emphatically. 'Absolutely none. There were no Palestinian gunmen in the area that day.'

There seemed so much more to say, and everyone in the room had something they wanted to tell us, but I could see that Andy and TFH were becoming restless. Andy seemed impatient and tetchy and kept looking at his watch. Finally he stepped out on to the balcony, looked down into the square and came back. 'Right,' he said briskly. 'Come on. It's time to go.'

Alison had disappeared for a moment, but now she was back, and as we began to move towards the door she came over to me. She was holding something wrapped in a plastic bag. 'We've been keeping these to give you,' she said.

'Thank you,' I said automatically, taking the bag and opening it. Inside there was a camera, a notebook and a small green canvas shoulder bag. I recognised the bag. It was Tom's.

FOUR

It was time now to see the place. Numbness enveloped me as though protecting me from napalm. It was my body's anaesthetic, and, strangely, I understood this at the time. What was I about to witness? I knew only that it was another step in confronting the reality of what had happened to Tom. So with Anthony, Andy, TFH and Inigo leading the way and Mohammed and the other ISMers following behind, I descended the stone staircase to where the crowd was still silently waiting. Our visit was clearly a significant event. We were the parents of a non-Palestinian, a Western European, who had reached out to save some Palestinian children. Members of the press surged forward to meet us and Anthony made a short statement.

'We have come here in search of the truth,' he said. 'We want to know who fired this bullet. We have asked the Israeli Defence Force for an open and honest dialogue and an exchange of information. We only want to discover the facts and we are determined to be fair and open-minded. It is, I know, what Tom himself would have wanted.'

Of course, I thought, it *was* what Tom would have wanted. Despite what we had just heard in that upper room, until we had firm evidence it was vital we keep an open mind.

We and the young ISMers climbed into the two vehicles for the journey to Kir Street, near the Egyptian border, where Tom had been shot. Mohammed leaned over to introduce me to another young Palestinian. 'This is Amjad,' he said. 'Whenever anyone is shot by the IDF you will find Amjad there. He has made it his job to rescue the wounded. Often he risks his own life. He also was with Tom on the day he was shot.'

'*Whenever* anyone is shot?' I thought to myself. It sounded almost matter of fact, a normal occurrence. What kind of existence was it, I wondered, that had produced the mixture of compassion and vulnerability that showed in this young man's eyes. Amjad, I later learned, was only seventeen, but he looked far older. In the coming weeks I was to discover more about his almost obsessional mission. He had developed a name for himself in Rafah, and when a slight figure in pyjamas appeared on television at the scene of a shooting, people immediately recognised Amjad.

As we drove towards Kir Street I realised we had an escort. The Palestinian Authority's military police had been waiting for us. They drove in front of us, jolting along, tightly packed into a rickety looking jeep or hanging perilously off the sides and back. Dressed in black and heavily armed, they looked ominous. As they bounced along at considerable speed, the guns hanging from their shoulders swung violently with every bump in the road. I wondered why they were coming with us – to control the crowds? Did we need protecting and if so what were they protecting us from? Looking at Mohammed I could tell he was angry. 'They shouldn't have come,' he said quietly. 'They are only attracting attention. They make the Israelis jittery.' The media followed us in a procession of cars and trucks.

Hundreds of people, including crowds of children, were running with us, moving along the pavements and from time to time blocking the road so that we had to stop. As we approached the street, Mohammed began pointing things out: over there the street called Salah El Din Street which runs parallel to the Egyptian border marked by Israel's huge new steel 'security wall'; over there the Israeli Defence Force watchtowers.

We parked and got out. The street itself, Kir Street, was wide, its barren but still inhabited buildings studded with holes, like colanders. It ran at right angles to the Egyptian border. At the border end was a square containing a crumbling mosque, into which Salah El Din Street also ran. Beyond that was wasteland – part of the so-called 'security zone' Israel was creating along the border by demolishing Palestinian homes. Overlooking the square – now also part of the security zone and in line for demolition – we could see, very clearly, the IDF watchtowers.

Mohammed pointed out to us the tank, motionless and menacing in some long grass, heavily camouflaged so that it was hard to see it at first. This was the tank that positioned itself in front of the mosque, and every night after curfew peppered the houses in the street with intimidating shots – shots, we were told, that had recently wounded two boys from a house nearby known as the Abu Jabr house. It was this routine violence and intimidation, we now knew, and the fact that the tank had been preventing people going into the mosque, that had caused the ISM to plan a peaceful demonstration, a plan which had brought Tom to this street on the day he was shot.

In the middle of the street was a mound of sand-covered rubble and tangled iron girders, the customary IDF barrier made from the ruins of demolished houses. This was where the children had been playing. 'They're like playgrounds for the children,' said Mohammed. 'They run up and down them. The IDF shoot from the watchtowers all the time for no reason, just to frighten, and if the shots are at high level the children go on playing. They are used to it. It's when they start shooting low that it gets scary.'

I tried to imagine the scene on that day. The group of children playing on the mound. A low bullet suddenly scuffing up the sand, and then another. The children scattering, a boy and two little girls hesitating, rigid with fear, not knowing where to turn. Tom, in his orange jacket, gesticulating to the boy, lifting him to safety, holding out his hands again as he came back for the girls. And then . . .

Slowly Anthony and I approached the mound. I felt frozen with terror at what I was about to see. The crowd moved and swayed with us, involved yet silent and respectful. Beautiful children with lovely spirited, open smiles, ran in and out of the crowd and jumped on and off the mound – among them the same children perhaps who had been playing on it that day. Amjad indicated a large lump of concrete near the foot of the mound. There was still blood on ground: Tom's blood. This was where he had fallen. Beside the mound was a building with a pitted garage door . . . bullet holes at eye level . . . its wall was spattered with blood. I felt a physical pain, as if my heart was breaking. At the end of a long tunnel in my mind, I could see Tom lying on the ground, hurt, bleeding. Anthony and I stood silently, looking, utterly bereft.

Tom, dearest Tom, I pray that you suffered no pain, that the shot which entered your head and shattered your quick brain did so too swiftly for you to feel anything. That simple human gesture of reaching out to those children, which made you vulnerable, was so typical of you.

The ominous top of the IDF watchtower rose menacingly at the end of the street, to the side of some derelict buildings and behind a massive wall, with the tank squatting further over to the right. Although you could discern no movement we were aware that the military could see us, that we were being observed through those darkened windows encircling the watchtower, though the spot where Tom was shot was not in the 'security zone'. I could feel the eyes of the crowd on us too, sympathetic yet also wary. We were people from another world, another place. We know suffering, their looks said. We've seen it all before. I was painfully aware of the number of disabled people among the crowd, people with thin faces and unseeing eyes, people who limped or moved on crutches, or nursed misshapen hands.

After a few minutes we moved cautiously out beyond the mound of rubble into the 'security zone' so that we could see the watchtower and the surrounding area more clearly. I couldn't understand why TFH and Andy were suddenly bristling with vigilance until they told us that many Palestinian civilians stepping into the zone had been shot. It made me wonder what policy allowed such casual shooting so near to a civilian area. But today the IDF had clearly been forewarned, and hundreds of Palestinians moved with us.

Anthony, with his lawyer's ability to apply himself to the task in hand, to concentrate on detail, began observing the scene from different angles and heights, trying to gauge what would have been in the sightlines of both the watchtower and the tank. Tom's height, both standing and crouching, the height of the mound of rubble, the block of concrete – he was taking them all into consideration, I knew, as he continued to measure and make notes. People crowded round, which made the task difficult. Others motioned them to stand away, but as soon as the crowd had parted it flowed back again, like sand.

A man came up to us and started pointing to the bloodstained wall. At first I couldn't understand what he was trying to tell me, then I realised he was pointing at the bullet holes, starting high and going lower, lower, lower. 'He's telling you they shoot low, they shoot children,' said Alice. Amjad stood on the mound, gesticulating: 'This is where Tom stood. This is where he reached out his arms.' Mohammed began telling Anthony and me again how Tom had fallen and how Sahir and Amjad had managed to lift him and carry him down the street away from the mound, while Alice screamed at them to try to staunch the blood. How they had laid Tom down and pressed a wad of cotton to the wound, how Alice tried mouth-to-mouth resuscitation, while Raph got out his mobile and his notebook and phoned the British Embassy, giving them Tom's name and passport number, shouting into the phone that a British civilian had been shot. 'Please will you tell the Israelis to stop shooting, please tell them to stop shooting,' he had pleaded over and over again. A young man called Nicola had made signals with his hand for the shooting to stop, and the tower had stopped shooting. Clearly whoever had fired the shot was aware of what had happened.

I looked at Alice. She was silent and very pale. I knew from Mohammed that only three weeks before she had been with Rachel Corrie when she died.

I turned to our interpreter and asked him about the little boy Tom had rescued. His name, he told me after some enquiries among the crowd, was Salem Baroum. Someone went off to find him, and minutes later he appeared, led by a woman I took to be his mother. Clearly she knew who I was, and the interpreter told me she wished to thank me. 'She weeps with you,' he said, 'that you have lost your brave son who saved her son. She prays with you. She knows that it is only because of your son that her son is alive.'

Little Salem hung back, withdrawn, behind his mother. He was a handsome, serious-looking child of about five. He was completely silent, utterly traumatised, I was told, by the shooting. He had not spoken a word since the previous Friday. I smiled at him and knelt down, taking his hand, speaking quietly to him, hoping the sound of my voice might reassure him, though I knew he could not understand me. He stood mute and rigid, gazing at me. On an impulse I put my arms round him and lifted him up. When there was a flash of cameras, it alarmed us both, and I could feel his body tauten. Perhaps it wasn't the right thing to do, but I was overcome by the thought that this was the last human being who had touched Tom before he was shot.

The women came closer but the men stayed on the edge of the group eyeing me warily, even with a kind of cynicism. Whatever they were feeling, I didn't blame them. These incidents, I now realised, were a daily occurrence for them. How different was our life experience, how different the backdrop to our own personal loss. But from the women I sensed empathy, solidarity. It made me feel guilty – it seemed the wrong way round. They wanted to talk, to tell me their stories through the interpreter. I learned of a son killed on the way to the supermarket. Another shot through a misted window as he took a drink of water. A mother shot as she hung out the washing to dry on the roof. An engineer picked off as he tried to mend a rooftop water tank riddled with bullet holes, which was the family's only source of water. These were some of the multitude of stories held within these shattered streets, within their homes, their families, only reaching the world occasionally through the reports of courageous foreign correspondents: days and nights of loss, intimidation, humiliation and destruction.

As they talked they seemed painfully resigned, without energy. 'This is the way we live', they seemed to be saying. 'This is how it is.' Yet underneath it all I felt the tremendous strength of spirit that I came so to admire among the Palestinians. I was struck by the contrast between the adults and the children, who hadn't yet lost their energy and their ability to smile. The older they got, the fewer smiles there seemed to be. Feelings seemed deadened and you could see it in their eyes.

I wanted to tell these women that I shared their loss, their exclusion, their humiliation. I wanted them to know that though Rafah was a place of tragedy for me, it was now inscribed on my heart, a never-to-be-forgotten part of my daily life and thought, linked by an unbreakable thread to my home and family far away in London. Were they wondering whether it had been worth-while telling me their stories? Would it matter to me? Could it make any difference?

We were being called back to the Embassy cars, and reluctantly I turned and walked away to join the others. TFH had arranged for us to call on our way back at the European Hospital in Gaza City, where Tom had first been treated, and he was insistent that we must be back at the Erez Crossing before dark. As we climbed in an old man with pleading eyes and reaching hands tried to prevent me from closing the door. I leaned towards him. What was he trying to tell me?

'Close the door,' commanded Andy.

I heard the clunk of the central locking system. I couldn't even wind down the window to wave goodbye. I could only stare in shocked silence at the old man through the bullet-proof glass. As our vehicles pulled away from the crowd I caught glimpses of faces. They looked fragile and vulnerable, accustomed somehow to being forgotten. During the years of conflict the world had repeatedly turned its back on them and you could tell that they were used to it.

I knew that I would never forget them. The image of the old

man, the whites of his eyes browned from the sheer hardship of life, is with me to this day. I had been in Rafah less than twenty-four hours, but what I had seen had shaken me to my foundations. Before I had only seen television's censored images. It was the first time I had truly come face to face with the obscenity of what oppression had done to this community. I felt a huge responsi-bility. I made an inner vow to return to Rafah, this town that had previously been wholly unknown to me, but next time with something to give.

The European Hospital was a modest, low-rise building in a relatively green and quiet area of Gaza City. Anthony, TFH and I were met in the entrance hall by a small group of doctors, one of whom introduced himself as Dr Jihad Abu Daya. We followed him into a meeting room where we all sat round a table and Dr Abu Daya, after expressing his sympathy in a most touching and sincere way, described to us the afternoon Tom had been brought in.

Directly after the shooting Tom had been taken by taxi to a small local hospital in Rafah, where they had been unequipped to treat him, and he had been sent on to the European Hospital by ambulance. 'When he arrived your son was bleeding very, very heavily from the wound in his head,' said Dr Abu Daya. 'We stopped the bleeding by compression and gave him fluid and many pints of blood. He had multiple fractures in his skull – the bullet entered the side of his head and exited at the back. His life was clearly in danger and he needed surgical intervention. Un-fortunately we were not equipped to make such an operation here. We took a number of CAT scans, however.'

We asked if the fractures could have been made another way, perhaps by something like a baseball bat. The doctor smiled. 'Let me show you,' he said.

Dr Abu Daya rose and we followed him once again to a small office further up the corridor. The blinds in the windows were lowered, and suddenly on a screen I saw the ghostly outline of

Tom's skull. As one scan followed another Dr Abu Daya described the damage and pointed to the concentrations of irregular sized dark marks that appeared on each. So transfixed was I by the sight of Tom's skull that it was hard for me to take in the detail of what he was saying, but I understood that these countless marks were fragments of metal, shards of the bullet with which Tom had been shot. The bullet had exploded on impact and these hundreds of tiny pieces of metal had lodged in his brain and caused terrible damage. My mind seemed to have travelled outside my body and I couldn't breathe. Voices, words, registered in a far-off space.

'We have never seen this kind of bullet before, and we think it may be a dumdum,' said one of the doctors.

'A dumdum bullet?'

'A bullet that explodes on impact. It does much more damage than an ordinary bullet would.'

Later we would learn from a ballistics expert that any bullet fired at such close range as this one explodes on impact — it need not be a dumdum. But these were doctors, not ballistics experts. One thing I knew — that the damage to Tom's brain was more extensive even than I had imagined. Here for the first time, even though imperfectly understood, was the medical evidence. For a while I sat silent with distress, dimly aware of the empathy of the doctors and of TFH. But gradually questions began to surface and I was struck by the calm and open way in which the doctors answered both Anthony and me. While Anthony continued to write in his notebook I asked for copies of all the CAT scans and medical notes. The doctors could not have been more human and helpful — I knew that they probably witnessed such cases every day. It was clear that they had put themselves at our disposal, and were prepared to spend as much time with us as we needed. The atmosphere felt very different from that in the Soroka Hospital — closer and more encircling. There, though I was aware of the technical sophistication, the efficiency of the care, I had somehow felt shut out, but here I immediately felt included by the doctors' warm humanity.

As we left we were handed copies of the CAT scans and Tom's medical notes. I noticed on the way back to the car park that TFH was carrying a black plastic bin liner, but I didn't ask what was in it.

The journey back through the desolate countryside and the grim wastes of the Erez Crossing was silent and subdued. Darkness was falling as we drew up outside the hotel, and suddenly I felt depression, like a stifling grey blanket, enveloping me as we got out of the Range Rover and TFH followed us into the lobby. So this was our reality now – a bleak hotel where no one met our eye in a country where no one in an official position had yet seen fit to acknowledge our existence, our family separated, and our son lying at death's door less than a mile away. I felt disorientated and at a loss. The day had shown us all too clearly that nothing in this chaotic situation was simple. But where were we to begin?

Now TFH handed me the black plastic bin liner. 'Tom's clothes,' he said. 'You'll need to keep them as evidence. I should ask the hotel to put them in the deep freeze.'

Upstairs in Anthony's room we sat on the bed. On the floor in front of us were the black plastic bin liner and the carrier bag Alison had given me containing Tom's spiral-bound notebook, his camera and his small green canvas bag.

Silently I opened the bin liner and began to remove its contents: first Tom's cotton trousers, slashed up the sides where they must have been cut off him; his T-shirt, similarly cut; his orange fluorescent non-combatant's jacket; his black photographer's waistcoat with its many pockets. Everything stiff with blood.

I felt in the waistcoat pockets and pulled out the familiar cigarette lighter and a packet of Camels. There was something so strangely ordinary about what I was doing. How many hundreds of times in the past had I pulled mud-caked clothing out of plastic bags, felt in the pockets before putting them in the washing machine? It's what mothers do, I thought. Yet now it was not mud, but the evidence of our son's shooting. Here was his blood.

In another pocket I found the Swiss Army knife, Anthony's last present to him. When he saw this Anthony turned and moved towards the window where he remained for some minutes, hunched over the sill. I felt desperately concerned for him, knowing how hard it was for him to talk about his feelings. It was all too much to bear.

We opened the small green canvas bag. This was the only luggage Tom had brought with him from Jerusalem, so he couldn't have imagined staying more than a couple of weeks. Silently we unpacked it and I was struck by the neatness and economy of the packing. Everything was absolutely organised – boxer shorts, T-shirts and socks tightly rolled, plasters and nail scissors packed away in one of the inside pockets. His foreign currency was in another, the money for different countries separately wrapped. There was a small pencil case with numerous pens – I remembered Tom had told us in one of his e-mails that they dried up in no time in this kind of climate.

I upended the black bin liner to make sure there was nothing left in it, and a small package fell out. It was Tom's watch, and, seeing it, a pang of the sharpest grief shot through me. I could see it on his wrist. He was never without it, and somehow it conjured him up as nothing else had.

Our brains and bodies were too blasted for us to do much else that night, though the phone kept ringing with calls from journalists of every nationality. There was a sense of urgency which was to become part of our daily life. Anthony answered the calls patiently, courteously and concisely. The message was always the same. We were seeking the truth, not revenge, and we were keeping an open mind.

After frustrating and ineffective telephone calls early in the day between Anthony and the British Passport Office over the renewal of Fred's passport, Ann, the mother of Fred's close friend Joe, had taken charge, and arrangements had now been made for Sophie and Fred to fly out the following night. We called Sophie. Her voice, when she answered, sounded faint and very far away.

'Hello, darling,' I said. 'Are you all right?'

'Yes. How's Tom?' I could hear the quaver in her voice.

How could I possibly describe at this distance what I had seen and experienced that day?

'It's a very modern, efficient hospital,' I said. 'Everything's being done that can possibly be done. Billy's at the hospital now. It's all quite complicated. I think you'll understand more when you see Tom.'

There was a pause. Then, 'Mum, I'm not sure I really do want to,' Sophie said. 'Not now anyway. Maybe I should come later. It sort of feels right being at home. I've got Catherine staying here with me and everyone's helping . . .' Her voice tailed off.

I understood. In a matter of a few days everything in Sophie's life had been turned upside down. We were all in deep distress and she was terrified, particularly at the though that Tom might be in pain. No wonder she was clinging to the secure, the familiar. The thought of seeing Tom was just too much to bear. But if she didn't come now, she might never see him again.

'Darling,' I said, 'you must do what feels right. But I think you and Fred need to come. Everything's so uncertain.'

'You're right,' she said, after a while, with typical directness.

We talked a little more about Fred, who was staying with friends, and about the arrangements for the following day. TFH would meet them both at Tel Aviv on Wednesday morning and drive them down to Be'ersheva.

' 'Night, Mum. Give my love to Dad and Bill,' she said finally in a small voice that stabbed at my heart.

' 'Night, darling,' I said, relieved that in forty-eight hours we would all be together, but devastated by the thought of what she and Fred had to face.

I went to bed deeply disturbed, going over and over the events of the day, my thoughts always returning to Tom, like a compass returning to the north. The noise in the corridor outside made sleep impossible. I knew it was Passover, and the seventh floor, on which we were sleeping, was full. In fact, it seemed to be the only floor of this big hotel that was being used. Children were running up and down, shouting and laughing. Groups of adults went backwards and forwards to the lift talking in loud voices. At one point there was a thump on my door, as if it had been hit by a football. I looked at the clock. It was well past midnight.

Suddenly outraged, I got out of bed, put on my dressing-gown and opened the door. As I stepped out into the corridor, a body cannoned into me, almost knocking me over, and a young boy of about ten took one look at me, turned, and skidded away across the polished floor. His father, dressed in Orthodox black coat and homburg was a few steps behind him, and I fully expected some kind of apology, some reproof to the child for running and for bumping into another guest so carelessly. But the man gave me not a single glance, carrying on up the corridor as if he simply hadn't noticed me. I stood there, astonished by the bad manners, the lack of acknowledgement that this was an inconsiderate way to behave when there were people staying in the hotel who might wish to sleep.

I closed my door, sat on the bed and turned on the bedside light. On a table by the telephone was the carrier bag that Alison had given me, containing Tom's camera and his notebook. I took out the little spiral-bound book and held it. It felt so precious I was almost unwilling to open it. Eventually I turned back the cover and there, on the first page, was Tom's careful, even handwriting. I had an image of him in his room at home, writing, always writing and recording, with his feet up on the window ledge. But these were words written in very different circumstances. The first pages described his days in Jerusalem, waiting to go into Gaza with the ISM. I would come back to those. Now I turned quickly to his arrival in Rafah. The place so haunted me, I seemed unable to leave it.

'Since I arrived I have been shot at, gassed, chased by soldiers, had "sound" grenades thrown within metres of me, been hit by falling debris and been in the way of a ten-ton D-9 bulldozer that didn't stop', I read.

'As we approached, I kept expecting a part of my body to be hit by an "invisible" force and shot of pain. It took a huge amount of will to continue. I wondered what it would be like to be shot, and strangely I wasn't too scared.'

It was so personal, so immediate, seeing Tom's handwriting, hearing his voice. This was Tom speaking, in the last days before speech was lost to him. I read on, traumatised by the sight of the words, unable to put the notebook down. In it Tom described his activities with the ISM during the previous week. On the first night he had slept in the home of a Dr Samir and his family, whose house was the only one left standing in an area bulldozed by the IDF, and who had refused to move. The family was subject to constant intimidation, and it was policy for ISM members to sleep in such houses as a gesture of solidarity. It was the house in which Rachel Corrie had stayed before she died.

'There is an Israeli tank less than 20 metres from my bed that was posted there two weeks ago,' Tom wrote. *'The room next to mine has several large-calibre bullet-holes in each wall, many of them having travelled through the brick . . . I asked Dr Samir if his children slept OK with the tank so close. He said, "For the first few nights they cried. Now it is OK. They are more used to it."'*

The journal conjured up pictures of Tom and other ISM members, highly visible in their orange peaceworkers' jackets, sitting guard while Palestinian plumbers fixed the sewage system which had been dug up by the Israelis.

'Gaza is the most densely populated place on earth', I read. *'1.2 million people in an area 10 km by 40 km, with 40 per cent of the "Palestinian Land" owned by settlers.'* This was followed by a page of mathematical calculations, and the conclusion: *'The average settler in the Gaza Strip owns 115 times as much land as the average Palestinian. The plan is to make life so bad that they all just get up and leave and the Israelis are using every trick in the book . . . They are creating their own holocaust, but using bureaucracy to cover it . . . What is going on is far beyond what is necessary, or even relative, to national security and it is all underhand.'*

As I read on I could feel Tom's passionate anger at what he was seeing, yet I could also hear him arguing with himself, playing devil's advocate, determined not to be carried away by propaganda from either side. He wrote of '*the frustration of being in the middle of various factions and their hype and being unable to ascertain what the truth is . . . in situations like this half-truths can build on each other exponentially to create a massive wrong conclusion*'. Though he liked Dr Samir enormously, did he really know the full story? he asked himself: '*The thousands of bullet-holes in south frontier houses may have been in response to direct fire. I know nothing about Dr Samir's history.*' I could feel the tension between what human decency and his own instincts were telling him, and his determination to be fair.

Anthony had mentioned to me that, in the car on the way to Heathrow before Tom had left for Iraq, they had been discussing the situation in Palestine, and Tom had actually been putting the Israeli point of view. It was part of Tom's nature to try to see both sides. As I finally turned out the light and lay down to attempt to sleep, along with the ever-present grief, I felt the most immense respect for his thinking and for what he'd done.

FIVE

Tuesday 15 April

I woke early and, as on every morning since the previous Friday, it took only a split second before reality closed in. After breakfast in the impersonal hotel dining room, Anthony and I prepared to go to the hospital. I felt disorientated – even the process of finding a taxi in this unfamiliar and unfriendly place was a mystery, and it was clearly no good appealing for help with anything to the staff on the reception desk, whose reactions seemed to range from unco-operative to rude. When I'd spoken to the girl on the desk about storing Tom's clothes in a freezer she had broken off, without apology, in mid-conversation to take a phone call. I stood waiting with the bloodied clothes in a bag. With media interviews being held in the foyer, the hotel staff must have known why we were in Israel; it was hard to understand this unfeeling blankness.

In the taxi Anthony and I worried again over the doctor's bizarre suggestion that Tom's injury was 'commensurate with a blow from a baseball bat'. Having seen the scans at the European Hospital it now seemed doubly incomprehensible. What on earth could it mean? Was the implication that Tom's wound had been caused by someone at close range – a Palestinian?

Yet there it was – 'gunshot wound' – written clearly on Tom's notes. And this was at an Israeli hospital experienced in dealing with gunshot wounds.

We felt deeply uneasy, and angry too, at what seemed like an attempt to mislead us. We were due to meet the medical staff that morning, and now we felt unsure about how to approach it.

I fully understood that we were feeling our way into another culture, and that this was likely to be uncomfortable. The 'benchmarks' were bound to be different and I had to keep a check on my own personal responses. But my sense of alienation, indeed irritation, was sharpened by the jarring sight of the blue guard posts at the entrance to the hospital. They were manned by the usual young armed soldiers – or were they military police? – clearly bored and uncomfortable in the already intense heat. Every visiting vehicle was stopped at the barrier and searched. The soldiers spoke peremptorily to our driver in Hebrew, checked his identification, opened the boot, peered inside the car. Before we were permitted to enter the hospital itself, we stood in a queue while my bag and Anthony's briefcase were opened and searched. I didn't question the need for security, but the sheer level of it everywhere we went had begun to seem almost provocative. Whose interests were being served, I wondered, by this state of advanced paranoia?

Again we mounted the stone stairs to the second floor, passed the rows of white-robed Arab men sitting smoking under the 'No Smoking' sign. Yesterday, on that terrible first visit, I had been almost too numb to feel fearful. I knew at some level that we had already lost Tom, and it was as if a part of myself was dying. Now I was filled with dread, partly at the thought of what we might learn from the medical staff about Tom's condition, partly because I knew I was in uncharted territory where I could not, at the moment, distinguish who was for us and who against – or, indeed, whether such divisions existed at all.

We found Billy in the waiting-room, drinking a cup of coffee with the same group of young people we had met there yesterday, amid the same confusion of sleeping bags and cast-off clothing. He was very quiet, even for Billy. Deep shock was still written on his face. He looked drawn and strained round the eyes, and I guessed he was not sleeping much. I also wondered whether he was drinking enough water in this hot climate. Though I had accepted that the hospital was where Billy was living for the present, and that this was where he wanted to be, the situation worried me. Yet I pushed these anxieties to the back of my mind. At present what energy I had was concentrated on Tom and I couldn't help it.

Anthony went to speak to the medical staff and returned to say that the consultant in charge of Tom's case, Professor Gurman, and his team, would meet us in half an hour. Tom's dressings were being changed; in the meantime we went in search of a quiet place where Anthony could settle with his laptop and his mobile phone. We found a secluded corner in the large hospital cafeteria, which looked out on to a pleasant garden in the centre of the building, aflame with red camellias and orange canna lilies. It was a place which would become a focal point for us during the coming weeks.

As I sat gazing out of the window, I realised that I was looking directly across at a grassy fenced-in compound – the helicopter pad where Tom had first arrived. Terrible pictures of him arriving in the dark, being rushed on a stretcher to the Accident and Emergency entrance with medical staff running alongside flashed into my mind. During our time at the hospital I could never pass the helicopter pad without feeling inwardly clamped by fear, and I found myself conflicted, alternately drawn to stare at it and then immediately blotting it out.

Anthony was single-minded about collecting witness statements from ISM members and others who had been in Rafah on the day of the shooting. One or two of them had by now left Israel and would have to be tracked down. He was keen to make contact with a young South African photographer, Garth Stead, who, we were told, had been present and had started filming seconds after Tom was shot. We had also received a call from a journalist called Sandra Jordan who had been filming in Rafah on that day for the Channel 4 series *Dispatches*. She had been in Kir Street within minutes of Tom's being shot and had filmed the subsequent terrifying scenes when he was transferred from Palestinian ambulance to Israeli helicopter. She was anxious to interview us and to provide any help she could.

Anthony's mobile rang constantly with calls from the international media asking for interviews, updates and our views on the situation. All we could say at present was that we had requested a meeting with the Israeli Defence Force through our Embassy in Tel Aviv, and had so far received no response. As I sat looking out on to the garden while Anthony took one call after another, it seemed to me that everyone was concerned to speak to us about Tom's shooting except those most closely involved – the Israeli government and the Israeli army. We had received no word of sympathy or sorrow for Tom; no official had come to meet us at the airport, the hotel or the hospital. Despite our requests for a meeting, so far there had been no reciprocity, no reaching out. It felt as if we were in a vacuum, with nothing to respond to or relate to. Was this a society so cocooned in a kind of membrane of unawareness, a society so insular and self-absorbed that it had no concept of how others see it, of why it was necessary to behave humanely? I was not looking for acknowledgement because our son was special in any way, but because he was a human being who had been seriously wounded, in all probability by the Israeli army. Why was it so difficult for the authorities to make a private statement, let alone a public one? Was so little value put on an individual life? It would have been a human response due to anyone in those circumstances, whether from Britain, Palestine or anywhere else. Yet such empathy was entirely lacking.

It was time for our meeting with the medical staff. Anthony, Billy and I were shown into a room inside the intensive care area where Professor Gurman, three other doctors and a nurse were waiting. Professor Gurman was tall and greying, with a slight beard, professional but kindly. We all sat at a table and Professor Gurman, with the help of the other doctors, described very clearly the operation they had carried out to remove some of the detritus from around the wound in Tom's head. Further operations would be needed, they told us, because, though they had managed to stop most of the bleeding, there was still bleeding from Tom's left ear.

All three of us had been deeply shocked and upset by the sight of Tom's terribly swollen head. We asked whether anything could be done to reduce the swelling.

'Unfortunately there is nothing we can do,' said Professor Gurman. 'The bullet entered above the left eyebrow and exited at the back of the skull. There is very severe damage to the left side of the brain and because of this there is enormous pressure. Now I am afraid this has also begun to affect the right side of the brain.'

At this point Billy rose quickly and left the room. I could see that he was in acute distress. My instinct was to follow him and hold him tight, but I was uncertain whether to go or stay.

Professor Gurman paused sympathetically for a moment. Then he said, 'I am not sure whether you quite understand that there is very little hope at all of any recovery. From the severity of your son's wound, we are surprised that he has lasted these few days. I am sorry to have to say this, but it is best to tell you the truth.'

We sat in silence. Then Anthony said, 'This wound was clearly caused by a bullet, was it not, as stated on the medical notes?' Professor Gurman inclined his head. 'So you will understand,' Anthony continued, 'if we ask you to retain any detritus, any shards of metal or relevant tissue that you remove during the operations. It will be important as evidence.'

I sensed a certain tension in the room, but Professor Gurman said, 'We will, of course, do what we can.' I could only guess what he and the other medical staff were feeling. I had no doubt, now, that they were highly professional, and that they would do their best to save the life of any patient, whether British, Palestinian or Israeli. Yet here they were faced with a highly contentious situation – a foreign national, a civilian, who had entered what they would term a war zone and had been shot by their own army. I felt they were choosing their words carefully, conscious that this was a high-profile case and that they must not put a foot wrong. They were all no doubt aware of the international media interest in Tom's shooting, of the political and diplomatic implications of the case. For some of them it must have raised personal conflicts – and how were we to know that there were not other pressures too?

We sought answers to many questions. Was there any possibility of improvement for Tom, however slight? Would he ever be in a condition to be moved? Had he any awareness at all of his surroundings? Did he feel pain? One of the young doctors explained that they had carried out a Glasgow Coma Scale Assessment. This test is used in traumatic brain injury to monitor the patient's level of consciousness. Eye, verbal and motor responses are tested on a scale from three to fifteen, anything below eight indicating a severe brain injury, and three being the worst, denoting that nothing more than the main organs were working. Tom was on three.

I was fighting back tears as we eventually left the room, and Anthony looked straight ahead of him. What we had heard seemed so final. Tom was never going to regain consciousness. His body was barely functioning. Yet a part of me still could not accept it, could not entirely give up hope.

We stood helplessly in the ante-room for a moment. Then Anthony said he must get back to the cafeteria and his computer – there was so much to do, so many calls to make and answer, so many witnesses to trace. This, I knew now, was his mission – to gather every shred of evidence he could. It was his way of coping with the situation, of doing his very best for Tom. Though shaped by his lawyer's training to question and assess, I knew it was not this that was driving him. For Anthony, as for both of us, uncovering the truth was a moral question. It was what he expected of himself, and was part of the person he was. And we both knew that Tom would have done the same.

I went in search of Billy and was told that he was in the Intensive Care Unit. A kind nurse called Netta, who spoke some English, helped me with the ritual that was to become so familiar: the washing of hands, the putting on of gloves and gown, then the slow, painful walk down the disinfectant-smelling ward, past all the anonymous beds with their tragic occupants to where, at the end, I could see Tom lying, still and pale, with Billy stationed beside him.

I stood gazing silently down at him – so near and yet so far. I was still too frightened to touch him in case I should dislodge some vital wire. I wanted to take his hand, but there was a clip on it and I had no idea what it was for. His face was covered by an oxygen mask.

Tom, how can I reach you now that you have no words – you to whom words have been so important, who used them so thoughtfully? What is left for someone who has no language? How can I reach you in your blank and solitary world? How can I comfort you?

I began trying to recall my research into particular neurological impairments and the highly complex functions of the different parts of the brain. Without the left side of his brain, he had lost the use of language, the ability to think mathematically, at which he had been so brilliant. But perhaps with the right side some awareness remained. Perhaps he might recognise the perfume I usually wore, and feel that I was near him. I must always remember to wear it. I must find some hand cream with a familiar scent – lavender perhaps – and massage his hands and feet when I dared. Yet if the parts of his brain associated with emotions were damaged, would he be able to feel comfort?

Billy and I sat silently on either side of Tom's bed. From time to time a nurse came to check the various dials and graphs. I had no way of understanding what was happening, what the nurse was seeing. All I could see was my son, lying utterly vulnerable. I knew that we could lose him at any moment. How had he clung on to life until now? Was he in pain? Could he feel pleasure?

Occasionally I looked across at Billy. He was quite still, his eyes always on Tom, though when a nurse arrived he became suddenly alert, with the kind of streetwise awareness I knew so well. I don't know how long we sat there together, but by the time I rose my whole body ached with concentration, with the weight of anguish and responsibility I felt. Billy looked far away, but I wondered if he felt this too.

I found Anthony still in the canteen. He had been joined by two of the human shields who introduced themselves as Michelle and Nathan. Michelle had a fine-boned face and olive skin, and looked Latin. Nathan was fair-haired and softly spoken. I quickly formed the impression of two sincere and thoughtful people. Anthony explained to me that they had been with Tom in Baghdad. They had left with him for Amman, and the three had spent a fortnight in Jordan in the Al Rweished refugee camp as volunteers, putting up tents and looking after Iraqi refugees. They had finally parted company in Jerusalem some days later, Tom to go to Rafah, Michelle and Nathan intending to go to the West Bank.

'We were walking along a road near Nablus when someone told us that a British national called Tom had been shot in the head in Rafah and was in hospital in Be'ersheva,' Michelle said. 'We knew it must be him and of course we came straight here.' There was an intensity about the way she spoke and her eyes filled with tears. I could tell that Nathan, too, was deeply shaken. They had all been through so much, and I was deeply moved at the affection and care this group felt for Tom and for one another. I was beginning to gain a very different impression of them from that put about by the Israeli media. These were no foolish, impulsive troublemakers, I could tell, but serious people with a social conscience and an awareness of human rights, and the integrity to take a stand.

So many things seemed to be happening simultaneously. Sophie told us of a letter from the Features Department of the *Guardian*, explaining that for a long time the paper had been campaigning for peace and equality in the Middle East, and that every time they heard of the death of an innocent person it stiffened their resolve to bring it to the world's attention in order to prevent it happening again. Recently they had published some e-mails Rachel Corrie had sent to her parents and it had provoked a huge response from around the world.

'I know Tom was doing photographic work in the region', the letter went on. 'And I wondered if, when you felt it was appropriate, you might consider running his work in the *Guardian*. I know he was there documenting the daily life of Rafah and we would really like to reprint his work in a similar way to our reproduction of Rachel's e-mails.'

I thought of Tom's camera, back at the hotel. There had barely been time even to look at it and I had put it and his journal aside.

'I have a huge amount of video footage of Tom to show you, taken during the seven weeks when we were together,' said Michelle. I believe you have Tom's camera, and I can help you select and e-mail photographs to the newspaper if you wish.'

So it was with Michelle, later that day, that we began to look at Tom's own photos taken in Rafah – and not only in Rafah. Anthony had now, finally, accessed e-mails and photographs in which Tom recorded a day he had spent in Gaza City on 9 April – two days before he was shot. The previous day two F16 rockets had been fired into the city in an attempt by Israeli Intelligence to target a group of Hamas and Fatah members who were travelling together in a car. The first rocket missed, but the second hit, killing everyone in the car and wounding three dozen civilians in the area, four of whom had later died.

Tom had got caught up that day in what was called the 'march for the martyrs'. There were pictures of the assassinated men's families and friends carrying the bodies wrapped in green Hamas flags through the streets, of running, shouting crowds and masked gunmen, '*It's kind of intimidating when you're the only non-Palestinian out of 850 and they're chanting: "Kill the Americans and Jews, drive them out of Palestine"*,' Tom wrote. I admired his boldness. He could have been mistaken for an American. Yet somehow I knew that in such a situation he would probably have been safe. Tom had such an unjudgemental way of looking directly at you with those friendly, intelligent, slightly challenging eyes. He had the true writer's desire to move through situations unseen, to observe and experience without disrupting the flow of events in his presence. Everything about him told you that that he was unthreatening and open-minded.

There were many more photos too, dozens of them, for, as Michelle showed us, Tom had concealed one photo beneath another as a security precaution. They showed Rafah's tragic, crumbling buildings with their gaping windows, tottering upper floors, shattered beams and trailing wires; ISM members standing in the path of a gigantic advancing bulldozer as it attempted to demolish a Palestinian house; and the smiling children of Dr Samir's extended family. *'Yesterday morning, two of the brothers were shot by snipers in the tower within two hours of each other,'* Tom wrote in one of his e-mails. *'Mustafa, 19, was hit in the leg outside the front of the house, but should be all right. Rushdie, 15, was shot in the throat while in the bathroom (through a misted glass window) and has been taken to a hospital in Gaza City. Ironically, his best hope for survival is if his family pays $4,000 (£2,500) and applies to take him to Israel for treatment. They don't have the money and Rushdie is still in critical condition.'*

And there was a photo of Tom that I loved. Someone else must have taken him, looking quizzically at the camera and wearing a cameraman's helmet with 'TV' on it. I cherished this image of him, so teasing and alive.

Sophie and Fred arrived early next morning, 16 April, delivered to the hotel by the unfailingly supportive TFH. As soon as the phone rang Anthony and I took the lift down to the lobby and found them standing by the reception desk with their rucksacks. They looked exhausted by the journey and clearly both terribly apprehensive. We hugged and hugged. I felt huge relief that the family was at least now in one place.

TFH had matters to attend to back in Tel Aviv, but we spoke

briefly. He told us that the Ambassador, Sherard Cowper-Coles, was pressing for a meeting with the IDF, so far without success. It seemed incredible to us that the army's only response to such a serious incident was total silence. We asked him to ask again. And again if need be.

'I don't think Sherard is hopeful of getting anywhere with them,' said TFH, 'but he'll go on trying. I'm in routine contact with the IDF but obviously this has to be dealt with at the highest level. I know the ISM aren't popular with them. The IDF people simply can't understand why someone like me doesn't support what the army's doing in the Occupied Territories. They've often said to me: "You're a soldier like us. You understand the problems an individual soldier has to go through" – things of that kind. They're impervious. For them there is no other point of view. There's nothing to discuss.'

'And what about No. 10?' Anthony asked. 'Will they be putting any kind of pressure on at governmental level?'

'Unlikely,' said TFH crisply. 'I don't think I'd better give you my views on that.'

So now we knew. Essentially we were on our own.

Fred and Sophie were both too tired and strung out to rest. We all tried to eat some breakfast and we heard how things had been in London since we had left. Media interest in Tom's case had been intense. Sophie had had to cope with the continual stream of calls from all the major television channels and had been interviewed by the national and local press. She had brought press cuttings for us to see, and the truthful and dignified way in which she had stood up to the ordeal didn't surprise me.

Fred, white as a sheet, sat very close and didn't say much. Hanging over us all was the knowledge that soon they must see Tom. I wanted to prepare them, yet I didn't want to frighten them. Knowing Tom was in a coma was one thing; seeing the reality was quite another. We described the Intensive Care Unit and the procedures for entering, told them that Tom was wired up to life-support machines, that Billy was staying at the hospital with a group of young people who had been in Rafah with Tom.

Billy wanted to be the one to take Fred in. He led him down the ward, past all the other patients. 'I didn't know which one was Tom,' Fred said later. 'I was only able to tell by recognising his arms.' Later, as we all stood round Tom's bed, I knew they had understood the worst. Fred, ashen-faced, looked silently down at his brother with an expression of such anguish and disbelief that it broke my heart. He was so shocked his body was rigid, he couldn't even shake. Sophie turned away in tears, utterly vulnerable, and buried her face on Billy's shoulder. There was nothing any of us could say.

Now we had somehow to find a way of existing in this new situation, this hostile terrain. The centre of our life was the hospital and at the centre of that was Tom. Each day we would set out, ferried by Ya'alon, a friendly Israeli taxi driver we'd got to know and who always seemed to be available to take us wherever we chose. He knew why we were in Israel and it was a relief not to have to answer questions or explain ourselves afresh every day. Ya'alon was an important peg in our daily organisation, and after the hotel, which was so devoid of any human warmth or connection, we appreciated his friendly willingness.

Once at the hospital we tended to separate, Anthony to the canteen to continue with his phone calls and investigations and to rendezvous with Michelle and Nathan who were helping him sort photographs and trace witnesses, Fred, Sophie and I to the Intensive Care Unit and its chaotic waiting room, where we would find Billy and the other ISM members, all of them taking turns to spend time with Tom. Very gradually, as the days passed, I began to know them a little. They were from various countries and all walks of life, and they all had their different reasons for being there. There were Joe and Laura, a couple of Americans who had been out in Israel with the ISM for several months; Phil, a lovely young Irishman who got on well with Billy and immediately seemed to understand what it must be like for Fred and took him under his wing; slim, dark-haired Alison, who had left a responsible job back in the UK; and Raph, an intense young Jewish man in his thirties, an Oxford graduate fluent in Hebrew and Arabic, who had been with Tom when he was shot. It was Raph who had phoned the Embassy on his mobile to tell them that a British national had been shot by the Israelis.

During those first long days, we would all take it in turns to spend the mornings around Tom's bed, leaving for a break at midday and returning in the late afternoon. We were all expecting he might stop breathing at any minute. There was a constant sense of yearning, searching for something to do that would help him. My body ached with the strain of watching – aware of all the worrying dials, of the lines and tubes that might become disconnected. Sometimes the regular bleep from one of the machines would change to a continuous sound. Usually it would bring a nurse quickly to Tom's bedside, a button would be pressed or a switch flicked, but if not I would rush, petrified, to find someone.

Tom's eyes were open. Occasionally he would blink, but he was unable to close one eye, and eventually they were both gently taped closed to try to prevent recurring infections. He would need another operation, we were told, to drain some of the fluid from the region of his ear. The hospital staff were at pains to explain to us, as gently as possible, that he could see and hear nothing. Yet despite what anyone told us I know we were all desperate for some sign that he was aware we were there. Fred remembers how Tom shook when Anthony's phone went off. 'I didn't believe it was coincidence,' he said. And when he squeezed Tom's hand, 'I felt sure he squeezed it back. I told Michelle and Sophie – Michelle believed me.'

Gradually I reached the point where I knew that it was safe to touch Tom, provided I didn't dislodge any of the equipment. We would take turns to massage his swollen hands and feet, and I was always on the alert for anything that might indicate he was in pain. He was subject to constant infections, and I could read the level of infection from the feel of his skin. I knew I must find a way of interpreting for him now he could not speak for himself.

Sophie had brought out a tape of songs and messages that Tom's friends had made for him, and she laid it close to his ear and played it to him one afternoon. I wasn't allowed to hear it. I could imagine the kind of messages that might be on it. I could see 'the boys', as we always called them, Tom's close inner circle, getting together on Primrose Hill to make the tape. They'd probably sworn at him and told him to get his act together, joking about it to push away the unbearable knowledge of how serious things were. A handful of our very close friends were keeping in touch by phone and thoughtfully took on the responsibility of keeping a wider circle of friends informed. But apart from that we were out of contact with England, living in limbo with no idea of when we might return.

SIX

Gradually evidence about Tom's shooting was accumulating. Anthony was obtaining witness statements from a number of the ISMers, as well as from the South African photographer Garth Stead, who had been filming ISM activities on that day. Any variations were minor and on the key facts they all told the same story. That the shot that had felled Tom could only have come from one of two IDF watchtowers on the Egyptian border, that it had not been a single shot, but one of a number, and that there had been no other gunfire in the area at that time. The 'gunman in fatigues' shooting a pistol at a watchtower, described by the IDF in their various statements, was clearly a fabrication. In his statement Garth Stead wrote:

> I am clear in my recollection of the gunfire that took place. I have some experience of firearms from family activities in South Africa (my father was in the defence force and an active member of the practical shooting club) and from various combat and similar activities I have covered as a journalist. While no expert, I can recognise different types of gunfire. I am confident that all the shots I heard while at the end of the street were rifle shots coming from the same direction into the street and that there was no other gunfire. I am certain that there was no pistol fire. At that distance I would have heard it and clearly distinguished it from the sniper rifle fire from the border tower.

Raph, in his statement, said:

I have been made aware of a suggestion that there was a gunman who was in the building on the other side of the square . . . and that he came out of this house and fired three pistol shots in the air and then two in the direction of the tower, immediately before Tom was shot and that it was him they intended to shoot. There was no gunfire audible from such a point being fired into the air or towards the tower. The shots which could be heard were easy to correlate with the concrete flying off the buildings and the dust flying off the earth mound. Other shots would have been recognisably anomalous.

Now Anthony was keen to visit Rafah again, to test these statements on the ground and to take photographs. Our first visit had been so bewildering, so traumatic, and the crowds had been so pressing that it had been difficult to photograph or get a proper view of the scene. So via TFH we got the all-clear to go into Gaza again. We talked it over with Sophie, Billy and Fred and there was no question: all three said they wanted to go. Any thought of protecting them would, I knew, have been unthinkable. They needed to see with their own eyes where their brother had been shot, to understand why he had been in Rafah and what he had been trying to do there. It was part of the coming to terms.

Michelle agreed to come with us this time. As a skilled photographer she would be indispensable, and she and Nathan were spending most of their time now assisting with Anthony's investigation. A shared love for Tom made everyone want to do whatever they could to help, and we worked alongside one another, using our different skills. Anthony and I valued this greatly.

We were all very quiet on that second journey. TFH and Andy escorted us as before, but even TFH's robust presence did nothing to dispel the dread we all clearly felt as we drove through the grey no-man's-land of the Erez Crossing and along the potholed roads towards Rafah. As the landscape unfolded and we passed through the Abu Houli checkpoint and beneath the looming IDF watchtowers on the Rafah road, I could see shock and disbelief on Sophie's and Billy's faces. As we approached the Yibnah district the desolation increased.

By now we were well aware of the IDF's rationalisation for all this destruction – to expose tunnels built by the Palestinians for smuggling weapons in from Egypt, and to deter suicide bombers. I felt deep sympathy for the Israelis living under this threat. Yet it wasn't the whole story. This level of destruction, however close to the border, simply could not be morally justified. What these bulldozers were aiming at was clearly total wipe-out. The army was behaving as if it had *carte blanche* to do as it chose.

Everywhere there was rubble and more rubble. The ground-floor walls of many of the houses had been pulled apart or pushed inwards, leaving a mound of debris mixed with personal posses-sions – a shoe, a saucepan, a piece of plastic tablecloth. Steel girders wrenched upwards out of the mess. And everywhere there were people, hordes of people, climbing round and over the rubble in a matter-of-fact way, as if this was what they did every day – which of course they did, in order to get on with their lives. Though Anthony and I had seen all this before, I know we were as shocked by it on this second visit as the rest of the family were. Yet we were all too preoccupied with thoughts of what we were about to see to say very much to one another. Under the layers of my own disbelief was the feeling that people, friends back in Britain, just wouldn't believe what we were witnessing. It might be a cliché, but I found myself saying inwardly, 'This needs to be seen to be believed.' But how could it all be conveyed? What could make people *feel* this situation, rather than complacently observe it on their TV screens? I had been guilty of that myself.

Again we parked at the end of Kir Street. If we had thought we would be able to make a quiet, private visit to the scene of the shooting, we were soon disabused. Drawn by the sight of the Embassy cars, a small crowd had appeared seemingly from nowhere and stood, watching quietly. Old men squatted in doorways surveying the scene. Children with mischievous smiles ran round us calling 'How are *you*?', 'What is your name?', 'How old are you?'. Yet, oddly, all this did not feel intrusive. It was not idle curiosity I felt from these Palestinian people who were virtual prisoners within their own territory, but a desperate need for connection. I felt a human warmth here, in such contrast to our experience in Israel, where no one met our eyes.

We walked slowly towards the spot, holding hands tightly. There was no need to point it out – there was still blood on the ground, dark bloodstains on the wall. When she saw them Sophie began to sob. I shall never forget the hopelessness and helplessness I felt at the sight of our three children holding one another, devastated by the loss of their brother, lost for words. Were they afraid to come to me because of my distress? This barrier of rubble seemed a thing of such significance, a border between life and death. One moment Tom had been standing here, whole and young and full of life, a thinking, feeling human being; the next he was lying on the ground, bleeding and unconscious, with no hope, no future. I think we were all seeing him as he had been and as he was now. It was not just our loss that we were weeping for, but all that he had lost – life, love, friendship, language, joy and imagination, the beauty of the world. And this was where it had happened.

Eventually we walked sombrely back to where the others were waiting. They had been joined now by Mohammed and Amjad, and by Alison, an older, Scottish ISM member we had met briefly on our first visit. While Michelle and Anthony set about photographing and taking measurements – again with some difficulty because of the crowd of people, which was increasing all the time – we stood in the shade of a crumbling balcony and talked. Mohammed told us again about Tom's arrival in Rafah.

'He didn't really talk very much, maybe because it was too hot,' he said. 'He was always drinking Coca-Cola. He got criticised by the others for it. They thought these companies were an emblem of capitalism. But Tom grinned. He didn't mind the teasing much.'

No one could have been less of a materialist than Tom, I thought, but he was not a hugely thoughtful consumer, and his unfortunate passion for Coke was irresistible.

Almost as soon as Tom arrived a call had come through about a house demolition, and they had all rushed to respond, snatching up orange jackets, loudhailers, torches and cameras.

'I never wear an orange jacket now,' said Mohammed. 'Since Rachel was killed I've begun to think it doesn't have any effect. You never know what the Israelis are thinking.'

'You mean people wearing orange jackets might actually be targeted?' I said, and Mohammed nodded.

'So is this what the ISM is doing?' said Sophie. 'Trying to save people's homes.'

'That's right,' said Mohammed. 'We can't stop the bullets and missiles and rockets; we can only place ourselves between these targeted homes and the Israeli army with their bulldozers and APCs.'

'APCs?'

'Armoured personnel carriers, a bit like a tank. An APC always comes along with a bulldozer. It waits in the background or suddenly it appears, driving in a threatening way towards you, very fast. It gives protection, kind of observing the area while the bulldozer is demolishing. These bulldozers weigh sixty tons, and I've seen them driving over people's homes.'

'What must you feel when you see this happening to the homes of people you know?' I asked.

'It's so painful,' said Mohammed. 'Good homes, crumbling like biscuits. Everything you worked for gone, not even photos left. Nothing can stop these bulldozers. They're just massive. Very cruel. Very powerful.'

Amjad told us, in his broken English, more about the two young brothers from what he called the Abu Jabr house, who had been shot two days before Tom. 'They live on the same street as my family – over there,' he said, pointing towards the border. 'That watchtower is right behind their house.'

On the evening of 9 April, Amjad told us, Rushdie, aged fifteen, had gone to get a drink of water and while he was drinking was shot through the neck, in front of his two young sisters. His mother presumed the soldier in the watchtower had seen her son through the window as he lifted the water to drink.

'He was bleeding real heavy. Everyone start to scream and call for help from the neighbours,' said Amjad. 'It was horrible. They take him first to the Rafah Hospital, and then to the Al Shifa Hospital in Gaza City. It's a half-hour drive, but the ambulance was held up at the Abu Houli checkpoint and it took very long. They kept giving him blood, and the ambulance got through in the end. He didn't die but he is in intensive care. The family is very sad, very worried.'

Later Mustafa, Rushdie's nineteen-year-old brother, went out to the shop and was shot in the leg. 'I think he got shot from the tank,' said Amjad. 'They took him to the hospital too.'

Alison told us that she and Tom had both stayed at the house of Dr Samir, whose name I recalled from Tom's journal, and at the house of Abu Jamil, both on the Egyptian border.

'Dr Samir's house was riddled with bullet holes, like all the buildings along the border,' she said, 'and one shell hole had gone right through two walls, so the family lived mostly in the back rooms for safety. Tom was very gentle and concerned, especially for the children. Dr Samir's kids loved him. He'd take their photos and show them the pictures on his digital camera, and lie on the floor playing noughts and crosses with them.'

When Tom learned that Abu Jamil's house was more directly under threat than Dr Samir's he asked to move there. 'I'm not sure whether it was testing himself against a challenge,' said Alison, 'or the feeling that he needed to be there with the people who were suffering the most.'

The two of them had provided cover, with other ISM members, while engineers mended water tanks that had been holed by Israeli fire. They had helped erect a banner on a threatened house saying that internationals were sleeping there.

'The Israelis shot it to ribbons. They used it for target practice,' said Alison, and I had a sudden picture of the ghostly banner at the ISM headquarters with its almost unreadable writing.

Alison had been near Tom when he was shot. 'The first call I got afterwards was from a man with a heavy Israeli accent who kept asking over and over if Tom was dead,' she said. 'I explained that he was on life support in Be'ersheva, so was still technically alive, though we had been told he was brain dead. I asked, "Who am I speaking to?" and he said "Err . . . Ron Brown". Then he said "So he is not dead? – then we will have to postpone our celebration." After that I cut him off. They hated people like Tom, because he was taking photographs of what they were doing.'

I turned away, feeling sick. It was one of the most chilling things I had yet heard.

TFH joined us and pointed out the extent of the so-called security zone at the end of Salah El Din Street, a barren no-man's-land extending one hundred metres to the border. 'It's hard to believe, but this was a thriving residential area,' he said. 'The Israelis claim they need to clear it for security reasons. I understand they've totally demolished nearly eight hundred homes in Rafah in the past thirty-one months.'

'Sometimes they have another strange kind of vehicle which digs vertically into the ground, looking for tunnels,' said Mohammed.

I looked up at the two armoured watchtowers, the tops of them clearly visible above the intervening buildings. There was absolutely no sign of movement, but we knew that the IDF was watching us through the horizontal slits near the top. What horrendous power and danger those watchtowers held. It would take only one false move, I realised – raising a hand, looking through binoculars, drinking a glass of water even – to call forth a shot from an IDF sniper.

About two hundred yards from the end of Salah El Din Street we could see the tank – the same tank that Tom had described, whose indiscriminate firing down the street and shooting of the two Palestinian boys the previous day had prompted the plan for a demonstration. How was it possible for people to live their lives with this daily level of threat, I asked myself. Yet people carried on because they had to. When you are living in such devastation, with the world looking the other way, at what point, I wondered, do you simply give up? At what point do you run out of hope, the essence of life?

Alison described the evenings she and Tom had spent with Dr Samir's family in the small backyard where Dr Samir tended a vine and some fruit trees: 'We would sit on the terrace drinking tea or coffee and talking a bit while Dr Samir's wife prepared the evening meal. You could almost believe in normal life then, because the wall screened off the border and the tank, which was usually parked nearby. Sparrows had nested in the bullet holes up above and you could hear them chirruping.' And this in the only house left standing for hundreds of yards around.

While we were talking, Anthony, Billy and Michelle had been at work. They crouched at different heights on the precise spot where Tom had been shot, working out the exact level at which his head would have been, then photographing the two watch-towers from various angles to gauge the line of vision from each. Anthony, surrounded by onlookers eager to help, was taking meticulous measurements and recording them in his notebook.

It was at this point that a British journalist, who must have got word that we had returned, appeared on the scene. Fred was standing a little away from the rest of us, watching Anthony, Billy and Michelle at work. The journalist went up to him and said something to him I couldn't hear. But I heard Fred's reply: 'My brother was doing something good, he was rescuing little children, and they shot him,' he said, looking far into the distance. 'They shot him, they shot my brother.' His face was white and swept of all expression. The memory of it comes back to me so often.

By now the heat of the day was intense in the barren, sun-baked street. We were all emotionally and physically exhausted, and Andy and TFH were clearly anxious to be on the move. So, saying goodbye to Mohammed, Amjad and Alison, we climbed into the Range Rovers for the long drive back to Be'ersheva. It was impossible to imagine that we wouldn't see them again, but we left feeling we'd had too little time with them. Yet again this had been a fact-finding mission. I wanted to return to talk with them at an ordinary human level.

That night my head was full of disturbing images: Dr Samir's family in their small garden, drinking coffee only yards from where a tank lay in waiting; a young boy raising a glass to his lips as an IDF sniper took aim; IDF bulldozers crushing Palestinian homes . . . I opened Tom's journal, which lay on my bedside table, and there in front of me was a passage about the death of Rachel Corrie. *'Being crushed by a bulldozer is not just losing your life. It is your body being pulled apart as people stand and watch. Your arm may be dislocated by the tons of metal grinding it against some piece of rusted metal wire, while one side of your face is crushed in and the skin and flesh torn away on the edge of the metal sheet designed to clear boulders and huge amounts of rubble quickly. You don't die immediately . . .'* But I couldn't read on.

Our days began to fall into some sort of pattern. My heart was wrung to see how the children gave themselves up to caring for Tom, each in their own way. One or other of us was constantly watching over him, sitting by his bed, hands near his on the coverlet. We would gently massage his hands and feet, searching for the smallest signs of consciousness or improvement. There were lighter moments too. Sophie remembers chatting to Tom, even teasing him, pretending there was booze in his drip, or that they'd brought him a pizza, threatening to take it away if he didn't wake up. This was the kind of playful relationship they'd had with Tom. It reminded them of what he would have laughed at, and by doing this they helped each other through. Yet though we were there together, surrounding Tom with all the love we had, we still felt isolated, cut off from one another by a private grief too deep to express; aware of my incapacity, I feared for all my children.

Our isolation was greatly eased by the presence of the ISMers – Raph, Phil, Alison (who I came to think of as Young Alison, to distinguish her from the older Alison we'd met in Rafah), Laura, Joe, and of Nathan and Michelle – who were still camping out at the hospital, anxious to stay near Tom. I often came across them in the waiting room or the canteen, talking on their mobiles to family and friends. They took turns to sit with us at Tom's bedside, and we would talk quietly – about Tom, about the shooting, about their own lives and plans. One day, when we were there alone, American Joe told me again of the horror of the day when Tom was shot.

'I heard a woman scream, turned to look thinking a child had been shot, and then saw the orange jacket on the ground,' he said. 'I rushed over as Amjad picked him up. I screamed for them to put him down and covered his head with cotton pads. A taxi appeared and they pulled him in, though we pleaded for them to wait for an ambulance. We caught a taxi and went straight to the hospital, me still clutching a bloody pad. He was stabilised and shipped off to Gaza City before I even knew what was happening, and I just sat outside the hospital clutching that pad, looking at all the blood on my hands for over half an hour.'

I still had a sense that information was coming at me so fast that it was passing over my head. But I needed to hear the ISMers' accounts, to share what they'd been through. They were con-scientious, thinking people, many of them working out what they wanted to do with their lives, and I respected their seriousness and sincerity. The more I got to know them, the less they seemed like the group of 'terrorists' portrayed by the Israeli press.

I also became aware of another figure, a quiet, dark man who seemed to be camped out in the waiting room. He was there when we arrived in the mornings and we would smile and nod. He seemed to know his way around and I sensed that he had been in the hospital some time. The ISMers told me he was a

Palestinian gynaecologist whose brother was dying in the Intensive Care Unit. He had been there for six weeks without leaving the hospital. He dared not go out because he had come with his brother from Gaza and didn't have a permit to be in Israel. Leaving the hospital was too risky because he could be arrested.

I was concerned by his isolation, this obviously intelligent young man, alone here with his dying brother, cut off from the outside world by these inhuman regulations, and I tried to find some Arabic newspapers for him. But I was too late. As I waited on the bench outside the Intensive Care Unit a few days later, the doors opened and a trolley was wheeled out with a body on it, covered with a sheet. Behind it walked the young gynaecologist. Our eyes met and he acknowledged me with a smile and a movement of his head. Then the trolley was whisked into the lift and he followed it. I heard later that he had been prevented from returning to Gaza with his brother's body. I felt both sorrow and outrage.

I began to understand that the row of white-robed men who sat smoking on benches outside the Intensive Care Unit were Palestinians from the Occupied Territories. Those who could pay brought their relations to be treated in Israel, for although the Palestinian health service did its best in their destroyed economy, the quality of care it could offer was inevitably greatly diminished. But what of those who could not pay, I thought. Especially those civilians wounded by the bullets of the IDF?

Sometimes, to my relief, some of the group would tempt Fred away to the canteen, or for a walk to the local shopping mall, and he would trot off, released for an hour or so. They all knew how close he was to Tom, and they did their best to amuse him and take his mind off things, especially Phil, the warm, sensitive young Irishman, and the ever thoughtful Michelle and Nathan. Already so used to his brothers' and sister's friends, Fred slotted easily into being with an older group.

It was during a conversation with Raph, the young Hebrew-speaker, that I learned more about Michal, the mysterious Israeli girl who had been at Tom's bedside when we first arrived. Her parents, Danny and Erella, lived on a kibbutz a bus ride from Be'ersheva, and they had come to the hospital on the night Tom was shot, having heard the news from Michal. Raph told me that Erella was a bereavement counsellor, and that she had offered her home on the kibbutz as a refuge to the traumatised group of young people who had gathered around Tom, some of whom had witnessed the murder of Rachel Corrie only days before. I had heard mention of 'the kibbutz' and had been aware that people sometimes disappeared for a day or two. Now I knew where they had gone.

'They're wonderful people, Danny and Erella, so generous and hospitable,' said Raph. 'Erella is there for anyone who needs her – it doesn't matter what nationality you are. You might like to come out there with us some time. It's a beautiful place. They don't mind how many people arrive – there's always food and talk and a floor to sleep on. It's like a bit of normal life after this place.'

Billy was the first to visit the kibbutz, but soon Sophie and Fred made the journey too. They came back with vivid descriptions of the peaceful surroundings and lush vegetation, of Erella's warmth and kindness, and of the evenings they all spent on the vine-covered balcony talking to Danny, an engineer on the kibbutz, about the situation in Gaza and on the West Bank. I could see getting out of the hospital had helped them to unwind. In fact over those early weeks Sophie visited several times and I saw that she and Erella hit it off wonderfully. I was grateful. I knew how much she missed the support of her London friends, how threatening, confusing and difficult she found the present situation.

I think that at this time I was still so shocked, so distanced from myself, that I was functioning almost automatically, and this must have been very difficult for Sophie, Bill and Fred. While Anthony spent his days dealing with the outside world and pursuing his investigations, I spent them in the Intensive Care Unit where Tom still lay, pale and unmoving. The orange brace remained around his neck, but the bandage round his head had been replaced by a smaller dressing, so that I could see more of his face. His head was still swollen, and it was impossible to bear the thought of the intense and painful pressure this must be causing. We were told that a section of his skull might have to be removed to relieve it, leaving his brain even more unprotected, and this seemed a terrible option. He would probably also need a tracheostomy.

Day after day I sat watching him, wondering how well I had really known him in the twenty-one years we had spent together. Only the past now seemed to have any meaning, and those twenty-one years were all concertinaed together, everything leading up to this point, nothing beyond it having any reality. Scenes and conversations flashed through my unfocused mind: the Saturday Tom had come home with 'Defy the Stars' tattooed on his arm – Romeo's challenge to fate from Tom's favourite Shakespeare play; the evening I had gone up to his room and found every piece of furniture covered with my best white linen, and every surface flickering with candles, awaiting the arrival of his girlfriend Libby. Tom, so romantic, so idealistic, and yet so grimly realistic too, vividly aware, as I knew now, of what he was letting himself in for when he arrived in Gaza. *'It is on the decision of any one Israeli soldier or settler that my life depends. I know that I'd probably never know what hit me. . . .'*

At night my mind could not shut down. The tension of watching with Tom, interpreting for Tom, my anxieties about the rest of the family and the strain of this alien environment registered in every fibre of my being. I felt it physically, emotionally, neurologically, chemically. Every part of me ached and I faced the mornings empty. One morning Sophie found me in the bathroom beside myself with grief, and was so upset that she phoned a friend of mine in London, who immediately phoned a friend in Jerusalem. Within hours a sympathetic doctor who lived in Be'ersheva was knocking at my bedroom door. We talked for a while and he gave me a prescription. I didn't take the pills, but I hung on to them, tremendously strengthened by this wonderful, direct support. At the same time I was distressed that for the moment Sophie and I seemed to have exchanged roles, and I knew it left her feeling terribly exposed. Before I had always coped, never given way. Now, seeing my vulnerability, feeling she had to care for me on top of everything else, it was too much.

At about this time we were disturbed to hear of a story that was going round the hospital. Anthony and I were approached rather hesitantly in the corridor by two young women who introduced themselves as Palestinian medical students. They expressed their sympathy, then told us that the other students in their classes were saying that Tom had been shot by a Palestinian. It had created bad feeling. Was it true?

We invited them to join us and we sat together on some shady benches beside the medical library. Anthony told them that this was not the case, that his researches indicated Tom had been shot by a member of the Israeli Defence Force while rescuing a small child from sniper fire. They asked us a number of questions and were obviously relieved by our answers. They told us they would pass the information on to their fellow students and Anthony volunteered to come and explain the situation to them if this would help. Where had this story come from, we wondered – from the misleading early press reports, or from somewhere else entirely?

During our second week in Israel TFH phoned to say that the British Ambassador, Sherard Cowper-Coles, and his wife Bridget would like to visit Tom and meet us. It was becoming increasingly obvious that we were getting nowhere through diplomatic channels in our attempts to meet the IDF, and we welcomed the chance to speak to the Ambassador face to face. The IDF had simply announced that it was conducting its own internal enquiry, a similar enquiry, we presumed, to the one that had completely exonerated the army over the death of Rachel Corrie.

In the late afternoon of 28 April the Ambassador and his wife arrived to meet us at the hospital, and we went immediately up to see Tom. We had been through so much in the preceding weeks that we were beyond formalities, and Sherard and Bridget greeted us not as diplomats but as one human being to another. They had five teenage children of their own, all away at boarding school in England, and I could see that they were both deeply affected by the sight of Tom. Much moved, Bridget turned to me while Sherard stood at the foot of the bed with Anthony, silent and appalled.

Afterwards they invited us all to dinner at a Chinese restaurant; in this informal family atmosphere we relaxed a little. It was comforting to be able to talk openly about what had happened to someone who was officially there to give us support. Sherard was an intelligent and experienced diplomat, approachable and very much his own man I felt, while Bridget was warm and empathetic.

But though Sherard's manner was more measured and less forthright than TFH's, what he had to say about the IDF, clearly based on experience, was hardly more encouraging.

'I'm afraid I really hold out very little hope of ever extracting a fully satisfactory account of what happened from them,' he said. 'We may end up with some mild general admission of a mistake having been made. But that would be set in the context of the ISM being hostile to Israel and having no right to be there in the first place, plus the threat to the IDF in Rafah.'

'But how *can* they justify these shootings of unarmed civilians?' I said, feeling anger rising. 'It's not just Tom and Rachel Corrie, is it? There was Brian Avery, that young American working with the ISM who was shot in the face in Jenin three weeks ago. Not to mention all the shootings of innocent Palestinians we've been hearing about.'

'The IDF have much looser rules of engagement than would be acceptable in, say, the British army,' said Sherard. 'They're permitted to fire on anyone they believe poses a threat. And there's no real culture of public accountability for soldiers.'

I remembered my conversation with TFH on the drive to Be'ersheva. I'd heard this before.

'However,' Sherard went on, 'it doesn't follow that we shouldn't keep up the pressure for an account of what happened. We owe this to ourselves and to Tom.' He spoke with obvious sincerity, yet I had an uncomfortable feeling that, as far as the Foreign Office was concerned, the pass had already been sold. It seemed to be accepted that the Israeli army was a law unto itself.

We went on to discuss Tom's condition and the possibility of bringing him back to England when he was sufficiently stable. British Embassy officials had already explored the cost of an air ambulance, which would be anything from £17,000 to £20,000. And then, of course, there was the matter of Tom's medical expenses. Although the Foreign Office would be happy to help with practicalities, he said, unfortunately it was unable to contribute financially in any way.

'What about the Israelis?' Anthony asked.

'Well,' said Sherard. 'Not surprisingly their style is to give as little as possible as late as possible. I suspect they may end up meeting the medical bills, if only because they can't stop treating Tom, and recovering the money from you could be difficult. But there could be a very nasty legal dispute – they might even prevent you from leaving the country.'

It felt extraordinary to be talking about Tom's life in this detached way, yet these were the practicalities. We had no idea when we would be able to return to the UK, and neither Anthony nor I could imagine going back to work in the present circumstances. There were the expenses of family travel and of staying in a hotel to meet, and meantime the everyday bills piled up in England. There were so many aspects to this situation – emotional, medical, financial, legal, diplomatic – and we had to consider all of them. I felt wrung out with trying to operate at so many different levels.

Sherard urged us to consider ways of raising money in the UK to bring Tom home, and we talked about how we could bring some good out of this evil thing that had happened – perhaps by establishing a trust in Tom's memory and setting up a website for information about the case which would be a point of contact for people who wanted to help.

We parted warmly, with Bridget suggesting I might come and spend a day or two at the Residence in Tel Aviv. 'It's quiet,' she said. 'We have a lovely garden, and you can just sit and relax.' I couldn't imagine being able to relax, but I was grateful for her kindness.

Next day Anthony received an e-mail from Sherard, setting out the points we had discussed. 'I see virtually no chance of anyone being able to conduct a meaningful independent enquiry,' he wrote. 'My advice would be to concentrate on getting answers out of the Israelis, and putting those alongside the statements you have, or are collecting, from ISM and Palestinian witnesses.'

Getting answers out of the Israelis? How on earth were we to do that? But at least Sherard had confirmed what we already knew: that although Her Majesty's Government might be willing to smooth our path in practical ways and in opening up important channels of communication with the Israelis, when it came to bringing the IDF to book it was going to be up to us. I would come to respect Sherard's judgement and perseverance with the Israelis. But I realised he was a diplomat and his hands were tied by No. 10.

SEVEN

We had very soon begun to appreciate the importance of the media in keeping Tom's story alive and – we hoped – exerting pressure on the IDF. There was no shortage of interest. On 17 April Tom's dramatic photographs appeared in the *Guardian*, and other cuttings, critical of Israeli action, filtered through to us, not just from the British press but from newspapers all over the world. Pictures of Tom were appearing everywhere, his bright orange vest vivid against the drab background of Rafah, indisputable evidence that IDF claims that they had mistaken him for a gunman in army fatigues were a lie.

The feeling of outrage at the shooting of Tom and Brian Avery and the killing of Rachel Corrie seemed to be worldwide. On 22 April the *Chicago Tribune* commented: 'Repeatedly the international community has caved in when faced with Israeli defiance. The difference between the docile international community, on the one hand, and individuals like Corrie, Hurndall and Avery, on the other, is that these individuals refused to be turned back. They left the safety of their lives to go unarmed, except with their principles, into harm's way, because they believed someone had to act where governments refused to do so.'

Joseph Algazy of the Israeli English-language newspaper *Ha'aretz* came to see us and published a long piece under the headline 'Dear IDF, Please Meet Us, Allow an Open Dialogue'. 'If I could write a letter to the IDF,' I told him, 'my letter would say: "Dear IDF, Please move on and let go of this negativity . . .

hear ordinary human anger, take responsibility where it is right that you do so . . . Allow this useless and perpetual dynamic of victimisation to shrivel to nothing, where it belongs . . . Please just put your head out of your faceless watchtowers and dark tanks and hear, feel, smell, breathe and taste the benefits of a more inclusive way of being." '

'Tom wanted to help the people here and we also want to contribute in some way to finding a solution that will put an end to this conflict,' Anthony told Algazy. 'From now on this is also our responsibility, just as it is the responsibility of the Israelis and the Palestinians.'

Among the many people who came to interview us were two dynamic French journalists in their early thirties who were making a television documentary about Tom's shooting. They could have been slightly older versions of Tom, fearless and energetic. On several occasions they had been locked up and detained by the Israelis while travelling out to film in the Occupied Territories. They told us numerous stories of these exploits, and of how they had managed to hide a mobile phone in order to keep in touch with the French Embassy. They were streetwise and full of nous, and had had enough experience of the IDF, they told us, to know what we were up against.

At the end of the day they suggested we all have dinner in Jerusalem and we called on the faithful Ya'alon to take us. It was thirty years since I had been in Jerusalem, and my heart leapt at the first glimpse of the Old City, standing on its hill, its pale walls glowing in the evening sunlight. Did we know the American Colony Hotel one of them asked, as we drew up outside a familiar leafy doorway.

How could he have known that the American Colony Hotel was part of my history? As soon as we walked into the cool reception area with its arched ceiling, mellow stone floor and antique blue wall tiles I was twenty-one again, dressed in a crushed red dress that I'd brought along for 'best' but which had languished for weeks at the bottom of my rucksack. 'You must visit the American Colony Hotel and meet Mrs Vester,' my father had said to me before I left England. So off we had gone, my friend and I, and ordered a cream tea with strawberries, which we ate in a courtyard which I thought then – and still do – must be the most beautiful courtyard in the world.

'Do you by any chance have a guest book for 1964–5?' I said now to the girl at the reception desk. I was overcome by a kaleidoscopic sense of different parts of my life coming together in a new pattern, of standing with my family in a place my father had known so well, a few days after my son had been shot. I longed to have something of my father, to see his familiar writing, to feel his steadfast, reassuring presence. 'My father used to stay here, and he knew Mrs Vester well, you see,' I said by way of explanation.

'Of course, we will look for you,' said the receptionist with a dazzling smile. It felt that nothing was too much trouble. Now we were in East Jerusalem, a predominantly Palestinian area, and we were being welcomed with Palestinian warmth.

'Would you like me to see if Mrs Vester is still up?' asked one of the waiters who was standing by the desk.

I couldn't believe it. I'd imagined that Mrs Vester had died long ago. She was related to the members of the old American colony who had settled in East Jerusalem in the nineteenth century and her name was synonymous with the hotel, which was still owned by the Vester family, though they no longer ran it. She and my father had become good friends during his visits to Jordan, and I'm sure they would have discussed the two main interests in his life – aspects of theology and saving the world's resources. Soon the waiter returned to tell me that Mrs Vester had gone to bed. But she would be at breakfast as usual, he said.

We talked late over dinner, and at some point one of the journalists left the table to make a phone call, returning to say that he had permission from his company to invite us to spend the night at the hotel. Billy declined, saying he would prefer to stay at the hospital. This was now the centre of Billy's life and he had made friends with several of the ISMers. I could tell that these friendships, and his grief over what had happened to Tom, had opened Billy's eyes and sharpened his awareness.

Next morning I saw Mrs Vester, seated at her own table, patrician, upright and immaculately dressed. Although she was in her nineties she was entirely on the ball and aware of the news, and had heard all about Tom. She and her son, who lived in London, had spoken about it, she said. She shook her head sadly. I knew from my father that she came from a colonial tradition based in care for the local community. The family into which she had married, the original American colony who came to Jerusalem from Chicago, was known for its charitable works, and the hotel they founded was always a place where Jews and Arabs could meet on neutral ground. Mrs Vester had retained that tradition, and in the middle of troubled East Jerusalem it still felt like an oasis of tranquillity. Talking to Mrs Vester I felt I had touched another world.

We sat in the lovely courtyard after breakfast, drinking our coffee, listening to the soothing sound of water splashing into a basin where goldfish swam hypnotically, catching the sunlight in flashes of red and gold. Above our heads were baskets of sharply scented geraniums, and around us carefully tended formal beds filled with pansies and tulips. Over in one corner of the courtyard was a piece of old stone pipe which had been made into a kind of sculpture. I remembered it from my last visit. I even had a photograph of my father, sitting beside it at one of the wrought-iron tables topped with hand-painted blue and green tiles. He was drawn to Palestinian art and craftsmanship, and would return home from Jordanian Jerusalem, as it was then, with glowing Palestinian pottery, butter dishes, ashtrays, mugs and glass from Hebron. I had inherited some of them, but there were only two pieces left now.

Doves cooed. Being here felt surreal. Everything was peace and warmth and colour, yet only miles away was the sterile grey ward of a hospital where Tom was lying, the violent mud-caked desolation of Gaza. I closed my eyes and held my face up to the morning sun slanting through the leaves of a jacaranda tree. Yet I dared not give myself up to the moment. *Dear Tom, it is not possible to believe you will never know this beauty, the sound of the fountain, the light on the stone, the shadows in the colonnade.*

This part of East Jerusalem was the last place where he had walked before he travelled down to Rafah. When I looked back on his life now, everything seemed to have been leading up to that point. It was almost as if I could have predicted it. Tom had always wanted to challenge, wanted to look – not look away as some of us do. I could see him in my mind's eye, loose-limbed and at ease, striding observantly through the narrow streets with his camera. Not far from here he had sat in a little rooftop café overlooking the Dome of the Rock, and wondered that there could be such peace in the middle of such turmoil.

'I saw children of ages between 5 and 15 fighting viciously, with sticks and shards of broken mirrors, throwing the sharpest rocks they could find at each other. This place is saturated with anger, resentment and frustration. You can feel it in the air. And it occurred to me; what would it do to the mind of a child growing up under these conditions? I can't imagine the number of tears they have cried and what they have thought they had to turn into just to survive.

'And then I came across a church and in it was the most serene atmosphere. In the centre of the Venetian-set slums and maze of alleys there was silence. The church of the Holy Sepulchre; the tomb of Jesus where he was crucified, etc. It drew me in, an agnostic verging on atheism, and it touched me. I'm not saying I came out a believer, but something really moved me, me, who am never moved.'

The maze of alleys drew me like a magnet. I wanted to be near to Tom, to hear what he had heard, see through his eyes, feel with his heart. It seemed important, too, that we should make the most of this visit; who knew when we would have a chance to see this historic place again? Fred was keen to look for a football and that seemed important, too, something ordinary for him to hold on to.

Sophie wanted to see the market, Anthony wanted to post a letter. So we set off.

Before long we were accosted by a guide. We tried to put him off. No, we didn't want a tour, we just wanted to post a letter, we told him.

'No, no – come. I will show you where postbox is,' he said. He was very insistent, in the way of all guides. We just wanted to be on our own, but none of us had the strength to resist. I was annoyed with myself for failing to stand up to him.

He led us towards the majestic Damascus Gate. Crowds were thronging in and out of the great dark archway leading through the massive grey stone wall into the Old City. This was the gate my father used, his door into old Jerusalem, and I wanted to stand there in the shadows and savour the place, but the man was hurrying us on. Down, down, down the wide stone steps we went into a cool well where the air was full of the sound of human voices, pungent with the smell of herbs and spices. Women crouched on the ground beside boxes of almonds and spring onions and vine leaves and dill, stalls overflowed with oranges and lemons, cauliflowers and cucumbers, all fresh and beautifully set out. From time to time narrow, high-sided barrows laden with fruit would come trundling towards us at an alarming pace, accompanied by warning shouts. On the back of each was a hook with an old tyre attached by a stubby chain. This was the braking system. When the stallholder needed to slow down he unhooked the tyre and stood on it – often only just in time.

Everywhere there was vibrant colour – trays of nougat and Turkish delight, displays of pottery, racks of Bedouin clothing. I noticed two young Israeli soldiers lounging against a stall selling cheap baby clothes, tensely observed by the stall's owners. And from time to time, through all this pulsating life, this connected-ness, this humanity, would walk a pair of men in the long black overcoats of the Jewish Orthodox, looking neither to right nor left, apparently entirely unconnected to their surroundings. They were just getting from A to B, but they seemed not so much single-minded as insulated. The sight of them made me ponder the apparent depth of separation between these two cultures. To me their demeanour was thought-provoking, incomprehensible.

Down and still down our guide led us, until we came upon a falafel shop which I seemed to recognise from thirty-odd years ago. Limited as his tastes were, Tom was notoriously difficult to feed, but I was sure he would have stopped there to buy falafels. Now we were being shepherded along narrow streets that led upwards towards small patches of sky, past moneylenders and moneychangers and shops full of lamps, musical instruments, tourist paraphernalia. We bought some Jerusalem plates – 'and this is for you, a gift,' said the shopkeeper, slipping in an extra plate with a picture of Yasser Arafat's face on it – and looked for a football for Fred. Our guide talked on. We were having the full tourist treatment and everyone was quietly grumbling. Sophie, I know, found it unbearable to see the groups of IDF soldiers crowding the holy shrines. Every bone in my body ached, my shoes were uncomfortable and my feet were hurting. It all felt unreal, inappropriate. Yet here we were, following this man as he whisked us round the sights, too dulled to bring this intrusive guided tour to an end.

Finally we were once more back at the Damascus Gate, and we said goodbye to our guide with some relief. It had been an uncomfortable experience, the very antithesis of what we had wanted. I had gone in search of Tom but I had not found him. To do so I knew I would sometime have to return, alone.

EIGHT

Sophie had decided to go home. I knew she was finding the situation in Israel isolating and stressful, but I felt sad that she was going, and concerned. We were all so preoccupied that it was hard for us to get together as a family and talk openly about the things that were on our minds, but I realised that Sophie felt she had already lost Tom. Yet Tom had not died, and she could not mourn. It was the tragic dilemma that faced all of us, and we all tried to deal with it as best we could. I sensed that Billy too, in his quiet, realistic way, had accepted the loss of his brother, but despite the doctors' insistent message that Tom would never recover, the rest of us clung to some sort of hope – for what? We didn't know.

So at the beginning of May Sophie left for London. She wanted to get on with raising funds to bring Tom home, so he could have his friends and family around him. She also badly needed the support of her own friends.

By this time we had managed to escape the hotel and move into a flat near the hospital generously lent to us by a lively, bright, human rights lawyer with whom we had been in contact. A group of human rights workers, lecturers at Be'ersheva University, had simply arrived one day and moved us in, even providing us with furniture, and we were touched and grateful. It was a slick, brand-new, purpose-built flat, furnished simply, with mattresses on the floor, and it was a great relief to be there after the noise, expense and chilling atmosphere of the hotel.

Sherard and Bridget kept in regular contact. Sherard was still negotiating behind the scenes with a General Eiland, the officer in charge of the army's enquiry into Tom's shooting, for a meeting between us and the IDF. So far he'd made no progress. The only glimmer we had had was through *Ha'aretz*, which reported an IDF spokesperson as saying the military authorities would 'meet with the Hurndall family, and on conclusion of investigations and the formulation of conclusions would present them to the relevant people'. We wondered what kind of investigation this could be – so far they had contacted none of the witnesses.

Now Bridget invited Fred and me to spend a few days at the Ambassador's Residence in Tel Aviv. So on the first Saturday in May an Embassy driver collected us from the flat, dropped us both at the Residence and took Sophie on to catch her plane. I felt that I should go to the airport with her, but my head was throbbing and my temples seemed gripped in an iron vice. All I wanted to do was lie down, and Sophie insisted that she would be fine. I stood on the steps watching the car with her gallant, determined figure waving in the back until it was out of sight. I hadn't the time or the emotional resources to respond to her needs. It was as if the carpet had been pulled from under my feet and I hardly recognised myself.

The Residence was a secluded single-storey building set among lush terraced gardens in a residential area of Tel Aviv. On the topmost terrace was a swimming pool, on the lowest level a basketball court and in the middle a lovely garden designed for diplomatic entertaining. Fred, a natural athlete, was able to have a break from the intensity and sadness of the hospital, racing between the pool and the court. Although he seemed carefree, he told me later he couldn't wait to get back to Be'ersheva and Tom. 'I needed to be with my big brother.'

Bridget and Sherard welcomed us, tactfully leaving me alone for most of the time to lie in the shade on the terrace outside my room. I longed for the warmth and kindness and peaceful surroundings to work some kind of magic, to disperse the tension in my back and shoulders, release the iron band around my head, but I had long passed the stage when I could let go. So I lay in a basket chair, trying to read or gazing through half-closed eyes at the bougainvillea that covered the wall, the vibrant purples and blues of the lilac and the jacaranda. But I wasn't seeing the flowers. My inner world was full of shifting monochrome images – Tom, lying deathly still on his hospital bed, the bloodstained ground in Rafah, my last glimpse of Sophie as she waved good-bye, concerned friends back home in London – round and round they went in my troubled brain, like an old film on a loop. When would we ever see home again? What would happen if no one in authority would meet us? Did we even exist in their eyes?

In the evenings we gathered for drinks and dinner on the marble-pillared verandah. It was here, I think, that Sherard and I discussed again the possibility of setting up a foundation in Tom's name. And it was here that I learned of the death of a young British cameraman called James Miller, shot in the neck by the IDF as he filmed for a television documentary on the children of Rafah.

According to *Ha'aretz*, as James and his team were preparing to leave a Palestinian home after curfew on the evening of 2 May, they realised they were trapped and could not leave without putting themselves in danger, though the soldiers were fully aware of their presence since they had been shouting over to them, even singing at them, during the day. So they had come out with the translator carrying a white flag and James walking close beside him, shining a flashlight at the flag, waving his arms and shouting to make sure the soldiers saw it. It was inconceivable that they had not seen it, but James was shot, nonetheless. The IDF were now claiming he had been caught in crossfire, yet several witnesses claimed there had been no other shooting at the time.

'The IDF is sorry at a civilian death, but stresses that a camera-man who knowingly enters a combat zone, especially at night, endangers himself,' said the predictable IDF spokesman. It was all painfully familiar. The young man with a concern for children, the tragedy, the excuse – no, my scepticism told me, the *lie*. It was no good beating about the bush. It had become impossible to believe these murders of peaceful civilians were accidental. This growing certainty was unbelievably shocking.

One evening Bridget and Sherard suggested I join them in a local bar to hear a well-known Israeli singer. I very much wanted to go, but at the last minute I knew I couldn't do it. It was just as well. At around midnight, a young British Muslim walked into Mike's Place, a bar only a few doors away from the one we had planned to visit, and blew himself up, killing three people. It was my first experience of suicide bombers. Israeli TV and Al Jazeera showed graphic footage of the resulting terrible human injury.

Reaction from the British government was swift and crystal-clear in its public condemnation. Jack Straw, the Foreign Secretary, announced in the Commons that he would give Israel every support in relation to the bombing and offered his condolences on behalf of the British public. The Chancellor, Gordon Brown, ordered the Bank of England to freeze all bank accounts belonging to the bomber's two suspected accomplices. Premises in England were raided and arrests swiftly made.

The Times reported that the raids 'followed a warning from Israel that the British Government must deal severely with Islamic extremists'. Yet the British government had not so far seen fit to make a public statement or put pressure of any kind on the Israeli government over its shooting of young British citizens. We were outraged, and we made our feelings clear to Sherard.

'I have expressed to the Embassy strongly my unease at the fact that immediately following the bombing at the bar in Tel Aviv and the killing of three Israelis, the British government jumped to give a statement of support for Israelis and to freeze funds and make arrests,' Anthony told the *Guardian*. 'There's an enormous difference between how the British reacted to British citizens' involvement in killing Israelis and the complete lack of cooperation and a complete silence over what happened to British nationals here.'

Only after this statement did we receive a communication from

Jack Straw, offering us a meeting when we returned to England. The Foreign Office belatedly stated, almost a month after the incident, that it was 'shocked and saddened by the shooting of Tom Hurndall' and was 'pressing the Israeli army for an investigation'.

Our hopes of a proper investigation were utterly dashed when we met Sandra Jordan, the young journalist working on the film about events in Rafah for *Dispatches*. Not long after my return from Tel Aviv she came to the flat in Be'ersheva and showed us the transcript of a conversation she had had with an IDF representative, Major Sharon Feingold. Much of the interview would have been laughable if its subject had not been so tragic. Under the pressure of Sandra Jordan's quiet but persistent questioning, it became clear that the major had not even troubled to identify the correct site of Tom's shooting. Her arrogance was breathtaking. Asked what evidence she had for the claim that the IDF had been fired at, Major Feingold replied: 'I don't think the onus is on us. I think the onus is on the Palestinian side – as I say we do not fire unless we are fired at. We have one of the highest standards of morals in the Israeli Defence Force.'

'But what independent evidence – witnesses – do you have that you were fired at that day?' Sandra persisted.

'We don't need witnesses,' replied Feingold, 'we, again as I say, have very strict instructions . . . The first responsibility that we have is to provide security for Israelis, secondly is to ensure that our soldiers are not targeted and if they are, they are there to protect themselves and this day, and every other day along the Israeli–Egyptian border, Palestinian gunmen are shooting.' And of the soldier who shot Tom: 'I am very proud that he followed the procedures and did exactly what he needed to do.'

Challenged to make public the army's internal recordings of conversations between the soldier and his commander and CCTV footage of the incident, Major Feingold clearly became rattled.

'I don't appreciate the fact that the IDF is being put on a stand or a pedestal on trial and has to prove that we are innocent,' she replied. 'I don't believe that the Israeli army has to be holier than the Pope in trying to prove that what we are doing is just. You will have to take my word when I say we are fired at and we return fire.'

So, case dismissed. In other words, the IDF saw itself as accountable to no one, a law unto itself.

Sandra Jordan was impressive. Slight, dark-haired and intelligent, with a deceptively low-key manner and a lilting Irish voice, she missed nothing and was clearly affected by what she had seen. She sat with us on the balcony of the flat and told us what had happened in the hours after Tom's shooting. Filming in Rafah that day, she had been on the scene within minutes, and had filmed Tom's transfers from hospital to hospital until he was finally airlifted out of Gaza to Be'ersheva. I still haven't watched the footage which finally appeared on *Dispatches*, and I don't think I ever will. Sandra's description of the horrors of that journey was enough, and I wept as she told us.

'After Tom was taken off in a taxi, I went with Joe and Alice and Amjad and some of the other ISM people to the hospital in Rafah and we all just waited around,' she said. 'We were stunned – completely silent. Amjad's clothes were covered in Tom's blood and Joe was still holding the cotton pads he'd used to try to staunch the bleeding.'

Sandra and her cameraman had followed the ambulance which took Tom on to the European Hospital in Gaza City where they waited until word came that he was to be transferred by helicopter to a hospital in Israel. I knew from talking to TFH that Andy Whittaker had phoned him that day while he was at a meeting of international defence attachés to say that a British national had been shot in Rafah. The US Defence Attaché Roger Bass, who was present at the meeting, had urged TFH to ask the IDF to evacuate the wounded man out of Gaza to a hospital in Israel.

Protracted negotiations had then taken place as Tom lay in a critical condition at the European Hospital. 'I was arguing and cajoling the IDF to agree and get moving and thought we had done a pretty swift job, but when I looked at the time it took it was about three to four hours – far too long for someone in his condition,' TFH had told me.

At the European Hospital Sandra learned that the transfer was to be made at Karem Shalom, one of the Israeli settlements near the border with Israel, and she made her way there. 'When the ambulance arrived it was horrific,' she said. 'There were all sorts of delays and difficulties because it was a Palestinian ambulance, but finally it arrived at the place where the helicopter was waiting. Someone signalled the driver to go ahead, but for some reason he went into reverse – I suppose he was thinking about how best to transfer the stretcher into the helicopter. People had gathered to watch, and suddenly there was complete hysteria – they thought it was some sort of terrorist ploy. Everyone was screaming and shouting, and Tom was just left unattended, I should say for the best part of an hour. It was so shocking – the degree of fear and mistrust. He was at death's door, but there was such confusion and paranoia he was completely forgotten. He could easily have died while all this was going on.'

Sandra had also interviewed a number of the ISMers who were there on that day, and was well aware of the picture of them put out by the Israeli media and the IDF ('I wouldn't say they were peace activists and I wouldn't call them non-violent,' Major Feingold had declared).

'You can see why the army don't like them,' Sandra said. 'They're in the front line in a way that even the UN isn't, and they see everything. They're the only people who will go and stand right in front of the bulldozers to prevent houses being demolished. The fact that they're peaceful and unarmed just adds to the aggravation.'

Ironically, it was not long after this meeting that we learned the International Solidarity Movement had been nominated for a Nobel Peace Prize.

'Although this nomination is for the ISM as a whole', read the citation, 'three young individuals merit particular recognition for the courage and resolve they displayed in their acts of non-violent civil disobedience in defence of peace and human rights in the Palestinian Occupied Territories.

'These individuals are Brian Avery and Tom Hurndall, who miraculously survived sniper shots to the head by Israeli forces while they were defending Palestinian civilians from Israeli troops, and Rachel Corrie, who was crushed to death by an Israeli Defence Force bulldozer while attempting to prevent the demolition of the home of an innocent Palestinian family.

'A Nobel Peace Price for the ISM would be a fitting testament to the fortitude and principle exemplified by the members of this organisation and these three individuals in particular.'

I felt immensely proud, but it was a deeply painful pride. Yes, Tom had 'miraculously survived', but he would never hear this praise.

Back in London Sophie had thrown herself into raising money for the 'Bring Tom Home' appeal. Before she left, the five of us had also discussed establishing another longer-term charitable fund with which we might do something positive for the people of Gaza. We decided to call one the Thomas Hurndall Fund and the other the Tom Hurndall Trust Fund, and there was a lot of work to do in setting them up.

Friends rallied round, offering their support, both practical and financial, as did the press – in particular the *Evening Standard* and our local paper, the *Camden New Journal*, which had followed Tom's story closely from the beginning. 'Help Bring Tom Home to Die' said the stark black headline. Contributions came from all over the UK. It was deeply affecting to know how many people had been touched by the story of Tom and what he had done.

On familiar ground again, Sophie dealt competently with the administration and talked confidently to the media, but I knew how fragile that carapace was. In mid-May she was asked to speak at a Free Palestine Rally in Trafalgar Square to mark the fifty-fifth anniversary of the creation of the State of Israel, and courageously she accepted, standing beside the actress Juliet Stevenson and Tony Benn to address a crowd of twenty thousand. She spoke passionately, from the heart, and friends told us later what a striking and emotional impact she had made standing there in her jeans and T-shirt, with her strong features and alive, expressive face framed by her glossy dark hair. She described vividly what had happened to Tom, and the situation in Gaza.

'If we don't take a stand to make the Israeli government accountable for its actions, then there will be no end to this terrible loss of life in Palestine. Help us exert pressure for proper accountability and an end to this indiscriminate loss of life,' she appealed to the crowd. 'Please contact the Foreign Secretary, Jack Straw, to reinforce our demand for an independent public enquiry. Help us to make a difference.'

Now Billy was talking of going home. We had been in Israel for over a month and during that time my second son had largely kept his own counsel, as was his habit, watching, hawk-like, at his brother's bedside, or sitting smoking and drinking coffee in the waiting room, listening to the conversations of the ISMers and sometimes joining in. Now, accepting that Tom was not going to recover, he felt it was time to go.

So a week after Sophie's departure Billy also left to join her at home. I knew I was going to miss his solid presence, his trenchant remarks and wry sense of humour. There is something utterly grounded and reassuring about Billy, though intensely vulnerable too. Yet I was almost relieved to see him go. All his concern was focused on Tom, and I wasn't even sure if he was eating and drinking. Under the unforgiving lights of the ward he looked strained, and I sensed an underlying panic, which the rest of us shared. In this limbo we were all beginning to feel disconnected.

We had been in Be'ersheva a month. Friends were starting to ask about our plans. One evening the phone rang and it was Tom's godfather, Max. 'Isn't it time you thought about coming home?' he said directly, after we had filled him in on what was happening. 'Tom could be in that state for a very long time.'

No doubt the authorities were hoping we would leave – our presence in Israel and all the media attention it attracted must have been a constant embarrassment to them. But we knew, and Sherard had also made the point, that we were in a much better position to force a meeting and to negotiate with the Israelis over the expenses of Tom's repatriation if we stayed. And leaving without Tom was unthinkable, absolutely out of the question.

But with Sophie and Billy back in London, we began to think more about how to bring Tom home. Touching messages reached us, reminding us of the life we had left behind. Ann Manly, wife of Guy Protheroe, the director of the English Chamber Choir, with which I had sung for many years, phoned to ask how we were and to say they were all thinking of us. 'Jocey,' she said, 'the choir would like to do a concert for Tom when you get back. Please think about it, and about the music. What would you like and what did Tom like?' Hearing this was truly heartwarming. But Ann's call put me in touch with another sense of loss. Music had always been central to my life. One of my greatest sources of comfort and inspiration, it affected the deepest part of me, but now I could not listen to it – could not hear it even. It had been entirely blotted out. There was no way of playing music in the flat, and I would not have done so even if it was possible. I once heard Daniel Barenboim comment that music brings peace because it 'enables you to have a dialogue with yourself'. It was a dialogue I could not bear to have.

Another friend told us that soon after Tom was shot there had been an announcement before a home match at Arsenal, and people had stood in silence, in tribute to Tom. Arsenal was our local team and all the boys were keen supporters. Anthony had taken Tom as soon as he was old enough and those had been some of their best times together. The two of them would set off on cold winter Saturdays or weekday evenings, Tom in his heavy biker's jacket with the red stripes on the shoulders, and bulky leather gloves.

I thought of Tom's friends – the two Adams, Daniel, Sam, Angie, Caelia, Antonia, Ollie, Cassie, Alex – his close-knit circle, some of whom had gone up on to Primrose Hill together to make that tape I hadn't been allowed to hear. They all loved Tom. We knew how hard it must be for them and trusted our messages were getting through.

We were very worried, too, about Tom's girlfriend, Kay. When Tom was shot she had been on her way back home from India and at the airport had accessed scores of e-mails from Sophie asking that she get in touch. It wasn't until she'd spoken on the phone to Sophie that she'd found out what had happened. Distraught and on her own, she had tried to change her flight to Tel Aviv without success, and had then returned to London.

These thoughts of home, the loving, empathetic messages we were receiving, threw into stark contrast the situation we were in. We were struggling so hard to remain impartial, not to lay blame or condemn anyone before all the evidence was in, even though it all seemed to be leading in one direction. Yet from time to time people would ask me, 'Do you hate us, do you hate the Israelis?' It seemed a bizarre question, and it made me recoil inwardly. How could anyone think that, just because the soldier who had shot our son belonged to an army whose policies we found shocking, we would therefore hate an entire people? Another question was: 'Are you a friend of Israel?' How could I reply? The question seemed to indicate a political immaturity, a black and white view that allowed for no subtler shades of opinion: 'You are either for us, or against us.' How could I explain that we didn't hate anyone, were nobody's special friends? We simply wanted to know the truth.

Sophie rang us one day to say that a Jewish friend in London had generously contributed to the 'Bring Tom Home' fund, but only on condition that the money 'wasn't put to any political use'. Sophie was shocked and hurt by this proviso from someone who

should have known us better. It seemed to be part of the same
siege mentality.

We were now well into May. A number of the ISMers were still
camping out at the hospital, unwilling to leave, perhaps not quite
knowing what to do next, paralysed by what had happened but
comforted to be involved. Apart from their sincerity and concern
for Tom, I was glad for Fred's sake that they were still there. I felt
he was spending too much time in the Intensive Care Unit. It was
such an unnatural situation for a twelve-year-old, but I knew he
was always watching for signs, that in his heart he couldn't give up
the idea that one day Tom might recover. Any other possibility
would have been too terrible to bear. Other people tried to
provide diversions for him. The human rights lawyer who had
lent us our flat and his Russian wife often invited him to their
home. They were exceedingly kind, and Fred liked their children,
but he was always slightly reluctant to go.

So I would always feel relieved when I heard the words, 'Mum,
we're going down to the Mall', or, 'Mum, we're getting the bus
out to the kibbutz', and I'd see him trotting off between a couple
of the group, arms linked on either side. I knew he was in safe
hands. We and the ISMers were like an extended family. Anyone
who went out of the unit to buy a cold drink would buy a drink
for everyone. Talk in the waiting room was quiet and serious.
They were all doing their best to support us and to help one
another.

Anthony was still deeply preoccupied with gathering witness
statements, sifting evidence, talking to the press, working at his
laptop in the canteen or back at the flat. Some of the witnesses had
now scattered and it was laborious work making contact since e-
mail connections were often difficult. By now his immediate
impulse to bring the facts of Tom's case to light had hardened into
a strategy – and a crusade. He wanted to follow through what
Tom had started, to make his sacrifice meaningful, and hoped by
establishing the facts of what had happened to Tom and the Abu

Jabr family, he could bring some openness and honesty to the Middle East situation. Tom's shooting and that of Mustafa and Rushdie two days before were part of a pattern, and Anthony was determined to engage with the media, government and law at every level to highlight this and so turn around the juggernaut of IDF policy. For him it was not an exercise in finger-pointing but his chance to contribute to peace in the area. He was utterly driven.

With Michelle's help we had now been able to uncover all the pictures in Tom's cameras. They were powerful and intensely personal, like his journal. I felt I was seeing through his eyes. This was what Tom had witnessed, these were the people he had stopped to talk to in the weeks before he was shot. Among the photos was one of a young smiling man taken on the bus from Amman to Baghdad. He was looking directly at Tom, and somehow you could see them relating. From press reports I recognised him as the cameraman James Miller. It seemed poignant that they had met and talked on this coach journey, perhaps shared the fear and adrenaline of possible death, discussed the effects of war on children. There were fearsome pictures of the ISMers confronting the bulldozers and APCs of the IDF (*'I'd heard that D-9 bulldozers were big, but this was fucking huge'*, Tom wrote in his journal. *'It towered up like a lookout tower or airport control tower'*). Looking at these gigantic machines rearing up in front of the unarmed peaceworkers, it was impossible to believe that Rachel Corrie's death could have been accidental, that neither the driver of the bulldozer nor the nearby APC had seen her. This, despite all the evidence, was what Major Feingold had brazenly claimed in her interview with Sandra Jordan.

Michelle and Nathan had met Tom in Amman and they had stuck together until they arrived in Israel. Among Michelle's many images of Tom, most of them taken in the Jordanian refugee camp they had travelled on to, there were two pictures that moved me particularly. One was of Tom playing football with a young Iraqi boy. He was about to kick the ball, swinging his long leg and twisting his body, with that particular set of the head that was so familiar. You could see from his expression and from the angle of his body that he was giving way to the little kid – it was so absolutely Tom. In the other he was showing his camera to another small boy, encouraging him to look, letting him hold it. It was a moment of real communication, a gesture of absolute trust.

By now Tom had had a tracheostomy; some of the time the oxygen mask was removed and he was able to breathe on his own. I sat with him every day, watching the slight rise and fall of his chest, alert for any variation in the pattern of his breathing, panic-stricken if it seemed to change. One afternoon when I was alone with him it suddenly appeared to me that he had stopped breathing. I put my face close to his, listening for the gasp that comes when someone asleep and dreaming stops breathing for a moment and then suddenly breathes in again. But it never came.

Suddenly all my control gave way and I ran down the ward, tears streaming down my face, desperate for help from someone – anyone. It felt to me at that moment as if Tom had been completely abandoned, as if no one cared any more whether he lived or died.

A young doctor was walking towards me and we almost collided. 'Are you still looking after Tom?' I asked him through my tears. 'He's stopped breathing. Are you just going to let him go?'

When we reached Tom's bed he was breathing again, but I was distraught. The young doctor seemed astonished, bewildered. 'Why are you crying?' he said.

The question astonished me. I thought I had lost my son.

Yet part of me had accepted that I had lost him already, that that fine brain of his was damaged beyond repair. It frightened me, in the heat of the night, that I could not conjure up pictures of Tom as he was growing up – Tom going to school, Tom with his friends, Tom writing, drawing, taking photographs, playing football. I knew he had done all these things, but I could no longer see them in my mind's eye. Was this normal – not being able to picture your child in this way? Was it just shock? Would these images ever be retrievable? It was as if a door had closed, a curtain had come down. I tried to speak to him, but there was silence. And I knew, in my heart, that Tom was not really alive.

At about four o'clock one morning, after a terrible, wakeful night, I got up and opened the sliding doors on to the balcony, looking across the night lights of Be'ersheva to the distinctive outline of the hospital on the horizon. The beauty of the night sky and the stars made me ache. Tom, too, had loved the Middle Eastern sky, had wondered that so much bitter conflict could co-exist with such beauty. I remembered so clearly another hospital, another early morning: Friday 27 November 1981, the day of Tom's birth. He was only a few days overdue, but Friday was the day of inductions and Anthony and I drove in early. Tom was born at five o'clock that afternoon. It had been a long day in the bustling labour ward, yet what I remembered now was the absolute stillness following Tom's birth, the joy as Anthony handed him to me. How keenly we felt our responsibility. All your instincts, as a parent, are focused on keeping your child alive. But what was the reason now for keeping Tom alive? Perhaps our responsibility as parents was to do the unimaginable, to enable our child to die.

Somehow I couldn't fit these responsibilities together in my mind. My reason fought with my emotions and I felt torn in two. I wandered aimlessly around, not knowing what to do, but aware I had to do something. Eventually I dressed, wrote a note for Anthony and set out towards the hospital. The sun was coming up and it was already warm as I walked along the main boulevard, but the heat was still bearable. I passed quickly through the security checks, went up the stairs and along the familiar wide corridors where, even at this hour, people were waiting in the treatment rooms on either side. I could hear the tap of footsteps on shiny lino floors, caught glimpses of medical staff grabbing a cup of coffee before going home after the night shift.

Professor Gurman's door was open, and he was already at his desk. I stood in the doorway, obviously distressed, and when he saw me he rose and came towards me.

'Please,' he said, indicating a chair, and pulling up another in front of me.

It was a minute or two before I was able to speak. 'When you bring a child into the world,' I said finally, 'you never expect to have to make the decision to end that child's life. Is this really what we have to do?'

Professor Gurman simply inclined his head, looking at me quietly. 'I can think of no greater sadness than the loss of a child,' he said at last. 'Does it help at all if I tell you that I too have lost a child? But in my case there was no decision to make. My son died in a motor accident.'

Suddenly we were no longer doctor and client, but simply two parents, sharing our desperate feelings of loss, and I listened with a different kind of sadness. He told me about his son and the circumstances of his death, I talked to him about Tom, and we both shed tears. It was a conversation that crossed all professional barriers, all cultural divides. I became aware that I was talking to someone who was in constant touch with the experience of death. People know about death in the Middle East, they face the reality of it every day, and it is one of the things that gives life there its vibrancy. In the West we are not forced to look death in the face in the same way. We barely acknowledge its existence. We take our lives very much for granted and because of it we lose something. It made me understand that an awareness of our own mortality is a gift, for it gives life itself, every minute of every day, such value.

I shall always be grateful to Professor Gurman for that conversation. I continue to carry it with me, though I doubt if he realised the impact it had on me at the time. Although we did not speak directly of Tom's future, I felt as if it had brought some kind of peace, some sort of resolution – an acceptance of what would be.

NINE

Someone else who helped me find some kind of peace during this time was Erella. We'd been hearing a lot about her and her husband Danny from our children and from the ISMers. Her home on the kibbutz seemed to have become a kind of family-run youth hostel and counselling centre rolled into one, an all-healing place where they could crash out and feel completely at home, and I grew curious about meeting this unusual person. Before there had been too many other priorities, but now the time felt right. So one morning, before it became too hot to breathe and the whole of Be'ersheva was covered in a pall of desert dust, we called Ya'alon who drove us out to the kibbutz.

As we drove through the Negev I remembered arriving at another kibbutz, in the Golan Heights, right on the border with Lebanon. It was 1972. I'd landed at Lod airport with a group of other volunteers and we'd been driven north for several hours through the clear starry night. At about midnight there was a feeling of getting closer to our destination – a change of speed and a sense of getting higher and higher, of having to hold on to the sides of the lorry as we revved and manoeuvred round the bumpy U-bends.

When we stopped on the border road with Lebanon I could hear voices talking in Hebrew, shouting orders. Glaring lights outlined armed soldiers milling around a parked tank and other military vehicles silhouetted against the pitch-black. 'There's a curfew,' someone explained. 'It starts at seven o'clock in the evening. So the military will have to escort us along the road to the kibbutz.' I'd never been in a society controlled by the military before; it felt strange and mildly alarming.

One day, when we were picking peaches within yards of the wire fence that marked the Lebanese border, my Scottish friend Sona let out a yell. She'd inadvertently put her hand on a poisonous snake. The kibbutzniks who were with us jumped into action, chopped its head off with a long knife and slung it over the fence. 'That's for Lebanon,' someone said. 'Lebanon can have that.' One could sense the tension.

I remember, too, being taken on a four-day trip down to the south of Israel and spending a night on the beach at Eilat. We lit a fire, heated supper and sat round on the sand singing Jewish songs of loss, hope and friendship. '*Shalom chaverim, shalom chaverim, lehidrahot, lehidrahot, shalom, shalom*,' we sang – 'Peace, my friend, we'll meet again.' Men's and women's voices mingled gently in the darkness by the fire, with the lights of Aqaba in Jordan twinkling across the Red Sea, in which we'd swum that day. Then, as now, I could feel the intense contrasts in this complicated country.

Now, more than thirty years later, I walked along the paved paths of this other kibbutz, lined with palm trees and giant succulents, past beds overflowing with roses and huge clumps of sweet-smelling herbaceous plants. It was blessedly quiet after the city, and the air seemed cooler and softer.

We went up some steps at the side of a low, cream-painted building and I saw coming down to meet us a sturdily built woman wearing a white T-shirt and baggy cotton trousers, with greying hair tied back in a ponytail and a face that was utterly alive. Erella didn't say anything. She just looked deeply at me with her extraordinary, searching eyes, put her arms round me and hugged me. Then she led me in, through a front door to which was pinned a quote by Gandhi – 'An eye for an eye leaves the whole world blind' – and asked if I would like to go and lie down.

I could feel a migraine coming on and there was nothing I

wanted to do more, but something in me held back. I had just met Erella. Little did I know how accustomed she was to seeing people walk through her door because of the death of someone close. So, unable to admit to myself how exhausted I was, I sat on the sofa, accepted a glass of water and tried to hold a conversation, while Danny took Anthony off to send some e-mails from his computer.

Erella told me that on the evening of Tom's shooting she, Danny and Michal had been coming out of the cinema in Be'ersheva when Michal received a call from a friend in Tel Aviv, concerned about a mutual friend who had been with a young English student who had been shot in Gaza. He was in a critical condition in the Soroka Hospital. It was eleven o'clock at night. Danny, Erella and Michal went straight there. Tom was in surgery and there were seven of his friends waiting in the hospital corridor, all in a terrible state.

'What made you go?' I said.

'I knew immediately I arrived that there was nothing I could do for Tom. He was in the best hands,' said Erella. 'But those other poor young people. Already they had seen that American girl killed by a bulldozer. They were in shock, far from home. I work with bereavement, and I gave them my phone number. I wanted to offer them some kind of help and support.'

Next morning as she was exercising on her walking machine she heard on Radio Kol Israel that an armed man in fatigues had been shot by the army in Rafah after he had aimed a pistol at a watchtower on the Philadelphi Road.

'I knew it was a lie,' said Erella passionately, 'a barefaced lie. My goodness, was I *angry*. But, then, we have come to expect this kind of random violence and dishonesty where the IDF are concerned. This is not a new story, believe me.'

Erella is one of those people who looks below the surface, who sees the complexities, the shades of grey. I found myself talking to her about who Tom was, about our feelings of isolation and astonishment at our treatment by the British government and the

IDF, our shock at what we had seen in Rafah, the hostility we often felt around us. It was such a relief to talk to someone for whom these issues were already familiar.

'*Oreach lerega roeh kol pega,*' said Erella at one point. 'It's a Hebrew saying and it means "A guest in a hurry sees all the worry". When you are in a place for a short time, you have to rely on your intuition. It makes you acutely aware of what's going on, what the key issues are. When you have experienced such a terrible tragedy as yours, your emotions are laid bare, and the pain of what you see is all the greater.'

Erella, in common with many Arabs and Israelis, often talks in sayings. It's a form of communication quite alien to us in the West. It gets directly to the heart of things. Whereas we are brought up to feel that analytical thinking – 'left-brain thinking' – is the best and really the only way to arrive at a judgement, the Middle Eastern way places more value on an intuitive awareness, an intense focus that goes straight to the core of a problem or a situation. It brings everything you know to bear without the intellectual filtering that often gets in the way of true understanding.

Another of Erella's favourite sayings is: 'Haste is of the devil'. It's an Arab saying, and to us Westerners, always rushing, always anxious about the fulfilment of our next goal or desire, it seems to express a general lack of efficiency. But as I came to learn from my time in the Middle East, what it really means is: 'Stop, savour the moment, feel what your senses are telling you'. It has nothing to do with efficiency or the lack of it. It is part of a deep respect for life.

As soon as I met her I felt this quality in Erella, an intense engagement with the moment, a capacity to enjoy what's around. Erella is a truly joyful person, and even in my distraught and desperate state my spirit responded and I began to relax. Later in the day it didn't feel right to be leaving. So Anthony went back to Be'ersheva and, too exhausted now to think about my inhibitions, I climbed into one side of Erella's big double bed and she climbed into the other. To her it was obviously entirely natural, and I later discovered that when any of her three grown-up daughters or her son came home, they shared her bed too; it was simply the Israeli way, the way of the Middle East. I lay awake for a while, listening to her deep steady breathing, trying to accustom myself to this unexpected situation. I hadn't yet got used to the total informality and spontaneity of life in Erella's family. But eventually, surprisingly, I slept.

Next day I felt worse. Talking to Erella had opened the door of my emotions one small crack, and the pain was terrible. It manifested itself as an appalling migraine. I could hardly see, and I sat on Erella's beautiful first-floor verandah where the breeze was soothing. Yet even in the midst of the pain I had a feeling of sanctuary, of being, for the first time since I had arrived in Israel, somewhere emotionally safe. There was nothing I needed to explain; Erella simply understood.

The apartment in Be'ersheva remained our base, but we visited the kibbutz after that on a number of occasions, sometimes singly, sometimes all together. Often Michelle was there, and she and Anthony would work side by side, Anthony on his computer and Michelle on Danny's, e-mailing questions, sending photographs, trawling the internet for information. Fred would just hang out, reading in the shade or kicking a ball, enjoying the freedom and the friendly atmosphere. Erella and Danny both loved Fred and did everything they could to amuse him and make him feel at home. When Sophie and Billy visited, Danny and Erella were very good at giving them the space just to be.

Often I would wander alone through the lovely gardens, drinking in the warm smell of the pine trees, losing myself among the paths that wound between lilacs and palms and oleanders, and abundant bougainvillea. Sometimes I would leave the path, lured by some seductive scent, or look upwards, my attention drawn by a minute movement – the lazy stretch of a cat's paw from a branch, the silver, indigo and black flash of a woodpecker. Everything here was fragrance and colour, order and contentment

– and yet, and yet, not far away was the horror of Gaza, the wounded, orphaned children whom Tom had photographed. And at intervals, above the branches of the pine trees, I would see a sinister black gunship moving purposefully across the Negev sky.

Erella and I would talk for hours on the verandah, shaded by an overhanging jacaranda tree, or in the light, creamy upstairs sitting room where the overhead fan whirred gently, lazily moving the heavy air around. I still retreat to that verandah in my imagination. All around the edge were pots of pink, purple and peach-coloured busy Lizzies and geraniums, and a clematis wound its way up a disused drain pipe in which a small bird had nested. Erella would sit attentively, talking, listening, smoking one of her roll-ups, getting up from time to time to answer the phone. People were always phoning. This home was a refuge for anyone in need, of any religion or no religion, any nationality.

At the back of the flat was a large square window covered with a mesh panel to keep out the mosquitoes. Sometimes I would slide the panel back, scattering light on the marbled floor, and gaze out to where the yellow and green of the Negev stretched away into the distance. Again it seemed incredible that not far from this peaceful landscape, a few miles only, war was being waged. One evening we drove out into this extraordinary countryside which had been coaxed from the desert. The flat cornfields and wide skies reminded me of East Anglia – except that here and there one would see an 'illegal' Bedouin settlement, a small cluster of tents with a few tethered camels. Danny explained to me that the government had rounded up the Bedouin in the south of the country into seven Arab 'villages', of which Rahat, on a potholed road between the kibbutz and Be'ersheva, was the largest.

'It goes against their culture,' said Erella. 'They like to be free, not right on top of their neighbours.' So these were the ones for whom the call of the desert was too strong to resist. This land was what they rightly owned, what they knew, and there was great dignity in their way of life. But at any moment these tented settlements could be broken up and their inhabitants forced back into a village.

Ever since meeting Erella's daughter Michal on that terrible first day in Israel, I had been haunted by what she had said to me as we stood beside Tom's bed: 'I am so sorry for my country'.

'All I can say,' said Erella, when we discussed it, 'is that more and more many of us here in Israel are tortured with guilt when we hear of the terrible things that are being done in our name, although there are many, many, many Israelis who have no idea what is going on, in Gaza mainly, but also in the West Bank. If you don't take the trouble to know then . . . you will never know the truth and, Jozaleen, let me tell you, *it is right there in our face.*' She emphasised these last words. 'We have *Ha'aretz* where there is open reporting but it's not widely read . . . what else . . .? For myself, I have moved beyond guilt. Why? Because I no longer feel that my country, my nation, my religion, is part of my identity.'

In 1985, she told me, she initiated a project to encourage Jewish-Israeli children and Israeli-Palestinian children to work in pairs, teaching one another about each other's language. It provided a rare chance, a bridge, for two cultures to reach out to one another. As part of her preparation she attended an adult workshop – eight Israeli-Jews and eight Israeli-Palestinians – during which they were each asked to choose four ways of defining their identity. They were given various definitions and asked to put them in order of priority. People thought hard and answered very seriously. The Israeli-Jews always began their definitions with the word 'Jewish'. The closer it came to Erella's turn the more anxious she became, because she knew that the way she saw her identity was light years away from this kind of thinking.

'When the facilitator finally reached me, I didn't want to answer. I said, "I suggest you forget me because what I say is only going to cause trouble." But the facilitator insisted. So finally I said, "Identity is something very serious, very basic. For me it has nothing to do with these labels. I believe my identity is made up both of my own 'self' and the 'self' of others, and both of them are equally important. I believe that I am a channel through which something much greater than me, something infinite, can pass — a cosmic wisdom if you like. I am part of this cosmic wisdom, and this cosmic wisdom is also within me."

'There was a moment's loaded silence, then the storm broke. The seven Jews started to shout at me hysterically: "What? Aren't you a Jew? Aren't you an Israeli? Aren't you a Zionist?" It had got to them deep down. It wasn't a joke. I looked at the eight Palestinians and they were clearly bewildered by all this shouting, they couldn't understand what I had said wrong.

'So I took a deep breath and I said, "Listen, as far as I know I am a Jew, an Israeli, a Zionist and not a Zionist, a woman, a mother, a partner, a kibbutznik, and many other things. These labels are just not part of my identity. They are only the tools we use to manifest our identity. If you confuse labels and identities you are making a tragic mistake. If we could only realise this, there would be no war. We are all one, all part of a greater wisdom, but the tools we use are different. If we accept this, there is no reason to kill one another." After that there was complete silence.'

As I listened to Erella I was thinking that Tom, too, with his inclusive way of being, had known he was part of that oneness, that greater whole.

Erella, I learned, had known great sadness in her life. Her intelligent, good-looking younger brother whom she adored had been paralysed by motor neurone disease and had died at twenty-four. Erella had cared for him during his illness, and his death had affected her profoundly. Danny had been her brother's best friend. Her mother, to whom she had been very close, had developed Alzheimer's, and Erella had cared for her too for many, many years.

A close friend of whom she often spoke had also known such sadness. Like me, Daniella had lost a son. His name was Tom and he was twenty-one. Erella told me that at the time of his death he and Ayelet, one of Erella's and Danny's daughters, had been boyfriend and girlfriend, and that his death had been a tragedy for Ayelet. On 4 February 1997, as darkness fell, he and seventy-two other young conscripts had boarded two helicopters to fly to an Israeli army base in southern Lebanon. Very close to the Lebanese border the two helicopters had collided, killing everyone on board. It was the worst military air disaster in Israeli history.

Daniella lived in a community called Neve Shalom, in Arabic Wahat al-Salam – 'Oasis of Peace' – about an hour's drive away, and one evening Erella took me to meet her. This community was founded by a Dominican priest in 1972, the year I first came to Israel, and is the only place in Israel where Jewish and Arab families have actually chosen to live together. As we drove away from the Negev, into the hillier countryside around Jerusalem, I was filled with anticipation and anxiety. I wasn't sure how I would feel meeting someone whose experience was so near to my own. I had so many questions to ask. But would we be able to talk, or would it be too painful for both of us?

As soon as we met, I realised there was no need for words. Everything important was said with our eyes in those first few moments. We sat on the balcony of Daniella's airy modern home looking out over the ordered lines of green vineyards. On a hill in the distance stood a red-tiled monastery surrounded by dark cypress trees, and the old road to Jerusalem cut through the valley below. Daniella told me that this valley had been the scene of a ferocious battle between Israel and Jordan during the 1967 war, in which Ariel Sharon had been badly wounded.

The huge orange sun sank towards the hill. We talked quietly, often drifting into a silence that felt perfectly natural. The shadows lengthened, the light began to fade. The loveliness and serenity of the scene reminded me of Tuscany. But as always the beauty tore into me; I could hardly bear it. It was a searing reminder of what Tom could never see. Daniella told me that when her son was killed she, too, had turned away from beauty – from nature, art, music. We were both singers, and music had been as important to her as it had been to me. But only now, six years after her son's death, had she felt able to rejoin the choir with which she sang.

I wondered despairingly if I would ever be able to sing again. Or stand beside the sea, or watch the sun set. Or listen to a beautiful piece of music. These were the things that had always inspired me. But inspiration involved feeling, and that was a terrifying prospect. Yet talking with Daniella I began to sense, however dimly, that Tom's tragedy, Tom's sacrifice, could become a source of inspiration. First, though, I would have to face the feelings, face the anger. For the first time since it had happened I was able to imagine that there might be a future, however far away it seemed.

It was dark when we rose to go. On a chest in a corner a lighted candle stood beside a collection of photographs and small mementos – pictures of Daniella's son. He even looked a little like Tom. 'I always keep the candle alight,' she said. 'It helps me to remember.'

TEN

Ever since our first visit to Rafah I had been haunted by the memory of Salem Baroum, the silent little boy whom Tom had rescued. I knew there would be many children like him in Rafah, marked for ever by the horror of what they had seen. In some ways this was familiar territory, for I was used to working with a wide range of traumatised children in the learning support unit. Some were refugees who'd fled their country in dangerous circumstances, many had suffered the death of a parent or sibling. Bedwetting, nightmares and withdrawn behaviour were common symptoms.

So I wanted to go back and find out how Salem was, and to see other Palestinians like Amjad and Sahir and Mohammed who had been caught up in our tragedy. Our last visit to Rafah had been so packed and public that there had been no real chance to have a genuine exchange. Anthony wanted to meet Dr Samir, with whose family Tom had stayed, and the family whose two sons had been shot by the IDF. We needed to have this human contact, to share their feelings, and experience what it was like for ordinary Palestinians to survive and live their lives in what seemed a grossly inhuman situation. We had been deeply moved to hear of a demonstration in which local people, many children included, had come to the spot where Tom had been shot to lay flowers. It showed the strength of Palestinians' feeling for these people who had travelled from all over the world to stand with them and show their solidarity and support.

Entering Gaza wasn't easy, however. We knew that each time we went we were putting the people who took us, as well as ourselves, at risk. I was astounded when TFH had told us that he was one of only two defence attachés, out of the fifty or so from different countries with embassies in Israel, who ever ventured into Rafah to report back to their governments on the situation. 'The Israelis often say to me, "Why do you want to go down there? We can tell you everything you want to know",' he'd said. So we hesitated, not entirely sure how much we could ask of the Embassy. But finally we called him, and a day was fixed.

'Don't bank on it, though,' he told us. 'We'll have to keep checking with the Consulate on the situation down there in Gaza over the next few days. My sources tell me that from next week the IDF will be requiring all foreign nationals, including relief workers, to sign waivers acknowledging that they are entering a danger zone and won't hold the army responsible if it shoots them. Wonderful, isn't it? I'll keep you posted.'

Early that morning he phoned to give us the all-clear, and after breakfast he and Andy were waiting in the Embassy Range Rovers at our regular meeting point outside the hotel. Fred could have stayed behind, but he chose to come. From time to time Anthony and I discussed the extent to which we should expose Fred, but we knew that mostly he needed to see for himself. Fred has never run from death. At the age of five he visited my father when he was dying and told me afterwards, 'I know Grandad's going to die. His feet were cold.'

As usual we made good time along the smooth roads to the Erez Crossing. We were becoming familiar with this ghastly landmark – the queue of patiently waiting cars, the bored young soldiers, the cages, the turnstiles, the faceless guard posts, the insulting sign welcoming us to the Erez Crossing in Hebrew and English. TFH was right. It did look like a concentration camp. At the very least, I now saw Gaza as a massive prison. Its only airport, Yasser Arafat International, had been closed, the borders were heavily guarded, and the Palestinians' every movement through them and within them was controlled by the Israeli Defence Force.

Once we were into Gaza the pace changed. Slowly negotiating the churned-up roads, the Range Rover overtook wildly over-loaded carts pulled by meagre looking donkeys. Not long before we entered Gaza City I caught a glimpse of blue, and realised we were driving along beside the Mediterranean. I had barely noticed it on our earlier visits, but now I was struck by the beauty of the coastline. Creamy waves lapped the sandy shore, but there was no one enjoying the beaches, no one swimming. You could still see the remnants of a previous life – the demolished seaside buildings, a children's playground that had been uprooted and broken up. It seemed utterly tragic that this lovely, healthful place, which could have attracted tourists and been a source of income to the Palestinians, was now closed to them, like everything else.

I asked TFH how long the airport had been out of action.

'The Israelis closed it at the end of 2000 and the IDF tore up the runway about a year later,' he said. 'This was at the beginning of the Second Intifada, after Sharon's visit to the Temple Mount in Jerusalem, and the Al Aqsa Mosque, which is one of the Muslims' holiest shrines. That visit was calculated to provoke. Basically the Israelis sealed Gaza off then and they've been systematically destroying the Palestinian economy ever since. The human cost is indescribable, and it's all done under the guise of self-defence. They used the uprising as an excuse for loosening up the army's rules of engagement too.'

'So what precisely *are* the rules of engagement now?' Anthony asked.

'That's the million-dollar question,' said TFH. 'Since the beginning of the Second Intifada the open-fire regulations in the Occupied Territories have been classed as "confidential information". They're given to soldiers verbally, not written down, as they used to be, and I gather certain battalion com-manders pitch in and add their own. A lot of the soldiers can't actually remember what they've been told. It's a recipe for confusion and it makes them trigger-happy. Hundreds of civilians are being shot who have nothing whatever to do with the fighting. I think there's no doubt that there's a shoot-to-kill policy for anyone entering the army's prohibited areas, regardless of the reason. The IDF always denies it, of course.'

As we entered Gaza City I noticed that the Range Rovers moved closer together. Again I was struck by the seething mass of humanity crisscrossing in the streets, an air of aimlessness and desperation that was hard to pin down. Sometimes the press of people was so intense that we slowed to a halt and were overtaken by a donkey cart. People stopped to stare as we went past and I was acutely aware of the wide gap between our lives and theirs as we sat cocooned in our armour-plated, air-conditioned vehicles.

Yet I also had the sense that Gaza had somehow managed to hang on to its identity as a living city. TFH told me there was a university there. Behind the scenes there was clearly a vigorous intellectual, legal and political life going on. I later discovered that Tom had not only photographed the Hamas funerals in Gaza City two days before he was shot, but had also visited the Palestinian Centre for Human Rights and spoken to the distinguished human rights lawyer Raji Sourani.

After picking up our interpreter, we drove on to the Abu Houli Crossing at the entrance to the Khan Younis refugee camp just outside Rafah, where we joined a long line of traffic waiting to go through. As we sat in the Range Rover, with little boys tapping at the windows, trying to hitch a lift or sell us nuts and sweets, I wondered what exactly the purpose of this particular checkpoint was. 'Well, with the refugee camp here this is a flashpoint and there are settlements around – see?' said TFH, pointing to clusters of buildings on the hills. 'It's a way of keeping control of the Palestinian population. And it stops the people in Rafah getting out.'

'So Rafah is really a prison within a prison,' I said.

'That's about it,' said TFH laconically.

The queue inched forward. When we were in sight of the rickety, leaning traffic light by the checkpoint tower we could just see, through the haze of sunlight and dust, that it wasn't working.

There was no other traffic control and the way through the checkpoint was on a single raised track, so it was hard to know what to do. We simply proceeded at snail's pace, following Andy who was following the car in front.

I heard nothing strange, but suddenly TFH, who had been chatting, broke off and picked up the phone. We stopped.

'Did you hear what I heard?' he said to the car in front.

The second time I did hear it – the distinct sound of a gunshot. 'I'm going to phone Joseph Levy,' I heard TFH say. He called a number: 'Blast! Engaged . . .' After a few moments' wait he tried again, then: 'Joseph, what the hell's going on? I've got civilians in the car . . .'

There was a pause while some kind of justification was clearly being offered by TFH's IDF contact. Then: 'How the hell does anyone know when to stop? The traffic lights aren't working. They're never working. Get a grip, Joseph. This is quite unacceptable. You knew we were coming through. I'll be coming back at the end of the day and I expect to go through absolutely smoothly. OK?' And TFH, clearly furious, ended the call.

By this time Andy had decided to get out of the car. 'For goodness' sake go very very slowly,' I heard TFH say. 'No sudden movements.'

Andy, in a white shirt with the sleeves rolled up, got gingerly out of the Range Rover and stood beside it with his hands up. Then he gestured towards the tower, as if to say, 'So what do you want us to do?'

That seemed to do the trick. A few seconds later a languid white hand appeared from the tower and dismissively waved us through.

Suddenly I felt livid. I wanted to shake the arrogant twenty-one-year-old I imagined was attached to that hand. 'Just get down from there and speak to us,' I wanted to say. 'All you need to do is explain what you want of us. Where's the dialogue? We followed the protocol. You could see our white number plates perfectly well, you knew who we were.'

Soon we were beneath the watchtowers on the outskirts of Rafah, then negotiating a route round the ugly mounds of rubble, topped with huge tangles of wire and bent girders, on our way to the Egyptian border. We had phoned Mohammed and he, Amjad and Sahir were waiting for us on the corner of Kir Street, three slight, dark-haired figures looking small and vulnerable in the midst of the now familiar devastation. I thought of the picture I had seen of Amjad, his face contorted with anguish, staggering under the weight of Tom's body as he and Sahir struggled to move him further down the street after the shooting. It was a tragic, shocking picture that made me think of Michelangelo's *Pietà* with its sense of human vulnerability, of our dependency on one another. Yet I knew that carrying the dead and wounded had become part of Amjad's everyday life.

We greeted one another affectionately, and as everyone stood talking for a moment Amjad and I began wandering down Kir Street, drawn irresistibly towards the place where Tom had been shot. I asked Amjad what he had been doing since last we met, and he began to tell me about his work with the Palestinian Progressive Youth Movement, a group that had developed links with the ISM and often put themselves at risk by acting with it, as they had on the day of the demonstration.

Amjad explained to me that the PPYM supported human rights, and tried to bring education and other opportunities to young people in Gaza. This meant that they were seen as a threat by the Islamic movement. Like the ISM they were non-violent, and when they demonstrated they tried to be practical, for example by giving blood to help the victims of the Iraq war.

By this time we had reached the mound, and I was suddenly aware that Andy was beside me. 'I really wouldn't go any further,' he said, putting his hand under my elbow and guiding me back towards the cars. He seemed distinctly jumpy.

Fred and I had bought a ball and some paper and coloured crayons in the mall in Be'ersheva to give to little Salem Baroum, so it was decided that we would split up. TFH would go with

Anthony and the others to visit the Abu Jabr house where the two boys were shot, while Andy and the interpreter would come with Fred and me to find Salem's family.

By this time the usual curious crowd of children and other onlookers had gathered and it had started to rain. The interpreter made enquiries and then led us, single file, through a maze of narrow, muddy alleyways until we reached a very small house only partly covered by a roof. A woman I recognised as Salem's mother came to the door with a man and several young children clustering behind her. She beckoned us warmly into a tiny, bare room and immediately offered us a cup of tea, which we drank sitting on chairs with the rain dripping in. I noticed that she was pregnant, and tried to imagine how she would cope looking after a newborn baby in such desperate circumstances. Salem's father stood silently by, watching us very seriously, bewildered, I felt, by our visit.

Onlookers, friends and neighbours had crowded in with us, and I felt sorry that we had descended on this family in such numbers. I had wanted this to be a quiet visit. Meantime, his father lifted Salem on to my knee. I spoke to the little boy gently as I put my arms round him, and felt his small body rigid against mine. Fred leaned over and with his head close to Salem's, very sweetly and lovingly offered him the ball and the crayons, looking into his face all the while. Salem took them but he didn't smile or show any interest. His expression was blank and his eyes were dull. Six weeks after the shooting, his mother said he could still not be persuaded to speak.

She and I talked a little more through the interpreter, but after twenty minutes or so Andy rose to go. Salem's mother and I took one another's hands and stood in silence for a long moment, simply looking at each other. Then I followed Andy out of the door and we all made our way back to Kir Street through the mud and debris of the alleys.

The sky was dark, the afternoon was drawing in and it was time to go. I wished we had had more time with Mohammed and

Amjad and Sahir, but I knew, as the car drew away and they receded into the distance, standing forlornly waving on the corner of Kir Street, that they were part of our lives now. I was certain we would see them again.

What Anthony had seen that afternoon had shocked him – families so fearful of IDF marksmen that they had abandoned most rooms in their houses. 'They daren't live at the front,' he said, 'and they daren't live on the top floor either because the army targets the top floors, so they live in one room on the ground floor at the back.' One of the sons from the Abu Jabr house was still in intensive care in Gaza City and the family was distraught.

By this time we had reached the approach to the Abu Houli Crossing and we joined a long line of stationary cars snaking back from the checkpoint. We sat waiting, waiting, but after about twenty minutes there was still no movement. Cars began turning round and going back in the direction they had come.

'What's the problem, do you think?' said Anthony.

'Absolutely no idea,' said TFH briskly. 'Could be waiting for a settler coming down the road from one of the settlements. Or the chaps in the checkpoint could be bored and just feel like being obstructive.'

A ratty looking jeep full of soldiers drove up beside the queue and parked at right angles to it. They looked as if they might know something, and my instinct was to lower the window and ask reasonably what was going on. But this was not England. The quietness was deceptive, and there was certainly no question of our getting out of the car.

'Right, I'm going to phone Joseph,' said TFH finally picking up the phone. 'What's the trouble *now*, Joseph?' I heard him say. 'We're sitting here at Abu Houli . . . right, well can you get us through?'

There was more conversation, then a brief word with Andy, TFH started the engine again, and we nosed out and drove very slowly up the inside of the queue. As always I felt uncomfortable as we overtook battered Palestinian cars in these large four-wheel-

drive vehicles flying the British flag, which TFH had been careful
to put up before we reached Abu Houli. No IDF soldier could be
in any doubt that this was a British vehicle. I think it was in all our
minds that we might be shot at again. We drove up and over an
alarmingly steep bank lurching diagonally down the other side,
then back on to the track, and within minutes we were through
the checkpoint. I looked back at the stationary line of vehicles
behind us, with their patient drivers and the little boys running
along the track in the humid heat and squeezing in and out of the
cars, and I felt a mixture of emotions – mortification at our
privileged treatment, anger and sadness on their behalf.

We reached the Erez Crossing and as we drove between the
bollards and across the sterile concrete it was as if we were
somehow leaving life behind. In Gaza there was desperation
but there was warmth – a determination to enjoy each minute
that was partly born out of that desperation. Now we were back
in a colder, more hard-edged world.

TFH had to be back in Tel Aviv, so at the crossing exit we
joined Andy in the other vehicle. I was just doing up my seat belt,
half-looking out of the window at the empty road in front of us as
we pulled slowly away when suddenly, out of nowhere, shot a
smart-looking Mazda heading directly and purposefully for us at
great speed. Andy's reaction was quick. He swerved up on to the
pavement, there was a screech of tyres, a jarring impact and we
were all thrown violently sideways as the oncoming car hit our
wing with a thud.

Andy was the first to recover. He got out and calmly walked
back to the other car, which had come to a halt a few yards away.
The rest of us sat there, dazed. Finally Anthony walked back to
join Andy, and after some conversation I saw him get out Tom's
camera and photograph the scene from various angles – for
insurance purposes, I presumed. Fred hopped out too and
reported that, surprisingly for such a heavy vehicle, the Range
Rover's wing was 'a real mess'. The impact must have been
considerable.

The Range Rover, one of a convoy of two diplomatic vehicles, and essential if we, and also James Miller's family, were to travel into Gaza, was now out of action. We travelled by taxi back to Be'ersheva, considerably shaken. I sensed that beneath his calm exterior Andy was as shocked as the rest of us. He had been able to get very little out of the Israeli driver, who appeared curiously unfazed. The whole incident seemed eerie, inexplicable. Or was it? The shots at Abu Houli, this rogue vehicle – it all seemed too much of a coincidence. Was this a way of preventing us from gathering evidence?

It was early one morning towards the end of May and we were getting ready to leave for the hospital, when the phone rang. Anthony answered but I could hear what the familiar voice at the other end was saying. It was Sherard.

'I've some news for you,' he said, after the usual greetings. 'I've got the Israelis' field report into the shooting here on my desk. They presented it to us yesterday. Obviously we'd like to discuss it with you and Jocelyn. Could you make it down here on, say, Thursday if we send a car for you?'

'So what are their conclusions?' Anthony said.

'Nothing very spectacular, I'm afraid,' said Sherard. 'I think there are some major discrepancies in the report – on the location, for instance – but it's probably better if we talk when you've seen the whole thing. We put forward our key demands, i.e. that they pay Tom's medical expenses and the cost of repatriation, your expenses, and some family compensation. They very reluctantly agreed to meet the medical expenses, and they did actually say they were considering a meeting. It's a lot better than we usually manage.'

Round about eleven o'clock on Thursday we took our seats on the Residence verandah with Sherard, Neil Wigan, a clean-cut young member of the Embassy staff, and the Consul, Mike Hancock. Lovely Middle Eastern morning light shone on the garden and the overhead fan whirred gently. I saw Bridget briefly on her way out; coffee was brought. Then TFH appeared with a sheaf of papers, which he laid on the table. I could read the writing on the top page. '*Thomas Hurndall's Injury*' it said in enormous yellow italics on a bright blue background. This presumably was the army's 'field report'. It looked a bit like something designed for children.

'Well,' said Sherard. 'Just to put you in the picture, we were given the report by the IDF on Monday. It was a PowerPoint presentation in Hebrew, which wasn't immensely helpful. Here's the English version they gave us. I'll be interested to see what you think of the whole thing.'

TFH handed us each a copy. We read in silence. It didn't take long. Few of the twenty-odd pages had more than half a dozen lines on them and the type was huge. The first ten pages were taken up with pro-IDF propaganda, justifying, in simplistic terms, Israel's presence and actions in the 'Military Installations Area' near the Philadelphi Road, and slating the ISM for its 'provocative and illegal activities'.

Then came a section headed 'The Incident', set out in bullet points. This outlined a scenario in which 'an individual aged about 20 dressed in camouflage fatigues', another 'bearded man aged about 30' and two children were seen simultaneously to 'exit' from a building. The first man fired three pistol shots into the air and then fired two shots at the IDF outpost, the outpost commander fired a single shot in return, the 'gunman' fell and was pulled back into the building, and there was then 'a large gathering during which the outpost was attacked with rocks'.

This was followed by five 'Possible Scenarios Explaining How Tom Hurndall Was Wounded'. They read thus:

- Mr Hurndall was hit by Palestinian fire or by a Palestinian gunman's stray bullet (the probability of this scenario is very low).
- The soldier at the outpost accidentally mistook the second adult at the scene for the gunman.

- The soldier at the outpost aimed at the gunman but hit the second adult at the scene.
- Mr Hurndall was hit by a bullet ricocheted off the wall opposite him.
- The gunman was Mr Hurndall (the probability of this scenario is very low).

Bewilderingly, in a separate 'Timeline of the Medical Evacuation' the IDF post also identified 'three figures planting what was presumed to be an explosive device' and the wounded man was brought to 'a nearby IDF outpost' where he received initial medical treatment. None of it added up, and it certainly bore no relation whatever to the facts as we knew them.

The conclusions of the 'report' were as follows:

- It is impossible to establish with certainty the cause of the injuries sustained by Mr Hurndall.
- It is likely that Mr Hurndall was hit by IDF fire.
- The commander of the outpost acted according to the rules of engagement for the area: an armed Palestinian fired at an IDF soldier who felt an immediate danger and therefore he shot a single bullet in response.

The document was accompanied by some meaningless grainy photographs and a 'location map'.

The whole thing was ludicrous, transparent, so unprofessional it was hard to know how to respond. Did they really think we would be content with this level of investigation, this so-called enquiry, backed up by no evidence of any kind? In any case, it made no sense. According to the location map, the notional gunman appeared to have come out of two entirely different buildings. And why would a Palestinian gunman attract attention to himself by firing shots into the air like a cowboy? In the no-go area he would have been shot immediately.

I looked at Anthony, and I could see that he was incandescent with rage. But he spoke quietly, pointing out that not only were the facts unquestionably wrong on the basis of the evidence we already had, but that the aerial map was out of date and that, anyway, the Israelis had got the wrong location. The point marked with a cross was about eighty yards from where Tom was actually shot.

'Yes, we spotted that,' said TFH.

Crucially, Anthony made the point that the claim of a single shot from the tower was an out and out lie. It was well established by a large number of witnesses – not only Palestinians, but international reporters – that there had been at least five shots and possibly as many as eight. And he brought up again the shooting of other civilians, including the boys in the Abu Jabr house.

It was agreed that Sherard would take up with the Israelis the fact that they had got the location wrong, and he promised to be in touch. I think we were both too stunned by the sheer inadequacy of the report and, indeed, the lies contained in it, to say very much after that. In the car on the way back to Be'ersheva we agreed it impossible to take it seriously. It was beyond being an insult.

Next day Sherard phoned. The Israelis had apparently had very little to say in answer to our criticisms.

'I think,' I heard Anthony say finally, in an ominously con-trolled voice, 'that this is such an obvious cover-up that it should be exposed. I think we should go to the press.'

Sherard, on the other end of the line, was clearly objecting.

'I'm not interested that it wasn't meant for publication,' Anthony said. 'The fact remains that it's a total fabrication. They shouldn't be allowed to get away with it.' Things were clearly becoming more and more heated, and I cringed as I heard Anthony say, 'They're quite simply liars.'

Eventually, after more heated exchanges, he said, 'All right. A few days, then I shall expose it to the press', put down the phone and walked over to the window, breathing audibly.

'Sherard wants to follow the diplomatic line,' he said finally. 'Keep quiet and work behind the scenes. He says it will be more effective. I don't agree. Why should we make it easy for the IDF? They *are* just a pack of liars.'

'Absolutely. So how did you leave it?' I said.

'I said I'd wait four days. But that's it.'

'Is Sherard thinking that they might still agree to a meeting? Is that perhaps why he's being careful?' I said.

'If they can produce something like that so-called "report" I don't really see the point of a meeting,' said Anthony, bitterly.

I'd been acutely aware of the toll our situation was taking on Anthony. He looked strained, but until now he had remained, on the surface anyway, controlled. I could see how affronted he was by the tissue of lies we had just been presented with.

Clearly, if we were going to take Tom home and pursue our case from England, we needed a lawyer in Israel to represent us. Several people recommended a well-known and highly regarded human rights lawyer, Avigdor Feldman, and we made an appointment to see him in his office in Tel Aviv. The office was in a back street, a plain building with a down-to-earth, hard-working look about it. I remember being mildly surprised at the modesty of the set-up. The office of someone of comparable standing in London would, I felt sure, have looked very different. We had been told that all the key human rights cases in Israel, such as that of Mordecai Vanunu, who had revealed to the world Israel's secret nuclear capacity, ended up on Avigdor's desk.

He came across his book-lined office to meet us and introduced his partner, Michael Sfarad, a young man in his thirties with an alert, intelligent manner and a friendly, open face. Avigdor was stocky, with rough red skin and iron-grey hair. He said very little, but what he said was to the point. I had the impression of an extremely busy man who knew how to conserve his energy, who knew precisely what he was talking about.

We discussed our situation, the IDF 'report' and various legal issues including the responsibility of the chain of command. Although it was not a priority at the time, we knew that at some stage we would need to pursue our case for compensation for Tom himself and for us. Expenses of every kind were piling up. I was in close touch with the school where I worked and my salary would be paid for a short while longer, but Anthony's practice in London was being manned by someone else, and neither of us had any idea what the future would hold as far as employment was concerned. When we showed Avigdor and Michael the field report, they simply shook their heads wearily. This was familiar territory. They told us that they were, at that moment, compiling a huge report on the IDF's shoot-to-kill policy. It was clear that they understood the workings of the IDF at a very deep level and were able to explain some of the legal precedents and procedures. As a lawyer Anthony was able to grasp more than I did, but it helped me to understand the picture.

I liked them both immensely. Michael told us that he himself had been in prison as a refusenik – he had refused to serve in the Occupied Territories – and I gathered that he spent a good deal of his time fighting for Palestinian human rights. It was agreed that when the time came they would represent us, though it was not clear at present how or when. We went away tremendously reassured to be in the hands of two people of such calibre.

Meantime, Professor Reichental, the head of the Intensive Care Unit, had been conducting his own private conversations with the IDF. I knew he had been doing his best to negotiate a repatriation arrangement for Tom, and Sherard, who was also in discussions about it with the IDF, seemed happy with this two-pronged approach. Sophie reported that many generous people were donating funds for the 'Bring Tom Home' campaign into a separate bank account, but we were still struggling with all the complexities of British charity law, which was difficult from a distance. Our plan was that as soon as Tom was stable enough to travel we would take him home, come what may, and I had already spoken to my own branch of NatWest in Belsize Park about a loan. The manager there was wonderfully responsive and kind; he bent over backwards to make available the £20,000 necessary to bring Tom home, should we need it.

Various helpful people had spent hours on the phone, exploring the possibility of hiring an air ambulance, but we were now told that it wouldn't in fact be the safest way for Tom to travel. With such a badly injured patient the longer journey on a small plane and the bumpier takeoff and landing could be dangerous, so it would be safer to take a scheduled flight. There would, of course, have to be an Israeli medical team to accompany him, including an anaesthetist, and accommodation would have to be found for them in London. The complications seemed endless.

There was also the immense problem of finding a London hospital willing to take Tom. Professor Reichental gave me the name of a contact at the Royal Hospital for Neurological Diseases in Queen Square, but finally, to my immense relief, our local hospital, the Royal Free in Hampstead, agreed to accept him. The biggest complication was the unpredictability of Tom's changing state. He was subject to frequent infections, and we had to wait for a window in which he was sufficiently stable to travel.

In the second half of May he had been moved from the Intensive Care Unit into a small neurological ward, which was really another kind of intensive care. In the next bed was an Israeli man who had suffered a brain haemorrhage. His wife came frequently to visit him from the kibbutz on which they lived. My heart went out to her, for it was obviously a difficult journey, but with tremendous generosity she always came laden with chicken and rice and piles of fruit which she insisted on sharing with us. It was one of those heartwarming contacts that meant so much.

Every day I sat by Tom, holding his hands. His head was still enormously swollen, though a small section of his skull on the left side had now been removed to ease the pressure. He lay there like a shadow, Tom, and yet not Tom. Sometimes I would sit beside him writing, knowing these were moments in which to think and record and remember. I felt he was drifting further and further away from us. *Tom, wait. We're going to take you home. You're going to be among your friends, and the people who love you. They need to say goodbye to you before you go. Wait Tom, dearest Tom.*

Professor Reichental clearly understood our anxiety to take Tom home. I had come greatly to like and respect this fatherly figure. He was dignified and cultured, close to retirement, and I sensed that he understood and empathised with our position.

One Sunday he invited us to tea at his home. We had spent a good deal of time that day with an unusually unpleasant, bullying journalist. He had interviewed us at length about Tom's shooting, but at three o'clock I had excused myself and had gone off alone to Professor Reichental's, leaving Anthony to finish the interview.

Another couple had been invited. I struggled to connect, but the pleasure for me was in being shown round Professor Reichental's beautiful garden as we talked about the various flowers and shrubs. It was restful and civilised, another world from the one I had just left.

I got back at about 7.30 to find the journalist still waiting for me. For some reason he wanted a picture of Anthony and me walking through the door of the ward. I had kept them waiting. So, tired as I was, I put my overall on as requested and we entered the ward. We had made it quite clear that in no circumstances would we permit photographs to be taken of Tom. As I walked through the door, with this man behind me, I realised that the door was about to swing back and hit his camera, so I held it briefly, then walked on towards Tom.

Suddenly I realised, to my horror, that this man was beside me at the foot of the bed, filming. Devastated, I put my hands out in front of me to shield Tom. A nurse appeared and said very clearly, 'Please stop. You are not allowed to do that', but the man simply went on filming.

When he finally lowered his camera, I said with suppressed

fury, 'I had no idea you were going to follow me in. How could you *possibly* feel it was OK to do that? You know we specifically asked you not to film in here.'

'But you held the door open for me,' he said brazenly.

When he had left I simply broke down. It had been such a sly, cheap trick, and I felt devastated. Here was Tom, more vulnerable than he had ever been in his life and needing my protection, and I had let him down. The press had always been so supportive of us; I was shattered by this betrayal.

A few minutes later, a friend, Anne Perkins, who writes for the *Guardian*, phoned. 'Anne,' I said through my tears, 'something terrible has just happened . . .' She was sensible and consoling. Anthony, too, was extremely angry and we complained to the television company. Later we heard that the journalist in question had had a difficult time justifying his behaviour to his bosses, and the film was never shown. But it was an episode that left its mark on me. After that I was always on my guard.

In the third week of May Professor Reichental told us that he thought Tom was stable enough to travel, and all the complex arrangements were finally made for us to fly back to London on 26 May. At last, at last, we were going to take Tom home. But before I could fully absorb the news, two unexpected things happened. Billy phoned to tell us he was planning to return to Israel. He realised he couldn't go into Gaza, but he was planning to travel to the West Bank under the umbrella of the ISM. He wanted to see and understand for himself what the IDF were doing, and was taking his video camera.

We were both appalled. But I realised, from his tone, that Billy, though only just eighteen, was now very much his own man and there was nothing we could do to stop him. Much as I trusted Billy's common sense, it seemed like a nightmare replay of what had happened with Tom. He arrived on 24 May, looking very calm and determined, and went straight out to the kibbutz. I could tell he had done a lot of thinking while we had been in Israel. Our second son had come out of himself and had begun to look at the world through another window. All I could do was phone the understanding TFH and implore him to keep an eye on him.

And on the day Billy arrived, Sherard phoned to tell us that the IDF had agreed to a meeting. They had arranged it for 26 May, the day we were due to fly home.

ELEVEN

Our meeting with the IDF was scheduled for 2.30 p.m. Peter Carter, the Deputy Ambassador who was accompanying us to Jerusalem, explained that we were going to save time by cutting through the West Bank and that we'd be driving pretty fast. 'We don't want to hang around more than is strictly necessary. One tends to attract attention in a vehicle like this,' he said.

There was an uneasy atmosphere in the car and no one spoke much. Anthony and I were preoccupied with the thought of this meeting for which we had waited so long, and Peter and Mike Hancock, another member of the consular staff who was with us in the car, were clearly on the alert for any sign of trouble. The lack of road signs in the West Bank didn't help. At one point we took a wrong turning and seemed to be climbing higher and higher until we reached a quarry-like dead end. Peter reversed rapidly and we found our way back on to the right road, but the feeling of being in unmarked territory was unsettling.

Now that the time for the meeting had come, it seemed almost an anticlimax. This should have been the day we took Tom home and in my heart I was already on my way to London. Somehow all the waiting had exhausted my anger. Anthony had had a sleepless night. When we'd first received news of it from Sherard, Anthony had felt that by this stage it was barely worth having this meeting with the IDF. The ludicrous field report had already shown them in their true colours, and it seemed to him pointless to waste time and effort changing the delicate arrangements for taking Tom home simply in order to meet them face to face.

Yet however insulting the IDF's behaviour, whatever their motive in scheduling this meeting for a time when they must have known that we were virtually on our way home, we couldn't quite bring ourselves to turn our backs. After all, apart from anything else there were still practical matters to be settled and Sherard had urged us to accept. So we were doing our best to psych ourselves up, build up the adrenaline again.

Nearer to Jerusalem we skirted the ancient city of Hebron. I remembered so well visiting it as a student with another volunteer from the kibbutz. We had taken a bus through the Jordanian countryside to visit the famous glass factory where, years before, my father had stood to watch the exquisite blue, green and brown Hebron glass being blown. It had felt good then to be following in his footsteps, seeing what he had seen – a little connection with home.

Returning to Jerusalem on the bus in the evening, to our open-air lodgings on the roof of the Armenian Monastery near the Via Dolorosa, I'd had the strange sensation that strands of my hair kept catching on something. I felt a regular, sharp little sting in my scalp and when I eventually turned round in annoyance I was just in time to catch the man behind me preparing to pluck out another strand. I was too nonplussed to say anything. I've wondered since why he was doing it. Was my fair hair unusual, or shouldn't I have had my head uncovered? Or perhaps he disapproved of my sawn-off jeans and skimpy polka-dot top. I cringe to remember how thoughtlessly we dressed in a country where women's culture was so different – despite all my father's warnings about cultural sensitivity.

Looking down at the old city, nestling in the valley, I was shocked to see what had happened since my last visit. Ugly, threatening tower blocks with darkened glass windows now covered the surrounding hills. I asked Mike what they were; he told me they were West Bank settlements. I was appalled. I had thought of settlements as groups of low-rise domestic buildings. I had never conceived of anything that looked like this. What on earth must it feel like to be the Palestinians living in the valley, with these Big Brother buildings glaring down on them? It was such a blatant and aggressive use of architecture to intimidate and oppress. I thought what a powerful positive effect beautiful architecture can have, and how it can also be used for entirely negative ends. These monstrous, swaggering buildings had clearly been designed to strike fear into a powerless minority. Their message was obvious: 'We don't want you here. We will watch your every move, control your comings and goings, and make life as difficult for you as possible.' As so often during the past few weeks, the word 'apartheid' came into my mind.

It was deeply painful to observe the erosion of this beautiful countryside. I thought how saddened my father would have been to see it and to witness such inhuman treatment handed out to a people he had come to admire and understand and who didn't deserve it. I was overcome by melancholy at the thought of this unending and apparently unresolvable conflict. It was impossible for these two peoples to shift the dark sands of history alone, yet all the words that were spoken now by the rest of the world, by the politicians and diplomats, had come to sound like empty clichés. I had come fresh and uninformed to the situation. I had no prior knowledge, no backlog of assumptions, only my pain at the loss of Tom, and I felt a sudden, urgent responsibility to use that in any way I could. At the same time I had a sick feeling in the pit of my stomach. We had waited so long for this chance to meet the IDF face to face. Would I be able to say what was really in my heart? Would we be able to do Tom justice?

As soon as we'd agreed to the meeting, Anthony and I discussed how we would approach it. To use the meeting to best effect we felt we needed to think very clearly about what we wanted to say and how to say it, and what precisely our demands were. We also wondered who we would be meeting and what level of official-dom there would be.

We'd decided that we both had different roles to play accord-ing to our individual personalities, and that it was important that

Tom, 3 years old, and me looking at photos together

Tom, 6 years old, in a fig tree in Portugal

A family cycling holiday in East Anglia

In the garden in North London; the Harwich Estuary; at Grandma's cottage gate

With Billy, Fred and Sophie

Tom Hurndall

The ISM banner later used for target practice by the IDF

Tom Hurndall

Schoolchildren demonstrating at a funeral in Gaza City

Tom Hurndall

Minutes after this picture was taken, the little boy throwing stones was shot in the shoulder by an APC

Tom Hurndall

Rafah: ISM volunteers Alison and Nicolai sitting on a 12 foot dirt roadblock to enable workers to fix the sewerage system in 'safety'

Tom Hurndall

Rafah: ISM volunteers demonstrating peacefully in front of a bulldozer, an APC and a digger to prevent house demolitions

Tom Hurndall

Rafah: children standing in the ruins of their demolished home

Working as a Red Crescent volunteer at the Al-Rweished refugee camp, Jordan

demonstration in Rafah: 'Palestinians and Internationals targeted by the Israeli Army'

Seconds after being shot, Tom is lifted from the ground by Amjad and Sahir; Nicolai is in the background

Clockwise from top left: Tom and Libby; Sam; Adam and Tom; Kay and Tom; Sam; Cassie

we both have the space to say what we had to say. Anthony, who, when it comes to legal matters is measured and rational, would deal with the practical and investigative side of things. He would tell the IDF very clearly that we wanted to know the truth and were seeking their full cooperation in gathering and sharing evidence. He would ask for confirmation that they would cover all Tom's medical expenses, the cost of bringing him home, and our own expenses, too – in other words, take responsibility for what had happened.

My contribution would be different. I was determined that they should know something of Tom as a person, and what this tragedy had meant to our family. I wanted to look them in the eye and show them that we were human beings, with lives that had been deeply affected by what they had done. I wanted them to understand that they couldn't simply ignore us, look through us, pretend we didn't exist.

We agreed that we wouldn't be accusatory or judgemental. What we wanted was to put them in touch with the pain they had caused us and demand that they make such practical reparation as they could.

The evening before the meeting we'd gone out to the kibbutz to talk to Erella. We felt we needed someone with her knowledge and human understanding to act as a sounding board, perhaps to give us insights into the way the IDF might be thinking. We sat in the cool of the verandah and talked over the way in which the IDF had made us feel transparent, non-existent. We discussed the extraordinary depth of their denial – of us, of what had actually happened, of everything – and how we might bring this out into the open, reflect it back to them. It was something that needed to be seen. Erella's realism gave us confidence. She urged us to focus on Tom's and our absolute right to be considered as human beings.

We came away feeling we'd cleared our minds. Anthony had worked out what he wanted to say, and I felt Erella had given me strength to confront the IDF with the human aspects of the situation. But I knew that I would probably be speaking a language they were not used to hearing, and I couldn't begin to imagine what their response would be.

As we drove through the outskirts of Jerusalem I recalled something TFH had said to me when we were talking about the IDF. 'The bottom line, always remember, is that Tom is seen as a gentile, a *"goi'im"* and therefore in the eyes of God worth less than a member of the Chosen Race,' he'd said. 'It's an appalling but true fact that's rarely talked about in public. To a huge extent it explains the savage nature of their operations against the Palestinians.' A tragic mirror image, I thought, of the way society had so often treated the Jews.

Before the meeting Peter and Mike took us to lunch at an elegant restaurant overlooking Jerusalem where they entertained us in true diplomatic style. We sat looking out over the distant roofscape of the Old City, talking idly. As so often, It felt terribly unreal, as if the parts of our world didn't really join up. Suddenly Peter looked at his watch, gave a sharp exclamation and took out his phone. 'Oh, hello, Danny,' he said. 'Yes, that's right. We're just on our way. We'll be with you in twenty minutes or so.'

The Ministry of Foreign Affairs was a large modern building in the centre of Jerusalem. We left the main road and drove through the usual barriers down a sweep of concrete into a grey-lit underground car park. A clean-cut man of middle height waiting at the entrance introduced himself as Danny Carmon, Head of the Ministry's Co-ordination Bureau. His manner was smoothly charming; as he and Peter greeted one another they might almost have been exchanging golf-course pleasantries. At one level I was intensely irritated, yet I also saw that this smooth, diplomatic approach was a way of oiling the wheels, of getting us through an awkward moment. But Anthony and I both stayed silent. We couldn't have felt more grave, and we showed it.

Danny Carmon led us along corridors and through a long open-plan office. A khaki-clad figure stood framed in a doorway at the end. The very sight of the military uniform was jarring, shocking, a symbol of everything we could no longer respect. The young soldier stood aside for us to enter, and my legs kept on walking though my head felt strangely separate. I picked up bits of a conversation between Peter and Mike behind me, and the sound of their familiar voices was reassuring.

There was a row of eight or nine people seated down one side of a long table. They rose as we came in and Danny Carmon, who appeared to be chairing the meeting, introduced them. It was hard to take in names but I understood that the soldier at the door, Major Biton, was in charge of the enquiry into Tom's shooting and presumably there to defend the infamous 'field report'. He looked about Tom's age. How on earth, I wondered, could someone so young have been given such a responsible job, with all its diplomatic and political implications? Also present were a legal adviser and a desk officer from the Ministry of Foreign Affairs, and an older army captain who was Deputy Head of the IDF Liaison and Foreign Relations Department.

Danny Carmon took his place in the middle of the table and we all sat down, with Anthony directly opposite him, me on Anthony's left and Peter and Mike on his right. Danny Carmon started by offering us a formal expression of sympathy. Anthony thanked him, and said that we appreciated this meeting.

'I'm afraid, however, that it is too little contact too late,' he said. 'We have had to cancel travel arrangements in order to be here, and we shall be leaving Israel within the next few days.'

'Why *has* it taken you so long to meet us?' I said, unable to contain myself as I looked at the row of impassive faces.

Carmon hesitated for a moment, then said rather quietly, 'Perhaps we need to reconsider our policy on this . . .'

Oh yes? What are the real chances of *that*? I thought.

Anthony then said very clearly, 'We haven't come here to criticise or point the finger, but we do want to get at the truth. I'm sure it's what we all want. Our aim is to exchange as much information as possible in order to build up a picture of what really happened on the day our son was shot. Israel used to be a country we all admired and respected. But that respect has been eroded by the way the IDF are conducting themselves now, and there is huge disappointment. We are saddened by the change in the world's perception of Israel.'

This produced an uncomfortable silence. Everyone on the other side of the table looked away, or fiddled with their papers. I had the impression that they weren't used to being held to account in this way. I knew that no family of a Palestinian victim would ever have been given the chance to confront them, and it clearly didn't feel good to have an English family, with all their advantages, doing so now.

Anthony explained that we were now planning to fly home with Tom in three days' time, on 29 May. He asked that Israel agree to cover Tom's medical expenses, the cost of repatriating him to the UK, and our own out-of-pocket expenses since the shooting, including loss of earnings. To cover the immediate cost of the flight, he told them, we planned to take out a loan.

Danny Carmon cleared his throat. 'I'm pleased to tell you that my government has already agreed to cover, *ex gratia*, all your son's medical expenses in Israel, and is positively contemplating a contribution to the cost of repatriation, although I have no final word on that yet. If we agree to contribute to repatriation, then we would naturally wish to be involved in the arrangements.'

'What would that mean, exactly?' Anthony asked.

'Well, for example, we would prefer you to fly by our own airline, El Al,' said Carmon, 'though I understand it may be difficult to change your arrangements at this late stage.'

'So if we were to fly, say, by BA?' said Anthony

'Then I am not sure we would be able to meet the additional cost,' said Carmon. 'Though naturally,' he added quickly, 'we would still consider a contribution as a goodwill gesture.'

A frozen fury was building inside me at the use of the word 'goodwill'. *Goodwill?* We hadn't yet even received an apology.

'However,' Carmon continued, 'we are most unlikely to be able to meet out-of-pocket expenses. Compensation of any kind is a legal issue which of course implies liability, and I hold out very little hope that my government will agree to that.'

Peter Carter now spoke for the first time. 'I would like to remind you, at this point,' he said, 'that Mr and Mrs Hurndall and their family are also seeking an apology for this tragic incident, and a full and open enquiry into the circumstances.'

'As you know, the Israeli Defence Force field report into the incident is now complete,' said Carmon, 'and the results have been passed to the Judge Advocate General's office. I believe you already know from the British Ambassador that the Judge Advocate General would like to see any further evidence you wish to offer before he makes any decision on the possibility of a judicial investigation.'

'Yes, and I understand he wants it by tomorrow, which I'm afraid is not possible,' said Anthony. 'The witness statements are almost complete, and there's a great deal of photographic and other evidence, but that deadline is unrealistic.'

Carmon looked at the young IDF officer. 'Could you approach the Judge Advocate General's office for an extension, Major Biton?' he said.

Anthony then spoke eloquently and at length of his hopes for a proper judicial enquiry, and our wish to use what had happened to improve the army's accountability and contribute to peace in the region. 'As I said earlier, we hold no grudges against the Israeli people,' he said finally. 'We ourselves have many Jewish friends in London. I must honestly say, however, that the results of my own investigation do not tally with the findings of the army's field enquiry. They are so very far from the facts as I understand them that to me they suggest a cover-up.'

The last word went through the meeting like an electric shock. Everyone suddenly moved and shifted papers uneasily. 'On the contrary,' said Carmon smoothly, 'I think it was an impressively frank and open enquiry. I cannot imagine there are many countries which would have gone to such lengths to establish the truth in similar circumstances. I can assure you there has been no cover-up. However, if new data has become available, then clearly the Judge Advocate General should have it.'

Here was a diplomat, cool as a cucumber, praising this blatantly superficial report and complacently imagining we would accept it. It shook me to the core, undermined all my assumptions about the way the world worked. But Anthony remained calm and courteous.

'To take just one example,' he said, 'the report claims that a single shot was fired from the watchtower at the time of the incident, whereas fifteen eyewitnesses state unanimously that there were at least five shots and possibly more than eight. How do you account for this difference?'

'Not true,' said Major Biton. 'The soldier in the tower fired only once.'

'And he was using a telescopic sight?' said Anthony.

'He was using a telescopic sight,' said Major Biton, 'but there was poor visibility from where that soldier was standing.'

'Which was . . .?'

The major went over to the whiteboard in the corner and with a thick black marker drew a crude picture of the tower. On it there was a single window, halfway up, which he marked with a large cross.

'That was the soldier's position,' he said. 'Because of the intervening buildings it would have been impossible for him to have seen your son.'

'But there is surely something wrong there,' said Anthony. 'The lookout windows are round the top of the tower. There is a surveillance platform at the top missing from your drawing. I have seen and photographed them myself, as did my son two days before he was shot. I have the pictures. From these windows there would have been perfect visibility.'

Major Biton simply shook his head, saying, several times, 'No, there was no visibility.'

'Then,' said Anthony, 'the proof will surely be in the CCTV footage. May we see that?'

'We have no CCTV cameras on that watchtower,' said Major Biton.

'But in my son's photographs one can quite clearly see the CCTV cameras fixed to a mast,' said Anthony.

The major had no answer to this. He stood silent for a moment, but then inspiration struck. 'Ah, yes,' he said, 'but those cameras are pointing towards the border, into Egypt.'

It was beginning to resemble a scene from Kafka. Even a civilian like myself could see that there would be no purpose in pointing the CCTV cameras over the Egyptian border when the scene of military action was in the security zone on the Rafah side. Yet again, they seemed to imagine we would be perfectly satisfied with this answer.

'In that case,' Anthony persisted, 'I should like to hear the relevant audiotapes from the two watchtowers and from the armoured personnel carrier which was stationed nearby. I understand that it's customary for you to keep video and audio records of these operations.'

I could see the major was getting flustered, but I felt not a jot of sympathy for him. Though he had seemed very confident at first, it was difficult to hold his own in the face of such cool persistence from someone so clear and determined. But he battled on.

'There was no armoured personnel carrier in the area on April 11 as far as I know,' he said. 'And as I've already said, there were no CCTV cameras in the watchtower that could have recorded the incident.'

'What about the second watchtower?' said Anthony.

'No, that had no cameras either,' said Major Biton after a moment's hesitation. 'It was still under construction and they hadn't yet been installed.'

'You haven't yet answered my question about the audiotapes. There must surely have been some record of what orders were given,' said Anthony.

'I will check on that,' said the major, 'but I think it's unlikely', and he scribbled something on a pad.

'I have to say,' said Anthony, 'that I find all this most extraordinary. Is it customary for you to have no record whatever of an
incident as serious as this?'

Nobody attempted to answer.

'As there seems no other way of checking, I would like to visit
the watchtower to see first-hand what the visibility from it is,' said
Anthony. 'I think I have a right to do that.'

The major looked down and shook his head. 'Again I will
check,' he said, 'but I'm afraid there are likely to be security
issues.'

'I am also troubled by the case of two Palestinian boys who were
shot within the same area within forty-eight hours of my son,' said
Anthony. 'Their names are Rushdie and Mustafa Jabr, and they
were shot without apparent provocation. To me these shootings
seem to demonstrate some kind of pattern. Too many unarmed
civilians are being shot for it to be entirely a coincidence, it seems to
me. I would like to see the IDF's comments on these incidents.'

It was clear that Anthony had mentioned the unmentionable.
The shooting of a young Englishman was one thing, but to
mention the shooting of young Palestinians was quite another. I
saw Danny Carmon's eyebrows lift slightly. Everyone else either
gazed silently into space, or fiddled with pens and pencils. I could
sense that Peter and Mike, on Anthony's right, were sitting very
still.

After an awkward pause Biton said, 'I personally know nothing
about these incidents, but again, I will make enquiries.'

I had sat through these exchanges with a feeling of disorientation, one that remains with me to this day. These people clearly
started out from a completely different baseline from ourselves. I
realised that they had genuinely imagined these monstrous eva-
sions would be enough to keep us quiet. And if this was what they
served up to us, what utter contempt Palestinians must be met
with if they ever attempted to put their case. If this was the
accountability of Israel's 'moral army', then it wasn't a morality I
could relate to.

There seemed little else that anyone could say. But I was determined that I was going to try to communicate our pain to them, as I had promised myself I would. I wanted to penetrate their ivory tower, make them understand the human consequences of what they had done. It was important they knew something of our life, of who we were and what we expected of ourselves and others. In the silence I spoke quietly.

'This is a terrible, terrible thing that's happened to our family,' I said. 'It's not just a tragedy for Tom and us. It's much more than that.'

They stared at me impassively.

'I mean,' I said, 'that shootings like this, of people who can't defend themselves, have an effect on all of us. They're not just a tragedy for the people involved. We are all eroded by them. They devalue life and make us lesser human beings. Such actions go to the core of all we believe about being civilised.'

No one moved. No one spoke.

'Our lives have been completely shattered,' I said. 'Tom and his siblings were very, very close. Sophie, my daughter, has had to leave her job as a researcher, my son Billy has had to take time out to be with his brother, and my son Fred, who is only twelve, hasn't been at school for seven weeks. No homework done. As for Anthony and I, we've had to take time out from our jobs with the uncertainty that brings, and this could have serious repercussions for the whole family. Those are just some of the ways our lives have been affected. What the loss of Tom has done to us emotionally I can't begin to describe. We are distraught, devastated. I can't at the moment see how we will ever recover.'

I thought of Rushdie and Mustafa's family and all the other Palestinian families who would never have a chance to say these things. I thought that at least we had jobs to leave, and roofs over our heads, and the freedom to come and go as we chose. My voice began to break and I could feel tears pricking my eyes and beginning to run down my face.

'When my son Tom came to Rafah he was a university student,

an exceptional young man with an enquiring mind who had all his life before him. I am talking about him in the past tense, because now that life has been taken away,' I said, my voice shaking. 'A bullet fired by one of your soldiers has put an end to it. When Tom was shot he was removing frightened small children from the line of fire. However you wish to interpret what happened, that is what it comes down to. He saw small children threatened by a soldier with a telescopic sight and he did the human thing. He held out his hands to them. What happened to him was utterly without humanity.'

Looking at the row of blank faces, I wanted to go on, to speak to them about the importance of seeing rather than turning away, of entering into dialogue rather than simply looking down the barrel of a gun. But the picture in my mind of Tom holding out his hands to those children was too vivid, too painful, and I choked.

There was still no reaction from the other side of the table. No one could look at me directly. It was as if I was speaking into air. I waited, imagining, I suppose, that someone would say something, but there was silence.

'And why did you shoot at us when we were last in Gaza?' I burst out finally. 'You knew who we were. We followed protocol. We were on our way to the place where Tom was shot. Is that the way you treat a grieving family – treat anyone?'

The embarrassment in the air was tangible. Danny Carmon said, 'I know nothing about this' and the others nodded in agreement – all except the major, who, after a muttered conversation with the captain said haltingly, 'Yes . . . I am . . . aware of that incident.' No expression of apology or regret. The IDF clearly hadn't seen it as an important matter, not something they would expect us to take up with them. I was aware again of the yawning gulf between our expectations and theirs.

After a pause, the lawyer, Daniel Taub, said, 'I think we would all like to say that we respect the way in which you have approached this whole situation.'

It was a small gesture, but at least it implied some empathy. The atmosphere eased somewhat. Danny Carmon raised his head, looked round the room and after a pause said: 'Well, I think we've covered all the various aspects. If no one has anything to add, we'll finish there. I shall be in touch as promised over the matters we've discussed and may I wish you a safe journey home.'

We all stood up. I felt lost, let down, unsure what to do. As people were gathering their papers the grey-uniformed captain came over to where we were standing with Peter and Mike.

'I'm sorry about the incident at the checkpoint. It was unfortunate,' he said.

I had to speak out. 'Thank you,' I said, 'but your army needs further training, Captain. If that soldier didn't know what he was doing, then he should have. We had followed all the correct protocol.'

He seemed extremely taken aback. We stood in awkward silence, then he said goodbye and moved away again. Peter and Mike were drifting towards the door, talking to Danny Carmon, and Anthony and I followed.

So our meeting with the IDF was over. Did they feel the way they had dealt with it was perfectly satisfactory? I realised now that they had come with no expectation that we would actually talk to one another, exchange information. Was dialogue a concept they understood? I thought of the young soldier shooting at us at the Abu Houli checkpoint, the IDF bulldozers driving over Palestinian homes, the shots aimed at small children playing in Rafah. In the coming months and years I would hear it said over and over again. Force was the only way the IDF seemed to know of dealing with conflict. Weapons did their speaking for them.

II

BE'ERSHEVA – LONDON

MAY 2003–JANUARY 2004

TWELVE

Thursday 29 May

I woke before dawn, but even if I'd wanted to there was no question of going back to sleep. This was the day when we were taking Tom home, a day I had thought would never come. Our bags were packed, the flat cleared, the last piece of documentation checked, the last address exchanged. I walked round the flat, gazing out of the windows at the lightening sky, looking over towards the hospital where I knew that, soon, they would be preparing Tom for the journey.

I thought of all the people we were leaving behind – our university friends from the human rights movement who had moved us into this flat; Professor Gurman and Professor Reichental and the staff at the hospital; TFH, and Sherard and Bridget; all the extended family of ISMers; Ya'alon and his taxi: all good, kind people who, in their different ways, had done their best to make life in Israel bearable for us. I thought, with a twist of the heart, of Amjad and Mohammed and Sahir and all the other people in Rafah, trapped behind the checkpoints, threatened by IDF guns and bulldozers, just trying to survive. And of course I thought about Erella. There had been barely time to say goodbye, but somehow there was no need. She and Danny were part of our life now, and we all took it for granted that we would stay in touch.

A few evenings before, our university friends had taken us for a farewell supper in Rahat, the Arab settlement I had often seen from the kibbutz. Though we were eating in the home of a family who were quite clearly very poor, they had laid on a huge, delicious, typically Arab meal for us of rice and coriander and chicken and stuffed vine leaves. They piled our plates high and I was overwhelmed by their generosity, their kindness, their openness, their good spirits. I wished I could have responded in the same way, but I was so tired with the strain of last-minute arrangements, the heat and the language barrier, that it was hard to do justice to the occasion, though both Anthony and I were deeply touched.

And now we were leaving all this behind. We'd decided it would be unfair to put Fred through the tension of travelling with Tom and he had flown to Heathrow the previous day, where he'd been met by Tom's girlfriend Kay and by Ann, the mother of his great friend Joe. I knew he was safe and happy with Joe's family, and I shall always be grateful to them for the way they supported us and opened their house to Fred. Some day, I hope, I shall find some way to repay them.

At 6 a.m. the Embassy driver arrived to take us to the airport, where Peter Carter and Mike Hancock were to meet us. 'Phew,' he said as we drove along the main boulevard, pretending to wipe his brow. 'Your Fred nearly had us in trouble yesterday.'

It seemed that when they'd arrived at the airport, security officials had taken Fred's bags apart and had come across the beautiful blue plates we'd bought on our day out in Jerusalem. I'd wrapped and packed them carefully, and in the middle of them, without thinking about it, I'd put the 'free gift' the shopkeeper had pressed on us – the plate with a huge picture of Yasser Arafat's face on it. This caused confusion and horror at the airport. It was put through the X-ray machine three times, Fred was closely questioned about where he'd got it, and his bags were obsessively searched all over again. How far could paranoia go?

We'd reached the crossroads by the hospital now, and as we stopped at the traffic lights an ambulance swept out at terrific speed. My heart lurched. I knew Tom was inside it. We'd been warned that he would be driven very fast to Tel Aviv to minimise the travelling time, which was dangerous for such a sick and vulnerable patient. I shall never forget the feeling of terrible, terrible sadness as we watched it race on into the distance and out of sight. Here we were at last, taking our son home. It was such a normal thing for parents to do, something we'd been doing all his life, but now it was all so totally, tragically different. Tom would never be part of ordinary life again, never speak to the friends who loved him, and whom he'd loved so dearly. They'd been through so much together. How would they be able to bear this new situation, I wondered, how would they react? It had been so difficult to keep in touch that many of them still had no idea of what had really happened. This was something new we would have to face. First we had had to bear the sharpness of Tom's shooting. Now we must endure the sharpness of bringing him home.

When we reached the airport the ambulance was waiting in a protected area of the car park. The anaesthetist and the nurse were standing talking in the sunshine. The side of the ambulance was open and Tom was lying on a stretcher inside. As I stood looking in at him, I could almost believe he was his old self. A piece of patterned cloth had been laid round his head, which hid the dressing on his terrible wound. I touched his hand, and his skin felt cool. Everything suddenly seemed more ordinary, more normal. Since Tom had left London in February the only place I had seen him had been in a hospital bed. Now it felt wonderful to see him lying there in the fresh air, with none of the paraphernalia of the hospital around him, just waiting for us to take him home.

As soon as we entered the airport building we were surrounded by the press. At hearings of the Israeli Parliament's law committee two days earlier Michael Eitan, the leader of Ariel Sharon's Likud party, had accused IDF soldiers of 'gross violations of human rights' in the Occupied Territories. He had demanded to know whether military leaders could tell him how many cases of human rights abuses there were a month, and, when he received evasive answers, had accused the army high command of indifference. This, from a former army officer, had caused a stir and had clearly focused new press interest on Tom's case. Anthony had just time to answer a few questions and reiterate that we would continue to press for justice, before Peter and Mike hurried us on towards the check-in.

After all our documents had been minutely inspected, a young soldier in the security section motioned us to one side and pointed to our luggage. 'We need to open your bags,' he said. I felt outraged. These soldiers knew very well our circumstances and what we'd been through, they could see that we had Embassy staff with us. How could they subject us to this? The young soldier rooted about, as if fairly uninterested, then picked up a black plastic bin liner that lay on top of my case and opened it. Inside it was another bin liner. He took that out and peered in, but quickly closed it again. Inside it were Tom's bloodstained clothes. It was vital we keep them, but once we'd moved to the flat there had been no cool place to store them, and by now the smell they gave off was horrific.

'What is that? What is in that bag?' he said.

'Those are clothes belonging to my son, who was shot by one of your soldiers,' I said, looking at him with burning eyes, my throat constricting, close to angry tears. It seemed such gross, even purposeful insensitivity. Were they trained not to show their own feelings or to respect other people's? That was our final contact with the Israeli military.

The El Al flight, a concession we were forced to make, was another ordeal. A small section at the back of the plane had been divided off with a tiny, flimsy curtain, the backs and arms of several rows of seats had been lowered and Tom's stretcher had been laid precariously across them. There was absolutely no privacy. Anybody walking down the central aisle could look over and see him. Clearly the Israeli government had wanted to keep its 'goodwill payment' for Tom's flight as low as possible.

Anthony and I sat next to Tom on one side, and the anaesthetist and the nurse sat close to him on the other, continually monitoring him and checking his pulse. I was rigid with tension as we took off, knowing that this was a dangerous moment for Tom, and even when we reached cruising altitude I couldn't relax. Anthony read quietly beside me, or looked out of the window as the map of Europe unfolded beneath us. From time to time I got up and went round to check with the medical staff that all was well, desperately needing reassurance. The plane was fairly full, with many Orthodox Jewish passengers travelling to London, and people walked up and down the aisle continually, peering over at us with undisguised curiosity. I felt we were a sort of show. It was a raw and shocking experience.

After what seemed an eternity we saw the English coastline, and the plane began its descent into Heathrow. I'd always had a feeling of warmth and security returning home from abroad, but this time I was on edge, worried about the landing and how it might affect Tom, not sure what would happen when we arrived. When the doors were finally opened and we were ushered off the plane, it was a relief to find a British ambulance team waiting. Tom's stretcher was lowered on to a trolley and we left him on the tarmac with the cheerful, competent ambulance men. Lying there in the midday sunshine, free of tubes and wires, he could almost have been asleep. I just remember seeing his long bare feet poking out from under the blanket before he was wheeled away and we followed the crowd towards the terminal.

A car was supposed to be meeting us, but somehow we were unable to make contact with it, so we took a taxi to the Royal Free, miraculously escaping the press. They were waiting inside the arrivals building, with their cameras pointing towards the tarmac where Tom was being transferred to an ambulance, and we simply walked out behind them.

It was extraordinary to drive through the London streets again, to feel the soft English breeze through the taxi window, to see the May sunshine on rows of Victorian houses, the blossom trees in the Hampstead front gardens. Everything was so familiar, yet we were seeing it with different eyes. It was as if we had lived another entire life in the seven weeks we'd been away.

To avoid the huge numbers of press who were apparently waiting at the hospital we had been asked to go in by a back door, where the Chief Executive's PA met us. We knew that a press conference had been arranged for us at 3.30 in one of the lecture rooms, and that the medical team who would be looking after Tom were to meet us first. Walking along the corridors, all the times I'd been here in the past came flashing back. This was where I'd brought the boys on occasion, where I'd come with Sophie when she'd broken her arm. The Royal Free was our local hospital and I was overcome with a sense of being on home ground. I felt so thankful that we had been able to bring Tom back to a place he knew, to enfold him here where his friends could have the chance to be with him, and – we would all have to accept it at some point – to say goodbye to him before he died.

The medical team were waiting for us in a small meeting room on one of the lower floors. As soon as we sat down I expressed my thanks to the hospital for having Tom, and for allowing us to take over one of their lecture rooms for a press conference. I felt awkward about this arrangement and wondered if it was usual. It had been made by someone in London whom we didn't know very well, and I had an uncomfortable feeling of being taken over, of somehow not being in control.

The doctors spoke quietly and sympathetically to us about Tom's medical condition, the need to do more neurological tests, run further scans. Then they began to talk about the importance of security, the need to have a guard on continuous duty outside Tom's ward, at least for the first few weeks, until things had 'settled down'. They were clearly somewhat apprehensive at the prospect of looking after such a high-profile patient, and it was only then that I began to understand what enormous public

interest there was in Tom's case. The doctors talked about the
extensive newspaper coverage there had been, and about reactions to the *Dispatches* programme. It seemed that Tom's story had
made an impact on people all over the UK.

As we entered the lecture room, I was aware for a moment of a
huge photograph of Tom projected on to a screen in front of us.
The sight of Tom's face in close-up threw me completely and I
stopped. There was a sudden loud clicking sound, and I felt
disorientated, very much taken by surprise, by flashing cameras.
We took our seats behind a table and when my eyes adjusted I
looked out at a sea of faces stretching to the back of the lecture
room. The place was packed, and people were standing inside the
doors. Waving microphones and cameras on rods were thrust
towards us.

'I'd like to ask Jocelyn. How's Tom?' called a voice from the
middle of the room.

It was such a simple, kind question, something that no one in
Israel had ever asked us. It made me feel that people really cared.
My voice was unsteady as I answered: 'Tom has a very, very
serious head wound. He is still in a coma, and sadly, he's unlikely
to recover. I'm afraid we must be realistic about that.'

'Nicola Woolcock from the *Daily Telegraph*,' said another
voice. 'What does the Israeli Defence Force have to say about
the shooting? I understand they've conducted their own enquiry.'

'On the basis of the evidence we've collected ourselves, the
report they've produced is a total fabrication,' said Anthony, with
great emphasis. 'We are conducting our own enquiry and we've
so far interviewed fourteen witnesses. We went out there with
open minds. We only wanted to discover the truth, but we've had
almost no cooperation from the Israeli army. What we do know is
that Tom was the third unarmed civilian to be shot in the same
area within forty-eight hours. The army seems to want to
intimidate and frighten people out of the area by a process of
terror. It is unaccountable and out of control.'

So now Anthony really had stated publicly what he thought of the field report. I wondered what Sherard would be thinking when he read the next day's papers.

'The army's so-called report consisted of twenty pages of very large print, and the majority of those were a history of the Israeli Defence Force,' I added.

There were numerous other questions. People wanted us to clarify what had actually happened on the day of the shooting, what we thought would happen next, whether anyone was likely to be brought to justice.

'And how have you both managed to deal with all this?' someone else asked. 'How are you feeling now? Do you blame yourselves for letting Tom go to the Middle East?'

How were we feeling? By this point I hardly knew. I could only think of seeing Tom settled in his new surroundings, and then getting home to Sophie and Fred.

'It's been a cruel seven weeks,' I said. 'We've been physically exhausted by all the emotion and the sadness of what's happened. All I can say is that I did what I could before Tom went to keep his eyes open to the dangers. Tom was someone who identified with other people's pain, and I'm enormously proud that he had this very strong desire to seek out injustice. We're extremely relieved to have him home and so grateful to the people who have helped. The support has been really staggering. Thank you so much.'

Finally it was over, and we took the lift to the seventh floor. Tom was lying in a corner of the Intensive Care Unit beside a large window that looked out over Belsize Park. Outside were the streets where he had walked, the houses of families he'd known all his life. This was where he'd hung out. This was his patch. The terrible underlying tension I'd felt every time I visited the Soroka Hospital melted away. Tom was here now, in his own place, among people who loved him. It felt so important that they would be able to come and share the precious time that was left. Though we had really no idea what would happen in the months ahead, I knew that being with Tom was all that really mattered now.

★   ★   ★

When Sophie opened the front door to us I hugged her and all the pent-up emotion and anxiety of the past days and weeks came flooding out. She had coped brilliantly while we were away, dealing with the press, fielding letters and enquiries, helping to set up a website in Tom's name. But she looked pale and very fragile.

We sat in the kitchen nursing mugs of tea, trying to anchor ourselves. There was so much catching up to do. Anthony described our meeting with the IDF and the progress of his investigation. I gave Sophie messages from Erella and various ISMers. Sophie told us of the huge support she'd had from her friends and even from the general public, amongst them journalists keen to keep the story in the public eye. And she told us how all Billy's mates had come round and cleaned and tidied his room before he got back. I knew we were all worried about Billy – too worried to say very much. We'd had word that he was filming the young soldiers' behaviour at checkpoints outside Nablus. So at least we all knew where he was and that the people he was with would be watching over him, knowing what had happened to his brother.

Our own friends had been amazing, dealing with bills, cleaning and servicing the car, organising practicalities. Sophie told us she'd also been contacted by Rachel Corrie's family in America, and they'd been talking and e-mailing. In particular she'd developed a rapport with Rachel's sister Sarah, who was slightly older than she was and whom she described as a 'wonderful person'. It had obviously been such a relief to them both to talk.

'Rachel's Mum Cindy told me that the day Tom was shot was the worst for her since the day Rachel was killed,' Sophie said. 'There were only three weeks in between and it was only 200 yards away. it was probably the same unit that killed James too.'

From all we'd read and heard about the Corries we had come to admire the dignified way in which they had dealt with their daughter's death, and especially the way they'd faced the subsequent smear campaign against Rachel and the ISM at home in

America. It seemed natural that I should make contact with Cindy, but I knew I couldn't do it yet. I wasn't ready to share that horror. What had happened to me? I thought. I was normally the kind of person who was able to go out to others, to feel their pain. I felt confused, as if I didn't recognise myself.

We rang Joe's home, where Fred had been staying, and spoke to Fred. 'Is Tom OK? Can I see him?' he asked immediately, and I could hear the little heartbreaking note of hope in his voice. Later, when he arrived home, he told us more about the scene at the airport, and the stir it had caused when he told the security officials rummaging in his bag that he didn't really know what was in it: 'My mother packed it.'

The phone was ringing continually while we sat at the kitchen table, and when we had talked ourselves out I went into the sitting room to listen to the messages. A harsh female voice immediately emanated from the handset. At first I couldn't believe what I was hearing. It was undisguised, obscene abuse. Tom was 'a fucking Nazi' and we were 'a load of fucking Nazi lovers'. I stood there in shock, and it wasn't until I heard the words 'I hope your fucking son will die a painful death' that I had the sense to put the phone down. I sat down on the sofa, feeling as if I had been violated, physically attacked. It was the kind of middle-class voice you might hear anywhere in north London, but there was something strangely familiar about it which I couldn't place. I decided to delete it. I hoped I wouldn't hear it again.

The rest of the tape was filled with supportive messages from well-wishers, including one from Afif Safieh, the Palestinian Delegate in London. When I phoned the number he had left I was immediately answered by Afif himself. He expressed his sympathy and concern, and asked if he and his wife Christ'l could come and meet us and visit Tom in hospital. The brief conversation with someone so warm and accessible, who seemed to understand our situation without my having to explain it, was like balm after that first appalling message. It was arranged that we would see them at the Royal Free at eleven o'clock next morning.

I sat alone downstairs for a long time after Anthony had left and Sophie had gone to bed, trying to put the day together in my mind, to make some sense of all that had happened. When I finally went upstairs I stood for a moment looking up at Tom's closed bedroom door. After Tom had left for Iraq I had had his room on the third floor redecorated and made into a bedsit, with a kitchenette and fridge. It was what he had always wanted – a place where he could boil a kettle, be a bit self-sufficient. I stood on the landing, knowing very well that the room was empty, that everything behind that door now was clean and bright and different. But in my heart Tom was still there, sitting in his old chair with his legs up on the windowsill, pen poised above the pad on his knees. '*Aren't you asleep, Tom? Want a cup of cocoa?*' He'd smile, pleased to be disturbed. '*Yeah. Thanks.*' I couldn't go in.

I wondered, yet again, whether I could have done anything to stop him going to Iraq. Probably not. Tom was someone who took calculated risks, the kind of challenging personality who gives an anxious mother nightmares. I thought of all the times I'd tried to stop him taking risks, tried to curb his enquiring mind to keep him safe. It was because I loved him so much, yet I realised that my caution has also been tinged with a kind of exasperation. Now I was beginning to understand my son at a deeper level, to see that he had taken risks because he was trying to know himself and the world better and because he hated injustice. I recognised that I had a hatred of untruth and injustice myself, which went very deep – we all did in the family. Now I was having to separate that out and learn to respect it in my son.

When we arrived at the hospital the next day we were met in the front entrance by Afif and Christ'l, and by a reporter from the *Hampstead & Highgate Express*. I warmed to Afif and Christ'l almost from the moment I saw them. Afif, with his ready smile, spoke eloquently and with genuine passion. Christ'l, fair-haired and elegant, was immediately empathetic. They both radiated wisdom and warmth and kindness, and I soon came to realise that they were a very special couple who were deeply loved and respected in diplomatic circles, not just in London but worldwide. They provided a link between three worlds – London, Palestine and Israel – and I would come to depend on them greatly.

We took the lift to the Intensive Care Unit and were standing around Tom's bed when we were met by the Senior Registrar, who led Anthony and me into his office. Since the previous day they had done more brain scans and neurological tests and the Registrar was at pains to tell us – as kindly as possible – that there was really no hope of recovery for Tom, or even any likelihood of improvement. We would ultimately have to decide what we wanted to do about Tom's future, he said, but meantime, of course, they would do everything they could to keep him comfortable and stable.

It wasn't as if we didn't know this already, but the little flame of consolation, the faint glimmer of optimism that I had felt on Tom's return to England and to the Royal Free was doused in a flash by these cool and realistic words. I was too weary, and it was all too raw. I wasn't ready to hear this again. When we re-emerged into the ward I could barely speak and Anthony was deathly quiet; he looked desolate.

Christ'l put her arms round me and Afif said: 'Come. Let's find somewhere quiet to sit down.' We found a café round the corner from the hospital and over coffee they encouraged both Anthony and me to talk. It was quite clear that Afif knew precisely what had happened in Gaza and it was like the shedding of a load to talk to someone of such obvious depth and maturity. He was not out to make political capital or to polarise the situation. He approached Tom's shooting as part of a much bigger picture. 'Just see this in terms of a fight for justice,' he urged. It was the way Afif and Christ'l expressed their humanity that was so striking – asking detailed questions about Tom, genuinely wanting to find out how we were, telling us about their own experiences, and giving us names of important contacts in the government.

Afif told us that he had been educated at the Ecole des Frères in Jerusalem, near the New Gate into the Old City, along with a group of friends that included the Palestinian writer Edward Said. Edward Said's was a name I barely knew then, though I remembered that one morning in Israel I had heard a voice on the radio speaking of the Middle East in such a poetic and insightful way that I had reached for a pencil and started taking his words down. The speaker was Edward Said, and after our meeting with Afif I began to search out his writings. They brought me a whole new awareness of the richness and resilience of Palestinian culture. So often the Palestinians are seen by the Western world simply as victims, as a hopeless, disorganised, downtrodden society, but reading Edward Said and talking to Afif I began to realise how utterly wrong this was.

'Under the worst possible circumstances,' Said wrote a few months later in an article on Rachel's Corrie's death, 'Palestinian society has neither been defeated nor has it crumbled completely. Kids still go to school, doctors and nurses still take care of their patients, men and women go to work, organizations have their meetings, and people continue to live, which seems to be an offence to Sharon and the other extremists who simply want Palestinians either imprisoned or driven away altogether. The military solution hasn't worked at all, and never will work. Why is that so hard for the Israelis to see?'

I had seen it, and I knew it was true. As we said goodbye to Afif and Christ'l that day, I had no idea what good friends they would become, or how they would guide us through the minefield of the coming months. But I did know, just from that one brief meeting, that Afif didn't simply represent the Palestinian cause. He represented the best of mankind.

Ten days later we received a letter from Yasser Arafat.

Dear Anthony and Jocelyn Hurndall,

Allow me my dear friends, to express my solidarity and sincere sympathy at these difficult moments that you are going through, due to the shooting of your dear son Tom. We believe that Tom was deliberately shot, in cold blood, by the Israeli army in Rafah two months ago, as he was defending Palestinian elderly, women and children. He was on a humanitarian mission in solidarity with our people, as part of an International campaign of peace by supporters from around the world, that supported the Palestinian people's just struggle to stop the vicious Israeli aggression and put an end to the Israeli occupation of our land and holy shrines . . .

I was touched by the private sympathy, but anxious that Tom seemed to be becoming a political icon, whereas to us he was simply Tom. Some journalists rewrote him in such a way that none of us recognised him. Sophie said later that, as he lay there in a coma, it felt as though he was being torn apart by people on both sides of the conflict.

THIRTEEN

Although we were home, normality seemed light years away. But Fred bravely went back to school part-time. Anthony, who had been given an extension for presenting his evidence to the Judge Advocate General in Israel, concentrated on finishing his report. In Israel we had both been completely focused on Tom's tragedy and our concern for our children. Now back in London, Anthony and I saw each other, either at home or at the hospital, almost every day. There was still an overwhelming amount to discuss and we supported one another. But we were all of us out of our minds with pain. We were trying to think of one another, but the very nature of grief made it impossible. We all found it hard to talk about the one thing that was on our minds.

Each day I went to the hospital, and Fred often called in there on his way home from school and sat quietly by Tom's bed listening to music. Almost as soon as Tom arrived in England there had been a change in his appearance. The external wound in his head had more or less healed now, the seepage of spinal fluid had stopped and so, more or less, had the bleeding from his ear. Quite suddenly the terrible swelling went down, leaving a raw, exposed, sunken area above his left temple with a ridge of bone where a section of his skull had been removed. It was agonising to see Tom in this state, but to me it was of the utmost importance that I put these feelings aside. Tom needed us to be strong for him, to help him bear everything. The disfigurement did not detract from his innate dignity. When I was with him I felt an overwhelming need to cradle his head, to stroke it.

Anthony was as distressed as I was. His feeling was that Tom would not wish others to be distressed by the sight of his wound, and at first he felt it should be covered. But to me the greatest respect we could pay Tom was to accept him as he was, wound and all, to share his cruel disfigurement with him. I felt there was no reason why we or anyone else should be protected.

One Sunday afternoon when we came back from the hospital Sophie looked pale and somehow disorientated – but we were all feeling disorientated, so I didn't pay too much attention. On Monday morning we were standing talking in the sitting room before she went to work, and she suddenly said rather vacantly, 'I don't know where to go.'

I was astonished. This was Sophie, my highly organised daughter. What did she mean?

As I opened my mouth to reply Sophie crumpled and sank to the floor. Her eyes were closed and her face was ashen. I managed to lever her on to the sofa and tried to give her some water, but she didn't respond. When she came to she seemed confused, and our neighbour, a GP, advised taking her to hospital. So within an hour I had not one but two children in the Royal Free. She was discharged within a couple of hours but when I brought her home she was almost too worn out to walk upstairs. It was just an indication, if I needed one, of the extreme strain she had been under. It was some days before she felt ready to return to work.

Since Anthony and I had been in Israel engaged with the struggle to bring Tom home I hadn't realised the extent of Sophie's emotional and physical exhaustion. She had been running the campaign which had developed beyond an appeal to raise funds for Tom's return and was now carrying on as a form of tribute to him, concerned with highlighting the plight of the many threatened families in Palestine and demanding accountability within the Israeli army. The non-stop interviews were emotionally draining, and the shock of Tom's return to the UK (Sophie felt she had in some ways said goodbye to Tom already), combined with seeing the cruel change in the wound on his head, brought about a complete physical collapse: her body simply shut down.

Gradually friends began phoning and arranging to visit. We had to explain that there was a twenty-four-hour guard on Tom's room, and we would need to add them to a list of visitors. I loved seeing them when our visits coincided because they were all, had been, a part of Tom. Some of them, when they came, brought CDs of Tom's favourite music to play him, others wrote personal, spirited messages on the large sheet of wallpaper on the wall opposite his bed.

Among the first people to visit was Tom's friend Sam. He and his mother Ann both adored Tom – most of the time, that is – and Ann was probably one of the adults outside the family who knew him best, his faults as well as his virtues. Tom had spent hours in Ann's kitchen, laughing and discussing everything under the sun, with Tom asking about Ann's life, and acting the mature adviser. I, in turn, was – and am still – devoted to Sam. To me it was as though he represented the emotional side of Tom. A talented musician, Sam is a liberating personality, able to express his feelings and to talk about them in an unusually articulate way. But there were times, as they were growing up, when neither Tom nor Sam was easy, and Ann and I had often laughed and commiserated about the challenges of bringing up our loveable sons.

Sam told me later that he had been in Dingwall's, a jazz bar in Camden Town when he heard the news of Tom's shooting. 'I was standing next to the bouncer, and I got this call on my mobile,' he said, 'and someone told me I just cried out, really loudly, "Oh, something terrible has happened to my friend!" Then we all went up to Alex's house and sat watching the news.'

Ann described to me the first time she went with Sam to visit Tom. Several of Tom's friends and their parents were visiting that day. They had collected at Belsize Park tube station and walked up the hill together. They couldn't all go in at the same time, and there were people already waiting outside the ward, including

Anthony and two of Tom's fellow students who had come all the way from Manchester.

'When we finally got in and I saw Tom lying there, with that terrible, terrible wound, I burst into tears,' she said. 'Sam said, "Just a minute, Mum." He went off and came back with a cloth to cover Tom's head. Then he bent down and started mopping Tom's face, stroking his hands so tenderly, rearranging the bed-clothes, trying to make sure he was comfortable. He was so concentrated, so concerned, it was heartbreaking. He was talking to Tom all the time: "Man, it's been about a week since I saw you. Everyone's thinking about you. Look, my Mum's come to see you . . ." It was as if Tom was at home and they were having an ordinary conversation.

'Then Sam put on a CD he'd brought. It was that song he and Adam wrote for Tom called 'Sleeping on the Floor'. Suddenly above the music I heard this strange kind of wailing. It was Sam, he was weeping his eyes out. Then he took hold of Tom's wrist and started dancing. Tom's wrist was like a twig, so, so thin, but Sam just held on to it as if they were dancing in a group, just like they'd always done, and he went on dancing to the rhythm, singing the words, except that his voice kept breaking. It was completely abandoned and unselfconscious, but it was so angry too. It was as if he just couldn't accept what had happened to Tom. I felt he was saying to him, "Come on, mate, you've got to get out of this." I just sat there watching them, with tears streaming down my face.'

All Tom's friends were different, of course, but perhaps the person who caused me most concern was Tom's close and oldest friend Adam. Adam is a very different kind of character, wry, witty, thoughtful, clever, less of an extrovert perhaps. He and Tom had known one another since they were small boys, attended the same prep school, been lost on a motorbike in the Egyptian desert together. Their outrageous wit and banter had often had us all in stitches, and he was part of the close group that surrounded Tom. He knew very well how difficult it was to dissuade Tom when he made up his mind to do something – I'd heard him describe it in an interview. Adam happens to be Jewish, and I wondered, still wonder, how he is dealing with Tom's loss. But I understood something of how angry he was when I heard that he had confronted the Israeli Ambassador outside our local cinema in Belsize Park. He must have discovered that the Ambassador was due to watch a film, and he'd joined a small crowd of demonstrators. Although he couldn't get near because of the security police, he shouted out at him to go and see his friend Tom Hurndall. 'Go, Adam!' I'd thought.

For the most part, however, Adam's anger was unexpressed and I didn't know how to help, though I had tried to get in touch.

And then there was Alex, one of Tom's closest confidants. Alex had lost his own brother in a car accident, and I knew that this tragedy had devastated his family. Tom had attended the funeral, and had always kept a newspaper report of the accident, with a photo of his good friend's younger brother, stuck on his bedroom wall. The family had shown enormous empathy for us and for Tom. The loss of Tom would surely revive terrible memories for Alex, and I was worried about how he would cope. And there were other friends, too, whom Tom had loved, who I knew less well. I thought of them in their grief, and hoped they were not feeling isolated.

My own friends, I think, tried to hide their distress at the sight of Tom. Guy and Ann, the director of the English Chamber Choir and his wife, arranged during these early weeks to meet me at the Royal Free to discuss their idea of a Concert for Tom. Though they were very controlled – for my sake, I'm sure – there was no disguising their shock, and it was the same with all my friends who came to the hospital. I knew the depth of their concern and affection, and I was grateful for their tact.

One still, bright morning, some days after our return, I was upstairs tidying and I started walking, almost without thinking, up the stairs to Tom's room. Until then I had avoided those stairs quite consciously. Now something had shifted, some defence had dropped. But I stood for a while, bracing myself, before opening the door.

Sunlight streamed through the window on to the newly laid oak floor and into the little kitchenette with its clean white surfaces. Where Tom's old writing desk had been there was a new beautifully carpentered built-in desk, with folding doors designed to hide the mess. Down one wall were spacious fitted cupboards, where his crowded wardrobe had once been. The only recognisable thing was his old chair. Tom's room, as I remembered it, was no more.

The Saturday before the shooting I had spent the day clearing it ready for the builders to come in. Almost every inch of the walls and ceiling had been covered by Tom with photographs of his family and friends. It was as if he wanted to be completely surrounded by the people he loved, by everything that had happened in his life, as if to remember every minute of it. There were pictures of us on holiday in East Anglia, his friends taken at school, in pubs, scuba diving, up on Hampstead Heath, much more recent photographs from university, pictures of Tom and Kay on holiday in Luxor, and in Paris by the Eiffel Tower. There were fading colour photos of my parents taken at my grandparents' much-loved holiday cottage on the Solway Firth. He had even found a photograph of Anthony and me sitting in a restaurant when we were engaged. It was a panoply of Tom's whole life. Painfully, lovingly, trying not to damage them, I had removed the staples and taken everything down. Now, standing in this unfamiliar room, this bright emptiness that should have been his to fill, all I could feel was the gaping hole of his absence. I couldn't find any meaning to it all and I moved aimlessly around the room, utterly bereft.

Eventually I got up and opened one of the new fitted wardrobes. There on the ceiling, which was still painted the familiar indigo blue, were some photographs I'd forgotten to remove. Tom's friends looked down at me, smiling, waving, making faces at the camera. A little bit of Tom was still there. That tiny remaining corner of his old room seemed as precious as some fragment of a medieval wall-painting. On one of the cupboard shelves was a stack of stationery, including a pile of the simple, buff, spiral-bound A5 writer's pads that Tom always had with him. I picked one up, saw him again in my mind's eye, with his feet up on the window-sill, pen poised. I leafed through it, gazed and gazed at it, wondering what he would have written on those empty pages.

On another shelf was a folder labelled 'Memories'. Some small, folded bits of paper fell out. On one was written 'Playing with Sophie when we were little'. On another 'When my mother says "Well done"'. It took my breath away, that sharp reminder that everything you say and don't say as a mother means something. *Oh Tom, did I say 'Well done' to you often enough? I pray that I did.*

Another buff folder held some English essays he had written at Winchester. There was a lyrical description of a ship at sea in the evening sunset with a glowing comment from his English master, a piece entitled 'A night out with the lads' in which he described how much he disliked drinking and how alien and 'out of it' he felt on such occasions. Underneath it were several more note-books, with dates on the front. Tom's diaries. I'd asked the builders to take everything down to the cellar, but Sophie must have brought them up again. The very sight of Tom's hand-writing affected me for days, and now, confronted with these diaries, I crumpled inside. Should I open them? The family had been at sixes and sevens over what to do about them, and we'd vaguely decided to put them away for a few years. Then it would be up to each of us to decide whether we wanted to read them.

Now I remembered that one day when I was at the Residence in Tel Aviv, Sophie had rung me, very excited, saying that she had found something beautiful that Tom had written. The date was November 2001. Tom would have been nineteen. The words jumped out at me:

What do I want from this life? What makes me happy isn't enough; all those things that satisfy our instincts complete only the animal in all of us. I want to be proud. I want something more. I want to look up to myself and when I die, I want to be smiling about the things I've done, not crying for what I haven't. I guess I want to be satisfied I know the answer to this question. Everyone wants to be different, make an impact, be remembered.

Since we'd got back, people I'd met had often asked me, 'So what was Tom doing in the Middle East?' I understood why they asked, but there were times when something in me bridled, and I found it difficult to answer. The implication from these often rather comfortable people seemed to be that Tom's journey had been just a young man's fancy, the kind of immature thing that he would ultimately grow out of. Looking at this diary I knew what I wanted to say: 'There are some people who don't just stay in their comfort zone, who don't think that we're here in this world just for ourselves. Tom was one of those. He was as pleasure-loving and party-going as any young man, but he also wanted to record the vileness of conflicts like this so you can sit in safety on your sofa and know about them. *That's* why he was in the Middle East.'

Some time later, a good friend sent me this passage from John Ruskin:

The greatest thing a human soul ever does in this world is to see something, and tell what it saw in a plain way. Hundreds of people can talk for one who can think, but thousands can think for one who can see. To see clearly is poetry, prophecy, and religion all in one.

★   ★   ★

In Highgate, Anthony was still working desperately on the final stages of his report. I knew he was frustrated at the length of time it was taking, but it was extraordinary that he could do it at all in the circumstances. I was keenly aware of how important this report was for Anthony. It was part of his tribute to Tom. Into it he channelled all his love and all his anger at the shoddiness and injustice of what had happened. His honesty, his painstaking pursuit of the truth, his determination to be even-handed, exposed the IDF's pathetic effort for the lying and self-serving exercise it was.

The tone of the report was calm and considered, the language clear and economical. It started by describing why Tom had been in Rafah and why the ISM had been in Salah El Din Street on that day, including the unprovoked shootings at the Abu Jabr house. It went on to give a clear picture of what had happened, based on the evidence of fourteen witnesses – nine ISM volunteers, two photographers, Khalia Hamra from Associated Press and the freelance photographer Garth Stead, and the three Palestinian witnesses, Mohammed, Amjad and Sahir. Neither the volunteers' nor the Palestinians' full names were given because, as Anthony tellingly put it, 'they are concerned at possible retribution from Israeli army and intelligence forces'.

Finally, point by point, it demolished the IDF's report, with all its inconsistencies and implausibilities, and Major Biton's attempt to defend it.

'The IDF acknowledge Tom was hit and taken to Soroka; that there was no other incident that afternoon,' Anthony had written. 'Beyond that their account does not tally in any way with the facts. Tom was shot in a different location, he was not exiting any building, he was not facing straight onto the security zone in front of the security wall, but behind a mound in a street eighty metres away. He was not wearing camouflage fatigues but an orange thigh-length jacket. He had no pistol. He was not pulled back into any building. He was not taken away in an ambulance. There is no similarity between the locations. The events described are two different events: one real and the other a fabrication.

'There is only one conclusion possible on the facts available. Given the admission that the commander was deliberately aiming at an identified adult, that no other adult was in view, and that Tom was wearing a clearly visible orange jacket, the conclusion has to be that the soldier shot Tom knowing his target to be either an international peace activist, who was part of an organisation considered to be impeding the activities of the IDF, or a photo-grapher recording such activities.

'General Eiland and the IDF chiefs of staff have sought to avoid responsibility by a straightforward fabrication. Their version does not accord with verifiable facts or with any possible interpretation of those facts.'

The report was supported by witness statements, photographs and clear location maps. It was cool, brilliant, unanswerable, a veritable sword of truth, cutting cleanly through all the IDF's lies.

During these first weeks at home we became aware that many concerned voices were being raised in Parliament over Tom's case. In early June we received a letter confirming that the Foreign Minister Jack Straw had agreed to our request for a meeting. It reiterated the well-worn claims. 'The government,' Straw assured us, had 'continually pressed the Israeli government for a full and transparent enquiry' into Tom's shooting, and had asked the Israelis to 'review their rules of engagement and to try to avoid further civilian casualties in the future'.

Before seeing Jack Straw in mid-June we had a meeting with Richard Burden, a Labour MP with a close and consistent interest in the Middle East, during which we showed him this letter. We were in the House of Commons when he challenged Jack Straw's Parliamentary Under-Secretary to clarify what precisely was meant in it by a 'full and transparent enquiry', and to reveal what Israel's response had been to the request for a review of the rules of engagement.

Around this time another Labour MP, Jeremy Corbyn, tabled an Early Day Motion, signed by twenty-nine MPs:

> That this House notes the shooting of 21-year-old Tom Hurndall whilst helping Palestinian children escape gunfire from an Israeli army watchtower in Rafah, Gaza; calls on Israel to conduct a full military police inquiry into the incident; supports the calls from Tom Hurndall's family for the Israeli military advocate-general to

start a prosecution against the Israeli commander who fired the
bullet; and sends its support to the family of Tom, who is in a
coma at the Royal Free Hospital from which he is not expected to
recover.

The government response was predictably anodyne, but it was
overwhelming to realise that there was a solid group of impressively well-informed and conscientious MPs who were behind us
in our passionate struggle to get justice for Tom, and who were as
appalled as we were by what the Israeli army was doing. We were
deeply grateful, but I must admit that at this point the heartbreaking day-to-day reality of visiting Tom made the world of
politics seem remote, and it was only later that I was able truly to
appreciate all that was being done.

'Remote' was certainly the impression we had of Jack Straw
when Anthony and I eventually went to meet him at the Foreign
and Commonwealth Office. Or perhaps 'disconnected' would be
a better word. Anthony was very clear that the purpose of this
meeting was to seek Straw's support in holding the Israelis to
account and calling for the soldier who fired the shot to be
prosecuted. We appreciated that this was a delicate issue, but
inwardly we were still smarting at the feebleness of the government's response, and the memory of Jack Straw's first statement
after Tom was shot, in which he had metaphorically shrugged his
shoulders with the observation that the Foreign Office had been
telling British nationals not to enter Gaza. I remember Sophie
shouted with outrage at that point and wanted to turn the
television off.

While I recognised the need to discourage teams of people
from entering the Occupied Territories and putting themselves
and British diplomats at risk, somehow it seemed an inappropriate
kind of statement to make directly after the shooting of a young
man – and especially cold for someone with a son of almost the
same age. I wanted Jack Straw to know that Tom was a thinking
young man who had gone down there not simply on a whim, but

to make a serious record of what was happening. I had brought along a small section of Tom's Rafah journals on Anthony's laptop, in which Tom described what he was seeing there, and his reasons for going. After all, I thought, if we're asking Straw to represent Tom's case to the Israelis, then it's important for him to have an idea of who Tom is.

We waited for what seemed ages in a high-ceilinged, dark-panelled room at the Foreign and Commonwealth Office until Jack Straw appeared and led us into his elegant office. After initial pleasantries, Anthony outlined our case and asked emphatically for government support.

When Anthony had finished speaking I opened the laptop and after a short explanation began to read from the journal. So absorbed was I in Tom's words that it was a while before I became aware of the pressure of Anthony's hand on my arm. I looked up and understood. There was something in Straw's expression that indicated that this was not appropriate, and I stopped immediately, feeling uncomfortable. But as we were finally ushered out amid further formal pleasantries, I was glad that I had done it. I was determined that Tom's voice should be heard. This was a human situation, and I knew that politicians, who take the enormous decision to go to war on our behalf, needed to be reminded of it.

Some good did come out of that meeting. Jack Straw passed us on to Baroness Symons, Minister of State at the Foreign and Commonwealth Office. This was a very different kind of encounter. Professional but extremely approachable, Baroness Symons was visibly moved when she heard the details of Tom's story, and clearly impressed by the weight of the evidence that Anthony showed her on his computer, including Garth Stead's photographs of the shooting. Soon after that she wrote a letter to Silvan Shalom, the Israeli Foreign Minister, informing him of our meeting, describing Anthony's report and the photographic evidence as 'powerful and disturbing' and urging the need for the Judge Advocate General to institute a Military Police Enquiry.

'You will know that this case continues to receive a great deal of media and parliamentary attention in the UK,' she wrote. 'I know you will agree that the family deserve full answers to their questions. Our Defence Attaché in Tel Aviv will be presenting the Hurndalls' evidence to the Judge Advocate General. I have agreed to see the family again when the Judge Advocate General has issued his report.' In other words – 'What your army has done is still under the spotlight here, and this family is not going to go away.'

Baroness Symons struck me as a very human person with an incisive and insightful mind, who was able to say difficult things in a challenging but acceptable way. We felt we'd found a real ally.

While Anthony was preoccupied with his report and with seeking the necessary legal advice to carry forward our demand for answers and recognition from the Israelis, and Sophie threw herself into the press campaign to keep the case alive, I spent my days at the Royal Free. It was the only place I wanted to be. As I woke each morning, my first conscious thought was how soon I could get to Tom. He had been moved from the Intensive Care Unit into an airy, light room on the neurological ward, and here his close friends came and went, most of them back from university for the summer. I realised that they were now looking for a response as intensely as we had done during the early days in Israel. Adam and Sam visited Tom together and sang and played to him. "We're sure he could hear us," they said. Often one or another of his friends would say to me wistfully, 'I'm sure Tom can see. I'm sure his eyes were following me.' Or, 'I'm sure Tom knows I'm there.' Kay, in particular, had a very stronge sense that Tom knew she was there, and had even moved his head to follow her round the room. To me it was a measure of his friends' love and longing, and of their disbelief. They simply weren't ready to accept the finality of what had happened.

I felt worried about Kay. She and Tom had shared so much and she was grief-stricken, but with her usual generosity she was now doing her best to take care of Fred, to whom she'd become very close. He would regularly go and see her after school, and they often visited Tom together. Cruelly, at around this time there was a fire at Kay's flat and she lost her computer with all Tom's e-mails on it, her camera equipment and many photographs. Though she did manage to rescue some pictures and mementos of Tom, she was devastated.

Though unnecessarily modest, Kay is a brilliant photographer, and she and Tom had been close for about a year – ever since the day he'd walked into the Hampstead photography shop where she was working. They'd travelled together, spent weekends in Paris, walking the streets till five in the morning, intoxicated with the excitement of it, missing the train home because they were having such a good time. Kay, who is quite a tomboy, had a picture of them sitting side by side on a parapet in Montmartre. They'd climbed over some official barrier to get there and they were gazing serenely out from this eyrie, relishing their secret view of Paris. They'd travelled to Egypt together in 2002, and among the photos they brought back was one of Tom playing chess on a boat going down the Nile, legs stretched out on deck, his head bent slightly to one side in an attitude of fierce con-centration as he considered his opponent's next move. Tom would always play chess with anyone who was willing.

Kay would later describe to me how they'd been resting on a bench outside a temple in Luxor and had been ambushed by a group of children.

'It was too much,' she said. 'There were at least fifteen of them, and they were all over me, asking me for my ring, my earrings, my pen – they were ready to grab anything. Tom just loved it, he thought it was really amusing, and he was down on one knee taking photographs. One of the little boys actually took something out of my pocket, and I got quite angry, but Tom said, "Oh don't. They're only kids." He was always so sympathetic. He loved kids.'

It hadn't always been easy for Tom's girlfriends. I knew that some of his friends had tended to close ranks against them. When I

looked at the messages on the whiteboard in Tom's hospital room
– 'Come on, get off your arse, Hurndall!', 'Wake up, mate!' – the
photographs of Tom and Sam and Ollie hamming it up in
Reservoir Dogs-style trilbies and dark glasses in some north London
street, it brought the atmosphere of their friendship back to me
with unbearable sharpness, like an overheard phrase of music, or
the drift of a familiar scent. It was a mixture of intelligent talk, and
teasing, and exuberant physicality – talented young men, growing
up and full of life. Many of Tom's friends, perhaps more especially
the girls, confided in him because he listened and understood.

Love affairs and female friendships had had to take place
alongside this closely guarded inner male circle. So I was aware
that Kay avoided the boys when she came to see Tom, as did his
first girlfriend Libby, and I realised how isolated they both must be
feeling.

Gradually we were getting to know the staff at the Royal Free. As
time went on, we could see that the obvious love and admiration
surrounding Tom, the visits and messages, were helping them see
behind Tom's shattered body to the person he had been. During
the long heavy hospital hours, one of the things we did was to fix
photographs to one of the walls. I was so anxious that the staff
should see him as a real person rather than simply as a body, and
now they could see a fuller Tom, more dimensions of him. One
of my nightmares was that when I was not there to interpret for
him they might not understand the small signals I had come to
recognise, and I felt that knowing him better might help.

I became very attached to one very special West Indian nurse –
I wish I could remember her name, but at that time my mind was
so confused and overloaded that many things slipped away. She
was of medium height, with a distinct physical presence, and
everything she did and said had a spiritual quality. She looked
beneath the surface of things, and I remember her saying to me
very gently one day: 'I can feel that Tom is a most unusual person,
and I know he has done something great that will be remem-

bered.' She gave me such comfort. In hospital everything tends to be reduced to the physical, and I was so grateful to talk to someone who recognised and acknowledged Tom's spiritual side.

I think it may have been this nurse who first told me about *Romeo and Juliet*, a play that had always had a particular resonance for Tom. It must have been on the syllabus at Winchester, and – much to my disapproval at the time – we'd noticed one day that he had a tattoo on his wrist. It was a stylised heart surrounding the words 'Defy the Stars', and he explained to us that it derived from a speech by Romeo in which he challenges fate with the words, 'Then I defy you, stars!' For Tom it summed up a whole philosophy of taking responsibility for your own life. He wanted to live every moment on his own terms. That philosophy affected everything he did, and it was clearly one of the things his friends remembered most about him, and wanted to acknowledge, for it seemed to go to the core of who he was.

And so a group of them had been coming to the hospital when no one else was there to perform *Romeo and Juliet* around Tom's bed. I think it consisted of Adam and Sam and a couple of others – Antonia, one of Tom's close female friends, and a very sensitive young man called Daniel whom I know Tom confided in and respected, and who was actually in the process of converting to Judaism at the time Tom was shot. ('Daniel,' Tom had written in an e-mail from East Jerusalem, 'you and I need to sit down and talk when I get back because being around activists 24/7 and being in Palestine is seriously messing with my head and I need someone I trust who knows about the situation to help me sift through all this mess out here as this is my first time doing this and it's getting really hard to be objective, plus some of the stuff I've been seeing is pretty heavy and it's just making me lose it.')

Performing the play took several visits, and there seems to have been a certain amount of musical accompaniment, with Sam on guitar. 'Yes, there really was quite a noise,' one of the nurses told me. 'At one point I had to come in and tell them to be quiet.'

I don't think the Royal Free had ever seen anything quite like it. All of Tom's friends, in their own particular ways, were paying tribute to him.

For all of us that early summer was both a precious and a painful time. We knew that there must be a limit to the limbo of Tom's existence, but we couldn't yet bear the thought of letting him go. Though we knew that Tom was never going to recover, we had no real idea of how long he was likely to continue as he was, or how we were going to deal with it.

I remember sitting in the garden and talking things over with Anthony and Sophie. I thought seriously about whether I could bring Tom home and look after him myself, but was this wholly unrealistic? My career had centred round working with various kinds of disability in school, but I had no direct experience whatsoever of looking after a severely disabled person. It was hard to imagine caring for Tom in his old room on the third floor, but could we perhaps convert the basement into a self-contained flat and have help from a series of carers? Or should we look around for suitable long-term homes? Converting the basement would be beyond our means, but we might make it part of our claim for compensation from the Israelis.

In July I attempted to return to work; but it was a post that required all of me and more, and I couldn't manage it. Half of me wanted to try to return to normality, but the other half knew I couldn't. Things simply weren't normal. Anthony looked drawn, pressured as he was by the need to finish his report and the need to resume his legal work. I felt pressured too, emotionally drained and physically depleted. I was dismally aware of my failure to respond to all the letters of sympathy from friends, and from the hundreds of other people unknown to us who had written and sent donations. I lay awake at night worrying about it and about Billy out in Nablus.

There were huge demands on Sophie too. She was interviewed by the media and spoke at university student unions around the country: given Tom's age, a great many students felt passionately about his plight. One of these was Nottingham, where Tom's first girlfriend Libby organised a spectacular Peace Festival to celebrate Tom's life. Libby told me later what an impression Sophie had made. 'Sophie spoke to the students in a way that most of them had never heard anyone speak before. To see a girl near enough their age standing up and speaking with that passion and clarity was something. She was of their generation and she gave a sense of how powerful people can be. So many things came out of that day. It gave an opportunity for a huge number of students to take part in something political.'

Yet though Sophie was managing to do all this, I knew she was in a fragile state.

So once again we put the matter of Tom's future on hold.

What disturbed us all was the question of whether Tom was in pain. No one seemed able to give us an answer to this – perhaps because there wasn't a straightforward one. We were told at various times that he felt no pain, and that he had no 'understanding' of pain. But occasionally he would make a sudden jerky movement, or turn his eyes upwards as if trying to connect with something or someone, and it was impossible then to believe that he had no feeling. I know we were all terrified by the spectre of 'locked-in syndrome' – that Tom might be able to see and hear but unable to communicate.

On 25 June, Anthony and I attended a meeting of the Ethics Committee at the Royal Free to discuss Tom's future treatment. We were welcomed by the Chairman, a consultant psychiatrist called Dr Geoffrey Lloyd, and introduced to the other members of the panel, which included a consultant neurologist, the director of nursing and the hospital chaplain. They asked sympathetically how we were coping. It was hard to answer such a question without breaking down, but I managed to say that I was trying hard to understand what had happened and wanted to ensure that something positive came out of all this suffering. Anthony added that we felt we had come to know Tom at a deeper level during the past ten weeks by reading what he had written. They encouraged us to speak about Tom and why he had been in Rafah, and Dr Lloyd asked us how we saw his further treatment.

'I'm just trying to think very hard what Tom would have wanted,' I said.

'And what do you think Tom's own view would have been?' asked Dr Lloyd gently.

I thought about all the things Tom had said and felt about living life to the full. *'Without happiness, pain is only a passing thing of interest, and without pain, what is happiness?'* That's what he'd written in his Rafah journal. Now he could feel neither. That acute intelligence, that engagement with life, was gone.

'I'm sure Tom wouldn't want to survive in his present condition,' I said. 'What we wonder is, whether he is suffering at all.'

Dr Lloyd thought for a moment. 'You can be certain Tom is not suffering,' he said, 'but given the nature of his injuries, there's very little prospect of any significant recovery. We're ensuring he has adequate nutrition, but he's likely to experience further infections, and the question is how actively we should treat them – with antibiotics, for example.'

This was something we had discussed with Sophie. Though she could not bear to come and see Tom, I knew that he was constantly in her mind and she was haunted by the thought of how his life might end. She had particularly wanted me to ask how long he would survive if he got pneumonia.

'That's a very hard question to answer,' said Dr Lloyd. 'Tom is still physically strong, and he might overcome it. But I think it's likely that complications would develop.'

Another thought that haunted all of us was that Tom might recover sufficiently to become aware of his condition. 'I couldn't bear that,' Anthony said. 'I would prefer him to remain as he is than have him suffer.'

Dr Lloyd told us that the likelihood of such a recovery was very small.

'There is no question of our withdrawing supportive care,' he said finally. 'The only question is, how actively you would like us to treat any infection that develops.'

'I don't think Tom himself would want to be treated, and I think many of his friends feel he wouldn't want to go on existing like this,' said Anthony. 'In fact the whole family is agreed about it.'

'So you're at one on this,' said Dr Lloyd.

I thought of Fred. I knew he was still hoping against hope that Tom would recover. Neither of us felt Fred should have to be involved in this decision. It would be too painful for him, and the panel agreed.

'So I think it's clear,' said Dr Lloyd, 'that if Tom develops an infection you would not wish us to treat it.'

What other course of action could there be? This decision seemed to bring us one step closer to a resolution for Tom, though I could hardly bear to think of what it would actually mean, or how prolonged this process would be.

Quite frequently now when I came home at night I found another hateful phone message. It was the same voice spewing out the same vitriol – filthy, abusive stuff about our being 'Nazi-lovers' that would have upset me more if I hadn't known, with utter certainty, that we were none of us racists, none of us anti-Semitic. We were emphatically not out to polarise the situation, or to get the Israeli people. This was not what our campaign was about. We were only interested in bringing the Israeli army and their government to account. It went without saying that both sides had suffered tragically. The Palestinians were the victims of the victims. But the casual shooting of civilians, the brutalising apartheid that was being practised on the Palestinians now could never be the answer. It could never be in the interests of either side.

Since I was a small child in Mauritius I had known what it felt like to be on the outside. My whole life and my career in education had been bound up with the effort to include those who exist on the margins, looking in. I knew that I mustn't allow my belief in my own integrity to be shattered by this disturbed and paranoiac woman. But I was also aware that inwardly I was balanced on a knife edge, and after a while I did call the police. They took the matter seriously and eventually traced the calls to two phone boxes in Belsize Park, though they were unable to identify the caller. It was shocking, somehow, to know that she was only down the road.

What a contrast these calls were to the understanding letters we received from thoughtful Jewish people who were clearly tormented by what was happening in Israel. As the parents of one of Tom's friends wrote to us: 'As you know we are Jewish and although not religious we have always been proud of our heritage. It is this which makes it so difficult for us to express ourselves to you. We share your view that the manner in which this whole matter has been treated by the Israeli authorities is reprehensible. It may be the Israeli way but it is most definitely so un-Jewish. The central tenet of Judaism is the concept of justice and that it must not only be done but be seen to be done. The barbarity of the last few years shows how far these standards have been eroded.'

It was just one of the many hundreds of letters we received at this time from all over the UK. They came from friends, and from well-wishers we'd never met, from people who had known Tom – teachers, fellow peace workers, the staff of the Jessops camera shop in Manchester where he had worked while studying – and from people of all nationalities who had simply read about him in the papers. These, and the love with which our friends surrounded us, helped us carry on. But inwardly I could feel only bleak despair. As another of our friends wrote: 'What a world we live in that this should have happened to such a brave, beautiful and principled young man.'

FOURTEEN

For some time now we'd known that Tom had left his big main rucksack in Amman, where he and Nathan and Michelle had stayed in a small hotel together before entering Israel. They gave us the hotel's name, and at some point Anthony had phoned its owner, Mr Al-Kayyali, who had assured him that the rucksack was there and that he would keep it safely in his attic until we could arrange for it to be collected.

Michelle told us that Tom and Mr Al-Kayyali had played a lot of chess together, and later Mr Al-Kayyali gave his impressions of Tom to a journalist from the *Camden New Journal*, who happened to be in Amman. 'He was, what can I say, a pure man, only thinking of others,' he said. 'He was shooted after saving one little child, he went back to help another one. He wanted to help the Palestinian refugees in Jordan and worked for the Red Crescent in the camps. So pure, so good!' Knowing the mischief that always surrounded Tom, and remembering how blue the air could be on occasion with his anecdotes at the supper table, I wasn't so certain about that last sentence. But Mr Al-Kayyali went on to say, 'You felt he knew the value of human life', and I certainly agreed.

From time to time the thought of the uncollected rucksack pushed its way to the front of my consciousness. In the event Mr Al-Kayyali solved the problem for us. In early July a photographer called Michael Burke phoned. 'I have your son's rucksack,' he said. 'The proprietor of the Al-Saraya Hotel in Amman asked me to bring it over to the UK for you. I'm so very sorry about what happened. Could I bring it round?'

We sat in the kitchen with Tom's big black rucksack on the floor between us. It became difficult to breathe. I could hardly bear to look at it. The last time I'd seen it it had been standing in Tom's room, ready and packed on the evening before he left for Baghdad. Now it was returning home with someone else. I felt betrayed. It should have been Tom sitting there on the sofa, telling me about Amman and the Al-Saraya Hotel, and the journalists who apparently hung out there on their way to and from Baghdad. 'Mr Al-Kayyali was very cautious about giving me the rucksack,' Michael Burke said. 'He wanted to be certain I would deliver it to you in person.'

When he'd gone I sat looking at the rucksack. I thought of all the places it had been with Tom, all the roads he'd walked along; all the bridges he'd crossed. He'd flown with it, taken it on trains, carried it through customs. I could see his tall rangy figure, slightly bent forward by its weight, smiling and holding up his hand to wave as he disappeared into the crowd. Tom had carried that rucksack everywhere; it was part of him. Now it seemed to me like an old friend that had let him down, and I wanted to grasp hold of it and say, 'What the *hell* were you doing? Tom always looked after you. Why didn't you look after him?' I felt angry with the ISM, too. What was this policy that had allowed Tom to confront bulldozers and tanks so soon after he arrived, thirsty and tired, from Jerusalem. *And why were you in such a hurry, Tom?* At that moment all my pent-up anguish came to the surface, and I could feel only fury at what Tom had put us all through.

I put the rucksack on the sofa and very slowly started to unzip the pockets. More unused little writer's notepads; pens. In one pocket was a photocopy of his passport, a list of emergency addresses of embassies, maps, cards of journalists and other people he'd met, details of places to eat and stay copied from the Lonely Planet guide. Every eventuality covered.

In another was a list of the human shields who were going to Baghdad, with James Miller's name on it, and an information sheet. It contained instructions on vaccinations and what to take:

money, clothes ('the Iraqis tend to dress well and would appreciate if we did also'), water purification tablets, a penknife . . . It was
the kind of list anyone going on an expedition might receive. But
this wasn't just an expedition:

> We have all decided, individually and for our various reasons, that
> this human shield action is an appropriate response from respon-
> sible human beings to the irresponsible threats of aggressive
> governments.
>
> There are significant risks for all of us taking part, and you
> should carefully consider the potential consequences before com-
> mitting yourself to this action. But if you're like many of us, you
> recognize a greater danger lies in our acquiescence in the face of
> injustice. And the more who recognize the absolute danger of
> doing nothing, the more will act toward making this world one
> they are proud to have made.

Tom, I now knew, *had* considered the potential consequences,
been prepared.

I unzipped the main compartment. In it were clothes – a single
sweater, T-shirts, some boxers, a few of pairs of baggy cotton
trousers. I knew that Tom sometimes concealed his notebooks
and pens by wearing a pair of short trousers with big pockets
underneath another pair. I remembered Nathan telling me how
he had patted him down to test the system out. Tom may have
been idealistic but when it came to dealing with hostile officials he
was also savvy. And he'd always been an economical packer. Kay
told me he'd been through her rucksack when they were preparing to go to Egypt and reduced the contents by about two-
thirds. 'It was partly because he knew he'd have to carry it for me,'
she said, laughing. 'But also he just knew I wouldn't need it all.'

So this, and the little canvas bag that he'd had with him in
Rafah, contained all he had taken to last him two to three months.
Automatically I started taking out the clothes, looking at them to
see if they needed washing. Wrapped in a T-shirt at the bottom

was something hard. Two more reporter's notebooks. I opened one, and there in front of me was Tom's careful writing: *'21st February 2003. It wasn't what you would expect as we came in to land. Thick cloud sent the intermittent flashes from the wing thudding back up the fuselage . . . Amman, Jordan . . .'*

With a lurch of the heart I realised that here were the missing pieces of the jigsaw: Tom's diaries covering the first part of his journey from the moment of his arrival in Amman with the human shields. . . .

Also at the bottom of the rucksack, written on a piece of lined paper and wrapped around a CD, was a note dated 22 February addressed to me – his final communication to me, now one of my most precious possessions. In it Tom asked me to forward the CD, containing a piece he'd written on the human shields, to the editor of *Pulp*, the Manchester Metropolitan University student magazine. He went on: *'. . . just so you know, I'm still in Amman and it's Saturday night. We're leaving on Monday morning and should be there in the evening and we have accommodation already set up. Everything is going great & the people all know exactly what they're doing. See you soon, love Tom.'*

'Everything is going great.' I sat for a very long time, not reading, just thinking about him, gazing from time to time at the notebooks. Such modest looking notebooks, yet the even writing on their pages held Tom's thoughts, a part of his mind. They seemed almost too precious to open. I remembered how I used to say to him, before he travelled anywhere, 'Tom, are you organised, do you know what you're doing at the other end?' Finally I phoned Anthony. 'Do you know what I've just found?' I said.

On a beautiful evening in early July we gathered in St Marylebone Parish Church for the Concert for Tom. It was one of those early summer evenings one dreams of – warm, serene, still. Late sunshine flooded in through the high windows, gilding the wood of the pews and falling in golden pools on the floor.

Anthony, Sophie and I sat in the upstairs balcony, watching people arrive. ('Please don't sit at the front. If we see you it will make us cry,' my friends from the choir had said.) That was a relief. Both Anthony and I feared that this concert might undo us. Fred sat below with Tom's friends. Looking down, it seemed as if the stream of arrivals would never end. Soon the church was packed, with people filling the balcony, too – there must have been at least five hundred. Many I recognised, but very many I did not. I so wished Billy could have been there, but he was still in the West Bank. We'd heard very little from him, though self-addressed packages had been arriving from time to time. As he'd promised, TFH had been 'keeping an eye' on him, and the founder of the ISM had been in touch. But I was still worried stiff.

So much love and thought had gone into the preparation of this concert. Ann and Guy, the members of the choir with which I had sung for so many years, and Tom's close friends had all contributed. As we sat waiting, the sound of Van Morrison's 'Brown-Eyed Girl' wound its way round the church and up into the vaulting. Then Sting's voice singing 'Shape of My Heart' and 'Fields of Gold', and Sinatra's, and the Eagles'. Adam and Sam and Alex had put together this selection of tracks Tom loved. It was the vibrant music that had filled our house, so difficult to hear now.

Then the English Chamber Choir filed in, all my friends who had surrounded me with such affection and support, and the concert proper began with Bach's beautiful setting of Psalm 117, *Praise the Lord*.

It's hard for me to convey the quality of that evening. Music speaks with its own voice, touching us in a way that is beyond words, and that is why I had been fearful. It was the first time since the tragedy that I'd truly opened myself to it, and I wasn't sure I could bear it. Yet for me the whole experience turned out to be one of consolation, of being enveloped by love.

All Tom's friends were there, and many of them took part – an astonishing array of talent led by Sam and Adam, both now doing degrees in music at Leeds. It made me smile just to think of El Loco, their band. Tom had been an occasional manager and roadie of El Loco.

Tom's long-time friend Simone, a violinist, gave an exquisite performance of Massenet's 'Meditation' from *Thaïs*. Laura, a member of the choir, sang 'On My Own' from *Les Misérables*. That was a must. Tom had loved *Les Mis* and had seen it several times. Then there was 'Era' by the French composer Eric Lévi. In 1995 the choir had recorded it at Abbey Road Studios under Guy's direction, and Tom had played it often, really loud.

And none of us will surely ever forget Sam on trumpet, accompanied by the renowned jazzman Eddie Harvey, playing Gershwin's 'Summertime'. It wasn't just a piece Tom had loved. As Sam played it, it was a lament for a lost friend, a cry of grief and loss and longing for times past that left us all stunned and tearful, and then – despite the request in the programme not to clap – spontaneously applauding. Nor shall I ever forget the sound of Adam's beautiful, steady voice as he sang, with such tenderness, the Eagles' 'Hotel California', with Sam accompanying on piano. As requested, we all joined in: *'Voices calling from far away . . . Some dance to remember, some dance to forget . . . You can check out any time you like, but you can never leave.'*

There was music from the Russian Orthodox tradition: Rachmaninov, Tchaikovsky; John Tavener's exquisite *Song for Athene*, written in memory of a young Greek girl killed in a road accident in London. I was completely absorbed, uplifted, and I know Anthony was too. It was strange, but I wondered what Tom would have made of it all.

And how fitting it seemed when Rageh Omaar – so familiar from his reporting of the Iraq war for the BBC – rose to read from Tom's journals. Truthful, passionate, angry, these were dispatches from a war zone. It was as if Tom was speaking to us directly, telling us about that last journey of his, from the moment he arrived in Amman with the other human shields, through the sandstorms and hardships of the refugee camp in Jordan, to his final days in Rafah, his first encounters with the monstrous bulldozers of the IDF, and the attacks on Dr Samir's house.

Rageh read clearly, with enormous feeling, and I wondered what his thoughts were. Tom, I sensed, would have greatly respected Rageh's journalistic savvy and the breadth of his experience as a foreign correspondent.

Later, Rageh wrote a moving piece about the Concert for Tom in the *Guardian*. It was called 'Company of a Stranger', and in it he described how he had several times visited the block of flats in Baghdad where Tom was staying, to interview the human shields – 'I may even have passed Tom on one of these occasions. Who knows?' Of the concert he wrote: 'It was both intimate and moving to hear the songs that made Tom Hurndall happy and, for me, a reminder that we sometimes don't realise the connections we have with people whom we think we do not know.'

That evening was full of connections, interweaving many different strands of Tom's life, like some beautiful fabric wrapped round us to warm and comfort us. His friend Antonia read from his e-mails, with their wry, affectionate, often playful messages to his friends softening the horrifying descriptions of what he was seeing: '*Hi! Another update. I'm now in Rafah, a few hundred metres from the Egyptian border. Within a couple of hours from our ride getting in, I had been shot at, shelled, tear-gassed, hit by falling brick/plaster, "sound" bombed, almost run over by the moving house called a D10 bulldozer, chased by soldiers and a lot else besides . . . on the downside: I didn't get a good night's sleep because I kept getting woken by the machine-gun fire that echoes around the area at night . . .*'

And Peter Best, a friend from the choir, eloquently read Tom's poem 'All the way along this line', in which Tom wrote of struggling to gain 'some semblance of control' over his own life:

> '*To find this focal point I must find a clear path*
> *Not only patches or clearings in the forest . . .*
> *Growing in maturity is facing what must be done,*
> *Not just responsibilities, as I am starting new*
> *And choosing my cards, not running from them.*'

At the end of that evening it was hard to express what I felt. I tried to thank everyone, but the speech I made seems terribly inadequate to me now.

Afterwards we all wandered over into Regent's Park which, through a contact of one of the choir members, had been kept open especially late for us, and sat on the grass in the balmy evening, eating the picnics we had brought. Surrounded by the quiet talk of friends, and of the many hitherto unknown people who came over to speak to us about Tom, I felt comforted and at peace. The horrors of the past two months receded briefly. As I sat watching the sun sink in a ball of fire behind the Nash terraces, somebody put a hand on my shoulder. It was the very special nurse who had given me such support during our visits to the Royal Free. 'When I heard about the concert, I had to come,' she said. 'I shall never forget Tom.'

One morning a few days after the concert I woke early, as usual, but feeling there was something different about the house. When I went downstairs there was no sign that anything had changed: the hall was empty; in the kitchen everything was as before. I was out in the garden at about ten o'clock when I turned suddenly at an unexpected sound and saw a tall figure at the garden door. It was Billy. *Billy was back.* 'Hello, Mum,' he said simply, smiling his sweet smile. I ran towards him and hugged him and hugged him, weeping, barely coherent with relief. I had been worried out of my mind about him, though I understood that we all had our own ways of trying to come to terms with what had happened. 'Don't you *ever* do that again,' was all I could say, over and over. I was hugging him for about the tenth time when Fred came up behind us, grinning from ear to ear, and snatched a photograph.

Oh! The relief at having Billy safe home again. He'd arrived back at Heathrow late the previous evening and had gone straight to the hospital, carrying his backpack and the rest of his luggage, to see Tom. That was Billy. No fuss, straight to the point. But I was immediately struck by the change in him. He had become far more outgoing and demonstrative, more self-confident and, as we were soon to discover, extremely well informed. As we all sat round the kitchen table later that day I could see that he was wanting to spare me some of the details of what he'd seen. With his new video equipment he'd been filming soldiers at the West Bank checkpoints. All he would say was that a lot of the footage was 'pretty distressing'.

He didn't have to tell me. I'd already read reports from the Israeli human rights organisation B'Tselem, so I knew a lot of it, and it made me incandescent – Palestinian women in labour prevented from getting to hospital, forced to give birth at checkpoints, sometimes losing their babies as a result; men and women kept waiting for hours in the hot sun for no good reason, unable to get to work; young children taunted and then fired at if they retaliated by throwing stones; university students subjected to verbal abuse on their way to university; the tyres of cars fired at if their drivers happened to lose patience after waiting hours and speak impolitely to the checkpoint soldiers.

Billy had shot many hours of film, which he'd sent on ahead of him – those were the regular packages that had kept arriving.

'Weren't the Israeli security suspicious that you had a video camera and no film?' Sophie asked.

'Oh, I had film on me,' said Billy. 'I'll show you a bit.' And he did. It couldn't have been more innocuous. It showed an adorable kitten, which Billy had filmed somewhere near Nablus.

'I think they may have been a bit surprised, but what could they do?' he said, grinning wickedly.

With all the relaxation of hindsight I thought that I needn't have worried. Billy would have taken care of himself, so organised, practical, always thinking ahead. I remembered him, as a thirteen-year-old, spending six summer-holiday weeks tiling the downstairs loo. He was absolutely determined to get it right, and he made a perfect job of it. With no training whatever he'd designed and built elegant fitted cupboards in the house when we moved. Billy's the person anyone who needs something doing always comes to. He's always been a problem-solver, brilliant at science at school. I hoped he was eventually going to follow that clever scientific brain of his. But at the moment we were all just getting by as best we could.

Having Billy back, with his understated humour, his dependability and thoughtfulness, it felt as if the sun had suddenly come out. I could see that he was especially aware of the need to be there for Fred. They'd had brushes in the past, when Fred had borrowed Billy's tools and hadn't returned them, for instance, but now Billy was adopting a more protective, fatherly role, and we felt concerned that it was a responsibility he didn't need at this point.

Yet I could tell from the way he spoke that beneath his apparently equable exterior Billy was extremely angry. Tom's shooting had politicised him, awoken him to the reality of what was happening in Israel. This, I thought, was the effect that such a family tragedy, such an injustice, could have on a young man – but how much more so if that young man was a Palestinian seeing his home destroyed, members of his family humiliated and shot. This was the way to breed enemies.

FIFTEEN

The long hot days of August came, and with them utter, blind exhaustion. We had been home for nearly three months now. I felt finished, played out, as if I was dragging myself along an interminable, dark tunnel without end. I had a sense that the family was fragmenting, each of us locked into our own particular nightmare, but I felt powerless to gather us together. As Cardinal Basil Hume so beautifully put it, 'Grief cannot be shared because it is mine alone'. We had always talked, and we still did, but now there were boundaries, no-go areas, things none of us could really bear to discuss. One of these was what we were going to do about Tom.

I couldn't concentrate on anything unless it was to do with Tom. Everything distressed me, as if I were missing several skins. When the end of term came I wondered whether I would be able to return in the autumn.

Anthony's completed report had now been delivered to the Foreign and Commonwealth Office, and Jack Straw had undertaken to forward it to the Judge Advocate General in Israel via the Embassy in Tel Aviv. Since this was a military matter, would it be TFH who delivered it? The thought was somehow comforting. So, in an exhausted and rather fatalistic frame of mind, we waited to see what would happen. Our hopes weren't high.

As part of our legal campaign to get justice for Tom, we, together with our lawyers, made a bid that summer to have the then Israeli Minister of Defence General Shaul Mofaz arrested under the provisions of the Geneva Convention when he visited London for a meeting with Tony Blair.

Our legal affairs in the UK were now being dealt with by Imran Khan, an eminent London solicitor well known for his human rights work on such high-profile cases as that of Stephen Lawrence. I took to Imran greatly. He was dark, slight, elegant and very quick, and had a concentrated depth to everything he did. To apply for an arrest warrant, however, we needed a barrister, and so, on a boiling summer day, we found ourselves in Furnival Chambers off Chancery Lane talking to the distinguished QC Michel Massih, who had pioneered the concept of prosecuting Israeli war criminals and had handled some of the most high-profile cases in the UK. His work in this field had established that under the Geneva Conventions Act, the UK had a positive duty to prosecute those suspected of committing grave breaches of the Geneva convention. We believed we had a good case.

Michel was a complete contrast to Imran. Silvery-haired, bewhiskered, larger than life and resplendent in a wonderfully flamboyant bow tie, he was theatrical, often outrageous – Imran told us he frequently had the courtroom in fits – but cut straight to the point. I later learned that he was part of the able and enlightened Palestinian community in London we were just beginning to meet through Afif and Christ'l, and, like Afif and Edward Said, had been educated at the Ecole des Frères in Jerusalem. He and Imran, and Michael Mansfield, who would later represent us, did a great deal of human rights work for which they took no payment – something for which we shall be eternally grateful to them.

Next day Anthony, Sophie and I sat in the stifling courtroom in Bow Street to see Michel make an application for a warrant to arrest Mofaz. Behind us sat a row of dark-suited men who were clearly from the Israeli Embassy.

The legal argument, which was not in effect rejected by the District Judge, was that there was evidence that Israel had a policy of targeted assassinations and that the Army committed several breaches of the Geneva Conventions with impunity. The defence team had presented the court with a well documented dossier

detailing the various breaches of the Conventions and which
supported our case that the murder of Tom formed part of a
pattern of behaviour by the Israeli army.

The Judge took time to consider the issue overnight. Next day
he dismissed the case not on the basis of insufficient evidence
linking Tom's murder to Mofaz, but on the technically narrow
point of 'immunity of a minister of state'.

But our action did create ripples, as did our attempt to arrest
another member of the Israeli Government when he visited
London – the Prime Minster Ariel Sharon. Those both inside
and outside the Palestinian community who, like us, were filled
with indignation at the brutality of IDF operations, were appre-
ciative of what we and this powerful legal team had done.

That August I read voraciously on the Middle East. The news
from Gaza was appalling – a four-year-old Palestinian boy shot
dead and two other small children injured by the army; another
eight-year-old shot twice in the head as she walked down the
street with her mother in the Khan Younis refugee camp to buy
a packet of crisps; a twelve-year-old girl shot in the head by
random IDF fire while sitting at her school desk . . . It was the
slaughter of the innocents. The heartbreaking list went on and
on. The Palestinian Centre for Human Rights reported that at
least 408 children had been killed by the Israeli army since
September 2000, mostly in the Gaza Strip, in Khan Younis and
Rafah. And the IDF command didn't even feel it needed to
justify or explain. The excuse trotted out repeatedly was that the
children had been 'caught in crossfire'. We knew what that
meant. As one journalist commented: 'The Israeli army's instinctive response is to muddy the waters when confronted with
a controversial killing.'

I thought of Rafah and couldn't get the women's faces out of my
mind. We too had suffered loss, but all through our time in the
Middle East we had known we could leave. We had something
better to go back to – a decent home, the possibility of work, the
support of friends, properly equipped hospitals. Yet these women

who had seen their children injured and murdered were trapped in intolerable conditions in the open-air prison the Israeli occupation had created. Even if children survived, the crippled Palestinian health service was no longer equipped to treat them. Physicians for Human Rights, a group of Israeli medical volunteers who went regularly into the Occupied Territories to bring medicines and give medical aid, reported that many Palestinians could now only get the care they needed at Israeli hospitals, but needed special permits to go to them and were often refused when they arrived.

I was terribly anxious too about Amjad and Mohammed and Sahir and the ISMers still hanging on in Rafah, despite the vicious attempts in Israel to smear the organisation's name and push them out. Billy had received an e-mail from Amjad in his fragmented English.

hi billy

how are you, i hope you are okey, also my freind here say hi, hi from injured Palestine to our friend in London. Please don't forget we all time thinking about people who's suffering also as us, all my friend and family know about Tom.

I know you can do more than us, you can write, you can speak. About us, the condation is very hard, they are killing us every day, they never don't.

My love to your family.

It was signed simply 'sad'.

Yes, we could write and speak. The media were still following Tom's case closely, Anthony was regularly quoted in the press and I gave interviews to the *Evening Standard* and BBC *Woman's Hour*, trying to draw attention to the atrocities in any way I could, while making clear my empathy for the Israeli victims of suicide bombers. But by the early weeks of August I felt I could barely carry on. I was on automatic pilot, struggling through the days. Coping but not coping. The only moments of respite I seemed able to find were at the old thatched cottage on the Essex/Suffolk border which Anthony had inherited from his mother, Gwen. Except for a brief time when Anthony and I had first separated, she and I had been close, kindred spirits, and it was soothing to be there among the things she had loved, walking round her garden with the Harwich Estuary glinting in the distance, trying to recall the hundreds of conversations we'd had, wondering what she would have been saying to me now.

I remembered so clearly sitting with her in that garden when Tom was a little boy, talking with some exasperation about his need to explore and challenge and always be on the move, his naughtiness which I found so wearing – the 'come and get me' look on his face when I called him, his insistence on climbing higher up a tree than I wanted him to go. Gwen heard me out sympathetically, and then she said, with absolute conviction: 'Don't worry. Tom's going to do something special with his life you know. You'll see, Jocey.'

Now I would arrive in the evening, and for an hour or two the quiet of this isolated countryside would soothe me – until I went to bed and the haunting would begin again: images of the Soroka Hospital, of those desperate pockmarked streets in Rafah, of Amjad and Sahir, covered in blood, struggling under the weight of Tom's body – I had reached that dangerous stage of emotional fatigue where I had lost the ability to sleep. Even at the cottage I was always half-awake, on the alert for a call to say that something had happened to Tom. I felt guilty for every moment I wasn't with him to interpret his needs, to protect him as I hadn't been able to do then.

Close friends, full of concern, suggested that a holiday might help. Their apartment in the Pas de Calais was free. Why not go there for a couple of weeks? But now we were confronted with the need to find another place for Tom. The Royal Free had made it clear from the start that he could stay there only temporarily – we had always understood that it was an acute hospital with no long-term beds. It was clear that bringing him home would be impossible, and, though we had been looking, we hadn't so far found a feasible nursing home. Since we had no idea how long Tom might survive, it was hard to know what we were looking for.

At last we were offered a bed by the Royal Hospital for Neurodisability in Putney. It had once been called the Royal Hospital for Incurables. I imagined what it must have been like to be a patient entering a place with such a name. At least sensibilities had moved on to that extent, I thought. It was a great deal further away than the Royal Free, but when we visited I was impressed by the dignified old building with its large, light, airy rooms and by the fact that this was a specialist hospital where everything possible would be done for Tom.

Yet the thought of seeing him moved once again was more than I could bear. My eye, my mind, my heart had been on Tom every moment of that fearful journey from Israel, and I felt less able to cope now than I had done then. And there was something so final about this move. Rationally I knew it was the right thing to do, but in my heart I felt we were abandoning him to this faraway place and I couldn't bear the thought of it. I was torn between the longing to shut myself away somewhere where there were no demands, and guilt at the thought of leaving. Anthony and I talked about it and we decided I should go to France. So, during the second week of August, Fred and I set off in the car, and on one of the hottest days of the year Anthony travelled in an ambulance to Putney with Tom.

The apartment was large and cool and very French: high ceilings and pale grey paint; terracotta tiles on the entrance hall floor, a big double front door with a knocker in the shape of a hand, a bay window looking out to sea. In the quiet you could hear the sea licking the shoreline. Half-buried in the sand of the dunes below were the concrete remains of old Second World War sea defences, all broken up now, with bits of rusted metal sticking crazily up. They reminded me of Gaza. Everything reminded me of Gaza.

We had been coming to this apartment almost every year since Sophie was six. As time went on we'd arrive in a car laden with bikes – or skateboards, or rollerblades, whatever was the sports fad that year. There was always the bliss of familiarity, the magic of that first morning when we would wake, relaxed in the unaccustomed quiet, and the children would run barefoot straight out on to the beach, or up the village street in search of their friends. The same group of them, mostly French but with a few English children thrown in, was always here in August. There would be days of blackberry picking, and pancake parties at different houses, and lying in the swing seat at the back, reading, or simply dreaming, gazing up at the sky. So safe. That seemed another world now. A golden age.

Before long Fred's French friends, Guillaume, Clement, Eugénie, were knocking at the door. They knew what had happened to Tom – one of them had even done a project about the shooting at school. The tragedy had been talked about in France. But they were too young to understand why Freddy didn't feel like coming out with them, didn't want to go and play football, run among the sand dunes, or climb about on the old concrete sea defences as they had always done. He preferred to stay quietly indoors. They called every day – *'Où est Freddy?'* – and hung about outside in a warm and friendly way, never giving up.

I spent much of the time swimming in the cool water or walking barefoot along the beach to Cap Gris Nez. At least my senses had time to regenerate a little, but I was utterly without energy, still, I see now, in a state of shock. All I could do was worry – that Tom might be in pain and no one at the new hospital would be able to read the signals, that no one would notice if he had cold hands or feet, or if he was too hot and needed a fan. I fretted that there would be no one there to explain things to them, as I would have done. Anthony assured me that he was in excellent hands. But in the end I was desperate to get back.

I found him lying in a spacious, airy room, with light streaming in through two vast Georgian windows. Immediately I came through the door I could see that something was terribly wrong. One side of Tom's body was moving and jerking convulsively in a way I had never seen before. I went quickly over to him and took his hand. It was burning. I felt his forehead; that was burning too. His face was contorted as if he was in agony. He must have a severe infection. Was that the reason for these dreadful convulsions which gripped his body and shook it, over and over, ceaselessly, exhaustingly? There seemed to be no one I could ask. Down the corridor I could hear the medicine trolley doing its slow rounds. Eventually I managed to find a nurse.

In my fear and anguish, my words came tumbling out. 'Look at him,' I pleaded. 'How long has he been like this? You can't just leave him in this terrible state. You must give him something. I know he's in pain. You've got to do something.'

She seemed taken aback. 'Please wait,' she said. She went away, and I sat holding Tom's burning hand, stroking his forehead, talking to him quietly, soothingly, as one does to a sick child – *Tom, my darling, my darling, it's Mum. I'm here. Don't worry. I'm here now, Tom, and I'm going to see you're all right. Mum's here, darling.* I'd no idea if he could even hear my voice, but I wanted him to feel my presence, perhaps sense the familiar tone.

After an age the nurse returned with the duty doctor. 'Can you please give him something,' I said. 'I know my son, and I can see he's suffering.'

The doctor looked at me searchingly. I had not then understood what a delicate ethical issue the giving of pain relief to terminally ill patients is. It was carefully explained to us later that once a patient has been given morphine, the body acclimatises to the drug and needs larger and larger doses for it to be effective. This in turn raises issues about the ending of life. But all I could think of now was helping Tom, and I knew, absolutely knew, that he was suffering.

'I think it's probable that he has no sense . . .' the doctor began.

I couldn't bear it. 'I don't care,' I said. 'If there's the slightest possibility he's in pain I think it's inhuman not to give him something.'

So Tom was given an injection, and gradually his face relaxed and the awful jerking subsided. It was a difficult beginning, nobody's fault, and was not typical of our relationship with the hospital staff, whom I soon came greatly to like and respect. With hindsight I can see that they had not yet had time to get to know Tom, just as we had not had time to get to know them. But driving back across London that night, through the crowds drinking on the pavements in the West End and the late-night theatre traffic, I wanted never to go away and leave him again.

Meanwhile, Danny and Erella had arrived for a visit. Erella and I had been phoning and e-mailing, and despite her positive approach to life I was always conscious of the unspoken message that underlay so much of what she said and wrote: 'I want to get out of here. But where can I go?' A number of people I'd met in Israel had said the same. So we had invited them to come and stay at the cottage, and I went on ahead to prepare before Anthony drove them down.

It was a thrill to see them arrive as the car swept through the gates and round the circular drive, but I found Erella, normally so bursting with warmth, in a bad way. She and Danny had been detained at Ben Gurion airport for four hours while Erella had been put through what amounted to an interrogation. Their luggage had been searched with a toothcomb, then 'lost', and she couldn't see properly without her disposable contact lenses. She was still smarting from the insult to her dignity.

'They even went through my hair,' she said, raising her hand to her long grey hair which she wore up in a bun. 'It was disgusting.'

This came on top of an aggressive security interview two weeks before they left.

'They kept on asking me why I wanted to support people who were not Jewish. "It is interesting that in your case only Palestinians need support," one of them said. They kept trying to push me into saying I was against the Jewish people.'

'And what did you say?'

'Well, this young man went round and round in circles, trying to force me to incriminate myself, until eventually I lost patience, and I said very loudly: "Now listen to me. You have hurt me very much. I am a Jewish person. This is my country, but I am everybody's friend, whatever their nationality. I am a bereavement counsellor, and if I see young people in need I support them, wherever they come from." Then I looked straight at him and said: "If you continue like this, I shall leave the room." '

When Erella throws down the gauntlet it is impressive.

'And what did he do?'

'Well, then he did stop,' said Erella. 'But at the airport they still went through everything. It was humiliating. What must it be doing to these young people that they are being taught to treat their own citizens in this way? It's sick, it's paranoiac. They are damaging themselves as much as they are damaging us.'

After a few days Erella began to recover as the peace of the cottage and walks in the countryside did their work. She and Danny both fell in love with the light, the wide skies and the broad, open fields of East Anglia. It was their kind of place. It was very hot, and we all sat in the shade and talked, or made lazy excursions to Constable country, to Flatford Mill and the little villages around, where we ate cream teas or drank long glasses of beer in pub gardens. I thought of the kibbutz and the way Erella had saved my sanity, and I was so grateful to be able to give her some kind of respite in return. It was a brief and lovely interlude, a break for both of us from the other fearful things that crowded in. But we knew it was merely an interlude. After they left I found a card from Erella and Danny. It said, 'You have a piece of Heaven'.

It was much more difficult now for Tom's close friends to see him – the journey across London took an hour and a half by car, and longer by train and bus. But there were other people who made contact that summer. Ned, who had been at the Hall School in Hampstead with Tom, phoned me asking if he could come round. At thirteen he and Tom had gone on to different schools and their ways had divided, but being friends so young had left a bond. Ned had just come down from Oxford. Now he sat on the floor in the sitting-room, clearly aghast. He had asked to see Tom's journals and he was both moved and appalled by what he was reading. From time to time he would stop and run his hand through his hair, gazing out of the window, as if seeing the scenes Tom was describing. He stayed all day, and over lunch he questioned me about Tom's motives for going, the conversations we had had before he left. Clearly the journals caused him to think very deeply, not only about the situation in Gaza but about the Tom he had known and the altogether more complicated person the journals revealed. 'I do wish I'd seen more of Tom,' he said as he left.

A friend of Tom's from his house at Winchester phoned to ask if he and two others could come and visit Tom in Putney. I met them in the reception area, three exquisitely mannered, attentive young men in suits and ties. I couldn't help thinking of Tom's London friends, 'the boys' I was so fond of, with their closeness and streetwise humour. Tom had such a wide variety of friends. I remembered these young men, and we sat and talked for a moment about what they were doing now. One of them had gone into the City, the others were just finishing at university. It moved me greatly to see them again and I could see Tom in each of them.

After a while I led them down the hall and through the big room where groups of people with varying degrees of disability were watching television, some making unintelligible noises as they watched. For anyone not used to spending time with severely disabled people the sight was disconcerting, but the boys were open, sensitive, empathetic. When we reached Tom's door the three of them hesitated, as if not wanting to intrude.

Tom was sitting upright, supported in a wheelchair. I knew this was almost more disturbing than seeing him lying down. One day, quite early on, I'd walked through Tom's door and very nearly collapsed. He was sitting on a special bed wearing a T-shirt and tracksuit bottoms, supported by two physiotherapists, his unseeing eyes gazing straight ahead. For some time I had not seen Tom sitting up, and the shock of it had been intense. The physiotherapists explained that it was better for his lungs if he sat upright. They were also testing to see if he had any residual sense of balance – I can't really imagine why. I sat there wincing as they gently moved him this way and that, looking for any sign of coordination or response.

The physiotherapists were sensitive and caring, but I sensed his distress, and it was as much as I could do not to rush at them crying 'Don't, oh please don't.' It was such a relief to me when he was back in bed. After witnessing a number of assessments and physiotherapy sessions I asked if he needed to be put through any more. I knew that the hospital was simply doing its best to understand Tom's condition, which was essential to making further decisions, but there seemed so little point in putting him through physiotherapy when he had so much to bear already, and when there was no hope.

Now I beckoned the boys to come in, and they stood round him. They didn't feel they had to say anything, but their shock and sadness were plain. One of them touched him gently. These were young men who had known Tom when he was active, funny, challenging, full of life. They'd played football together, sat in class together, enjoyed loud music. Now they looked down at the wreck of the person he had once been, and I could see they were remembering. Each of them had known him well. They were a part of him, and he was a part of them. The relationship was clearly still there. And yet Tom wasn't. I was moved by their visit and filled with an agonising sense of loss – Tom's loss, the loss of possibility.

Late that summer, too, we met Rachel Corrie's parents for the first time. We had dinner together in a homely Italian restaurant off Sloane Square, and it was an emotional meeting. As Sophie said afterwards: 'They're the only people I know who really understand. Losing a member of your family in a freak accident is one thing, but it's another to have someone you love deliberately murdered by a soldier who's quite certain he's going to get away with it.'

Cindy and Craig Corrie were on their way back from a memorial ceremony for Rachel in Rafah, near the spot where she had died. They had stayed in Dr Samir's house – the house where Tom had slept and which Rachel had died protecting – and they described how they had all been sitting quietly having a meal when the IDF drove a bulldozer straight at the house. It was a piece of outright intimidation. 'They knew we were there,' said Craig, 'and they went on doing it until I phoned the US Embassy. The noise was unimaginable. And these poor guys in Rafah have to go through this all the time.'

As to the IDF 'report' into Rachel's death which had entirely exonerated the army, Craig said in his measured way but in a voice unsteady with anger: 'They said the doctor who did the autopsy said that her death was probably caused by tripping on debris or perhaps by being covered by debris. Well, that statement is not in the autopsy. They must have gone back to get that statement, and of course I would like to ask the doctor how many times he's seen somebody with I've forgotten how many broken ribs, breaks in her spinal column and crushed shoulder blades and cut lungs just from tripping.' The Corries had been told the report was secret, only to discover that the Israeli government was covertly distributing it among members of the US Congress to prevent an independent investigation.

I found Cindy and Craig deeply sympathetic. We shared so much – the loss of our children, shock at our unexpected treatment by the Israeli government and by the governments of our own countries, a determination to bring this tragic cause to the attention of people in the West. Above all, we wanted to do something tangible for the people of Rafah, and especially the children. The Corries told us of a Youth and Cultural Centre in Rafah, providing health care and activities for the children in the refugee camps, which was to be named after Rachel. We talked of our hopes of setting up a learning support project for disabled children as a memorial to Tom.

They shocked us with descriptions of the persecution they had suffered in the US following Rachel's death – the personal attacks, the anonymous letters and phone calls, the smearing of Rachel's name by the media and on pro-Israeli websites, the vicious attempts to discredit the work of the ISM. By comparison we felt we had been lucky. For us, the British media had been a channel of communication and by and large had treated us with consideration and compassion. And, whatever our feelings about the official government line, we knew that a substantial body of MPs was behind us. Even the obscene phone caller had been silenced after I'd managed to break into the stream of abuse to say: 'When you give me your name we can have a mature discussion. But I don't talk to people who aren't prepared to give me their name.' After that the calls had stopped.

Later that week we took the Corries to see Tom. I remember the loving atmosphere they created, the gentle way Cindy bent to touch Tom's shoulder, the care and attention with which they looked at the photographs ranged round the room. Cindy had brought a photograph of Rachel, which we put beside Tom's bed. She told me: 'When Tom was shot I just felt like Rachel had been killed all over again.'

I was gradually getting to know the staff at the Royal Hospital and the hospital routines. Three or four days each week I drove there, knowing that I would come back home in the evening utterly depleted. Being there tore my soul, yet it was where I wanted to be. I slept fitfully, waking every few hours, lying waiting for the daylight when I knew I could get into the car and go to Tom. I felt his need calling to me, his utter dependence and vulnerability drawing me, much as the need of a newborn child keeps its mother in a constant state of semi-wakefulness through the night. I wanted to do everything for him, protect him, cherish him, care for him. I learned from the nurses how to cut his nails, how to pat his forehead very gently, how to clean his teeth while the nurse held the suction tube. I cut his hair, which still grew so thickly around the terrible wound.

I spent long hours sitting beside him, gently massaging his feet and the stiffening fingers of his long hands. Sometimes I talked to him about the happy times we'd had – the mischief he and Billy had got up to in France, climbing high up on the old rusting sea defences when I'd told them not to – Tom's defiant side. And the days at the East Anglian cottage when they rode together round the garden on the motor lawnmower with its chunky trailer, collecting firewood, or helped Anthony chop up a fallen tree and store the logs in the woodshed across the lawn. *Tom, can you remember when you first went to school – the Montessori school in Ashley Road? Sophie loved it, but you just wouldn't sit still on those little squares of carpet to listen to Lucy, that lovely teacher of yours. And you wouldn't do what you were supposed to do with the wooden bricks. You wanted to glue them together. When Lucy closed the school she gave each of you a present, and yours was a bag of bricks, with the message: 'Dearest Tom, these are for you to do with what I would never allow you to do. Love Lucy.'*

Often I put music on the CD player and sat listening as the sound of Bach or Mozart or Sinatra or Sting filled the room. I had read somewhere that hearing was the last of the senses to go. One day at the Royal Free one of the nurses had helped me place my arm beneath Tom's shoulders, and I had cradled him through the whole of *Les Misérables*, tears blinding me as I remembered how the music would go on the minute he fell out of bed. Now as I cradled him, I could feel his bones digging into my arms, he was so thin. And all the time I told him how much we loved him, how proud of him we were – of his bravery, his humanity, his hatred of injustice. *Tom my darling, this terrible suffering of yours has not been wasted. You saved those little children's lives in a place that has become known for the taking of life. People all over the world will remember you and thank you for what you've done.*

Sometimes I just sat quietly, gazing out of the big windows at the well-kept gardens outside. Familiar snatches of poetry, of hymns, of things I'd read to comfort myself, ran through my head.

'Do not go gentle into that good night . . . Rage, rage against the dying of the light . . .' Those were words that Tom knew and had read aloud at his grandmother's funeral.

Sometimes I sat simply struggling to conjure up Tom as he had been, to enter into that magic realm of memory where the past is as vivid as the present. It was not that I could not remember things he had done. I could recall them by an effort of will, but somehow the colour had been drained from them, the intensity had been wiped away. And without such memories, what would I have left when Tom was gone? I tried to explain this to Anthony. 'I'm sure it will all come back in time,' he said reassuringly.

Anthony was able to come to the hospital most days. He would often come late in the evening, giving me the chance to go home and get some rest. Billy came regularly too, as did Kay, and Fred often came with Anthony or me. But still Sophie could barely bring herself to visit. For her I knew there was no point, since she didn't believe Tom had any consciousness at all.

Someone who did come to the hospital was Libby. When Tom was eighteen he and Libby had been in an intensely close relationship and she had continued to be an important person in his life. Libby had been at boarding school when they met and the fact that the relationship was a little clandestine had been part of its charm. Tom, the romantic, would drop little parcels off at her front door – some sweets, a minidisc of their favourite songs he'd compiled for her, a rough sketch. I think her parents were anxious at first about the visits from this tall teenager, but they soon came to realise that Tom didn't drink or do drugs and would always return Libby home safely. Now her father was always with her when she came to the hospital.

Libby's memories of Tom were so vivid. She told me that on their first date he'd taken her to one of the ponds on Hampstead Heath at night. He'd brought two sleeping bags, some candles, wine, and hot chocolate for when it got cold. 'We spent the whole night talking until the sun came up over the pond and we could see its smoothness like glass,' she said. 'Needless to say, he had me hook line and sinker after that. I thought he was wonderful.'

Sometimes they'd hop over the wall into the local park at night, dodging the park wardens, playing on the swings. At the beginning it was all lighthearted fun, but in the end the relationship became too intense to last. Yet for Libby he was always a rock. If he knew she was upset he would stand quietly at the end of her road. 'It was the most beautiful thing anyone has ever, ever done for me,' she said. 'It gave me such protection and peace of mind. One night it was snowing and he was just standing there, in his long dark coat, blowing on his hands. I can picture his silhouette against that little bit of wall any time.'

Now, for all of us, the change in Tom's appearance was shocking. It was as if his whole being had sunk in on itself. We were convinced he was in pain. And yet his young man's body was strong, unable to give up. I wished his death could be quick and merciful, yet how could I let him go into that place where I could not follow? *Lord, now lettest thou thy servant depart in peace* . . . *Tom, my darling, how are we ever to let you go?*

SIXTEEN

When Tom was first shot we'd been told that he was unlikely to survive the night. Since then the time had expanded to another day, another week, another month, another year even – nobody really had any idea how long. But as October came, and the old trees in the hospital gardens began to lose their leaves, I became aware of a shadow, something intangible that told me death was approaching, however slowly. When I got home from the hospital at night I paced about, unable to rest, possessed of a kind of desperate, unreal energy. There was so little I could do.

My close friend Julia urged me to come away with her for a week to the Scilly Isles. At first I was doubtful. 'What if something happens?' I said. 'What if Tom suddenly gets worse?' 'Then we'll come straight back,' she said.

So in the end I went, and it was perhaps one of the most important decisions I made at that time. That week enabled me to gather strength, both physically and emotionally, to clear my mind a little, and to regain some slight sense of the person I had once been.

We stayed on St Agnes in a guesthouse run by a warm and intelligent young couple who took great pains to make us comfortable. From my bedroom I could see a brilliant white lighthouse against the skyline, and each morning I woke to the golden sunshine of an Indian summer, the screaming of gulls and the distant sound of the sea.

I was overwhelmed by the wild beauty of St Agnes. The island is joined to another tiny island, called Gugh, by a sand-bar, and

Julia and I would often walk there at low tide and stand gazing into the turquoise blue water, so clear you could see the white pebbles on the sea floor. One day we went to the lush subtropical gardens on Tresco and I could feel myself drawing peace and strength from this salty old garden, with its steps and statuary and distant views of the sea. Everywhere on these islands I found beauty, and there was barely a moment when I did not think of Tom. I phoned Anthony regularly and he told me Tom had a temperature, which was not at all unusual, though it worried me.

Sometimes Julia and I would walk over to the other side of St Agnes, to Wingletown Bay, where the huge Atlantic breakers crashed on jagged black rocks far out to sea, and I would lose myself in the inevitability of the sea's movement, its vastness, its force. No one stood a chance against that gigantic swell, those tons of unrelenting water. The scene that kept flashing before my mind's eye was the first chapter of *Jane Eyre*, in which Jane hides from her bullying stepbrother behind a red velvet curtain in the drawing room bay window and pores over Bewick's *History of British Birds*, with its wonderful engravings of seabirds and ship-wrecks on wild coasts. The sight of the great rolling breakers made me think that mankind is very small, and that the forces of good have to speak very loud if they are to be heard. I felt the shortness of life – not only Tom's, but the brief time any of us has on this earth. It made every action seem important, the responsibility to be a force for good, however small, vital.

When we returned home there was still no word from Israel about an enquiry. It was almost six months now since Tom had been shot. Anthony was frustrated, and Sophie and Billy were angry. At the end of September, Sophie and Billy had both made fiery speeches at an 'End the Occupation of Iraq' rally in Trafalgar Square, and while I was away they had written and delivered a letter to the Israeli Ambassador in London, describing the family's 'anguish and deep disappointment at the lack of response to their request for a fully transparent inquiry into the shooting of Tom'. 'We do not accept,' they wrote, 'that there can be a reasonable excuse for delaying or refusing such an inquiry which, under the norms of international law, the family have every right to expect.'

The news from the Middle East was worse than ever. Twenty people had been blown up in Haifa in a suicide bombing by a member of Islamic Jihad, and Israeli reprisals followed swiftly – not only against Syria, which was accused of harbouring terrorists, but against the Palestinians penned up in the Gaza Strip, always an easy target when Israel had a point to make. On 10 October at midnight eighty Israeli tanks, accompanied by military bulldozers and helicopters, burst into the Rafah refugee camp and began shooting, shelling and demolishing homes and firing gas grenades. As the Palestinians fled, eight people, including three children, were killed and sixty-five injured. Some people were so badly wounded they had to have limbs amputated. Two of the children had their heads blown off. By the end of the incursion 120 homes had been demolished and 1,500 people left homeless.

The IDF had cut off Rafah's electricity and water supplies, and the whole of Gaza was under closure. Access routes to Israel and Egypt were sealed, and all main internal roads were closed, so that ambulance drivers were being forced to carry critically ill patients over rough, unpaved back roads. Anyone trying to avoid the checkpoints was fired on, and it was reported that the army had opened fire on Palestinian medics attempting to help the wounded.

The official pretext, as usual, was that the army was looking for tunnels used by arms smugglers, but a few weeks before, on Kol Israel Radio General Samiya of the IDF Southern Command had been more honest. The army's aim, he said, was to totally rase all houses and structures within a strip of 300–400 metres of the Egyptian border so as to create a *fait accompli* and ensure that this evacuated strip remained under Israeli rule in any permanent agreement.

On 13 October we received an e-mail from the ISM in Rafah:

It is now six months since the horrific day when Tom was shot and your suffering continues, as does the suffering of the Palestinian people. Rafah has just been invaded by Israeli occupation forces and Yibnah and Block 'J' were sealed off. The place where Tom fell was occupied by the tanks of the army responsible for shooting him. Just today, 19-year-old Zuky Alshareef was shot in the neck and killed in Kir Street in the same place as Tom. Tom has become part of this land. He will never be forgotten. His memory will live on in Rafah's children. We wish you strength and courage and hope that you will take comfort in the thought that justice and peace must, eventually, prevail.

More e-mails arrived from Amjad. His English made them hard to decipher, but we understood that his home had been demolished and the family were sleeping on a school floor. Yet they kept going back. It was the only home they knew, and besides, they had nowhere else to go. On 20 October Amjad wrote to tell us that a nineteen-year-old neighbour had gone back to look at his own derelict home and had been shot in the head by the IDF.

When this happend I was home [Amjad went on] and I took him by a car of my friend to elnajar hospital. He is died now. I think you will ask why I was home: because I miss my home and I went to see it with my father, but my father told me I dont want to leave my home. Never I cant leave my home. He is told me this is my house I came to from Bet Daras in 1948, how can I leave my house, and I see him starting to crying and I left him.

The thought that Amjad's father had now been violently driven from the home to which he had come as a dispossessed refugee in 1948 was unbearable.

Mohammed e-mailed to tell us he had gone to look for Dr Samir and his family and had been shocked to find their house abandoned. All the doors and windows had gone and a channel about four or five metres wide had been dug all the way round it. Frightened people in the neighbourhood told him that on the last day of the invasion the army had told the family that if they didn't leave, the house would be demolished on top of them. After the horrors of the preceding days, this must have been too much even for the lion-hearted Dr Samir.

I felt a white-hot fury at what was being done to the people of Rafah, and the resounding silence from the Judge Advocate General on the subject of an enquiry into Tom's shooting, despite consistent pressure from our lawyer Avigdor Feldman in Tel Aviv, only made me more furious. I wrote a letter to Tony Blair which Sophie and I delivered personally to Downing Street, asking for a meeting, and urging him to challenge US support for Israel's actions.

How loud do I have to shout [I wrote] and what language do I have to find to say that this is unacceptable in a civilized society? Mr Blair, I am asking you to challenge Mr Bush's support of this deeply immoral regime which is cruel beyond human under-standing and which I have seen for myself at first hand: the illegal demolition of houses, the destruction of olive groves, the process of depriving people of the possibility of earning a living, the closure of checkpoints, the cutting off of water and electricity, curfews, humiliation, terror . . . so it goes on. In short, the dehumanization of a people. Mr Bush's statement that 'Israel has the right to defend itself' says it all and clearly demonstrates views that collude with the perception of Israel as the victim. If ever there was a level of aggression that far outstrips justification and provocation, then here it is.

I wrote to everyone I could think of – the editors of news-papers, sympathetic MPs such as Andrew George and Frank Dobson, even to Cherie Blair. Surely, as a mother herself, I thought, and someone involved in defending human rights, she must be as appalled by this inhumanity as I was. As Christ'l pointed out, the Prime Minister's wife had recently met some Israeli victims of suicide bombings, and meeting me might help to provide a counterbalance. I also agreed to appear on a BBC TV discussion programme called *Hard Talk* in which I was asked some searching questions about Tom's motives for being in Rafah, and what had happened since. I found such appearances an ordeal, but fortunately, perhaps, I was in a state of such controlled fury that I was able to forget my nerves. All I had to do was to think of what Tom had lost and it gave me an unearthly energy.

The programme made me think even more deeply about Tom, and why he had been in the Middle East. I knew he had gone as a photojournalism student, eager to witness and photograph what was going on. But there was more to it than that. It was Tom's nature to seek the bigger picture, to understand and share other people's experiences. You could see it in his eyes from a very early age, in the way he carried himself, which was sharply observant but somehow unassuming.

In fact at this stage I didn't manage to meet either Tony or Cherie Blair, from both of whom I soon received cautiously phrased letters. But after *Hard Talk* I received dozens of e-mails and letters of support, many from distressed Jewish people living in this country. 'I am a mature man and an ex-soldier but I feel like crying with shame, anger and humiliation at the Israeli government's atrocious and unforgiveable treatment of your family,' wrote one.

> Please believe me when I tell you that there are many, many thousands of Jews, such as myself, in the UK and Europe and even in Israel itself who abhor the policies and actions of the Sharon administration.
>
> After the Second World War, the decimated remnants of European Jewry had a dream, as did Martin Luther King, that all men are born equal. In Israel, that dream has turned into a nightmare so horrific that it can well provide the spark – and may indeed already have done so – that will lead the entire world into another era of darkness.

Then out of the blue, in the last week of October, we heard from the Foreign and Commonwealth Office that the Judge

Advocate General in Israel had ordered a military police investigation into the circumstances of Tom's death. It was not what we had hoped for, which was an immediate criminal prosecution. Once again, it seemed, the army was about to investigate itself, and we were not surprised when we learned from Avigdor Feldman, our lawyer in Tel Aviv, that his request to see the full report of the enquiry when it was completed had been refused on the grounds that it was 'confidential'. 'But I do assure you that in the circumstances an enquiry like this is quite unprecedented,' said the man from the Foreign Office.

In the same week we received a cheque for £8,370 to cover the cost of Tom's repatriation, accompanied by a letter from the Israeli Ambassador reminding us that this sum was made 'as an *ex-gratia* payment and without any admission of liability by the State of Israel or the Ministry of Defence as to Mr Hurndall's injury'. It represented only a fraction of the cost of bringing Tom home, but I paid the cheque into the bank and waited for it to clear so that I could transfer the money to the Thomas Hurndall Fund bank account.

I could barely believe it when, a week later, I received a letter telling me that the cheque had bounced. 'Insufficient funds' was the reason given. It was so improbable, so absurd almost, that it was hard even to be angry. I wrote a letter which was published in the *Guardian*, suggesting that, since funds were so tight, perhaps Israel should channel less funding towards the construction of illegal 'security' fences and the development of remote-control bulldozers and more towards the rebuilding of wantonly destroyed Palestinian homes.

The response from the Embassy was not an apology, but an attempt to cover up with a public statement that the cheque had already been cashed – the implication being, I suppose, that we were trying to pull a fast one – plus a long defence of Israel's policies in the Occupied Territories. After some chilly communication the cheque was finally re-presented and cleared, but, as in all our dealings with Israeli officialdom, the incident left a bitter taste.

★   ★   ★

I felt at this time that I was leading parallel lives – the public one and the intensely private and painful one that continued day by day at the hospital. In a way, one fuelled the other. Tom's nightmare was ongoing, yet there was so little I could do to help him that I think the despair and distress I felt were translated into a determination to make a difference anywhere else I could. I wrote e-mails to Amjad, and was relieved when I heard from the ISM that money had been raised to enable his family to rent a flat. Amjad himself was desperate to get out of Gaza – who wasn't? – and his e-mails were becoming increasingly depressed. '*If any body can help me just send me massage, love from your sun Amjad.*' It was heartbreaking. His ambition was to come to England and we wanted to help him, but I knew this was more than I could cope with just now.

The whole family was feeling the weight of Tom's suffering and we were all responding differently. I could see the pressure of it in everyone's eyes. Sophie had decided to move away from home to live in a friend's flat, and I had to accept her need for distance. I thought often of the old days, when all the children were at home, and how easy affection had been. I remembered Billy plaiting Sophie's hair as she sat at the kitchen table, the ribbing and the laughter. I remembered how Sophie used to say to Fred, 'I love you more than the stars and the moon and the mountains.'

Fred was quiet and sad and when we were not at the hospital he spent a lot of his time in Tom's room, which seemed to give him comfort. Billy, in his usual practical and thoughtful way, had decided he would transform Fred's old room at the back of the house to make it more inviting. He'd taken out the ceiling to give it greater height, installed three roof windows and built on a little balcony. Now he was building a platform bed. It was a wonderful piece of work, fun and imaginative, and it tore at my heart to see the way he was trying to take care of Fred.

Anthony and I were both spending more and more time at the hospital. All I could do was to sit with Tom, holding his hand, gently dabbing his face, talking to him, hoping that the warmth of my body, the sound of my voice, the smell of my perfume, the tinkling of my bangles, would somehow reach him and comfort him in his prison. During those long hours I told Tom everything. I told him what was happening to the family and to his friends, and about what was happening in Gaza. I told him about our meeting with the Corries. I told him about the letter I'd just received telling me that the Students' Union at the London School of Economics had recognised what he had done by voting him its Honorary Vice-President. I told him how much we loved him and admired him and talked of him, and that he would always, always, be in our hearts. I told him these things not because I believed he could hear me, not because I needed to pour my heart out, but out of love and a feeling of deep respect for him and what he had done. I wanted to do everything right for Tom.

His breathing was very shallow now and his bones were visible beneath the translucent skin. Often he jerked his head, his hands clammy, his forehead damp with sweat. We were all certain that he was in pain, that this could not go on. At first I had thought of Tom as being in purgatory, in a kind of no-man's-land between life and death. But purgatory, I remembered having studied Dante's *Il Purgatorio*, was a place where you had a chance to gain something, a step on the way to something else. Dante's ideas of the relationship between celestial influences and human responsibility made me think of Tom's tattoo. Tom had already been engaged by such ideas, but he could never pursue them now. This was not purgatory, it was hell – *L'Inferno*.

The hospital was aware of our deep distress, and it was arranged that Anthony, Sophie and I should have a meeting to discuss Tom's future care and the likelihood of recovery with Patti Simonson, the hospital social worker, and with Professor Andrews, Director of the hospital. By this time Anthony and I both believed that, as parents, we had a serious responsibility to speak for Tom, to ask that he should not go on suffering. It wasn't that

Tom simply had no quality of life; it was worse than that, it was a totally negative quality. The gift of life had come to seem even more precious to me during the past six months, but I knew that Tom's condition was not life.

Patti explained to us carefully that, though consultation with the family was crucial, the decision to allow Tom to die was not ours to make. Nor did it lie in the hands of the hospital and the Primary Care Team; it rested with the court.

Professor Andrews, a kindly, greying man with an encouraging manner, was clearly aware of how difficult this meeting was for us. Like Dr Lloyd of the Royal Free's Ethics Committee, he asked us: 'What do you think Tom would have wanted?'

I told him of the passage in Tom's journals where he describes, in brave and unsparing detail, what precisely would have happened to Rachel Corrie as she was crushed by an IDF bulldozer, and says that with such a maimed and unrecognisable body he would not have wanted to survive. We discussed whether this passage might constitute a kind of advance directive, and Professor Andrews asked us to send it to him.

As we sat at the table in Patti's office in the hospital on that warm November day, everything around me seemed very distant and unreal. I was asking whether my child should be allowed to die. A part of me could not believe that this was happening, and yet I knew that if we asked that Tom should be kept alive it would be not for him, but for us.

Yet I had no idea, before this meeting, of the legal complexities that this would involve. Firstly, we were told, an application would have to be made by the Primary Care Trust to the Family Division of the High Court to withdraw food and hydration from Tom. Under British law there could be no merciful injection. Since Tom was breathing on his own, there was no life-support machine to turn off. This application would have to be accompanied by a report on his condition from an independent medical expert, and by a witness statement from someone speaking on Tom's behalf. If the application was granted, Tom would be moved to a house in the hospital grounds and we, his family, would be able to live there with him until he died. We would have to watch him die of thirst.

I remember Anthony looking at Professor Andrews and asking, 'How long is this likely to take?', and Professor Andrews replying, 'Normally ten days to two weeks.'

We all sat gazing at him, unable to speak. 'Isn't there *any* other way?' I said finally.

'No, there isn't. This is where British legislation stands,' he said. He was clearly a humane man in a painful position. This was a high-profile case, and the hospital could not afford to put a foot wrong. But the idea that we had to put Tom through this agonising process in the year 2003 seemed barbaric, incredible. Why could the law not acknowledge that increasing doses of morphine would probably kill him anyway, and agree that his misery should be ended now? I tried to imagine what it would be like for Fred — for all of us — to watch Tom die of dehydration. All I could say as we left was: 'Professor Andrews, if you ever want me to speak publicly in favour of giving a lethal injection, about the need for all this to be done differently, then I will.'

Short of taking Tom to a country like Holland or Switzerland, which seemed unthinkable in his condition, there appeared to be no other way. So the hospital set wheels in motion, and a week later, in the presence of Anthony and Sophie, I made a witness statement on Tom's behalf to a sympathetic young lawyer, Kiran Bhogal, setting out my belief that it was 'not, in the existing circumstances, in Tom's best interests for him to be given life-sustaining medical treatment measures (including ventilation, nutrition and hydration by artificial means)'. It was a long and very personal statement, and in it I strove to give as full and truthful a picture as I could of Tom's present state and an interpretation of what his own wishes would have been. 'What I am clear about is this; that this is not what Tom would have wanted,' I said. 'I am trying to meet his wishes even though in my heart I would always want him to be there. To be mature and rational I need to let Tom go for Tom's sake.'

Anthony, Sophie and I had agreed what Tom would have wanted beforehand, and we all signed. As we left the solicitor's office I was overwhelmed by the weight of what we had just done. I said to Anthony, 'I feel as though I've just killed Tom.'

It was horrifying to see the *Evening Standard* headline a few days later 'Let Human Shield Boy Die'. The press had got hold of the story, and the *Daily Mail* and other national newspapers trumpeted the fact that we were applying for permission to 'turn off Tom's life-support machine'. I was devastated. It felt like the grossest intrusion into something deeply personal, as if my innermost soul had been invaded, and I paced the house at night, distraught, unable to sleep. Suddenly all our anguish was public property, the agonising decision we had made reduced to a few crude and simple sentences. Soon we began receiving letters from the pro-life lobby. On the whole they were polite, but I was sickened by their holier-than-thou tone. These were from people, I was certain, who had never experienced the pain of seeing their child in Tom's condition. For whose sake were they asking us to keep him alive? To me it felt like arrogance. The hospital, too, was unhappy with this unwanted publicity.

As October turned into November we felt we were living in a state of suspension, simply hanging on, waiting for the inevitable, but not knowing how or when it would happen. Everyone was beginning to think of Christmas preparations. All I had in mind was that this would be our last Christmas with Tom.

The twenty-seventh of November was a day I had been dreading: Tom's birthday. He was twenty-two. It was a family tradition on birthdays and special occasions to have a hydrogen-filled balloon bearing a special message floating above the kitchen table, attached to the fruit bowl. The last time I'd bought a balloon for Tom had been the previous September, on the day he was going off to university. I remembered rushing out and coming back with one in the shape of an enormous champagne bottle with the message 'Good Luck Tommo' on it. It had been such a happy day, full of anticipation. We'd all sat down to coffee and croissants, with Tom – typically – still filling out his university bank form. Then, etched into my memory, was the picture of Tom and Billy hugging and hugging as they said goodbye like a couple of young bears, exuberantly lifting one another off the ground in a rocking motion.

Today, on this saddest of birthdays, I'd gone to the Party Shop, the same shop I'd been going to for years to buy a balloon for Tom. I chose one in the shape of a star, with the words: 'To dearest Tommo, with all the love we have. Mum, Dad, Sophie, Billy and Fred.' As I walked across the hospital car park carrying the balloon I met Anthony walking with Tom's godfather Max, who was just leaving. It was always warming to see Max. We had all been friends since university. He was part of our life, our past, a cheering, positive presence. But that day there seemed very little to say.

Tom was looking extraordinarily peaceful. Winter sunshine flooded in through the big windows and he lay in a kind of halo of light. He was so frail now he seemed hardly there. I kissed him and tied the balloon to the foot of his bed. Then I lit a candle, and put some framed verses from the Koran sent to him by a Palestinian organisation on the shelf behind his bed.

Outside the Foreign Office that evening, at a candlelit ceremony to mark Tom's birthday organised by the London branch of the ISM, Sophie and I cut a cake decorated with the words 'Blessings to Tom'. There were balloons and banners tied to the railings, supporters sang 'Happy Birthday', and the police and Foreign Office security guards stood tolerantly by as Foreign Office staff leaving work were offered symbolic pieces of cake.

I had dreaded this part of the day most of all – I think we all had, fearing that we wouldn't be able to hold up in public. But in fact we felt cheered and buoyed up by all the kindness and support. There were crowds of young people there, including

Raph, whom we had got to know well at the hospital in Be'ersheva and who was now working in London. Afif and Christ'l came, warm and supportive as ever, and so did our solicitor Imran Khan and other members of the Palestinian community. As Fred said thoughtfully, when asked by someone how he felt: 'I'm not really upset about today. I'm kind of happy. It seems strange and I've been thinking about why, but I'm not too sure.'

After the cutting of the cake we moved on to the LSE, where Sophie was taking part in a discussion panel. I was presented with an engraved glass panel on a stand marking Tom's Honorary Vice-Presidency of the Students' Union. As I rose to express my gratitude everyone stood in tribute to Tom and applauded. It was deeply moving.

The evening ended with the screening of two films – *Human Shields*, which followed the experiences of the ISM in Rafah and Tulkarem in the weeks after Tom's shooting, and Sandra Jordan's *The Killing Zone*, her horrific Channel 4 documentary covering the day Tom was shot. Sandra was there, and it was extraordinary to see her again in this very different setting. We had shared an experience in Gaza that few other people could understand. But before the films were shown I stole away. I couldn't watch.

SEVENTEEN

We all wondered how we were going to get through Christmas. In the end Billy, Fred, Anthony and I decided to go to the cottage, while Sophie arranged to spend it with her friends in London. It was the first Christmas we hadn't all been together. The cottage had always been a place of comfort and consolation for us, but as we prepared for Christmas it was hard to find consolation anywhere – even in all the loving thoughts and messages that poured through the letterbox. The world seemed drained of hope and colour.

As I shopped among the Christmas crowds, carol singers were singing of 'peace on earth and mercy mild'. But where was the peace in the world? Where was the mercy? I couldn't make sense of anything. I went about automatically, preparing food, writing cards, wrapping presents. It all seemed entirely without meaning.

We drove down to the cottage on Christmas Eve, unpacking the car in the clear frosty air, making up the beds, lighting the fire, chopping wood, going through all the familiar rituals, trying to keep ourselves busy in order not to think too much. On the news we heard that the Israeli army had again raided Rafah, killing at least ten people and destroying more than one hundred homes, some, reportedly, with the residents still inside. Mixed in my mind with all the comforting images of Christmas – the stable, the holy family, the shepherds and the wise men, all set against the traditional, peaceful background of the Holy Land – were ghastly pictures of what was happening there now. I thought of Amjad and his father and their demolished home, and homeless Dr

Samir, whose children Tom had so loved. And I thought of Tom arriving in Jerusalem, walking into the Old City and seeing young children in the street fighting one another viciously with sticks. As he'd written in his journal: '*Now I'm here at the heart of the Holy Land and the reason I am here is because of war. This place is saturated with anger, resentment and frustration. You can feel it in the air.*'

We had heard no more from Kiran Bhogal, the young lawyer who was dealing with the hospital's application to end Tom's life, since the application was before the court and we were due to attend a hearing in January. But as I went through the motions of Christmas I was thinking all the time about how I could help the family through the ordeal that was to come. I wanted Billy and Sophie and Fred to be able to associate Tom's dying with some kind of beauty rather than with pain and horror. I thought of lighting candles, buying lovely flowers. But in the end I knew I would be trying to make something beautiful out of something barbaric that should never be happening – something deeply uncivilised and grossly disrespectful, not just to Tom but to all those close to him. Tom was going to die, one way or another, but our other children would have to carry on, and I felt deeply concerned about the effect all this was going to have on them.

That Christmas neither Anthony nor I went to Midnight Mass. It was something from which I normally drew spiritual strength, a feeling of togetherness and continuity. But this year there were too many other people's needs to consider.

On Christmas Day we got up early and Anthony, Billy and Fred drove to London to see Tom, while I stayed and cooked Christmas lunch. At about three o'clock they were back, very subdued. Anthony said that Tom was breathing badly and seemed feverish. The dosage of morphine had been increased now to every four hours. We managed to get through lunch and then wrapped up warm and went for a walk along the darkening lane, gasping and stamping in the icy cold. After that we got out the board games and played Risk and Scrabble in front of the fire until it was time to go to bed, trying not to remember the fun of past Christmases – the laughs, the banter, the outrageous remarks, the sheer bursting life when Tom had been with us.

Back in London on 30 December I read that the IDF had shot five more Palestinians in Rafah, one of them a young man carrying the coffin of his brother who himself had just been shot. The radio informed me that George Bush had 'strongly condemned' the actions of the suicide bombers who had killed four IDF soldiers at a bus stop just outside Tel Aviv.

Next morning the phone rang early. It was the Foreign Office, with news that an IDF soldier had been arrested for Tom's shooting. When interrogated, he had confessed to knowing that Tom was an unarmed civilian. He had not yet been charged, but the Foreign office would keep us informed.

That evening, as I sat with close friends in front of the fire, listening to the church bells ringing in the new year, I was seized with fresh outrage at the thought of the Christmas carnage in Rafah, at George Bush's complicity in Israel's barbarous actions, at the silence of our leaders. And I thought of the words of Edmund Burke: 'All that is necessary for the triumph of evil is that good men do nothing.'

Occasionally people had suggested to me that I'd become 'politicised', but for me this was a wider issue than politics. It was to do with morality and human values and our responsibility towards each other. By this time I was studying the Israeli/Palestinian conflict with a passion, and everything I'd read and seen told me that the Israeli response was cynical and disproportionate. Anthony and I had both reached this conclusion quite independently and by different routes, and for both of us it had been reached with great internal struggle. With all the clarity of youth, Sophie and Bill had reached the same conclusion far sooner.

Now, towards midnight, I sat down and poured out my feelings in a piece which appeared that week in the *Guardian*.

When will those responsible accept that it is illegal to collectively and obsessively punish a whole community? [I wrote] Does Tony Blair regard the children of Palestine as children of a lesser God? Does he accept that his inaction is tantamount to complicity in the process of destroying any peace initiative in the Middle East? Mr Blair, you now know that a British citizen has been shot in cold blood while trying to shepherd children from the live bullets of an IDF sniper. Are you now ready to openly condemn these actions?

Each day now we could see that Tom was growing weaker. He had developed pneumonia and his breathing was laboured and shallow, however many times his chest was cleared. The morphine was having less and less effect, and he shifted restlessly as if in pain. I sensed as I sat beside him that he had now entered a shadowland, a place nearer to death than to life. Yet the will to live in his young body was so strong, it still could not surrender. I could only pray *O God, release my child.*

On the first Monday in the new year I asked one of the doctors how much longer he thought Tom had.

'I don't think it will be very long now,' he said.

I asked what that meant.

He thought carefully and then said, 'About a week.'

It had taken so long to reach this point, we had been told so many different things at different times, that the calm, precise answer came like a blow. For some months now I had felt almost beyond tears; now I felt dislocated from the world, hurled into a bottomless black morass which sucked me down. I longed for Tom to be free of all this horror, but I could not imagine a world in which he was not physically there, in which I could not see him and touch him. And in such a little time, I would have to face that. This was the very worst. All the manifestations of his physical being seemed so precious now – the T-shirts and tracksuits piled up neatly on the shelves, his toothbrush, his shampoo, the small possessions we had brought with him to the hospital.

Billy and Fred came often – Fred pale and accepting and

terribly brave. Sophie came, and Kay, Libby and Antonia. I called one of Tom's little inner group of friends, 'the boys', and explained that we were close to losing Tom. When they visited they stood looking at him in a kind of loving disbelief, still somehow unable to accept that the Tom they had grown up with and hung out with could be leaving them in this way. I racked my brains to think what my other responsibilities were – who else should I be telling? What would I live to regret if I didn't do it now? But everything outside the hospital room faded into irrelevance. I could really only think of Tom.

On 12 January Anthony and I were both with him in the afternoon. Anthony was standing beside the bed and I was sitting with my hand beneath Tom's arm when I felt a kind of energy in his body, and something changed in his face, which was illuminated almost with a look of recognition. Anthony saw it too. It was as if, with an enormous effort of will, Tom was summoning up all the last energy he had to be with us. Though his eyes were unable to focus, I had the sense that he was looking down at me as I sat in the chair beside him. I just kept holding him and repeating, 'Look, Tom darling, this is Mum. We're here. Mum and Dad are here. We love you very much. You're doing so well. Well done, Tom, well done, darling.' And I do believe – perhaps I want to believe – that at some level there was recognition.

That evening when we got home there was a message from the Foreign Office to say that the soldier who had been arrested for Tom's shooting had been charged with aggravated assault. He was also being charged with obstruction of justice for shooting Tom and then seeking permission from his commander to kill him on the grounds that he was carrying a gun. A second soldier was under arrest for allegedly corroborating his account.

Next day, 13 January, was my birthday, and I went to the hospital early. Anthony and Fred had been there through the night. I leaned over the bed and put my face beside Tom's on the pillow so that I could hear the beating of his heart, feel the quick rise and fall of his breathing. How often I had soothed him like this when he was a small child, unable to sleep. I told him about the soldier, and I promised him that we would make sure justice was done, that we would hold the army's chain of command to account. I told him that all his suffering had not been in vain and that what he had done had touched and inspired people across the world. I told him what a good person he was. And again and again I told him how proud we were of him and how much we loved him.

Oh Tom, my darling, you must go now into a place where I cannot follow. I must let you go, but you know that in my heart I will never leave you. You'll be at my shoulder, always. You are my son; my child.

Billy came and we went to the canteen where, with great sweetness, he gave me a card and a birthday present – a little Walkman for me to listen to music on. It was so typical of him to remember. With all the surrounding trauma my birthday seemed so unimportant, but it was deeply touching to me that he had thought of it. We went back to Tom's room and Billy put on some of Tom's favourite music. Anthony phoned to say he would come in the evening. We sat there all day, with Billy holding Tom's hand in his quiet, peaceful way.

By late afternoon I sensed that Tom had reached some turning point, and I knew that I must tell Father Hubert, our local parish priest. Father Hubert was an old friend. He had known Tom since he was a child, had prayed for him, said Masses for him, though Tom had stopped going to church years ago. I knew Billy wouldn't like it – Billy and Sophie had both rejected Catholicism in their teens – but in my distress it was all I knew how to do. It had nothing to do with my own faith. I needed the comfort of Father Hubert's spiritual presence. Tom, I knew, had been a spiritual person, though not bound by any creed. He had been inclusive, respectful of everyone's beliefs. Now I wanted Father Hubert to bless him on his journey, to help me let him go.

When I phoned Father Hubert he was about to say Mass, but he put everything aside and at 5.30 he came. This wonderful eighty-year-old had made the long journey by tube and on foot from the station, and when he came into the room his presence was like a benediction. I felt his immense strength and calm. There was no need for words. When he arrived Billy left the room abruptly. This made me so sad, but I understood, and I hoped that one day Billy himself would understand.

Father Hubert said nothing, but he took my hands in his firm dry ones and held them. He stood for some time looking down at Tom with great love. Then, from his small bag he took out a prayer book, and another for me, and in his strong quiet voice began the prayers for the departing: *'I commend you, my dear brother, to almighty God, and entrust you to your Creator. May you return to him who formed you from the dust of the earth . . .'*

He made the sign of the cross with oil on Tom's forehead, beside the livid wound: *'Through this holy anointing may the Lord in his love and mercy help you with the grace of the Holy Spirit. May the Lord who frees you from sin save you and raise you up . . .'*

The beautiful, enduring words were like a bell gently tolling in celebration of Tom's life. I stood looking down at his dear face, so closed now, so remote, and felt a deep thankfulness for the twenty-two years we had had him with us. And such pain as I have never felt before or since, and such loneliness.

It was dark when Father Hubert left. I wanted to drive him to the station but he wouldn't hear of it. I walked with him to the main entrance, and again we stood silently with my hands in his before he disappeared into the night.

I walked back along the quiet corridor. The canteen was closed, but I sat down in it and took out my mobile phone. I knew Anthony would be here soon, but there were other people I felt I should send messages to – people who needed to know that Tom would not be with us long. I was just starting when the phone rang. It was one of Tom's nurses. Almost without hearing what she was saying I picked up my things and fled up the stairs and along the corridor towards Tom's room.

The nurses were standing round his bed. I flung my coat on the floor and ran towards Tom. Someone put a hand on my arm, and I heard someone else say: 'He's gone.'

I stood looking down at my dead child. And I knew that I was also looking at a young man who had lived a worthwhile life, and whose heart had been in a good place. Whatever his human frailties Tom had essentially been a deeply good person, a courageous person who had risked himself for others, and who had made a difference. And all I could say was, 'Well, done, Tom. Well done.' Over and over I kept repeating it as I held him. 'Well done, darling, well done.'

The nurses must have wondered why I was saying it but I couldn't explain. I was thinking of that precious little bit of folded paper in his 'Memories' file on which Tom had written: 'When my mother says "Well done".'

III

LONDON – ASHKELON
MAY 2004–AUGUST 2005

EIGHTEEN

On the morning of 10 May 2004 I stood in the courtroom of the IDF Southern Command at the Kastina Junction Military Base near Ashkelon, about sixty kilometres from Tel Aviv. It was the first day of the trial of the soldier who had shot Tom. I'd arrived in Tel Aviv from the kibbutz the evening before and been driven down to the base early that morning with Neil Wigan from the British Embassy. It was a bleak place, a cluster of low, functional buildings set in scrubby desert land on the outskirts of the town of Ashkelon and surrounded by a high wire fence. Outside, in the dried-earth parking lot, we'd met up with Karin Loevy, an able young woman lawyer from Avigdor Feldman's practice who spoke fluent English and would be attending the whole trial. Since it was a criminal military trial she would have no direct part to play and nor would we. But to us she would be a vital link, keeping us informed on all the legal issues. The trial could last many months, we'd been told, since the court would convene quite spasmodically, sometimes for only one or two days a month.

I had been adamant that a member of the family would be present on this first day, and it was agreed I should go. It was a statement. I wanted the IDF to know that we were still on the case, that we were watching them, and that we weren't going to go away.

It was a small, wood-panelled courtroom. I couldn't have been more than a few yards from the accused soldier when he was led in. Though he had not been publicly identified, I knew that his name was Sgt Taysir Walid Heib, that he was a Bedouin, and that he was twenty years old. He entered with a strange shuffling gait and I was shocked when I heard the clunk of leg irons. He was in uniform and handcuffed to another soldier, a woman who looked even younger than he was. In fact none of the small group guarding him looked more than nineteen or twenty. Although he was so close to me, I didn't meet his eye, then or at any other time during the trial. Though I was conscious of what I was doing, it was an almost instinctive reaction – an indication, however slight, to the defence lawyers and above all to the whole Israeli Defence Force that we were convinced he was only a tiny cog in a much bigger wheel.

We had asked to see the full evidence of the military police investigation and the IDF had responded with a three-page summary that raised more questions than it answered. But we knew from what Taysir had been telling the press that the full evidence contained crucial transcripts of statements about IDF rules of engagement made under questioning by him and his fellow soldiers. It was possible these transcripts might shed light on a whole culture of random killing in an army that had declared itself 'the most moral army in the world'. We were determined to see the full evidence, and we were ready to take our case to the Supreme Court if necessary.

In many ways Taysir was an ordinary looking young man. He had strong Bedouin features, with what appeared to be a scar down one cheek and another on his forehead. When the leg irons and handcuffs were removed, he slouched on a chair between his guards. There was none of the professional formality between them that I would have expected. This was a military trial, and it all felt very much 'in-house'. Occasionally he and the guards would exchange a remark in Hebrew, and even laugh, like any group of teenagers. It was hard to believe they were in court, and that the case was one of manslaughter.

I looked at the soldier from my place at the front of the courtroom with a strange mixture of feelings. Here was the man who had shot my son – knowingly, the evidence indicated, a sniper taking aim with cool precision through his telescopic sight. Here was the man who had lied, who, we now knew, had made five conflicting statements in an effort to save his skin, and had finally attempted to withdraw his confession.

I thought, too, that he was a boy who had been given too much leeway by his commanding officers, functioning within a culture that, in a literally unwritten and unspoken way, seemed to give out the message that it was acceptable to shoot unarmed civilians in cold blood. A pawn in a much larger and more terrible system designed by people much further up the military hierarchy. Who was he, I wondered; where had he come from, what was the track that had taken him to that desolate guard post on the Egyptian border? I didn't just feel anger and contempt. I had a powerful need to know who this young man was, what were the factors that had brought him to this point, what had gone through his mind as he pulled the trigger. The immorality of such an act was incomprehensible to me, but I desperately wanted to understand.

The defence and prosecuting counsel were already in court and Karin pointed them out to me. Hila Gurney, the IDF prosecuting counsel, was quite a severe looking young woman, dressed in military uniform with her hair scraped back. I guessed she was only in her twenties, and wondered how someone so young could be acting for the prosecution in such a politically sensitive and high-profile case. Her assistant, Oren Lieber, looked pleasant and even younger. But from the moment Hila spoke she came across as competent, alert and highly professional, with a confident but not overconfident presence. However, we already understood the limitations of her brief. She was here simply to establish the guilt or otherwise of this particular soldier, but nothing beyond that. There would be no discussion of any wider issues, of how much responsibility for Tom's shooting should be borne not just by this single soldier, but by the chain of command. Indeed, as I was to discover, whenever anything came up that was remotely connected with the army's rules of engagement – or 'national security' as it was called – we would be required to leave the court.

The main defence lawyer, Ilan Bombach, seemed a very different kettle of fish, a puffy-faced, self-important looking man in a civilian lawyer's black gown, whose bleached-blonde miniskirted fiancée sat not far from us casting vacuous glances at me.

The three military judges entered and took their places on a raised dais behind a low wooden bench-desk. The charges against Taysir were read out: manslaughter, obstruction of justice, submitting false testimony, obtaining false testimony, and unfitting behaviour. Another soldier had been arrested on a charge of giving false testimony on Taysir's behalf, but there was no sign of him, and I presumed he would be having a separate trial.

As the charges were read out Taysir sat sprawled on the bench, occasionally crossing and recrossing his legs, looking deeply bored. His entire body language indicated what a waste of time he thought all this was, and that he was certain he was going to be cleared. And why should he think otherwise? The IDF chain of command supported its soldiers, did it not? No indictments had been made against the driver of the bulldozer which had killed Rachel Corrie. No soldier had been called to account and prosecuted for the killing of James Miller. And since the beginning of the Second Intifada thousands of Palestinian civilians had been shot and injured by the army without the soldiers' behaviour being seriously challenged by the IDF itself.

The main issue under discussion that day and the following one was whether the statements already made by Taysir under questioning were admissible as evidence. He was now claiming that these statements, which had led to his indictment, had been made under duress.

He spoke only to confirm his name and rank; the exchanges were between the defence and prosecuting counsel, and we saw very quickly what the pattern was to be. Hila's approach was quick, economical and to the point, whereas Ilan Bombach's was slow, pedantic and overblown. He read laboriously from his sheaf of notes, questioning the minutest details: how many breaks had Taysir been allowed during questioning, for precisely how long, what exactly had he been given to eat, how much water had he been allowed . . . the list went on and on *ad absurdum* until the main point was lost in repetitions and technicalities and even the judges seemed exasperated. Bombach was clearly clutching at straws as he saw each objection calmly and directly countered by Hila.

In fact what seemed to take up much time in court was the fact that Taysir had previously been convicted on drugs charges, something the IDF seemed to take more seriously than killing a civilian. It was also claimed that Taysir could neither read nor write Hebrew and had a poor grasp of the language. His comprehension was also poor, due to a learning disability, and he was therefore confused about the rules of engagement.

The court's noisy air conditioning made it hard to hear, the sound of Bombach's irritating and insistent voice with its circular questioning was draining, and it was a relief to us all when the lunch break came and we could go outside. Journalists asked for my reactions. I thought about Taysir and his appearance in court – pathetic somehow, as if he was incapable of grasping what he'd done, or the gravity of the situation. Some of the Israeli press had already dwelt on the fact that he was an Arab, a Bedouin – basically one of Israeli society's outcasts, as I was beginning to understand – i.e. not 'one of them'. They implied that Tom would never have been shot by an Israeli Jewish soldier, but we were far from convinced. As far as I was concerned this soldier had been trained by the IDF, was operating under their rules of engagement and was their responsibility. And I could only say what I had already said on the BBC *Today* programme – that we hadn't come this far to attend a show trial, that we believed there were systemic problems within the IDF, and that there were still many questions to be answered.

★   ★   ★

At the end of two interminable days of objections from Bombach, the court was adjourned for a month to consider the admissibility of Taysir's evidence. I had spent the two nights of the trial in a hotel in Tel Aviv and now, as ever, I was grateful to be driven further south to the kibbutz by Neil Wigan, where I was to stay for the next ten days. My eyes felt as if they had sand grains in them, and my head throbbed from the strain of trying to take in what was going on in court at every level. I'd felt like a sea anemone, receiving sensations through countless filaments. I knew it was going to take some time to make sense of all these facts, issues and impressions.

What a relief it was to sit once more with Erella in the green haven of her verandah, with the smoke from one of her roll-ups rising lazily in the evening air. People naturally unburden themselves to Erella, and I found myself going over with her once more the terrible time after Tom's death, when all the family's pent-up anger rushed to the surface and I felt most of it was directed at me. For all of us our grieving had been stalled by everything else that was going on. Now for the first time our loss had begun to seem like a reality. It was a time of insanity. Everything seemed out of control. It's still hard to think about, but it is part of Tom's story, part of our desperate individual battles to come to terms with his loss.

Now I felt the need to look back to what I believed I'd given Tom. It was easy to remember the mistakes I'd made, the things I would have done differently. But at least I felt that I had not tried to make him into something he was not. I'd had faith in him, encouraged him to search for his star. '*Much of the morality I hope I have I believe comes from your example . . . my decision to help out in a refugee camp is a result of the ideals you and other people gave me.*' Tom had written that in his Middle East journal. It was a surprising but comforting thought.

Next day, as we sat down to the customary delicious meal of salads and fruits in the kibbutz's communal dining room, Erella introduced me to a pleasant, serious looking man in his late thirties who lived on the kibbutz and was currently doing research for a Ph.D. on an aspect of Jewish Thought. His name was Ehud. It emerged that he had been a refusenik and had spent time in an Israeli prison for it. There, he told me, he had met three Bedouin soldiers, members of the same unit in Rafah in which Taysir had served. I asked what he knew about this unit.

'Well,' Ehud said, 'the Rafah unit is different because it's a Bedouin unit, so it's not made up of conscripts. Legally, being Arabs, Bedouins are not obliged to do military service, so these are volunteers, people who have made up their minds to be professional soldiers.'

'Why on earth would a Bedouin want to fight for Israel considering how Israeli society treats them?' I said.

'They hope it will bring them some sort of social acceptance, prove that they're "good" citizens,' said Ehud. 'Basically they do it to better themselves.'

'And does it?'

'No,' said Ehud. 'They're still discriminated against when they leave the army, and some of their own people despise them, because they're shooting their own brothers after all. They're confined to this special unit and it's treated very differently from the rest. There's no progression; a Bedouin could never, say, become a pilot. Normally combat units rotate – they do a few months in one area and then they're moved to another front. But the Bedouin unit doesn't rotate. It's been in the Rafah zone for years. It's really the worst zone because it's right on the Egyptian border. The place is absolute hell.'

Ehud reflected for a moment and then went on: 'Soldiers like the one who shot Tom probably come from the poorest Bedouin villages in the north, the unofficial ones not recognised by the government – no water, hardly any electricity, walking several kilometres to school for a few years and then leaving school early. Soldiers like these are not seen as human. They just serve the army's purposes. Their life has little value.

'The three Bedouin soldiers I met in prison were all there on drugs charges. But what can soldiers do with this horrible routine – being shot at and shooting all the time? If they want to preserve their sanity it's very logical they will use drugs as a form of escape. From what I heard in prison it's absolutely routine.'

'There seem to be longer sentences for using drugs than for shooting Palestinians,' I said.

'The army doesn't mind if soldiers shoot Palestinians,' said Ehud. 'They're just "doing their job". If they're charged it's always said that it "happened in a war zone", or that the victim was "caught in crossfire".'

After talking to Ehud, I couldn't sleep. There was something so disturbing, so barbaric about what I had just heard. More than ever now I was convinced that Tom was the victim of a victim, that it was the people, the policy-makers, who had put Taysir in this position who should be on trial in the courtroom in Ashkelon.

As ever, the news coming in from Gaza was appalling. Seven IDF soldiers had been killed in Rafah, and in revenge forty-five homes had been bulldozed and more than forty people killed. In what seemed an unbelievable act of barbarity, Rafah's little zoo had been flattened by IDF bulldozers, the animals butchered or crushed.

'People are more important than animals,' the zoo's co-owner was reported as saying. 'The zoo was the only place in Rafah where children could escape the tense atmosphere. There were slides and games for them. We had a small swimming pool. Why would they destroy that?' The destruction of the zoo and its animals had particularly angered Billy.

As usual the official explanation was that the army was hunting down Palestinian fighters and weapons-smuggling tunnels running under the border from Egypt. But the zoo was away from the border, in the al-Brazil district. An IDF spokesman put the devastation in Rafah down to 'explosive devices' activated by terrorists. But that was not the story that eyewitnesses or foreign correspondents told.

Israeli aircraft were now flying low, using sonic booms to

terrorise civilians in the Gaza Strip. Women were giving birth prematurely, people were having heart attacks, suffering burst eardrums. It was equally shocking to read of Israeli complaints that these sonic booms could be heard in some parts of Israel, frightening children and keeping them awake at night.

I received a devastating e-mail from Amjad. On 13 May, at 2.30 a.m., Amjad's mother had been knocked unconscious by an explosion very near his home and he had taken her to hospital. When he returned, the electricity had gone out all over Rafah, and there was shooting 'from everywhere' – the tank, the tower and an Apache attack helicopter flying overhead. Amjad went to look for the group of friends who had been with him and saw them near a local supermarket. But then, he wrote,

> I saw the Apache sent to them a bomb and I was very stressed and I went quickly but where are they? I did not see them head or face, just I saw some hands here, some heads there, it was the first time for me to see like this. I tried to carry some from there but I wasn't strong. I tried to be but I didn't. Today morning I was thinking about them, and I blacked out and was taken to hospital and now I can't move normally and am afraid and worried, today my friends, tomorrow it may be me. Where is the justice? I want to let everyone know about the martyrs.

Amjad listed their names and ages – eight young Palestinian men blown to bits, some of them Amjad's schoolfriends. The oldest was twenty-three.

I had last seen Amjad in London, not long after Tom's death. During that period his e-mails had been becoming more and more desperate and eventually, with the support of the Labour MP Jeremy Corbyn, I had written a letter to the Consulate in Gaza offering to sponsor Amjad and inviting him to stay. Though I was barely functioning at the time, I felt it was the least I could do.

Within days of his arrival Sophie and I had taken him to a meeting on the Israeli occupation of Palestine held in a committee

room at the House of Commons. We were anxious for him to
know that there were people in England who cared about what
was happening in Rafah, and wanted to do something about it. At
the end of the meeting I had introduced him to the assembled
MPs and everyone had risen to their feet and applauded him.

When we got outside into Parliament Square Amjad had let
himself go, punching the air in a gesture of irrepressible excitement and triumph. By then it was quite late, but there was no
curfew, no fear of snipers, no military helicopters flying overhead.
Amjad's expression said it all. It was the first time he had walked
down a street without fear. Next day, he'd set off into London on
his own and simply walked and walked. He'd wanted to experience every moment of his new freedom, to live it, breathe it in.

But within days the contrasts and contradictions were too
much for Amjad and he'd become increasingly angry, disorientated and disillusioned. 'They do nothing but talk. We die, they
talk,' he would say furiously when we watched the news. In the
week before Tom's funeral he'd decided to return home. It was
painful to watch his struggle to make this decision – one I felt he
shouldn't have to make. But it was the only life he knew.

Now I couldn't bear to think of him, grieving and terrified.
Amjad, who so longed to take hold of his life, but who had such
an impossible life, who could easily, even now, be dead. I rang
him on a poor connection from the kibbutz. As he answered, I
could hear shooting in the background. He told me he was out in
the street near his house. I knew that street well.

'Please, go back inside, Amjad,' I implored him.

'It's no good,' he shouted over the noise. 'It make no difference
inside or out. Inside they shoot at you too, or bulldoze your house
with you in it.'

He sounded distraught. His father and mother were both ill –
how could one be well in a situation of such stress? Anything I
could say was wholly inadequate. 'I miss you and your family so
much,' he said several times. And 'I never stop thinking about
London.'

'Dear Amjad, please take care. Keep safe,' I begged him as we said goodbye. But it seemed an empty thing to say.

An Israeli withdrawal from Gaza and from some of the West Bank settlements was being discussed under a new plan proposed by Ariel Sharon. Erella took me to a demonstration in support of withdrawal in Rabin Square in Tel Aviv. It was a huge gathering, about 150,000-strong. Erella pointed out to me groups from various Israeli peace organisations – B'Tselem, Machsom Watch ('Women Watching at Checkpoints'), Peace Now, Ta'ayush ('Living Together').

It was an impressive gathering, but when the official speakers, who included the former Prime Minister Shimon Peres and a retired Israeli general, took the platform, what struck me most was that for them this withdrawal plan really seemed to have little to do with the Palestinians. It was all about what would benefit Israel. Where, I thought despairingly, was the human feeling, the justice, that would take the concept of withdrawal much further and ensure the Palestinians had equal human rights, access to water, and freedom from fear? I felt I learned a lot that day about the mentality of those in power in Israel.

A few days later we went in coaches to a much smaller demonstration in the Negev, at the Kissufim checkpoint not far from Rafah. This was a protest against the recent horrible incursions and killings in Rafah, and the atmosphere was very different – infinitely more human. Members of the Israeli Parliament, the Knesset, were there, and it was a pleasure to bump into the human rights lawyer who had so generously lent us his flat in Be'ersheva. People spoke spontaneously, and at some point someone handed me a microphone and I talked briefly of what had happened to Tom and of his desire to build bridges, of the challenge of bringing the IDF to account, of my pity for the sufferings of both the Palestinians and the Israelis, and of the need to search for true reconciliation.

★   ★   ★

Afif had put me in touch with a member of the Knesset, Dr Ahmad Tibi, who represented the Palestinian interest, and towards the end of my stay on the kibbutz I went to Jerusalem to meet him. His car collected me at the hotel, and I was driven up the winding streets to the Knesset, a monolithic flat-roofed modern building set on one of the hillsides on which Jerusalem is built.

As soon as his assistant pushed open the door of Dr Tibi's office, I could see he was a man firing on all cylinders. A television at one end of the room was on, and proceedings in the Knesset competed with the news on Al Jazeera, Sky and numerous other cable channels. Dr Tibi, a powerful looking man in his fifties, was speaking on the phone as he sprang up to meet me, and to my astonishment he said something into the phone and then handed it to me, saying, 'It's President Arafat. He would like to speak to you.'

I was mildly taken aback. I asked him how he was – at that point he was incarcerated by the Israelis in the Muqata, his compound in Ramallah – and he said something like 'Complex times!' He told me how sorry he was about Tom, and that he had a picture of him on his wall. 'You are doing great things in the UK, speaking out,' he said, 'and I want to thank you.' I wasn't sure how I felt. We'd been uncomfortable that Arafat had claimed Tom as a martyr for the Palestinian cause, but at another level I understood it as an act of desperation. It was a way of drawing attention to an unbearable situation, which seemed to be what martyrdom was about.

After Dr Tibi and I had talked a little, his secretary took me into the Knesset's main chamber. I suppose I was expecting the relatively controlled atmosphere of the House of Commons, but as we came though the door I was hit by a babel of angry voices. Members were on their feet shouting and screaming at one another, others were moving about the floor. Was it always like this or had I just chanced upon a moment of madness? There must surely have been more rational voices struggling to be heard, but it seemed like a marketplace. At one point Dr Tibi's secretary made a scoffing noise and I asked her why. Pointing out one woman Member of the Knesset she said, 'She's just said that the Palestinians are not human beings.' And at my shocked look: 'Oh yes, it's said all the time. Sometimes these right-wing MKs call the Palestinians cockroaches.'

When Dr Tibi moved to the dais, he welcomed me and spoke about what had happened to Tom. Realising I was in the chamber, an Israeli journalist came up to me and began asking me how I felt about suicide bombers. I could tell there was a hidden agenda here, for as soon as I condemned suicide bombing unequivocally, and expressed empathy with Israeli victims, she lost interest and moved away.

My departures from Israel were always intense, vulnerable times and I was grateful next day for the presence of the Israeli driver from the British Embassy who would always wait and see me through the various security procedures until it was time to board the plane. On this occasion we had passed smoothly through several when suddenly we were surrounded by a group of officers from Israeli Security. The next hour was one of the most unpleasant and intrusive I have ever experienced. A woman took my handbag and briefcase from me without a word. Absolutely no explanation was given and, as ever, no one made eye contact. My luggage was fetched back from the aircraft hold, and every-thing was taken apart. Fingers were rubbed along every hem and seam of my clothing, wrapped presents were unwrapped and examined, every item of my make-up was opened and minutely inspected, my Chanel perfume held up and observed from every angle. Oddly, someone asked me if my hairdryer was working and as I'd used it that morning I replied, 'Yes, it is.'

In a back room everything, including my jewellery, was sorted into boxes. My shoes were taken away from me, and I was told I was going to be body-searched. I objected, but the driver, who had stayed with me, said: 'Just go along with it. Let them.' 'What possible reason could they have to behave like this?' I said. He leaned towards me and said with emphasis: 'They say these instructions have come from the very top.' Realising I could easily miss my plane, I gave in. But when the woman had finished going through my hair I couldn't contain my fury. 'It's not enough that you kill my son,' I said. 'You behave like this with a mother?' They stared back with their trained, impassive gaze. But I thought I detected a flicker of embarrassment on the face of the young woman who had searched me. It seemed I was being given a very clear message by the authorities. 'We don't want you in Israel, and we're going to make things very uncomfortable for you if you come.'

In the grand scale of things the incident was unimportant and back home I quickly unpacked my bag. It was like revisiting the scene of a violation. It took me a few days to realise that my hairdryer was broken and that the pad on which I had noted the contact details of many people, and on which I had made crucial notes about the trial, had mysteriously disappeared.

There was a terrible hollowness at the heart of the house now which couldn't be filled. I was worried about every member of the family but felt powerless to intervene, and I was struck once again by the loneliness of grief. We all have choices as to how we respond to death, and what transformation we undergo – W.B. Yeats called it 'a terrible beauty' – and to a degree we were energised, taking up the cause of justice for Tom and for others who had suffered. Much of the time we tried to clutch at ordinary life from within the political and media furore that surrounded us. Anthony concentrated on a new project, developing a way of improving access to justice. Sophie seemed far away, wrapped in a cloak of self-protection that I felt unable to penetrate, while Fred was grieving in a silent, withdrawn way that broke my heart. Billy I could see had in some way been given a new direction by our tragedy. Just as I distracted myself from the pain of it by trying my best to use it to influence events, he too was preoccupied with what was happening in Israel. He was thinking of moving away from home to live with friends and I knew how much Fred would miss him.

Seeing one another only seemed to add to the pain. When we did get together, what seemed to comfort us most was sharing memories of Tom. It helped, too, when other people talked to us about him – his old friends, his new friends, anybody who had known him. It was as if we were all having to re-create Tom for ourselves, to build up a picture of him that we could hold on to. For us and for Tom's friends, putting together all these different memories somehow helped us to get closer to him, to know him better. Tom's friends had been incredibly important to him. *'I get paranoid sometimes, as does everyone,'* he had written in his diary, *'but there is nothing better than knowing how much my friends care about me. It is an incredible feeling when I suddenly realise what good friends they are, that they love me as I do them, and that I'm worth it.'*

I found comfort in talking to Mohammed, who had arrived in London at about the same time as Amjad and was now applying for asylum – his work in Rafah as a Palestinian peace activist made it far too dangerous for him to return. In his intelligence and self-awareness Mohammed reminded me of Tom. He had already succeeded in getting out of Rafah to spend four years away from his family studying for a degree in Bangladesh – an incredible achievement – and now he was hoping to study engineering in England. To me he was a vital link with Tom's last days in Rafah. He had been one of the last people to see Tom alive.

Thoughtful friends would ask me how we were. I didn't want to burden them, although I did confide in a few close friends, and in Erella, of course. With Erella one barely needed words. I'd learned from her that the most truthful thing to say was 'I am all right at this minute.' Inwardly it was frightening. Tom was with me night and day and I found myself remembering the small, sometimes quite mundane things. I saw him taking off his black and red biker's jacket as he walked into the house and throwing it over the banister. It was so stiff and heavy it invariably fell off.

'Hang it up, Tom,' I'd say. How often had I said that? I saw him harnessing his energy as he got ready to sprint – it was one of my loveliest memories, Tom ran like a gazelle. I remembered the time in Cornwall when he and 'the boys' had noticed some seals swimming about in the water near the jetty where they were standing. Everyone was aghast when Tom jumped in among them. Afterwards I asked Tom why he'd done it and he'd simply smiled and answered exuberantly: 'I wanted to swim with seals.'

NINETEEN

At the beginning of June the military judges in Israel were still considering whether the evidence given by Taysir was admissible in court, and we waited to see when the trial would be resumed. Billy was keen to attend it. But Peter Carter, the Deputy Ambassador, had taken me out to dinner when I was in Tel Aviv, and at the end of it had said: 'I have to tell you that Danny Carmon at the Foreign Ministry says Billy will not be given permission to enter Israel.'

'On what grounds exactly?' I asked.

'They're not explicit, but I imagine they're thinking about his trip to the West Bank,' said Peter.

I was outraged. 'Would it be possible to arrange a meeting with Danny Carmon?' I asked. 'I've got several things I'd like to discuss with him.'

As indeed I had. There was the matter of compensation and damages, still unacknowledged and unsettled. There was the question of openness and transparency, a promise so often made by Israel but never kept. There was the matter of a formal apology from the Israeli government – something they seemed to feel was of no importance. And now there was this insult to Billy. The whole family felt affronted.

So once again I'd found myself at the Ministry of Defence with Peter, confronting Danny Carmon, whose smooth and smiling presence I remembered from our meeting with the IDF a year earlier. I put my points to him and was met with the customary diplomatic stonewalling. When it came to Billy he simply refused to give me specific reasons for his exclusion, and I found this extraordinarily callous.

'It's important to Billy to attend this trial; it should be taken as a moral right,' I said. 'For him it's part of coming to terms with Tom's death, and excluding him is just a further cruelty. It is unacceptable that you do not give reasons.'

But it was no good. Carmon simply took refuge behind the all-purpose phrase that he had 'taken note of what I'd said'.

Billy, of course, was furious when he heard the news, and was all for setting off for Israel as soon as the trial resumed. Both he and Sophie felt that if he was turned away the resulting publicity would be making a point, but I was horrified by the idea. After my experiences with Israeli Security, I had no illusions. I felt sure they would have no compunction in targeting Billy. They had repeatedly shown that they did not care that we had already lost a member of the family, and I was adamant that, for Billy's own protection, his decision needed to be taken with the knowledge and support of the FCO and our Israeli lawyers. For a while I was on tenterhooks, but fortunately Billy's innate common sense won the day, and he decided not to go.

The trial resumed briefly in mid-June. Over the phone Karin told me that the courtroom was packed with pro-IDF activists, who arrived in busloads waving Israeli flags and placards reading 'Save Our Soldiers' and 'No Human Shields in War-Zones'. They were there at the instigation of the Israeli Law Centre, Shurat HaDin, which was organising a legal campaign on behalf of Taysir and his family. Karin told me that Shurat HaDin's vocal Director, Nitsana Darshan-Leitner, was telling the press that the trial was a farce. 'Hurndall's family reached out to British officials and human rights organisations to apply pressure on the Ministry of Defence to in turn put pressure on the IDF to find a soldier to blame and they chose this soldier', she was reported as saying. There was more poisonous propaganda from her about the terrorist activities of the ISM and the bias of the

British press. On 16 June the court was again adjourned after further arguments about the manner in which Taysir had been questioned.

At about this time an all-party delegation of British MPs and a member of the House of Lords – Huw Irranca-Davies, Crispin Blunt and Baroness Northover – visited Rafah, and on their return reported with shock that they had been shot at by the IDF, only yards from the place where Tom had been shot. 'It is absolutely appalling,' Crispin Blunt told the *Guardian*. 'If Israeli soldiers are prepared to do this to people who are clearly with the UN it is no surprise that so many Palestinians have been killed. This demonstrates that the Israelis do not want witnesses to what is happening in Gaza and the West Bank.'

To me, privately, he said: 'I can understand why Tom did what he did. There were children playing at that spot when we were there.'

July and August dragged by with very little for Karin to report. On 23 September the court reconvened and the commander, or *Magad*, of Taysir's regiment was called to the witness box. According to Karin he spent most of his time trying to defend himself and Taysir. He argued that if Tom had been standing where the prosecution claimed he was, the bullet that shot him could not have come from the watchtower – a line of houses would have intervened. The implication was that the shot had been fired by a Palestinian, or possibly, as the commander also implied, by a Palestinian disguised as an ISMer.

That particular watchtower, we knew, had since been moved by the IDF to another position, and before this we had been refused permission to view it from the inside to check for ourselves the line of vision and confirm one way or another the assertions now being made by the commander, despite Anthony's repeated requests. However, it soon became clear that the map he produced in court had been out of date even at the time Tom was shot, which undermined his evidence.

★   ★   ★

That same month I came face to face with Tony Blair. We met at a dinner hosted by the seventeen Arab League Ambassadors at the 2004 Labour Party Conference in Brighton, which the public service union UNISON had sponsored me to attend. I had been invited to the dinner by Afif, who was sitting with Christ'l on the Prime Minister's table, and after dinner he beckoned to me and to David Freeman, a lawyer with a close interest in the Middle East, and introduced us to Cherie Blair. When she tapped her husband on the shoulder and he turned and gave me his strong, firm handshake I came straight to the point, telling him I was very hurt that he hadn't yet publicly condemned the shooting of Tom.

He looked at me with light, glass-blue eyes that couldn't seem to decide whether they were looking at me or beyond me, and raised his hands and shoulders in a helpless gesture as if to say 'I didn't know I was meant to'. We talked for a few more minutes about Tom and the conclusions he was coming to in the days before he was shot. Blair listened attentively, but I found his gaze disorientating because I couldn't gauge its focus. Later, as he left the room, he looked back and nodded to me. No words, but a gesture of acknowledgement.

And while the West remained silent, in Rafah the horror continued. On 5 October a thirteen-year-old girl called Iman al-Hams was shot dead as she walked to school. An internal IDF 'debriefing' immediately after the incident found that the company commander who shot her 'had not acted unethically'. 'Anything that's mobile, that moves in the zone, even if it's a three-year-old, needs to be killed', he was recorded as saying.

It turned out that Iman had not been shot once only. Soldiers from the company told the press that the commander had 'confirmed the kill' – an appalling IDF phrase meaning that he'd pumped her body full of bullets from close range. Only after this disclosure, and the soldiers' release of a communications tape showing that another soldier had warned the commander that the victim was 'a little girl' did the IDF promise a military police investigation. And what would that lead to in terms of a conviction, I wondered cynically.

In November Dr Chapman, the pathologist who had conducted Tom's autopsy, travelled to Israel to give evidence about Tom's medical condition. According to Karin, Dr Chapman was a model witness: clear, concise and extremely polite. A colleague of Ilan Bombach had by now taken over and his defence team were crudely attempting to prove that he had not followed the procedures laid down by the Royal College of Pathologists during the post-mortem, and were questioning his report. Their information had been gleaned from the internet. Dr Chapman courteously pointed out that he had contributed to the drawing up of these particular procedures. They were trying to break the causal link between the shooting and Tom's death but the questioning was clearly going nowhere, and the judges cut it short.

Karin also described one extraordinary incident. There was a break in the hearing while the commander who had shot Iman al-Hams appeared briefly in court. Taysir apparently lounged in his seat talking to his guards and chewing gum. At some point the prosecution asked him not to chew gum, at which he let out an earsplitting screech and rushed from the building. The guards ran after him and he was brought back. He was rude and sulky, like a spoilt child wanting to make an impression, said Karin.

In December Taysir took the stand. Karin told us his answers were so absurdly contradictory it was obvious he was lying. Although he was a crack shot – we already knew he had won an award as a marksman – she felt he was a person with a very poor level of comprehension. The judges did their best to get him to open up about what had actually happened, but he kept returning to what he had *reported* had happened, almost as if he couldn't tell the difference.

Taysir had at first said that he'd seen someone in uniform running towards the lookout post, and that he hadn't fired at him but 'far away from him just to frighten him'. He'd never had him in his telescopic sights. After the shot he'd seen him fall, but not as if he'd hit him. Then he claimed that he had fired ten centimetres from Tom's left ear but that Tom had moved.

Under further questioning he admitted that he had lied in his original testimony – that the person was not wearing a uniform. But he could not bring himself to say that he was actually wearing an orange vest – just that he had 'something round his neck'. He had not attached any significance to this.

The prosecutor then asked why, if it was not important, he had lied to the military investigator about what Tom was wearing. Taysir had no answer.

He said that after firing the shot he had turned away to do something with his gun, and when he looked back there was no sign of the person. He admitted that he had then phoned his commander – after he had already shot Tom – and told him there was someone in uniform with a weapon coming towards him, and asked for permission to shoot, which was given.

'So you gave a false report to the company commander?' the prosecutor had asked.

'I did not give a false report,' he replied. 'He might have had a weapon under his clothing. People fire freely there. The army fires freely in Rafah.'

After that, he said, there were no more shots. He knew he had not hit Tom – it must have been someone else. Asked why he had lied, he said it was because he was afraid and under pressure. His testimony was utterly confused.

What was clear was that Taysir was trying to emphasise that he had only been doing what was expected of him. He said his commanders had told him, and everyone else, to shoot anyone in the area they called the security zone, between the houses and the watchtower. It was standard procedure. 'I did what we were told, and that is that everyone entering the security zone must be taken out.' I was concerned that no one seemed to have pointed out that Tom was, in fact, a considerable distance outside the security zone when he was shot. He knew the dangers only too well.

When asked if he knew the rules of engagement Taysir said he hadn't discussed them with his superiors and hadn't seen them. 'In any case they are written in Hebrew and everyone knows I have problems with Hebrew.'

In early January we heard from Karin that Pinhaus Zuaretz, the brigadier in charge of the Southern Gaza district, was about to give evidence, and the defence were planning to play their trump card by calling their own medical witnesses. I knew I had to attend. I was also anxious to see Amjad and to bring news of Mohammed to his family. So I applied for a permit to go down to Rafah again. This time I planned to go alone.

I flew into Ben Gurion airport on a grey January day. It felt very much like flying into London on a winter's day, except that the ground was parched dark by the heat of summer. That day it looked muddy and the runway was wet. Rivulets of rain sparked across the mud-splattered port window, and I thought of Tom's description in his journal of his arrival in Amman: '*It wasn't what you would expect as we came in to land. Thick cloud sent the intermittent flashes from the wing thudding back up the fuselage, penetrating only a few metres, and the ground was only a wall of mist. You could see the raindrops momentarily frozen in their horizontal paths.*'

In those few words he'd said it all. I was seized by a deep sadness, which shocked me by its sudden onslaught. I told myself it would have been strange if I hadn't felt vulnerable arriving in Israel. And I knew that in the past months I had barely been able to grieve. It had been impossible at home – there were too many distractions, too many responsibilities. I'd found myself intentionally looking for activities to deflect the pain, knowing full well what I was doing. Now suddenly I was alone, and face to face with my grief.

At my hotel in the centre of Tel Aviv I was given a room with a view of the sea. The overcast, rainy sky merged with the dark water, and you could barely see the horizon. I stood looking out at the waves, my head already filled with troubling questions.

How was I going to deal with the coming days in court? Could I ever forgive Taysir for what he had done? I wished the pounding water would wash through my head and give me some relief.

I left the hotel and crossed the main boulevard in search of a restaurant. As I sat down the news was on and I could pick out the word 'Falestini' used over and over again. I knew it was the Hebrew word for Palestinians. As I left, Don McLean's 'American Pie' was playing in the background:

. . . *Singin' this'll be the day that I die, This'll be the day that I die* . . .

I couldn't get it out of my head all evening. Many a time I'd heard this track emanating from Tom's room.

I woke at 6.30 and when I drew back the curtains the dawn was bright and fresh. The sun shone on the rocks, which were golden brown with seaweed, and the water spilled over them, glossing them momentarily as if with a clear varnish. There was blue sky over the windy sea. Near the shore the water was a pale khaki, broken only by explosions of white spume, but further out it changed sharply to a dark, dull indigo, as if a line had been drawn across the water. The wind caught the surface, flinging the spray joyously back, and I watched, comforted as always by the sea's mysterious rhythms.

At 8 a.m. the Embassy car arrived to collect me. This time I was accompanied by Adam Sambrook, the Hebrew-speaking member of the Embassy staff who had been attending the trial with Karin. On the way to Ashkelon I asked him what his impression of the soldier was, and of the defence team.

'Well,' he said, 'he's brighter than his lawyers are trying to make out, but certainly not the sharpest tool in the box. One of the defence's claims has been that he was too thick to understand the rules of engagement. As you've seen for yourself, his lawyer was really pedantic, but now they've brought in someone else.'

'What the hell,' I said, 'were they doing putting someone who couldn't understand the rules of engagement in charge of a lookout post in a heavily populated civilian area? Had they even tried to brief him?'

'Good question,' said Adam. 'They also claim that he doesn't speak very good Hebrew, but it's certainly as good as mine.'

As we walked into the courtroom we met the prosecution lawyer Hila. Apparently Taysir had not shown up that day. He had been on 'home leave', and no one knew quite where he was – not even the military police. It seemed extraordinary to me that someone accused of manslaughter should be allowed to go home in the middle of his trial. The defence were clearly embarrassed, and even the judges seemed at a loss.

The court rose to give the defence a chance to try to get in touch with their client. When it reconvened Hila whispered to us that apparently Taysir hadn't known the court was sitting today – he had expected to be contacted. There was further discussion about whether the trial could go ahead without him. The defence had been planning to call a medical witness, Dr Lazary, to challenge Dr Chapman's testimony. But after prolonged discussion, the judges announced that they had no authority to hear evidence without the accused being present, and the court was adjourned for a further two weeks.

Erella had invited me to stay with them at the kibbutz, and Adam and the Embassy driver took me there and dropped me by the now familiar pathway in the grounds. It was late evening by the time we arrived, and I walked slowly along the path in the velvet dark, drawing in deep, refreshing breaths of balmy air which carried the scent of herbs and new-mown grass. As I mounted the steps to Erella's apartment, I could hear the faint notes of the Moonlight Sonata. Danny was playing the piano. After the courtroom at Ashkelon the kibbutz felt like a haven, and I stood for a moment at the top of the steps, thinking how lucky I was to have found it, how fortunate to have the friendship of Danny and Erella, before the door opened and Erella enfolded me in her arms.

As always we sat up late, talking of the trial, of the situation in Gaza and the West Bank, of the isolation Erella herself so often felt, and of Tom. 'It's very rare,' I said at one point, 'that people can both feel the pain, the emotion of a situation and at the same time stand back and observe themselves objectively in that situation. Tom seemed to be able to do that.'

'It's the basis of meditation,' said Erella, 'to break down the barrier between the observer and the thing observed, to both actively meet your feelings and simultaneously stand back from them. Emotions are both strong and impermanent, so it's a very difficult thing to do. That's why Tom was so unusual.'

Later, speaking of Israel's actions in the Occupied Territories, Erella said passionately: 'It's so difficult. I am someone who sees what's going on, and I am facing such loneliness because of it. It's the price I have to pay for seeing: terrible loneliness. I've had it for most of my life – it's not as if I've just woken up after a certain number of years and discovered my country is lying. I've known it for a long time. It makes me sick.'

Next morning, Erella told me she had had a dream. She was with a group of people standing next to a very poor man who had a little tray of goods for sale. He kept reaching out to them desperately, trying to sell them something, but Erella was the only one of the group who noticed. No matter how hard she tried to draw their attention to the vendor they completely ignored him. Erella woke in tears. That dream, we agreed, seemed to be not only about Erella, but about Tom – about all those people who have the imagination to feel others' pain, who do not turn away from it, and the anguish they feel because others refuse to see it. And of the loneliness that can bring.

One evening, after a supper of Danny's famous roasted vegetables, for some reason I asked Erella and Danny about the Hatikva, the Israeli national anthem. It was a moment I shall never forget. They both began quietly singing and though I didn't know the Hebrew words, I joined in and hummed the tune. The solemn anthem spoke of courage and dignity, and hope for a peaceful homeland. I wondered what had happened to Israel, and to that courage and dignity and desire for peace, which had come out of so much suffering. Now, Erella told me, she could hardly bear to sing it – she felt too disillusioned.

I was still trying to get a permit to go down to Rafah. By the end of January I'd heard no more, and I spoke briefly to a young lieutenant at the Erez Crossing over an indistinct, crackling line. I tried to explain my movements – the necessity for me to be in Tel Aviv the following week so that the Embassy could take me to Ashkelon for the next stage of the trial, my anxiety to return to London as soon as the next stage of the trial was over – on 9 February an exhibition of Tom's photographs organised by Anthony with the assistance of Kay and others was to open at the Frontline Club, the foreign correspondents' club in Paddington. The bleak but predictable response from the lieutenant was that my permit application had not yet been processed.

The court reconvened for the umpteenth time in the first week of February. Adam Sambrook met me in Tel Aviv and drove me down. This was the day on which the defence called their first 'independent' medical expert witness, Dr Lazary, and his appearance in court was an experience I shan't forget.

Dr Lazary was a small, bumptious man whose views seemed to take no account of the facts contained in Dr Chapman's painstaking post-mortem report. His claim was that Tom's death had nothing directly to do with the shooting – that he had died as the result of major negligence on the part of the British hospital. In fact he believed, he said, that the negligence was so severe that it actually amounted to criminality.

It was hard to sit and listen to this poorly informed man talking on so smugly and confidently, and it was difficult to follow the drift of his argument. He appeared to have no grasp of the progress of Tom's condition following the shooting – what he was describing bore no relation to what I had actually observed, sitting at Tom's bedside, month in, month out, and from time to time it was all I could do to stop myself getting up and telling him how it had really been. He seemed unable to produce any real evidence to back up his claims. How, I wondered, could he possibly suggest that there was no causal connection between the shooting and Tom's death when we all knew that the bullet had destroyed a large part of Tom's brain?

I sat there tense with fury. But when we reached the point where Dr Lazary began to imply that the family had been complicit in Tom's death – I think it was even suggested that we might have put a pillow over his head – and that had he, Dr Lazary, been looking after Tom he would probably have recovered to the point where he was able to communicate, I could only shake my head in disbelief. I could stand it no more. I rose and left the courtroom, my high heels audibly clacking on the bare floor.

I stood outside shaking, unable to stop the tears. Adam came and joined me and we sat down on a bench. At one point I glanced back into the court, to where the soldier was sitting. He was watching me, and for a split second our eyes met. It was the nearest thing to human communication we had during the course of the trial. Eventually Karin emerged. 'Don't worry,' she said. 'The judges were not impressed with Dr Lazary. I don't think his testimony has been much help to the defence.'

Towards the end of the day a further witness was called by the defence – an impressively bright and articulate young soldier who was in charge of the IDF's maps. His brief had been to establish whether there was a line of vision between the watchtower and the point where Tom was standing when he was shot, and he had been given several sets of coordinates to work from. His evidence was highly technical, but I understood that the coordinates, which he had been given by the defence team itself, indicated that there was either no line of vision, or only a partial line of vision between those points and the watchtower. But it emerged in court that none of these coordinates represented the exact point where Tom had fallen.

However, among the documents the young soldier had been

given was a photograph of Tom lying on the ground beside the distinctive lump of concrete. This had enabled him to establish accurately the point where Tom had been standing when he was shot and he had taken it upon himself to work out a further set of coordinates. These calculations proved beyond doubt that there had been a clear line of vision between Tom's position and the watchtower.

This was a vital piece of evidence for the prosecution, and I was deeply touched by the young man's honesty and integrity. It seemed that the defence team had scored yet another spectacular own goal.

When I got back to the kibbutz I found that my permit for Rafah had come through. Erella and Danny were away, but Ehud called in and I told him about the trial and about my plan. He looked apprehensive. I rang Anthony.

'Is that really a good idea?' he said. 'Do you have to go down to Rafah now? If you do you're probably going to miss the opening of Tom's exhibition.'

'I know,' I said, 'but it's something I have to do while I'm here. I've promised Amjad. And I want to see Mohammed's family. Mohammed's cousin has said he'll meet me at the border. And I have to visit the site again.'

'Well, just be careful . . .' said Anthony doubtfully. But I could tell he wasn't happy.

One of Anthony's particular interests is photography and it had seemed natural that he should stay in London to finalise arrangements for the exhibition while I attended the trial. The effort he had put into this exhibition was a measure of his care and love for his son. The opening would be a big moment, and I felt hopelessly torn. Yet I knew it was important that I make this journey.

I spent the night in Be'ersheva and next day took a taxi to the Erez Crossing, stopping at a small flower shop to buy two bunches of flowers. It was raining and there was very little traffic on the roads. When we reached the high metal gates of the crossing I got out and paid the taxi driver, and suddenly all the strain of the previous days hit me. Before, I'd always been protected, with a member of the Embassy staff to see us through. Now I was just another person on foot. Flowers in hand, I walked towards the low checkpoint building.

I knew that inside it there were three channels – civilian, diplomatic and VIP. I ignored these classifications and walked up to the desk. Behind it I found the usual group of laid-back eighteen-year-olds, slouching and chatting, supremely unconcerned that anyone might be waiting. They already had my details and I had a contact number at the Embassy to ring, but even so I felt a little knot in my stomach, a lurch of uncertainty about whether they would let me through. There were very few people about. The soldiers looked at my papers without much interest, and after a few minutes indicated that I could proceed.

I walked on, through another door, past what looked like cattle pens where a few Palestinian men were standing huddled together waiting, and into a long tunnel with a corrugated-iron roof, lit by a few dim bulbs and the grey light from a long gap high up in the concrete wall. The floor was earth, and at intervals off to the side there were areas filled with rubbish. It was a horrible place. There was no light at the end of the tunnel, and I walked on into the freezing dimness, carrying my flowers. Then suddenly the tunnel curved, and round the bend I could see a distant light and a figure, a Palestinian guard. As I approached, the figure took on more definition, and out of this desolation came a welcoming smile. The feeling of warmth and relief was overwhelming.

Mohammed's cousin, also named Mohammed, was waiting for me, and we took a taxi along the now familiar road, through Gaza City and the bleak rubble of the Khan Younis refugee camp. Amjad had been adamant about wanting to come to the Erez Crossing to meet me, but I remembered how we had been shot at at the Abu Houli checkpoint, and knowing what a perilous flashpoint it could be, I felt worried about him. 'Please don't come. It's dangerous,' I insisted. He'd taken a lot of persuading, and I knew he was a little hurt.

When I met him in the Palestinian Progressive Youth Movement's sparsely furnished little office, he greeted me shyly. We weren't in London now. He looked somehow calmer and more mature. But he was still the same old Amjad, with his sweet boyish smile and zest for life, and that sense he always gave me of a compassionate spirit triumphing over suffering. It was good to see him, and before long he had relaxed and was asking me about Billy and Fred and Sophie and Anthony, and inviting me to lunch with his family.

I knew immediately we entered Amjad's house that this visit from his London friend was a significant event. We sat on mattresses in Amjad's room, which I was told he had tidied specially for the occasion. The family all smiled and made a gentle joke of it. 'He's thrown everything into the cupboards,' said his father, a delightful older man with the same warm brown eyes as Amjad.

His mother and sisters were hard at work in the kitchen, bringing in huge dishes of rice and pungent smelling chicken with coriander. His father asked me about London, and told me how he had worked for the British under the Mandate, and come to this house in 1948. 'Now it has been made good again, and I am happy,' he said. From time to time he would pick out a particularly choice piece of chicken and place it thoughtfully on my plate saying 'Have a bit.' I was wet and exhausted, my feet were freezing, and my back was aching from the unaccustomed position. But inwardly I thought I had rarely felt such human warmth as I felt in this desolate place.

After lunch I gave Amjad's mother one of the bunches of flowers I had brought. Then Amjad and I walked together to the place where Tom had been shot. I'd notified the army that I was coming, told them I'd wear an orange scarf around my neck so they could identify me from the watchtower. At intervals I phoned the IDF number and they would ask me sharply, 'Where are you now? Which road?', and I would try to describe our position among the bombed-out buildings. If anything it all looked worse than before. It seemed incredible that people were still actually living here.

We approached the barrier of rubble and the huge block of concrete. As always, beautiful children were running up and down the mound, jumping and laughing and calling to one another. Amjad and I stood together for a moment, simply looking. Then I laid the other bunch of flowers in the place where Tom had fallen, where I thought his head would have been. The group of lovely children stood together around the spot. Our eyes met and they smiled.

We were silent as we left, but after about twenty yards Amjad pointed out a derelict looking building riddled with bullet holes. 'School for deaf people,' he said. 'Are they still using it?' I asked. It was hard to believe. 'Many deaf people in Rafah,' said Amjad. 'From the bombs and planes making boom,' and he put his fingers in his ears. How good it would be, I thought, to be able to do something for this poor school.

There was now just time to see Mohammed's family. His mother and his four sisters welcomed me like a long-lost friend, pressing food upon me and thanking me over and over for helping Mohammed. Under the terms of his asylum, Mohammed could not return to Gaza for several years, and I saw from the look in his mother's eyes how much she missed him. She gave me some special seeds for making tea that she knew Mohammed liked, and I tried to describe a little of his life in London, and how he was.

It was hard to leave, but it was beginning to get dark and I knew the Erez Crossing closed at eight. Mohammed's cousin was to come back with me, and Amjad insisted on accompanying us as far as Gaza City, where he said he would stay with friends. When it came to it, it was difficult to say goodbye – I had learned so much about him and his life. So I pressed his arm, and he quickly got out of the taxi, waved and disappeared into the night.

It was completely dark when we reached the Erez Crossing. I

said goodbye to Mohammed and showed my papers to the Palestinian guards who were sitting in the open behind a rickety looking trestle table at the entrance to the tunnel, attempting to keep warm with a small cooking ring on an extension lead, which hissed as the raindrops hit it. One of them picked up the phone and there was a terse conversation with the soldiers on the Israeli side. Then they bade me a friendly goodbye and I started down the tunnel.

It was empty and eerie. I tried to walk as purposefully as possible, to give myself courage. I could hear dripping water. Wires without light bulbs hung down. The only light came from the glare of the watchtowers through a gap along the top of the tunnel twenty feet or so up. I rounded the bend – put there to prevent Israelis and Palestinians shooting at each other from either end – and there, suddenly, in front of me were huge steel gates, about fifteen feet high. Through the bars I could see the cattle pens I'd spotted on my way out, and more huge steel-barred gates beyond. I pushed at one of the gates in front of me, but it didn't budge. I stood there feeling increasingly angry – not because I was wet and cold and tired, but because the whole thing suddenly struck me as so outrageous, so arrogant, so unnecessary. I stood there for a good ten minutes. I could hear voices in the distance, and from time to time I called out 'Hello! Is anybody there?'

Eventually a rasping voice over a loudspeaker said, 'Wait!' Then, 'Push the gate.' I pushed it but nothing happened. 'The other one,' came the irritable voice. Nothing happened again. 'No, the other one,' from the exasperated young voice. It was completely disorientating. I went back to the first gate, pushed it, it opened, and I went through.

Now I was in a kind of cage with an electronically controlled and locked gate behind me and a gate in front of me, and steel pens at the side. The voice came over the loudspeaker again, but this time I couldn't understand what it was saying, so I just carried on walking until I was taken up short by an order: '*Stop!*' This was followed by something else, but still I couldn't make it out. 'I can't understand you!' I said to the loudspeaker, naively imagining someone could hear me. But no – this was a one-way conversation. Eventually I deduced what they wanted and took my coat off. Another faceless order was shouted. I put my arms out and turned round. Then I was told to walk forward.

Now I was up against another set of massive gates. I rattled them, but they didn't open. I called out 'Hello!', but no one answered. Eventually a young soldier appeared, sauntering towards me, taking his time. I was furious. I could have been his mother. 'Can't you just open the gate?' I said. He said nothing, simply handed me a glove through the bars without explanation. 'What's this for?' I said. 'This isn't the way to treat people. You need to explain.' I was carrying a plastic bag with the seeds Mohammed's mother had given me, and a tracksuit for myself that she had insisted I take. He pointed to the bag and said: 'Put this glove on and rub it round the things in that bag. Then give it back to me.'

I was fuming, but did as I was asked. Another, more mature-looking soldier joined us. 'Look at me,' I said. 'Do you honestly think I've got something in here that would harm anybody?' Neither of them said anything, but the older soldier looked slightly apologetic.

By this time I was aware that an elderly Palestinian man had come up behind me. I looked back at him, but he gazed down at the ground, avoiding my eyes. I felt desolate for him. What must he be feeling about being seen going through this barbaric and humiliating ritual? I imagined he was going over into Israel to do nightshift work. Each time he must have to face this procedure and one of these arrogant young soldiers.

'Can't you open the gate?' I said.

'You'll have to wait until he's been through the system,' the young soldier said. Finally the gate was opened and the Palestinian and I went through together. I longed to communicate to him my empathy and my disgust. For a moment he raised his head and I saw his face. It was deeply furrowed – the face of someone who has been in a war zone, defeated, only half-alive.

The older soldier must have seen my look. 'Soon we're going to have a better system,' he said ingratiatingly, 'where internationals go through a separate door.'

The gulf between our understanding was so great there seemed nothing to say, but I gazed steadily back at him.

'Yeah, yeah,' said the young soldier, with a kind of ironic bravado. 'We're all wrong, the Israeli army. It's all our fault.'

TWENTY

I arrived in London just too late for the opening of Tom's exhibition at the Frontline Club, but on seeing it next day with Anthony I was bowled over. It was as if I was in Rafah again – the hideously destroyed buildings with their protuberances of rusting steel girders, the bleak, litter-strewn streets. And I was stabbed with thoughts of Amjad, and of all the ravaged people we'd met there who were trying to make a life against all the odds.

Anthony had chosen the venue carefully. One of the Frontline Club's aims is to promote freedom of expression and to support those working at the sharp edge of journalism, and its members include some of the best photographers, journalists and camera-men in the world. It gives off a tremendous sense of vigour and immediacy, of leaving no stone unturned to bring back the truth. Tom, I knew, would have loved its intellectual energy; it was a place, I felt, that might well have become part of his professional life if he had lived. Now I felt incredibly proud and moved to see his pictures on the exposed brick walls.

Anthony had collated three thousand images on various discs and cartridges taken during Tom's months in the Middle East. Many of them were different versions of the same picture, and in London Anthony and Kay had struggled to sort them. Eventually they had reduced them to nine hundred, and with huge difficulty and the help of a picture editor from the *Sunday Telegraph* from these we had selected twenty-one.

Looking now at the blown-up mounted photographs of tanks bearing down on the peaceworkers I could hear the earsplitting noise of metal against metal and feel the terrifying vibrations of the revving engines. One powerful photo showed Raph walking calmly past a tank at full throttle, spewing out a cloud of poisonous fumes, almost burying him from sight.

I stood for a long time gazing at the picture of a wistful child leaning pensively against the ruined wall of his demolished home. All Tom's anger, all his shock at the thought of those children's futureless lives, were in that photograph. It was an extraordinarily humbling feeling to be looking through his eyes, almost as if searching to understand his judgement. Inside me a respect grew, and a kind of realisation that this was what he had gone to the Middle East to find.

The week after I left Israel, Pinhaus Zuaretz, the brigade commander whose name I had first heard mentioned in early January, was called to Ashkelon to give evidence, and Karin described the scene in court. She told me Zuaretz held a very senior position in the army, the equivalent probably of a British brigadier-general. It was his responsibility to ensure that soldiers were trained in the rules of engagement. And he it was, I learned from one of the foreign correspondents, who had helped reformulate the IDF's rules of engagement after the Second Intifada to permit soldiers to shoot children as young as fourteen.

Zuaretz, so Karin told me, was a man with a deceptively easy and friendly manner. He had clearly been called by the defence to bolster Taysir's testimony, to give him a character reference, as it were. And that is what he did. He praised him warmly and at length, calling him an excellent soldier. This was interesting, since we already knew that Taysir had been convicted of taking drugs while on duty. It had also emerged during the trial that he had been convicted of illegal use of a weapon after using a field near his home as a shooting range. It seemed that off-duty firearms regulations were very strict.

More strangely still, Zuaretz said that he had believed Taysir's original testimony. This I couldn't understand, since from very early on it was clear that Taysir had lied and given contradictory versions of the event. Zuaretz said he had been disappointed to discover that Taysir had lied. The picture he attempted to draw, in defiance of all the evidence, was of a soldier dealing with a crisis professionally and appropriately.

'But this is fantasy,' I said to Karin on the phone.

'It's just the way the IDF behave,' said Karin. 'Commanders always tend to back up their soldiers.'

In fact Zuaretz turned out to be a better witness for the prosecution than for the defence. When examined about whether there was a line of vision from the watchtower to where Tom was standing, at first, on the basis of the court's outdated material, he said that there was not. However, when the prosecution showed him more accurate pictures proving that there had been a line of vision, he was forced to agree.

The final expert witness called by the defence was a forensic pathologist, Dr Chen Kugel, an opinionated young army doctor with a dramatic manner who appeared in court in military uniform. When I heard this I was astonished. Could he really be said to be unbiased? The line Dr Kugel took, based on hospital reports, was that Tom could not have been in a vegetative state since he was breathing unaided and had certain basic reflexes, and so should have been treated with antibiotics. He claimed that Tom's death had not been caused by pneumonia, but by an overdose of morphine – a decision for which we, his family, and the English doctors were responsible.

I was outraged that Dr Kugel, like Dr Lazary, was attempting to break the causal link between the shooting and Tom's death, and to shift the blame on to the English doctors who had given Tom such outstanding care. It was preposterous.

Karin told me there had been a revealing exchange when the prosecution team pointed out that they had originally approached Dr Kugel for an opinion with a view to his appearing as an expert witness for the prosecution, and had shown him various medical documents. During these conversations he had expressed entirely different opinions from the ones he had just proffered in court. In the event Dr Chapman had been able to attend, and the idea of using Dr Kugel was dropped. Dr Kugel seemed furious that his fickleness had been exposed. It left me questioning a system that allowed expert witnesses to change their 'considered' professional opinions according to the side for which they were giving evidence. What view would the judges take?

A few days after the second anniversary of Tom's shooting, an Israeli military court acquitted an IDF lieutenant of the killing of the English cameraman James Miller, though there was little doubt, in my view, that he had been knowingly targeted. Evidence had been tampered with, and the soldier had apparently changed his account of the incident six times. Just what had happened with Tom – it was still the same old story. And even though the Israelis were set to pull out of Gaza in August, they would maintain their stranglehold. They would still control the borders, the territorial waters and the air space, and had even reserved the right to invade. Gaza would still be a prison, its borders hermetically sealed, its economy trampled and squeezed out of existence.

I remembered a tragic description I had read of an old man standing on the beach in Gaza with a box of oranges – his sole means of livelihood – beside him, throwing them, hopelessly, one by one into the sea. He was prevented from exporting his oranges to Israel, and rather than let them rot in his orchards, he preferred to do this. The utter waste of it all.

Yet amazingly, among our friends in Rafah, humanity still prevailed. On the anniversary of Tom's shooting I received an e-mail from the family of Dr Samir:

Dear Tom family, we will never forget the time when Tom first came at our house with Alison. He was high-spirited and so generous with his care and concern. Probably we were to him just a family that needs his support. He played with our children and

take many photos of them. He lost his life for children, and instead
of them. At this anniversary we share with you the pain and agony
of losing him. He will remain deep in our hearts. May God bless
his soul and replace this sad memory with happy one.

The trial had now been going on for almost a year. Anthony had
decided he would fly to Israel for the verdict, which was due on
27 June, and Billy was determined to go with him. Peter Carter
had been trying to obtain permission for him from the Israeli
Foreign Ministry and eventually we received the following
communication: Billy could enter Israel if the Embassy guaranteed that he would leave within twenty-four hours; if an Embassy
official accompanied him throughout; and if Billy provided a
letter signed by himself and a lawyer stating that he would not
attempt to enter the Gaza Strip, and that he would do nothing
illegal.

To us it seemed insulting beyond belief. There was no good
reason why Billy should be barred from Israel, and the government had made no attempt to provide one. Billy, however, wasn't
about to accept such conditions. 'The bastards!' was his reaction.
He was adamant that he was going to go, and Anthony and I were
fully behind him, though we had no idea what the outcome
would be. Anthony called me just as they boarded the aircraft and
I phoned the Foreign Office to ask them to notify the Embassy in
Tel Aviv that Billy and Anthony were on their way.

'Well,' I said to the smooth young Foreign Office duty officer
at the other end of the line, 'if they refuse to let Billy in we will let
the media know.'

'Oh, I shouldn't do that,' he said quickly. 'It won't do your
cause any good.'

I bit my tongue, but something snapped inside me. Unlike the
FCO, we didn't have to work with the Israelis on a day-to-day
basis. We were free agents. 'I think by now we've learned that, if
it hadn't been for the media, if we had simply relied on diplomatic
channels, we would never have got as far as we have,' I said.

I doubted there was any chance that when their plane touched down in Tel Aviv at three o'clock in the morning Billy might somehow be able to get through, but we did hope the Israelis might respond to the absurdity of the situation. Vain hope! Anthony phoned very early to say they had been stopped by Israeli Security and Billy had been detained at the airport.

'I told them that either Billy and I stayed together or we left together,' Anthony said, 'but they told me that was impossible. Although Billy was standing right beside me, my passport had been stamped and I was now in Israel. So I'm afraid I had no alternative but to leave him.'

Anthony was clearly furious. He had been in touch with Karin who had spoken to Billy, suggesting that she should go to court straight away on his behalf with a request that he should be able to attend the trial without conditions. Billy agreed, but the request had to go through many judicial stages, ending with the Attorney General. By the time a reply came it was too late, in any case, for Billy to reach the court in Ashkelon.

The request was turned down on the vague grounds of 'security'. This, we had been told, was common practice with the Israeli security service, Shin Bet. Very rarely do they give specific information on why an individual is being denied entry – even in matters of life and death. Though Billy had no record of lawlessness whatever, the fact that they had shot his brother to them gave him an immediate motive for revenge. The Israeli Deputy Ambassador would later say on Channel 4 News that they had denied him entry because they feared 'trouble'.

So Billy spent the day at the airport in a room with another detainee, with the Embassy keeping in touch by phone. When lunchtime came and food was brought, Billy put a mischievous note on the glass panel of the door saying 'Gone to lunch. Back in ten minutes'. This 'trouble' caused confusion among the young soldiers of Israeli Security, who are not known for their sense of humour.

★　　★　　★

On the afternoon of 27 June 2005, Taysir Walid Heib was convicted of manslaughter. He was also convicted of obstruction of justice, submitting false testimony, obtaining false testimony and unbecoming behaviour. The long and impressively thorough ruling found that he had lied repeatedly about events in Rafah on 11 April 2003 and that he had shot Tom with clear knowledge of the consequences. The judges stated categorically that it was Taysir's shot that had caused Tom's death – they found no evidence of medical malpractice, and they completely accepted Dr Chapman's report. There was no doubt Taysir had broken the rules of engagement and had 'brought Israel into disrepute'.

As Taysir was led from the court he tried to break loose from his guards and lashed out in fury at the crowd of foreign journalists – there were very few Israeli journalists in court. Interviewed outside the courtroom Anthony looked drained. I thought of all the exhausting months he had spent pursuing this investigation and producing his report – doing the work that the Israeli justice system should have done.

'Does this amount to justice, Mr Hurndall?' the BBC journalist James Reynolds asked him.

'It amounts to limited justice,' Anthony said. 'We're very pleased that it has got to this stage as we were told at the outset that there was no way we would get the Israelis to turn their story round. My concern is that the crime was not actually fairly laid at this soldier's door. He is a scapegoat, a pawn in a larger system. As a Bedouin he has been laid at the sacrificial altar of Israeli policy, one of very indiscriminate shooting and very little accountability. We don't feel that the underlying policy has been addressed.'

'So what is your response to the verdict?' James Reynolds asked.

'In terms of this particular soldier it is the correct verdict on the evidence that has been presented,' Anthony replied. 'It might have been appropriate to bring a murder prosecution, but we haven't seen all the evidence, though we have asked to do so repeatedly. Maybe there should have been further prosecutions, and indeed we think this goes much higher up the chain of command.'

'What is your feeling for the Israeli government today?' Reynolds asked.

'Great disappointment,' Anthony replied. 'Israel is a democratic and open society in many respects, but it has great failings which the government is failing to face up to. It has behaved irresponsibly, and been oppressive and dishonest.'

'And finally, Mr Hurndall, do you have a message for the Israeli people?' Anthony was asked.

He answered. 'I would say to them, you are a great people but there are matters that you seriously have to address, both about the way the army handles itself in Gaza and the West Bank, and the way it deals with a number of other issues. We sincerely hope as a family that you will address these so that you can find peace and security.'

On 11 August 2005, Taysir Walid Heib was sentenced to eight years in prison – the longest sentence imposed on a soldier for killing a civilian since the Second Intifada broke out in 2000, the previous maximum having been twenty-one months for 'conduct unbefitting a soldier'. The prosecution had asked for the maximum sentence for manslaughter of twenty years, but the court held back, saying that a heavier sentence would only lend credence to claims that Taysir had been made a scapegoat.

Before the judge pronounced sentence he spoke the following words:

> Sergeant Wahid Taysir caused a soul to leave this world. He spilt the blood of a young man in the bloom of youth, causing the loss of an entire world. When that young man was alive, there was no one else like him, and there will never be anyone like him again.

The Israelis immediately claimed the case as a triumph for Israeli justice. But I thought of the peaceworker Brian Avery, shot in the face by the IDF, and of the United Nations worker Iain

Hook, killed by an Israeli marksman in the Jenin refugee camp, of James Miller, and Rachel Corrie, all of whose cases had been dismissed. I thought of Amjad's dead friends, and of little Iman al-Hams, and of the 3,600 unnamed Palestinian civilians and 600 children whom Amnesty reported had been killed by the Israeli army since September 2000, not to speak of the thousands who had suffered injuries without proper access to medical care. None of these people had received any justice. This couldn't be the end of it. We must try to salvage some good from all the pain we'd suffered, that we'd seen for ourselves, fight on to bring the faceless men in charge of Israeli army policy to account. Do it for Tom.

AFTERWARDS

It is October 2006 and I am sitting looking out at the garden. The garden has been my summer project. I wanted to create a place of beauty where all Tom's family and friends could relax and be together, a place where we would all exchange stories of Tom. Jay, a friend from the choir, created a design with diagonal raised beds which I had built using old stock bricks, and I filled them with fragrant climbing roses, evergreen jasmine, lavender and so much else that there is hardly a square of earth still visible. Cream and pink honeysuckle, deep pink tea roses and several types of clematis cover the walls. I gave one corner a flavour of the Middle East, with canna lilies, oleander and grevillea, and designed a wrought-iron garden table with green and blue hand-painted Palestinian tiles brought back from Jerusalem to remind me of the American Colony Hotel.

We've all found healing in the garden. Kay, who has become an important part of our lives, has created a special corner with miniature dark pink sedums. Fred enjoys it from the balcony Billy built for him. Sophie has always loved fragrant flowers and Anthony, not known as a keen gardener, has taken an interest. Even the cat has found a favourite spot amongst the ferns behind an ornamental urn.

But now the summer is over, and I'm sitting looking out, surrounded by files of documents and press cuttings, thinking about all that has happened during the past eighteen months, since the conviction of Taysir.

The inquest into Tom's death was finally held in London, at

Camden Coroner's Court, in April 2006. It had had to wait for
the outcome of Taysir's trial. We were fortunate to be represented
by Michael Mansfield, QC, and Imran Khan. I found the dynamic
Michael Mansfield extremely warm and likeable and greatly
admired his laser-sharp brain. It was inspiring to see these two
lawyers working together, as I know they regularly do.

The jury returned a unanimous verdict of Unlawful Killing, as
it had done a few days earlier at the inquest of James Miller. On
my desk is the jury's statement:

> We the Jury unanimously agree that Mr Thomas Peter Hurndall
> was shot in Rafah in Gaza between 3.30 p.m. and 4.30 p.m. on
> 11.4.2003. He was shot intentionally with the intention to kill
> him. The Jury would like to express their dismay at the lack of
> cooperation from the Israeli authorities during this investigation.

The Israeli authorities had refused to allow the Metropolitan
Police to travel to the site of the shooting, and refused to release
vital documents for the Coroner's investigation directly to him, or
to attend the inquest. Yet even so, it had been clear to the jury
that Tom had been shot intentionally, in cold blood, within an
army culture where soldiers were not held to account for killing
civilians, where those in command were too quick to believe a
soldier's story, or turned a blind eye.

I think Anthony and I were surprised at the devastating effect
the inquest had on both of us. Reading from Tom's journals, as
I did in court, seeing the film of Tom's shooting which was
shown, hearing Anthony read from his report, brought it all
back. As Anthony said afterwards, although it was three years
now since Tom was shot, it had been impossible for us to deal
properly with what happened. We had had to put a part of
ourselves aside just in order to carry on. 'I have tried to keep
myself forensically impartial,' Anthony told a journalist, 'partly
to ensure I got to the truth but also to protect myself. The
process has put my feelings into something like deep freeze. I

thought the inquest would provide an end to it but it is just going on.'

What the inquest did, however, was to bring the case into the public eye again with huge media coverage, and to strengthen political support. The *Independent* devoted its front page to an extract from Tom's journal under the headline 'A Death Foretold'. The Labour MP Richard Burden, whose close involvement we had so much appreciated, tabled an Early Day Motion in the House of Commons, which was signed by more than a hundred MPs, expressing renewed concern over Israel's failure to investigate the cases of innocent civilians killed by the IDF, and urging Israel to comply with international law and to withdraw from all the Occupied Territories.

In July Anthony, Fred and I were in the House of Lords to hear Baroness Northover question the Attorney General, Lord Goldsmith, about the possibility of bringing prosecutions in the UK over the deaths of Tom and James Miller, as suggested by the Camden coroner. I knew it was good that Fred should hear that people still cared about his brother, and about the cause for which he had died. He sat gripped by the proceedings and wanted to stay and stay.

And we have had our own meeting with the Attorney General, who is pursuing Tom's case with the Israeli authorities to ascertain whether there should be other arrests. To this day we have received no official public apology from the Israeli authorities.

I look with anger and despair at the press cuttings describing Israel's actions in the Gaza Strip during this past summer. A Palestinian family blown up during a day out on the beach – an act denied by the IDF, though an independent ballistics expert found that 'the crater size, the shrapnel, the types of injuries, their location on the bodies' left little doubt that this family was killed by an Israeli shell. The orgy of destruction and killing in Gaza in retaliation for the kidnapping of Corporal Gilad Shalit.

The fact that thousands of Palestinians are still held without trial
in 'administrative detention' in Israel is rarely mentioned, though
in July 150 distinguished British Jews, including Harold Pinter,
Lynne Reid Banks and Miriam Margolyes, publicly expressed
their horror at 'the collective punishment of the people of Gaza',
and urged the public to write to the British government and to
the Israeli Embassy: 'Presenting this as an isolated hostage-taking
incident ignores Israel's regular snatching of Palestinians from
their homes,' they wrote. As the outstanding Israeli journalist
Gideon Levy put it in *Ha'aretz*: 'We kidnapped civilians and they
kidnapped a soldier, we are a state and they are a terror organisation.'

I am keen to pursue the project we have been discussing with
the union to which I belonged for thirty years, the National
Union of Teachers, to set up a scheme in Gaza in Tom's name to
give learning support to children with disabilities. I couldn't forget
the sight of the School for the Deaf in Rafah in its poor, war-torn,
crumbling building, and of so many disabled people, especially
children. But for the present anyway we can't get into Gaza, and
the people in Gaza can't get out.

But there was good news, too. In July I received an exuberant e-
mail from Amjad to say that he had passed his exams. Now he is
even more desperate to come to England, but it's difficult, and I
remember how much his last visit disturbed him. It's so painful for
me to think about Amjad. There are days when I know I should
e-mail him, but it would be cruel to get up his hopes of leaving
Rafah. I suppose this is a pattern that's easy to get into – turning
away from situations that are too dreadful to think about. But after
what I have seen, I know I must not turn away, which is why I
have written this book.

Mohammed is in London studying for a master's degree in
engineering, and comes to the house often. One summer Sunday
not long ago he and some friends from a Palestinian dance group
were performing at a local street party. They came back for tea in

the garden afterwards and I listened with amazement to the tragic stories they all had to tell. There was not one amongst them who had not lost a member of his or her family. They were all embarked on advanced courses, studying for PhDs and master's degrees. When I asked them what they planned to do afterwards, the answer was the same. 'It's terrible to be separated from our families, but we don't want to go back. We want a life. Gaza is a prison and the Israelis want us to leave.' I felt for Mohammed's mother on hearing such things.

Mohammed has taken to London. He makes us laugh with his grasp of slang, his urban body language and his street cred. He, Billy and Fred have become close. Recently Mohammed came with Anthony and me to see Fred play football for Winchester – Tom's old school, where Fred is now very happily into his second year. The sight of Mohammed in this safe and tradi-tionally beautiful English setting, among green meadows and ancient grey school buildings, was a vivid reminder of the daily conflict and insecurity with which he had lived. After the match, Mohammed ran on to the pitch in true Palestinian style and lifted six-foot Fred right off the ground, and suddenly I had a vision of Tom picking Fred up and throwing him over his shoulder as he used to do. Fred, who's become used to the expressive ways of the Middle East, didn't mind a bit, though I expect other boys might have.

As for the rest of us, our lives are very gradually beginning to settle – but in quite a different form from before. I constantly think of snow globes, those glass toys that you shake to create a snowstorm. Eventually everything settles, as things have slowly begun to do for us. We've all changed, found new strengths and different priorities. I think we've all become more public people, more politically aware, able to speak out in a way I certainly never would before. Sophie has always been articulate, and in speaking out strongly about the Middle East and the policies of our government she has in a sense found a new platform for her abilities. She now has an interesting new job helping charities and voluntary organisations develop their communications effectively. Billy, with his creative scientific brain, is hoping to do a physics degree at Leeds University. Anthony is reshaping his legal practice. For myself, this year has been a search – for Tom and for a greater understanding of the person he was. I knew that I must do this if I was ever to be whole, and able to be there for the family again.

In March this year I went back to Jerusalem. I wanted to retrace Tom's steps, to find the rooftop café where he had sat, Coke in hand, writing his journal, to visit the Church of the Holy Sepulchre, which had made such a deep impression upon him.

I was staying at the crumbling and characterful 'New' Imperial Hotel near the Jaffa Gate, and on the first morning I set off into the Old City, making my way uncertainly through the maze of alleyways with their pale, glowing, almost translucent flagstones, avoiding the carts that came rumbling towards me, trying not to get into conversation with all the shopkeepers and storeholders who wanted to stop me and show me their goods.

Within a very short time I was lost, and as I stood wondering what to do I heard a voice: 'Lady, you look sad. I am a Bedouin and I know. What are you looking for?' It was one of the shopkeepers. He came out of his shop and I explained my mission. 'I know the place you mean,' he said. 'I will take you there.'

We walked along silently together until we came to a staircase between the stalls in the Suk Aftimos. I thanked him and he laid his hand on my arm: 'Everything has a beginning and an end,' he said. 'We have a saying in Bedouin' – he pointed to his forehead – 'that it was written that your son should die. You could have talked to him, argued with him, but it would not have been different. You must look to the future, allow yourself to breathe, get on with your life.' Then he waved and was gone.

I mounted the staircase, which gave on to a wide roof terrace with tables and chairs. There were big clay pots with plants, and in a corner a stack of hookahs. It was wonderfully quiet. I went and leaned on the terrace railing and there below me in the morning

sunlight was the gold Dome of the Rock and the grey dome of
the Holy Sepulchre, just as Tom had described them. The roofs of
Old Jerusalem stretched away, red tiles, creamy domes, hundreds
of small balconies and water tanks. Here and there a dark cedar
tree poked up, and I could hear the different sounds of birds.
Tom's presence was so strong. If I turned round he would be
there, sitting at a table with his long legs stretched out, smoking a
hookah, writing in his notebook with that very peculiar concentration of his.

I thought about the Bedouin's words, which seemed to have
come from a place of deep suffering, and all that they meant. It
came to me strongly that it was precisely because Tom was aware
of death that he was so vividly and passionately alive; his journal
showed that. And that given the person he was, there was really
nothing I could have done to stop him.

Then I made my way to the Church of the Holy Sepulchre.
Standing in its great silent, dim interior, I thought about Tom,
wondered where he had walked, where he had sat. On my right
and left were side chapels, Catholic, Russian Orthodox, some
simple, some glitteringly ornate. Eventually I chose a simple little
chapel, unfrequented and slightly out of the way off one of the
transepts, and sat down on the stone seat. It seemed to be a space
without distractions, without a name, a spiritual space with no
particular allegiance and the one that was truest to Tom.

It was very quiet, and I sat and let the atmosphere of the church
seep into me. I could almost physically feel the pulls of the
different religious dogmas which we human beings use and abuse
for our own purposes. Yet somehow this building seemed to
incorporate the essence of what was good in them all. It was a
place of division, and yet of unity, a place that penetrated deep
into the soul, so powerful and serene that it had caused Tom, an
agnostic leaning towards atheism, to buy a crucifix. Within its
stillness I lit a candle for him and sat for a long time, watching its
small light burning steadily against the dark.

*   *   *

A few weeks ago I left London and drove north. Ever since
Tom died I had longed to go to some wild and lonely place
where I could lose myself in the power and vastness of the sea.
After my last visit to Rafah, when I had been utterly demolished by the destruction I had seen, the need to be somehow
cleansed by the sea had become an overwhelming urge. I had a
yearning to go to Scotland, with its reassuring links to my
childhood, and especially to Fingal's Cave, that mysterious place
which had inspired the young Mendelssohn to write music of
such haunting beauty. I wanted to scream my grief and anger to
the waves and let them do my struggling for me, to encounter a
force so great that it would give me a perspective, an understanding of what had happened and how it fitted into the larger
scheme.

So on a calm, sunny day I arrived in Fionnphort and took a
little motor boat past Iona to Staffa. As we drew nearer to the tiny
island its extraordinary cliff face came into focus, gigantic grey-
green basalt columns, crowned with rock of a rougher texture,
with the sea foaming around the mysterious entrance to Fingal's
Cave. There were only a few of us in the boat, and we climbed
out and made our way gingerly along the rocky path down to the
yawning black opening.

Once inside I stood in awe. The cave was like a cathedral, with
great Norman pillars and internal arches, and suddenly I was back
at Tom's memorial service in Westminster Cathedral. Round the
edge of the cave were more clusters of basalt pillars which had
been cut off by some natural cataclysm and which formed a kind
of path. They looked like groups of people, very solemn and still,
and as I stepped along them it seemed to me that I was walking
beside all the people who had come to pay tribute to Tom, and
that their love and respect for him was somehow holding me,
supporting me.

At the end of the transept were more basalt columns, like the
pipes of a massive organ, and I stood very still, listening to its
sounds – the many-layered ethereal music of the ocean, the

echoing roar, the irregular deep surges and sucking noises, the wilder explosions as the water hit the rocks.

As I looked down into the crystal water I could see that the pillars changed from grey to pink, right down to the bottom of the volcanic rock, and suddenly out of the water the small dark shape of an otter appeared, slid between the rocks and disappeared below me. I thought of all the eruptions of the earth's crust, the geological upheavals, the fragmentations that had gone to form this place. And now it was a whole, compacted together by some mighty force, and stronger than before. And I thought that perhaps, after all this life-changing upheaval that had been like some volcanic fire, my own fragmented self might be put together again, and be stronger. One day I would be able to remember Tom and celebrate his life without the intense, racking sadness I felt now, with happiness even. Somehow this ancient place gave me hope. I didn't cry out to the sea as I had thought I would. I sang. Quietly to myself, the overture to *Fingal's Cave*, which is called in Gaelic the Cave of Melody.

When we got back into the boat the wind had got up and there was a lashing rain. Holding on tight I gave in to the tossing of the boat, feeling the crash of the waves on the bow, and the whipping rain and wind on my face. I was glad the weather had changed. I wanted the elements to cleanse me, to blow through my head. Looking back at Staffa as it receded into the distance I felt certain that there must be some grand design, some force and intelligence that had shaped it – a design of which we were all a part if we could only know it.

Next day I took the ferry back to the mainland. I drove along the North West Coast and then turned inland towards Glencoe. On either side of me rose mountains of an intense emerald green which swelled into a bowl as I approached Glencoe. It had been raining and streams were gushing down the mountainsides, over the great boulders, and I longed to get out, to bury my face in the clear mountain water, to breathe the clean air, but something powerful forced me on.

Nearer to the pass the mountains began to close in. As I entered the pass, I began to feel an almost physical pressure, as if a great force was bearing down on me. Again I wanted to stop, but I somehow knew I must go on, through the narrow passage in the mountains. My face was wet with tears, and I heard a voice, which was my own, calling out 'Thomas! Thomas!' It was an anguished, involuntary cry that came from the depths of my being, like the cry of birth. I remembered the travail of Tom's birth, the moment of first holding him, vulnerable and restless, and the overwhelming feeling of wanting to protect and nurture him. Now I knew that I must let him go and return to life, that it was part of loving to be able to let go. *What will survive of us is love.* I thought of Tom's 'Rules for Life', which he'd written in his teens, and I seemed to hear his voice saying to me, *None of us deserves this life, and one single minute on this planet is an undeserved blessing.*

And I drove on through the pass until finally the mountains parted and I found myself on a plateau, with fresh green countryside opening out before me.

ACKNOWLEDGEMENTS

When I embarked on my diary while sitting beside Tom in hospital it never occurred to me that I would one day feel moved to write and publish a book about him. That I have now done so is thanks to a multitude of talented people to whom I owe a great debt.

My deepest gratitude is to Hazel Wood, who held my hand throughout the writing process. Hazel, from whom I learnt so much, has been invaluable in harnessing and giving shape to my thoughts, emotions and the events of the story.

My thanks to Victoria Millar for her sensitive and acute judgment, to Mary Morris for her diligent attention to the final details, and to so very many other hugely able and inspiring people at Bloomsbury.

I shall be eternally grateful to Andrew Nurnberg, my literary agent, for believing in and nurturing the book, for his unending encouragement and for guiding me through the unfamiliar world of publishing with great expertise.

My thanks to Colonel Tom Fitzalan Howard, former British Defence Attaché in Israel, who led me through and commented on the minefield of military and diplomatic matters with absolute integrity, breadth and patience.

My thanks to Kay Fernandes, professional photographer and researcher, whose outstanding flair, skill and painstaking care continues to fill me with awe. It was Garth Stead, as the foreign photographer present at the scene, who helped to expose the truth which British and Israeli governments could not ignore.

My sincere thanks to a host of spectacularly helpful people in 'Palestine', Israel and the UK who guided us through the different processes and who made a difference. Many I have interviewed and, where relevant, a few people have been kind enough to check sections of the text. These include lawyers, Parliamentarians, diplomats, those involved in Tom's medical care, Union members, representatives of NGOs and aid agencies and those who were with Tom in the Middle East. Some cannot be named for their own security – subject to potential threat both from their own and other governments. To name just a few: Imran Khan,

Matthew Ryder, Danny Friedman, Michael Mansfield QC, Michel Massih QC, David Freeman, Avigdor Feldman, Karin Loevy, Kiran Bhogal, Michael Sfarad, Phil Shiner, Richard Burden MP, Jeremy Corbyn MP, Crispin Blunt MP, Sir Gerald Kaufman MP, Andrew George MP, John Austin MP, Dr Ahmad Tibi MK, Baroness Elizabeth Symons, Baroness Lindsay Northover, Baroness Jenny Tonge, Baroness Shirley Williams, Lord Navnit Dholakia, Sir Sherard and Lady Bridget Cowper-Coles, Peter Carter, Scott Simpson, Afif and Christ'l Safieh, Professor Reichental, Professor Gabriel Gurman, Netta (whose surname I never knew), Professor Keith Andrews, Professor Derick Wade, Dr C. Chapman, Dr Roy McGregor, Patti Simonson, Steve Synott, Sulieman Mleahat, Belinda Coote, Chris Doyle, Gillian Watts, Linda Ramsden, Nathan Chapman, Michelle de Mello, Phil Callan, Joseph Carr, Alison Phillips, Raphael Cohen.

There are many people in the media to whom we owe much. I am particularly indebted to the following enlightened foreign correspondents and writers upon whose extensive knowledge I depended: Lyse Doucet, Chris McGreal, Rageh Omaar and Sandra Jordan. Simon Block, playwright, helped me with his insight and tremendous wit to know Tom more deeply. Antony Wood shed light on many tricky decisions.

I'd like to thank Guy Protheroe, Director of the English Chamber Choir, and his wife Ann Manly, and my friends in the English Chamber Choir, from the bottom of my heart for the exquisite music at the 'Concert for Tom', Tom's funeral and memorial service, for their warmth and for helping me to return to music.

My warmest thanks to my dear cousin, Vari Havard-Millar, and my truly wonderful friends Patricia and Charles Brims, Jamil Bullata, Erella and Danny Danievsky, Elisabeth Eidinow, Mike Evans, Vicky Farmer, Ian and Janet Harrison, Jo Fitzalan Howard, Max Hughes, John and Catherine Jardine, Didi Al-Khalil, Ehud Krinis, Anne Perkins, Ann Ritchie, Diana and Harold Rose, Julia Singer, Anne Stoneham, Ann Sullivan, Sarah Taylor, Mike Torbe and Olivia and Patrick Whitworth for accompanying me and keeping my feet on the ground throughout this journey. I shall never forget their affection, the spirit of our conversations, our walks across Hampstead Heath, our laughter and gentle quietness.

Above all, I would like to thank Anthony for helping me to remember all manner of details, our thoughts, observations and the order of events, and for endeavouring to explain to me, repeatedly, the bewildering legal mazes. Without his meticulous report the picture would have been vastly different.

My deepest wish in writing this book is that, with the healing passage of time, Tom's dear friends and our extraordinarily courageous children, Sophie, Bill and Fred, will smile at the thought of him and always remember Tom's love for them.

SOME CURRENT NGOs AND AID AGENCIES

UK:
The Amos Trust: www.amostrust.org
The Council for Arab–British Understanding (CAABU): www.caabu.org
Christian Aid: www.christian-aid.org.uk
The Israeli Committee Against House Demolitions (ICAHD UK): www.icahduk.org
Jews for Justice for Palestinians (JFJFP): www.jfjfp.org
Medical Aid for Palestinians (MAP): www.map-uk.org
Palestine Solidarity Campaign (PSC): www.palestinecampaign.org
War on Want: www.waronwant.org

Palestine:
Al-Haq: www.alhaq.org
MIFTAH: www.miftah.org
Palestinian Centre for Human Rights (PCHR): www.pchrgaza.ps
Palestinian Human Rights Monitoring Group (PHRMG): www.phrmg.org
Palestinian NGOs network (PNGO): www.pngo.net

Israel:
Architects for Human Rights: www.bimkom.org
Breaking the Silence: www.shovrimshtika.org
B'Tselem: www.btselem.org
Gush Shalom: www.gush-shalom.org
Machsom Watch: www.machsomwatch.org

The Olive Tree Movement: www.o-t-m.org
Parents Circle: www.theparentscircle.com
Physicians for Human Rights: www.physiciansforhumanrights.org
Rabbis for Human Rights: www.rhr.israel.net
Yesh Din: www.yesh-din.org
Yesh Gvul: www.yesh-gvul.org

Israel and Palestine:
Combatants for Peace: www.combatantsforpeace.org
One Voice: www.blog.onevoicemovement.org
Ta'ayush: www.taayush.org

International organizations and other sources of information:
The Alternative Information Centre (AIC):
    www.alternativenews.org
Amnesty International: www.amnesty.org
Electronic Intifada: www.electronicintifada.net
Occupation Magazine: www.kibush.co.il
Open Bethlehem: www.openbethlehem.org
PLO Negotiations Affairs Department: www.nad-plo.org
United Nations Office for the Coordination of Humanitarian
    Affairs (OCHA): www.ochaonline.un.org
US Campaign to End Israeli Occupation:
    www.endtheoccupation.org

THE TOM HURNDALL EDUCATION FUND

The National Union of Teachers, along with Education Action International (Charity No: 1003323), has established a fund in memory of Tom with the aim of making provision for vulnerable, disabled children in Gaza. It wil be managed by the Canaan Institute for Education Development in Gaza.

Education Action International (TH Education Fund)
14 Dufferin Street
London EC1Y 8PD
UK

Tel: 00 44 (0)20 7426 5800

Email: info@education-action.org

A NOTE ON THE AUTHOR

Jocelyn Hurndall was born in Winchester in 1951. In the early 1970s she worked as kibbutz volunteer on the Israeli/Lebanese border and travelled through the West Bank to Jerusalem, where her father had worked as a pioneer of wave energy in the early 1960s. She began a career as a teacher in 1974, eventually becoming Head of Learning Support in a multi-cultural school. She lives in London with her family.

Change and Continuity in the 2016 and 2018 Elections

In Memory of Paul R. Abramson

Change and Continuity in the 2016 and 2018 Elections

John H. Aldrich
Duke University

Jamie L. Carson
University of Georgia

Brad T. Gomez
Florida State University

David W. Rohde
Duke University

FOR INFORMATION:

CQ Press

An Imprint of SAGE Publications, Inc.

2455 Teller Road

Thousand Oaks, California 91320

E-mail: order@sagepub.com

SAGE Publications Ltd.

1 Oliver's Yard

55 City Road

London EC1Y 1SP

United Kingdom

SAGE Publications India Pvt. Ltd.

B 1/I 1 Mohan Cooperative Industrial Area

Mathura Road, New Delhi 110 044

India

SAGE Publications Asia-Pacific Pte. Ltd.

18 Cross Street #10-10/11/12

China Square Central

Singapore 048423

Library of Congress Cataloging-in-Publication Data

Names: Aldrich, John H., author.

Title: Change and continuity in the 2016 and 2018 elections / John H. Aldrich, Jamie L. Carson, Brad T. Gomez, David W. Rohde.

Description: Los Angeles : SAGE/CQ Press, 2020. | Includes bibliographical references and index.

Identifiers: LCCN 2019010859 | ISBN 9781544356778 (pbk. : alk. paper)

Subjects: LCSH: Presidents—United States—Election, 2016. | United States. Congress—Elections, 2016. | United States. Congress—Elections, 2018. | Voting—United States. | Elections—United States.

Classification: LCC JK526 2016 .A54 2020 | DDC 324.973/0932—dc23

LC record available at https://lccn.loc.gov/2019010859

This book is printed on acid-free paper.

Acquisitions Editor: Scott Greenan

Editorial Assistant: Sam Rosenberg

Production Editor: Gagan Mahindra

Copy Editor: Michelle Ponce

Typesetter: C&M Digitals (P) Ltd.

Proofreader: Rae-Ann Goodwin

Indexer: Amy Murphy

Cover Designer: Janet Kiesel

Marketing Manager: Amy Whitaker

19 20 21 22 23 10 9 8 7 6 5 4 3 2 1

CONTENTS

PART II • VOTING BEHAVIOR IN THE 2016 PRESIDENTIAL ELECTION

PART III • THE 2016 CONGRESSIONAL ELECTIONS

PART IV • THE 2016 AND 2018 ELECTIONS IN PERSPECTIVE

TABLES AND FIGURES

Tables

Figures

PREFACE

On November 8, 2016, Republican Donald Trump was elected president of the United States despite losing the popular vote. Trump's Electoral College victory over the Democratic nominee, former Secretary of State Hillary Clinton, marked the first time since 2000 that the popular vote winner did not also win a majority of votes in the Electoral College. The Democrats gained two Senate seats in 2016, but this was insufficient for them to regain majority control of the upper chamber. The Democrats also gained six seats in the House of Representatives, but the Republicans maintained a sizable majority and thus control of that body.

In the short term, the reemergence of unified partisan control of government created new opportunities for a Republican majority in adopting key aspects of political agenda. Yet with recent legislative struggles in Congress and a new president besieged by his inability to deliver on major campaign promises—somewhat unusual circumstances for a first term president with unified government—Democrats remain cautiously optimistic about winning back control of government in the future. Democrats have now won the popular vote in six of the last seven presidential elections. The party currently draws support from a coalition of the highly educated, women, African Americans, and Latinos. The latter two groups are expected to increase as a share of the U.S. population over the next twenty years, and electoral participation among both groups has increased steadily in recent years. Yet any talk of a long-term electoral advantage for the Democrats presupposes that current voters will maintain their loyalties to the two political parties and that group allegiances will be stable over time. The past shows that this can be a tenuous assumption.

Is America in the midst of an electoral transformation? What were the sources of Trump's victory in 2016, and how do they differ from Republican coalitions of the past? Does his victory signal a long-term positive trajectory for Republicans' chances in presidential elections? And are the electoral forces at play in presidential elections similar to those that structure congressional elections? These are the sorts of questions that we seek to answer here.

OUR ANALYSIS

In our study of the 2016 elections, we rely on a wide variety of evidence. Because the bulk of our analysis focuses on individuals' voting decisions, we rely extensively on survey evidence—four surveys in particular. In studying voter turnout, we employ the Current Population Survey (CPS) conducted by the U.S. Census Bureau. The CPS provides information on the registration and voting behavior of more than 131,000 individuals from more than 80,000 households. In examining voting patterns, we rely heavily on a survey of more than 24,500 voters interviewed as they exited the voting booths; this survey, conducted by Edison Research for a consortium of news organizations, is commonly referred to as the "pool poll." We employ pool poll data in our analysis of the 2018 congressional midterm elections as well. These data were also collected by Edison Research and reflect a combination of exit and telephone interviews with more than 19,000 voters. In studying the party loyalties of the American electorate, we also analyze data from the General Social Survey (GSS) conducted by the National Opinion Research Center at the University of Chicago, which measured party identification twenty-seven times from 1972 through 2008, usually relying on about 1,500 respondents.

Our main source of survey data is the 2016 American National Election Studies (ANES) survey based on 1,181 face-to-face and 3,090 web-based interviews conducted before the 2016 election and 1,059 face-to face and 2,590 interviews conducted after the election, using the version of the data released for analysis on May 2, 2017. This 2016 ANES is part of an ongoing series funded mainly by the National Science Foundation. These surveys, carried out originally by a team of scholars at the University of Michigan, began with a small study of the 1948 election; the first major study was in 1952. The ANES investigative team has studied every subsequent presidential election, as well as all thirteen midterm elections from 1954 to 2002. The 2016 ANES was conducted jointly by Stanford University and the University of Michigan. In the course of our book, we use data from all thirty-one surveys conducted between 1948 and 2016.

The ANES data are available to scholars throughout the world. Although we are not responsible for the data collection, we are responsible for our analyses. The scholars and staff at the ANES are responsible for neither our analyses nor our interpretation of these data. Similarly, the organizers and researchers of the CPS, GSS, and national pool poll bear no responsibility for our analyses or interpretation.

ACKNOWLEDGMENTS

Many people assisted us with this study. We deeply appreciate the hard work of our research assistants, Ryan Williamson and Aaron Hitefield at the University of Georgia, Mark Dudley at Duke University, Jessica Sullivan at the North Carolina School of Science and Mathematics (serving on a mentorship program at Duke) and now at Duke, and David Macdonald at Florida State University. Ryan assisted with the data analysis for Chapters 2, 6, 7, 8, 9, and 10 while Aaron assisted with Chapter 11 in the revised edition; Mark provided special assistance in integrating the 2016 ANES with earlier election studies; and David assisted with the data analysis for Chapters 3, 4, and 5.

In our study of turnout, we were greatly assisted by Michael P. McDonald of the University of Florida, who for several years has provided scholars with a valuable resource on voter turnout. McDonald's website, the United States Elections Project (http://www.electproject.org), presents detailed national- and state-level estimates of voter turnout based on both voting-age and voting-eligible population estimates.

Several years ago, Russell J. Dalton of the University of California at Irvine and the late Robert W. Jackman of the University of California at Davis helped us locate information about cross-national estimates of voter turnout. Abraham Diskin of the Hebrew University of Jerusalem helped us locate turnout data for Israel and provided us with updated data for this volume. Corwin D. Smidt at Michigan State University exposed us to several recent studies on religion and politics. And we thank Gary C. Jacobson of the University of California, San Diego for sharing his data on 2016 House and Senate race types.

We are grateful for support from the Department of Political Science at Duke University, the Department of Political Science at the University of Georgia, the Political Institutions and Public Choice Program at Duke University, and the Department of Political Science at Florida State University.

At CQ Press we are grateful to Charisse Kiino and Monica Eckman for encouragement and Michael Kerns for help in the early editorial stages of the 2016 volume and Lauren Schultz for her efforts on the 2018 midterm volume. We are especially grateful to them for finding reviewers who had assigned our book in the past, thereby allowing us to receive input from instructors and, indirectly, from students. The reviewers were Suzanne Chod (North Central College), Abbie Erler (Kenyon College), Alison Howard (Dominican University of California), Brad Lockerbie (East Carolina University), and Thomas R. Marshall (University of Texas Arlington). We are grateful to Christine Dahlin and Gagan Mahindra, our production editors, Zachary Hoskins and Sam Rosenberg for their editorial assistance, and Erica DeLuca for her efforts in marketing our book. Pam Schroeder and Michelle Ponce did an excellent job of copyediting the manuscript.

This book continues a series of books that we began with a study of the 1980 elections. In many places, we refer to our earlier books, all of which were published by CQ Press. Some of this material is available online through the CQ Voting and Elections Collection, which can be accessed through many academic and public libraries.

Like our earlier books, this one was a collective enterprise in which we divided the labor. With the volume preceding this one, however, membership in the collective changed. With David Rohde's retirement from the writing and data analysis, Jamie Carson was invited to join the authorship team. Brad Gomez had primary responsibility for the Introduction and Chapters 3, 4, 5, and 12; John Aldrich for Chapters 1, 6, 7, and 8; and Jamie Carson for Chapters 2, 9, 10 and 11. Aldrich, Carson, and Gomez collaborated on Chapter 13.

Finally, we dedicate this book to our friend and colleague, Paul R. Abramson of Michigan State University who passed away on February 12, 2018. Paul coauthored seventeen volumes in the *Change and Continuity* series, beginning with the first volume in 1980. Though he retired from writing on this series prior to the 2016 edition, Paul's influence remains. We are indebted to him for his contributions to this project. Paul and his wife, Janet, lost their beloved son, Lee, in 2016 to his long, brave fight with ALS (Lou Gehrig's Disease). Lee also contributed to these volumes from time-to-time with assistance in gathering data. Paul's wife, Janet, and their daughter, Heather, remain in our thoughts. Shalom, friends.

We appreciate feedback from our readers. Please contact us if you disagree with our interpretations, find factual errors, or want further clarification about our methods or our conclusions.

John H. Aldrich
Duke University
aldrich@duke.edu

Jamie L. Carson
University of Georgia
carson@uga.edu

Brad T. Gomez
Florida State University
bgomez@fsu.edu

David W. Rohde
Duke University
rohde@duke.edu

ABOUT THE AUTHORS

John H. Aldrich is Pfizer-Pratt University Professor of Political Science at Duke University. He is author of *Why Parties? A Second Look* (2011) and *Before the Convention* (1980) and coauthor of *Why Parties Matter: Political Competition and Democracy in the American South, 1832-2012* (2018), and he has also published numerous articles, chapters, and edited collections. He is past president of the Southern Political Science Association, the Midwest Political Science Association, and the American Political Science Association.

Jamie L. Carson is UGA Athletic Association Professor of Public and International Affairs II in the Department of Political Science at the University of Georgia. His research interests include congressional politics and elections, American political development, and separation of powers. He is coauthor of *Ambition, Competition, and Electoral Reform* (2013) and *Electoral Incentives in Congress* (2018) and has published articles in the *American Political Science Review, American Journal of Political Science, Journal of Politics,* and other journals.

Brad T. Gomez is Associate Professor of Political Science at Florida State University. His research interests focus on voting behavior and public opinion, with a particular interest in how citizens attribute responsibility for sociopolitical events. His published work has appeared in the *American Political Science Review, American Journal of Political Science, Journal of Politics,* and other journals and edited volumes.

David W. Rohde is Ernestine Friedl Professor of Political Science and director of the Political Institutions and Public Choice Program at Duke University. He is coeditor of *Why Not Parties?* (2008) and *Home Style and Washington Work* (1989), author of *Parties and Leaders in the Postreform House* (1991), and coauthor of *Supreme Court Decision Making* (1976).

INTRODUCTION

Presidential elections in the United States are partly ritual, a reaffirmation of our democratic values. But they are far more than rituals. The presidency confers a great deal of power, and those powers have expanded during most of the twentieth century and into the twenty-first century. It is precisely because of these immense powers that presidential elections have at times played a major role in determining public policy and in some cases altered the course of American history.

The 1860 election, which brought Abraham Lincoln and the Republicans to power and ousted a divided Democratic Party, focused on whether slavery should be extended to the western territories. After Lincoln's election, eleven southern states attempted to secede from the Union, the Civil War broke out, and, ultimately, the U.S. government abolished slavery completely. Thus an antislavery plurality—Lincoln received only 40 percent of the popular vote—set in motion a chain of events that freed some four million black Americans.

In the 1896 election, Republican William McKinley defeated the Democrat and Populist William Jennings Bryan, thereby beating back the challenge of western and agricultural interests to the prevailing financial and industrial power of the East. Although Bryan mounted a strong campaign, winning 47 percent of the popular vote to McKinley's 51 percent, the election set a clear course for a policy of high tariffs and the continuation of the gold standard for American money.

Lyndon B. Johnson's 1964 landslide over Republican Barry M. Goldwater provided the clearest set of policy alternatives of any election in the twentieth century.[1] Goldwater offered "a choice, not an echo," advocating far more conservative social and economic policies than Johnson. When Johnson received 61 percent of the popular vote to Goldwater's 38 percent, he saw his victory as a mandate for his Great Society programs, the most far-reaching social legislation since World War II. The election also seemed to offer a clear choice between escalating American involvement in Vietnam and restraint. But America's involvement in Vietnam expanded after Johnson's election, leading to growing opposition to Johnson within the Democratic Party, and four years later, he did not seek reelection.

Only the future can determine the ultimate importance of the 2016 election. Some scholars argue that American elections have become less important with time, and there is some truth to their arguments.[2] Yet elections do offer important choices on public policy, choices that may affect the course of governance—even if only in the short term.

Despite the continued, fifteen-year-long presence of American combat forces in Afghanistan, the 2016 presidential election focused mainly on economic issues. Nearly a decade removed from the Great Recession of 2007–2009, the U.S. economy had experienced a prolonged period of economic growth, but growth had been slow and uneven. The average annual growth rate in real GDP between 2010 and 2016 was 2.1 percent, well below the average 3.1 percent growth rate experienced during the decade before the economic collapse or the 3.2 percent growth rate experienced in the 1990s.[3] Between 2009 and 2016, corporate profits in the United States had grown by nearly 50 percent, and the Dow Jones Industrial Average signaled a bullish stock market, increasing a staggering 12,000 points over the seven-year period.[4] But these corporate gains were not always felt in the pocketbooks of average citizens. By election day 2016, the U.S. unemployment rate had declined to 4.6 percent, well below its 2009 high mark of 10 percent and similar to 2007 levels. But the number of long-term unemployed individuals was higher than prerecession levels and so too was labor force participation, meaning that many Americans who could not find jobs simply withdrew from the labor market.[5] Real median household income in the United States declined in four of the seven years between 2009 and 2016, and economic inequality in the United States, which has increased markedly since 1980, reached levels not seen since the 1920s.[6]

These economic issues provided the backdrop for one of the most remarkable electoral events in U.S. history—one not soon to be forgotten. For the first time ever, one of the major American parties nominated a candidate with no prior political or military experience, Donald J. Trump. Trump, the Republican Party nominee, was no stranger to the American public; the billionaire New York real estate developer had been a fixture on Americans' televisions and tabloid magazines since the early 1980s, and for fourteen seasons, he hosted a reality TV show, *The Apprentice*, on NBC. And now he was an American Silvio Berlusconi, a billionaire populist, speaking for the "common man" against the "rigged system."[7] Trump argued that America's economic woes were the product of unfair international trade deals, taxation, and illegal immigration. According to Trump, "[America's] politicians have aggressively pursued a policy of globalization—moving our jobs, our wealth, and our factories to Mexico and overseas."[8] Trump's antifree trade message was counter to conventional Republican Party doctrine, and he promised to renegotiate America's trade deals with China and "tear up" the 1994 North American Free Trade Agreement (NAFTA) with Mexico and Canada.[9] Trump's views on taxation were more in step with his party, favoring significant reductions in corporate tax rates, a lowering of the top individual tax rate from 39.6 percent to 33 percent, and a repeal of the estate tax. Perhaps his most noted (and divisive) policy position was on the issue of immigration. Even before announcing his candidacy, Trump had warned conservatives in his party against comprehensive immigration reforms that would create a path to citizenship for illegal immigrants already in the United States: "They're taking your jobs. You better be careful."[10] Instead Trump promised, "I will build a great, great wall on our southern border. And I will have Mexico pay for that wall."[11]

For the most part, Democratic Party nominee Hillary Clinton's economic positions were more in line with her party's typical positions. Clinton called for increased government spending for job training programs and community college education; the former First Lady, senator, and secretary of state argued that spending in these areas could help retrain workers who had lost jobs in manufacturing industries. Clinton's position on taxation was antithetical to Trump's, arguing that "we need to get the wealthy and the corporations to pay more for their fair share."[12] Clinton also argued that Trump's trade policy would start a trade war with China. But Clinton was forced to take a more nuanced approach to trade policy than perhaps she would have liked. For instance, as secretary of state, Clinton had originally supported America's participation in the Trans-Pacific Partnership (TPP), calling it the "gold standard" of trade agreements. But after fighting back a primary challenge from Vermont Senator Bernie Sanders, a socialist and only recent affiliate of the Democratic Party, she withdrew her support from the TPP rather than risk alienating Sanders's supporters: "I oppose it now. I'll oppose it after the election, and I'll oppose it as president."[13] Clinton's position on immigration also contrasted sharply with Trump's. Clinton claimed that the U.S. border with Mexico was "the most secure border we have ever had" and that Trump's plan for a wall across the entire border was pure "fantasy."[14] And Clinton supported immigration reform efforts to provide lawful status to the children of illegal immigrants and a path to citizenship for undocumented immigrants who did not provide a security threat.

Another issue on which the candidates differed was on the future of the central legislative achievement of the Obama administration, the Affordable Care Act of 2010, commonly known as "Obamacare." The legislation marked the most significant change to the nation's health care system since the creation of Medicare and Medicaid during the 1960s. It mandated that all individuals who are not currently insured or already covered under government insurance programs buy a private health insurance policy or pay a penalty (a "tax" according to the United States Supreme Court). And to lower the costs of policies, Obamacare promoted the creation of state-level health insurance exchanges to foster competition among insurance providers and grant subsidies to low-income individuals and families to offset costs. Clinton hoped to amend the program, among other things, expanding the tax credits individuals could receive to offset out-of-pocket health expenses, increasing funding for community health centers, and increasing government control over drug price increases.[15] Trump offered few details about how he would reform the health care system other than his oft-stated pledge to "immediately repeal and replace Obamacare."

The contrast between the two candidates who squared off in the 2016 presidential election could not have been sharper, both in style and substance. On the Republican side was a highly confrontational political novice who often engaged on the political trail in both bombast and profanity, pledging to "make America great again" and claiming during his nomination acceptance speech that "I alone can fix it." On the Democratic side was the ultimate political insider, a policy wonk who had not only served a president but also had been married to one. However, for all of their differences, Trump and Clinton had one thing in common—Americans didn't seem to like either one. On the eve of the election, the Gallup Poll reported that the candidates suffered from the lowest favorability ratings recorded by the company since it starting asking the question back in 1956. According to Gallup, 52 percent of Americans viewed Clinton unfavorably, whereas a record 61 percent found Trump unfavorable.[16] Yet, despite the public's consternation, the election went on . . . just as the Constitution mandates. On November 8, 2016, Donald J. Trump was elected president of the United States, winning a comfortable Electoral College victory despite losing the popular vote to Clinton, 48.2 to 46.1 percent.

To be sure, the 2016 presidential campaign was unusual; from the rise of an unorthodox candidate to the presence of a woman at the head of a party's ticket (a historic first), and there were missing e-mails, stolen e-mails, FBI investigations (of both candidates we would learn later!), charges of Russian interference, and abhorrent conversations recorded on buses. Yes, 2016 was unusual (or, at least, one might hope)!

But none of this means that the election itself was unusual. Indeed, as we hope to show, the 2016 election was, in many ways, the product of electoral continuity. Although American parties have become more ideologically disparate over the past few decades, no party holds a clear advantage. The 2016 election marked only the second time since Franklin D. Roosevelt that one of the parties, the Democrats, won the popular vote in three straight elections—the Republicans did so in 1980, 1984, and 1988. But the popular vote balance was so close that it became feasible for the second-place finisher in the popular vote, Trump, to capture the Electoral College and the White House. Once considered a historical aberration, this divergence between the popular vote and electoral vote has now happened in two of the last five U.S. elections.

With the election of Republican majorities in both the House and Senate, along with Trump's victory, 2016 brought unified partisan control of government. Whereas unified government has not been the norm in modern American politics, it is important to note that the Republican majorities in both the House and Senate were relatively small. The Republicans lost six House seats in 2016, bringing their majority down to twenty-three seats (roughly 5 percent of the chamber). Senate Republicans also lost seats (two) in 2016 but maintained a slim, two-seat majority. Although the election outcome did advantage the Republican Party, it would be difficult to claim that the GOP now holds an electoral advantage. Indeed, with only small majorities in both houses of Congress, there is no guarantee that President Trump will be able to push through his legislative agenda with ease. The first two years of Trump's administration have borne this out. Consider Trump's campaign promise to quickly repeal and replace Obamacare. During the Obama presidency, and knowing full well that the president would veto their efforts if necessary, Republicans voted on fifty-four separate occasions to repeal all or part of the Affordable Care Act.[17] Yet, with unified Republican control, the Congress has failed to repeal the law. In March 2017, during what should have been the new president's "honeymoon period," House Speaker Paul Ryan (R–WI) cancelled a vote to replace Obamacare (a full repeal was not in the offing to the consternation of some conservatives) because he did not have the votes.[18] Although the House would eventually pass a replacement bill in May, the Senate failed to pass a similar bill in July by one vote.[19] An apparently final attempt for the year in the Senate was pulled from consideration in September after the Republicans failed to receive commitments for at least a bare fifty-vote majority. Congress did eventually pass a sweeping tax reform proposal in early 2018, but the remainder of the year demonstrated that majority status alone is not sufficient for legislative success.[20] Now that the Democrats have gained control of the House following the 2018 midterm election, the Trump agenda clearly is in peril.

Is America in the midst of an electoral transformation? What were the sources of Trump's victory in 2016, and how do they differ from electoral coalitions of the past? Does his victory signal a long-term negative trajectory for Democrats' chances in presidential elections? And are these electoral forces similar to those that structure congressional elections, especially given the results of the 2018 midterms? These are the sorts of questions that we seek to answer here.

This book continues a series of eighteen books that we began with a study of the 1980 elections. Our focus has always been both contemporary and historical. Thus, we offer an extensive examination of the 2016 presidential and 2016 and 2018 congressional campaigns and present a detailed analysis of individual-level voting behavior, examining those factors that lead citizens to vote as well as those that affect how they vote. We also aim to place the 2016 and 2018 elections in proper historical and analytical contexts.

CHANGE AND CONTINUITY

Elections are at once both judgments on the issues of the day and the product of long-term changes in the relationship between the political parties and voters. For example, Democrats' aspirations for an emerging electoral majority following their 2012 presidential victory were not unfounded. If one is to believe the projections of the U.S. Census Bureau, many of the social groups that have supported Democrats in recent elections, particularly Latinos, are growing as a percentage of the overall U.S. population. And turnout among these groups has increased in recent decades. So, for some Democrats, their party's future success in presidential elections over the next few decades seemed all but assured. Then Donald Trump won, and the questions became: Was 2016 the dawn of an emergent Republican majority? Had Trump realigned the American party system?[21]

It is not uncommon for winning parties to make hyperbolic claims about the "historic" nature of their victories or to assert that their win was a sign of impending electoral dominance. Indeed, in 2008, Democrats were exuberant over Obama's sizable victory over John McCain and were even more pronounced in their claims of a bright Democratic future. Some observers saw the election as restoring Democrats to their status as the majority party, which they had enjoyed between 1932 and 1968. Lanny J. Davis, a former special counsel to President Clinton, wrote following the 2008 election, "Tuesday's substantial victory by Barack Obama, together with Democratic gains in the Senate and House, appear to have accomplished a fundamental political realignment. The election is likely to create a new governing majority coalition that could dominate American politics for a generation or more."[22] Two years later, the Democrats lost sixty-three seats, and their majority status in the House of Representatives—the largest seat change since 1946—and six seats in the Senate, where they maintained a slim majority.[23]

In 2004, following incumbent President George W. Bush's victory over Democrat nominee, John Kerry, scholars speculated about a pro-Republican realignment. Indeed, speculation about Republican dominance can be traced back to the late 1960s, when Kevin P. Phillips, in his widely read book, *The Emerging Republican Majority*, argued that the Republicans could become the majority party, mainly by winning support in the South.[24] Between 1969, when his book was published, and 1984, the

Republicans won three of the four presidential elections, winning by massive landslides in 1972, when Richard M. Nixon triumphed over George S. McGovern, and in 1984, when Ronald Reagan defeated Walter F. Mondale. In 1985, Reagan himself proclaimed that a Republican realignment was at hand. "The other side would like to believe that our victory last November was due to something other than our philosophy," he asserted. "I just hope that they keep believing that. Realignment is real."[25] Democratic victories in the 1992 and 1996 presidential elections called into question the claims of a pro-Republican realignment.

Obviously not all elections are transformative. So how is electoral change—not simply the ebbs and flows from election to election but changes in the fundamental factors that link parties and voters—to be understood?

For generations of political scientists, theories of electoral change have centered on the concept of political realignment.[26] Political scientists define *realignment* in different ways, but they are all influenced by V. O. Key, Jr., who developed a theory of "critical elections" in which "new and durable electoral groupings are formed."[27] Elections like that in 1860 in which Lincoln's victory brought the Republicans to power, in 1896 in which McKinley's victory solidified Republican dominance, and in 1932 in which the Democrats came to power under FDR are obvious candidates for such a label.

But later, Key argued that partisan shifts could also take place over a series of elections—a pattern he called "secular realignment." During these periods, "shifts in the partisan balance of power" occur.[28] In this view, the realignment that first brought the Republicans to power might have begun in 1856, when the Republicans displaced the Whigs as the major competitor to the Democrats and might have been consolidated by Lincoln's reelection in 1864 and Ulysses S. Grant's election in 1868. The realignment that consolidated Republican dominance in the late nineteenth century may well have begun in 1892, when Democrat Grover Cleveland won the election, but the Populist Party, headed by James D. Weaver, attracted 8.5 percent of the popular vote, winning four states and electoral votes in two others. In 1896, the Populists supported William Jennings Bryan and were co-opted by the Democrats, but the electorate shifted to the Republican Party. The pro-Republican realignment might have been consolidated by McKinley's win over Bryan in 1900 and by Theodore Roosevelt's victory in 1904.

Though the term *New Deal* was not coined until Franklin Roosevelt's campaign of 1932, the New Deal realignment may have begun with Herbert C. Hoover's triumph over Democrat Al Smith, the first Roman Catholic to be nominated by a major political party. Although badly defeated, Smith carried two New England states, Massachusetts and Rhode Island, which later became the most Democratic states in the nation.[29] As Key points out, the beginnings of a shift toward the Democrats was detectable in Smith's defeat.[30] However, the "New Deal coalition" was not created by the 1932 election but after it, and it was consolidated by Roosevelt's 1936 landslide over Alfred M. Landon and his 1940 defeat of Wendell Willkie. The New Deal coalition structured the distribution of party support within the electorate during the earliest decades of the post–World War II period, and its decline and eventual replacement are important to understanding the changes and continuities of modern electoral politics.

Past partisan realignments in the United States have had five basic characteristics. First, realignments have traditionally involved changes in the regional bases of party support. Consider, for instance, the decline of the Whig Party and rise of the Republicans. Between 1836 and 1852, the Whigs drew at least some of their electoral support from the South.[31] The last Whig candidate to be elected, Zachary Taylor in 1848, won sixty-six of his electoral votes from the fifteen slave states. In his 1860 victory, Lincoln did not win a single electoral vote from the fifteen slave states. Regionalism may be less important to future electoral changes, however. Today television and other media have weakened regionalism in the United States, and politics is much more nationalized. Two-party competition has diffused throughout the country, and the issues on which the parties compete tend to be more national in scope.[32]

Second, past party realignments have involved changes in the social bases of party support. Even during a period when one party is becoming dominant, some social groups may be moving to the losing party. During the 1930s, for example, Roosevelt gained the support of industrial workers, but at the same time, he lost support among business owners and professionals.

Third, past realignments have been characterized by the mobilization of new groups into the electorate. Indeed the mobilization of new voters into the electorate can result in significant electoral volatility.[33] Between Calvin Coolidge's Republican landslide in 1924 and Roosevelt's third-term victory in 1940, turnout among the voting-age population rose from 44 percent to 59 percent. Although some long-term forces were pushing turnout upward, the sharp increase between 1924 and 1928 and again between 1932 and 1936 resulted at least in part from the mobilization of new social groups into the electorate. Ethnic groups that were predominantly Catholic were mobilized to support Al Smith in 1928, and industrial workers were mobilized to support Franklin Roosevelt in 1936.

Fourth, past realignments have occurred when new issues have divided the electorate. In the 1850s the Republican Party reformulated the controversy over slavery to form a winning coalition. By opposing the expansion of slavery into the territories, the Republicans contributed to divisions within the Democratic Party. Of course, no issue since slavery has divided America as deeply, and subsequent realignments have never brought a new political party to power. But those realignments have always been based on the division of the electorate over new issues.

Last, most political scientists argue that partisan realignments occur when voters change not just their voting patterns but also the way they think about the political parties, thus creating an erosion of partisan loyalties. During the Great Depression in 1932, for example, many voters who thought of themselves as Republicans voted against Hoover. Later, many of these voters returned to the Republican side, but others began to think of themselves as Democrats. Likewise, in 1936, some voters who thought of themselves as Democrats disliked FDR's policies and voted against him. Some of these defectors may have returned to the Democratic fold in subsequent elections, but others began to think of themselves as Republicans.

Not all scholars believe that the concept of realignment is useful. In 1991, Byron E. Shafer edited a volume in which several chapters questioned its utility.[34] More recently, David R. Mayhew published a monograph critiquing scholarship on realignment, and his book received widespread critical acclaim.[35] Mayhew cites fifteen claims made by scholars of realignment and then tests these claims. He argues that many of these claims do not stand up to empirical scrutiny, questions the classification of several elections as "realigning," and suggests that the concept of realignment should be abandoned.

Although we agree with some of the claims made by Mayhew, we see no reason to abandon the concept completely. Some electoral changes may correspond to the critical election-realignment dynamic—a long period of stability in the party system is altered by a rapid and dramatic change, which leads to a new, long-term partisan equilibrium. Using biological evolution as a theoretical analogue, Edward G. Carmines and James A. Stimson argue that partisan realignments of this type are similar in form to the evolutionary dynamic known as cataclysmic adaptation.[36] But the authors note that biological examples of the cataclysmic adaptation dynamic are extraordinarily rare and suggest that critical election realignments are likely to be rare also.

Carmines and Stimson articulate two additional evolutionary models of partisan change. The authors argue that Key's secular realignment dynamic is consistent with the model of Darwinian gradualism. In this view, electoral change does not result from a critical moment but instead is "slow, gradual, [and] incremental."[37] As noted in Key's original work, the secular realignment dynamic "operate[s] inexorably, and almost imperceptibly, election after election, to form new party alignments and to build new party groups."[38]

The third model of partisan change espoused by Carmines and Stimson is consistent with the "punctuated equilibrium" model of evolution.[39] In this dynamic process,

the system moves from a fairly stationary steady state to a fairly dramatic rapid change; the change is manifested by a "critical moment" in the time series—a point where change is large enough to be visible and, perhaps the origin of a dynamic process. Significantly, however, the change—the dynamic growth—does not end with the critical moment; instead it continues over an extended period, albeit at [a] much slower pace.[40]

In our view, the punctuated equilibrium model best captures the dynamic nature of electoral change in the United States since the 1960s.

The 1960s were a critical moment in American politics. The events of the decade were the catalysts for fundamental changes in the rules that govern political parties and the partisan sentiments that would govern voters for years to come.[41] Of particular interest is the transformative power of the issue of race. By 1960, the national Democratic Party's sponsorship of civil rights for African Americans had created a schism between the more-liberal elements of the party and white southern Democrats. But it had also allowed the party to chip away at black voters' allegiance to the Republican Party, "the party of Lincoln." The partisan loyalties of African Americans had been shaped by the Civil War, and black loyalties to the Republican Party—where and when allowed to vote—lasted through the 1932 election. By 1960, a majority of African Americans identified with the Democratic Party, but there was still a substantial minority of Republican identifiers. Between 1960 and 1964, however, African American loyalties moved sharply toward the Democrats. The civil rights demonstrations of the early 1960s and the eventual passage of the 1964 Civil Rights Act solidified the position of the Democratic Party as the party of civil rights. By late

1964, more than 70 percent of African Americans identified as Democrats, a level of loyalty that persists today. The change in partisanship among blacks and the subsequent mobilization of black voters following the passage of the 1965 Voting Rights Act provided the rapid, critical moment that disrupted the stable equilibrium created by the New Deal Coalition. And, as the punctuated equilibrium dynamic suggests, the electorate continued to change in a direction set forth by the critical era of the 1960s, but it did so at slower rate, and it continues to have ramifications for politics today.

The political events of the 1960s also had an effect on white partisanship, but the change was neither immediate nor decisive. From the mid-1960s to the mid-1970s, there was a substantial erosion in party loyalties among whites. The proportion of the white electorate who considered themselves "independent" increased noticeably. By 1978, nearly 40 percent of whites said they were either pure independents or independents who "leaned" toward one of the two parties, nearly double that found in the late 1950s and early 1960s.[42] These changes led some scholars to use the term *dealignment* to characterize American politics during the period.[43] The term was first used by Ronald Inglehart and Avram Hochstein in 1972.[44] A dealignment is a condition in which old voting patterns break down without being replaced by newer ones. Yet, beginning in the 1980s, the proportion of whites claiming to be pure independents declined as whites nationally began to lean toward the Republican Party. In the once "solid Democratic South," whites have become decidedly Republican. Voters appear to be aligned.

Despite these changes, the Republicans have never emerged as the majority party among the electorate. Democrats, however, saw a growth in political loyalties between 2004 and 2012, and in 2016, the party once again emerged as the majority party among two party identifiers, albeit a small majority.[45] This is not to say that Republicans cannot win, of course; it simply means that the GOP has entered recent elections at a numerical disadvantage. Democrats' electoral gains have largely been the product of the critical events of the 1960s, which established them as the party of civil rights. As America's nonwhite population has increased—more than half of the growth in the U.S. population between 2000 and 2010 was due to an increase in the nonwhite population—Democrats have been the beneficiaries. For instance, roughly two out of every three Latino voters in the United States identify with the Democratic Party, and 54 percent of Latino voters say that Democrats have more concern for them, compared to only 11 percent who say that Republicans do.[46] America's racial and ethnic minorities continue to view the Democrats' adherence to the civil rights agenda of the 1960s as providing them with a natural political home, and America's whites are increasingly more likely to side with the Republicans. In our view, the 2016 elections do not represent a fundamental change in America's electoral politics. Instead, the 2016 elections continue to reflect electoral alignments set in motion by a critical era that occurred nearly a half century ago.

VOTERS AND THE ACT OF VOTING

Voting is an individual act. Indeed the national decision made on (or before) November 8, 2016, was the product of more than 230 million individual decisions.[47]

Two questions faced Americans eighteen years and older: whether to vote and, if they did, how to cast their ballots. These decisions, of course, are not made in isolation. Voters' decisions are influenced by the social, economic, and information contexts in which they live; they are influenced by the political attitudes that they have acquired throughout their lifetime; and they are influenced by the voting decisions they have made in the past.[48] Voters' decisions are also constrained by America's electoral rules and two-party system—these are the primary sources of continuity in our political system.

How voters make up their minds is one of the most thoroughly studied subjects in political science—and one of the most controversial.[49] Voting decisions can be studied from at least three theoretical perspectives.[50] The first approach is *sociological* in character and views voters primarily as members of social groups. Voters belong to primary groups of family members and peers; secondary groups such as private clubs, trade unions, and voluntary associations; and broader reference groups such as social classes and religious and ethnic groups. Understanding the political behavior of these groups is central to understanding voters, according to Paul F. Lazarsfeld, Bernard R. Berelson, and their colleagues. Social characteristics determine political preferences.[51] This perspective is still popular, although more so among sociologists than political scientists.[52]

A second approach places greater emphasis on the *psychological* (or, more aptly, attitudinal) variables that affect voting. The "socio-psychological model" of voting behavior was developed by Angus Campbell, Philip E. Converse, Warren E. Miller, and Donald E. Stokes, scholars at the University of Michigan Survey Research Center, in their classic book *The American Voter*.[53] The Michigan scholars focused on attitudes most likely to have the greatest effect on the vote just before the moment of decision, particularly attitudes toward the candidates, the parties, and the issues. An individual's party identification emerged as the most important social-psychological variable that influences voting behavior. The Michigan approach is the most prevalent among political scientists, and party identification continues to be emphasized as one of the most influential factors affecting individual vote choice, although many deemphasize its psychological underpinnings.[54]

A third approach draws heavily from the work of economists. According to this perspective, citizens weigh the costs of voting against the expected benefits when deciding whether to vote. And when deciding for whom to vote, they calculate which candidate favors policies closest to their own policy preferences. Citizens are thus viewed as rational actors who attempt to maximize their expected utility. Anthony Downs and William H. Riker helped to found this *rational choice* approach.[55] The writings of Riker, Peter C. Ordeshook, John A. Ferejohn, and Morris P. Fiorina are excellent examples of this point of view.[56]

Taken separately, none of these approaches adequately explain voting behavior; taken together, the approaches are largely complementary.[57] Therefore, we have chosen an eclectic approach that draws on insights from each viewpoint. Where appropriate we employ sociological variables, but we also employ social-psychological variables such as party identification and feelings of political efficacy. The rational choice approach guides our study of the way issues influence voting behavior.

SURVEY RESEARCH SAMPLING

Because of our interest in individual-level voting behavior, our book relies heavily on surveys of the American electorate. It draws on a massive exit poll conducted by Edison Research for the National Election Pool, a consortium of six news organizations, as well as surveys conducted in people's homes by the U.S. Census Bureau, and telephone polls conducted by the Pew Research Center. But our main data source for 2016 is the 1,181 face-to-face and 3,090 web-based interviews conducted before the election and 1,059 face-to-face and 2,590 interviews conducted after the election as part of the ANES Time Series Survey.[58] Originally conducted by the Survey Research Center (SRC) and CPS at the University of Michigan, the ANES surveys have been conducted using national samples in every presidential election since 1948 and in every midterm election between 1954 and 2002.[59] The 2016 ANES was conducted jointly by Stanford University and the University of Michigan, with funding by the National Science Foundation. Since 1952, the ANES surveys have measured party identification and feelings of political effectiveness. The CPS, founded in 1970, has developed valuable questions for measuring issue preferences. The ANES surveys are the best and most comprehensive for studying the issue preferences and party loyalties of the American electorate.[60]

Readers may question our reliance on the ANES surveys of just over 4,200 people when some 230 million Americans are eligible to vote. Would we have similar results if all adults eligible to vote had been surveyed?[61] The ANES uses a procedure called multistage probability sampling to select the particular individuals to be interviewed. This procedure ensures that the final sample is likely to represent the entire population of U.S. citizens of voting age, except for Americans living on military bases, in institutions, or abroad.[62]

Because of the probability procedures used to conduct the ANES surveys, we are able to estimate the likelihood that the results represent the entire population of noninstitutionalized citizens living in the United States. Although the 2016 ANES survey sampled only about one in every 55,000 voting-eligible Americans, the representativeness of a sample depends far more on the size of the sample than the size of the population being studied, provided the sample is drawn properly. With samples of this size, we can be fairly confident (to a level of 0.95) that the results we get will fall within three percentage points of that obtained if the entire population had been surveyed. For example, when we find that 52 percent of respondents approved of the job Barack Obama was doing as president, we can be reasonably confident that between 49.7 percent (52 − 2.3) and 54.3 percent (52 + 2.3) approved of his performance. The actual results could be less than 49.7 percent or more than 54.3 percent, but a confidence level of 0.95 means that the odds are nineteen to one that the entire electorate falls within this range. The range of confidence becomes somewhat larger when we look at subgroups of the electorate. For example, with subsets of about five hundred (and the results in the 50 percent range) the confidence error rises to plus or minus six percentage points. Because the likelihood of sampling error grows as our subsamples become smaller, we sometimes supplement our analysis with reports of other surveys.

Somewhat more complicated procedures are needed to determine whether the difference between two groups is likely to reflect the relationship found if the entire population were surveyed. The probability that such differences reflect real differences in the population is largely a function of the size of the groups being compared.[63] Generally speaking, when we compare the results of the 2016 sample with an earlier ANES survey, a difference of three percentage points is sufficient to be reasonably confident that the difference is real. For example, in 2008 during the final year of the George W. Bush presidency and during the onset of the "great recession," only 2 percent of respondents said that the economy had improved in the last year; in 2016, 28 percent did. Because this difference is greater than three percentage points, we can be reasonably confident that the electorate was more likely to think the national economy was improving in 2016 than they were to think it was improving back in 2008.

When we compare subgroups of the electorate sampled in 2016 (or compare those subgroups with subgroups sampled in earlier years), a larger percentage is usually necessary to conclude that differences are meaningful. For example, 35 percent of whites who did not complete high school favored Hillary Clinton; among those who graduated high school but did not continue their education, 33 percent favored Clinton. We cannot be confident this is real, however, because the subsample sizes are quite small—only seventy-seven people are in the first category, whereas there are 463 people in the latter. With subsamples of this size, we would need to see a difference of thirteen points to be confident in the results. Thankfully, the relatively large sample size that we obtained in 2016 by using the full (face-to-face and Internet) sample means that statistical confidence in our subgroup comparisons is much easier to achieve. For instance, among voters, we have 2,131 men and 2,392 women.[64] With subsamples of this size, a three-point difference is large enough to conclude that the gender difference was real. However, it is important to recognize that in previous years, our sample sizes (face-to-face only) were much smaller. Generally speaking, comparisons of men and women using data from previous ANES studies require a difference of five percentage points. Similarly it is important to be mindful of racial differences in the sample. In 2016, our full sample contains 4,563 whites (71.6 percent) and 598 blacks (9.4 percent). Thus, to be confident in racial difference, we require a spread of more than four percentage points. When using data from previous years with smaller sample sizes, a difference of at least eight percentage points is needed to conclude that differences between whites and blacks are meaningful.

This discussion represents only a ballpark guide to judging whether reported results are likely to represent the total population. Better estimates can be obtained using the formulas presented in many statistics textbooks. To make such calculations or even a rough estimate of the chances of error, the reader must know the size of the groups being compared. For that reason, we always report in our tables and figures either the number of cases on which our percentages are based or the information needed to approximate the number of cases.

PLAN OF THE BOOK

We begin by following the chronology of the campaign itself. Chapter 1 examines the battle for the Democratic and Republican Party presidential nominations. Three major Democratic candidates and twelve major Republican candidates campaigned for the chance to square off in the general election. As is typical when no incumbent president stands for reelection, both parties featured heated contests for the nomination. In Chapter 1, we discuss the regularities in the nomination process that explain why some candidates run and others do not. We then examine the rules governing the nomination contests, and we also assess the importance of campaign finance. The dynamics of multicandidate contests and the concept of momentum to discuss nomination contests in the 1970s are covered in Chapter 1 as well.

Chapter 2 moves to the general election campaign. Because of the rules set forth by the U.S. Constitution for winning presidential elections, candidates must think about how to win enough states to gain a majority (270) of the electoral vote (538 since 1964). We examine the Electoral College strategies adopted by the campaigns. There were three presidential debates and one vice presidential debate, and we discuss their impact. Last, we turn to the end game of the campaign, the battle over turnout. We examine the "ground game" undertaken by each campaign in an effort to get out the vote, and we will examine how these strategies differ from previous presidential campaigns.

Chapter 3 turns to the actual election results, relying largely on the official election statistics. Our look at the electoral vote is followed by a discussion of the election rules, noting that the U.S. plurality vote system supports "Duverger's law." We examine the pattern of results during the eighteen postwar elections as well as those in all forty-seven elections between 1832 and 2016. We then analyze the state-by-state results, paying particular attention to regional shifts in the elections between 1980 and 2016. We focus special attention on electoral change in the postwar South because this region has been the scene of the most dramatic changes in postwar U.S. politics. Finally we study the results of the last five presidential elections to assess the electoral vote balance.

Chapter 4 analyzes what is perhaps the most important decision of all: whether to vote. We examine the dynamics of electoral participation in U.S. politics, particularly changes in turnout during the postwar period. Although turnout grew fairly consistently between 1920 (the year women were enfranchised throughout the United States) and 1960, it fell in 1964 and in each of the next four elections. We show that the decline in turnout during this period coincides with steep declines in partisan attachment and political efficacy in the electorate. As partisan attachments have increased in recent decades, turnout has risen, but it remains lower than its 1960 high. Turnout is low in the United States compared with other advanced democracies, but it is not equally low among all social groups. In Chapter 4 we examine social differences in turnout in detail, using both the 2016 ANES survey and the Current Population Survey conducted by the U.S. Census Bureau.

In Chapter 5, we examine how social forces influence the vote. The ANES surveys enable us to analyze the vote for Clinton and Trump by race, gender, region, age, education, income, union membership, and religion. The impact of these social factors has changed considerably in the postwar period as the New Deal coalition broke down and new partisan alignments emerged after the critical era of the 1960s. We show that minorities—specifically blacks and Latinos—are now central to the modern Democratic coalition.

Chapter 6 examines attitudes toward both the candidates and the issues. We begin by examining voters' feelings toward the candidates before turning our attention to their appraisals of the candidates' personal traits. We then attempt to assess the extent to which voters based their votes on issue preferences. We conclude that voters' issue concerns were particularly important in determining their vote choices in 2016.

We then examine how "retrospective evaluations" influence voting decisions. Existing research suggests that many voters decide how to vote on the basis of past performance. In other words voters decide mainly on the basis of what the candidates or their parties have done in office, not what they promise to do if elected. In Chapter 7, we show that retrospective evaluations, particularly those related to the performance of the economy, were a powerful reason underlying citizens' vote decisions. Perhaps most interesting, we find that just one in four American voters in 2016 thought that the country was on the right track.

In Chapter 8, we explore the impact of party loyalties on voting using the ANES data. Since the 1980s, there has been a substantial shift in whites' partisan loyalties—particularly in the South—toward the Republican Party. The clear advantage Democrats once held among whites dissipated. Although the 2008 election that initially brought Obama to office saw a resurgence in whites' Democratic identification, that advantage proved temporary as whites' party loyalties reverted to near parity in 2012. Remarkably, the Democrats were able to reestablish an advantage in party loyalties in 2016. This is a striking (and unusual) finding, not just because the Republican won the Electoral College vote but also because Clinton won the popular vote by only a few percentage points, hardly a sweep toward the Democratic Party. We examine partisanship among whites and blacks separately, tracking change from 1952 to 2016. This analysis reveals that the patterns of change among whites and blacks have been markedly different. We also compare Latino partisanship in recent elections. Finally, we take a close look at the role of party loyalties in shaping issue preferences, retrospective evaluations, and voting preferences. We find that the relationship between party identification and the vote was very strong in every U.S. election since 2000, including 2016.

In Chapters 9 and 10, we are reminded that election day 2016 featured many elections. In addition to the presidential election, there were twelve gubernatorial elections, elections for thousands of state and local offices, as well as thirty-four elections for the U.S. Senate and elections for all 435 seats in the U.S. House of Representatives.[65] We focus our analysis on the 2016 House and Senate elections, which are by far the most consequential for national public policy.

Chapter 9 examines the pattern of congressional outcomes for 2016 and brings to light those factors that affect competition in congressional elections. We review the pattern of incumbent success in House and Senate races between 1954, the first Democratic victory in their forty-year winning streak, and 2016. Despite citizens' low levels of trust in government and the large portion of voters who believed the country was heading in the wrong direction, congressional incumbents were returned to office in droves. In the House, 96.4 percent of incumbents were reelected in 2016, whereas the success rate for Senate incumbents was 93 percent—not the "anti-Washington" fervor that one might infer from the outcome at the presidential level. We examine the interplay of national and regional factors in structuring congressional election outcomes. And, of course, we give particular attention to the critical factors of candidate recruitment, incumbency, and campaign finance. Finally, we speculate on the future of congressional elections and party polarization in Congress in 2018 and beyond.

Chapter 10 explores how voters make congressional voting decisions. Using the same ANES surveys we employed to study presidential voting, we examine how social factors, issues, partisan loyalties, incumbency, and retrospective evaluations of congressional and presidential performance influence voters' choices for the House and Senate. We also try to determine the existence and extent of presidential "coattails," that is, whether Democrats were more likely to be elected to Congress because of Obama's presidential victory.

Chapter 11 examines the 2018 congressional midterm elections. We begin by discussing the pattern of outcomes, showing that, despite anti-incumbent sentiments, nearly 90 percent of incumbents who sought reelection were successful. We also discuss the record turnout in the election—50.3 percent of eligible voters—which is the highest recorded in any midterm election since 1914 when senators were first directly elected by the people. We examine the 2018 results in terms of historical trends, especially given the record number of women running, and compare the actual results with those that political observers expected. We briefly discuss academic models of congressional elections, paying particular attention to the economy and to public approval for Trump's performance as president. As we argue in Chapter 11, voters in 2018 were substantially different from those who went to the polls in 2016. Exit polls in both years suggest that the electorate in 2018 was younger, more Democratic, and more liberal. These changes do not necessarily reflect demographic shifts, since such changes are highly unlikely to occur in two years. The tendency of the electorate to be more Democratic and more liberal reflects differential turnout between presidential and midterm elections, not changes in the party loyalties of the electorate or their ideological location. The dramatic increase in turnout relative to 2014, when it was only 36.1 percent, is likely a function of strong disapproval of President Trump, especially in light of what happened two years earlier during the 2016 presidential election.

In Chapter 12 we note that the alternation of partisan victories between presidential and congressional midterm elections is a product of the long-term partisan balancing that has become a feature of American politics. While Democrats seem to be advantaged in presidential elections, Republicans have the advantage during midterms (the last two elections aside). The reason, again, is differential turnout. But, as we demonstrate in Chapter 12 using a simple statistical analysis, midterm elections outcomes have little to no bearing on future presidential outcomes. This stands in sharp contrast to the claims sometimes made by election night pundits and politicians from the winning party, who argue that midterm victories serve as an ominous sign for the losing party's chances for victory in the next presidential election. By this account, the Democratic victories in the House in 2018 should diminish President Trump's chances of reelection in 2020. We show that this claim has no empirical merit. Rather, the long-term factors that influence American electoral politics suggest the 2020 presidential election is likely to be highly competitive. We then assess the Democratic Party's prospects in 2020, examining the potential field of candidates for the party's nomination and how recent changes in the party's convention balloting rules might affect the nomination process. We also assess President Trump's prospects for renomination and the likelihood that he will be challenged as the Republican standard bearer.

Finally, in Chapter 13, we attempt to place the 2016 and 2018 elections in the proper historical context. Although we examine changes and continuities in American elections over the course of the nation's history, the great advantage of our analysis is its use of high-quality surveys of the electorate over the last sixty years. This wealth of data provides extraordinary insights regarding the political preferences of the America people, how those preferences have varied with time, and how they relate to voting behavior. Thus, we explore the long-term changes and continuities in the politics of American national elections.

PART ONE

THE 2016 PRESIDENTIAL ELECTION

CHAPTER ONE

THE NOMINATION STRUGGLE

Presidential nomination campaigns are the contests through which the two major political parties in the United States select their presidential nominees. As they have done since 1832 (Democrats) and 1856 (Republicans), the delegates who are chosen to be seated at the national party conventions do the actual selecting. However, since about 1972, both parties have used public campaigns for popular support as a way of selecting and/or instructing most delegates to the convention on how they should vote. Many people think of these primary contests as formal elections, just like those in general elections in the fall. Whereas presidential primary elections are, indeed, run by the government, they are actually designed solely to help each political party select delegates to choose its presidential nominee, and that applies only to the roughly half of the states that use primary elections to select or instruct their delegates.[1] States that use the alternative means, caucus or convention procedures, instead of primaries (see what follows) do so without involving the government at all. Presidential nominations are thus a mixture of public and private selections, and they are conducted at the state level only, even though their ultimate outcome is to select the two major parties' nominees for the only national offices that Americans elect.

In this, America is nearly unique. In almost no other country have the leaders of the major political parties' leaders ceded so much control over candidate selection to the general public. While now and then there are primary elections run by political parties in other nations, they are rare, typically isolated to one or a few parties, and are often used only once or twice before being discarded. American nominations, on the other hand, have run this way for Democrats and Republicans since the 1970s and have become entrenched in the public's and the political leaderships' minds. It would be very difficult for a party to nominate someone the public did not support at near or actual majority levels in the primary season. The leadership has, in that sense, ceded its control over its own party to the general public.[2] In turn that has empowered the media who seek to inform the public and the many activists, supporters, and financial donors of the presidential nomination campaigns who provide the wherewithal for most candidates to have any chance of reaching the public to win their support.

The 2016 campaigns in many respects were like all of those since the 1970s, that is, in the era of the "new nomination system," as we call it. As we shall see there were perhaps a surprising number of similarities between the two campaigns of 2016 and their predecessors. Most people, however, when they speak of 2016, talk with wonder about specific and individual aspects of the campaigns regardless of the similarities to other contests. They ask "How could someone like Donald J. Trump win the Republican nomination?" and (if they disliked the outcome) "Why couldn't Republican leaders prevent his nomination?" On the Democratic side the question more often seemed to be "Why didn't Hillary R. Clinton win nomination more easily and quickly instead of appearing unable to reach out to larger numbers of Democrats?" or (if the outcome was viewed as negative) "How could the party fail to nominate someone more at the heart of the Democratic Party and end up with someone who so epitomizes the 'establishment' in this anti-establishment year?" As we will see the answers to these questions are that the two parties' campaigns largely unfolded in replication of the many and well-established continuities established since the empowering of the public and consequent loss of party leadership control over nominations. But it is the unique properties of the two winners, especially in comparison to their major party opponents, that made the two campaigns unlike previous ones and in sometimes very important ways.

In short, reforms in the late 1960s and early 1970s brought about a new form of nomination campaign, one that required public campaigning for resources and votes. The new nomination system has shaped many aspects of all contests from 1972 onward, and we examine the similarities that have endured over its more than forty-year existence. Each contest, of course, differs from all others because of the electoral context at the time (e.g., the state of the economy or of war and peace) and because the contenders themselves are different. And in the new nomination system, the rules change to some degree every four years as well. The changes in rules and the strategies that candidates adopt in light of those rules combine with the context and contenders to make each campaign unique.

WHO RAN

A first important regularity of the nomination campaign is that when incumbents seek renomination, only a very few candidates will contest them, and perhaps no one will at all. In 1972, although President Richard M. Nixon did face two potentially credible challengers to his renomination, they were so ineffective that he was essentially uncontested. Ronald Reagan in 1984, Bill Clinton in 1996, George W. Bush in 2004, and Barack Obama in 2012 were actually unopposed. They were so, in large part, because even a moderately successful president is virtually undefeatable for renomination. Conversely Gerald R. Ford in 1976 and Jimmy Carter in 1980 each faced a most credible challenger.[3] Ford had great difficulty defeating Reagan, and Carter likewise was strongly contested by Democratic senator Edward M. Kennedy of Massachusetts.[4] Of course Obama was ineligible to run for a third term in 2016, and so there was no incumbent running in either party. President Trump may well run for reelection in 2020 or perhaps join the few incumbents who chose not to run for reelection even though eligible, such as Harry S Truman in 1952 and Lyndon B. Johnson in 1968.

The second major regularity in the nomination system concerns the contests—such as those in 2016—in which the party has no incumbent seeking renomination.

In such cases a relatively large number of candidates run for the nomination. For our purposes we count candidates as "running" if they were actively campaigning on January 1, 2016 (or entered even later, although none did this time). That definition means that there were twelve major candidates who sought the Republican Party's nomination in 2016. There were actually quite a few more in 2015—by most counts seventeen—although that means that five were sufficiently "defeated" (or at least believed their chances of winning were too remote) so that they dropped out before January 1, 2016.[5] By our counting procedure there were three Democratic candidates in 2016.[6] Thus, in this section, we will be considering fifteen major party contenders. The numbers are higher on the Republican side and lower on the Democratic side than usual but not substantially out of the ordinary in either case.

Since 1980 there have been thirteen campaigns in which there was no incumbent seeking a major party's nomination, and the number of major candidates that were in the race as the year began varied remarkably little: seven in 1980 (R); eight in 1984 (D); eight (D) and six (R) in 1988; eight in 1992 (D); eight in 1996 (R); six (R) and two (D) in 2000; nine in 2004 (D); eight in both parties' contests in 2008; eight in 2012 (R); in addition to the twelve Republicans and three Democrats in 2016. Thus most such races featured at least six candidates. Only 2000 (D) and 2016 (D) had noticeably fewer, whereas 2016 (R) had a third more candidates running than the next most crowded field (2004, D).[7] We will discuss why there were fewer candidates in those two races, but note that both had larger numbers of declared candidates before our January 1 date for counting (as did most other races).

The three candidates on the Democratic side were: Hillary Clinton, who most recently served as secretary of state in the Obama administration;[8] Bernie Sanders, senator from Vermont; and Martin O'Malley, former governor of Maryland. The large number of Republicans was somewhat unusual in that the list included three candidates who had held no previous political office experience and very unusual in that such candidates (such as Ben Carson and Carly Fiorina in 2016) generally fare poorly, whereas Trump went on to win the nomination and election. There were also three incumbent senators (Ted Cruz, TX; Marco Rubio, FL; and Rand Paul, KY), two incumbent governors (John Kasich, OH; and Chris Christie, NJ); three former governors (Jim Gilmore, VA; Jeb Bush, FL; and Mike Huckabee, AR), and a former senator (Rick Santorum, PA). See Table 1-1 for these and other details we will discuss shortly. We have so far illustrated two regularities: few or no candidates will challenge incumbents, but in most cases many candidates will seek the nomination when no incumbent is running. In this 2016 is not particularly exceptional.

A third regularity is that among the candidates who are politicians, most hold or have recently held one of the highest political offices. This regularity follows from "ambition theory," developed originally by Joseph A. Schlesinger to explain how personal ambition and the pattern and prestige of various elected offices lead candidates to emerge from those political offices that have the strongest electoral bases.[9] This base for the presidential candidates includes the offices of vice president, senator, governor, and of course, the presidency itself. Note that even with a large number of contenders, there were no sitting members of the U.S. House who chose to run for the presidential nomination in 2016. House members do not have as strong an electoral

Table 1-1 Candidates for Nomination to the Presidency by the Democratic and Republican Parties, 2016, With Various Aspects Pertinent to Their Candidacy

	Name	Last Political Office	Withdrawal Date[a]	Campaign Expenditures (in Millions of Dollars)[b]	Independent Expenditures (in Millions of Dollars)[c]
Democrats	Clinton	Sec of State	None	$187	$12
	O'Malley	Gov (former)	1-Feb	$6	$0.40
	Sanders	Sen (current)	12-Jul	$213	$6
Republicans	Bush	Gov (former)	20-Feb		$87
	Carson	None	4-Mar	$6	$5
	Christie	Gov (current)	10-Feb	$8*	$22
	Cruz	Sen (current)	3-May	$85	$27
	Fiorina	None	10-Feb	$11	$4
	Gilmore	Gov (former)	12-Feb	$0.40	NA
	Huckabee	Gov (former)	1-Feb	$4	$3
	Kasich	Gov (current)	4-May	$19	$21
	Paul	Sen (current)	3-Feb	$12	$5
	Rubio	Sen (current)	15-Mar	$52	$49
	Santorum	Sen (former)	3-Feb	$0.30	$0.20
	Trump	None	None	$62	$44

Source: Compiled by authors.

[a]Information obtained from the *New York Times*, http://www.nytimes.com/2016/65/election/2016-presidential-candidate.

[b]Information obtained from the Federal Election Commission, http://www.fec.gov/disclosurep/pnational.do—and various subpages from there; accessed March 20, 2016.

[c]Information obtained from OpenSecrets,org, https://www.opensecrets.org/outside-spending/summ.php?cycle-2016&disp-C&type-P.

base from which to run for the presidency, and they may well have to abandon a safe House seat to do so. As a result few House members run, and fewer still are strong contenders. The most prominent exception to the strong electoral base of ambition theory—Trump having had no experience in politics—will be at the center of our account of the unique features of his victory.

Most candidates in 2016, as in all earlier campaigns under the new nomination system, emerged from one of the strong electoral bases. Table 1-2 presents the data for 2016 and for all campaigns from 1972 to 2016 combined. More than two-thirds of the presidential candidates had already served as president, vice president, senator, or governor; another one in eight was a member of the U.S. House. In 2016 those ratios were largely true again, although no member of the House from either party was still a candidate as 2016 opened.[10] Many of the presidents in the early years of the nation were chosen from the outgoing president's cabinet (especially the sitting secretary of state) and other high level presidential appointees, but the cabinet is no longer a common source of presidential candidates, and the same is true for the nation's many mayors.[11] About one in seven candidates run for president without ever holding any elective office. That percentage was a little higher in 2016 as one in four of the

Table 1-2 Current or Most Recent Office Held by Declared Candidates for President: Two Major Parties, 1972–2016

Office Held	Percentage of All Candidates Who Held That Office	Number, 1972–2016	Number, 2016
President	6	8	0
Vice President	3	4	0
U.S. Senator	36	53	5
U.S. Representative	12	18	0
Governor	24	35	6
U.S. Cabinet	3	5	1
Other	6	9	0
None	10	14	3
Total	99	146	15

Sources: 1972–1992: Congressional Quarterly's Guide to U.S. Elections, 4th ed. (Washington, D.C.: CQ Press, 2001), 522–525, 562. 1996: Paul R. Abramson, John H. Aldrich, and David W. Rohde, Change and Continuity in the 1996 and 1998 Elections (Washington, D.C.: CQ Press, 1999), 13. 2000: CQ Weekly, January 1, 2000, 22. 2004: CQ Weekly, Fall 2003 Supplement, vol. 61, issue 48. The 2008–2016 results were compiled by the authors.

Republican candidates in 2016 (and no Democrats) had not held office previously. The big change, then, was not in the numbers but that one of those relatively politically untested contenders actually won the nomination in 2016, whereas few had left any visible mark at all on the contests in earlier years.

A fourth regularity, also consistent with ambition theory, is that of the many who run in nomination contests without incumbents, only a few put their current office at risk to do so. In 2016 only two senators, Paul and Rubio, were up for reelection. Paul withdrew on February 3, after the first contest of the campaign (the Iowa caucuses). Rubio said he would not run for reelection as a senator, but perhaps because the Florida senatorial primary was so late (August 30), he reentered the senatorial contest after withdrawing from the presidential race and won renomination and then reelection to the Senate.[12]

THE RULES OF THE NOMINATION SYSTEM

The method that the two major parties use for nominating presidential candidates is unique and includes an amazingly complicated set of rules. To add to the complication, the various formal rules, laws, and procedures in use are changed, sometimes in large ways and invariably in numerous small ways, every four years. As variable as the rules are, however, the nomination system of 1972 has one pair of overriding characteristics that define it as a system The first is that whereas delegates actually choose their party's nominee, it is the general public, at least those who vote in the primaries and attend the caucuses, that chooses the delegates and often instructs them as to how to vote. The second characteristic is that the candidates, as a consequence, campaign in public and to the public for their support, mostly by heavy use of traditional media, such as television and newspapers, and, increasingly, social media, such as Facebook and Twitter. The dynamics of the technology of the media make campaigning in the media dynamic as well. Obama pioneered fund-raising and campaign contacting on social media in 2008 and 2012. Trump adroitly used the "free media" of television and newspaper coverage in lieu of buying campaign ads on them, and he pioneered the use of Twitter, especially, in 2016.

The complexity of the nomination contests is a consequence of four major factors. The first of these, federalism, defines the state as the unit of selection for national nominees and has been central to party nominations for nearly two centuries now. The second factor is the specific sets of rules governing primaries and caucus/convention procedures—established at the level of the national party in terms of general guidelines and then more specifically by state parties and/or state laws—these rules are at the heart of the nomination system of 1972. These rules govern delegate selection (and sometimes dictate instructions for delegates' presidential voting at the convention). The third factor is the set of rules about financing the campaign, which are also the oft-revised products of the reform period itself, starting in 1972. The fourth factor is the way in which candidates react to these rules and to their opponents, strategies that grow out of the keen competition for a highly valued goal. These factors are described in more detail in the sections that follow.

Federalism or State-Based Delegate Selection

National conventions to select presidential nominees were first held for the 1832 election, and for every nomination since then, the votes of delegates attending the conventions have determined the nominees. Delegates have always been allocated at the state level; whatever other particulars may apply, each state selects its parties' delegates through procedures adopted by state party organizations whether they choose to use caucuses and conventions, by state law, or the party organization wants to use a primary election, or both. Votes at the convention are cast by a state's delegation, and in general the state is the basic unit of the nomination process. Thus there are really fifty separate delegate selection contests in each party.[13] There is no national primary, nor is there serious contemplation of one.

The fact that there are more than fifty separate contests in each party creates numerous layers of complexity, two of which are especially consequential. First, each state is free to choose delegates using any method consistent with the general rules of the national party. Many states choose to select delegates for the parties' conventions via a primary election. States not holding primaries use a combination of caucuses and conventions, which are designed and run by each political party and not by the state government. Caucuses are simply local meetings of party members. Those attending the caucuses report their preferences for the presidential nomination and choose delegates from their midst to attend higher-level conventions such as at the county, congressional district, state, and eventually national levels.

The second major consequence of federalism is that the states are free (within the bounds described as follows) to choose when to hold their primaries or caucuses. These events are thus spread out over time, although both parties now set a time period—the delegate selection "window"—during which primaries and caucuses can be held. Both parties began delegate selection on February 1, 2016, with the Iowa caucuses (a month later than in 2012), Republicans closed their delegate selection process with five states (CA, MT, NJ, NM, and SD) holding primaries on June 7, whereas Democrats in DC held a primary on June 14. The Republicans, concerned about how long the Romney nomination in 2012 took to unfold to victory, not only favored this shortening of the length of the primary season but also tried to regulate front-loading even further. In particular they required that states holding their primaries before March 15 had to use some kind of proportional allocation method so that the delegates awarded to candidates were to some degree proportionate to the votes those candidates received in the primary or caucus. It was not until March 15 that states could use the winner-take-all (WTA) rule, such that the candidate with the most votes wins all that state's delegates.[14] WTA rules are often favored by GOP states, due to the larger impact that state's delegation might have on the race, concentrating their vote on a single candidate.[15]

The Nomination System of 1972: Delegate Selection

Through 1968 presidential nominations were won by appeals to the party leadership. To be sure public support and even primary election victories could be important in a candidate's campaign, but their importance stemmed from the credibility they would give to the candidacy in the eyes of party leaders. The 1968 Democratic nomination, like so many events that year, was especially tumultuous.[16] The result was that the Democratic Party created a committee, known as the McGovern-Fraser Commission, which proposed a series of reforms that were proposed to the Democratic National Committee between 1969 and early 1972 and then finally adopted by the party convention in 1972. The reforms were sufficiently radical in changing delegate selection procedures that they, in effect, created a new nomination system. Although it was much less aggressive in reforming its delegate selection procedures, the Republican Party did so to a certain degree. However, the most consequential results of the Democratic reforms for our purposes—the proliferation of presidential primaries and the media's treatment of some (notably the Iowa) caucuses as essentially primary-like—spilled over to the Republican side as well.

In 1968 Democratic senators Eugene J. McCarthy of Minnesota and Robert F. Kennedy of New York ran very public, highly visible, primary-oriented campaigns in opposition to the policies of President Lyndon B. Johnson, especially with respect to the conduct of the Vietnam War. Before the second primary, held in Wisconsin, Johnson surprisingly announced, "I shall not seek and I will not accept the nomination of my party for another term as your President."[17] Vice President Hubert H. Humphrey took Johnson's place in representing the presidential administration and the policies of the Democratic Party generally. Humphrey, however, waged no public campaign; he won the nomination without entering a single primary, thereby splitting an already deeply divided party.[18] Would Humphrey have won the nomination had Robert Kennedy not been assassinated the night he defeated McCarthy in California, effectively eliminating McCarthy as a serious contender? No one will ever know. Democrats including Humphrey himself did know, however, that the chaos and violence that accompanied Humphrey's nomination clearly indicated that the nomination process should be opened to more diverse candidacies and that public participation should be more open and more effective in determining the outcome. He thus offered a proposal to create the McGovern-Fraser Commission, as it was popularly called, which was accepted by the Democratic National Committee.

The two most significant consequences of the reforms were the public's great influence on each state's delegate selection proceedings and the proliferation of presidential primaries. Caucus/convention procedures, however, also became timelier, were better publicized, and in short, were more primary-like. Today the media treat Iowa's caucuses as critical events, and the coverage of them is similar to the coverage of primaries—how many "votes" were "cast" for each candidate, for example. Indeed the party organizations formally recognized this fact. The Iowa Republican Party, for example, held a secret balloting among caucus attenders that determined how the delegates to subsequent levels of conventions were to be allocated among supporters of the candidates.[19] Iowa Democrats, in their turn, conducted a standing "vote" of attenders to the same effect.

Whereas the McGovern-Fraser Commission actually recommended greater use of caucuses, many of the state party officials concluded that the easiest way to conform to the new Democratic rules in 1972 was to hold a primary election. Thus the number of states (including the District of Columbia) holding Democratic primaries increased from fifteen in 1968 to twenty-one in 1972 to twenty-seven in 1976, and the number of Republican primaries increased comparably. The numbers peaked in 2000, when forty-three states conducted Republican primaries, and Democratic primaries were held in forty states. In 2016 there were thirty-nine primaries on each side. Thus it is fair to say that the parties' new nomination systems have become largely based on primaries or in more primary-like conventions.

The only major exception to this conclusion is that about 15 percent of delegates to the Democratic National Convention were chosen because they were elected officeholders or Democratic Party officials. Supporters of this reform of party rules (first used in 1984) wanted to ensure that the Democratic leadership would have a formal role to play at the conventions of the party. These "superdelegates" may have played a decisive role in the 1984 nomination of Walter F. Mondale, in the nomination of Obama over Clinton in 2008, and again for Clinton's nomination in 2016, when she, like Mondale and Obama, at one point had a majority of the non-superdelegates but not a majority of all delegates.[20] Each candidate needed only a relatively small number of additional superdelegates to commit to vote for them to win the nomination. All three received those commitments soon after the regular delegate selection process ended, and with that, they were assured the nomination.[21]

The delegate selection process has, as noted, become considerably more front-loaded.[22] The rationale for front-loading was clear enough: the last time California's (actual or near) end-of-season primary had an effect on the nomination process was in the 1964 Republican and the 1972 Democratic nomination contests. Once candidates, the media, and other actors realized, and reacted to, the implications of the reformed nomination system, the action shifted to the earliest events of the season, and nomination contests, especially those involving multiple candidates, were effectively completed well before the end of the primary season. More and more state parties and legislatures (including, for a while, California's) realized the advantages of front-loading, bringing more attention from the media, more expenditures of time and money by the candidates, and more influence to their states if they held primaries sooner rather than later.

Soon, however, other factors started to affect state decisions. First, the rewards for early primaries were concentrated in a relatively small number of the very earliest primaries. And as we have noted, the national parties regulated which ones could go when and threatened to penalize states that violated the national party decisions. Indeed Michigan and Florida were actually penalized in 2008 and 2012 for holding their contests too early in the season. In addition the very early presidential primaries forced states to make an increasingly difficult choice. If they held their presidential primaries early in the year, they had to decide whether to hold the primary elections for all other offices at the same time, which was proving quite a bit earlier than made sense for candidates for local, state, and even national congressional posts, or to pay the costs of running two primaries, one for the president and one much later for all other offices.[23] Some states like California, for example, which were not able to reap the major benefits of being among the very earliest of events, chose to return to late in the season.

If the rationale for front-loading was clear by 1996, when it first became controversial, the consequences were not. Some argued that long-shot candidates could be propelled to the front of the pack by gathering momentum in Iowa and

New Hampshire and could, before the well-known candidates had a chance to react, lock up the nomination early. The alternative argument was that increasing front-loading helps those who begin the campaign with the advantages associated with being a front-runner, such as name recognition, support from state and local party or related organizations, and most of all, money. The dynamic of this adjustment, described in the following paragraphs, can be seen clearly in Figure 1-1, which reports the week in which the winning candidate was assured nomination in contested nomination campaigns since 1976.

Indeed as the primary season has become more front-loaded, the well-known, well-established, and well-financed candidates have increasingly dominated the primaries. Senator George S. McGovern of South Dakota and Carter won the Democratic nominations in 1972 and 1976, even though they began as little-known and ill-financed contenders. George H. W. Bush, successful in the 1980 Iowa Republican caucuses, climbed from being, in his words, "an asterisk in the polls" (where the asterisk is commonly used to indicate less than 1 percent support) to become Reagan's major contender and eventual vice presidential choice and his successor to the presidency. And Colorado senator Gary Hart nearly defeated former Vice President Mondale in 1984. In 1988 the two strongest candidates at the start of the Republican race, George H. W. Bush and Bob Dole, contested vigorously, with Bush winning, while

Figure 1-1 Length of Multicandidate Campaigns: Two Major Parties, 1976–2016

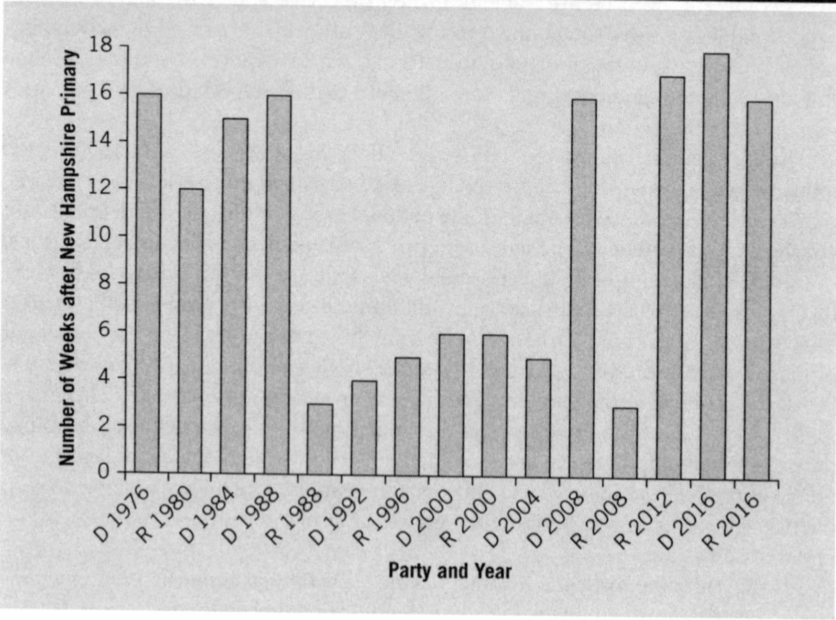

Source: Compiled by authors.

their presence basically locked other lesser-known contenders out. Gov. Michael S. Dukakis of Massachusetts, the best-financed and best-organized (albeit little known) Democrat, won the nomination surprisingly easily. Bill Clinton's victory in 1992 appeared, then, to be the culmination of the trend toward an insuperable advantage for the strongest and best-financed candidates. Clinton was able to withstand scandal and defeat in the early going and eventually cruise to victory.

The campaign of former Democratic senator Paul Tsongas of Massachusetts in 1992 illustrates one important reason for Clinton's victory. Tsongas defeated the field in New Hampshire, and as usual, the victory and the media attention it drew opened doors to fund-raising possibilities unavailable to him even days earlier. Yet Tsongas faced the dilemma of whether to take time out of daily campaigning for the public's votes so that he could spend time on fund-raising or to continue campaigning in the upcoming primaries. If he campaigned in those primaries, he would not have the opportunity to raise and direct the funds he needed to be an effective competitor. Front-loading had simply squeezed too much into too short a post-New Hampshire time frame for a candidate to be able to capitalize on early victories as, say, Carter had done in winning the nomination and election in 1976. The events of 1996 supported the alternative argument—that increased front-loading benefits the front-runner—even though it took nearly all of Dole's resources to achieve his early victory that year.[24]

This lesson was not lost on the candidates for 2000, especially George W. Bush. In particular he began his quest in 1999 (or earlier!) as a reasonably well-regarded governor but one not particularly well-known to the public outside of Texas (although, of course, sharing his father's name made him instantly recognizable). He was at that point only one of several plausible contenders, but he worked hard to receive early endorsements from party leaders and raised a great deal of money well ahead of his competition. When others sought to match Bush's early successes in this "invisible primary," they found that he had sewn up a great deal of support. Many, in fact, withdrew before the first vote was cast, suddenly realizing just how Bush's actions had lengthened the odds against them. Bush was therefore able to win the nomination at the very opening of the primary season. Incumbent Vice President Al Gore, on the other side, also benefited from the same dynamics of the invisible primary made manifest by front-loading, although in the more classical role of one who began the nomination season as the odds-on favorite and therefore the one most able to shut the door on his opposition well before it was time for most voters to cast their ballots.[25]

In 2004 there was no strong leader of the contest before the Democratic campaign began. Howard Dean burst on the scene and rather surprisingly into a lead before dropping nearly as suddenly.[26] As a result there was a period of uncertainty in the shape of the contest, followed by solidifying support around long-time senator John Kerry, who thereby benefitted more from lack of anyone able to compete strongly against him than any rule.

The pre-primary period on the Republican side in 2008 was quite variable, with first McCain, then Giuliani, then Romney surging to the front. McCain's campaign was considered all but dead in the water by that point, but it regathered strength before 2007 ended. There was, then, no strong front-runner in the GOP; the campaign was wide open. In fact some pundits imagined former Arkansas Governor Mike Huckabee had become a favorite to win, and so McCain's victory in the Iowa caucuses was a genuine surprise (at least from the perspective of, say, October 2007). On the Democratic side, Hillary Clinton was a clear front-runner. In retrospect it was also clear that Obama had developed an impressive organization both by mobilizing support across the nation and by fund-raising, especially through adroit use of the Internet. Thus once his organizational strength became publicly visible, it was no surprise that he and Clinton easily defeated their rivals. Having boiled down to a two-candidate contest, each had carved out their own bases of support, and neither could decisively defeat the other. Obama did have a slight lead throughout much of the primary season, but because of the superdelegates, it was too slight a lead to be able to secure an outright majority of delegates until after the primary season ended. As heretofore unbound superdelegates determined their choices, they soon favored Obama sufficiently to put him over the top.

The 2012 Republican contest had some similarities to 2008, with Romney moving from his also-ran slot to replace McCain as the candidate who early on seemed strong, lost steam, and then resurged back to victory. One effect of the modest reversal in front-loading was that Romney, even though ahead, was not able to completely shut the door on his opposition until much later in the season. Simply too few delegates were selected as early in 2012 as in, say, 1980. This extended length of time had several effects. The most important appears to have been that the slowing of the delegate selection process, although still relatively highly front-loaded, permitted Romney's opponents to run negative campaigns against him, quite possibly hurting his ability to shape his own image and providing fodder for attacks in the general election campaign before the campaign had selected enough delegates for him to claim what proved to be a rather straightforward nomination victory.

Much the same appeared to happen again in 2016 on the Republican side. The unusual nature of someone like Trump emerging as the leading contender (even after losing the Iowa caucuses but righting his campaign and its dynamic growth in New Hampshire) led to calls for the remaining candidates (fairly soon into the season, the race reduced effectively to Trump versus Cruz, Kasich, and Rubio) and the "Republican establishment" to figure out a way to stop Trump. When that failed to happen, the divided opposition allowed Trump to build his delegate lead to victory.[27] On May 3, the night of the Indiana primary, his last major opponent, Ted Cruz, withdrew his candidacy, although Trump was still short of having a majority of delegates on his side. But from that night onward, he was unchallenged and thus the "presumptive nominee." Thus continued active opposition until May did yield a longer period in which Republicans were criticizing the eventual nomination, sometimes quite strenuously, in spite of a relatively straightforward and convincing win by Trump.

The slowed rate of delegate selection also affected the Clinton-Sanders contest on the Democratic side. Clinton, as she had in 2008, began her quest for nomination as a very strong front-runner, especially after those who appeared likely to be among her strongest opponents, Senator Elizabeth Warren (MA) and Vice President Biden, decided not to run. Of the remaining actual candidates, Sanders effectively had the liberal wing of the party on his own, and the race narrowed almost immediately to a two-person contest. In such races it is typically the case, as here, that both candidates have their own constituency in their party's base and are thus difficult to defeat. That is to say that these races—in 2016 like 2008 and others before them—take a long time to resolve. Even when Clinton had secured an outright majority of delegates (which was at the end of the season anyway), Sanders failed to concede and thus continued to be able to criticize Clinton and to remain a holding place for liberal Democrats who were disenchanted with her.

These effects can be seen in Figure 1-2, which reports the cumulative selection of delegates. As can be seen there, 1976 (the first primary season defined by the rules adopted at the 1972 Democratic convention) shows a slow, gradual increase in the number of delegates selected. It is not until week thirteen, just over a month before the season ends, that 50% of the delegates were selected, and even later that a sufficiently large proportion of the delegates had been selected to make a majority likely to be held by the leading candidate, if he or she faced any opposition at all. The 2000 season was dramatically different, with the 50% mark being reached in week six (indeed reaching nearly two-thirds of the delegates selected by that week). Finally the slight retreat from such heavy front-loading in 2016 is visually apparent, but it is also apparent that it is rather slight, looking far more like the 2000 apogee than the 1976 perigee.

The final consequence—and possibly the most important for differentiating the nomination system of 1972 from its predecessors—is "momentum," the building of success over time during the extended campaign period, such that every nomination has, so far, always been decided before the convention balloting and always going to the candidate who won the greatest support from the party's electorate.

The most significant feature of the nomination process, from the candidates' perspectives, is its dynamic character. This system was designed to empower the general

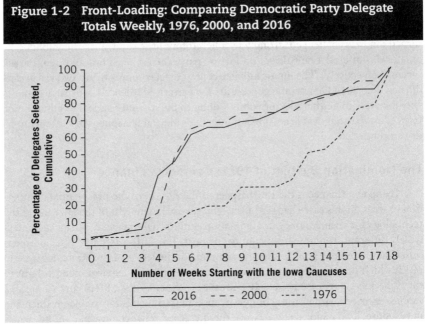

Figure 1-2   Front-Loading: Comparing Democratic Party Delegate Totals Weekly, 1976, 2000, and 2016

Source: Compiled by authors.

public, giving it opportunities to participate more fully in the selection of delegates to the national party conventions. The early state delegate selection contests in Iowa and New Hampshire allowed largely unknown candidates to work a small state or two using the "retail" politics of door-to-door campaigning to achieve a surprising success that would attract media attention and then money, volunteers, and greater popular support. In practice this was exactly the route Jimmy Carter followed in 1976.

John H. Aldrich developed this account of "momentum" in campaigns, using the 1976 campaigns to illustrate its effect. He first showed that there is no stable balance to this process.[28] In practical terms he predicted that one candidate will increasingly absorb all the money, media attention, and public support and thereby defeat all opponents before the convention. He further showed that the tendency for this process to focus rapidly on a single winner increases the *more* candidates there are. This finding was just the opposite of the original speculation and, indeed, what at the time seemed obvious: the greater the number of candidates, the longer it would take to reach victory. But commonsense was not a helpful guide in this case. Like other contests with large numbers of contenders, the Republican race of 2016 illustrates the power of momentum. Trump did not start off the campaign with a large lead in popular support, but he built that over the course of the campaign, eventually all but crushing even his strongest opponents and forcing their mostly early exits.

There is one exception to this pure "momentum" result: the possibility of an unstable but sustainable balance with two candidates locked in a nearly precise tie. Early campaigns offered two illustrations compatible with two candidates in (unstable) equipoise, the 1976 Republican and 1980 Democratic contests. In both the 1984 Democratic and 2008 Democratic contests, the campaigns began with a large number of candidates. Each featured a strong, well-financed, well-known, well-organized candidate (former Vice President Mondale and Hillary Clinton, respectively) who, it turned out, was challenged strongly by a heretofore little-known (to the public) candidate who offered a new direction for the party (Sen. Gary Hart and Sen. Barack Obama, respectively). The multicandidate contest quickly shrank to just two viable candidates. The 2016 Democratic contest fits the pattern of balanced two-party contests very nicely, with neither bloc of voters willing to move from Sanders to Clinton nor from Clinton to Sanders in any great numbers, as inevitably happens in a momentum-driven contest.

The Nomination System of 1972: Campaign Finance

Campaign finance is the third aspect of the reform of the presidential nomination process. In this case changes in law (and regulation in light of the law) and in the technology for raising money in nomination contests have made the financial context widely different from one campaign to the next. The 2016 campaign was no exception. These candidates were able to learn some of the lessons from strategies tried in 2012, which was the first run under a new (de-)regulatory environment in light of the Supreme Court case popularly known as *Citizens United* (2010), and so in 2012 candidates tried a large variety of new or modified strategies for campaign financing in response. Two major changes were the increased reliance on what are known as independent expenditures by a number of candidates, and Trump's strategy, which focused less on raising money but instead in getting the media to cover his campaign much more highly than those of other candidates. This was a strategy he believed to be a more effective use of "free" media than what impact higher expenditures for purchasing time on the paid media would offer.

Our story begins, however, with the Federal Election Campaign Act of 1971 and especially amendments to that act in 1974 and 1976. The Watergate scandal during the Nixon administration included revelations of substantial abuse in raising and spending money in the 1972 presidential election (facts discovered in part in implementing the 1971 act). The resulting regulations limited contributions by individuals and groups, virtually ending the power of individual "fat cats" and requiring presidential candidates to raise money in a broad-based campaign. The federal government would match small donations for the nomination, and candidates who accepted matching funds would be bound by limits on what they could spend.

These provisions, created by the Federal Election Commission to monitor campaign financing and regulate campaign practices, altered the way nomination campaigns were funded. Still, just as candidates learned over time how to contest most effectively under the new delegate selection process, they also learned how to campaign under the new financial regulations. Perhaps most important, presidential candidates learned—although it is not as true for them as for congressional candidates—that "early money is like yeast, because it helps to raise the dough."[29] They also correctly believed that a great deal of money was necessary to compete effectively.

The costs of running presidential nomination campaigns, indeed campaigns for all major offices, have escalated dramatically since 1972. But a special chain of strategic reactions has spurred the cost of campaigning for the presidential nomination. The *Citizens United* case accelerated the chain reaction by creating a much more fully deregulated environment.

When many states complied with the McGovern-Fraser Commission reforms by adopting primaries, media coverage grew, enhancing the effects of momentum, increasing the value of early victories, and raising the costs of early defeat. By 2008 very few candidates were accepting federal matching funds because doing so would bind them to spending limits in individual states and over the campaign as a whole, and these limits were no longer realistic in light of campaign realities. By 2012, only one candidate, former Louisiana Governor Buddy Roemer, applied for federal funding, and his candidacy was considered sufficiently hopeless that many debates did not even bother to include him among the contestants. No major candidates accepted matching funds in 2016.

Much money was being raised, however. Through May 2008, for example, the fund-raising totals for the three major contenders were $296 million for Obama, $238 million for Clinton, and $122 million for McCain.[30] By the same point in 2012, Romney reported raising $121 million, with Paul having raised $40 million, Gingrich $24 million, and Santorum $22 million. See Table 1-1 for reports on campaign expenditures in 2016. Note that, for example, Clinton and Sanders spent much more than Romney raised in 2012.

The 2008 campaign also marked a dramatic expansion in the use of the Internet to raise money, following on the efforts of Democrat Howard Dean, the former governor of Vermont, in 2004 (and, to an extent, McCain in 2000). Ron Paul, for example, raised more than $6 million on a single day, December 6, 2007, through the Internet. But Obama's success in 2008 served as the model for future campaigns, such as the $55 million he raised in February at a critical moment for the campaign.[31]

The *Citizens United* decision in 2010 changed the landscape dramatically. In the narrow it overturned the 2002 Bipartisan Campaign Reform Act and held that corporations and unions could spend unlimited money in support of political objectives and could enjoy First Amendment free speech rights, just as individuals could. These organizations, however, continued to be banned from direct contribution to candidates and parties. The case, and especially a subsequent one decided by the U.S. Court of Appeals in light of this case, spurred the development of what are known as "super PACs," which are political action committees that can now accept unlimited contributions from individuals, corporations, and unions and spend as much as they like so long as it is not in explicit support of a candidate or party's election campaign or coordinated with their campaign organization.[32]

According to data from the Center for Responsive Politics, expenditures on behalf of the three major nomination contenders were quite large. In 2012 about $14 million was spent on behalf of Romney, $19 million for Gingrich, and $21 million for Santorum. Data from Open Secrets are reported in Table 1-1 for the 2016 campaign. Note that the expenditures on behalf of many candidates, especially Republicans, had as much, or even more, spent on behalf of their campaigns than they spent themselves.[33] These organizations altered the terms of the campaign in that their expenditures had to be independent of the candidates and their (and their party's) organizations. It is therefore not necessarily the case that the candidate and, in the fall, the party will retain total control over the campaign and its messages.

Another consequence of these changes is that what were previously dubbed "fat cats" are once again permitted. The 2012 exemplar was Sheldon Adelson, a casino magnate and a strong supporter of Israel. He contributed $10 million to the Winning Our Future super PAC in support of Newt Gingrich, contributing about half that total before the South Carolina primary and the other half before the next primary in Florida. His public support is rare, however. Most of the super PACs are funded and led by small numbers of individuals, and we often do not know their names.

Note that in 2016, although Trump did raise and spend a good deal of money, much of his expenditures came later in the game, and he made a very public case for not spending a dime of his own money until late into the campaign. Certainly he spent much less than either of the two major Democrats, both of whom raised sums comparable to the Obama-Clinton race in 2008. But he did spend much more than his opponents, with only Rubio being at all close behind. And, of course, he eventually received a lot of support from super PACs, even though Bush also had a great deal spent on his behalf (even if ineffectually). The lessons are that money is very helpful, that early money still must be better than that raised late, that candidates are still trying to figure out the best configuration in this largely deregulated campaign finance regime, and that, as Trump's approach shows, it is not money that is important, but what it will buy. We will discuss his campaign strategy in a little while, but this also raises the final lesson for the future, that if candidates come to rely on super PACs, they risk control over their campaign, or they simply agree to adopt the stances of their party or its backers as their own. This concession to the party and its "image" is greatly strengthened due to the dramatic increase in partisan polarization that began around 1980 and continues to increase today.

STRATEGY AND THE CANDIDATES' CAMPAIGNS IN 2016: THE ELECTORAL SETTING AND HOW THE CANDIDATES WON THEIR NOMINATIONS

The Strategic Context: One of the most dramatic changes of the last half century has been the increase in partisan polarization, which generally means an increasing similarity of attitudes and preferences within each party and a substantial increase in divergence of opinion between the two parties. The leading indicators of this increase in partisan polarization have been among the party elites and especially their elected officeholders.[34] What is less clear is whether the electorate has followed polarization among elites (or, even less obviously, led elite polarization), and if so, how much the electorate has followed (or led). Some argue that there has been little change for decades, especially on such key measures as issue and ideological preferences. In this view polarization in the electorate is relatively small, with the result that the electorate continues to be basically moderate in its views.[35] Others point to at least some increased polarization in preferences between partisan identifiers, particularly among the more attentive and engaged in politics, such as those among the most likely to participate in primaries and caucuses.[36]

The clearest evidence of partisan polarization in the electorate lies in divergences between the two parties in other ways than their attitudes toward issues and even their ideological views. For example, Marc Hetherington and Jason Husser showed that there has been a dramatic decline in trust across party lines, whereas Shanto Iyengar and colleagues have shown that emotional responses have become much more polarized along party lines in the electorate.[37] Finally Gary Jacobson demonstrated that the so-called approval ratings of presidents (something we analyze in Chapter 7 in detail) went from having only a modest amount of partisan differences to becoming deeply divided by party.[38]

Here we illustrate that the context for the 2016 presidential nomination campaign has become much more deeply polarized along party lines than it was in 1980 in terms of overall affective evaluations of the candidates running for the presidential nomination. The ANES ran nation-wide surveys in January 1980 and in January 2016.[39] These years turn out to be especially appropriate ones for this look at partisan polarization of candidate evaluations for two reasons. The 1980 presidential election, as it happens, was the year in which elite partisan polarization turned and began its sharp increase, and thus we have data from the beginning and (current) end points of elite polarization. In addition both parties' nominations were strongly competitive. In both years the Democrats witnessed a strong two-person contest that lasted throughout the primary season. In both years the Republicans chose over a larger number of candidates that more quickly ended with Reagan and Trump's victories, respectively, but were nonetheless hotly contested in January. Especially on the Republican side, contenders argued for their candidacy in part by claiming to be supported by Democrats.

The survey data reported in Figures 1-3 and 1-4 show an increase in partisan polarization in the electorate in two ways. The figures report data using the so-called candidate thermometers, which ask how "warmly" or "coolly" the respondent feels toward the candidate, where 100 is the warmest possible feeling, 50 is neutral (neither warm nor cool), and 0 is the coldest possible feelings toward that candidate.[40] Figure 1-3 reports the difference between how the average Democrat and average Republican evaluated that candidate.[41] This is probably the most direct measure of partisan polarization of candidate evaluations. Those who are concerned about partisan polarization often point to the decline in the ability to work across party lines—the decline in bipartisanship—which is compounded by an apparent growth in emotional hostility to those on the other side of party lines. In Figure 1-4, therefore, we report the percentage of partisans who rate the relevant candidate of the opposite party positively (i.e., warmly or above 50 degrees). Even if there are large gaps in evaluations, as in Figure 1-3, the ability to see the opposition candidate positively bodes more favorably for bipartisanship.

The two figures have strong and reinforcing findings. In 1980, although each party felt more positively toward its own candidates than did those identifying with the other party, the difference between the two parties was fairly muted, with

Figure 1-3 Difference in Average Thermometer Rating: Selected Candidates, January 1980 and 2016

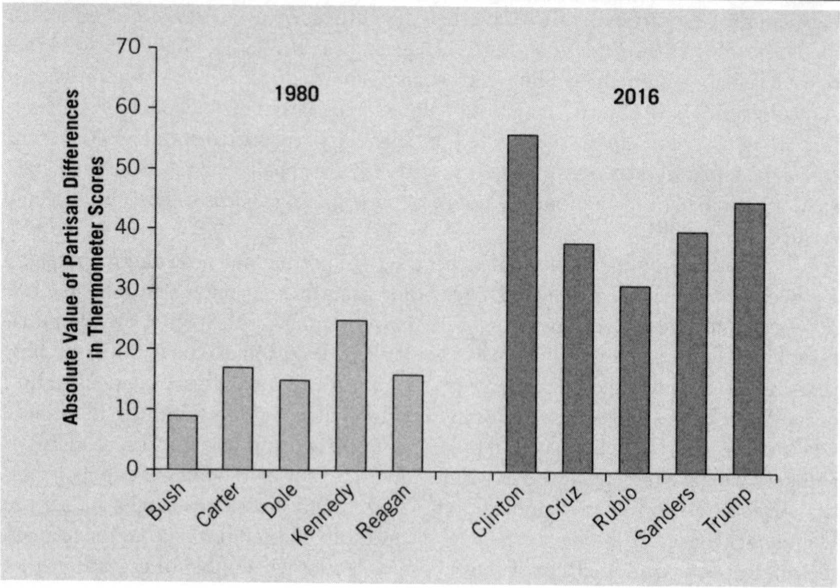

Source: Authors' analysis of "feeling thermometers" is from the respective ANES surveys.

Note: Data are weighted.

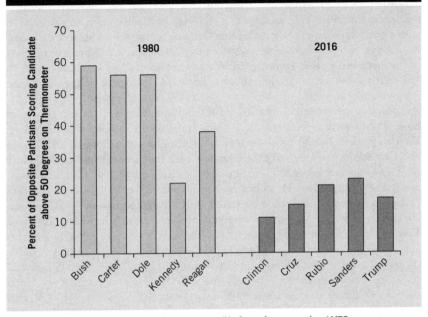

Figure 1-4 Warm Feelings from Opposite Partisans: Selected Candidates, January 1980 and 2016

Source: Authors' analysis of "feeling thermometers" is from the respective ANES surveys.

Note: Data are weighted.

differences typically under 20 degrees on the 100-point scale. Only evaluations of Kennedy were higher, at 27 points. None of these were as large as the smallest partisan gap in 2016, and the partisan polarization between the two eventual nominees was great—more than 40 points for Trump and more than 50 for Clinton. Perhaps even more dramatic, in 1980 *majorities* of the opposition felt warmly toward Carter and toward eventual vice presidential nominee Bush, with Reagan evaluated positively by many Democrats. Conversely, in 2016, none of the candidates were evaluated positively by a quarter of the opposition, and fewer than one in five partisans felt warmly toward the candidate who eventually won the other party's nomination. There was very little chance that either party could nominate a candidate with any appreciable support among the opposition in 2016, quite unlike Reagan's success in winning over "Reagan Democrats" in his campaigns and presidency.[42] Even at the start of the campaign, that is, the contenders were in a strategic context that rewarded focus on one's own party with no incentive to build toward a cross-party coalition, either in open primary states or for the general election—or thereafter when in office. The public has become deeply divided emotionally over our electoral contests even before they have barely begun in a way that simply was not true a generation ago.

Whereas, therefore, it is always true that nomination politics leads candidates to focus on their party to win, this was truer in 2016 than ever before. How, then, did the candidates win? We begin with Democrats. Hillary Clinton started both the 2008 and 2016 campaigns in the enviable position of an unusually well-known candidate in the public, with many areas of support in the Democratic electorate already won and with a great deal of support from leading Democrats and those with access to funding sources. Her position was thus well-defined with appeal to moderate Democrats, women (especially older women), African Americans, and those who have long been "Clintonians." As such if she had a vulnerability in the Democratic primary electorate, it was on the party's left.

Sanders was able to clearly fashion his appeal to that very constituency, even though not nearly as well-known to Democratic voters in January. He had long been on the left. Indeed his original election as mayor of Burlington, VT, was as a Socialist, and he had long served in Congress as an Independent who caucused with the Democrats but retained his independent status. Only recently had he formally and publicly affiliated as a Democrat, making his potential nomination viable. Unlike earlier nomination contests, few contested for the liberal portion of the Democratic electorate, with the apparently strongest contenders, especially Senator Elizabeth Warren (MA), declining to run. Given his late and, in some measures, begrudging entry into the Democratic Party, he lacked the close interactions and shared service to the party leadership that Clinton had with so many of them. And both his lack of seeking support from Democratic donors (Vermont did not require the same level of campaign expenditures as larger states) and his vocal stance against super PACs and other organizations that serve as sources of campaign resources, he also faced obstacles to expanding upon his electoral base. And, indeed, that is how the campaign worked out.

Perhaps the biggest surprise of the Democratic campaign was how Sanders was able to make a strong appeal, especially to younger voters on the left, and to turn college students, among others, into active supporters. As a further result, Clinton, even as she emphasized the more liberal parts of her agenda and adopted more left-wing positions on key issues, was unable to expand her base on the left, as Sanders was demonstrably a liberal (even socialist) candidate, and she was forced to publicly change her stances to try to reach Sanders's supporters. Conversely Sanders had too little standing among Democratic leaders (such as superdelegates) or more moderate Democrats in the public, nor even among the large constituency of African Americans. Thus he too was unable to cut into Clinton's strengths and expand his base of support.

Clinton won the Iowa caucuses (a real victory, given her loss there in 2008) and held Sanders to a relatively small victory in New Hampshire, sitting next door to Sanders's home (see Table 1-3 for delegates won by these two candidates over the nomination campaign). Of course that meant that Sanders did reasonably well in Iowa and won New Hampshire, cementing him as a credible candidate, able to be considered by voters over the long haul. Still, his inability to shake much of her support meant that in the March 1 "Super Tuesday" primaries, most of which were in the South and thus featured two sources of Clinton strength, moderate white Democrats and African Americans, followed by her largely similar victories in the large, industrial states of the "Rust Belt," meant that Sanders fell behind in the count of delegates won, even as he very slowly approached her standing in the public opinion polls. Because the Democratic rules require some form of proportional selection of delegates (i.e., roughly in proportion to the percentage of votes received), Clinton's delegate lead became simply insurmountable.

As noted earlier, however, it took Clinton until June for her to win an absolute majority of the delegates and thus achieve victory, a victory strengthened by heavy support of superdelegates, those party leaders with whom she had so long worked. In short two candidates with clear and distinct appeals were able to hold their own support, but both were unable to expand into that of the opponent. As a result the early lead Clinton had in public opinion polls (8 points in the February CBS/*New York Times* [NYT] poll) held steady throughout the season (the same poll in May had her with a 7-point lead), and that relatively small lead in the national polls became a small but winning majority in the delegate count as state after state selected its delegates.

The Republican side was, of course, rather different in many ways. Still, Trump held a 17-point lead over Cruz, his closest competitor in the January (and February) CBS/NYT poll that in April, just before Cruz withdrew, stood at 13 points. Once delegate selection started, that is, all the sound and fury of Republican candidates attacking each other on increasingly personal grounds had at best minor effects on Trump's public standing and lead in the delegate count. To be sure, in 2016 or 2017, many different Republicans got their day in the sun, but none were able to close the Trump lead.

Perhaps surprisingly Trump lost to Cruz in Iowa (and nearly fell to third place there) but righted his ship in New Hampshire, South Carolina, and virtually everywhere thereafter, consistently winning most of the states with pluralities (only occasionally with actual majorities) but picking up the bulk of the delegates in state after state. Trump did lose two large states, Ohio and Texas, and with those losses in votes, he also lost even larger percentages of their delegates, but these were divided between Kasich and Cruz, respectively (each winning their home states). Even so, Trump was able to carry many other larger states (perhaps most significantly, Rubio's home state of Florida). While opponents considered ways to unite their forces to maximize leverage against Trump, no plan was able to be worked out. Further, after the earliest states had chosen, the Republican Party rules permit states to use WTA rules so that the candidate who wins more of the larger states wins a far higher percentage of the delegates needed to win nomination. Thus Trump was able to move consistently and smoothly toward victory, as can be seen in Table 1-4, which reports the results of each Republican contest.

This relatively placid and straightforward account of how Clinton and Trump won nomination belies the media frenzy that accompanied both campaigns—and especially these two candidates in particular. These circumstances are those that most remember, even though their consistent and largely unchecked (and apparently uncheckable) drives to victory are the real story of how to win nominations in the post-1972 nomination system.

Still, both were tagged with problems (quite reasonably understood as of their own doing) that would dog their campaigns throughout the spring, summer, fall, and in Trump's case, into the White House itself as we discuss in subsequent chapters. Clinton was tarnished with three charges that yielded appearances of corruption— the financing of the Clinton Foundation, the events that led to the deaths of four

Table 1-3 Democratic Nomination Results, 2016: Bound Delegates Won in State Primaries and Caucuses—Clinton and Sanders

Date	State	Clinton	Sanders
1-Feb	Iowa	23	21
9-Feb	N.H.	9	15
20-Feb	Nev.	20	15
27-Feb	S.C.	39	14
1-Mar	Ala.	44	9
	Ark.	22	10
	Colo.	25	41
	Ga.	73	29
	Mass.	46	45
	Minn.	31	46
	Okla.	17	21
	Tenn.	44	23
	Texas	147	75
	Vt.	0	16
	Va.	62	33
5-Mar	Kan.	10	23
	La.	37	14
	Neb.	10	15
6-Mar	Maine	8	17
8-Mar	Mich.	63	67
	Miss.	31	5
15-Mar	Fla.	141	73
	Ill.	79	77
	Mo.	36	35
	N.C.	60	47
	Ohio	81	62
22-Mar	Ariz.	42	33
	Idaho	5	18
	Utah	6	27

Date	State	Clinton	Sanders
26-Mar	Alaska	3	13
	Hawaii	8	17
	Wash.	27	74
5-Apr	Wis.	38	48
9-Apr	Wyo.	7	7
19-Apr	N.Y.	139	108
26-Apr	Conn.	28	27
	Del.	12	9
	Md.	60	35
	Pa.	106	83
	R.I.	11	13
3-May	Ind.	39	44
10-May	W.Va.	11	18
17-May	Ky.	28	27
	Ore.	25	36
5-Jun	P.R.	37	23
7-Jun	Calif.	254	221
	Mont.	10	11
	N.J.	79	47
	N.M.	18	16
	N.D.	5	13
	S.D.	10	10
14-Jun	D.C.	16	4

Listed numbers are for bound delegates.

Source: Kevin Schaul and Samuel Granados, "The Race to the Democratic Nomination," *Washington Post*, October 10, 2017, https://www.washingtonpost.com/graphics/politics/2016-election/primaries/delegate-tracker/democratic/, accessed June 1, 2017.

Americans in Benghazi, Libya, and her use of a private e-mail account while she was secretary of state (and possible misuse of classified material). The latter, of course, continued right up to election day itself. In the spring, as well as in the fall, Trump regularly referred to her as "Crooked Hillary," and his audiences chanted "Lock her up! Lock her up!" Trump made a series of what we would ordinarily have imagined to be candidacy-ending gaffes, but (just as Clinton's poll numbers stayed fixed at a high level in the nomination campaign) no matter how vindictive (calling Cruz's wife "ugly"), mean-spirited ("Little Marco"), lascivious,[43] factually inaccurate, or seemingly outrageously racist his words, Trump simply marched toward victory in the spring. Or, as he put it himself, "I could stand in the middle of 5th Avenue and shoot somebody, and I wouldn't lose voters," Trump said in Sioux City, Iowa, January 24, 2016.[44] Yet these unique features of these two candidates seemed to have had little effect on their nomination campaigns.

National Party Conventions: As we noted earlier the purpose of the state primary or caucus convention procedures is to select who will be the delegates from that state to attend their national party convention and/or to instruct those delegates on how to vote for presidential nomination. The delegates are those entrusted with voting on all the convention's major pieces of business. These include resolving any remaining problems that arose in selecting one state's or another's delegations, adopting rules that will govern the party for the next four years, voting on the proposed party platform, and choosing the presidential and vice presidential nominees. Thus the delegates are entrusted with essentially all of the party's major decisions. But, as we have already seen with respect to the presidential nomination, they may cast the formal ballots—and it could well be some day that they will in fact play active roles—but their decision making is so tightly constrained that they almost invariably have no real choices to make. Their choice for presidential nominee is constrained by the vote of the public in their state.[45] The presidential nominee selects a candidate she or he would like to see serve as a running mate, and it has been a very long time since there was any real opposition to that choice.[46]

Party platforms once were regularly contended, as this was the one time when the party leadership could interact and work out just what the party stood for. Although this has not been true in recent years, both parties have had protests over the platform committee's proposals on one issue or another (e.g., the change in the 1980 Republican platform from its long-held stance of endorsing an Equal Rights Amendment to the Constitution for women to opposing it), whereas the last truly contended (nearly violently contended) battle over a platform plank was the debate over the Vietnam War in the 1968 Democratic Convention.

Instead of the traditional role of party conventions serving as the one time the party gathers from around the nation to debate and decide party business, the conventions have changed in recent decades to serve as major public presentations of the party to the nation. This leads the party and its leadership to seek to downplay internal divisions (although when they are really there, they are typically not able to be completely hidden) and present a united front to the public. Their other central role is to serve as the end of the intra-party competition of nominations and the transition to the general election campaign. The acceptance speeches of the nominees (and certainly of the presidential nominee) are generally used to showcase the major themes of the candidates for the general election campaign.

In 2012 the conventions were held late in August, which put the Republicans, especially, at a disadvantage as their nominee was restricted in spending in opposition

Table 1-4 Republican Nomination Results, 2016: Bound Delegates Won in State Primaries and Caucuses—Trump, Cruz, Rubio, and Kasich

		Trump	Cruz	Rubio	Kasich
1-Feb	Iowa	7	8	7	1
9-Feb	N.H.	11	3	1	4
20-Feb	S.C.	50	0	0	0
23-Feb	Nev.	14	6	7	1
1-Mar	Ala.	36	13	1	0
	Alaska	11	12	5	0
	Ark.	16	15	9	0
	Ga.	42	18	16	0
	Mass.	22	4	8	8
	Minn.	8	13	17	0
	Okla.	13	15	12	0
	Tenn.	33	16	9	0
	Texas	48	104	3	0
	Vt.	8	0	0	8
	Va.	17	8	16	5
5-Mar	Kan.	9	24	6	1
	Ky.	17	15	7	7
	La.	25	18	0	0
	Maine	9	12	0	2
6-Mar	P.R.	0	0	23	0
8-Mar	Hawaii	11	7	1	0
	Idaho	12	20	0	0
	Mich.	25	17	0	17
	Miss.	25	15	0	0
10-Mar	V.I.	1	0	0	0
12-Mar	D.C.	0	0	10	9
	Wyo.	1	23	1	0

(Continued)

Table 1-4 (Continued)

		Trump	Cruz	Rubio	Kasich
15-Mar	Fla.	99	0	0	0
	Ill.	54	9	0	6
	Mo.	37	15	0	0
	N.C.	29	27	6	9
	M.P.	9	0	0	0
	Ohio	0	0	0	66
22-Mar	Ariz.	58	0	0	0
	Utah	0	40	0	0
5-Apr	Wis.	6	36	0	0
9-Apr	Colo.	0	30	0	0
19-Apr	N.Y.	89	0	0	6
26-Apr	Conn.	28	0	0	0
	Del.	16	0	0	0
	Md.	38	0	0	0
	Pa.	17	0	0	0
	R.I.	12	2	0	5
3-May	Ind.	57	0	0	0
10-May	Neb.	36	0	0	0
	W.Va.	30	0	0	1
17-May	Ore.	18	5	0	5
24-May	Wash.	41	0	0	0
7-Jun	Calif.	172	0	0	0
	Mont.	27	0	0	0
	N.J.	51	0	0	0
	N.M.	24	0	0	0
	S.D.	29	0	0	0

Listed numbers are for bound delegates.

Source: Kevin Schaul and Samuel Granados, "The Race to the Democratic Nomination," *Washington Post*, October 10, 2017, https://www.washingtonpost.com/graphics/politics/2016-election/prima ries/delegate-tracker/republican/, accessed June 1, 2017.

to President Obama by the rules of the nomination season. Thus they were especially keen to hold their convention earlier in 2016. They choose to hold it in Cleveland July 18–21, whereas the Democrats held theirs in Philadelphia July 25–28.[47]

Trump selected the governor of Indiana, Michael Pence, to be his running mate on July 15. Pence is as understated as Trump is flamboyant and has had considerable experience in politics to balance Trump's outsider status. He has particularly deep religious beliefs, which guide many of his policy positions and, of course, appeals strongly to the large and important religious right in the party. That he hails from a combined Rust Belt, agricultural Midwestern state balanced the ticket, as is a common tradition, counterbalancing a New York City, high-rolling businessman with little formal connections to religion. Whereas the Trump and Pence nominations (and adoption of the party platform) went smoothly enough, there were moments of contention. Perhaps the most obvious was Cruz's unwillingness (often described as "defiance") to endorse Trump's nomination on prime-time television, which resulted in loud booing and heckling. Trump, for his part, stuck pretty closely to the script of his acceptance speech, which outlined a dark vision of contemporary America, leading those who agreed to the conclusion (he hoped) that one needed to vote for him to reverse course.

Clinton, for her part, selected Senator Tim Kaine, Virginia, as her running mate. This choice had less ticket balancing as compared to selecting a candidate from the liberal wing of the party, such as Sanders or Senator Elizabeth Warren (both of whom had featured speeches—Warren gave the keynote address). Although perhaps not quite as similar as Senator Al Gore was to Bill Clinton, Kaine was less about uniting the party (although he certainly did not divide it) than about trying to win the general election. Any worries about major disruption from the left wing were unfounded, and thus the convention presented a united image to the public and allowed Clinton to use her acceptance speech to complete the uniting and begin the general election campaign.

CHAPTER TWO

THE GENERAL ELECTION CAMPAIGN

Once they have been nominated, candidates choose their general election campaign strategies based on their perceptions of what the electorate wants, the relative strengths and weaknesses of their opponents and themselves, and their chances of winning. A candidate who is convinced that he or she has a dependable lead may choose very different strategies from those used by a candidate who believes he or she is seriously behind. A candidate who believes that an opponent has significant weaknesses is more likely to run an aggressive, attacking campaign than one who does not perceive such weaknesses.

After the 2016 conventions Hillary Clinton maintained a modest lead over Donald Trump in national polls (although many polls were within the margin of error). Most political observers thought that Clinton would win the election and that the stark differences in campaign styles for the two candidates would make a difference. Chapters 4 through 8 of this book will consider in detail the impact of particular factors (including issues and evaluations of President Obama's job performance) on the voters' decisions. This chapter will provide an overview of the fall campaign—an account of its course and a description of the context within which strategic decisions were made.

THE STRATEGIC CONTEXT
AND CANDIDATES' CHOICES

One aspect of the strategic context that candidates must consider is the track record of the parties in recent presidential elections. In presidential races the past is certainly not entirely prologue, but it is relevant. From this perspective the picture was slightly more encouraging for the Republicans than for the Democrats. From 1952 through 2012 there had been seventeen presidential elections, and the Republicans had won ten of them. On the other hand the Democrats had won three of the last five races since 1996, and in 2000 they secured a narrow popular-vote margin despite falling short in the Electoral College.

The nature of the American system for electing presidents requires that we examine the state-by-state pattern of results. U.S. voters do not directly vote for president or vice president. Rather they vote for a slate of electors pledged to support a presidential and a vice-presidential candidate. Moreover, in every state except Maine and Nebraska, the entire slate of electors that receives the most popular votes is selected. In no state is a majority of the vote required. Since the 1972 election, Maine has used a system in which the plurality-vote winner for the entire state wins two electoral votes. In addition the plurality-vote winner in each of Maine's two House districts receives that district's single electoral vote. Beginning in 1992 Nebraska allocated its five electoral votes in a similar manner: the statewide plurality-vote winner gained two votes, and each of the state's three congressional districts awarded one vote on a plurality basis.[1]

If larger states used the district plan employed by Maine and Nebraska, the dynamics of the campaign would be quite different. For example, candidates might target specific congressional districts and would probably campaign in all large states, regardless of how well they were doing in the statewide polls. But given the WTA rules employed in forty-eight states and the District of Columbia, candidates cannot safely ignore the pattern of past state results. A state-by-state analysis of the five presidential elections from 1996 through 2012 suggests that the Democrats had reason to be hopeful about the effort to win the 270 electoral votes required for victory.

Figure 2-1 States That Voted Democratic in at Least Four Out of Five Elections, 1996–2012, with Number of Electoral Votes

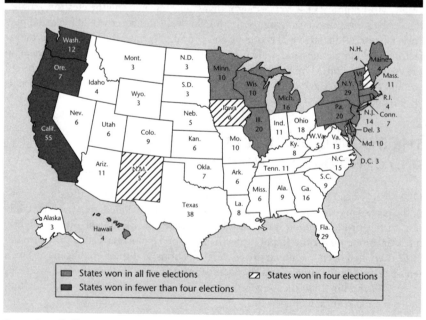

Legend:
- States won in all five elections
- States won in fewer than four elections
- States won in four elections

Source: Compiled by authors.

As Figure 2-1 reveals eighteen states plus the District of Columbia voted Democratic in all five of these elections. Only fifteen states were equally loyal to the GOP. (See Chapter 3 on long-term voting patterns.) These perfectly loyal states provided a prospective balance of 242 electoral votes for the Democrats to only 121 for the Republicans. Less problematic for the GOP candidates were the next groups of states. Nine states had voted Republican in every election but one, with a total of eighty-five electoral votes. Balancing these were only three states with fifteen electoral votes that had supported the Democrats in four of the five contests. Thus if each of these state's political leanings were categorized solely on the basis of the last five elections, one might expect that 257 electoral votes were likely to go to the Democrats in 2016, whereas only 206 were as likely to go to the Republicans, placing Clinton fifty-one votes ahead of Trump and only thirteen votes short of the number required to win.

If this past pattern had completely controlled the 2016 election, the GOP ticket would have been at a serious disadvantage. But, of course, things were not that simple, and many factors made Republican chances considerably better than they looked based on these numbers. Most obviously they had *won* two of the four previous elections, and the loss in 2008 occurred in the context of the worst economic downturn since the Great Depression, for which many blamed President Bush and his party. Moreover, the economic recovery over the past few years had been modest, and many potential voters were unhappy with the president's performance generally and his stewardship of the economy in particular.

Although most observers thought Clinton had a distinct advantage once Trump secured the Republican nomination, both campaign organizations viewed the same set of states determining the outcome of the election. These would be the "battleground" states, where both campaign organizations would concentrate the lion's share of their time, money, and effort. Indeed, even before the beginning of 2016, the two parties had already focused their attention on a set of twelve or thirteen states, and most of the other states would be largely ignored until election day.[2] The larger states in this group—particularly Florida, Michigan, Ohio, and Pennsylvania—would be the main focus of their efforts. Many of the non-battleground states, on the other hand—even large ones like California, New York, and Texas—would see little evidence that a presidential campaign was in progress. A state perspective through the lens of the Electoral College would dominate the strategy of the 2016 campaign.[3]

POLITICAL CONTEXT, OVERALL STRATEGY, AND OPENING MOVES

The strategic choices of candidates and parties are shaped by the particular context of the election. One feature of that context is whether an incumbent is running. Races without an incumbent, like the one in 2016, are very different from those where an incumbent is seeking reelection. In many respects the 2016 presidential race was one of the most bizarre and unprecedented elections in American history. Donald Trump, a political novice, became the presumptive nominee on May 3, when Ted

Cruz withdrew from the race following his defeat in the Indiana primary. Trump later secured enough delegates to officially clinch the Republican nomination for president on May 26, 2016, after besting fourteen other candidates in the primaries. When Hillary Clinton clinched the Democratic nomination two weeks later, she made history as the first woman ever to win a major party's presidential nomination but only after a long and grueling struggle against Vermont senator Bernie Sanders. The fact that both Trump and Sanders had done so well early in the campaign reflected a mix of populist anger and rhetoric that would continue to influence the general election campaign.

Clinton had a distinct fund-raising advantage over Trump in the fall campaign. As of July 21, 2016, the Clinton campaign had raised $264.4 million compared to the $89.0 million raised by the Trump campaign. Super PACs also contributed a large sum of money to Clinton's presidential campaign by this time, totaling nearly $122 million. By comparison the Trump campaign had only received about $5.2 million from super PACs in late July. This trend would continue throughout the fall campaign as Clinton continued to outraise and spend more money than her Republican opponent. When the electoral dust settled, Clinton would ultimately have nearly a 2:1 spending advantage over Trump in the general election campaign.[4]

Much of the $1.2 billion that the Clinton campaign would ultimately spend during the fall was directed toward television advertising and the get-out-the-vote operation. Her campaign believed that mobilizing voters to go to the polls was key and that being able to outspend her opponent was critical in this strategy. By contrast the Trump campaign raised only about $646.8 million from individual contributors and super PACs (which was less than any major party presidential nominee since John McCain in 2008). Trump's ability to dominate media headlines and his prolific use of Twitter in an attempt to control the narrative of the campaign were clearly factors in his ability to keep the polls close despite spending considerably less than Clinton in the fall campaign.[5] One estimate suggests that he may have received as much as $2 billion worth of free media coverage from the beginning of his campaign through February 2016.[6]

Both candidates faced highs and lows after the primary elections. One of the Trump campaign's biggest challenges came about a month before the Republican National Convention when Donald Trump fired Corey Lewandoski, his initial campaign manager. Lewandoski had been instrumental in Trump's early wins during the primaries, but influential party officials, such as RNC Chairman Reince Priebus, routinely criticized his controversial and divisive campaign style. Lewandowski lacked experience running a national campaign, and many of his critics within the party organization felt that his strategies for fund-raising and staffing the campaign were insufficient to wage a competitive operation against Hillary Clinton, who was clearly excelling in both of these areas. "Republicans across the spectrum welcomed [Lewandoski's] firing as a positive step, but they suggested that it needed to be followed by consistent changes in performance from the candidate himself."[7]

On July 1, the Trump campaign hired Kellyanne Conway as a political advisor, who had previously worked as a super PAC strategist for Ted Cruz's campaign. Conway was a veteran GOP pollster and long-time political strategist who had experience working with Republican lawmakers. Trump had previously offered Conway a job in 2015, but she turned down the offer to work on behalf of Ted Cruz instead. Conway decided to join the Trump campaign in early May once Cruz dropped out of the presidential race. She was initially brought on board in her long-time capacity of advising Republicans on how to better appeal to female voters.[8] On August 17, 2016, Conway was named as Donald Trump's campaign manager, making her the first woman to ever be selected to run a Republican presidential campaign. On the same day Steve Bannon, former Breitbart news executive, was appointed as the CEO of Trump's campaign. Bannon has a long history of populist rhetoric, including criticizing the establishment wing of the Republican Party, but is perhaps best known for his tireless crusade against the Clintons.[9]

Amid the controversy and shake-ups within the Trump campaign, Clinton was dealing with her own challenges stemming from a year-long FBI investigation. On March 2, 2015, the *New York Times* reported that Clinton had used a private email server when she was serving as secretary of state during the Obama administration.[10] Clinton defended her use of the private server several days later, claiming it was for convenience, so she could use one device for both business and personal use. On August 11, 2015, the Clinton campaign revealed that her server had been turned over to the Justice Department as per their request. More than nine months passed before the State Department's inspector general issued a report highly critical of Clinton's use of a private email server saying that "she had not sought permission to use it and would not have received it if she had." The report, which had been issued to Congress, undermined some of Clinton's previous statements and gave new political fodder to Republicans and the Trump campaign.[11]

Based largely on the inspector general's report, Hillary Clinton was interviewed by the FBI in Washington, DC, for more than three hours on July 2, 2016, about her previous use of the private email server. Three days later FBI Director James Comey, who had been at the center of the investigation since 2015, announced that the FBI would not recommend that Clinton be indicted on any charges but called her behavior "extremely careless" with respect to how she handled classified information during her time as secretary of state.[12] Clinton and her Democratic allies praised the decision by Comey, whereas Trump and his followers were highly critical of the outcome, referring to it as a "total miscarriage of justice."[13] Many Democrats hoped this would put an end to the discussion of emails and private servers, but the topic continued to remain relevant throughout the campaign and would resurface in a big way later on in the fall.

Selecting the Vice Presidents

Most political scientists agree that the presidential candidate's choice of running mates has little or no effect on the outcome of the election because most voters are inclined to vote primarily on the basis of which candidates are at the top of the ticket (and typically along party lines). Nevertheless, the selection of a candidate's vice presidential nominee often receives considerable attention by the media because it invites potential speculation about geographical or ideological balancing on the ticket.[14] The process also tends to occur a few days before the national conventions during the summer, when news coming out of the campaigns is far less regular and the media are looking for anything newsworthy to report upon.

In the days leading up to Donald Trump's choice of a vice presidential candidate, there was considerable speculation about who he would select for the position. Among some of the possible contenders discussed early in the summer were Ohio Governor John Kasich, Oklahoma Governor Mary Fallin, New Jersey Governor Chris Christie, and former U.S. House Speaker from Georgia, Newt Gingrich.[15] Although there were potential advantages and disadvantages with respect to each of these picks, many within the establishment wing of the party felt that most of these candidates would be in a good position to mitigate some of the more controversial aspects of the Trump candidacy. At the same time the "right" candidate for vice president might help ensure that Republican voters would not stay home on election day, a worry that had concerned party loyalists ever since Trump had sailed through the Republican primaries.

Just prior to the Republican National Convention, Trump seemed to narrow his choice down to one of three potential vice presidential nominees—Christie, Gingrich, and Indiana Governor Mike Pence. Pence had not been part of the initial discussion of potential nominees earlier in the summer, but he had gained some traction after a series of meetings with Trump, where the two seemed to hit it off. Trump had planned to wait until the convention to announce that Pence was joining the ticket but ended up making the official announcement the Friday before the convention started. Many establishment Republicans were thrilled with the selection of Pence because he was viewed as a "safe" choice who had been a consistent voice of conservative orthodoxy since his early days in talk radio. Pence's selection was also viewed by many as an attempt to shore up support, especially among social conservatives, who remained somewhat skeptical of Trump as the Republican candidate for president and perhaps an opportunity to win over voters in many of the Rust Belt states. According to one initial report, "In tapping Pence, Trump adds to the GOP ticket a politician with ties to the Koch brothers and other influential donors who have so far stayed away from Trump."[16] Pence's prior experience in office may have also helped to appease those Republicans who worried about Trump's lack of executive experience.

On the Democratic side Hillary Clinton waited until the Republican convention ended before naming her own choice for vice president. In the weeks leading up to the conventions, five different individuals had regularly been discussed as potential Clinton nominees for vice president—Virginia senator Tim Kaine, Ohio senator Sherrod Brown, New Jersey senator Cory Booker, Agriculture Secretary Tom Vilsack, and Massachusetts senator Elizabeth Warren. Some of these individuals, including Vilsack, were viewed as a safe choice by the Clinton campaign, whereas others—like Kaine and Brown—were considered at or near the top of the list given the strategic advantage that might come from having someone from states like Ohio and Virginia, which were very much in play in the presidential election.[17]

In the end Clinton went with the individual that potentially could offer her the greatest strategic advantage on the Democratic ticket, especially in carrying the state of Virginia—Senator Tim Kaine. Other than Vilsack, Kaine was easily among the safest choices for Clinton, and most within the Democratic Party readily acknowledged this. Given his strong ties to the party and his past electoral success in the state of Virginia, Kaine's selection as Clinton's nominee for vice president made a lot of strategic sense. Additionally his fluency in Spanish was definitely a plus in Clinton's attempt to reach out to Hispanic voters.[18] Interestingly enough Bernie Sanders spoke out the day after the announcement indicating that he would have preferred seeing Clinton select Elizabeth Warren as her running mate rather than Kaine. His comments seemed to reflect others' views from within the left wing of the party who were clearly disappointed by Clinton's selection.[19]

FROM THE CONVENTIONS TO THE DEBATES

The Conventions

The Republicans held their convention in Cleveland, Ohio, from July 18 to 21, amid potential protests and turmoil both inside and outside the convention hall. Many worried that the protests outside the convention would be large and unruly but ultimately proved to be much smaller than anticipated.[20] On the first day of the convention, tensions within the Republican Party became apparent when officials were forced to adopt the rules of the proceedings by a loud voice vote. Anti-Trump forces within the chamber sought to further derail the proceedings, but things quickly settled down, and no further disruptions were immediately apparent. Perhaps the most conspicuous event at the convention was the sheer number of notable Republicans who willingly chose not to attend, including George W. Bush and his brother Jeb along with John Kasich and John McCain. "From the party's former presidents to the host state governor, many leaders were staying away from the convention stage, or Cleveland altogether, wary of being linked to a man whose proposals and temperament have sparked an identity crisis within the GOP."[21]

This potential identity crisis was further illustrated when Ted Cruz spoke on the third night (July 20) of the convention. Cruz had been an outspoken critic of Donald Trump during the presidential primaries, and many within the party wondered if he would be willing to set aside his differences with the presumptive nominee and publicly endorse him for president. Much of his rhetoric echoed his comments from the campaign, especially when it came to issues such as health care, immigration, religious freedom, and taxes. Near the end of his convention speech, however, he stopped short of endorsing Trump when he offered the following remarks: "If you love our country, and love our children as much as you do, stand, and speak, and vote your conscience, vote for candidates up and down the ticket who you trust to defend our freedom, and to be faithful to the Constitution."[22] Many within the party viewed the "vote your conscience" comment as an implicit rejection of Trump as the nominee, which served to further highlight the divisions within the Republican Party rather than signify unity as is typically the case at national conventions.[23]

Trump's acceptance speech the following night was a mix of fiery rhetoric and partisan imagery that marked a significant departure from the optimistic tone characterizing Republican convention speeches dating back to the presidency of Ronald Reagan. Early in his speech he remarked, "Our convention occurs at a moment of crisis for our nation. The attacks on our police, and the terrorism in our cities, threaten our very way of life. Any politician who does not grasp this danger is not fit to lead our country." Trump reiterated that he would be the voice of American citizens who felt that they had been left behind over the past eight years. He also said he would take the necessary steps to keep America safe and bring back prosperity to the nation.[24] Finally Trump emphasized that he would present the facts "plainly and honestly. . . . So if you want to hear the corporate spin, the carefully crafted lies and the media myths, the Democrats are holding their convention next week. Go there."[25]

The Democratic National Convention met in Philadelphia, Pennsylvania, the following week. Just prior to the convention, however, WikiLeaks released a large number of hacked emails from the Democratic National Committee suggesting that DNC chairwoman Debbie Wasserman Schultz may have taken steps to help Hillary Clinton win the Democratic primary. These allegations led to significant fallout among Democrats, especially those who had supported Bernie Sanders in the primaries, as some of the emails made several disparaging remarks about Sanders and his campaign manager, Jeff Weaver. The outrage over the emails was enough to force Wasserman Schultz to announce she would be stepping down after the Democratic National Convention in light of her involvement in the scandal.[26] The timing of the email leaks did little to support the Democrats' message of unity following the chaos and discord at the Republican convention the week before.

Once the Democratic National Convention got under way on July 25, it was clear that the rhetoric would be significantly different from the message at the Republican convention the previous week. The speakers, which included a number of prominent Democrats such as former President Bill Clinton, vice presidential nominee Tim Kaine, and President Barack Obama made a strong case for why the country needed to select Hillary Clinton to be the next president. Many viewers agreed that one of the most memorable and impassioned speeches was given by First Lady Michelle Obama on the third night of the convention. In her remarks she mentioned that "this election and every election is about who will have the power to shape our children for the next four or eight years of their lives." She continued by adding, "I am here tonight because in this election there is only one person who I trust with that responsibility, only one person who I believe is truly qualified to be president of the United States, and that is our friend Hillary Clinton."[27]

On the following evening Hillary Clinton made history as she became the first woman to accept the nomination for president of the United States. Her speech was a sharp contrast to the one given by Donald Trump the week before. Clinton emphasized the need for unity as well as putting aside our differences: "We have to decide whether we all will work together so we all can rise together." She also contrasted her message from that of her Republican opponent, who she mentioned was trying to divide the nation for political gain. In her own words, she stated, "That's why 'Stronger Together' is not just a lesson from our history. It's not just a slogan for our campaign. It's a guiding principle for the country we've always been and the future we're going to build."[28] According to the Nielsen ratings, approximately 33.7 million people tuned in to watch Clinton's convention speech, which was just shy of the 34.9 million who had watched Trump's speech the week before.[29]

It is often the case that nominating conventions provide a short-term boost in the polls to the candidate of the party holding them. After all, the party and its candidate receive a lot of attention, and they largely control what is seen and heard during the convention. In 2016, with the conventions so close together, it is difficult to be sure of the effects, but data from a CNN/ORC poll conducted immediately after the convention gave Trump a bounce of six points, three points ahead of Clinton in a head-to-head matchup.[30] Shortly after the Democratic National Convention wrapped up on July 28, an NBC News poll had Clinton leading Trump by eight points (50 to 42 percent) after a narrow lead several days prior following the conclusion of the Republican convention.[31] Clinton continued to maintain a small but modest lead over Trump during the month of August, when he received a growing amount of negative news coverage.

A series of news stories over the next four weeks would lead to a disastrous August for the Trump campaign. The downward spiral began on the third night of the Democratic convention when Trump tweeted, "If Russia or any other country or person has Hillary Clinton's 33,000 illegally deleted emails, perhaps they should share them with the FBI!" The campaign was forced to deny that Trump had "encouraged" a foreign nation to interfere with the U.S. election, a concern that would continue to hound them for the foreseeable future. The following evening the parents of Army Captain Humayun Khan, who had been killed in 2004 by an Iraqi suicide bomber, spoke at the Democratic convention and questioned whether Trump had even read the U.S. Constitution before pulling out a pocket-size version and stating, "I will gladly lend you my copy."[32] Trump could not resist the temptation to respond, and the situation continued to escalate over the next few days with most of the media criticism clearly directed at Trump's mishandling of the situation.

Following campaign rallies in both Ohio and Pennsylvania, Trump then suggested that the election might be "rigged" against him, a charge that he would bring up again later in the campaign. He also referred to Clinton at one of the rallies as "the devil" before suggesting that a crying baby be removed from a campaign event (to which he responded later that he was only kidding).[33] Then, in an August 2 interview with the *Washington Post*, Trump implied that he was not yet ready to endorse House Speaker Paul Ryan or Senator John McCain in their GOP primaries, which only served to further illustrate the deep divisions within the Republican Party.[34] During a press conference following Trump's remarks, President Obama declared Trump "unfit to serve as president" and "woefully unprepared to do this job." He also challenged Republican leaders to withdraw their support for their nominee in light of the latest series of critical news stories.[35]

Two days later a new series of polls showed that Clinton had a growing lead over Trump in states such as Florida, Michigan, New Hampshire, and Pennsylvania. Then, on August 5, a new *Atlanta-Journal Constitution* poll showed that Clinton was leading Trump in Georgia, a state that had supported every Republican presidential candidate since Bill Clinton in 1992.[36] Republicans were growing increasingly nervous at this point about Trump's chances of winning, but he showed little or no signs of greater discipline on the campaign trail. The following week a new CNN poll released on August 8 suggested that Clinton had a ten-point national lead over Trump, which further cemented mounting concerns within the Republican Party over Trump's candidacy.

Trump did little to assuage his critics when he spoke at a campaign rally in Wilmington, North Carolina, the following day. During the speech, he remarked, "Hillary wants to abolish—essentially abolish the Second Amendment. By the way, if she gets to pick, if she gets to pick her judges, nothing you can do, folks." After the crowd started booing, Trump added, "Although the Second Amendment people, maybe there is. I don't know."[37] Not surprisingly, Trump's remark set off a firestorm of protests among Democrats who quickly denounced suggestions of violence against Hillary Clinton or liberal judges. It also attracted the attention of the Secret Service, who takes any type of threat against presidential candidates very seriously. Clinton's running mate, Senator Tim Kaine, said that Trump's statement offers "a window into the soul of a person who is just temperamentally not suited to the task."[38] Even Republicans remarked that Trump's comment was a very poor joke at best.

Still reeling from his comment about the "Second Amendment people," Trump continued to push ahead by claiming that Obama and Clinton were the "cofounders" of ISIS and that any fallout was clearly their fault. It took several days before Trump backed off of this provocative claim and began referring to it as "sarcasm." At the same time he continued to mention that the election was "rigged" and that the media was completely biased against him.[39] When asked if he might adjust his approach during a CNBC interview in light of poll numbers that continued to trend downward, Trump rejected this suggestion and said that his plan was to "[j]ust keep doing the same thing I'm doing right now." He went on to add that "[a]nd at the end, it's either going to work or I'm going to, you know—I'm going to have a very, very nice, long vacation."[40]

Just days after insinuating that he could actually lose the election, Trump announced the most serious shake-up in his campaign staff since Lewandowski was fired as campaign manager in June. As noted earlier in the chapter, Trump brought Steve Bannon on board as the new CEO of his campaign, which many viewed as a strong signal that Trump wanted to continue to pursue a more aggressive style. Bannon had previously served as the executive chairman of Breitbart News, which had a reputation for hard-hitting conservative news. He also promoted senior adviser Kellyanne Conway to campaign manager. Whether or not these two actions would help to right the ship were not yet clear, but many within the Republican Party believed that it could hardly make things worse at this point in the campaign.[41]

Although August proved to be problematic for the Trump campaign, Clinton had to deal with two events in early September that generated much more media attention than her campaign probably would have expected. At a New York City fund-raising event held on September 9, Clinton remarked, "You know, just to be grossly generalistic, you could put half of Trump's supporters into what I call the basket of deplorables. Right? They're racist, sexist, homophobic, xenophobic, Islamophobic—you name it. And unfortunately there are people like that. And he has lifted them up." The following day Trump responded to Clinton's statement by tweeting, "Wow, Hillary Clinton was SO INSULTING to my supporters, millions of amazing, hard working people. I think it will cost her at the Polls!"[42] Clinton's "basket of deplorables" comment may have had a deleterious effect on the polls as the Trump campaign repeatedly used a clip of this statement in campaign ads throughout the fall.

At an event two days later commemorating the victims of the September 11 terrorist attacks, Clinton was recorded nearly collapsing afterward and was helped into her van by Secret Service agents. Two hours later she emerged from her daughter Chelsea's Manhattan apartment looking refreshed and ready to return to the campaign. Later that day her doctor reported that she was being treated for pneumonia and dehydration. This event in particular renewed concerns about whether Clinton was healthy enough to serve in office. "The incident, which occurred after months of questions about her health from her Republican opponent, Donald J. Trump, and his campaign, is likely to increase pressure on Mrs. Clinton to address the issue and release detailed medical records, which she has so far declined to do."[43] This issue would continue to come up during the next few weeks as questions of Clinton's health and "stamina" would be raised by the Trump campaign.

The Debates

In the days leading up to the first presidential debate, the presidential race had tightened up considerably, with Clinton clinging to a narrow two-point lead. Both candidates saw an opportunity for turning their polls around during the debate held at Hofstra University. In preparation for the first debate, Clinton maintained a lighter campaign schedule so that she could review prior debate performances by Trump and brush up on the important issues that would likely come up in the debate. "For her prep sessions, Clinton has reportedly surrounded herself with a team of strategists, including Ron Klain, former chief of staff to Vice President Joe Biden, and Karen Dunn, a Clinton adviser and former White House aide."[44] She also sought a variety of media and communication specialists such as Jim Margolis, Mandy Grunwald, and campaign chairman John Podesta, who could help her focus her message during the debate.[45]

In contrast to Clinton, Trump seemed to favor a different style of preparing for the first debate. When asked about his strategies for debating Clinton, Trump often seemed to rely on his comfort and past exposure to the media spotlight. In one of the more revealing statements about his debate preparation, Trump mentioned, "Obviously I will be practicing, but I don't want to put so much practice in that all of a sudden, you're not who you are."[46] In a story reported by National Public Radio on the debate, it was suggested, "One way Trump may have been preparing already is by giving a number of scripted speeches on the campaign trail in recent weeks, as opposed to the freewheeling style he adopted at rallies through most of the campaign. Those speeches have allowed Trump to practice delivering more measured and detailed versions of his pitch to voters."[47]

During the actual debate a number of topics were addressed ranging from jobs, gender, national security, and taxes. Early on in the debate, when Trump was asked to clarify a remark he had made that Clinton lacked a certain presidential "look," he responded by saying, "She doesn't have the stamina. To be president of this country, you need tremendous stamina. You have to be able to negotiate." In response to this specific critique, Clinton remarked, "As soon as he travels to 112 countries and negotiates a peace deal, a cease fire, a release of dissidents, an opening of new opportunities in nations around the world, or even spends 11 hours testifying in front of a congressional committee, he can talk to me about stamina." To this she added, "He tried to change from looks to stamina, but this is a man who has called women pigs, slobs and dogs."[48]

Throughout the course of the debate, both candidates managed to get in a few memorable one-liners when answering questions and discussing their specific policy positions. When asked if he would release his tax returns, Trump repeated the refrain that he was facing a routine audit that precluded him from distributing this information. The moderator challenged this assertion, to which Trump responded by saying that he would go against his lawyers' wishes and release his returns if Clinton agreed to release approximately 33,000 emails that had been deleted from her private server.[49] Later on in the debate, when discussing his plans to lower taxes on wealthy Americans while also mixing in additional critiques of Clinton, she remarked, "I have a feeling that by the end of this evening, I'm going to be blamed for everything that's ever happened," to which Trump replied, "Why not?"[50]

The audience for the first presidential debate was substantial. In total approximately 84 million viewers tuned into the thirteen stations that carried the debate live, making it the most watched presidential debate in American history. In reality the viewership was even higher because many individuals ended up watching the debate online.[51] By the next morning the media consensus was that Clinton was the winner of the first debate. According to a Gallup poll released later in the week, "Americans who saw the debate believed Clinton was the runaway victor, 61 percent to Trump's 27 percent."[52] Clinton also seemed to dominate Trump on several dimensions. "On all the characteristics Gallup asked voters about, Clinton prevailed over Trump: she appeared to be more inspiring (46 percent to Trump's 34 percent), was more likable (55 to 36 percent), appeared presidential (59 percent to 27 percent), and exhibited a better understanding of the issues (62 to 26 percent)."[53]

Next in the debate sequence was the vice-presidential debate held on October 4. Not surprisingly, it received far less attention than the presidential events. Trump's running mate, Mike Pence of Indiana, sought to soften his image and "put a calmer, gentler face on the 2016 Republican ticket."[54] Senator Tim Kaine, in contrast, used the forum to remind voters about all of the negative comments Trump had made on the campaign trail and asked Pence to explain them. As a former talk-radio host, Pence was able to deflect most of Kaine's criticisms, and a CNN/ORC poll that came out days later suggested that 48 percent of those who tuned into the debate thought Pence had won compared with only 42 percent saying Kaine won.[55] In the end, however, it did little to move poll numbers for the two presidential candidates, as is typically the case.[56]

Just days before the second presidential debate, a shocking news story broke that turned out to be the first "October surprise" in the campaign. "Trump's campaign was sent reeling on Friday after a private tape was published in which the reality TV star bragged about groping, kissing and attempting to have sex with married women—and said he was entitled to do so because he's a 'star.'"[57] The *Washington Post* first reported the story, indicating that the video was from a 2005 *Access Hollywood* interview that host Billy Bush conducted with Trump.[58] Following the release of the shocking video, described by some as the worst October surprise that any campaign has ever suffered, there were immediate calls for Trump to step down as the Republican nominee. Numerous insiders expressed concerns that they did not know how their candidate could survive this.[59]

In response to the firestorm of criticism that erupted, Trump issued a rare apology late Friday evening. "I never said that I'm a perfect person nor pretended to be someone I'm not. I've said and done things I regret and the words released today on this decade old video are one of them. Anyone who knows me knows these words don't reflect who I am. I said it, I was wrong, and I apologize." Had Trump stopped there, the fallout might have been very different. But Trump continued with the following controversial remarks, "I've said some foolish things but there's a big difference between the words and actions of other people. Bill Clinton has actually abused women and Hillary has bullied, attacked, shamed, and intimidated his victims."[60]

Not surprisingly these extra remarks set off additional protests that did little to silence critics of Donald Trump in the days ahead. In fact as many as nine different women came forward following the release of the tape claiming that Trump had assaulted them at some point in the past.[61] Although some within the Trump campaign questioned the timing of these charges and accusations, they forced Trump and his team to immediately go on the defensive. Trump responded to the growing criticisms by tweeting, "The media and establishment want me out of the race so badly—I WILL NEVER DROP OUT OF THE RACE, WILL NEVER LET MY SUPPORTERS DOWN."[62]

Two days later the second presidential debate took place in St. Louis, Missouri. Still stinging from news stories surrounding the tape, Trump elected to go on the offensive by inviting several women who had made sexual harassment accusations in the past against Bill Clinton to attend the debate and sit in the front row. The subject of the 2005 tape came up early on in the debate, and Trump continued to downplay his comments—"It's just words, folks"—whereas Clinton used his remarks to remind the audience how little respect he had for women. She also added, "He never apologizes for anything to anyone."[63] Later on in the debate, when Clinton stated it was a good thing Trump is not in charge of the law, Trump responded, "Because you'd be in jail."[64] In the aftermath of the debate, the public's view of the results were much closer than after the first debate, with respondents to an NBC poll choosing Clinton as the winner by 44 to 34 percent.

The final presidential debate, on October 19, was supposed to focus on entitlements and the debt, immigration, the economy, and the Supreme Court, but the discussion quickly veered off into Russian influence in the campaign, whether the election was rigged, and the candidates' fitness to be president. At one point, while discussing Russia's role in the presidential election, Clinton remarked, "Russia is trying to influence the election. Putin would prefer to have a puppet," to which Trump immediately responded, "You're the puppet." Later on in the debate, when asked repeatedly by the moderator whether Donald Trump would accept the results of the election, he simply responded by saying, "I will look at it at the time. I will tell you at the time. I will keep you in suspense."[65] Finally, while Clinton was answering a question about social security taxes at the end of the debate and remarking that her "social security payroll contributions will go up as will Donald's assuming he can't figure out how to get out of it," Trump leaned into the microphone and stated, "Such a nasty woman." This comment served to undermine his earlier remarks about respecting women and became a rallying cry for women in the waning days of the campaign.[66] According to a CNN/ORC poll, Clinton was the winner of the debate by a thirteen-point margin, giving her a clean sweep over Trump in all three presidential debates.[67]

The consensus among political scientists is that presidential debates usually do not have a significant impact on a race.[68] The most prominent explanation is that by the time the debates occur, the vast majority of voters have made up their minds and are thus unlikely to have their position reversed by the event. There are, however, a few exceptions where some analysts perceive a greater impact. These include 1960 (Kennedy vs. Nixon), 1976 (Ford vs. Carter), 1984 (Reagan vs. Mondale), and 2012 (Obama vs. Romney).[69] Robert Erikson and Christopher Wlezien took a systematic look at the ten presidential elections with debates (1960 and 1976–2008), comparing the poll standings of candidates before and after the debates. They found that with one exception, the pre-debate polls were closely matched by the post-debate polls (the exception was 1976, when Carter was already in decline before the debates and the decline persisted). They conclude that debates do not have as great an impact as the conventions (the effect of which they find to be substantial) but that they may have as much or more effect than other campaign events.[70]

It appears, however, that 2016 may be another exception. Data from Real Clear Politics (which averages results for all major polls over a time interval) shows that on September 26, the day of the first debate, Clinton had a 2.3 percent lead in the poll averages, while on October 19 (the last debate's date), Clinton led by 6.5 percent.[71] That amounted to a four-point swing in favor of Clinton during the course of the debates, which initially suggested that Trump might have a difficult time turning the tide around before the election.

THE END GAME AND THE STRUGGLE OVER TURNOUT

The Final Two Weeks

In the days following the third debate, both candidates continued to campaign in swing states around the country, repeating their respective messages about how each of them offered a better alternative for the country than their opponent. Clinton seemed to capitalize immensely on her final debate performance as a ABC News tracking poll that came out a few days following the third debate showed her leading Trump 50 percent to 38 percent in a four-way race (with Libertarian Party nominee Gary Johnson earning 5 percent and Green Party nominee Jill Stein earning about 2 percent in the poll). The poll reflected the highest level of public support for Clinton of any survey taken by ABC News during the fall and the lowest for Trump.[72] Some analysts interpreted this new poll as evidence that Clinton was making inroads among voters that had traditionally supported Trump throughout the fall campaign.[73]

The good news for the Clinton camp ended up being short-lived, however, as potentially unsettling news broke just eleven days before the election. "The FBI on Friday dropped a bombshell on Hillary Clinton's campaign less than two weeks before Election Day, with Director James Comey telling lawmakers that the agency is reviewing new evidence in its investigation into her use of a private email server as secretary of state."[74] The new evidence was prompted by an investigation into an unrelated case where the FBI discovered emails that could be relevant to Clinton's case. Although Comey did not elaborate on where the emails originated from, it was later learned that they were discovered "out of the probe into (former Congressman) Anthony Weiner, the estranged husband of Clinton aide Huma Abedin who is under investigation for allegedly sexting a teenage girl."[75] According to a *New York Times* story, the FBI seized several devices from Weiner as part of their ongoing probe and discovered the additional emails.[76]

News of the renewed FBI investigation into Clinton's emails broke as she was on the way to a campaign event in Iowa, where she waved off reporter's questions as she was getting off the plane. "Clinton's campaign initially appeared blindsided by the development."[77] Nevertheless, it did not take long before her surrogates began hitting back about the news, especially given the close proximity to the November election. Clinton's campaign chairman, John Podesta, referred to the timing of the announcement as "extraordinary." In an interview on MSNBC, Brian Fallon, Clinton's national press secretary said, "It boggles the mind why this step was taken today. As it is, we now have the worst of all worlds here. He aired this in an extraordinary step and the public doesn't have any way to judge the significance of this and what it has to do with Clinton."[78] Tim Kaine, Clinton's running mate, also mentioned that he found the FBI's handling of the renewed investigation as "very, very troubling" and that the FBI "should give a clear accounting of what's going on right now."[79]

While the Clinton team was scrambling to deal with the late-breaking October surprise, Trump took full advantage of the situation when the news broke. During a campaign rally in New Hampshire, Trump led off by saying, "Hillary Clinton's corruption is on a scale that we have never seen before. We must not let her take her criminal scheme into the Oval Office. I have great respect for the fact that the FBI and the Department of Justice are now willing to have the courage to right the horrible mistake that they made."[80] Trump's comments were met with cheers of "lock her up," a now common refrain at his campaign rallies. He continued his remarks by adding, "This was a grave miscarriage of justice that the American people fully understood, and it is everybody's hope that it is about to be corrected."[81]

In the days following Comey's announcement, the polls for the presidential race began to tighten up significantly. What started out as a five-point advantage for Clinton on the day the story broke quickly turned into a narrow one-point lead over Trump according to polling trends on Real Clear Politics.[82] Clinton continued to try to downplay the story in the days before the election, whereas the Trump campaign repeatedly emphasized it at campaign rallies around the country. When FBI Director Comey announced on November 6, two days before the election, that his agency's review of the new emails did not change his previous conclusion that Clinton should not be prosecuted for her behavior, many on both sides wondered if the damage had already been done.[83]

Mobilizing the Vote

In 2004 the Republicans had a distinct advantage with respect to mobilizing and turning out voters on election day. The Democrats significantly reversed this trend in 2008, leading to the highest turnout in a presidential election since 1968.[84] Four years later the Democrats' voter identification and mobilization efforts took a big leap forward in terms of both technology and effort.[85] When Jim Messina took on the job of Obama's campaign manager, he said: "We are going to measure every single thing in this campaign."[86] Messina "hired an analytics department five times the size that of the 2008 campaign."[87] These analysts believed that the product of their efforts—their data—was the principal advantage President Obama had over his opponent, and they guarded it diligently.

In 2016 both parties continued using new data analytic techniques to mobilize voters, but this strategy has become increasingly difficult as the country has become more polarized. In the past campaigns sought to persuade undecideds to go to the polls, while they simultaneously reached out to loyal partisans to vote. More recently, however, candidates and parties have had to adapt to a new reality in light of the decreasing number of "swing voters." "The goal is now to mobilize the most loyal voters rather than lure in the undecided or persuade the other party's voters to change sides."[88] One direct consequence of this change is that an increasing number of voters tend to be stronger partisans who are less likely to defect than independents or those who only weakly lean toward one party in particular.

The shift away from persuasion to one of increasing turnout among loyalists had vastly different effects across the two campaigns. "For the Trump campaign, this mobilization strategy meant trying hard to inspire disenchanted working-class whites in heavily Republican areas, giving them something to get excited about in Donald Trump's anti-establishment white identity politics."[89] Trump did not attempt to reach out to voters who were not already disposed to vote for him as his campaign recognized the futility of such effort. Clinton, on the other hand, sought to repeat the success of the Obama campaign in 2008 and 2012 in getting voters to turn out on election day. "For Democrats, this meant investing in large-scale get-out-the-vote operation on the premise that the 'Obama coalition' of black and Hispanic voters and young educated whites could be sustained by enough field offices and data analytics."[90]

Whereas the Trump campaign was relying largely on the support of white voters to win the election, Clinton and her surrogates recognized the value of reaching out to a broad coalition of ethnic voters, including Hispanics. Even before Trump emerged as the Republican nominee, the Democrats had been laying the groundwork to attract new Hispanic voters by spending millions of dollars in outreach efforts. Clinton also saw an advantage in carefully positioning herself on immigration, especially when it came to the issue of how to deal with undocumented immigrants. "From the beginning of her campaign, Mrs. Clinton and her team saw untapped potential in the 27 million Hispanics who would be eligible to vote in 2016, a 26 percent increase since 2012."[91] Although turnout among Hispanics is traditionally lower than among other groups, the task was perhaps easier in 2016 in light of Trump's repeated assertions about illegal immigration as well as his description of immigrants as "murderers and rapists." Indeed her efforts appeared to pay off during the initial weeks of early voting. "Energized by anger at Mr. Trump and an aggressive Democratic campaign to get them to the polls, Latinos are turning out in record numbers and could make the difference in the outcome in several highly contested states."[92]

One can see the differences in the candidates' campaign strategies as reflected by their placement of presidential campaign field offices during 2016 as shown in Figure 2-2 (data from 2012 is included for comparison purposes). For instance Clinton had 511 field offices across the country in forty-nine different states with Wisconsin being the only exception. In twenty-seven of these forty-nine states, she had only one field office, presumably because these states were not considered competitive electorally. In contrast Trump had only 145 field offices across the country in eighteen total states. In five states he had only one office, and in thirty-two he had none. Although the pattern for the placement of Trump's field offices is less clear, it appears that many were located in the Midwest or mid-Atlantic region, where the Trump campaign believed those states were in play.[93] Overall the 2016 placements reflect a significant decline from the 2012 campaign, in which both candidates had more field offices— Obama had a total of 755 offices across the country, whereas Romney had 283, nearly twice as many as Trump in 2016.

As noted earlier Clinton had a distinct fund-raising advantage over Trump in the general election, which continued into the final month of the presidential campaign. This, in turn, led many to believe that Clinton would have an edge in getting voters to the polls. During the third quarter of 2016, Clinton's joint fund-raising with the Democratic National Committee yielded slightly more than $261 million based on Federal Election Commission reports. "By comparison, the equivalent Trump Victory Fund, which coordinates with the Republican National Committee and state parties, raised less than one-quarter of Clinton's haul—$61 million."[94] Nevertheless, Trump did receive a tremendous amount of free media coverage over the course of the primary and general election campaign as a result of his "celebrity" status. "According to data-driven analytics firm mediaQuant, Trump received around $5 billion in free media coverage, more than twice that garnered by Clinton."[95] How that much free coverage from the media would translate into increased voter turnout was unclear in the days leading up to the election.

The Final Days

As noted the Real Clear Politics average of polls showed Clinton with slightly more than a five-point lead over Trump two weeks before the election. Once news broke of the FBI's renewed interest in Clinton's emails, however, the presidential race immediately began to tighten up. By November 3, Clinton's lead over Trump had been reduced to 1.3 percent. Then, over the next few days, Clinton began to open up a small lead, and on election day, she led by a margin of 3.2 points in the poll average. It was hardly a safe cushion, and the outcome remained in doubt, but many Democrats felt a growing confidence that Clinton would eventually win. The fact that the race had tightened up considerably gave both candidates reason to be optimistic, and the campaigns launched the final effort to appeal to voters in the last days before the election.

As is often the case, presidential candidates maintain a rigorous schedule during the last weekend before an election in an attempt to deliver their personal message to voters one last time. "Hillary Clinton and Mr. Trump used the final Saturday before Election Day to make their closing pitches to voters, with Mrs. Clinton in South Florida and Philadelphia and Mr. Trump dashing to four states across three time zones—the sort of barnstorming tours presidential candidates have traditionally made in the last 72 hours before Election Day."[96] Both candidates and their surrogates also spent a considerable amount of time in New Hampshire just prior to the election given its status as an important swing state.[97]

During the closing days of the campaign, Clinton avoided discussing her emails as well as Comey's decision to reopen the investigation so close to election day. Instead

Figure 2-2 Location of Presidential Campaign Field Offices, 2012 and 2016

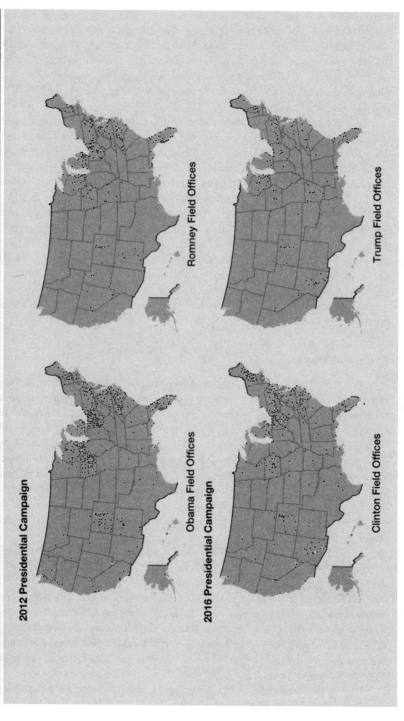

2012 Presidential Campaign

Obama Field Offices

Romney Field Offices

2016 Presidential Campaign

Clinton Field Offices

Trump Field Offices

Source: Field office information and addresses were gathered by the authors from the official campaign websites on the weekends before the respective election days. The authors used Google Maps to identify the longitude and latitude coordinates for each office.

she spent most of her time on the campaign trail talking about salient issues such as raising the minimum wage, providing affordable child care, and granting tuition-free college education for the middle class. She also sought to reassure voters that in light of the harsh rhetoric used throughout the fall campaign, it was important for the next president to find a way to bridge the growing divide in this country. "We will have some work to do to bring about healing and reconciliation after this election. We have to begin listening to one another and respecting one another."[98]

Trump's message in the final days sought to reiterate many of the same themes that he had emphasized throughout the campaign. In addition to reiterating the claim that Hillary was "too corrupt" to be president, he discussed the importance of cutting taxes on businesses to help stimulate the economy, increasing funding for the military, terminating NAFTA, and building the wall along the Mexican border. Trump also reemphasized the need to deal with what he perceived as the growing immigration problem in the country. At one campaign stop over the weekend in New Hampshire, he declared, "And we will keep radical Islamic terrorists the hell out of our country."[99]

DID THE CAMPAIGN MAKE A DIFFERENCE?

It is appropriate to ask whether the general election campaign made any difference, and the answer depends on the yardstick used to measure the campaign's effects. Did it determine the winner? Did it encourage voters to go to the polls? Did it affect the choices of a substantial number of voters? Did it put issues and candidates' positions clearly before the voters? Would a better campaign by one of the major party candidates have yielded a different result? Did the campaign produce significant events that will have a lasting impact on American politics? We cannot provide firm answers to all of these questions, but we can shed light on some of them.

Regarding the outcome and voters' decisions, it seems clear that the campaign did indeed have an effect.[100] As noted the relative standing of the candidates ebbed and flowed from the conventions to November, and these changes seemed to be linked in part to events in the campaign. Both candidates clearly got a boost from their respective conventions, but Clinton's seemed to last longer, especially given the series of gaffes that Donald Trump and his campaign endured during the month of August. Clinton also seemed to do well in each of the three debates after a rough start in September. However, the renewed investigation by the FBI into Clinton's emails with less than two weeks until the election clearly affected the closeness of the race, especially because the FBI did not seem to be investing equal time into allegations that Russia might be trying to influence the presidential election. In the final few days of the campaign, most of the undecideds seemed to move toward Trump, which may have played a key role in him carrying states like Michigan, Pennsylvania, and Wisconsin in the Rust Belt.[101]

Perhaps the best evidence of the campaign's impact relates to turnout. As noted earlier many Republicans thought they had an advantage in 2016 because the Democrats had controlled the White House for the previous eight years and the electorate would be less favorable to them than it had been in either 2008 or 2012. Although Trump's missteps throughout the fall left a number of Republicans worried about the election outcome, the returns coming in at and around 9:00 p.m. on election night seemed to suggest the race would be a lot closer than expected. In key states such as Michigan, North Carolina, Ohio, Pennsylvania, Virginia, and Wisconsin, the race was simply too close to call based on exit poll data, suggesting that much of the previous polling in these states had been mistaken. If turnout among white voters was higher than expected across these states and African Americans and Hispanics did not turn out in as great of numbers as some anticipated, there was a chance that Trump could turn the tide in the election. In the end this is what happened as exit polls showed Trump won the white vote by a record margin (58 to 37 percent) and turnout among ethnic groups and women was lower than expected.[102]

The success of the presidential candidates' mobilization effort is indicated by the turnout data compiled for 2012 and 2016 by Michael McDonald of the University of Florida.[103] The data show that the national turnout rate increased by 1.6 points, from 58.6 percent to 60.2 percent. The increase, however, was not equal across the battleground states. Table 2-1 lists the thirteen battleground states and their turnout in the two elections. In seven of the thirteen states, turnout increased relative to 2012, whereas it declined in the remaining six. Trump ended up winning a majority of the battleground states—including key Rust Belt states that traditionally vote for the Democratic candidate—which is surprising given the limited number of field offices in many of these states relative to Clinton and despite lingering concerns about his ability to win. At the same time it appears that Trump did better in states with slightly lower-than-average turnout.[104]

There is also the question of whether a better campaign by a candidate, specifically by Clinton, would have led to a different result. Many observers expressed the view that a better campaign by Clinton could have carried the race. "In anointing Clinton, the Democrats went all in with a candidate despised by a good portion of the country. . . . Warning signs of trouble came early and often in her campaign, but she failed to heed them. She was overly cautious, effectively staying on a course of political destruction rather than learning from mistakes along the way."[105] Critics also claimed that her campaign did not go far enough in attempting to reach out to voters who had supported Sanders over her in the primary by making a bolder vice presidential pick such as Sanders or Elizabeth Warren. "Failing to fire up her own side only exacerbated how much she fired up her opposition. . . . Her incendiary 'basket of deplorables' and other remarks flourished on the internet and fit into the narrative of people who spread an anti-Hillary gospel."[106]

Some were even of the dubious opinion that had Sanders won the Democratic primary, he might have had a better shot of defeating Trump in the election. When asked by the *Washington Post* several days after the election if he could have beaten Trump, Sanders responded by simply saying, "I hesitate to be a Monday morning quarterback. In my heart of hearts, I think there's a good chance I could have defeated Trump, but who knows."[107] When his wife Jane was asked the same question the week before on CNN, she replied, "Absolutely, but it doesn't matter now."[108] Not everyone shared these opinions about Sanders's likely victory over Trump in the election, however. At least one postelection commentary criticized this perspective by saying that most of the candidates that Sanders endorsed ended up underperforming in the

Table 2-1   Change in Turnout in Battleground States and Nationally, 2012–2016

	Turnout 2012	Turnout 2016	Change 2012–2016
National	58.6	60.2	+1.6
Colorado	70.6	72.1	+1.5
Florida	63.3	65.8	+2.5
Iowa	70.6	69.0	−1.6
Michigan	65.4	65.7	+0.3
Minnesota	76.4	74.8	−1.6
Nevada	56.5	57.3	+0.8
New Hampshire	70.9	72.5	+1.6
New Mexico	54.8	55.2	+0.4
North Carolina	65.4	65.2	−0.2
Ohio	65.1	64.2	−0.9
Pennsylvania	59.5	63.0	+3.5
Virginia	66.6	66.1	−0.5
Wisconsin	72.9	69.4	−3.5

Source: Data are from the United States Elections Project, http://www.electproject.org/, accessed February 7, 2017.

election, which says a lot about how he might have done himself had he been on the ballot instead of Clinton.[109] Moreover, this perspective fails to account for the fact that Clinton won the popular tally by more than 2.86 million votes but ended up losing the Electoral College as a result of near misses in states like Michigan, Pennsylvania, and Wisconsin, where she failed to spend time or money in the waning days of the campaign.[110]

Additionally campaigns without an incumbent are usually close, and close elections can go either way. One should not expect the positives from Obama's performance to easily transfer to Clinton, his former secretary of state. Nevertheless, Clinton did carry the popular vote despite failing to achieve a majority in the Electoral

College (like Al Gore did in 2000). This was the seventh presidential race with no incumbent since the Second World War (the others were 1952, 1960, 1968, 1988, 2000, and 2008). The elections of 1960, 1968, and 2000 were closer races in terms of the popular vote, and even though Bush's father won fairly easily in 1988, he had trailed in the polls that year as well.

Finally, and perhaps most consequential for the outcome of the election, Clinton seemed to be at a strategic disadvantage as a result of having to run against Sanders in the primary and having both Gary Johnson and Jill Stein in the race during the fall campaign. Many Democrats who had strongly supported Sanders, especially younger voters, seemed to reluctantly embrace Clinton once she won the Democratic nomination. In the fall Johnson and Stein were polling as high as 8 and 4 percent, respectively, in some pre-election polls, which may indicate that voters were looking for candidates other than Clinton and Trump to support in the election. The fact that Johnson earned at least 2.4 percent of the vote in very close states like Pennsylvania and Michigan may have been just enough to shift the Electoral College vote in favor of Trump.

CHAPTER THREE

THE ELECTION RESULTS

In the closing days of the bitter campaign, it appeared that Hillary Clinton held an electoral advantage. Analysis of early voting patterns in several swing states suggested that Clinton's ground game advantage was paying dividends—registered Democrats were turning out at higher rates than registered Republicans.[1] Donald Trump, who had been calling the election "rigged" in the weeks leading to election day, responded to reports of early voting trends with additional skepticism: "Do you think these ballots are properly counted," Trump asked supporters in Colorado; "do you think?"[2] The polls also suggested a Clinton victory was on the horizon. The average (mean) of ten national public opinion polls conducted during the final week of the campaign showed Clinton with 46.8 percent of the vote and Trump with 43.6 percent, a seemingly comfortable lead for the Democratic nominee.[3] Indeed these ten polls were decidedly pointed in Clinton's favor: six predicted a Clinton victory of greater than four percentage points, three predicted a Clinton victory in the one to three point range, and only one national poll predicted a Trump victory (by a margin of three points). A series of academic models were similarly predictive of a Clinton electoral victory.[4] In October 2016, James E. Campbell published the results of eleven statistical forecasts for the presidential election.[5] The median prediction from these models projected that Clinton would win 51.1 percent of the two-party vote. Nine of the eleven models forecasted a Clinton win, whereas only two predicted Trump's popular vote victory. Importantly, none of these polls or models of the election predicted the Electoral College outcome, only the popular vote.

All eyes were on New York on election day, November 8, as for the first time since 1944 both major party nominees hailed from the same state.[6] Both candidates held last-minute campaign events that bled into election day before returning to New York to cast their ballots. Clinton had taken part in an election-eve rally in Philadelphia that featured her husband, as well as President Obama and First Lady Michelle Obama, and was punctuated by musical performances by Jon Bon Jovi and Bruce Springsteen.[7] She then jetted to Raleigh, North Carolina, where she was joined by Lady Gaga for a 1:00 a.m. rally.[8] Trump made his final campaign stop shortly after midnight in Grand Rapids, Michigan, a state that last voted for a Republican presidential candidate in 1988. It was his eleventh campaign stop in two days, a trip that covered seven states and three time zones.[9] Despite being the oldest two candidates to ever square off in a presidential contest, Clinton and Trump both sprinted to the proverbial finish line before returning to their respective homes in the wee hours of election day morning.[10] And both were back at it within hours. Clinton and her husband arrived at the Douglas Grafflin Elementary School in Chappaqua, New York, at 8:00 a.m. to vote. She described casting a ballot for herself as "the most humbling experience, you know, I know how much responsibility goes with this and so many people are counting on the outcome of this election."[11] Trump and his wife, Melania, arrived at P.S. 59 in midtown Manhattan a few hours later to cast their votes. Trump joked with reporters that it was a "tough decision" and then noted presciently, "We'll see what happens; it's going to be an interesting day."[12]

The campaigns' election night parties were held a mere twenty-five blocks from each other.[13] Trump supporters—many of whom were wearing the campaign's now ubiquitous, red "Make American Great Again" baseball caps—had gathered at the New York Hilton Midtown. But the lasting images of the night are likely those that were witnessed at the Clinton campaign party at the Javits Convention Center on Manhattan's West Side, where excitement turned to shock and then despair. The Clinton supporters' optimism as the night began was not unfounded; the electoral map seemed to present a very difficult path to victory for Trump. The toss-up states on the electoral map were Florida, Iowa, North Carolina, and Ohio—three of these had voted Democrat in the last two elections, whereas North Carolina supported Obama in 2008 but not in 2012. The Trump campaign believed that Michigan, Pennsylvania, and Wisconsin were also in play, but these states had voted Democrat in each election since 1992. There are, of course, various routes to an Electoral College victory, but the numerical advantage that Clinton garnered from "safe" Democratic states meant that she needed far fewer of the toss-up states to win than Trump required.[14] Expectations started to give way to reality around 10:21 p.m., however, when Ohio was called for Trump. At 11:07 p.m., North Carolina went Trump's way, followed soon thereafter by Florida and Iowa.[15] Early returns from the other toss-up states—all of them!—were also leaning toward Trump. Around 2:00 a.m., Clinton's campaign chairman, John Podesta, took the Javits Center stage to inform the shocked and tearful crowd that their candidate did not plan to speak and that "everybody should head home."[16] Forty minutes later, Clinton called Trump to concede the race.

Donald Trump had pulled off a shocking and decided Electoral College victory, capturing 304 electoral votes to Hillary Clinton's 227. But the Electoral College outcome does not adequately capture the level of political division within the 2016 electorate. Indeed Trump became the fourth presidential candidate to win the Electoral College without winning the popular vote.[17] In the final tally, Clinton won a 48.2 percent plurality of the popular vote, while Trump won 46.1 percent. Discontent with the two major-party candidates was made evident by the fact that independent and third-party candidates garnered 5.7 percent of the total popular vote in 2016, four percentage points higher than in 2012. Leading the way were Libertarian Gary Johnson, who garnered 3.3 percent of the national popular vote, and Green Party nominee, Jill Stein, who won 1.1 percent.[18] Clinton's popular vote margin of 2.1 percentage points makes 2016 the ninth closest presidential election in U.S. history and the closest since 2000, when Democrat Al Gore claimed a 0.51 percentage point popular vote victory over Republican George W. Bush, only to lose the Electoral College.

Table 3-1 presents the official 2016 election results by state and includes those for Maine's two congressional districts and Nebraska's three districts.[19] Clinton won

Table 3-1 Presidential Election Results by State, 2016

State	Total Vote	Clinton (Dem.)	Trump (Rep.)	Other	Two-party Differential		Total Vote (%)	
							Dem.	Rep.
Alabama	2,123,372	729,547	1,318,255	75,570	588,708	R	34.4	62.1
Alaska	318,608	116,454	163,387	38,767	46,933	R	36.6	51.3
Arizona	2,573,165	1,161,167	1,252,401	159,597	91,234	R	45.1	48.7
Arkansas	1,130,635	380,494	684,872	65,269	304,378	R	33.7	60.6
California	14,181,595	8,753,788	4,483,810	943,997	4,269,978	D	61.7	31.6
Colorado	2,780,247	1,338,870	1,202,484	238,893	136,386	D	48.2	43.3
Connecticut	1,644,920	897,572	673,215	74,133	224,357	D	54.6	40.9
Delaware	443,814	235,603	185,127	23,084	50,476	D	53.1	41.7
Florida	9,420,039	4,504,975	4,617,886	297,178	112,911	R	47.8	49.0
Georgia	4,114,732	1,877,963	2,089,104	147,665	211,141	R	45.6	50.8
Hawaii	428,937	266,891	128,847	33,199	138,044	D	62.2	30.0
Idaho	690,255	189,765	409,055	91,435	219,290	R	27.5	59.3

(Continued)

71

72

Table 3-1 (Continued)

State	Total Vote	Clinton (Dem.)	Trump (Rep.)	Other	Two-party Differential		Total Vote (%)	
							Dem.	Rep.
Illinois	5,536,424	3,090,729	2,146,015	299,680	944,714	D	55.8	38.8
Indiana	2,734,958	1,033,126	1,557,286	144,546	524,160	R	37.8	56.9
Iowa	1,566,031	653,669	800,983	111,379	147,314	R	41.7	51.1
Kansas	1,184,402	427,005	671,018	86,379	244,013	R	36.1	56.7
Kentucky	1,924,149	628,854	1,202,971	92,324	574,117	R	32.7	62.5
Louisiana	1,994,065	780,154	1,178,638	35,273	398,484	R	39.1	59.1
Maine[a]	747,927	357,735	335,593	54,599	22,142	D	47.8	44.9
Maryland	2,781,446	1,677,928	943,169	160,349	734,759	D	60.3	33.9
Massachusetts	3,325,046	1,995,196	1,090,893	238,957	904,303	D	60.0	32.8
Michigan	4,799,284	2,268,839	2,279,543	250,902	10,704	R	47.3	47.5
Minnesota	2,944,813	1,367,716	1,322,951	254,146	44,765	D	46.4	44.9
Mississippi	1,209,357	485,131	710,746	13,480	225,615	R	40.1	58.8

State	Total Vote	Clinton (Dem.)	Trump (Rep.)	Other	Two-party Differential		Total Vote (%) Dem.	Rep.
Missouri	2,808,605	1,071,068	1,594,511	143,026	523,443	R	38.1	56.8
Montana	497,147	177,709	279,240	40,198	101,531	R	35.7	56.2
Nebraska[b]	844,227	284,494	495,961	63,772	211,467	R	33.7	58.7
Nevada	1,125,385	539,260	512,058	74,067	27,202	D	47.9	45.5
New Hampshire	744,296	348,526	345,790	49,980	2,736	D	46.8	46.5
New Jersey	3,874,046	2,148,278	1,601,933	123,835	546,345	D	55.5	41.4
New Mexico	798,319	385,234	319,667	93,418	65,567	D	48.3	40.0
New York	7,721,453	4,556,124	2,819,534	345,795	1,736,590	D	59.0	36.5
North Carolina	4,741,564	2,189,316	2,362,631	189,617	173,315	R	46.2	49.8
North Dakota	344,360	93,758	216,794	33,418	123,036	R	27.2	63.0
Ohio	5,496,487	2,394,164	2,841,005	261,318	446,841	R	43.6	51.7
Oklahoma	1,452,992	420,375	949,136	83,481	528,761	R	28.9	65.3
Oregon	2,001,336	1,002,106	782,403	216,318	219,703	D	50.1	39.1
Pennsylvania	6,165,478	2,926,441	2,970,733	268,304	44,292	R	47.5	48.2

(Continued)

73

Table 3-1 (Continued)

State	Total Vote	Clinton (Dem.)	Trump (Rep.)	Other	Two-party Differential		Total Vote (%)	
							Dem.	Rep.
Rhode Island	446,144	252,525	180,543	13,076	122,473	D	56.6	40.5
South Carolina	2,103,027	855,373	1,155,389	92,265	300,016	R	40.7	54.9
South Dakota	370,093	117,458	227,721	24,914	110,263	R	31.7	61.5
Tennessee	2,508,027	870,695	1,522,925	114,407	652,263	R	34.7	60.7
Texas	8,969,226	3,877,868	4,685,047	406,311	807,179	R	43.2	52.2
Utah	1,131,430	310,676	515,231	305,523	204,555	R	27.5	45.5
Vermont	315,067	178,573	95,369	41,125	83,204	D	56.7	30.3
Virginia	3,984,631	1,981,473	1,769,443	233,715	212,030	D	49.7	44.4
Washington	3,317,019	1,742,718	1,221,747	352,554	520,971	D	52.5	36.8
West Virginia	714,423	188,794	489,371	36,258	300,577	R	26.4	68.5
Wisconsin	2,976,150	1,382,536	1,405,284	188,330	22,748	R	46.5	47.2
Wyoming	255,849	55,973	174,419	25,457	118,446	R	21.9	68.2
District of Columbia	311,268	282,830	12,723	15,715	270,107	D	90.9	4.1
United States	136,669,237	65,853,516	62,984,825	7,830,896	2,868,691	D	48.2	46.1

Source: Federal Election Commission, "Official 2016 Presidential General Election Results," January 30, 2017, https://transition.fec.gov/pubrec/fe2016/2016presgeresults.pdf. Based on reports of the secretaries of state of the fifty states and the District of Columbia.

[a]In Maine the statewide plurality vote winner gained two votes, and each of the state's two congressional districts was awarded one vote on a plurality basis (the official results reported by congressional district do not match the official state-wide totals reported):

Maine

747,927	357,735	335,593	54,599	22,142	D	47.8	44.9
1st District	392,107	210,979	154,127	27,001	56,852	D	53.8	39.3
2nd District	351,834	143,739	180,818	27,227	37,079	R	40.9	51.4

bIn Nebraska the statewide plurality vote winner gained two votes, and each of the state's three congressional districts was awarded one vote on a plurality basis (the official results reported by congressional district do not match the official state-wide totals reported):

Nebraska

844,227	284,494	495,961	63,772	211,467	R	33.7	58.7
1st District	282,338	100,132	158,642	23,564	58,510	R	35.5	56.2
2nd District	291,680	131,030	137,564	23,086	6,534	R	44.9	47.2
3rd District	270,034	53,290	199,657	17,087	146,367	R	19.7	73.9

roughly 65.8 million votes, a total that is similar to the 65.9 million votes won by Barack Obama four years earlier. Yet, compared to Obama in 2012, Clinton and the Democrats saw declines in two-party vote share in 45 of the 50 states, by an average decrease of 5.1 percentage points. Trump won roughly 62.9 million votes nationally, nearly 3 million fewer votes than Clinton. However, Trump's popular vote total demonstrated gains for the Republican Party. Trump garnered just over 2 million more popular votes than the 2012 Republican nominee, former Massachusetts Governor Mitt Romney. And in half of the states carried by Obama in 2012, Trump improved the Republican's two-party vote share by an average increase of 2.2 percentage points.

Despite her favorable popular vote margin, Clinton lost six of the twenty-six states won by Obama in 2012, costing her the Electoral College and the presidency.[20] As Figure 3-1 shows, Trump won 304 electoral votes to Clinton's 227.[21] Among the 538 electors chosen to represent their states in the Electoral College, there were a record seven "faithless electors" who cast ballots contrary to their states' popular votes—five who were faithless to the Democratic nominee and two to the Republican.[22] Nevertheless, Trump's 304 electoral votes easily surpassed the 270 votes needed for election. Trump carried thirty of the fifty states and received one electoral vote for winning Maine's second congressional district. Trump won each of the twenty-four states that Romney won for the Republicans in 2012. Trump's average two-party vote share margin in these twenty-four states was 22.6 percentage points—only Arizona and North Carolina were within a five-point margin. To this electoral coalition Trump was able to add Florida, Iowa, Michigan, Ohio, Pennsylvania, and Wisconsin—states that comprise a total of 99 electoral votes. Although he won Iowa and Ohio rather comfortably, Trump's margin in the remaining four states was extraordinarily thin. Trump's electoral margin in Florida was 1.2 percentage points, and he won Michigan, Pennsylvania, and Wisconsin by an average of only 0.57 points. Indeed in Michigan, Trump bested Clinton by only 10,704 votes. No matter how close his victories in these battleground states may have been, it is remarkable that Trump was able to put all of these states in the Republican column, especially when one considers that the GOP has not won Michigan or Pennsylvania since 1988 and Wisconsin since 1984.

THE ELECTION RULES

Rules matter. And this is certainly the case in U.S. presidential elections.[23] Electoral rules, specifically those pertaining to the Electoral College, structure the nature of party competition and voter behavior, they influence the strategic actions of candidates (as we saw in both Chapters 1 and 2), and as was the case in 2016, they sometimes dictate who wins and who loses. Whereas Hillary Clinton won the popular vote, Donald Trump won the Electoral College and was elected president. Simply put the rules governing U.S. presidential elections do not guarantee that the candidate who receives the most votes wins. In addition to the 2016 election, on four other occasions in American history—the elections of John Quincy Adams in 1824, Rutherford B. Hayes in 1876, Benjamin Harrison in 1888, and George W. Bush in 2000—the plurality winner of the popular vote failed to achieve a majority in the Electoral College and lost the presidency.[24] Confusion or a lack of knowledge about the electoral rules that

Figure 3-1 Electoral Votes, by State, 2016

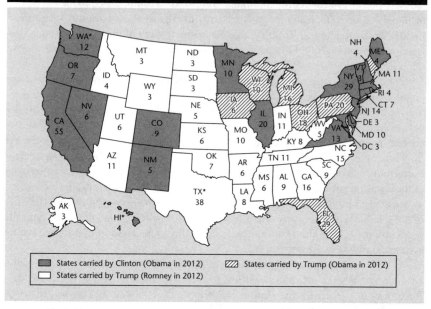

Legend:
- States carried by Clinton (Obama in 2012)
- States carried by Trump (Romney in 2012)
- States carried by Trump (Obama in 2012)

Source: Federal Election Commission, "Official 2016 Presidential General Election Results," January 30, 2017, https://transition.fec.gov/pubrec/fe2016/2016presgeresults.pdf. Based on reports of the secretaries of state of the fifty states and the District of Columbia.

Note: Donald J. Trump won 304 electoral votes; Hillary Clinton, 227.

*Trump was awarded one electoral vote from Maine for winning the state's second congressional district. In 2016 there were seven "faithless electors": a Democratic Party elector from Hawaii cast a ballot for Bernie Sanders; a Republican Party elector from Texas cast a ballot for John Kasich, and another voted for Ron Paul; and in Washington three Democratic electors cast ballots for former Secretary of State Colin Powell, a Republican, and another voted for Faith Spotted Eagle, a Native American activist.

govern the United States can cause consternation among voters, and calls for Electoral College reform (or its elimination) resound when the outcome of the electoral process does not seem to coincide with the general wishes of the electorate, but the rules are well defined.[25]

As we saw in Chapter 2, voters do not vote directly for president. Rather they vote for a slate of electors pledged to support certain presidential and vice presidential candidates. In every state except Maine and Nebraska, the slate that receives the most popular votes (a plurality) is awarded all of the state's electoral votes. In no state is a majority required to win. In 2016 Trump won majorities in twenty-three of the thirty states he carried; Clinton won majorities in thirteen of the twenty states in which she led voting. Plurality winners are most likely to occur when a prominent independent or third-party candidate (or candidates) is on the ballot. In 2016 a robust 5.7 percent of the national popular vote went to candidates outside of the two main parties, result-ing in plurality winners in fourteen of the fifty states. Compare this to 2012, when only 1.7 percent of the national popular vote went to candidates outside of the two main parties, or 2008, when the independent/third-party vote share was 1.4 percent. In 2012 both Obama and Romney won majorities in each of the states in which they were victorious. In 2008 Obama won a majority in all but two of the twenty-eight states he carried.

The plurality rule, winner-take-all system usually transforms a plurality of the popular vote into a majority of the electoral vote. And it takes a majority of the elec-toral vote (currently 270 votes) to produce a winner. If no candidate wins a majority of the electoral vote, the U.S. House of Representatives, voting by state delegations, chooses among the three candidates with the highest number of electoral votes. Yet the House has not chosen a winner since 1825. In forty-four of the forty-eight elec-tions from 1828 to 2016, the candidate with the most popular votes has won a majority of the electoral vote. During this period there were fourteen elections in which a can-didate won a plurality of the national vote—but not a majority—and won a majority of the electoral vote.[26] So why does the plurality rule, winner-take-all system typically produce a majority winner? The answer lies in the tendency for plurality rule voting systems to yield a two-party system.

The U.S. plurality vote system is a confirmation of Duverger's Law, a proposition advanced by French jurist and political scientist Maurice Duverger in the 1950s.[27] According to Duverger, "the simple-majority single-ballot system favours the two-party system."[28] Indeed Duverger argued that "the American procedure corresponds to the usual machinery of the simple-majority single-ballot system. The absence of a second ballot and of further polls, particularly in the presidential election, constitutes in fact one of the historical reasons for the emergence and the maintenance of the two-party system."[29]

According to Duverger, this principle applies for two reasons. First, a plurality vote system produces a "mechanical factor": third parties may earn a large number of votes nationally but fail to gain a plurality of the votes in many electoral units. Scholars agree that this effect is important, except in countries where smaller parties have a geographic base. Second, some voters who prefer a candidate or party they think cannot win will cast their votes for their first choice between the major-party candidates, which Duverger labels the "psychological factor." This behavior is called "sophisticated" or "strategic" voting and in Britain is referred to as "tactical" voting. William H. Riker defines strategic voting as "voting contrary to one's immediate tastes in order to obtain an advantage in the long run."[30] Whether strategic voting occurs to any significant extent is controversial, yet evidence suggests that a substantial number of voters who preferred a third-party or independent candidate in the 1968, 1980, 1992, 1996, and 2000 elections wound up voting for one of the major-party candidates instead of voting their "sincere" preferences.[31] As we will see in Chapter 6, it seems highly likely that a substantial number of voters in 2016 who preferred a third-party candidate voted for one of the major-party candidates instead.

The plurality rule system thus places a heavy burden on third-party or indepen-dent candidates. Even a relatively successful third-party candidate typically receives a far smaller share of the electoral vote than of the popular vote.[32] Here it is useful to review the fates of the four most successful third-party and independent candidacies (in popular vote results) since World War II: George C. Wallace won 13.5 percent of the popular vote in 1968, John B. Anderson won 6.6 percent in 1980, and H. Ross Perot won 18.9 percent in 1992 and 8.4 percent in 1996. Despite relatively high levels of popular support among these candidates, only Wallace was able to win enough votes in a state to obtain electoral votes. Wallace came in first in five states (winning majorities in Alabama and Mississippi) and gained forty-six electoral votes (including one from a faithless elector from North Carolina). Yet Wallace won only 8.5 percent of the electoral vote, significantly less than his popular vote share.[33]

The rules had a direct and clearly discernable effect on the outcome of the 2016 election, and the rules also create the conditions that have led to major-party dominance; they help shape the strategies that campaigns employs, and they also constrain the choices that voters make. Choosing the president by presidential electors is a central part of these rules, and a strong case can be made for eliminating the Electoral College.[34] Some critics, such as presidential scholar George C. Edwards III, argue in favor of direct election of the president. Direct election would force candidates to campaign nationally (although candidates would likely concentrate their efforts in densely populated, urban areas) and would promote equality by making every vote in every state count. Moreover, direct election would eliminate questions of fairness that arise when popular-vote winners do not win the presidency. The main obstacle to adopting a direct election system is that it requires a constitutional amendment, which is unlikely because gaining approval of three-fourths of the states would be difficult in a system that overrepresents the smaller states.[35]

An alternative reform would retain the Electoral College but would diminish its importance by establishing a compact among states that would guarantee that electors would vote for the national popular-vote winner regardless of the outcome within their own state. This compact would come into effect only after it is enacted by states collectively possessing a majority of the electoral votes. As of July 2017 ten states and the District of Columbia with a total of 165 electoral votes (roughly 61 percent of the 270 electoral votes needed) had agreed to the National Popular Vote Interstate Compact.[36] Because an interstate compact requires congressional approval, there would still be an additional hurdle, but only a majority of both chambers is required to approve an interstate compact, not the two-thirds supermajority to initiate a constitutional amendment.

As described earlier Maine and Nebraska both have district systems for choosing electors, and widespread state-level adoption of this method is often put forward as a way of reforming the Electoral College. The district system does away with the winner-take-all rule for assigning electors and makes it possible for candidates to split a state's electoral vote. However, this method does not guarantee that electors will be divided in proportion to candidates' popular-vote shares. Indeed, because partisan majorities in state legislatures typically gerrymander congressional district lines to make the districts uncompetitive and unbalanced in their favor, the adoption of the district method would likely bias Electoral College outcomes relative to the popular vote.[37] A study by *The Cook Political Report* shows that had there been a uniform application of the district method in 2016, Donald Trump would have been elected.[38] Trump won more congressional districts than Clinton (230 of 435) while carrying

30 states for a total of 290 electoral votes. Clinton would have received 248 electoral votes based on 205 congressional district wins, twenty state popular-vote wins, and the District of Columbia. Obviously this result is in line with the real Electoral College outcome, but note that neither method is consistent with the national popular vote. Moreover, the district method is not always in line with the Electoral College. In 2012 Barack Obama won the popular vote (51.1 percent) and the Electoral College (332 electoral votes to Mitt Romney's 206), yet the district method would have resulted in a Romney victory because he carried 226 of 425 districts and twenty-four states, a total of 274 electoral votes.[39] Widespread adoption of the district system is unlikely, however, because most states do not want to diminish their potential influence by making it likely that their electoral votes will be split.

THE PATTERN OF RESULTS

Political observers often focus their attention on those factors that make a particular election appear unique. The 2016 election certainly featured many events that were unprecedented in American electoral history. Indeed one headline in a major newspaper referred to the presidential contest as "unusual, unexpected, strange, weird, and . . . bizarre."[40] Yet systematic analysis also requires that commonalities be observed. Thus the 2016 election can be placed in perspective by comparing it with previous presidential elections. Three conclusions emerge. First, the election further demonstrates the competitive nature of postwar elections in the United States, which exhibit a relatively even balance between the two major parties. Second, although 2016 provided the Democrats with their third consecutive popular vote win, postwar elections continue to display a pattern of volatility. Third, although incumbent presidents seem to have an electoral advantage, incumbent parties do not.

Perhaps the most remarkable feature of American presidential elections in the postwar period is the competitive balance between the two major parties. In the eighteen elections held since World War II, the Republicans have been victorious in ten, whereas the Democrats have won eight. If one considers popular vote winners, the score is tied eight to eight. The Republicans have been slightly more successful in establishing electoral majorities, winning a majority of the popular vote in seven of these elections (1952, 1956, 1972, 1980, 1984, 1988, and 2004). The Democrats have won a popular-vote majority only four times, including both of Obama's victories (1964, 1976, 2008, and 2012). The average (mean) level of popular support shows the competitive balance: the Republicans have won 48.7 percent of the popular vote, and the Democrats have won 47.0 percent. This division of popular support also demonstrates the dominance of the two major parties in presidential elections. During the postwar period, third-party and independent candidates have only garnered an average of 4.4 percent of the popular vote.

Examining electoral history is like looking at clouds: if you look hard enough, you'll find something that looks like a pattern. Yet, with a few important historical exceptions, electoral history is best described as volatile. This is especially true in the postwar period, where competitive balance would appear to place a party's chances at winning the presidency at 50-50.[41] Evidence of electoral volatility should give pause to pundits and partisans alike who are too quick to label any one election, such as 2016, as the dawn of a new era of electoral dominance. Declarations such as this seem ill-advised and ill-informed.

Table 3-2 presents presidential election results since 1832, the first election in which political parties used national nominating conventions to select their candidates. From 1832 to 1948 there are four instances in which the same party won three elections or more in a row. Scholars often associate these episodes with partisan realignments. Walter Dean Burnham, for instance, identifies the elections of 1860, 1896, and 1932 as realigning elections during this period.[42] From 1948 to 2004, however, despite the election of five two-term presidents, the same party won three elections in a row only once (the Republicans in 1980, 1984, and 1988). The 2008, 2012, and 2016 elections marked three consecutive popular vote victories for the Democrats, but the party's inability to secure an Electoral College win in 2016 is greater evidence of partisan balance and electoral volatility than one party's advantage.

The postwar period is an era of sustained electoral volatility. From 1952 to 1984, neither party was able to win more than two elections in a row. The Republicans won 1952 and again in 1956, the Democrats won in 1960 and 1964, and the Republicans won in 1968 and 1972. In all three sets of wins, the second win was by a larger margin than the first. Volatility increased in 1980, when the Democrats, who had won the White House in 1976, failed to hold it. The 1980 and 1984 elections reverted to the pattern of back-to-back party wins when Ronald Reagan was reelected in a landslide.[43] Then in 1988 George H. W. Bush's election gave the Republicans three elections in a row, breaking the pattern of postwar volatility. But the Republicans could not sustain their control of the presidency. The Democrats recaptured the White House with Bill Clinton's victory in 1992. Clinton was reelected in 1996, and he did so by capturing a larger popular-vote margin than in his first election. George W. Bush's defeat of Al Gore in 2000 continued the postwar volatility, and Bush, who finished second in the popular vote in 2000, improved his vote share in 2004. Obama's victories in 2008 and 2012 gave some Democrats hope that a period of Democratic Party dominance had emerged. Yet Obama's reelection was achieved with a smaller popular-vote margin than his first (unlike all other reelected incumbents during the postwar period) and did not carry with it the legislative majorities generated in 2008.[44] Hillary Clinton's popular vote plurality in 2016 fell short of Obama's electoral majorities and demonstrated a softening of electoral support for the party. By capturing an Electoral College majority, Donald Trump was able to recapture the White House for the Republican Party and add to the pattern of volatility.

The electoral volatility of the postwar period is not without precedent. In fact two periods in the nineteenth century were more volatile. From 1840 to 1852 the incumbent party lost four consecutive elections—a period of volatility between the Democrats and the Whigs. This occurred again from 1884 to 1896, when the Republicans and the Democrats alternated elections. Both of these periods, however, were followed by party realignments. In 1854, just two years after the decisive defeat of the Whigs, the Republican Party was founded, and by the 1856 election the party's nominee, John C. Fremont, came in second behind James Buchanan, the Democratic winner.[45] By 1860 the Republicans had captured the presidency, and the Whigs were extinct.[46] Although many Whigs, including Abraham Lincoln himself,

Table 3-2 Presidential Election Results, 1832–2016

Election	Winning Candidate	Party of Winning Candidate	Success of Incumbent Political Party
1832	Andrew Jackson	Democrat	Won
1836	Martin Van Buren	Democrat	Won
1840	William H. Harrison	Whig	Lost
1844	James K. Polk	Democrat	Lost[a]
1848	Zachary Taylor	Whig	Lost
1852	Franklin Pierce	Democrat	Lost
1856	James Buchanan	Democrat	Won
1860	Abraham Lincoln	Republican	Lost
1864	Abraham Lincoln	Republican	Won
1868	Ulysses S. Grant	Republican	Won[b]
1872	Ulysses S. Grant	Republican	Won
1876	Rutherford B. Hayes	Republican	Won
1880	James A. Garfield	Republican	Won
1884	Grover Cleveland	Democrat	Lost
1888	Benjamin Harrison	Republican	Lost
1892	Grover Cleveland	Democrat	Lost
1896	William McKinley	Republican	Lost
1900	William McKinley	Republican	Won
1904	Theodore Roosevelt	Republican	Won
1908	William H. Taft	Republican	Won
1912	Woodrow Wilson	Democrat	Lost
1916	Woodrow Wilson	Democrat	Won
1920	Warren G. Harding	Republican	Lost
1924	Calvin Coolidge	Republican	Won
1928	Herbert C. Hoover	Republican	Won

Election	Winning Candidate	Party of Winning Candidate	Success of Incumbent Political Party
1932	Franklin D. Roosevelt	Democrat	Lost
1936	Franklin D. Roosevelt	Democrat	Won
1940	Franklin D. Roosevelt	Democrat	Won
1944	Franklin D. Roosevelt	Democrat	Won
1948	Harry S. Truman	Democrat	Won
1952	Dwight D. Eisenhower	Republican	Lost
1956	Dwight D. Eisenhower	Republican	Won
1960	John F. Kennedy	Democrat	Lost
1964	Lyndon B. Johnson	Democrat	Won
1968	Richard M. Nixon	Republican	Lost
1972	Richard M. Nixon	Republican	Won
1976	Jimmy Carter	Democrat	Lost
1980	Ronald Reagan	Republican	Lost
1984	Ronald Reagan	Republican	Won
1988	George H. W. Bush	Republican	Won
1992	Bill Clinton	Democrat	Lost
1996	Bill Clinton	Democrat	Won
2000	George W. Bush	Republican	Lost
2004	George W. Bush	Republican	Won
2008	Barack Obama	Democrat	Lost
2012	Barack Obama	Democrat	Won
2016	Donald J. Trump	Republican	Lost

Source: *Presidential Elections, 1789–2008* (Washington, D.C.: CQ Press, 2009); 2012–2016, compiled by authors.

[a]Whigs are classified as the incumbent party because they won the 1840 election. In fact their presidential candidate, William Henry Harrison, died a month after taking office and his vice president, John Tyler, was expelled from the party in 1841.

[b]Republicans are classified as the incumbent party because they won the 1864 election. (Technically Lincoln had been elected on a Union ticket.) In fact after Lincoln's assassination in 1865, Andrew Johnson, a war Democrat, became president.

became Republicans, the Republican Party was not just the Whig Party renamed. The Republicans had transformed the political agenda by capitalizing on opposition to slavery in the territories.[47]

The 1896 contest, the last of four incumbent party losses, is usually considered a critical election because it solidified Republican dominance.[48] Although the Republicans had won five of the seven elections since the end of the Civil War, after Ulysses S. Grant's reelection in 1872, all their victories had been by narrow margins. In 1896 the Republicans emerged as the clearly dominant party, gaining a solid hold in Connecticut, Indiana, New Jersey, and New York, states that they had frequently lost between 1876 and 1892. After William McKinley's defeat of William Jennings Bryan in 1896, the Republicans established a firmer base in the Midwest, New England, and the Mid-Atlantic states. They lost the presidency only in 1912, when the GOP was split, and in 1916, when the incumbent, Woodrow Wilson, ran for reelection.[49] The Republicans would win again in 1920, 1924, and 1928.

The Great Depression ended Republican dominance. The emergence of the Democrats as the majority party was not preceded by a series of incumbent losses. Instead the Democratic coalition forged in the 1930s relied heavily on the emerging working class and the mobilization of new groups into the electorate.

As the emergence of the New Deal coalition demonstrates, a period of electoral volatility is not a necessary condition for a partisan realignment. Nor perhaps is it a sufficient condition. In 1985 Ronald Reagan himself proclaimed that his reelection was indicative of a realignment. Political scientists were skeptical about that claim mainly because the Democrats continued to dominate the U.S. House of Representatives. George H. W. Bush's election in 1988 suggested that Republican dominance indeed might have arrived. But Clinton's 1992 victory called this thesis into question, and his 1996 victory cast further doubts on the idea that a realignment had occurred. After the 2000 election, the Republicans held control of the House, the Senate, and the presidency for the first time since 1953, although they temporarily lost control of the Senate between June 2001 and January 2003.[50] But the closeness of the election called into question any claim of Republican dominance. The Democrats regained the presidency—by a comfortable margin—with Obama's victory in 2008, and they also won relatively large majorities in both houses of Congress, only to lose control of the House and a sizable portion of their advantage in the Senate in the 2010 midterm elections. The election of 2012 gave Obama and the Democrats another four years in the White House, but Congress remained under divided party control. Following the 2016 election the Republicans control the White House and both houses of Congress. Yet, just as unified political control of government following the 2008 election did not launch a period of Democratic dominance, it is unlikely that unified government under the Republicans signals the dawn of GOP ascendancy. No party currently dominates American politics. Volatility persists.

One clear pattern that does emerge when one examines presidential elections across history is that incumbent candidates appear to have an advantage. Between 1792 and 2016, in-office parties retained the White House about two-thirds of the time when they ran the incumbent president but only won half the time—a coin flip—when they did not run an incumbent.[51] Obama's victory in 2012 made him the third straight incumbent president to win reelection. In fact eight of ten postwar incumbent presidents seeking reelection have won, with Ford losing in 1976 and Carter in 1980. The 1976 and 1980 elections were the only successive elections in the twentieth century in which two incumbent presidents in a row lost. The only other elections in which incumbent presidents were defeated in two straight elections were in 1888, when Benjamin Harrison defeated Grover Cleveland, and in 1892, when Cleveland defeated Harrison. With no incumbent on the ballot in 2016, the presidential election was seemingly either party's to win. In Chapter 7, we examine voters' evaluations of presidential performance and how it relates to voting.

STATE-BY-STATE RESULTS

The modern electoral map is a conglomeration of Republican "red states" and Democratic "blue states." Yet this color pairing has no real historical meaning and, in fact, has only become convention in recent years.[52] In 1976, for instance, election-night news coverage on NBC classified Republican (Ford) wins in blue and Democratic (Carter) victories in red. ABC News featured an electoral map that colored Democratic states in blue and Republican states in yellow.

Whereas the colors on the electoral map may be meaningless, the political geography of presidential elections most certainly is not. Because states deliver the electoral votes necessary to win the presidency, the presidential election is effectively fifty-one separate contests, one for each state and one for the District of Columbia. With the exception of Maine and Nebraska, the candidate who wins the most votes in a state wins all of the state's electors. Regardless of how a state decides to allocate its electors, the number of electors is the sum of its senators (two), plus the number of its representatives in the U.S. House.[53] Since 1964 there have been 538 electors and a majority, 270, is required to win. In 2016 the distribution of electoral votes ranged from a low of three in Alaska, Delaware, Montana, North Dakota, South Dakota, Vermont, Wyoming, and the District of Columbia to a high of fifty-five in California.

Because each state, regardless of population, has two electoral votes for its senators, the smaller states are overrepresented in the Electoral College and the larger states are underrepresented. The twenty least-populated states and the District of Columbia were home to roughly 10.5 percent of the U.S. population according to the 2010 Census, but these states had 16.5 percent of the electoral votes. The nine most-populated states, which had 52.2 percent of the population, had only 44.8 percent of the electoral vote.

Even though smaller states are overrepresented in the Electoral College, presidential campaigns tend to focus their resources on larger states unless pre-election polls suggest that a state is unwinnable. Consider the two most populous states, California and Texas. California's fifty-five electoral votes represent one-fifth of the votes needed to win the Electoral College. Texas has thirty-eight electoral votes, one-seventh of the votes necessary to win. Clearly both are vital for building an Electoral College victory. Yet pre-election polls suggested landslide wins for Clinton in California and Trump in Texas, and neither campaign spent significant time or money in either state. During the general election campaign (from the end of their respective conventions to election day), neither presidential candidate made a public appearance in California, and

Trump visited Texas only twice.[54] Florida, North Carolina, Ohio, and Pennsylvania, on the other hand, were competitive, large states with a total of eighty-two electoral votes at stake, and both candidates visited the four states more than any other. Clinton made twenty-one public appearances in Florida, for instance. Trump, who spent more time on the campaign stump overall, made twenty public appearances each in Florida, North Carolina, and Pennsylvania.[55] Trump won all four states.[56]

States are the building blocks of winning presidential coalitions, but state-by-state results can be overemphasized and may sometimes be misleading for three reasons. First, although much attention is given to battleground states, the nature of broadcast and social media coverage means that candidates must run national campaigns. Candidates can make appeals to specific states and regions, but those messages are likely to be reported across geographic boundaries. Thus, whereas battleground contests and regional bases of support may color a campaign's message and strategy, most campaigns seek to form a broad-based coalition throughout the nation. Indeed, given that forty-four of the forty-eight elections between 1828 and 2016 have resulted in the candidate with the largest number of popular votes also winning a majority of the electoral votes, it would appear that successful campaigns have always been national rather than regional in scope.

Second, comparing state-level election results over time can be misleading and may even conceal change. To illustrate this point we compare the results of two close Democratic victories—John Kennedy's defeat of Richard Nixon in 1960 and Jimmy Carter's defeat of Gerald Ford in 1976—that have many similarities. In both 1960 and 1976, the Republicans did very well in the West, and both Kennedy and Carter needed southern support to win. Kennedy carried six of the eleven southern states—Arkansas, Georgia, Louisiana, North Carolina, South Carolina, and Texas—and gained five of Alabama's eleven electoral votes, for a total of eighty-one electoral votes. Carter carried ten of the eleven southern states (all but Virginia) for a total of 118 electoral votes. Yet the demographic basis of Carter's support was quite different from Kennedy's. In 1960 only twenty-nine percent of African Americans in the South were registered to vote compared with sixty-one percent of whites. According to our analysis of the American National Election Studies, only about one in fifteen of the Kennedy voters in the South was black. In 1976, 63 percent of African Americans in the South were registered to vote compared with 68 percent of whites.[57] We estimate that about one in three southerners who voted for Carter was black. A simple state-by-state comparison would conceal this massive change in the social composition of the Democratic presidential coalition.

Third, state-by-state comparisons do not tell us why a presidential candidate received support. Of course such comparisons can lead to interesting speculation, especially when the dominant issues are related to regional differences. Following the 2016 election, for example, some observers speculated that Trump's victory, particularly in states such as Michigan, North Carolina, Ohio, and Pennsylvania, could be attributed to manufacturing job losses in those states.[58] Yet exit polls from these states show that voters who reported that the economy was the "most important issue facing the economy" were actually more likely to vote for Clinton than Trump.[59] Inference based solely on who won the state may be fallacious and lead to mischaracterizations of the electorate. Indeed similarly constructed inferences often lead to hyperbolic comparisons of "red states" versus "blue states," creating an illusion of a deeply divided electorate.[60] State-level election results should not be used to infer voters' preferences; for this we must examine individual-level survey responses—as we do in later chapters.

With these qualifications in mind, we now turn to the state-by-state results. Figure 3-2 shows Trump's margin of victory over Clinton in all states. As noted earlier both of the parties maintain regional bases of strong support, whereas relatively few states are competitive and truly in play. A continuing base of strength for the Democrats was the Northeast, sweeping eight of the nine states in the region (by an average popular vote margin of 15.3 points).[61] The Democrats have dominated the Northeast in presidential elections since Bill Clinton's election in 1992.[62] But Hillary Clinton was unable to hold the region's second-largest electoral prize, Pennsylvania, which Trump won by a slim 0.72 points. Despite the party's electoral strength in the Northeast, the region is proving to be a precarious base of electoral support for the Democrats. Whereas comparison of vote shares across the last seven elections suggests that the region has not waned in its support of the Democratic Party, the region

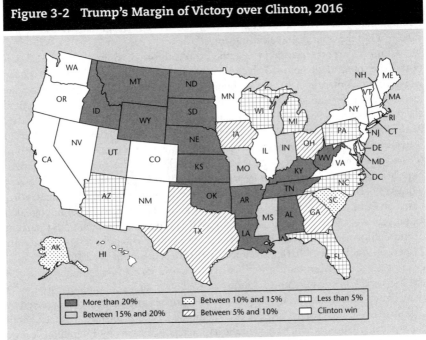

Figure 3-2 Trump's Margin of Victory over Clinton, 2016

Legend:
- More than 20%
- Between 15% and 20%
- Between 10% and 15%
- Between 5% and 10%
- Less than 5%
- Clinton win

Source: Federal Election Commission, "Official 2016 Presidential General Election Results," January 30, 2017, https://transition.fec.gov/pubrec/fe2016/2016presgeresults.pdf. Based on reports of the secretaries of state of the fifty states and the District of Columbia.

Note: We classify Maine as being carried by Clinton in 2016. Clinton actually won the statewide race and one of Maine's two congressional districts, thus winning three of the state's four Electoral College votes.

is declining in population and thus carries less weight in the Electoral College. In 1992 the region offered 106 electoral votes. In 2016 that number was only ninety-six, and by one estimate—based on U.S. Census population projections—by the 2024 election, the Northeast's share of electoral votes will decline further to ninety-one.[63] Whether the region continues to vote consistently for the Democratic Party remains to be seen.

Clinton's coalition was not restricted to one region. Outside of the Northeast she carried seven other states, as well as the District of Columbia, by ten percentage points or more, including the electorally rich states of California and Illinois. Clinton's sizable victories in Oregon and Washington continue the Democrat's dominance in those states, which have voted Democratic in each of the last eight presidential elections. Clinton also won pluralities in Nevada and Colorado, although her victories in each did not approach the comfortable majorities secured there by Obama in both 2008 and 2012. Yet Clinton's ability to keep these states in the Democratic column is notable because Nevada had voted Democrat only twice (for Bill Clinton in 1992 and 1996) between 1964 and 2008, and Colorado voted Democrat only once (1992) during that time frame. Clinton was also able to maintain Virginia for the Democrats. Until Obama's victory there in 2008 and 2012, Virginia had not voted Democratic since Lyndon Johnson's 1964 landslide, although the state had been inching toward the Democratic column because of the suburban growth from D.C. But the rest of the South remained unfertile ground for the Democrats in 2016. Clinton was only able to capture 13 of the South's 160 electoral votes.

Clinton's largest electoral prize came from California, where she won 61.7 percent of the vote and the state's 55 electoral votes. In fact California was the only state in which Clinton's margin of victory was bigger than Obama's in 2012. The Golden State has now voted for the Democratic candidates in each of the last seven presidential elections. Between 1952 and 1988, the state voted for the GOP presidential candidate in nine of the ten elections. But in those elections, California did not differ much from the country as a whole: its average level of Republican support was the same as that of the nation as a whole. One reason for this political change is the state's growing Latino population, which increased from 19 percent in 1980 to 39 percent in 2016, overtaking whites to become California's largest ethnic group.[64] According to Mark Baldassare, based on exit polls in 1990, only 4 percent of California voters were Latino; by 2000 14 percent were.[65] In 2016 exit polls indicate that Latinos accounted for 31 percent of the California electorate. Of those voters 71 percent voted for Clinton and only 24 percent for Trump.[66] Perhaps California's greatest effect on the 2016 presidential election is its contribution to the disparity between the national popular vote and the Electoral College outcome. Clinton received a whopping 4.3 million more votes than Trump in California. That surplus of votes alone is greater than that received by Trump in his seven most decisive victories combined.[67] If California were taken out of the vote tally, Trump would have won the national popular vote by 1.4 million votes.[68] Thus California's place in the 2016 election helps demonstrate the logic inherent in the Electoral College, an institution designed by the founders to prevent regional candidates from dominating a national election.[69]

As noted previously Trump's narrow victories in Michigan, Pennsylvania, and Wisconsin—all by less than one percentage point—brought three reliably Democratic states back into the Republican's win column. All three of these states supported Reagan in both 1980 and 1984, and Michigan and Pennsylvania sided with George H. W. Bush in 1988. In the six elections that followed, all three states voted for the Democratic nominee, although not always by comfortable margins. These states represented a substantial haul for Trump, totaling 46 electoral votes (17 percent of the 270 needed for victory). Other states that Trump was able to win, such as Florida and Ohio, are far more variable electorally. Since 1992, for instance, neither state has voted for a presidential candidate of the same party more than twice in a row. Unsurprisingly, these states are typically defined as among the most competitive from election to election. And Ohio continues to be a bellwether for the nation; the Buckeye State has voted for the presidential (Electoral College) winner in every election since 1960, when it voted for Richard Nixon over John F. Kennedy.

The remaining states captured by Trump in 2016 are the core of the Republican electoral coalition. These twenty-two states, which Trump won by an amazing average margin of 23.6 percentage points, all voted Republican in each of the last five presidential elections.[70] Thirteen of these states (Alabama, Arkansas, Idaho, Kansas, Mississippi, Nebraska, North Dakota, Oklahoma, South Carolina, South Dakota, Utah, and Wyoming) have voted Republican in every election dating back to 1980. The problem for Republicans, generally, is that the twenty-two solidly Republican states tend to be smaller in population and result in 180 electoral votes. Texas, with its thirty-eight electoral votes, is the largest state in this coalition, followed by Georgia with sixteen electoral votes, but five of these states have only three electoral votes each. To make the point clearer, consider the subset of thirteen states that have voted Republican since 1980. These thirteen states cumulatively represent sixty-seven electoral votes. This is not much of an advantage when we recall that Democratic-leaning California alone has fifty-five votes.

The region that offered Trump his greatest electoral reward was the South. One hundred forty-seven of Trump's electoral votes were from the South, nearly half of his total (48.4 percent). In the last half century, the South has been transformed into the base of the Republican Party, and this transformation is the most dramatic change in postwar American politics. Clinton's only victory in the South was in Virginia. In 2008 and 2012 Obama cut into the Republican's southern base by winning both Florida and Virginia, and in 2008, he also carried North Carolina. In each of those elections, however, Obama would have won the Electoral College without winning a single southern state. The same is true of Bill Clinton's victories in 1992 and 1996. Yet it is infeasible for the Republicans to win the presidency without southern electoral votes.

Republican strength in the South and Democratic advantage in the Northeast does not mean that sectionalism has beset the country. Indeed regional differences in presidential voting have declined in the postwar period and are currently low by historical standards. This can be demonstrated by statistical analysis. Joseph A. Schlesinger has analyzed state-by-state variation in presidential elections from 1832 through 1988, and we have updated his analyses through 2016.[71] Schlesinger measures the extent to which party competition in presidential elections is divided along geographic lines by calculating the standard deviation in the percentage of the Democratic vote among the states.[72] The state-by-state variation was 10.35 in 2016, slightly higher than the 10.29 deviation in 2012 and the 9.54 deviation in 2008. This suggests that states were slightly more divided in their support for Trump in 2016 than in recent elections.[73]

Schlesinger's analysis clearly reveals the relatively low level of state-by-state variation in the postwar elections.[74] According to his analysis (as updated), all fifteen of the presidential elections from 1888 to 1944 displayed more state-by-state variation than any of the seventeen postwar elections. To a large extent, the decline in state-by-state variation has been a result of the transformation of the South and the demise of local party machines, which has allowed partisan cleavages to become more consistent across states and allowed party competition to increase across the country.[75]

ELECTORAL CHANGE IN THE POSTWAR SOUTH

The South is a growing region that has undergone dramatic political change. Even though five of the eleven southern states have lost congressional representation since World War II, Florida and Texas have made spectacular gains. In the 1944 and 1948 elections, Florida had only eight electoral votes, but in the 2016 election, it had twenty-nine. In 1944 and 1948, Texas had twenty-three electoral votes; in 2016 it had thirty-eight. Since the end of World War II, the South's electoral vote total has grown from 127 to 160. The South gained seven electoral votes following the 2010 Census and projections suggest that it may gain an extra four by 2024.[76]

The political transformation of the South was a complex process, but the major reason for the change was simple. As V. O. Key, Jr., brilliantly demonstrated in *Southern Politics in State and Nation* in 1949, the main factor in southern politics is race. "In its grand outlines the politics of the South revolves around the position of the Negro.... Whatever phase of the southern political process one seeks to understand, sooner or later the trail of inquiry leads to the Negro."[77] And it was the national Democratic Party's sponsorship of African American civil rights that shattered the party's dominance in the South.[78]

Between the end of Reconstruction in 1877 and the end of World War II, the South was functionally a one-party system. Unified in its support of racial segregation and in its opposition to Republican social and economic policies, the South was a Democratic stronghold—the "Solid South." Indeed in fifteen of the seventeen elections from 1880 to 1944, all eleven southern states voted Democratic. Between 1896 (the first election after many southern states adopted the "white primary") and 1944, the average Democratic Party vote share in presidential elections was 71.6 percent.[79] The only major defections were in 1928, when the Democrats ran Alfred E. Smith, a Roman Catholic. As a result the Republican candidate, Herbert Hoover, won five southern states. Even then six of the most solid southern states voted for Smith, even though all but Louisiana were overwhelmingly Protestant.

After Reconstruction ended in 1877, many southern blacks were prevented from voting, and in the late nineteenth and early twentieth centuries, several southern states changed their voting laws to further disenfranchise blacks. The Republicans effectively ceded those states to the Democrats. Although the Republicans garnered black support in the North, they did not attempt to enforce the Fifteenth Amendment, which bans restrictions on voting on the basis of "race, color, or previous condition of servitude."

In 1932 a majority of African Americans in the North remained loyal to the Republicans; although by 1936 Franklin D. Roosevelt had won the support of northern blacks. But Roosevelt made no effort to win the support of southern blacks, most of whom remained disenfranchised. Even as late as 1940, about 70 percent of the nation's blacks lived in the states of the old Confederacy. Roosevelt carried all eleven of these states in each of his four victories. His 1944 reelection, however, was the last contest in which Democrats carried all eleven southern states.

World War I led to massive migration of African Americans from the agrarian South and into the industrial North, where—given the absence of laws restricting their suffrage—many would enjoy the franchise for the first time. The influx of African Americans alarmed some Democratic politicians in the North, who would likely see their electoral prospects decline unless they were able to siphon a share of African American voters who were loyal to the party of Lincoln. In 1932 African American voters in most major cities in the North voted for Herbert Hoover by a roughly two-to-one margin.[80] To appeal to African American voters, many northern Democrats encouraged their party to adopt a supportive position toward civil rights. By 1948 President Harry Truman was making explicit appeals to blacks through his Fair Employment Practices Commission, and in July 1948 he issued an executive order ending segregation in the armed services.[81] These policies led to defections from the "Dixiecrats" and cost Truman four southern states in the 1948 election; he still won the seven remaining southern states by an average margin of 26.2 points. In 1952 and 1956 the Democratic candidate, Adlai E. Stevenson, de-emphasized appeals to blacks, although his opponent, Dwight Eisenhower, still made inroads in the South. In 1960 Kennedy also played down appeals to African Americans, and southern electoral votes were crucial to his win over Nixon.[82] Kennedy also strengthened his campaign in the South by choosing a Texan, Lyndon Johnson, as his running mate. Clearly Johnson helped Kennedy win Texas, which he carried by only two percentage points.

If Johnson as running mate aided the Democrats in the South, Johnson as president played a different role. His explicit appeals to African Americans, including leading the Civil Rights Act into law in 1964, helped end Democratic dominance in the South. Barry Goldwater, the Republican candidate, had voted against the Civil Rights Act as a member of the Senate, creating a sharp difference between the two candidates. Goldwater carried all five states in the Deep South.[83] The only other state he won was his native Arizona. In 1968 Hubert Humphrey, who had long championed black equality, carried only one southern state, Texas, which he won with only 41 percent of the vote. He was probably aided by George Wallace's third-party candidacy because Wallace, a segregationist, won 19 percent of the Texas vote. Wallace carried Alabama, Arkansas, Georgia, Louisiana, and Mississippi, while Nixon carried the remaining five southern states. Nixon won every southern state in 1972, and his margin of victory was greater in the South than in the rest of the nation. Although Carter won ten of the eleven southern states in 1976 (all but Virginia), he carried a minority of the vote among white southerners.

In 1980 Reagan won every southern state except Georgia, Carter's home state. In his 1984 reelection victory, Reagan carried all the southern states, and his margin of victory in the South was greater than his margin outside it. In 1988 George H. W. Bush was victorious in all eleven southern states, and the South was his strongest region. Four years later, in 1992, Clinton, a native of Arkansas, made some inroads in the South and somewhat greater inroads in 1996. All the same the South was the only predominantly Republican region in 1992, and in 1996 Bob Dole won a majority of the electoral vote only in the South and mountain states. In 2000 the South was the only region in which Bush carried every state, and more than half of his electoral votes came from that region. Bush again carried every southern state in 2004, along with all of the states in the Mountain West. As was the case four years earlier, more than half of his electoral votes came from the states of the old Confederacy. Despite slippage in 2008 and 2012, Republicans have won every southern state in five of the twelve elections (1972, 1984, 1988, 2000, and 2004) between 1972 and 2016.

Although the transformation of the South is clearly the most dramatic change in postwar American politics, the 2016 election underscores that the Republicans do not hold the same level of dominance in the region that the Democrats once enjoyed. The average Republican vote share in the South between 1972 and 2016 was 54.1 points—much smaller than the 71.6 vote share that we reported earlier for the Democrats from 1896 to 1944. Florida is highly competitive. Bill Clinton won the Sunshine State in 1996, and in 2000 George W. Bush carried the disputed contest by a negligible margin. Obama narrowly won Florida in both 2008 and 2012, and Trump won the state by 1.2 percentage points. Trump won North Carolina by 3.7 points, but it too remains competitive. The state narrowly voted for Obama—by a 0.3 percentage-point margin—in 2008 and for Romney—by a slim two-point margin—in 2012. Although Virginia did not vote Democratic between 1968 and 2004, the growing number of suburbanites in northern Virginia has made the state more competitive, and the Democrats have now captured the state in three straight elections. Even in Georgia Democrats see Atlanta and its close-in suburbs as fertile ground to make the state competitive.[84] Clinton carried Georgia in 1992, and McCain won by only 5.2 percentage points in 2008. Republicans have an advantage in the South, to be sure, but Democrats are competitive in few a southern states, thus allowing the South to keep its place of prominence in modern presidential politics.

Some scholars predict that the South will play a part in the next major transformation in American politics, one they argue could make the Electoral College less competitive. John Judis and Ruy Teixeira contend that shifting demographics, specifically a growing professional class and an increase in America's nonwhite population, are setting the stage for an "emerging Democratic majority."[85] Central to this argument is that in the next two decades, the proportion of Latinos in the electorate is likely to double.[86] Latino growth in the South, where African Americans already compose a large share of the electorate, could greatly benefit the Democrats. Three southern states—Arkansas, North Carolina, and South Carolina—were among the top five states in Hispanic population growth between 2000 and 2010 according to the U.S. Census.[87] And Texas (19 percent) and Florida (8 percent) already have the second- and third-largest Hispanic populations, respectively. It is assumed by Judis and Teixeira that further growth in the Latino population could make Texas a Democratic-leaning state and Florida a safe Democratic state by the 2024 election cycle, giving Democrats, who already hold advantages in the electorally rich states of California and New York, an easier path to victory in the Electoral College.[88]

We have heard predictions of impending electoral realignment before, and as in the past, we encourage caution when evaluating these claims.[89] As noted earlier, after his reelection in 1984, Ronald Reagan proclaimed that his victory represented a Republican realignment. Indeed some scholars went so far as to argue that the Republicans held an electoral vote "lock."[90] But the Democrats won two consecutive elections in the 1990s. The scenario outlined by Judis and Teixeira offers reason for optimism for the Democrats and pessimism for the Republicans. Yet there are two major assumptions undergirding this scenario that complicate things for the Democrats. First, it should not be assumed that Latino voting participation will increase proportionately with Latino population growth; it has not thus far. As noted in a Pew Research Center report, the "[n]umber of Latino eligible voters is increasing faster than the number of Latin voters in presidential election years."[91] Hispanics were 24 percent of Florida's population but only 18 percent of voters on election day. In Texas Hispanics were 39 percent of the population but only 24 percent of the electorate.[92] For Democrats to make real substantial gains in the near future, voter participation among Latinos—particularly those in Texas—must grow at a faster rate to become commensurate with the group's share of the population. Second, it should not be assumed that Latinos will continue to support Democrats at the same levels. The Latino vote is not monolithic and has changed somewhat over time (we will have more to say about Latino political preferences in Chapter 8). For instance, Cuban Americans in Florida, many of whom fled their homeland to escape Fidel Castro's dictatorship, have long been a reliable voting bloc for Republicans. "In Florida, Cubans were about twice as likely as non-Cuban Latinos to vote for Donald Trump" in 2016.[93] But recent evidence shows that second- and third-generation Cuban Americans are more liberal and more likely to vote Democratic than the elder generation.[94] This is good news for Democrats, of course, but it also serves to remind both parties that old loyalties are not easily maintained and that voters respond to changing issues and interests, not simply on the basis of ethnicity. However, this battle for Latino votes plays out, it appears the South will be the focus of both parties' attention for many elections to come.

THE ELECTORAL VOTE BALANCE

Elections often conclude with the winning party making hyperbolic claims of electoral mandates and partisan realignments. However, as we have seen, comparing presidential elections results over time suggest that party competition for the presidency is high in the postwar period. Today's presidential elections are national in scope, and the Electoral College provides no significant barrier to either political party. Moreover, Andrew Gelman, Jonathan N. Katz, and Gary King present compelling evidence that since the 1950s partisan biases created by the Electoral College are negligible.[95]

Despite Trump's victory in 2016, short-term factors suggest that Democrats are currently advantaged. Since 1988 the Democrats have won the presidency in four of seven elections and the popular vote in six out of the seven. But the recent past is not always a guide to the future. Consider the fact that in the six elections between 1968 and 1988, the Republicans held the advantage, winning five of the six and several by significant margins.[96] Republican strength in the 1980s was soon replaced by Democratic victories in the 1990s. Yet because competition for the presidency has always rested upon some assessment of a candidate's relative strength in each of the states, recent election results often guide how parties develop future electoral strategies.[97] In Figure 3-3, we illustrate how the states have voted in each of the last five elections.

Figure 3-3 creates an illusion of Republican dominance. Twenty-two states have voted Republican in each of the past five elections—an impressive number, to be sure. But the geographic expanse of these Republican states belies their electoral power. These solidly Republican states only tally 180 electoral votes (33 percent of all available electoral votes). Texas with thirty-eight electoral votes is the only large state among the twenty-two, and five of these states have the minimum of three votes. Two other states, Indiana and North Carolina, have voted Republican in four of the five elections, accounting for twenty-six electoral votes. Both states voted for Obama in 2008. The Republicans have won Florida and Ohio (forty-seven electoral votes combined) in three of the last five elections, but both voted for Obama in 2008 and 2012. In total these twenty-six "Republican states" represent 253 electoral votes, seventeen votes shy of the 270 needed to win the Electoral College.

Figure 3-3 Results of the 2000, 2004, 2008, 2012, and 2016 Presidential Elections

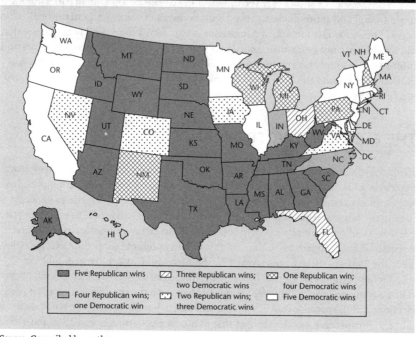

Source: Compiled by authors.

This leaves Democrats with twenty-four states and the District of Columbia, which total 285 electoral votes, exceeding the majority needed. Of these, fifteen states and the District of Columbia have voted Democratic in five straight elections. Although seemingly less impressive than the twenty-two states held comfortably by the Republicans, the solidly Democratic group represents 285 electoral votes (53 percent of all the available electoral votes). Five states—Michigan, New Hampshire, New Mexico, Pennsylvania, and Wisconsin (55 electoral votes collectively)—have voted Democratic in four of the five elections. And four states—Colorado, Iowa, Nevada, and Virginia (34 votes in sum)—have voted Democratic on three of the last five occasions.

If we were solely to use these five elections as the basis for determining battleground states for 2020, it would be a narrow field of play. Only six states fall into the "three-out-of-five" categories: Colorado, Florida, Iowa, Nevada, Ohio, and Virginia (three voted for Clinton; three voted for Trump in 2016). In this hypothetical, the Democratic candidate in 2020 would only have to win Florida to win the Electoral College. Indeed with 251 electoral votes on the safer side of their ledger, the Democrats could reach 270 electoral votes with a wider variety of coalitions than the Republicans. The Republicans, on the other hand, start with only 206 electoral votes in the safe column and cannot create a winning electoral coalition without Florida. Even with Florida in the win column, the Republicans would need a minimum of three additional states in their coalition to reach 270. Of course the odds of a Republican victory were just as long in 2016.

Undoubtedly the current electoral map presents a challenge for the GOP. But this is not the first time in recent history that the Electoral College map has appeared so uninviting for one of the parties and generally uncompetitive. Figure 3-4 illustrates over-time changes in the electoral balance of the Electoral College. Similar to Figure 3-3, we calculated how each of the states voted in the prior five elections but did so for each election from 1988 to 2016.[98] We then categorized states that voted for the same party in three of the five previous elections as "highly competitive." States that voted for the same party in four of the five elections were labeled "sometimes competitive," and those that voted for the same party in each of the five were labeled "uncompetitive."[99]

The figure shows that the number of uncompetitive states has more than doubled since the 2000 election. Thirty-eight of the fifty states currently appear to be uncompetitive, having voted for one of the two parties consistently over each of the last five elections. This rise coincides with a decline in the number of highly competitive states, which as noted earlier is now down to six (in 1996 the number of highly competitive states was twenty-six!). This alone would suggest a lack of electoral competition. But perhaps the clearest message conveyed by the figure is that the current electoral vote balance is likely subject to change . . . indeed, perhaps rapid change. The competitive balance in 1988 was similar to what we see today. Following that election, only eight states were considered highly competitive, and twenty-six were uncompetitive. Yet the challenge confronting Democrats following the 1988 elections was arguably more daunting than that confronting Republicans today. Whereas there are thirty-eight uncompetitive states following the 2016 elections, sixteen are Democratic and twenty-two are Republican states. In 1988, however, twenty-five of the twenty-six

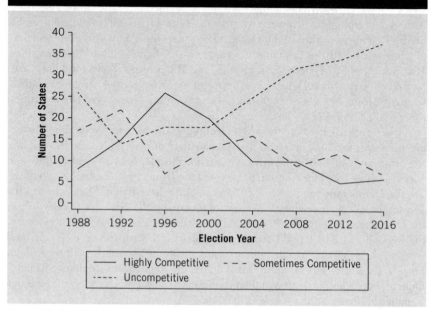

Figure 3-4 Competitive Balance in the Electoral College, 1988–2016

Source: Calculated by the authors.

uncompetitive states were Republican states. Based on the electoral vote balance alone, no one could have reasonably predicted Democratic victories in 1992 and 1996.

To assess the future prospects of the major parties, we must go beyond analyzing official election statistics. Although these statistics are useful for understanding competitive outcomes and future party strategies, they tell us little about why Americans vote the way they do or whether they vote at all. To understand how social coalitions have changed over time, as well as the issue preferences of the electorate, we must turn to surveys. They reveal how Trump was able to win election despite the public's relatively positive assessment of the Obama presidency. Furthermore, to determine the extent to which Americans really are polarized along party lines, we must study surveys to examine the way in which the basic party loyalties of the American electorate have changed during the postwar period. Thus, in the next five chapters, our study turns to survey data to examine the prospects for continuity and change in American electoral politics.

PART TWO

VOTING BEHAVIOR IN THE 2016 PRESIDENTIAL ELECTION

CHAPTER FOUR

WHO VOTED?

More than 136 million Americans cast ballots in the 2016 presidential election—more than any prior election in U.S. history. Yet this number is less impressive when one considers that some 93 million Americans who were eligible to vote did not.[1] Overall the turnout rate in 2016 was 54.7 percent of the population (59.3 percent if we count only those eligible to vote), a one percentage point increase from the 2012 election but roughly 2.2 points lower than 2008, the last presidential election without an incumbent on the ballot.

Voter turnout in the United States is lower than in any other Western industrialized democracy. In Table 4-1, we present average turnout rates during the postwar period for twenty-five democracies, including the United States.[2] Clearly there is much variation in turnout among these democracies. And although it is not our goal to provide a full accounting of these differences, several points are worth noting.[3] Australia and Belgium, which have the highest turnout rates shown in Table 4-1, are among several democracies with laws that enforce some form of compulsory voting. Although the penalties for not voting are relatively mild, compulsory voting obviously increases turnout.[4] A country's electoral system has also been shown to affect voter turnout rates. In democracies that use some form of proportional representation (PR) system, political parties have an incentive to mobilize the electorate broadly because every vote contributes to a party's proportional share. In plurality rule, winner-take-all systems, such as the United States and Britain, many electoral units are not competitive, and get-out-the-vote efforts are likely to be of little value.[5] Differences among party systems may also encourage the lower social classes to vote in some societies and do little to encourage them to vote in others.

No matter whether one is examining turnout in legislative or presidential elections, the United States clearly lags behind other industrialized democracies in voter participation. To be fair, U.S. congressional elections, especially midterm elections, are not wholly comparable to parliamentary elections in these other democracies. In the United States, the head of government is elected separately from the legislature. The president, for instance, remains in office regardless of the outcomes of the congressional midterms. In parliamentary systems, the head of government, typically a prime minister, is dependent upon the performance of his/her legislative party in

Table 4-1 Voter Turnout in National Elections, 1945–2017 (Percent)

Country	National Parliamentary	Presidential
Australia (28)	94.8	
Belgium (22)	92.1	
Luxembourg (15)	90.0	
Malta (18)	89.4	
Austria (21)	89.0	(13) 85.2
Italy (18)	88.1	
Iceland (21)	88.0	(8) 92.2
New Zealand (24)	87.4	
Denmark (26)	86.1	
Sweden (21)	85.5	
Netherlands (22)	85.0	
Germany (18)	83.1	
Norway (18)	79.9	
Greece (20)	77.1	
Israel (21)	76.4	
Finland (20)	74.1	(11) 73.5
Spain (13)	73.2	
United Kingdom (19)	73.0	
Ireland (19)	71.7	(7) 56.9
Canada (23)	71.4	
Portugal (15)	71.4	(9) 63.6

Country	National Parliamentary	Presidential
France (19)	71.3	(10) 81.1
Japan (27)	68.1	
Switzerland (18)	54.6	
United States (36)	44.6	(18) 55.4

Source: All countries except United States: mean level of turnout computed from results in International Voter Turnout Database, http://www.idea.int/data-tools/data/voter-turnout. U.S. turnout results: 1946–2010: U.S. Census Bureau, *Statistical Abstract of the United States, 2012* (Washington, D.C.: Government Printing Office, 2012), Table 397, 244, https://www.census .gov/prod/2011pubs/12statab/election.pdf. U.S. results for 2012, 2014, and 2016 were calculated by authors; total votes cast in U.S. House elections obtained from Clerk of the House of Representatives, "Statistics of the Presidential and Congressional Election," http://history.house .gov/Institution/Election-Statistics/Election-Statistics/; voting-age population estimates obtained from Michael P. McDonald, United States Elections Project, http://www.electproject.org/home/ voter-turnout/voter-turnout-data.

Note: For all countries except the United States, turnout is computed by dividing the number of votes cast by the number of people registered to vote. For the United States, turnout is computed by dividing the number of votes cast for the U.S. House of Representatives (or for president) by the voting-age population. Numbers in parentheses are the number of parliamentary or presidential elections. For all countries with bicameral legislatures, we report turnout for the lower house.

parliamentary elections. Even in a semipresidential system such as France, the president may be forced to replace his prime minister and cabinet as a result of a National Assembly election. Yet, even when the president is on the ballot, turnout for U.S. House elections during the eighteen presidential elections since World War II was only 51.4 percent, which is substantially lower than that of any democracy except for Switzerland. Indeed turnout for U.S. presidential elections ranks well below voting rates in Austria, Finland, France, Iceland, and Portugal. Voter participation in U.S. presidential elections is roughly equivalent to presidential turnout in Ireland, where the presidency is essentially a ceremonial position.

Although not evident in Table 4-1, it is important to note that voter turnout in most democracies has declined significantly over the postwar period. Indeed, by our analysis, seventeen of the twenty-five democracies have experienced a statistically significant decline in voter participation, by an average of roughly 2.4 percentage points per decade.[6] Great Britain, for instance, has seen turnout declines as large as twelve percentage points in recent elections. In our sample of democracies, average parliamentary turnout during the 1990s was 78.3 percent ($N = 67$); average turnout since then has dropped roughly five percentage points to 73.8 percent ($N = 114$). This average remains substantially higher than turnout in U.S. national elections.

In comparative perspective the low turnout rate of the United States can be explained in part by institutional differences. But this does little to explain the tremendous amount of individual-level variation in voter turnout that occurs within the United States. If roughly 55 percent of Americans participate in presidential elections, that means 45 percent *do not*. Thus, before discovering how people voted in the 2016 election, we must answer a more basic question: who voted? The answer to this question is partly institutional because federal and state laws in the United States—both historically and still today—often serve to inhibit (and sometimes facilitate) individuals' ability to vote. Political parties also play a role in affecting individuals' turnout decisions because parties' electoral strategies help define which voters are mobilized. And, of course, personal characteristics, such as an individual's socioeconomic status, political predispositions, and feelings of efficacy, contribute to someone's decision to go to the polls. Using survey data from the 2016 American National Election Study, we will consider how each of these factors affected who voted in the most recent presidential election. Before doing so, however, it is important to place the study of voter turnout in the United States in a broader historical context.[7]

VOTER TURNOUT, 1789–1916

As noted by the historian Alexander Keyssar, "At its birth, the United States was not a democratic nation—far from it. The very word democracy had pejorative overtones, summoning up images of disorder, government by the unfit, even mob rule."[8] Between 1789 and 1828 popular elections were not the norm in the United States. The Constitution did not require the Electoral College to be selected by popular vote, so many state legislatures simply appointed their presidential electors. Indeed, as late as the election of 1824, six of the twenty-four states appointed their slate of electors. Because U.S. senators were also appointed by state legislatures, voting in national elections was essentially limited to casting ballots for members of the House of Representatives.[9] Even then voter participation was strictly limited. Race exclusions and property requirements, combined with the lack of female suffrage, effectively narrowed the eligible electorate during this period to white male landowners.[10] As a result of this limited electoral competition and restricted suffrage, voter turnout rates during this period are the lowest in American history.

The presidential election of 1828 is the first election in which the vast majority of states chose their presidential electors by popular vote, thus making it the first for which meaningful measures of voter turnout can be calculated.[11] Historical records can be used to determine how many people voted in presidential elections, but constructing a measure of the turnout rate requires us to choose an appropriate denominator. Turnout in presidential elections is typically determined by dividing the total number of votes cast for president by the voting-age population.[12] But, given limited voting rights, should the turnout denominator be all people who are old enough to vote? Or should it include only those who were eligible to vote? The answer will greatly affect our estimates of turnout in presidential elections through 1916 because voting rights differed significantly among the states during this time. Women, for instance, were eligible to vote in a handful of states before the ratification of the Nineteenth

Amendment in 1920.[13] Clearly women should be included in the turnout denominator in states where they had the right to vote, but including them in the states where they could not vote would grossly deflate our estimates of turnout.

In Figure 4-1 we present two sets of estimates of turnout in presidential elections from 1828 through 1916. The alternative estimates reflect the difference in the choice of denominator used to measure the turnout rate. The first set was compiled by Charles E. Johnson, Jr., who calculated turnout by dividing the number of votes cast for president by the voting-age population. The second set is based on calculations by Walter Dean Burnham, who measures turnout by dividing the total number of votes cast for president by the number of Americans eligible to vote (the voting-eligible population). Burnham excludes African Americans before the Civil War, and from 1870 on, he excludes aliens where they were not allowed to vote, basing his estimates on what he calls the "politically eligible" population. But the main difference between Burnham's estimates and Johnson's estimates is that Burnham excludes women from the turnout denominator in states where they could not vote.

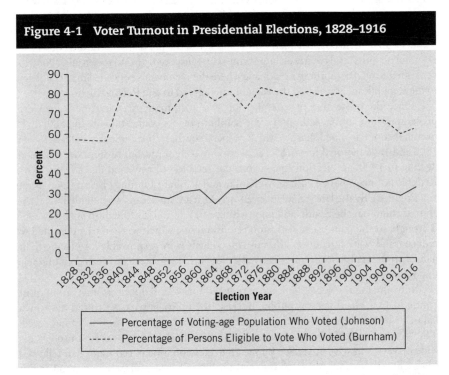

Figure 4-1 Voter Turnout in Presidential Elections, 1828–1916

——— Percentage of Voting-age Population Who Voted (Johnson)
- - - - - Percentage of Persons Eligible to Vote Who Voted (Burnham)

Sources: Estimates of turnout among the voting-age population based on Charles E. Johnson, Jr., *Nonvoting Americans,* series P-23, no. 2, U.S. Department of the Census (Washington, D.C.: Government Printing Office, 1980), 2; estimates of turnout among the population eligible to vote based on calculations by Walter Dean Burnham, "The Turnout Problem," in *Elections American Style,* ed. A. James Reichley (Washington, D.C.: Brookings, 1987), 113–114.

Note: Johnson's estimate for 1864 is based on the entire U.S. adult population. Burnham's estimate for that year excludes the eleven Confederate states that did not take part in the election.

Most political scientists would consider Burnham's calculations more meaningful than Johnson's. But whichever set of estimates one employs, the pattern of change is very similar. One clearly sees the effect of the advent of mass political parties and reemergence of two-party competition on voter participation. There is a large increase in turnout after 1836, when both the Democrats and Whigs began to employ popular appeals to mobilize the electorate. Turnout jumped markedly in 1840, during the "Log Cabin and Hard Cider" campaign in which William Henry Harrison, the hero of the Battle of Tippecanoe (1811), defeated the incumbent Democrat, Martin van Buren. Turnout waned somewhat after 1840, only to increase by roughly ten percentage points in 1856 after the Republican Party, founded in 1854, polarized the nation by taking a clear stand against slavery in the territories. In Abraham Lincoln's election in 1860, four out of five eligible white men went to the polls.

Turnout vacillated during the Civil War and Reconstruction era. The presidential election of 1864, held just weeks after General Sherman's Union troops seized Atlanta, saw a decline in turnout. Voter participation increased in 1868, but the turnout rate declined sharply in the 1872 election, the first to take place after African Americans were granted suffrage by the ratification of the Fifteenth Amendment.[14] Voter participation peaked in the 1876 contest between Republican Rutherford B. Hayes and Democrat Samuel J. Tilden. Although Tilden won a plurality of the popular vote, he did not win an electoral majority, and twenty electoral votes were disputed. To end the ensuing controversy, an informal compromise was made where the Democrats conceded the presidency to the Republican, Hayes, and the Republicans agreed to end Reconstruction.

Once the protection of federal troops was lost, many African Americans were prevented from voting. Although some southern blacks could still vote in 1880, their overall turnout dropped sharply, which reduced southern turnout as a whole. Between 1880 and 1896 national turnout levels were relatively static, but turnout began a long decline in 1900, an election that featured a rematch of the candidates from 1896, Republican incumbent William McKinley and William Jennings Bryan (Democrat and Populist). By the late nineteenth century, African Americans were denied the franchise throughout the South, and poor whites often found it difficult to vote as well.[15] Throughout the country, registration requirements, which were in part designed to reduce fraud, were introduced. Because individuals were responsible for placing their names on the registration rolls before the election, the procedure created an obstacle that reduced electoral participation.[16]

Introducing the secret ballot also reduced turnout. Before this innovation most voting in U.S. elections was public. Because the political parties printed their own ballots, which differed in size and color, any observer could see how a person voted. The "Australian ballot"—as the secret ballot is often called—was first used statewide in Massachusetts in 1888.[17] By the 1896 election nine in ten states had followed Massachusetts's lead.[18] Although the secret ballot was designed to reduce fraud, it also reduced turnout.[19] When voting was public, men could sell their votes, but candidates were less willing to pay for a vote if they could not see it delivered. Ballot stuffing was also more difficult when the state printed and distributed the ballots. Moreover, the Australian ballot also proved to be an obstacle to participation for many illiterate voters, although this was remedied in some states by expressly permitting illiterate voters to seek assistance.[20]

As Figure 4-1 shows, turnout trailed off rapidly in the early twentieth century. By the time the three-way contest was held in 1912 among Democrat Woodrow Wilson, Republican William Howard Taft, and Theodore Roosevelt, a Progressive, only three in five politically eligible Americans were going to the polls. In 1916 turnout rose slightly, but just over three-fifths of eligible Americans voted, and only one-third of the total adult population went to the polls.

VOTER TURNOUT, 1920–2016

With the extension of suffrage to all women by constitutional amendment in 1920, the rules that governed eligibility for voting became much more uniform across the states. This makes it easier to calculate turnout from 1920 onward, and we provide estimates based on both the voting-age and voting-eligible populations. As suffrage becomes more universal, these two populations grow in similarity (and the large gap between the measures that is evident in Figure 4-1 dissipates). Indeed these alternative measures of voter turnout produce fairly similar estimates, although differences have increased since 1972. In the modern period we prefer focusing on turnout among the voting-age population for two reasons. First, it is difficult to estimate the size of the eligible population. Walter Dean Burnham and coauthors Michael P. McDonald and Samuel L. Popkin have made excellent efforts to provide these estimates.[21] Even so Burnham's estimates of turnout differ from McDonald and Popkin's, with the latter reporting somewhat higher levels of turnout in all five elections between 1984 and 2000. One difficulty in determining the eligible population is estimating the number of ineligible felons.[22] Incarceration rates, which have grown markedly during the last four decades, are frequently revised, and the number of permanently disenfranchised is nearly impossible to measure satisfactorily.[23] According to McDonald, in 2016 more than 1.4 million prisoners were ineligible to vote, as were 2.2 million on probation and more than 508,000 on parole.[24]

Second, excluding noneligible adults from the turnout denominator may yield misleading estimates, especially when U.S. turnout is compared with turnout levels in other democracies. For example, about one in ten voting-age Americans cannot vote, whereas in Britain only about one in fifty is disenfranchised. In the United States about one in seven black males cannot vote because of a felony conviction. As Thomas E. Patterson writes in a critique of McDonald and Popkin, "To ignore such differences, some analysts say, is to ignore official attempts to control the size and composition of the electorate."[25]

In Table 4-2, we show the percentage of the voting-age population who voted for the Democratic, Republican, and minor-party and independent candidates ("other candidates") between 1920 and 2016. The table also shows the percentage that did not vote as well as the overall size of the voting-age population.

Hillary Clinton won 48.2 percent of the popular vote in 2016, a plurality, but this number does mean that her supporters composed a comparable portion of the voting age population. As Table 4-2 shows, it is more likely for a majority of American adults to stay away from the polls on election day than support any one candidate. In all the elections between 1920 and 2016, except 1964, the percentage that did not vote

Table 4-2 Percentage of Adults Who Voted for Each of the Major-Party Candidates, 1920–2016

Election Year	Democratic Candidate		Republican Candidate		Other Candidates	Did Not Vote	Total	Voting-Age Population
1920	14.8	James M. Cox	26.2	Warren G. Harding	2.4	56.6	100	61,639,000
1924	12.7	John W. Davis	23.7	Calvin Coolidge	7.5	56.1	100	66,229,000
1928	21.1	Alfred E. Smith	30.1	Herbert C. Hoover	0.6	48.2	100	71,100,000
1932	30.1	Franklin D. Roosevelt	20.8	Herbert C. Hoover	1.5	47.5	100	75,768,000
1936	34.6	Franklin D. Roosevelt	20.8	Alfred M. Landon	1.5	43.1	100	80,174,000
1940	32.2	Franklin D. Roosevelt	26.4	Wendell Willkie	0.3	41.1	100	84,728,000
1944	29.9	Franklin D. Roosevelt	25.7	Thomas E. Dewey	0.4	44.0	100	85,654,000
1948	25.3	Harry S. Truman	23.0	Thomas E. Dewey	2.7	48.9	100	95,573,000
1952	27.3	Adlai E. Stevenson	34.0	Dwight D. Eisenhower	0.3	38.4	100	99,929,000
1956	24.9	Adlai E. Stevenson	34.1	Dwight D. Eisenhower	0.4	40.7	100	104,515,000
1960	31.2	John F. Kennedy	31.1	Richard M. Nixon	0.5	37.2	100	109,672,000
1964	37.8	Lyndon B. Johnson	23.8	Barry M. Goldwater	0.3	38.1	100	114,090,000
1968	26.0	Hubert H. Humphrey	26.4	Richard M. Nixon	8.4	39.1	100	120,285,000
1972	20.7	George S. McGovern	33.5	Richard M. Nixon	1.0	44.8	100	140,777,000

Election Year		Democratic Candidate		Republican Candidate	Other Candidates	Did Not Vote	Total	Voting-Age Population
1976	26.8	Jimmy Carter	25.7	Gerald R. Ford	1.0	46.5	100	152,308,000
1980	21.6	Jimmy Carter	26.8	Ronald Reagan	4.3	47.2	100	163,945,000
1984	21.6	Walter F. Mondale	31.3	Ronald Reagan	0.4	46.7	100	173,995,000
1988	23.0	Michael S. Dukakis	26.9	George H. W. Bush	0.5	49.7	100	181,956,000
1992	23.7	Bill Clinton	20.6	George H. W. Bush	10.8	44.9	100	189,493,000
1996	24.1	Bill Clinton	19.9	Bob Dole	4.9	51.1	100	196,789,000
2000	24.8	Al Gore	24.5	George W. Bush	1.9	48.8	100	205,813,000
2004	26.7	John F. Kerry	28.1	George W. Bush	0.6	44.6	100	220,804,000
2008	30.0	Barack Obama	26.0	John McCain	0.8	43.2	100	230,917,000
2012	27.4	Barack Obama	25.2	Mitt Romney	0.9	46.5	100	240,926,957
2016	26.3	Hillary Clinton	25.2	Donald J. Trump	3.1	45.4	100	250,055,734

Sources: Voting-age population, 1920–1928: U.S. Census Bureau, Statistical Abstract of the United States, 1972, 92nd ed. (Washington, D.C.: Government Printing Office, 1972), Table 597, 373. Voting-age population, 1932–2000: U.S. Census Bureau, Statistical Abstract of the United States, 2004–2005, 124th ed. (Washington, D.C.: Government Printing Office, 2004), Table 409, 257. Voting-age population, 2004–2016: Michael P. McDonald, United States Election Project, http://www.electproject.org/home/voter-turnout/voter-turnout-data. Number of votes cast for each presidential candidate and the total number of votes cast for president: Federal Election Commission, "Official 2016 Presidential General Election Results," January 30, 2017, https://transition.fec.gov/pubrec/fe2016/presgeresults.pdf.

Note: The names of the winning candidates are italicized.

easily exceeded the share cast for the winning candidates. In 2016 only 26.3 percent of American adults could be counted as a Clinton voter (25.2 percent of the adult population cast ballots for Trump). In both absolute and proportional terms, fewer Americans voted for either Clinton or Trump than voted for Obama in 2012 or 2008. Of course, it was Trump who won the Electoral College and the presidency. Yet the proportion of Americans who supported Trump in 2016 was well below the average for all winning presidential candidates before 2008 (29.1 percent).

Figure 4-2 illustrates the percentage of the voting-age population that voted for president in each of these twenty-five elections as well as the percentage of the politically eligible population between 1920 and 1944 and the voting-eligible population between 1948 and 2016.[26] The extent to which these trend lines diverge depends on the percentage of the voting-age population that is eligible to vote. In eras when few people were ineligible, such as between 1940 and 1980, it makes very little difference which turnout denominator one employs. Today, however, there is a much larger noncitizen population, and incarceration rates are nearly 2.5 times higher than they were in 1980. Back in 1960, when turnout peaked, only 2.2 percent of voting-age Americans were not citizens; in 2016 8.4 percent were not. In 1960 only 0.4 percent of Americans were ineligible to vote because of their felony status; in 2016, 1.3 percent was ineligible. Thus as Figure 4-2 shows, in 1960 there was very little difference between turnout among the voting-age population and turnout among the voting-eligible population. In the 2016 election 136,669,237 votes were cast for president. Because the voting-age population was 250,055,734, turnout among this population was 54.7 percent. But, according to McDonald, the population eligible to vote was only 230,585,915. Using this total as our denominator, turnout was 59.3 percent. If we use McDonald's measure to calculate turnout in all eighteen postwar presidential elections, turnout would rise from 55.4 percent to 58.2 percent. However, U.S. presidential turnout would still be lower than turnout in parliamentary elections in any country except Switzerland and lower than in presidential elections in any country except Ireland.

Turnout among the voting-age population generally rose between 1920 and 1960. Two exceptions were the elections of 1944 and 1948, when turnout decreased markedly due to social dislocations during and after World War II. Campaign-specific conditions sometimes account for increases in turnout in certain elections. In 1928, for instance, it is plausible to attribute the jump in voter turnout to the candidacy of Alfred Smith, the first Catholic candidate to receive a major-party nomination. The increase in 1936 partly reflects Franklin Roosevelt's efforts to mobilize the lower social classes, especially the industrial working class. The extremely close contest between Republican Vice President Richard Nixon and the second Catholic candidate, Democrat John F. Kennedy, may account, in part, for the high turnout in 1960, when it rose to 62.8 percent of the voting-age population and was slightly higher among the politically eligible population.[27] The presidential election of 1960 produced the highest level of turnout among voting-age adults in American history. Yet the turnout percentage for the politically eligible population in 1960 was far below the typical levels found between 1840 and 1900. Moreover, the U.S. turnout in 1960 was still well below the average level of turnout in most advanced democracies (see Table 4-1).

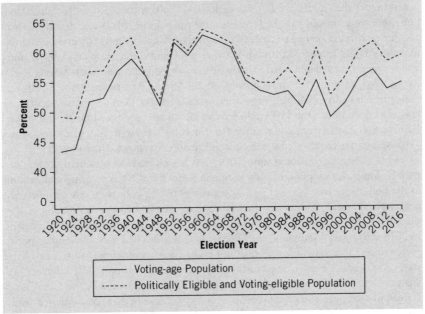

Figure 4-2 Percentage of Voting-Age Population and of the Politically Eligible and Voting-Eligible Population Voting for President, 1920–2016

Voting-age Population
Politically Eligible and Voting-eligible Population

Sources: Voting-age population, see Table 4-3 in this volume. Politically eligible population, 1920–1944: Walter Dean Burnham, "The Turnout Problem," in *Elections American Style*, ed. A. James Reichley (Washington, D.C.: Brookings, 1987), 113–114. Voting-eligible population, 1948–2000: Michael P. McDonald and Samuel L. Popkin, "The Myth of the Vanishing Voter," *American Political Science Review* 95 (December 2001): 966. Voting-eligible population, 2000–2016: Michael P. McDonald, United States Election Project, http://www.electproject.org/home/voter-turnout/voter-turnout-data.

Although short-term forces drove turnout upward in specific elections, long-term forces also contributed to the increase in turnout during this period. Three examples—not an exhaustive list certainly—help illustrate how long-term forces affect turnout. First, women who came of age before the Nineteenth Amendment, perhaps out of habit or long-held social expectations, often failed to exercise their right to vote once suffrage was granted. But women who came of age after 1920 were more likely to turn out, and as this younger generation of women gradually replaced older women in the electorate, turnout levels rose.[28] Second, because all states restrict voting to citizens, immigrants enlarge the voting-age population but do not increase the number of voters until they become citizens. After 1921, however, as a result of restrictive immigration laws, the percentage of the population that was foreign-born declined. Over time this led to an increase in turnout as a percentage of the voting-age population. Finally, levels of education rose markedly throughout the twentieth century, a change that acts as an upward force on turnout. Americans who have attained higher levels of education are much more likely to vote than those with lower levels of education.

From 1960 to 1980 voter turnout in the United States declined with each election, followed by a variable pattern through 2016. Turnout among the voting-age population in 1960—the highest in the modern period—was roughly eight percentage points higher than it was in 2016. (To match the 1960 turnout rate, more than 20 million more voters would have had to have gone the polls in 2016!) The decline in turnout during this period occurred even though there were several institutional changes that should have increased turnout. Between 1960 and the century's end, the country underwent changes that tended to increase turnout. After passage of the Voting Rights Act of 1965, turnout rose dramatically among African Americans in the South, and their turnout spurred voting among southern whites too. Less restrictive registration laws introduced since the 1990s also have made it easier to vote. The National Voter Registration Act, better known as the "motor voter" law, went into effect in January 1995, and it may have added 9 million additional registrants to the rolls.[29]

One recent institutional innovation that has altered the way many voters cast their ballots is the adoption of early voting in many states.[30] Early voting makes going to the polls more convenient by allowing voters to cast ballots on one or more days before election day.[31] Texas was the first state to use early voting in 1988. Since then the number of states adopting early voting laws has increased in every election period. In 2016 thirty-seven states and the District of Columbia had laws allowing in-person early voting. The remaining states offer some form of absentee voting, and three states, Colorado, Oregon, and Washington, conducted voting strictly by mail.[32] We analyzed the 2016 Current Population Survey (CPS) conducted by the U.S. Census Bureau to determine the extent to which voters made use of these convenience-voting mechanisms in 2016.[33] Figure 4-3 shows that early voting varies greatly among the states. Nationally, 38.6 percent of Americans reported voting early. The three states with vote-by-mail reported rates of early voting greater than 80 percent, while at the lower end, eleven states (all of which have absentee voting only) reported rates of less than 10 percent.[34]

And yet despite all of the institutional changes related to voting since the 1960s, turnout has not increased. Except for a small increase in turnout in 1984, turnout among the voting-age population clearly declined in each election between 1960 and 1988, falling most between 1968 and 1972.[35] Turnout then rose almost five points in 1992, perhaps as a result of Ross Perot's third-party candidacy.[36] But in 1996 turnout fell some six percentage points, reaching only 48.9 percent. In 2000, 2004, and 2008, turnout rose. Both George W. Bush elections were expected to be close going into election day, and this may have stimulated voter participation. In 2008 Barack Obama's historic campaign as the nation's first African American nominee from a major party excited many minority and young voters. Although few people expected that election to be close, the Obama campaign ran an inventive ground game, incorporating many Internet-based technological advances in their attempt to get out the vote. Although some observers expected a large increase in turnout in 2008, it rose only 1.4 percentage points. But it rose nevertheless. Unfortunately, the increased levels of voter turnout between 1996 and 2008 were not extended or sustained in 2012, when turnout declined by roughly three percentage points, whereas 2016 only made up a third of that decline.

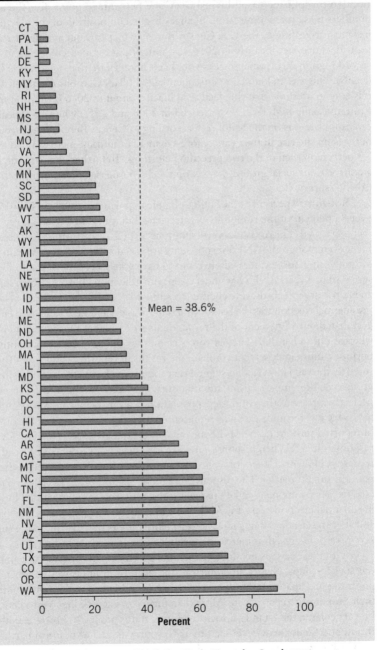

Figure 4-3 Percentage of Voters Who Voted Early, by State, 2016

Mean = 38.6%

Source: U.S. Census Bureau, 2016 Current Population Study, November Supplement.

Note: Data are weighted.

VOTER TURNOUT AMONG SOCIAL GROUPS

In 2016 turnout increased by just over one percentage point. But the aggregate numbers mask many interesting nuances in the composition of the electorate. For instance, according to the U.S. Census Bureau, voter turnout among African Americans declined significantly in 2016, dropping by seven percentage points from its record high in 2012, when blacks voted at a higher rate than whites (see below for details). This was undoubtedly consequential to Hillary Clinton's campaign. Of course it is easy to presume that the decline in black turnout in 2016 is simply a regression from unusually high levels experienced in 2008 and 2012, when an African American candidate was on the ballot. Yet, according to Census Bureau figures, black turnout was on the rise in the years before Obama's candidacy, increasing an average of 3.3 percent in each of the two preceding elections. To further compare voter turnout among various social groups, we rely on the 2016 American National Election Study (ANES) survey.[37]

Roughly 59 percent of the voting-eligible population turned out in 2016, but just over 85 percent of the respondents interviewed in the postelection survey reported that they voted. The ANES surveys commonly overestimate turnout for three reasons. First, even though the ANES respondents are asked a question that provides reasons for not voting, some voters falsely claim to have voted, perhaps owing to social pressure.[38] In past years ANES has undertaken vote validation efforts in which state voting and registration records were checked to authenticate respondents' claims—the 2012 presidential election was the last for which this was done. These validation efforts suggest that about 15 percent of the respondents who say that they voted did not do so, whereas only a handful of actual voters claim they did not vote. Importantly, for our purposes, most analyses that compare the results of reported voting with those measured by the validation studies suggest that *relative* levels of turnout among most social groups can be compared using reported turnout.[39] Second, the ANES surveys do not perfectly represent the voting-age population. Lower socioeconomic groups, which have very low turnout, are underrepresented. Discrepancies between the distribution of reported turnout in the ANES and actual turnout are exacerbated by low survey-response rates.[40] When response rates are low, surveys like the ANES tend to over-represent higher socioeconomic groups and those who are interested in the survey's political subject matter. The response rate for the 2016 ANES was 50 percent for the face-to-face component and 44 percent for the Internet component.[41] Third, during presidential election years, the ANES attempts to interview respondents both before and after the election. Being interviewed before the election may provide a stimulus to survey respondents, thus increasing turnout among the ANES sample.

With these caveats in mind, we examine differences in voter turnout among various social groups. Nearly all empirical studies of turnout (as well as other forms of political participation) note the importance of individuals' social environments on their propensity to participate. More than forty years ago, Sidney Verba and Norman Nie articulated the "standard socioeconomic status model."[42] More recently, Verba, Brady, and Schlozman developed their "resource model of political participation," by which they argue that individuals' resources, particularly time, money, and civic skills, facilitate political participation.[43] Individuals high in socioeconomic status are also more likely to be located in social networks that encourage participatory norms. In the following sections we examine patterns of voter participation among various social groups.

Race, Gender, Region, and Age

Table 4-3 compares reported turnout among social groups using the 2016 ANES survey. To many observers the 2016 election reflected growing levels of resentment among white Americans toward a political system that in their view, seemed to cater to minorities and immigrants and an economic system that valued global trade and devalued the domestic manufacturing jobs usually held by working-class whites.[44] Trump's populist message seemed tailored to these voters. But did white voters flock to the polls in disproportionate numbers in 2016? What about turnout among other social groups; what can we say about their levels of voter participation? Was voter turnout in 2016 significantly different than in years past?

Our analysis begins by comparing African Americans and whites.[45] In both the 2008 and 2012 election studies, whites and blacks reported voting at equal rates. In 2016, however, white respondents reported voting at a higher rate than that of blacks, a difference of four percentage points. Data from the CPS also suggest that whites were more likely to vote in 2016 than blacks, 65.3 percent to 59.6 percent. This gap, it is important to note, is more attributable to a decrease in black turnout than an upswing in white turnout. Whether one is using the ANES or the CPS, white turnout between 2012 and 2016 increased only minimally—by one percentage point. Black turnout, on the other hand, declined precipitously. According to the ANES, reported turnout among blacks decreased from 87 percent in 2012 to 84 percent in 2016. Both figures are likely inflated due to overreporting among ANES survey participants. Estimated turnout rates from CPS are lower generally and suggest a steeper decline: in 2012, CPS estimated black turnout to be 66.6 percent, dropping to 59.6 percent in 2016.

Of course, voter turnout levels among black voters were not always close to those of whites, and this marks a significant change in voting behavior (and American politics generally) over the last half century. In 1964, the year prior to the passage of the Voting Rights Act, the CPS reported whites were 12.2 percentage points more likely to vote than blacks. By 2004 this difference was reduced to 5.4 percent.[46] As noted earlier, in 2012, for the first time, black turnout was estimated to be higher than white turnout, although the gap was not large. The reversion of black voter turnout to roughly 2004 levels is a statistic worth watching because black voters are a sizable component of the Democratic Party's electoral coalition.

Roughly 11 percent of the 2016 ANES sample (face-to-face and Internet) is composed of self-identified African American respondents, making it possible to make within-group comparisons. As with earlier ANES surveys, blacks with higher levels of education are more likely to vote than those with lower levels of education. Blacks with college degrees were ten percentage points more likely to vote than those with only a high school diploma, and turnout among younger blacks continues to lag behind older generations. In 2016 the ANES shows a slightly higher turnout for black women than men, a difference of 2.7 percentage points; exit polls indicate that black women were 7 percent of the electorate, whereas black men were 5 percent. Perhaps the most influential variable for predicting voter turnout among blacks is income. By our estimate, using the ANES, blacks in the upper quartile (top 25 percent) of income are roughly 20 percentage points more likely to vote than those in the bottom quartile (lowest 25 percent).[47]

Table 4-3 reveals that turnout among Latinos was lower than turnout among whites and African Americans. This is consistent with the historical record. Low levels of Latino turnout have typically been attributed to lower levels of education, income, and English language skills, and some have demonstrated differences between native- and foreign-born Latinos—although evidence varies on this issue—as well as ethnic group.[48] ANES data reveal the importance of education as a predictor of Latino participation; college graduates were 10.5 percentage points more likely to vote than Latinos with only a high school degree. Yet, unfortunately, while the 2016 ANES sample includes roughly 12 percent Latinos, data regarding their ethnicity (e.g., Mexican-American, Puerto Rican, etc.) were not publicly available at the time of this study. To examine differences among Latinos, we turn to the CPS. The Census Bureau data show that Latinos (47.6 percent) were significantly less likely to vote than blacks (59.6 percent) and non-Latino whites (65.3 percent) and, for the first time since 1996, were slightly less likely to vote than Asian Americans (49.3 percent). The data also show that foreign-born, naturalized Latinos were eight percentage points more likely to vote than native-born Latinos. And ethnicity seems to matter as well, but these differences may be confounded by political geography. Turnout among Mexican Americans (the lowest among Latino groups) was roughly 9.5 percentage points lower than that of Cuban Americans. This difference is likely attributable to Mexican Americans, many of whom live in California and Texas, residing in uncompetitive states, whereas many Cuban Americans live in the battleground state of Florida. Overall, though, Latino turnout in 2016 was roughly equal to that experienced in 2012 (a difference of 0.2 percent).

The 2016 presidential election was the first to feature a woman as one of the major party nominees, and gender differences in voter turnout might be expected. To be sure women have voted at higher rates than men for some time now. The 1980 election was the last year in which the ANES surveys show white males to have a clear tendency to report voting more often than white females. Early ANES surveys show a clear decline in the turnout differential that advantaged men. In 1952, 1956, and 1960, the average male advantage was just over ten points, whereas in the 1964, 1968, 1972, and 1976 elections, the gap narrowed to an average of just over five points. This pattern of a long period of male advantage in turnout followed by a long period of female advantage has also been evident in midterm elections. In the 2008 election white women were seven points more likely than white men to report voting, the largest female advantage in any of the presidential elections we studied prior to that year.[49] But the gender gap in voting may have declined some in 2012. The 2012 ANES shows that white women were only four points more likely to vote than white men, a gap that is comparable to that found in that year's CPS.

The data for 2016 presents a somewhat mixed view of the gender gap in turnout. The ANES suggests that among whites, gender differences in turnout might have declined even further than that shown in 2012: 88 percent of the study's white female respondents reported voting compared to 87 percent of white men. The gender differences found in the 2016 CPS, however, are a bit larger. Among non-Hispanic whites,

Table 4-3 Percentage of Electorate Who Reported Voting for President, by Social Group, 2016

Social Group	Did Vote	Did Not Vote	Total	(N)[a]
Total electorate	85	15	100	(3,254)
Electorate, by race				
African American	84	16	100	(366)
White	88	12	100	(2,273)
Other	77	23	100	(598)
Latinos (of any race)	73	27	100	(381)
Whites, by gender				
Female	88	12	100	(1,187)
Male	87	13	100	(1,069)
Whites, by region				
New England and Mid-Atlantic	89	11	100	(440)
North Central	87	13	100	(547)
South	86	14	100	(604)
Border	87	13	100	(196)
Mountain and Pacific	90	10	100	(485)
Whites, by birth cohort				
Before 1946	95	5	100	(316)
1947–1956	93	7	100	(392)
1957–1966	89	11	100	(515)
1967–1976	84	16	100	(328)
1977–1986	85	15	100	(325)
1987–1994	77	23	100	(245)
1995–1998	81	19	100	(110)
Whites, by level of education				
Not high school graduate	67	33	100	(132)
High school graduate	85	15	100	(578)
Some college	87	13	100	(689)
College graduate	93	7	100	(510)
Advanced degree	94	6	100	(350)

(Continued)

Table 4-3 (Continued)

Social Group	Did Vote	Did Not Vote	Total	(N)[a]
Whites, by annual family income				
Less than $15,000	77	23	100	(193)
$15,000–34,999	82	18	100	(333)
$35,000–49,999	86	14	100	(248)
$50,000–74,999	87	13	100	(406)
$75,000–89,999	92	8	100	(221)
$90,000–124,999	90	10	100	(355)
$125,000–174,999	94	6	100	(230)
$175,000 and over	91	9	100	(208)
Whites, by union membership[b]				
Member	90	10	100	(361)
Nonmember	87	13	100	(1,906)
Whites, by religion				
Jewish	99	1	100	(57)
Catholic	90	10	100	(477)
Protestant	91	9	100	(763)
None	81	19	100	(483)
White Protestants, by whether born again				
Not born again	92	8	100	(333)
Born again	91	9	100	(426)
White Protestants, by religious commitment				
Medium or low	92	8	100	(321)
High	90	10	100	(303)
Very high	96	4	100	(127)
White Protestants, by religious tradition				
Mainline	96	4	100	(328)
Evangelical	90	10	100	(216)

Source: Authors' analysis of the 2016 ANES survey.

[a]Sample includes both face-to-face and Internet respondents. Numbers are weighted.

[b]Respondent or family member in union.

the CPS estimates a 3.8 percentage-point gap in turnout, with women (60.1 percent) voting at a higher rate than men (56.3 percent). Exit polls also found a similar gender difference in turnout, estimating that white women composed 37 percent of the electorate and white men accounted for 34 percent.

Surveys are not needed to study turnout in the various regions of the country. Because we have estimates of both the voting-age population and the voting-eligible population for each state, we can measure turnout once we know the number of votes cast for president. According to McDonald's estimates, turnout among the voting-age population ranged from a low of 38.3 percent in Hawaii (42.2 percent of the voting-eligible population) to a high of 69.4 percent in Minnesota (74.2 percent of the voting-eligible population). But regional differences as a whole were small. According to our calculations, among the voting-age population in the South, 52.9 percent voted; outside the South, 55 percent did. Among the voting-eligible population, 59.2 percent of southerners voted; outside the South, 60 percent did. There are small regional differences among whites. As the data in Table 4-3 show, 86 percent of southern whites said they voted; this estimate is lower but not significantly different from the estimates for whites outside the South. We used CPS state-level estimates to calculate white non-Latino turnout in the eleven southern states. The CPS estimates turnout in the South to be 55.5 percent and 59.4 percent turnout outside the South. This relatively small difference (3.9 percent) reflects a fundamental change in postwar voting patterns since the Voting Rights Act of 1965. The one-party South was destroyed, electoral competition increased, and with blacks enfranchised for the first time since the turn of the twentieth century, turnout increased among whites as well. Outside the South, turnout has declined.

Young Americans are more likely to have higher levels of formal education than their elders, and one might thus expect them to have higher levels of turnout. But they do not. Voter participation tends to increase with age, and this is supported by the ANES data presented in Table 4-3. This relationship is often attributed to changes in the life cycle; as people get older, settle down, and develop more community ties, they develop a greater appreciation for the role of government and politics in their lives, and they participate more.[50] Others argue that the effect of "life-changing" events may be overstated and that the greater likelihood of voter turnout with age is a product of greater political learning as people grow older.[51] Whatever the cause the relationship between age and voter turnout is evident in each of the studies we examined.

In both 2008 and 2012 the Obama campaign expended great effort trying to mobilize young voters. But this effort had limited success at best. Exit polls report that in 2008, eighteen- to twenty-nine-year-olds composed 18 percent of the electorate; in 2012 that number was 19 percent. These numbers represent a modest increase from the 2004 election, where the youngest cohort of voters represented 17 percent of the electorate. In the 2016 primary campaign, the youth vote was most energized by the candidacy of the seventy-four-year-old, Bernie Sanders, than by Trump or Clinton.[52] With Sanders out of the race and without the concerted efforts to mobilize young voters as during the Obama campaigns, some may have wondered if the so-called Millennials would turn out to the polls in the general election.[53] Exit polls suggest that young voters once again composed 19 percent of the electorate, as they did in 2012. However, it is important to remember that exit polls are not nationally representative but instead tend to focus on competitive states. Thus to examine voting participation among young people more broadly, we examined Census Bureau estimates. The CPS reports turnout by age group, with eighteen- to twenty-four-year-olds being the youngest cohort for which estimates are provided. The 2016 CPS estimates turnout for this cohort to have been 39.4 percent, a small increase (although within the margin of error) of the 38 percent estimated in 2012. In the thirteen battleground states we identified in Chapter 2, the CPS reports that turnout among Millennials was approximately 43.7 percent; in non-battleground states, it was only 35.6 percent (a difference of 8.1 percentage points). However, it is important to put these numbers into perspective. Young voters, even those in battleground states, are far less likely to vote than their elders. According to CPS estimates, nationally, adults who were forty-five years old or older participated in the election at a rate of 64.1 percent, roughly 1.6 times more likely than the youngest cohort. Thus age continues to be an important predictor of voter turnout rates in the United States.

Income and Union Membership

Jan Leighley and Jonathan Nagler argue that there is no better measure of an individual's social class than income, and income is strongly linked to voter participation.[54] The 2016 ANES shows that respondents' family income is related to reported turnout. White respondents with family incomes less than $15,000 were over thirteen percentage points less likely to vote than those with incomes over $90,000. We found strong relationships between income and validated turnout in 1980, 1984, and 1988 and between income and reported turnout in all the presidential elections between 1982 and 2012. Earlier analyses of ANES data also demonstrate a strong relationship between family income and turnout in all the presidential elections between 1952 and 1976 and all the midterm elections between 1958 and 1978.[55] Previous CPS surveys have also shown a strong relationship between income and turnout, and the data for 2016 are no different. The CPS data show that turnout among all respondents with incomes less than $15,000 was 36.9 percent, whereas turnout among those with incomes greater than $100,000 was 74.5 percent.

Surveys over the years have found a weak and inconsistent relationship between union membership and turnout. Being in a household with a union member may create organizational ties that encourage voting. And unions have also been an important mobilizing agent for the Democratic Party, which for a significant portion of the postwar period relied on white working-class support as part of its electoral coalition. Yet Leighley and Nagler argue that the small and sporadic empirical association between union membership and turnout may result from union mobilization efforts increasing turnout among members and nonmembers alike. To support their claim they provide evidence that the decline in union membership since 1964 has resulted in a decrease in voter turnout among low and middle-class income groups regardless of membership. Exit polls show that voters from union households made up eighteen percent of the electorate. The 2016 ANES shows the effect of union membership to be small, with members reporting turnout at a slightly higher rate (3 percent more) than nonmembers. In both 2008 and 2012, we found no difference in turnout between union members and nonmembers.

Religion

Religion continues to play a powerful role in American public life.[56] A 2014 survey by the Pew Research Center shows that 82 percent of Americans say that religion is an important part of their lives, and over half say they attend religious services on at least a monthly basis.[57] Religious individuals tend to have strong social networks, which facilitate the transmittal of political information and ease the costs of voting.[58] Churches also serve as direct and indirect vehicles for voter mobilization.[59]

In the earlier postwar years, Catholics were more likely to vote than Protestants, but these differences have declined.[60] The low turnout of Protestants, clearly documented by ANES surveys conducted between 1952 and 1978, resulted largely from two factors.[61] First, Protestants were more likely to live in the South, which was once a low turnout region. And, second, Protestants were more likely to be black, a group that had much lower turnout than whites. We have always compared turnout or reported turnout by comparing white Catholics with white Protestants. Except for the 1980 election, when there were no differences between Catholics and Protestants, Catholics were more likely to vote when vote validation measures were used (1984 and 1988). Catholics were also more likely to report voting in the five elections between 1992 and 2004, but in 2008 and 2012 Protestants and Catholics were equally likely to turn out. The 2016 ANES inquired about respondents' religious affiliations and practices, and as seen in Table 4-3, Protestants and Catholics once again reported turning out in roughly equal rates. Exit polls estimate that Protestants composed 27 percent of the electorate, whereas Catholics were 23 percent.[62] Fifteen percent of the electorate did not profess a religion.

Between 1952 and 1996 Jews had higher reported turnout than either Protestants or Catholics in six of the seven presidential elections as well as in five of the six midterm elections between 1958 and 1978. We found Jews to have higher levels of turnout or reported turnout in all seven elections between 1980 and 2012. In 2016, although exit polls estimated that Jewish voters represented only 3 percent of the electorate, the ANES suggests that Jews were nearly ten percentage points more likely to vote than Protestants or Catholics—the highest turnout level among any religious group.

For nearly three decades, fundamentalist Protestants have been a pivotal player in American politics. As we will see in Chapter 5, fundamentalist Protestants are conservative on social issues, such as abortion and same-sex marriage, and tend to throw their support overwhelmingly toward Republican presidential candidates. Indeed Christian conservative churches and organizations expend considerable resources mobilizing voters through get-out-the-vote efforts and attempt to galvanize supporters through the circulation of voter information guides.[63] In examining turnout among white fundamentalist Protestants since the 1992 election, we have found that the success of these groups in mobilizing their supporters has varied from election to election. In 2016 we found no statistically significant difference in reported turnout between Protestants who say they are born-again Christians and those who say they are not.[64]

Lyman A. Kellstedt argues that religious commitment is an important factor contributing to voting behavior.[65] Using multiple indicators we were able to construct a measure of religious commitment using the ANES.[66] To score "very high" on this measure, respondents had to report attending church at least once a week. In addition they had to say that religion provided "a great deal" of guidance in their lives and to believe that the Bible is literally true or the "word of God." In 1992, 1996, 2000, and 2004, respondents who scored very high on this measure were the most likely to report voting, but in 2008 there was only a weak relationship between religious commitment and whether white Protestants said they voted. We lacked the data necessary to measure religious commitment in 2012. The 2016 ANES shows that white Protestants with very high religious commitment are about four to six percentage points more likely to vote than those with lower levels of commitment. The 2016 exit polls show that 33 percent of voters said they attended church weekly or more; 16 percent of the electorate reported attending monthly; 29 percent declared they attend religious services only a few times a year; and 22 percent identified as never attending religious services.

Most white Protestants can be classified into two categories, mainline and evangelical, which according to Pew Research Center's Religious Landscape Survey, make up more than two-fifths of the total U.S. adult population.[67] As R. Stephen Warner has pointed out, "The root of the [mainline] liberal position is the interpretation of Christ as a moral teacher who told his disciples that they could best honor him by helping those in need." By contrast, says Warner, "the evangelical interpretation sees Jesus (as they prefer to call him) as one who offers salvation to anyone who confesses in his name." Liberal or mainline Protestants stress the importance of sharing their abundance with the needy, whereas evangelicals see the Bible as a source of revelation about Jesus.[68]

In classifying Protestants as mainline or evangelical, we rely on their denomination. For example, Episcopalians, Congregationalists, and most Methodists are classified as mainline, whereas Baptists, Pentecostals, and many small denominations are classified as evangelicals.[69] In 1992, 1996, 2000, 2008, and 2012, white mainline Protestants were more likely than white evangelicals to report voting. And we find similar evidence in 2016 with mainline Protestants being six percentage points more likely to report voting than evangelicals. These results are scarcely surprising because mainline Protestants have higher levels of formal education than evangelicals. Only in 2004, when fundamentalist churches launched a massive get-out-the-vote effort, were white evangelicals as likely to report voting as white mainline Protestants.

Education

Surveys consistently reveal a strong relationship between formal education and electoral participation. The tendency for better-educated citizens to be more likely to vote is one of the most extensively documented facts in the study of politics. Indeed in their classic study, *Who Votes?*, Raymond E. Wolfinger and Steven J. Rosenstone note the "transcendent power of education" as a predictor of voter turnout.[70] Better-educated Americans have higher levels of political knowledge and political awareness; they also are more likely to possess the resources—money, time, and civic skills—that reduce the information costs of voting.[71]

The 2016 ANES reveals a strong relationship between formal education and voter turnout. Whites who did not graduate from high school were nearly twenty-six percentage points less likely to report voting than those who graduated college. The 2016 CPS also found a strong relationship between education and reported voter turnout. Among all citizens (i.e., regardless of race) with less than a high school education, only 34.3 percent reported voting, and among those with only a high school diploma, 51.5 percent said they cast a ballot. Among those citizens with some college-level education, 63.3 percent reported voting, and among college graduates, turnout was 76.3 percent.

Earlier we noted that education was also strongly associated with voter turnout for African Americans and Latinos. According to the 2016 ANES, blacks with less than a high school education turned out at a reported rate of 86.2 percent (a number likely inflated by few observations fitting into this category), whereas those with a high school diploma reported turning out at a 79.8 percent rate. Turnout among African Americans with some college education was 88.7 percent, and among those with a college degree, it was 91.2 percent. Turnout differences among Latinos at varying levels of education were quite sharp. Latinos with less than a high school education turned out a reported rate of 72.4 percent; the rate was 71.2 percent among Latinos who are high school graduates. Turnout among Latinos with some college education was 65.6 percent, and for those with a college degree, turnout was 88.3 percent.

CHANGES IN TURNOUT AFTER 1960

The postwar turnout rate peaked in 1960. According to the U.S. Census Bureau, in that year, only 43.2 percent of whites and 20.1 percent of blacks twenty-five years and older were high school graduates. By 2010, 87.6 percent of whites and 84.2 percent of blacks were high school graduates. In 1960 only 8.1 percent of whites and 3.1 percent of blacks were college graduates. By 2010, 30.3 percent of whites and 19.8 percent of blacks had obtained college degrees. The growth in educational attainment is a remarkable change in American society, and this social transformation plays a central role in one of the longest-standing empirical puzzles in the study of political behavior, a puzzle Richard A. Brody labels the "puzzle of political participation."[72] Given that education is a strong predictor of voter turnout at the individual level, why did national turnout levels decline between 1960 and 1980, and why did they stabilize, roughly speaking, thereafter, during a time when education levels rose dramatically?

Political scientists have studied the postwar changes in voter turnout extensively over the past several decades. Given the influence of education on turnout, one would expect increasing levels of education would lead to a substantial increase in turnout over this time, and certainly not a decline in voter participation of any degree, as happened between 1960 and 1980. This suggests that any stimulating effect of education on voter turnout was likely offset by other factors that depressed it. Some scholars argue that the decline in turnout was a function of social forces, such as the changing age distribution of the electorate and a decline in social institutions generally. Others point to institutional changes, such as the expansion of suffrage to eighteen-year-olds or to the ways in which the political parties conduct their campaigns as sources for the decline in voter turnout. Still others argue that the decline in voter turnout reflected changes in political attitudes that are fundamental for encouraging political participation.

The research by McDonald and Popkin provides one important part of the explanation for why turnout among the voting-age population has declined during the past half century. The percentage of noncitizens among the voting-age population in the United States has increased markedly from less than 2 percent in 1960 to 8.5 percent in 2010.[73] Moreover, in 1960, fewer than half a million people were incarcerated or were convicted felons, whereas in 2012 about five million were. This has resulted in an expansion in the number of ineligible voters in the United States. These changes would tend to reduce turnout among the voting-age population. Of course neither the growth in noncitizens nor the increased number of disenfranchised felons is so large (large though these changes are) as to be sufficient for explaining the entire decline in turnout from 1960 onward. Moreover, these factors have increased at a higher rate in recent decades, but turnout no longer appears to be in decline.

In a comprehensive study of the decline in turnout between 1960 and 1988, Ruy Teixeira identifies three of the social forces that contributed to declining levels of voter participation.[74] After 1960 the electorate became significantly younger as the post-World War II baby boomer generation (those born between 1946 and 1964) came of age. Thus the largest cohort in the electorate consisted of baby boomers, who were of an age when participation is lowest. Of course, boomers are considerably older today and now reside in the age cohort that is most likely to turnout, so they should be fueling an increase in participation. Teixeira also cites the decline in the percentage of Americans who were married, and married people are more likely to vote than those who are unmarried. He also points to declining church attendance as contributing to the decline in voter turnout.[75] Teixeira argues that the decline in church attendance, which reduces Americans' ties to their communities, was the most important of these three factors in reducing turnout and suggests that voter participation would have declined even further had education not been a countervailing force.[76]

Steven J. Rosenstone and John Mark Hansen also develop a comprehensive explanation for the decline in turnout. Using data from the ANES, they examine the effect of expanded suffrage (estimating that the inclusion of eighteen-, nineteen-, and twenty-year-olds in the 1972 elections likely caused about a one percentage point decline in turnout) and reduced voter registration requirements on voting. They found that reported turnout declined eleven percentage points from the 1960s to the 1980s. Yet their analysis also demonstrates that the increase in formal education was the most important factor preventing an even greater decline in voter participation. They estimate that turnout would have declined sixteen percentage points if it had not been for the combined effect of rising education levels and liberalized election laws.[77] Next we discuss another institutional change that they argue contributed substantively to the decline in turnout—a change in the way political parties conduct electoral campaigns.

Most analysts agree that attitudinal changes contributed to the decline in electoral participation. Indeed our own analysis has focused on the effects of attitudinal changes, particularly the influence of changes in party loyalties and the role of what George I. Balch and others have called feelings of "external political efficacy"—that is, the belief that political authorities will respond to attempts to influence them.[78] These are the same two fundamental attitudes analyzed by Teixeira in his first major study of turnout, and they are among the attitudes examined by Rosenstone and Hansen.[79] We found these attitudes contributed to the decline in turnout from 1960 through 1980, and they have remained influential in every presidential election we have studied from 1980 to 2016.[80]

To measure party identification, we use a standard set of questions to gauge individuals' psychological attachment to a partisan reference group.[81] In Chapter 8, we examine how party identification contributes to the way people vote. But party loyalties also contribute to *whether* people vote. Strong feelings of party identification contribute to one's psychological involvement in politics.[82] Moreover, party loyalties also reduce the time and effort needed to decide how to vote and thus reduce the costs of voting.[83] In every presidential election since 1952, the ANES studies have shown that strong partisans are more likely to vote than weaker partisans and independents who lean toward one of the parties. And in every election since 1960, independents with no partisan leanings have been the least likely to vote.

Partisanship is an important contributor to voters' decisions to turn out, but the strength of party loyalties in the United States has varied over time. Between 1952 and 1964 the percentage of self-identified "strong partisans" among the white electorate never fell below 25 percent. It then fell to 27 percent in 1966 and continued to fall, reaching its lowest level in 1978, when only 21 percent of voters identified strongly with one of the two major parties. In more recent years party identification has risen; indeed, by 2004, it had returned to 1952–1964 levels. After a temporary decline in 2008 due to a decrease in Republican loyalties, the percentage of whites who were strong party identifiers rose to just over 30 percent in 2012 and reached 37.4 percent in 2016.[84]

Feelings of political efficacy also contribute to voter participation. Citizens may expect to derive benefits from voting if they believe that government is responsive to their demands. Conversely, those who believe that political leaders will not or cannot respond to popular demands may see little reason to engage in political participation.[85] In fourteen of the sixteen elections between 1952 and 2012, Americans with high levels of political efficacy were more likely to vote than those at lower levels of efficacy.[86]

From 1960 to 1980 feelings of political efficacy dropped precipitously, and they remain low and in decline today. In 1956 and 1960, 64 percent of whites reported high levels of political efficacy, with only 15 percent scoring low. In 2016 few Americans felt that that government responded to their needs. Indeed efficacy was at an all-time low. Only 21.6 percent of whites scored "high" on our measure of political efficacy, and 52.3 percent scored "low." Incredibly the portion of respondents with low levels of political efficacy increased roughly seven percentage points since 2012.

The steepest declines in partisan attachment and political efficacy occurred between 1960 and 1980, contemporaneous with the sharpest decline in voter participation. Our analysis of voter turnout during this two-decade period suggests that the combined impact of the decline in party identification and the decline in beliefs about government responsiveness accounts for roughly 70 percent of the decline of electoral participation. The ANES reports a decline in validated turnout among white voters of 10.3 percentage points between 1960 and 1980. By our estimates, if there had been no decline in either partisan attachments or external political efficacy, the decline in turnout would have been only 2.9 percentage points.[87] In previous volumes we have noted the persistent role these attitudes play in predicting voter turnout in subsequent election years. Whereas party loyalties have rebounded to 1952–1964 levels, Americans' feelings of efficacy remain anemic, thus preventing a substantial increase in turnout levels. Using a rather simple algebraic procedure, we can estimate the percentage of whites in 2016 who would have reported voting for president had strength of partisanship, and external political efficacy remained at 1960 levels.[88] Our estimate suggests that reported turnout among whites in 2016 would be 1.5 percentage points higher if not for these attitudinal changes.

In Table 4.4 we present the joint relationship between strength of party identification, feelings of efficacy, and reported electoral participation in the 2016 presidential election. As we have found in the past, strength of party identification and feelings of political efficacy are weakly related, but both contribute to turnout. Reading across each row reveals that strength of party identification is positively related to reported electoral participation, but the strength of this relationship has been weaker in the past two elections relative to years we have studied. The difference in reported voting among whites with strong partisanship and those describing themselves as independents who lean toward a party is six percentage points for those high in efficacy and eight points for those low in efficacy. These differences were much smaller in 2012, but in 2008, we reported differences of fifteen percentage points for those high in efficacy and thirty-four points for those low in efficacy. Reading down each column, we see a consistent relationship between feelings of political efficacy and reported voting within each partisan group—on the magnitude of six to nine percentage point differences. This suggests that the record-low level of political efficacy in 2016—52.3 percent report "low" levels of efficacy—was distributed among strong, weak, and nonpartisans alike and that efficacy had a strong relationship with decisions to turn out. This finding is similar to what we found in 2012, when political efficacy was at a then record low (50 percent scored "low"). In 2008, by comparison, we found a strong relationship between feelings of efficacy and reported turnout in only one partisan group: independents who lean toward a political party. In that year 43.7 percent of respondents reported low feelings of political efficacy.

A comprehensive analysis of the role of attitudinal factors would have taken into account other factors that might have eroded turnout. For instance, as has been well documented, there has been a substantial decline in trust during the past four decades, a decline that appears to be occurring in a large number of democracies.[89] In 1964, when political trust among whites was highest, 77 percent of whites trusted the government to do what was right just about always or most of the time, and 74 percent of blacks endorsed this view.[90] Political trust reached a very low level in 1980, when only 25 percent of whites and 26 percent of blacks trusted the government. Trust rebounded during the Reagan years, but it fell after that, and by 1992 trust was almost as low as it was in 1980. After that, trust rose in most elections, and by 2004, 50 percent of whites and 34 percent of blacks trusted the government. But trust dropped markedly among whites during the next four years, and it dropped somewhat among blacks. In 2008, 30 percent of whites and 28 percent of blacks trusted the government.[91] In 2012, after the first term of the first black president, 19 percent of whites—a sharp decline—and 40 percent of blacks—a sharp increase—trusted the government in Washington to do what is right. Among Latinos, trust declined by six points over the course of Obama's first term from 36 to 30 percent. In 2016 trust in government

Table 4-4 Percentage of Whites Who Reported Voting for President, by Strength of Party Identification and Sense of External Political Efficacy, 2016

Score on External Political Efficacy Index	Strength of Party Identification							
	Strong Partisan		Weak Partisan		Independent Who Leans toward a Party		Independent with No Partisan Leaning	
	%	(N)	%	(N)	%	(N)	%	(N)
High	97	(236)	91	(140)	91	(118)	66	(34)
Medium	88	(201)	89	(134)	91	(129)	66	(50)
Low	93	(454)	82	(314)	85	(300)	75	(150)

Source: Authors' analysis of the 2016 ANES survey.

Note: The numbers in parentheses are the totals on which the percentages are based. Sample includes both face-to-face and Internet respondents. Numbers are weighted.

was in marked decline among all groups. Only 8.6 percent of whites profess trust in government, whereas 20.8 percent of blacks and 17.8 of Latinos did.

Although the decline in trust in government would seem to be an obvious explanation for the decline in turnout since the 1960s, scholarship shows little evidence supporting this. In most years Americans who distrusted the government were as likely to vote as those who were politically trusting. In the past two elections, the evidence has been mixed. In 2012 we found some evidence for a relationship between trust in government and turnout. Respondents who trusted the government in Washington to do what is right were nine percentage points more likely to vote than those who expressed no trust in government. This relationship was not dependent upon the race of the voter. In 2016 trust in government—or, better put, the lack thereof—seemed to motivate white voters but not blacks or Latinos. For blacks and Latinos we see no statistically significant relationship between trust in government and voter turnout. However, among whites, those who claimed to "never" trust the government were roughly seven percentage points more likely to vote than those who trusted the government "most of the time" or "always." Whether these disaffected voters turned out to vote for Donald Trump, a candidate who pledged to "drain the swamp," that is Washington, warrants investigation in Chapter 7.

ELECTION-SPECIFIC FACTORS

Focusing on long-term stable factors related to voting, such as social demographics and partisan attachments, might give one the impression that election-specific factors may not matter. Yet in any election there will be political and nonpolitical circumstances that affect voting. Among the nonpolitical factors shown to affect voter turnout is election day weather. Bad weather is likely to increase the physical costs of voting and make it more difficult for potential voters to get to the polls. A study by Brad T. Gomez, Thomas G. Hansford, and George A. Krause, which examined county-level voter turnout in every presidential election from 1944 to 2000, showed that for every inch of rain a county received above its thirty-year average rainfall, turnout declined by nearly one percentage point.[92] In close elections a nonpolitical factor like weather could have real political consequences by keeping voters in some localities away from the polls and potentially changing electoral outcomes.[93]

Politics matters, too, of course. Not all elections are competitive, and one factor that stimulates voter turnout is the expected closeness of the outcome.[94] According to the rational choice theory of voting developed by Anthony Downs and refined by William H. Riker and Peter C. Ordeshook, a person's expected benefit from voting increases in close elections because the probability that one's vote will directly affect the outcome is higher.[95] Close elections also make it easier for potential voters to become politically informed as heightened media coverage, television advertising, and interpersonal discussion of politics help create an information-rich environment. And parties and candidates are more likely to engage in get-out-the-vote efforts when election outcomes hang in the balance.

In Chapter 2 we identified the thirteen battleground states in the 2016 election.[96] Early predictions suggested these states might have close elections. According to the 2016 CPS, average voter turnout (voting-age population) in these thirteen states was 60.0 percent, whereas the average in non-battleground states was 54.6 percent.

At the individual level, perceptions of the closeness of the presidential election may vary from person to person. These perceptions may be informed by the actual competitiveness of the election in the individual's state, or they may reflect the expected outcome of the Electoral College. But people sometimes espouse a distorted view of the competitive nature of the election. As Rosenstone and Hansen note, "[t]his may reflect ignorance, excitability, wishful thinking, accurate assessments of the leanings of friends and localities, or sober recollections of the inconstancy of public opinion polls."[97] Our analysis of the ANES shows that the percentage who thinks the election will be close varies greatly from election to election. For example, in 1996, only 52 percent of whites thought the election between Bill Clinton and Bob Dole would be close, but in 2000, 88 percent thought the contest between Gore and Bush would be close. In 2008 there were clear racial differences in individuals' perceptions of the competitiveness of the election. Among whites 82 percent thought the election would be close; among blacks only 69 percent did. These racial differences were remarkably persistent in 2012. In 2016, 72.6 percent of ANES respondents thought the election would be close. Racial differences in perception were once again evident; 75 percent of whites thought the election would be close, whereas 62.2 percent of blacks and 64.8 percent of Latinos thought so. These racial and ethnic differences may be a function of differences in partisan attachment. Republicans (78.7 percent) were significantly more likely than Democrats (63.8 percent) to think the election was going to be close. To the extent that perceptions of closeness are related to decisions to turn out, these partisan differences suggest that Democrats may have been overconfident in their party's chances to win and, perhaps, less motivated to go to the polls.

The most direct way that campaigns attempt to influence turnout is through get-out-the-vote efforts. Modern campaigns expend exorbitant amounts of money and effort trying to bring their voters to the polls. Campaigns employ local phone banks and door-to-door canvassing; they use direct mail and social networking technology and even old-fashioned political rallies all in an effort to stimulate voter interests. But to what effect? Over a decade ago political scientists Donald Green and Alan Gerber began a research agenda aimed at answering this question. Green and Gerber use field experiments to gauge the effectiveness of voter mobilization tactics.[98] The field experiments typically use voter registration rolls to randomly assign a subset of voters into "treatment" and "control" conditions. Those assigned to the treatment group are exposed to the specific get-out-the-vote tactic being tested, whereas those in the control group are not.[99] After the election the voter rolls are reexamined to determine whether voter turnout was higher among those in the treatment group than those in control group, thus providing evidence that the mobilization tactic *caused* an increase in turnout. Green and Gerber's work, as well as that undertaken subsequently by others, suggests, among other things, that voters tend to respond best to personalized methods and messages, such as door-to-door canvassing, than impersonal techniques, such as "robocalls."[100] Pressure from one's social network is also important in mobilizing voters to the polls. In one of their most well-known experiments to date, Gerber and Green, joined by Christopher Larimer, find that voters are more likely to turn out—by an increased probability of 8.1 percentage points—when they are told prior to election day that their decision to vote will be publicized to their neighbors. This experiment not only demonstrates the effectiveness of social pressure in mobilizing voters; it provides supporting evidence for the argument that the historic decline in turnout could have been caused in part by the concomitant decline in Americans' willingness to join associational groups, such as fraternal organizations and churches.

Unlike these experimental designs, it is difficult to estimate the *causal* effect of mobilization on turnout using surveys. Consider the fact that campaigns often contact voters based on how likely they are to vote. Can we really say that mobilization causes turnout, or does the potential for turnout cause mobilization? Because the survey environment typically measures whether the individual was contacted by a political party and the individual's reported turnout contemporaneously, it is hard to establish for certain which variable came first. Thus an analysis of the relationship between whether an individual was contacted by a political party and their reported turnout using the 2016 ANES is likely to only establish correlation, not causation.[101]

The longitudinal nature of the ANES does offer interesting insights into changes in the mobilization of the electorate, however. Most notably the percentage of Americans who say they have been contacted by a political party increased after the 1960 election. In 1960, 22 percent of the electorate said a political party had contacted them.[102] By 1980, 32 percent said they had been contacted. The upward trend abated in 1992, when only 20 percent said they had been contacted by a political party. The percentage that said they had been contacted by a political party grew in 1996 and in 2000, and it increased slightly between 2000 and 2004. It grew again somewhat in 2008, when 43 percent said they had been contacted, with whites somewhat more likely to claim they were contacted (45 percent) than blacks (38 percent). In 2012, 39 percent of the electorate said a political party had contacted them, a decrease from four years earlier. This number dropped precipitously in 2016, when only 31.8 of respondents reported contact by one of the parties. That party contact went down in 2016 may not be a surprise to close observers of the campaigns. Much was made during the general election season about the limited resources dedicated by the Trump campaign to the mobilization "ground game."[103] Indeed our estimates show that Republicans were more than three percentage points less likely to be contacted by a party than Democrats, 32.9 to 36.2, respectively. The study of party contact rates over time may shed further light on changes in turnout. Similar to education, increased levels of party contact over time may have prevented the decline from being even greater.

DOES LOW VOTER TURNOUT MATTER?

Many bemoan the low levels of turnout in U.S. elections. Some claim that low rates of voter participation undermine the legitimacy of elected political leaders. Seymour Martin Lipset, for instance, argues that the existence of a large bloc of nonparticipants in the electorate may be potentially dangerous because it means that many Americans have weak ties to the established parties and political leaders.[104] This may increase the prospects of electoral instability or perhaps political instability generally. Others argue that the low levels of turnout, at minimum, increase the probability that American elections produce "biased" outcomes, reflecting the preferences of an active political class while ignoring those who may be alienated or disenfranchised.

Turnout rates may also increase the electoral fortunes of one party over the other. Conventional wisdom holds that because nonvoters are more likely to come from low socioeconomic-status groups and ethnic minorities—groups that tend to vote Democratic—higher turnout benefits the Democrats. James DeNardo, using aggregate election data from 1932 to 1976, and Thomas Hansford and Brad Gomez, using aggregate data from 1948 to 2000, provide evidence that increases in turnout enlarge the vote share of Democratic candidates, although the nature of the relationship is more complex and weaker than one might assume.[105]

Elected officials appear convinced that their reelection fates depend on the level of turnout.[106] Over the past several decades, at both the national and state level, legislators have debated a number of laws aimed at making it easier (or sometimes harder) for citizens to vote. Bills that make it easier to register to vote, such as the 1993 motor voter law, and bills that promote convenience voting mechanisms, such as early voting or vote by mail, have typically divided legislators along strict party lines with Democrats supporting efforts to expand the electorate and Republicans opposing them.

More recently Republicans have led in the push to require voter identification at the polls, typically by requiring the presentation of a government-issued identification card, such as a driver's license. At the time of the 2016 election, these bills had passed in thirty-four states.[107] After the 2012 election, North Carolina, which had a Republican legislature and governor, passed a strict voter identification requirement. In addition to requiring people to show photo identification, the North Carolina law condensed the number of early voting days, abolished same-day registration, and eliminated out-of-precinct voting. Supporters of the North Carolina bill argued that the bill attempted to increase the integrity of elections; opponents of the bill argued that the aim of the bill was voter suppression, particularly minority voters.[108] In July 2016 the Fourth Circuit Court of Appeals struck down the North Carolina law, stating that the state legislature had acted with "discriminatory intent" and that the law targeted the state's black voters with "almost surgical precision" to reduce their voter participation.[109] In May 2017 the U.S. Supreme Court rejected the state's appeal of the case.[110]

In our analyses of the 1980, 1984, and 1988 presidential elections, we argued that among most reasonable scenarios, increased turnout would not have led to Democratic victories.[111] In 1992 increased turnout coincided with the Democratic victory but not a higher share of the Democratic vote. Our analyses suggest that Bill Clinton benefited from increased turnout but that he benefited more by converting voters who had supported George H. W. Bush four years earlier.[112] Despite the six percentage point decline in turnout between 1992 and 1996, Clinton was easily reelected. Even so there is some evidence that the decline in turnout cost Clinton votes.[113]

In view of the closeness of the 2000 contest, it seems plausible that a successful get-out-the-vote effort by the Democrats could have swung the election to Al Gore. In 2004 turnout rose by over four percentage points, regardless of how it is measured. But Bush won with a majority of the popular vote, even though his margin over Kerry was small. Our analyses suggest that the Republicans were more successful in mobilizing their supporters than the Democrats. Some argue that the GOP gained because in eleven states proposals to ban same-sex marriages were on the ballot. But, as we have shown, turnout was only one point higher in the states that had these propositions on the ballot than in the states that did not.[114] Bush won nine of the eleven states with such a proposition, but of those nine states only Ohio was closely contested, and turnout increased by nine percentage points there.

In 2008 many argued that Obama's victory was aided by the mobilization of new voters, particularly blacks, Latinos, and eighteen- to twenty-five-year-olds. But we found little evidence of turnout effects in the 2008. The ANES data suggest that Republican identifiers were more likely to vote than Democrats in 2008, and Obama would have enjoyed an increase in support had Democrats and Republicans voted at the same rate. However, we found no additional evidence that higher turnout would have benefited Obama.[115]

As was the case in 2008, Obama was able to win the 2012 election in spite of Republican identifiers turning out at a higher rate than Democrats. Our analyses showed that if we assume that each of the Democratic identifiers had turnout as high as Republican identifiers and assume that the additional Democrats drawn to the polls would have vote the same way as the Democrats who did not, Obama would have gained about 1.5 percentage points.

As argued originally by the authors of *The American Voter*, if nonvoters and occasional voters hold preferences that differ from those of regular (or core) voters, then variation in turnout is likely to have meaningful electoral implications.[116] Thus, in Table 4-5, we examine whether respondents reported voting for president in 2016, according to their party identification, their positions on the issues (the "balance-of-issues" measure), and their evaluations of the performance of the incumbent president

(Obama), which party is best able to handle the important problems facing the country, and their beliefs about whether the country is going in the right direction (the summary measure of "retrospective" evaluations).

Although Hillary Clinton won the popular vote, her party did not win the turnout battle. Table 4-5 shows that strong Republicans were more likely to vote than strong Democrats by four percentage points, and independents who felt close to the Republican Party were more likely to vote than those who leaned toward the Democrats by three percentage points. Among weak identifiers, the Democrats had the advantage but only by two percentage points. If we assume that each of the low-turnout groups had turnouts as high as each of the comparable high-turnout groups, and assume that the additional voters drawn to the polls voted the same way as actual voters, we estimate that Hillary Clinton would have gained about 1.5 percentage points to her popular vote total—whether this would have affected Clinton's Electoral College fortunes is difficult to determine.

In Chapter 6, we examine the issue preferences of the electorate. For every presidential election between 1980 and 2008, we built a measure of overall issue preferences based on the seven-point scales used by the ANES surveys to measure the issue preferences of the electorate.[117] But we have found little or no evidence of issue differences between those who vote and those who do not.

In 2016 our overall measure of issues preferences is based on scales measuring the respondent's position on six issues: (1) reducing or increasing government services, (2) decreasing or increasing defense spending, (3) government health insurance, (4) government job guarantees, (5) government helping blacks, and (6) protecting the environment.[118] As Table 4-5 shows partisan differences on the balance-of-issues scale do not contribute significantly to differences in voter turnout. Respondents who are strongly Republican on the issues were one percentage point more likely to report voting than those who are strongly Democratic. Respondents who were moderately Democratic were four points more likely to vote than those who were moderately Republican on the issues. Those who were slightly Republican on the issues were equally likely to vote as those who lean toward the Democrats on the issues. Based on our simulation, if the differences in turnout based on issue preference were leveled out, Clinton would have gained about 1.3 percentage points to her popular vote total.

In Chapter 7 we discuss the retrospective evaluations of the electorate. Voters, some analysts argue, make their decisions based not just on their evaluation of policy promises but also on their evaluation of how well the party in power is doing. In past studies we used a summary measure based on presidential approval, an evaluation of the job the government was doing dealing with the most important problem facing the country, and an assessment of which party would do a better job dealing with this problem. Across each of the elections that we have studied, the relationship between retrospective evaluations and turnout has been weak, at best, and often nonexistent.

In 2016 we employed a summary measure based on the respondent's approval of the president, the respondent's evaluation of how good a job the government had been doing over the last four years, and the respondent's belief about whether things in the country are going in the right direction or are on the wrong track. Although 53 percent of voters approved of President Obama, they overwhelmingly

Table 4-5 Percentage of Electorate Who Reported Voting for President, by Party Identification, Issue Preferences, and Retrospective Evaluations, 2016

	Voted	Did Not Vote	Total	(N)
Strong Democrat	90	10	100	(747)
Weak Democrat	84	16	100	(453)
Independent, leans Democratic	84	16	100	(351)
Independent, no partisan leaning	67	33	100	(358)
Independent, leans Republican	87	13	100	(376)
Weak Republican	82	18	100	(392)
Strong Republican	94	6	100	(563)
Electorate, by scores on balance-of-issues measure				
Strongly Democratic	92	8	100	(323)
Moderately Democratic	88	12	100	(327)
Slightly Democratic	81	19	100	(495)
Neutral	81	19	100	(465)
Slightly Republican	81	19	100	(609)
Moderately Republican	84	16	100	(555)
Strongly Republican	93	7	100	(478)
Electorate, by scores on summary measure of retrospective evaluations of incumbent party				
Strongly opposed	91	9	100	(999)
Moderately opposed	77	23	100	(396)
Slightly opposed	80	20	100	(189)
Neutral	76	24	100	(392)
Slightly supportive	86	14	100	(449)
Moderately supportive	89	11	100	(248)
Strongly supportive	90	10	100	(525)

Source: Authors' analysis of the 2016 ANES survey.

Note: Sample includes both face-to-face and Internet respondents. Numbers are weighted. Chapter 6 describes how the balance-of-issues measure was constructed, and Chapter 7 describes how the summary measure of retrospective evaluations was constructed. Both measures differ slightly from those presented in previous volumes of *Change and Continuity*, so care should be given when comparing to earlier election studies.

(72.5 percent) believed that the nation was headed on the "wrong track." On our summary scale roughly half of the respondents, 48.8 percent, had negative views of recent governmental performance; 37.2 percent had a positive view. Yet, interestingly, those who were supportive were more likely to vote on balance. Whereas those with the strongest views turned out in roughly equal proportions, those who were slightly or moderately supportive of the incumbent party were nine percentage points more likely to vote than those who opposed the incumbent party slightly or moderately. Thus, in our simulation, evening out turnout differences based on retrospective evaluations brings more voters with negative views of the recent past into the equation. Nevertheless, adding more voters to the tally, even those with a pessimistic view of things, would have aided the Democratic candidate, Clinton. If turnout differences between retrospective subgroups are eliminated, Clinton would have gained 1.1 percentage points.

In most elections higher turnout is unlikely to affect the outcome. But in close elections, like that held in 2016, variation in voter turnout is most likely to have an effect on who wins or loses. In our analyses the largest and most consistent turnout effects that we see are associated with differences in voter participation among party identifiers. Consistent with other scholarship we found that higher turnout benefits the Democrats but only to a small degree.[119] Moreover, we have found limited evidence in our analyses to support the argument that low voter turnout biases election outcomes on the basis of issue preferences or retrospective evaluations. Because in most presidential contests increased turnout would not have affected the outcome, some analysts might argue that low turnout does not matter.[120]

Despite this evidence we do not accept the conclusion that low turnout is unimportant. We are especially concerned that turnout is low among the disadvantaged. Some observers believe this is so because political leaders structure political alternatives in a way that provides disadvantaged Americans with relatively little political choice. Frances Fox Piven and Richard A. Cloward, for example, acknowledge that the policy preferences of voters and nonvoters are similar, but they argue that this similarity exists because of the way that elites have structured policy choices:

> "Political attitudes would inevitably change over time," they maintain, "if the allegiance of voters from the bottom became the object of partisan competition, for then politicians would be prodded to identify and articulate the grievances of and aspirations of the lower-income voters in order to win their support, thus helping to give form and voice to a distinctive political class."[121]

We cannot accept this argument, either, mainly because it is highly speculative and there is little evidence to support it. The difficulty in supporting this view may in part stem from the nature of survey research itself because questions about public policy are usually framed along lines of controversy as defined by mainstream political leaders. Occasionally, however, surveys pose radical policy alternatives, and they often ask open-ended questions that allow respondents to state their own preferences. We find no concrete evidence that low turnout leads American political leaders to ignore the policy preferences of the electorate.

Nevertheless, low turnout can scarcely be healthy for a democracy. As we have shown much of the initial decline in U.S. voter turnout following the 1960s could be attributed to decreases in partisan attachment and external political efficacy. Partisan identification has largely returned to 1960s levels, but turnout has not increased proportionally. Feelings of political efficacy have continued to decline and, as we reported, were at an all-time low in 2016. If turnout remains low because an ever-growing segment of the American public believe that "public officials don't care much what people like me think" and "people like me don't have any say about what the government does," then concern seems warranted.

CHAPTER FIVE

SOCIAL FORCES AND THE VOTE

Although voting is an individual act, group characteristics influence voting choices because individuals with similar social characteristics may share similar political interests. Group similarities in voting behavior may also reflect past political conditions. The partisan loyalties of African Americans, for example, were shaped by the Civil War. Black loyalties to the Republican Party, the party of Lincoln, lasted through the 1932 election, and the steady Democratic voting of southern whites, the product of those same historical conditions, lasted even longer, at least through 1960.

It is easy to see why group-based loyalties persist over time. Studies of pre-adult political learning suggest that partisan loyalties are often passed on from generation to generation.[1] And because religion, ethnicity, and to a lesser extent, social class are often transmitted across generations as well, social divisions have considerable staying power. The interactions of social group members also reinforce similarities in political attitudes and behaviors.

Politicians often make group appeals. They recognize that to win an election, they need to mobilize the social groups that supported them in the past while attempting to cut into their opponents' bases of support. These group-based electoral coalitions often become identified at election time with the particular candidate being supported and the nature of the particular campaign, creating what we might think of as "Trump voters" or "Clinton voters," for example. Yet group-based electoral coalitions tend to be relatively stable from one election to the next, so it is perhaps best to think of these social-group loyalties as the basis for partisan coalitions, for example, "Republican voters" or "Democratic voters." Indeed political scientists often identify periods of significant electoral change, "realignments," by virtue of observing dramatic and lasting shifts in group-based support from one party to another. Thus examining the social forces that influence voting behavior is a crucial aspect for understanding change and continuity within an electoral system.

To place the 2016 presidential election within the context of recent electoral history, we examine the evolution of the Democratic Party's broad and diverse electoral coalition from its zenith in the years following the New Deal to its eventual unraveling and how the subsequent shifting of white political loyalties structures the major parties' bases and electoral competition today. It is sometimes said that Democrats tend to think in group terms more than Republicans, but it is most certainly the case that both of the major parties count on the support of core groups as part of the electoral bases. Yet the historical alteration of the Democratic Party's group-based coalition provides an important examination of how partisan allegiances change over time and how this has changed both parties' electoral fortunes. Beginning with the election of Franklin D. Roosevelt in 1932, the Democrat Party brought together sometimes disparate groups, a "coalition of minorities" that included both union and nonunion working-class households, both African Americans and native white southerners, and both Jews and Catholics. Yet by the late twentieth century, the coalition was in decline. African Americans maintained, even strengthened, their loyalty to the Democrats, but southern white conservatives have drifted to their more natural ideological home on the right and are now more likely to identify with the Republican Party. Working-class voters are a cross-pressured group who sometimes side with the Democrats on economic issues but sometimes agree with Republicans on social issues.[2] Union membership in the United States has declined greatly, making it difficult for the party to mobilize working-class voters. Jewish voters remain loyal to the Democrats, but non-white Catholic voters now support the two major parties at the roughly the same rate, and churchgoing Catholics now lean toward the Republican Party. And a growing Latino population appears to be joining the Democratic coalition.

The 1992 and 1996 presidential elections provide an example of the fragile nature of the Democratic coalition. Bill Clinton earned high levels of support from only two of the groups that made up the New Deal coalition formed by Roosevelt—African Americans and Jews. Most of the other New Deal coalition groups gave fewer than half of their votes to Clinton. Fortunately for him, in a three-way contest (it included independent candidate Ross Perot), only 43 percent of the vote was needed to win. Despite a second candidacy by Perot, the 1996 election was much more of a two-candidate fight, and Clinton won 49 percent of the popular vote. He gained ground among the vast majority of groups analyzed in this chapter, making especially large gains among union members (a traditional component of the New Deal coalition) and Latinos. In many respects the Democratic losses after 1964 can be attributed to the party's failure to hold the loyalties of the New Deal coalition groups.

In 2008 Barack Obama's victory returned a Democrat to the White House. His victory marked the first time since 1976 that a Democrat won the presidency with a majority of the popular vote. But Obama did not restore the New Deal coalition. Obama gained nearly a fourth of his total vote from black voters. This was possible because black turnout equaled white turnout and because blacks voted overwhelmingly Democratic. Yet, among the groups that we examined, only blacks and Jews (a small segment of the electorate, to be sure) gave a clear majority of their vote to Obama. Obama had only a slight edge among white union members, and he split the white Catholic vote with the Republican nominee, John McCain. Among white southerners, a mainstay of the New Deal coalition, Obama won only a third of the vote.[3]

In 2012 the coalitional divisions of 2008 were accentuated slightly. As noted in Chapter 4, 2012 marked the first time in the nation's history that turnout among African Americans exceeded that of whites. Combined with the group's extraordinarily high level of support for Obama, we estimated that blacks were between 23.7 and 24.4 percent of Obama's reelection electorate. No other Democratic presidential winner has received as large a share of his vote from the black electorate than Obama.

Conversely, Obama lost support from southern whites and non-Latino Catholics, core groups that were once part of his party's electoral coalition.

HOW SOCIAL GROUPS VOTED IN 2016

Table 5-1 presents the results of our analysis of how social groups voted in the 2016 presidential election.[4] Among the 2,564 respondents who said they voted for president, 48.8 percent said they voted for Hillary Clinton, 44.0 percent for Donald Trump, and 7.2 percent for other candidates—results that are within roughly two percentage points of the actual results (see Table 3-1). The American National Election Studies (ANES) are the best source of data for analyzing change over time, but the total number of self-reported voters is sometimes small. This can make group-based analysis tenuous if the number of sample respondents within a group is exceedingly small. Therefore, we will often supplement (sometimes by necessity) our analysis with the exit polls (pool polls) conducted by Edison Research for a consortium of news organizations.[5] For the 2016 exit polls, 24,558 voters were interviewed. Most were randomly chosen as they left 350 polling places from across the United States on election day. Respondents who voted absentee or voted early were contacted via telephone, totaling 4,398 telephone interviews in all.[6] For comparison we will sometimes reference the 2012 exit polls, for which 26,565 voters were interviewed.

Race, Gender, Region, and Age

Political differences between African Americans and whites are far sharper than any other social cleavage.[7] According to the 2016 ANES, 90 percent of black voters supported Clinton (see Table 5-1), similar to the pool poll, which indicates that 89 percent did. Clinton's level of support among black voters in 2016 was smaller than Obama's level of support (98 percent) as reported in the 2012 ANES, although the differences are negligible according to the exit polls. Based on the ANES survey, we estimate that 20.1 percent of Clinton's vote came from blacks; our analysis of the pool poll suggests that 22.2 percent did. These estimates are smaller than those associated with Barack Obama's 2012 electorate, which as we noted earlier, composed roughly 24 percent of his electoral coalition. This reduction in the proportional share of African Americans in the Democratic candidate's coalition appears to be driven primarily by the decline in voter turnout among blacks from 2012 to 2016 (see Chapter 4). Nevertheless, this is a sizable, and relatively high, contribution to the Democratic electorate and suggests that the party is heavily reliant on black voters for their electoral fortunes. Clinton's electorate is estimated to have been between 54.5 (exit poll) and 59.2 (ANES) percent white.

In comparison, African Americans comprised a very small portion of the Trump coalition. Based on the ANES estimates only 6.4 percent of blacks voted for Trump, 8 percent according to the exit polls. These estimates suggest that between 1.5 to 2.1 percent of all Trump voters were black, approximately 1 to 1.3 million of Trump's 63 million voters. Four years earlier, the Republican nominee, Mitt Romney, constructed an electorate that was estimated to be 1.9 percent black, thus roughly comparable to

Table 5-1 How Social Groups Voted for President, 2016 (Percent)

Social Group	Clinton	Trump	Other	Total	(N)[a]
Total electorate	49	44	7	100	(2,564)
Electorate, by race					
African American	90	6	4	100	(275)
White	39	54	7	100	(1,854)
Other	64	26	9	99	(422)
Latino (of any race)	69	23	8	100	(255)
Whites, by gender					
Female	41	53	7	101	(967)
Male	37	55	8	100	(872)
Whites, by region					
New England and Mid-Atlantic	53	43	4	100	(377)
North Central	38	56	7	101	(442)
South	24	69	7	100	(473)
Border	40	51	9	100	(168)
Mountain and Pacific	46	45	10	101	(393)
Whites, by birth cohort					
Before 1946	32	66	3	101	(286)
1947–1956	44	53	4	101	(329)
1957–1966	36	57	8	101	(423)
1967–1976	36	56	9	101	(259)
1977–1986	47	43	10	100	(267)
1987–1994	35	50	15	100	(176)
1995–1998	60	35	6	101	(83)
Whites, by level of education					
Not high school graduate	35	58	7	100	(77)
High school graduate	33	62	6	101	(463)
Some college	30	63	8	101	(564)
College graduate	42	48	10	100	(437)
Advanced degree	64	31	5	100	(306)

Social Group	Clinton	Trump	Other	Total	(N)[a]
Whites, by annual family income					
Less than $15,000	30	63	7	100	(140)
$15,000–34,999	39	51	10	100	(259)
$35,000–49,999	37	57	6	100	(201)
$50,000–74,999	38	58	5	101	(335)
$75,000–89,999	36	58	6	100	(186)
$90,000–124,999	39	51	10	100	(292)
$125,000–174,999	45	48	6	99	(205)
$175,000 and over	53	39	8	100	(169)
Whites, by union membership[b]					
Member	49	47	4	100	(311)
Nonmember	37	55	8	100	(1,542)
Whites, by religion					
Jewish	79	20	2	101	(54)
Catholic	37	56	7	100	(405)
Protestant	31	63	6	100	(645)
None	61	28	11	100	(363)
White Protestants, by whether born again					
Not born again	46	48	6	100	(285)
Born again	18	75	6	99	(358)
White Protestants, by religious commitment					
Medium or low	45	50	5	100	(272)
High	27	64	9	100	(256)
Very high	7	90	3	100	(112)
White Protestants, by religious tradition					
Mainline	44	52	5	101	(294)
Evangelical	19	76	5	100	(175)

Source: Authors' analysis of the 2016 ANES survey.

[a]Sample includes both face-to-face and Internet respondents. Numbers are weighted.

[b]Respondent or family member in union.

Trump's.[8] Based on the ANES we estimate that Trump's electoral coalition was 84.5 percent white; the exit poll estimate is 87.8 percent white. But this figure is not atypical for Republican presidential nominees. In 2012, for example, it is estimated that 90 to 93 percent of Romney voters were white, larger than the Trump electorate. Clearly, while the Democratic Party is increasingly reliant on black voters as a part of their coalition, the Republican Party is almost wholly dependent upon white voters.

The Democrats continue to hold a decided edge among Latino voters, but Clinton's level of support among Latinos was less than that received by Obama in 2008 and 2012. In his initial election, Obama garnered 75 percent of the Latino vote, and he did equally well in his reelection. As seen in Table 5-1, the ANES reports that Clinton received 69 percent of the Latino vote, a figure in line with the level of Latino support received in 2004 by Democratic nominee John Kerry, who won support from 67 percent from the group. The exit polls suggest that Clinton won 66 percent of the Latino vote. Latinos, of course, are not a homogeneous group.[9] Cuban Americans in South Florida, for example, have traditionally voted Republican, although younger generations now lean Democrat. Unfortunately, we cannot examine differences among Latino groups using the ANES. The pool poll, however, shows that Cuban American voters in Florida split 54 percent to 41 percent in Trump's favor; four years ago, the poll reported that the group voted 50–47 percent in Romney's favor. The data do not allow us to examine the voting behavior of other Latino groups.

Based on data from the ANES and the pool polls, we estimate that Latinos (of all ethnicities) composed roughly 14.2 to 15.1 percent of Clinton's 2016 electorate, depending on the data source, and between 5.2 to 6.7 percent of the Trump electorate. The exit poll estimate for Trump's Latino electorate size (6.7 percent) actually marks a small, one percentage point increase of Romney's Latino electorate (5.7 percent) in 2012. Trump's level of support among Latinos is likely surprising to many given that during the campaign, candidate Trump threatened to build a wall on the Mexican border, deport undocumented immigrants, and described Mexican immigrants as "bringing drugs; they're bringing crime; they're rapists."[10] The battle over the Latino vote is a potentially important one. The U.S. Census predicts that the size of the Latino electorate could grow by as much as 40 percent in the next twelve years. If Latinos' current rate of support for the Democrats were to continue, we estimate that nearly one in five Democratic votes will be cast by Latinos by 2028. This puts tremendous pressure on Republicans. The GOP already lags well behind Democrats in support among Latinos and African Americans; about 34 to 37 percent of Clinton's voters came from these two groups, whereas somewhere between 6.7 to 8.8 percent of Trump's voters did. If Republicans cannot make inroads with these two minority groups, they will be forced to increase their support—through increased turnout and vote share—from white voters.

Gender differences in voting behavior have been pronounced in some European societies, but they have been relatively weak in the United States.[11] Gender differences, whereby men disproportionately support the Republican Party and women the Democratic Party, emerged in the 1980 election and have been found in every election since. According to the exit polls, the "gender gap" was eight percentage points in 1980, six points in 1984, seven points in 1988, four points in 1992, eleven points in 1996, twelve points in 2000, seven points in 2004, seven points in 2008, and ten points in 2012. According to the 2016 exit polls, 54 percent of women and 41 percent of men voted for Clinton, a gap of thirteen points. Among whites Trump received a majority of votes from both men and women, although men were significantly more likely to support him. Trump received 52 percent of the white female vote and 62 percent of the white male vote, for a gap of ten points.

As the gender gap began to emerge, some feminists hoped that women would play a major role in defeating the Republicans.[12] But as we pointed out more than three decades ago, a gender gap does not necessarily help the Democrats.[13] For example, in 1988, George H. W. Bush and Michael Dukakis each won half of the female vote, but Bush won a clear majority of the male vote. Thus Bush benefited from the gender gap in 1988. However, two decades later the role of gender was reversed. In 2008 Obama and McCain split the male vote, whereas Obama won a clear majority among women. By the same logic, then, Obama benefited from the gender gap in 2008. During the intervening elections, Clinton benefited from the gender gap in both 1992 and 1996, and George W. Bush benefited in 2000 and 2004.

Unlike the pool polls, the 2016 ANES (see Table 5-1) finds evidence of a much smaller gender gap in voting. We find a small, two percentage point difference between white women and men in their support for Trump. Like the exit polls, the ANES shows that a majority of white men and women voted for Trump. Hillary Clinton, despite being the first female major party nominee for president, received only 41 percent of the vote from white females, who gave Trump 53 percent of their vote. Among all women voters, Clinton received 55.4 percent of the vote. Thus a significant portion of her support among females is driven by minority women.

As for marital status, in all of our analyses of ANES surveys between 1984 and 2012, we found clear differences between married women and single women.[14] Among all women voters who were married, 42.7 percent voted for Clinton; among those who were never married, 70.2 percent did—a 27.5 point difference. This difference remains large, 16.1 points, if we limit our analysis to white women. Interestingly the 2016 election is one of the few where we see a large marriage gap among men. Among all men, married voters were nineteen points less likely to vote for Clinton than men who had never been married. Indeed the majority of married men (52.3 percent) voted for Trump, whereas the majority of single men (54.3 percent) supported Clinton. This overall difference cannot be attributed wholly to racial differences. Among white men, married voters were 14.6 percentage points less likely to vote for Clinton than those who have never married.

Since the 2000 election, exit polls have shown that sexual orientation is related to the way people vote. In 2000, 70 percent of the respondents who said they were gay, lesbian, or bisexual voted for Gore; in 2004, 77 percent voted for Kerry; in 2008, 70 percent voted for Obama; and in 2012, 76 percent voted for Obama. Although it is difficult to confirm, Obama's ability to increase his support among the LGBT community may have resulted from his actions as president. Obama signed legislation repealing the "don't ask, don't tell" law, which allowed gays to serve in the military so long as they were not open about their sexual orientation, and in May 2012, he unexpectedly declared his support for the legalization of same-sex marriage.[15] In the 2016 exit polls, 5 percent of respondents said that they were gay, lesbian, bisexual, or transgender. Of these voters, 77 percent said they voted for Clinton, thus matching the level of support received by Kerry in 2004 and Obama in 2012. In the five ANES surveys that have inquired about sexual orientation, self-acknowledged homosexuals made up approximately 4 percent of the electorate.[16] In 2016, 5.3 percent of the ANES respondents said they were gay, lesbian, or bisexual.[17] Among homosexual or bisexual voters ($N = 149$), 76 percent voted for Clinton. This is down from the 83 percent of the vote that Obama earned from this group.

As described in Chapter 3, in the 2016 election the political variation among states was higher than in 2012 (and greater than in any election since 1964), suggesting that states were slightly more divided in their support for Trump in 2016 than in recent elections. And there were clear regional differences among white voters. As Table 5.1 shows, Trump garnered electoral majorities from white voters in three of the five regions. Trump, like all recent Republican nominees, fared best in the South, where he won 69 percent of the white vote (consistent with Romney's share in the region four years earlier). Clinton won only 24 percent of the vote among white southerners. The exit poll shows that she fared only marginally better among whites in the one southern state she carried, Virginia, where she captured 35 percent of the white vote. Obama won 38 percent of the vote in Virginia in 2012, a state he too won outright; thus it does not appear that Clinton improved her position among white Virginians despite the presence of the commonwealth's former governor and current U.S. senator on the ballot as her running mate. Trump also won majorities in the border region on the South and in the north central states, but Clinton won a plurality in the Mountain and Pacific region and a majority in the New England and mid-Atlantic region. Exit polls were taken in thirteen of the twenty-two states that define these two regions, and our analysis of these state-level results shows that Clinton outpolled Trump among whites in only four of these states—California, Maine, Oregon, and Washington.

Between Ronald Reagan's election in 1980 and Bill Clinton's reelection in 1996, young voters were more likely to vote Republican than their elders, and the Democrats did best among Americans who came of age before World War II (born before 1924). This was not the case in the 2000, 2004, 2008, and 2012 elections. In these elections the ANES surveys show that Republicans did well among white voters who entered the electorate in the 1980s and who may have been influenced by the pro-Republican tide during the Reagan years. Yet among white voters, those who entered the electorate in the mid-1990s or later, Democrats outgained Republicans. If Democrats were optimistic about their future because of these trends among young voters, they were no doubt ecstatic about Obama's exceptional performance among young adults in 2008. According to the 2008 ANES surveys, Obama won 57 percent of the vote among whites born between 1979 and 2000 (those who were between the ages of eighteen and twenty-nine at the time of the election). The ANES shows Obama lost ground among young white voters in 2012. But Obama remained quite strong among younger nonwhite voters. Indeed, among all voters, Obama won clear majorities with voters thirty-nine years old and younger.

The ANES shows that Trump won majorities from each of the four oldest cohorts (forty and over). Except for eighteen- to twenty-one-year-olds, who were decidedly pro-Clinton, the younger cohorts, overall, were competitive. Among white voters thirty-nine years old or younger, Clinton won a plurality of the vote, 45.3 to

Trump's 43.7 percent. Interestingly the younger cohorts were significantly more likely than older cohorts to cast a ballot for third-party candidates. In 2016, 11 percent of whites under the age of thirty-nine voted for someone other than Clinton or Trump. The pool poll also shows a relationship between age and voting behavior, but unlike the ANES, these polls suggest that whites of all ages supported Trump more than Clinton (although it should be noted that the cohorts are defined differently by the survey organizations). The pool poll shows that Trump fared best among older whites (forty-five and older), earning roughly 60 percent of the vote; he won a plurality of whites (47 percent) between eighteen to twenty-nine years old.

Social Class, Education, Income, and Union Membership

Traditionally the Democratic Party has fared well among the relatively disadvantaged. It has done better among the working class, voters with lower levels of formal education, and the poor. Moreover, since the 1930s most union leaders have supported the Democratic Party, and union members have been a mainstay of the Democratic presidential coalition. We have been unable to measure social class differences using the 2012 and 2016 ANES surveys because the occupational codes we use to classify respondents as working class (manually employed) and middle class (non-manually employed) are restricted access for privacy concerns and unavailable at the time of this writing. But we do have substantial evidence that class differences as defined by occupation have been declining—a trend found in other advanced democracies.[18] Differences between the more educated and the less educated were relatively strong in 2016, as were income effects.

In 1992 and 1996 Bill Clinton fared best among whites who had not graduated from high school, whereas both George H. W. Bush and Bob Dole fared best among whites who were college graduates (but without advanced degrees). In 1992 Clinton won more than half of the major-party vote among whites with advanced degrees, and in 1996 he won almost half the major-party vote among this group. In 2000 there was a weaker relationship between education and voting preferences, and in 2004 Kerry did best among whites in the highest and lowest educational categories. The 2008 ANES survey found only a weak relationship between level of education and the vote among whites. Moreover, the only educational group among which Obama won a majority of the vote was the small number who had not graduated from high school. In 2012 the ANES showed no discernible relationship between educational attainment and vote choice among whites. Romney won majorities among whites from all levels of education, but he did slightly better among those with a high school degree and those with some college.

In Table 5-1, we see the relationship between education and vote choice in the 2016 ANES. The evidence shows that Trump won clear majorities among whites who had not completed high school, high school graduates, and those with some college. Clinton did much better among whites with a college degree and won a majority of the vote from whites with postgraduate degrees. Indeed, if we collapse these two top categories, we find that Clinton won a majority (51.1 percent) from all whites with college degrees. Thus here we see partial evidence in support of the recent claim that support for Democratic candidates among whites tends to be limited to those who are educated and living in urban areas.[19] Unfortunately we cannot fully test this claim because data identifying whether respondents live in rural or urban areas is not publicly provided by the ANES. The 2016 exit polls—which, again we remind readers, are not nationally representative—also show a strong relationship between education and vote choice among whites. Trump won 18 percentage points more support from those whites without college degrees than he did from those with college degrees.

Scholars such as Jeffrey M. Stonecash and Larry M. Bartels argue that voting differences according to income have been growing in the United States.[20] We find little evidence to support this claim, however. Instead we find evidence that the relationship between income and voting has varied considerably in recent decades and in no discernible pattern. In his victories in 1992 and 1996, for example, Clinton clearly fared much better among the poor than among the affluent. The relationship between income and voting preferences was weaker in both 2000 and 2004, although whites with an annual family income of $50,000 and above were more likely to vote for Bush. In 2008 the ANES data revealed a strong relationship between the respondent's family income and voting choice. Like Clinton's victories, Obama did better among those with lower incomes than those who were wealthier. Among whites with annual family incomes below $50,000, a majority voted for Obama. In all income groups above that level, a majority voted for McCain. Moreover, among whites with family incomes of $150,000 and above, over three in four voted Republican. The 2012 ANES showed a weak negative relationship between annual family income and voting for Obama. In fact, across all income categories except for those making between $125,000 and $174,999, Romney won a majority of the white vote. Obama's majority among this high-income group is perhaps a bit surprising given the expectation many have that wealth is positively related to support for the Republican Party.

The 2016 ANES shows a relationship between income and vote choice similar to that seen in 2012. Once again, the Republican nominee, Trump, did best among whites in the six lowest income categories, winning majorities from all income groups under $125,000. Clinton won a majority among the top earners in our sample, and among top two income categories combined, she won a 48.7 to 44.3 plurality. If we include voters of all races and ethnicities in the analysis, the relationship between income and the vote appears to flip, with low-income voters being more likely than the more affluent to support Clinton. The exit polls, which do not report a breakdown of income and vote share based on race, support this general finding. Thus, as was the case in 2012, it appears that much of the relationship between social class—in this case, measured by income and education—and the vote is conditioned by race and ethnicity.

According to the ANES surveys, Bill Clinton made major gains among white union households between 1992 and 1996. But the 2000 ANES survey shows that Gore slipped twelve percentage points from Clinton's 1996 total, whereas George W. Bush gained sixteen points over Dole's. The 2004 ANES survey shows that Bush made no gains among union households but gained six points among nonunion households. In 2008 the ANES survey shows a five-point loss for the Democrats among white union households but a seven-point gain among nonunion households. Four years later Obama's vote share among white voters in nonunion households declined markedly, a five percentage point drop. This allowed Romney to dominate Obama among nonunion households: 61 to 38 percent.

Our estimates show that despite his appeals to working-class whites and union members, particularly, Trump did no better among union members than Romney did four years earlier, capturing 47 percent of the vote.[21] And Trump's level of support among nonunion whites was lower (55 percent) than Romney's (61). Yet, among union workers, Clinton performed approximately 4 points lower than Obama in 2012, winning a 49 percent plurality. Among nonunion whites, Clinton's 37 percent share was roughly equal to Obama's. Four percent of union workers voted for a third-party candidate in 2016. The exit polls also suggest that Clinton won union voters (51 percent), whereas Trump won nonmember households (48 percent).

Religion

Religious differences have long played a major role in American politics.[22] In the postwar period, Catholics tended to support the Democrats, whereas white Protestants, especially those outside the South, tended to favor the Republicans. Jews consistently voted more Democratic than any other major religious group. Yet the religious cleavages of old, partly reflecting ethnic differences between Protestants and Catholics, do not necessarily hold today. As noted by David E. Campbell, "the last thirty years have seen a re-sorting of the parties' electoral coalitions along religious lines."[23] As ethnic differences have faded through assimilation and as social and moral issues have become more politically salient, religious denomination plays a smaller role in defining partisan loyalties. Indeed the role of religion in modern politics is not so much about denomination as it is about what Campbell calls "religious devotional style" or religiosity. Today Christian voters who classify themselves as devout in their beliefs and practices—regardless of denomination—tend to support the Republican Party.[24] This has allowed the Republicans to benefit electorally from a "coalition of the religious," which brings together groups that are sometimes theologically and politically disparate (if not antagonistic), evangelical Christians, traditionalist Catholics, and Mormons.[25]

In the 2016 election Hillary Clinton won a plurality of the Catholic vote (47.6 to 45.3 percent), much smaller than Barack Obama's majority (55.1 to 44.9 percent) with the group four years earlier against Mitt Romney. But Clinton's plurality support among *all* Catholics belies her relationship with *many* Catholic voters, as well as the Church hierarchy, and says much about ethnic changes among American Catholics.[26] Roughly three in ten voters in 2016 was a self-identified Catholic, but the "Catholic vote" is hardly a monolith. White Catholics voted in favor of Donald Trump, awarding him 55.9 percent of the vote to Clinton's 30.8 percent. Obama did markedly better among white Catholic voters four years earlier, when the 2012 ANES showed that he garnered 47.2 percent of the white Catholic vote to Romney's 52.8 percent. Obviously Clinton's primary source of support among American Catholics was from Latinos, who represent about a third of all Catholics in the United States (and also a third of Catholic voters in the 2016 ANES).[27]

Although the Republican Party has been successful among white Protestants, it has been more successful among some than others. The Republican emphasis on traditional values may have special appeal to Protestants who share them. George W. Bush's policies such as limiting funding for embryonic stem cell research, calling for an amendment to the U.S. Constitution to ban same-sex marriage, and appointing conservatives to the federal courts may have appealed to Christian conservatives. But Romney's Mormon faith and previous support for abortion rights—although he has consistently opposed same-sex nuptials and stem cell research—may have given some socially conservative evangelical Protestants cause for concern. In 2016 the question was whether white Christian conservatives would lend their support to Donald Trump, a nominal mainline Protestant who has been married three times and was secretly recorded making lewd comments about his own treatment of women

We focus here on differences among white Protestants. For example, for the 1992, 1996, 2000, 2008, and 2012 ANES surveys, we examined differences between white Protestants who said they were "born again" and those who had not had this religious experience.[28] In all five surveys, white born-again Protestants were more likely to vote Republican than those who were not. In 2016, 47.6 percent of the white Protestants who said they had not had this religious experience voted for Trump; among those who said they were born again, 75.3 percent voted for Trump. Among born-again Protestants, Clinton only received 18.4 percent of the vote. The 2016 pool poll also asked Protestants if they considered themselves born again or not. According to this survey, among born-again Christians—roughly one-fourth of all Protestants— Trump outpolled Clinton 80 percent to 16 percent. Finally white Protestants affiliated with evangelical denominations were 24 percentage points more likely to vote for Trump than those who were affiliated with mainline congregations.

As we noted earlier Campbell argues that the role of religion in modern politics is not so much about denomination as it is about "religious devotional style" or religiosity. The point is similarly made by Lyman A. Kellstedt, who argues that religious commitment has an important effect on voting behavior.[29] According to the 2012 ANES, religious commitment was strongly associated with voting for the Republican nominee, Mitt Romney. Figure 5-1 presents the results from the ANES for all Protestants and Catholics voters, and religious commitment appears to have mattered in 2016.[30] Trump won nearly 90 percent of the vote from those voters who held a "very high" religious commitment; among whites who had low levels of religious commitment, Clinton won 49.8 to 42.3. This division is particularly pronounced among Protestants. White Protestants with very high religious commitment were approximately 40 percentage points more likely to vote for Trump than those with low religious commitment. White Catholics with "high" levels of commitment were 18 percentage points more likely to vote for Trump than white Catholics with low commitment.[31]

HOW SOCIAL GROUPS VOTED DURING THE POSTWAR YEARS

Although we found sharp racial/ethnic and religious differences in voting, most other social differences in voting behavior were relatively modest in 2016. How does this election compare with other presidential elections? Do the relationships between social variables and the vote found in 2016 result from long-term trends that have changed the importance of social factors? To answer these questions, we will examine the voting behavior of social groups that were an important part of the Democrat's New Deal coalition during the postwar years. Understanding the nature of this broad coalition and its subsequent collapse helps place current American politics into a broader historical perspective—and, in our view, this helps us understand better that the politics that brought Donald Trump to office in 2016 are not very different from (indeed are a product of) the politics of the recent past. Our analysis, which will begin with the 1944 election between Roosevelt and Thomas Dewey, uses a simple measure to assess the effect of social forces over time.

In his lucid discussion of the logic of party coalitions, Robert Axelrod analyzed six basic groups that made up the Democrat's New Deal coalition: the poor, southerners, blacks (and other nonwhites), union members (and members of their families), Catholics and other non-Protestants such as Jews, and residents of the twelve largest metropolitan areas.[32] John R. Petrocik's more comprehensive study of the Democratic coalition identified fifteen groups and classified seven of them as predominantly Democratic: blacks, lower-status native southerners, middle- and upper-status southerners, Jews, Polish and Irish Catholics, union members, and lower-status, border-state whites.[33] A more recent analysis by Harold W. Stanley, William T. Bianco, and Richard G. Niemi analyzes seven pro-Democratic groups: blacks, Catholics, Jews, women, native white southerners, members of union households, and the working class.[34] Our own analysis focuses on race, region, union membership, social class, and religion.

The contribution that a social group can make to a party's coalition depends on three factors: the relative size of the group in the total electorate, its level of turnout compared with that of the total electorate, and its relative loyalty to the political party.[35] The larger a social group, the greater its contribution can be. For example, African Americans make up 11.3 percent of the electorate; the white working class makes up about 30 percent. Thus the potential contribution of blacks is smaller than that of the white working class. Historically the electoral power of blacks was limited by their relatively low turnout. But black turnout has increased substantially in recent elections and has been comparable to white turnout. Moreover, because blacks vote overwhelmingly Democratic, their contribution to the Democratic Party can be greater than their group size would indicate. And the relative size of their contribution grows as whites desert the Democratic Party.

Race

We begin by examining racial differences, which we can trace back to 1944 by using the National Opinion Research Center (NORC) study for that year.[36] Figure 5-1 shows the percentages of white and black major-party voters who voted Democratic for president from 1944 to 2016. (All six figures in this chapter are based on major-party voters only.) After emancipation and the passage of the Fifteenth Amendment, most blacks voters—when not deprived of their voting right under Jim Crow—tended to vote for the Republican Party, the "Party of Lincoln." By 1932, however, those old allegiances had begun to change, and the GOP could no longer count of the solid support of black voters. Although most African Americans voted Democratic from 1944 to 1960, a substantial minority voted Republican. Yet the political mobilization of blacks, spurred by the civil rights movement and by the Republican candidacy of Barry Goldwater in 1964, evaporated black support for the Republican Party, and the residual Republican loyalties of older blacks were discarded between 1962 and 1964.[37]

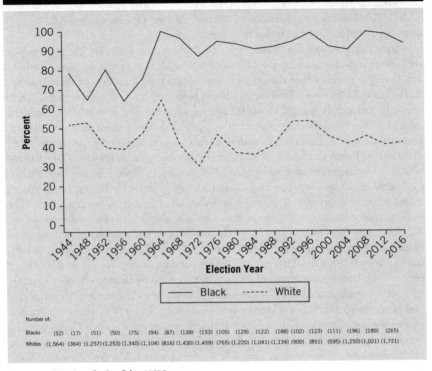

Figure 5-1 Major-Party Voters Who Voted Democratic for President, by Race, 1944–2016 (Percent)

Number of:																		
Blacks	(52)	(17)	(51)	(50)	(75)	(94)	(87)	(138)	(133)	(105)	(129)	(122)	(188)	(102)	(123)	(111)	(196)	(189)	(265)
Whites	(1,564)	(364)	(1,257)	(1,253)	(1,340)	(1,104)	(816)	(1,430)	(1,459)	(765)	(1,220)	(1,041)	(1,134)	(900)	(851)	(595)	(1,250)	(1,021)	(1,721)

Source: Authors' analysis of the ANES surveys.

Note: Numbers are weighted.

Although the Democrats made substantial gains among blacks, they lost ground among whites. From 1944 to 1964 the Democrats gained a majority of the white vote in three of six elections. Since 1964 the Democrats have never again won a majority of the white vote. However, in a two-candidate contest, a Democrat can win with just under half the white vote, as the 1960, 1976, 2008, and 2012 elections demonstrate. (Of course, in 2016, Hillary Clinton won the popular vote while only capturing 39.2 percent of the white vote. But her relatively low levels of support among white voters also hurt her in several states, such as Pennsylvania and Wisconsin, which cost her in the Electoral College.) In the three-candidate contests of 1992 and 1996, Bill Clinton was able to win with only about two-fifths of the white vote.[38]

The gap between the two trend lines in Figure 5-1 illustrates the overall difference in the Democratic vote between whites and blacks. Table 5-2 shows the overall level of "racial voting" in the six elections from 1944 to 2016 as well as four other measures of social cleavage.

Table 5-2 Relationship of Social Characteristics to Presidential Voting, 1944–2016

	Election Year (Percentage-Point Difference)																		
	1944	1948	1952	1956	1960	1964	1968	1972	1976	1980	1984	1988	1992	1996	2000	2004	2008	2012	2016
Racial voting[a]	27	12	40	25	23	36	56	57	48	56	54	51	41	47	47	49	54	57	51
Regional voting[b]																			
Among whites	—	—	12	17	6	-11	-4	-13	1	1	-9	-5	-10	-8	-20	-10	-14	-16	-22
Among entire electorate (ANES surveys)	—	—	9	15	4	-5	6	-3	7	3	3	2	0	0	-10	1	-11	-2	-11
Among entire electorate (official election results)	23	14	8	8	3	-13	-3	-11	5	2	-5	-7	-6	-7	-8	-8	-10	-9	-6
Union voting[c]																			
Among whites	20	37	18	15	21	23	13	11	18	15	20	16	12	23	12	21	8	15	11
Among entire electorate	20	37	20	17	19	22	13	10	17	16	19	15	11	23	11	18	6	10	9

(Continued)

Table 5-2 (Continued)

	Election Year (Percentage-Point Difference)																		
	1944	1948	1952	1956	1960	1964	1968	1972	1976	1980	1984	1988	1992	1996	2000	2004	2008	2012	2016
Class voting[d]																			
Among whites	19	44	20	8	12	19	10	2	17	9	8	5	4	6	–6	3	3	—	—
Among entire electorate	20	44	22	11	13	20	15	4	21	15	12	8	8	9	2	4	4	—	—
Religious voting[e]																			
Among whites	25	21	18	10	48	21	30	13	15	10	16	18	20	14	8	19	15	16	7
Among entire electorate	24	19	15	10	46	16	21	8	11	3	9	11	10	7	2	5	9	7	13

Sources: Authors' analysis of a 1944 NORC survey, official election results, and ANES surveys.

Notes: All calculations are based upon major-party voters. — indicates not available.

[a] Percentage of blacks who voted Democratic minus percentage of whites who voted Democratic.

[b] Percentage of southerners who voted Democratic minus percentage of voters outside the South who voted Democratic. Comparable data for region were not available for the surveys conducted in 1944 and 1948.

[c] Percentage of members of union households who voted Democratic minus percentage of members of households with no union members who voted Democratic.

[d] Percentage of working class that voted Democratic minus percentage of middle class that voted Democratic. The data for occupation needed to classify respondents according to their social class for 2012 and 2016 are restricted for privacy concerns.

[e] Percentage of Catholics who voted Democratic minus the percentage of Protestants who voted Democratic.

From 1944 to 1964 racial differences in voting ranged from a low of twelve percentage points to a high of forty points. These differences then rose to fifty-six percentage points in 1968 (sixty-one points if Wallace voters are included with Nixon voters) and did not fall to the forty percentage point level until 1992.[39] Racial voting was higher in the 1996, 2000, and 2004 contests but increased markedly in the elections of Barack Obama. In 2008 there was a forty-four percentage point gap between blacks and whites, and in 2012 that gap increased to fifty-seven points, matching the record high level of racial voting found in 1972. Obama's elections exhibit the highest levels of racial voting in any elections in which the Democratic candidate has won. In 2016 racial differences in voting contracted only slightly, by six points, to a fifty-one percentage point gap. Thus America has not experienced a racial gap in voting of less than forty percentage points since 1964, more than a half century ago.

Not only did African American loyalty to the Democratic Party increase sharply after 1960, but black turnout rose considerably from 1960 to 1968 because southern blacks were enfranchised. And while black turnout rose, white turnout outside the South declined. Between 1960, when overall turnout was highest, and 1996, when postwar turnout was lowest, turnout fell by about fifteen percentage points among the voting-age population.[40] Between 1996 and 2008, turnout in the United States rose by roughly eight percentage points. In the 2000 and 2004 election, turnout among whites and blacks increased at approximately the same rate. Yet in the 2008 and 2012 election, the groups moved in opposite directions, with black turnout continuing to rise and white turnout declining to the point where black turnout exceeded white turnout in 2012. Yet the trend lines reversed course between 2012 and 2016. As noted in Chapter 4, black voter turnout declined by seven percentage points, whereas white turnout increased 1.2 percentage points.

From 1948 to 1960 African Americans never accounted for more than one Democratic vote in twelve. In 1964, however, Johnson received about one in seven of his votes from blacks, and blacks contributed a fifth of the Democratic totals in both 1968 and 1972. In the 1976 election, which saw Democratic gains among whites, Jimmy Carter won only about one in seven of his votes from blacks, and in 1980, one in four. In the next three elections, about one in five Democratic votes were from blacks. In 1996 about one in six of Clinton's votes came from black voters, and in 2000 about one in five of Gore's votes did. In 2004 between a fifth and a fourth of Kerry's total vote was provided by black voters. Both Gore and Kerry came very close to winning, even with this heavy reliance on African American voters. In both 2008 and 2012, black voters accounted for about one-fourth of Obama's total vote. No Democratic presidential winner had ever drawn this large a share of his total vote from these voters. Hillary Clinton received about one in five of all of her votes from blacks, lower than the share received by Obama but comparable to that received by the Democratic nominees in 1984, 1988, 1992, 2000, and 2004. Thus it is fair to say that Obama's elections aside, the size of the Democratic Party black electoral base has been relatively consistent over the past three decades.

Region

White southerners' desertion of the Democratic Party is arguably the most dramatic change in postwar American politics . . . and the most consequential for the electoral fortunes of the Republican Party. As we saw in Chapter 3, regional differences can be analyzed using official election statistics, but these statistics are of limited use in examining race-related differences in regional voting because election results are not tabulated by race. Consequently we rely on survey data to document the dramatic shift in voting behavior among white southerners.

As Figure 5-2 reveals, white southerners were somewhat more Democratic than whites outside the South in the 1952 and 1956 contests between Dwight Eisenhower and Adlai Stevenson and in the 1960 contest between John Kennedy and Richard Nixon.[41] But in the next three elections, regional differences were reversed, with white southerners voting more Republican than whites outside the South. In 1976 and 1980, when the Democrats fielded Jimmy Carter of Georgia as their standard-bearer, white southerners and whites outside the South voted very much alike. But since 1980 southern whites have been less likely than nonsouthern whites to vote Democratic, by an average difference of 12.6 percentage points. In 1984 and 1988 white southerners were less likely to vote Democratic than whites from any other region. In 1992 and 1996 Bill Clinton and his running mate, Al Gore, were both from the South. Even so, George H. W. Bush in 1992 and Bob Dole in 1996 did better among white southerners than among whites from any other region.[42] In 2000 the Democrats ran the southerner Gore, with Joseph Lieberman of Connecticut as his running mate. The Republican candidate, George W. Bush, the governor of Texas, was also a southerner, and his running mate, Dick Cheney, who had become a resident of Texas, moved back to Wyoming to reestablish his residence.[43] In 2004 the Democrats ran John Kerry, the junior senator from Massachusetts, although John Edwards, his running mate, was from North Carolina. But in both these contests, the Democratic vote in the South was low, and the Democrats did substantially better outside the South. In both 2008 and 2012, neither party ran a southerner on its ticket. In Obama's 2008 election, the Democrats made gains among both white southerners and among whites outside the South. But, as Figure 5-2 shows, the Democrats' support among whites in both regions receded in 2012. In 2016 both Hillary Clinton and Donald Trump were residents of New York. Although Clinton could claim a connection to the South, having been the First Lady of the State of Arkansas for eleven years, this was of little help to the Democratic nominee. Regional differences among whites set a record high for the modern period in 2016, with white southerners being twenty-two percentage points less likely to vote Democratic than white nonsoutherners.

Regional differences among whites from 1952 to 2016 are summarized in Table 5-2. The negative signs for 1964, 1968, 1972, and 1984–2016 reveal that the Democratic candidate fared better outside the South than in the South. As we saw in Chapter 3, in 1968 Wallace had a strong regional base in the South. If we include Wallace voters with Nixon voters, regional differences change markedly, moving from –4 to –12.

Table 5-2 also presents regional differences for the entire electorate. Here, however, we present two sets of estimates: (1) the ANES results from 1952 to 2016 and (2) the results we computed using official election statistics. Both sets of statistics indicate that regional differences have been reversed, but these results are often different and in many cases would lead to substantially different conclusions. The 2004 election provides a clear example. According to the 2004 ANES survey, voters in the South

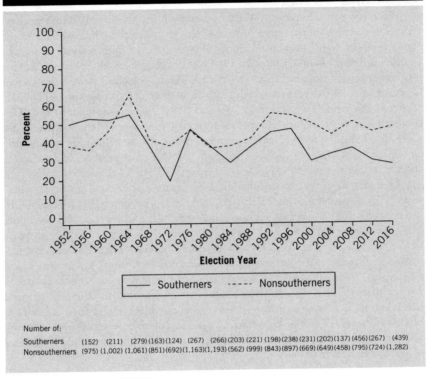

Figure 5-2   White Major-Party Voters Who Voted Democratic for President, by Region, 1952–2016 (Percent)

Number of:
Southerners   (152) (211) (279)(163)(124) (267) (266)(203)(221)(198)(238)(231)(202)(137)(456)(267) (439)
Nonsoutherners (975) (1,002) (1,061)(851)(692)(1,163)(1,193)(562)(999)(843)(897)(669)(649)(458)(795)(724)(1,282)

Source: Authors' analysis of ANES surveys.

Note: Numbers are weighted.

were as likely to vote Democratic as voters outside the South. But we know that this result is wrong. After all Bush won all the southern states, whereas Kerry won nineteen states outside the South as well as the District of Columbia. In fact the official statistics show that southerners were eight points more likely to vote Republican than voters outside the South. In this case, the ANES results, which are based on a sample of eight hundred voters, overestimated the number of Democratic voters in the South. This should remind us of a basic caution in studying elections: always turn to the actual election results before turning to the survey data.

Surveys are useful in demonstrating the way in which the mobilization of southern blacks and the defection of southern whites from the Democratic Party dramatically transformed the Democratic coalition in the South.[44] According to our analysis of ANES surveys, between 1952 and 1960 Democratic presidential candidates never received more than one in fifteen of their votes in the South from blacks. In 1964 three in ten of Johnson's southern votes came from black voters, and in 1968 Hubert Humphrey received as many votes from southern blacks as from southern whites. In 1972, according to these data, George McGovern received more votes from southern blacks than from southern whites.

Black voters were crucial to Carter's success in the South in 1976; he received about a third of his support from African Americans. Even though he won ten of the eleven southern states, he won a majority of the white vote only in his home state of Georgia and possibly in Arkansas. In 1980 Carter again received about a third of his southern support from blacks. In 1984 Walter Mondale received about four in ten of his southern votes from blacks, and in 1988 one in three of the votes Michael Dukakis received came from black voters. In 1992 and 1996 Clinton won about a third of his southern support from African Americans. In 2000 four in ten of the southern votes Gore received came from blacks. A southern running mate helped Kerry very little among southern whites in 2004. According to the ANES survey, about half of Kerry's votes in the South came from blacks.

Our analysis of the 2008 ANES survey indicates that about a third of Obama's votes in the South came from black voters. And blacks were crucial to the three southern states he carried, because he won a minority of the white vote in those states. In 2012 Obama's electorate in the South was roughly 38 percent black, an increase of five percentage points from his first election. This reflects a combination of factors, including increased turnout among blacks, lower turnout among whites, and a decrease in Obama's vote share among whites. Obama won two southern states in 2012. Hillary Clinton won only one southern state, Virginia, in 2016. We estimate that Clinton's electorate in the South was 41 percent black, larger than the share of blacks in Obama's electorate but primarily a product of lower levels of support among southern whites. By comparison we estimate that blacks represented only 1.3 percent of Trump's electorate in the South.

Union Membership

Figure 5-3 shows the percentage of white union members and nonmembers who voted Democratic for president from 1944 to 2016. Over the course of the postwar period, Democrats have enjoyed a higher level of support from union members than nonmembers, but this has not always resulted in a majority of union votes. In all six elections between 1944 and 1964, the majority of white union members (and members of their households) voted Democratic. In 1968 Humphrey won a slight majority of the union vote, although his total would be cut to 43 percent if Wallace voters were included. The Democrats won about three-fifths of the union vote in 1976, when Jimmy Carter defeated Gerald Ford. In 1988 Dukakis appears to have won a slight majority of the white union vote, although he fell well short of Carter's 1976 tally. In 1992 Bill Clinton won three-fifths of the major-party union vote and won nearly half the total union vote. In 1996 the ANES data show him making major gains and winning 70 percent of the major-party vote among union members. In 2000 Gore won a majority of the union vote, but he was well below Clinton's 1996 tally. In 2004 Kerry did slightly better than Gore among white union voters, but Bush did somewhat better among nonmembers. Because there are more nonmembers than members, this shift worked to Bush's advantage. In 2008 the Democrats' support among white union members declined from 2004 levels, but Obama nonetheless won a small majority of white union voters. Obama made significant gains among nonmembers in 2008, obviously a net benefit for the Democrats. Obama maintained his majority support among white union members in 2012, again winning about 53 percent of the white union vote. But Obama's support from whites from nonmember households dropped precipitously, by roughly six points.

Hillary Clinton's support among union members was slightly less than that received by Obama in his two elections. Nevertheless, Clinton won a majority of white union voters, 51.4 percent, while receiving 40.4 percent support from nonunion whites. Clearly unions continue to be an important vehicle for mobilizing white voters' support for the Democratic Party, but the gap in support from union versus nonunion voters has contracted some since the heyday of the New Deal coalition.

Differences in presidential voting between union members and nonmembers are presented in Table 5-2. Because in 1968 Wallace did better among union members

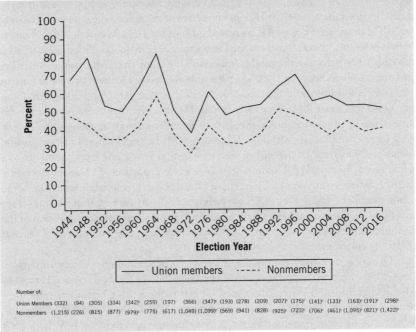

Figure 5-3   White Major-Party Voters Who Voted Democratic for President, by Union Membership, 1944–2016 (Percent)

Number of:
Union Members (332) (94) (305) (334) (342)ᵉ (259) (197) (366) (347)ᵉ (193) (278) (209) (207)ᵉ (175)ᵉ (141)ᵉ (133)ᵉ (163)ᵉ (191)ᵉ (298)ᵉ
Nonmembers (1,215) (226) (815) (877) (979)ᵉ (775) (617) (1,049) (1,099)ᵉ (569) (941) (828) (925)ᵉ (723)ᵉ (706)ᵉ (461)ᵉ (1,095)ᵉ (821)ᵉ (1,422)ᵉ

Source: Authors' analysis of ANES surveys.

Note: "Union members" indicates that the respondent is a union member or lives in a union household. "Nonmembers" indicates that the respondent is not a union member nor lives in a union household. Data are weighted.

than nonmembers, including Wallace voters, with Nixon voters reducing union voting from thirteen percentage points to ten. Union voting was highest in 1948, a year when Truman's opposition to the Taft-Hartley Act gained him strong union support.[45] Union voting was low in 1992 and 2000, when white union members were only slightly more likely to vote Democratic than nonmembers. Because Bush did better among nonmembers in 2004, the differences between members and nonmembers rose to twenty-one points. Differences between members and nonmembers were sharply reduced in 2008, reaching the lowest level in any of the preceding seventeen elections, although the differences were expanded—due to a loss in vote share among white nonunion households—during his reelection bid in 2012. In 2016 the gap in member/nonmember voting differential decreased by four percentage points with symmetrical forces seemingly at play; union members lowered their support for the Democratic nominee by two points, whereas nonmembers increased their support by two points. Table 5-2 also shows the results for the entire electorate, but because blacks are about as likely to live in union households as whites, including blacks has little effect in most years.

The percentage of the total electorate composed of white union members and their families has declined during the postwar years. White union members and their families made up 25 percent of the electorate in 1952; in 2016, according to the ANES survey, they made up only 16 percent.[46] Turnout among white union members has declined at about the same rate as turnout among nonunion whites. In addition, in many elections since 1964, the Democratic share of the union vote has been relatively low. All of these factors, as well as increased turnout by blacks, have reduced the contribution of white union members to the Democratic presidential coalition. Remarkably, through 1960, a third of the total Democratic vote came from white union members and their families; between 1964 and 1984 only about one Democratic vote in four; in 1988, 1992, and 1996 only about one Democratic vote in five; and in 2000 only about one Gore vote in six. In 2004, with a drop in Democratic support among whites who did not live in union households, the share of Kerry's vote from union households rose back to one vote in five. Although Obama recorded a small majority among union voters in 2008, only 10 percent of his votes in that year came from members of a white union household.[47] Union voters were a larger portion of Obama's electorate in 2012; by our estimation 16.1 percent of Obama's votes nationally came from white union members. Using the ANES we estimate 12.3 percent of Clinton's votes were cast by white union members, a four percentage point shift in the composition of the Democratic electorate. By comparison white union members composed 9.7 percent of Trump's electorate.

Of course, as with all groups, the union vote is not monolithic. Voters from union households were an important part of the electorate in the battleground states of Michigan, Ohio, and Wisconsin. Based on exit polls in those states and regardless of race, it appears that Clinton won a majority of the union vote in Michigan and Wisconsin, whereas Trump won a majority of union voters in Ohio. In Wisconsin it is estimated that 21 percent of all voters were union members; of these Clinton won 53 to 43 percent. By our estimate, 24 percent of Clinton's voters in Wisconsin were from union households (19.1 percent of Trump voters). Clinton also did well garnering union support in Michigan, where roughly 28 percent of the electorate belong to unions. Of these voters Clinton won 53 to 40 percent. In Michigan 31.4 percent of Clinton voters were union members (23.6 percent of Trump voters). Despite this support, of course, Clinton lost both states. She also lost Ohio, but in the Buckeye State, union voters were decidedly pro-Trump. The billionaire Republican won 54 percent of union voters to Clinton's 41 percent. Approximately one quarter of all Trump voters in Ohio were union members; one-fifth of Clinton's voters were.

Social Class

The broad social cleavage between manually employed workers (and their dependents) and non-manually employed workers (and their dependents) is especially valuable for studying comparative behavior.[48] For this reason we present the results of our analysis in Figure 5-4, even though we are not yet able to analyze the ANES results for 2012 and 2016 due to a lack of available data. The figure shows the percentage of white major-party voters who voted Democratic among the working class and the middle class in all the presidential elections between 1944 and 2008.

Figure 5-4 White Major-Party Voters Who Voted Democratic for President, by Social Class, 1944–2008 (Percent)

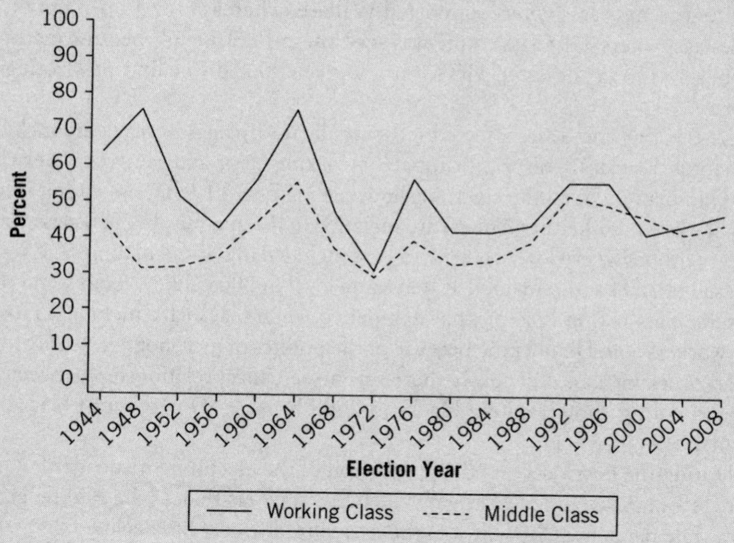

Number of:
Working class	(597)	(134)	(462)	(531)	(579)ᵃ	(425)	(295)	(587)	(560)ᵃ	(301)	(473)	(350)	(393)ᵃ	(279)ᵃ	(224)ᵃ	(149)ᵃ	(115)ᵃ
Middle class	(697)	(137)	(437)	(475)	(561)ᵃ	(454)	(385)	(675)	(716)ᵃ	(376)	(634)	(589)	(569)ᵃ	(507)ᵃ	(540)ᵃ	(379)ᵃ	(271)ᵃ

Source: Authors' analysis of a 1944 NORC survey and ANES surveys.

Note: Numbers are weighted.

In all fourteen presidential elections between 1944 and 1996, the white working class voted more Democratic than the white middle class. But as Figure 5-4 shows, the percentage of white working-class voters who voted Democratic has varied considerably from election to election. It reached its lowest level in 1972, during the Nixon-McGovern contest. Carter regained a majority of the white working-class vote class in 1976, but he lost it four years later. Bill Clinton won only two-fifths of the vote among working-class whites in the three-candidate race of 1992, although he did win a clear majority of the major-party vote among working-class whites. The 1996 election again featured a strong third-party candidate, but Clinton won half of the working-class vote and a clear majority of the major-party vote among this group. In 2000 Gore won only two-fifths of the vote among working-class whites, and 2000 is the only election during these years in which the Democratic presidential candidate did better among middle-class whites than among working-class whites. Support for the Democrats among the white working class increased slightly in 2004, but their vote share among the middle class declined, and John Kerry failed to win a majority among either group. The 2008 ANES is the last survey for which we have data on working-class and middle-class voting. Figure 5-4 shows that Obama improved his party's standing among working-class and middle-class voters in 2008, gaining around three percentage points among each group, but he failed to win a majority from either.

Although levels of class voting have varied over the last six decades, they have clearly followed a downward trend, as Table 5-2 reveals.[49] Class voting was even lower in 1968, if Wallace voters are included with Nixon voters, because 15 percent of white working-class voters supported Wallace, whereas only 10 percent of white middle-class voters did. Class voting was very low in 1972, mainly because many white working-class voters deserted McGovern. Only in 2000 do we find class voting to be negative.[50]

Class voting trends are affected substantially if African Americans are included in the analysis. Blacks are disproportionately working class, and they vote overwhelmingly Democratic. In all the elections between 1976 and 1996, class voting is higher when blacks (and other nonwhites) are included in the analysis. In 2000 class voting is positive (although very low) when blacks are included in our calculations. Class voting increased in 2004 and remained at that same level in 2008. The overall trend toward declining class voting is somewhat dampened when blacks are included. However, black workers vote Democratic because of the politics of race, not necessarily because they are working class. Obviously there was no statistical relationship between social class and voting choice among blacks in 2008 because 99 percent of blacks voted Democratic.[51]

During the postwar years the proportion of the electorate made up of working-class whites has remained relatively constant, whereas that of the middle class has grown. The percentage of whites in the agricultural sector has declined dramatically. Turnout fell among both the middle and working classes after 1960, but it fell more among the working class. Declining turnout and defections from the Democratic Party by working-class whites, along with increased turnout by blacks, have reduced the total white working-class contribution to the Democratic presidential coalition.

In 1948 and 1952 about half the Democratic vote came from working-class whites, and from 1956 through 1964, this social group supplied more than four in ten

Democratic votes. Its contribution fell to just over a third in 1968 and then to under a third in 1972. In 1976, with the rise in class voting, the white working class provided nearly two-fifths of Carter's total, but it provided just over a third four years later in Carter's reelection bid. In 1984 more than a third of Mondale's total support came from this group, and in 1988 Dukakis received more than two in five of his votes from this group. In both 1992 and 1996, working-class whites provided three in ten votes of Clinton's total, but in 2000 this group accounted for only about a fifth of Gore's votes. In 2004, with a drop in middle-class support for the Democratic candidate, Kerry received just under a fourth of his vote from working-class whites. Obama obtained only 15 percent of his votes from white working-class voters, a significant departure from 2004 and far below the group's contribution to the Democratic coalition in the early postwar years.

The white middle-class contribution to the Democratic presidential coalition amounted to fewer than three in ten votes in 1948 and 1952, and just under one-third in 1956, stabilizing at just over one-third in the next five elections. In 1984 Mondale received fewer than two in five of his votes from middle-class whites, and in 1988 Dukakis received more than two in five. In 1992 more than two in five of Clinton's total votes came from this group, rising to a half in 1996. In 2000 Gore received two-fifths of his total vote from middle-class whites, and in 2004 Kerry received just over two-fifths. In 2008 Obama received around 37 percent of his votes from middle-class whites. In all of the elections between 1984 and 2008, the Democrats received a larger share of their vote from middle-class whites than from working-class whites. The increasing middle-class contribution stems from two factors: (1) although objectively the middle class is shrinking, the percentage of individuals who classify themselves as "middle class" has increased, and (2) class differences are eroding.[52] The decline in class differences is a widespread phenomenon in advanced industrialized societies.[53]

Of course our argument that class-based voting is declining depends on the way in which we have defined social class. Different definitions may yield different results. For example, in a major study depending on a far more complex definition that divides the electorate into seven social categories, Jeff Manza and Clem Brooks, using ANES data from 1952 to 1996, conclude that class differences are still important.[54] But their findings actually support our conclusion that the New Deal coalition has eroded. For example, they found that professionals were the most Republican class in the 1950s, but that by the 1996 election they had become the most Democratic.

Religion

Voting differences among major religious groups have also declined during the postwar years. Even so, as Figure 5-5 reveals, in every election since 1944, Jews have been more likely to vote Democratic than Catholics, and Catholics have been more likely to vote Democratic than Protestants.[55]

As Figure 5-5 shows a large majority of Jews voted Democratic in every election from 1944 to 1968, and although the percentage declined in Nixon's landslide over McGovern in 1972, even McGovern won a majority of the Jewish vote. In 1980 many Jews (like many Gentiles) were dissatisfied with Carter's performance as president, and some resented the pressure he had exerted on Israel to accept the Camp David

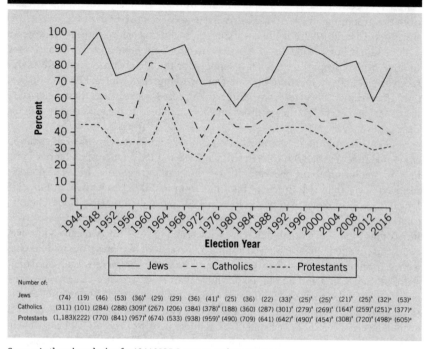

Source: Authors' analysis of a 1944 NORC survey and ANES surveys.

Note: Numbers are weighted.

Accords, which returned the Sinai Peninsula—captured by Israel in 1967 during the Six Day War—to Egypt. A substantial minority of Jews supported third-party candidate John Anderson that year, but Carter still outpolled Reagan. Both Mondale in 1984 and Dukakis (whose wife is Jewish) in 1988 won a clear majority of the Jewish vote. The Jewish Democratic vote surged in 1992, with Clinton winning nine in ten major-party voters. With Lieberman, an observant Jew, as his running mate, Gore, too, won overwhelming Jewish support in 2000. Bush was strongly pro-Israel in his foreign policy, but Kerry won solid support among Jewish voters, although there may have been some Republican gains. In 2008 some Jews may have had reservations about Obama's commitment to Israel's security, but even so he may have made slight gains among Jewish voters. The data show that Obama's support among white Jewish voters dropped significantly in 2012 to 59.8 percent. Obama had a rocky relationship with the Israeli prime minister, Benjamin Netanyahu, during his first term, and the decline in his support among Jewish voters between 2008 and 2012 may reflect these tensions. Hillary Clinton was able to regain high levels of Jewish support in 2016. According to the ANES Clinton won 80.1 percent of the Jewish two-party vote. Obviously, on the whole, Jewish voters' loyalty to the Democratic Party remains very strong.

A majority of white Catholics voted Democratic in six of the seven elections from 1944 to 1968. The percentage of Catholics voting Democratic surged in 1960, when the Democrats fielded a Catholic candidate, John Kennedy, but Catholic support was still very high in Johnson's landslide four years later.[56] In 1968 a majority of white Catholics voted Democratic, although Humphrey's total is reduced from 60 percent to 55 percent if Wallace voters are included. In 1976 Carter won a majority among white Catholics, but the Democrats did not win a majority of the major-party vote among white Catholics again until 1992. In his 1996 reelection Clinton again won over half of the major-party vote among white Catholics. Four years later, George W. Bush outpolled Al Gore among white Catholics. Even in 2004, when the Democrats ran a Catholic presidential candidate, Bush outscored Kerry among white Catholic voters. Based on 2008 ANES data, Obama won half the vote among white Catholics. He won slightly less than half in the 2008 pool poll. Obama's two-party vote share among white Catholics declined, however, in 2012, falling to 47.2 percentage points. Hillary Clinton's white Catholic support in 2016 declined even further to 40 percent of the two-party vote share. Catholics had once been firmly footed in the Democrats' New Deal coalition, but the party's support for abortion rights—first formally espoused in the 1976 party platform—places it odds with the Catholic Church and many of the faithful.[57] As we noted earlier, much of the Democrats' support from white Catholics comes from those who are less devout in their religious practices as well as the Latino Catholic population. Nevertheless, on average, Democrats continue to do better among white Catholics than among white Protestants.

Our measure of religious voting shows considerable change from election to election, although there was a downward trend from 1968 to 2000, when religious differences reached their lowest level. Religious differences were somewhat higher in both 2004 and 2008 (see Table 5-2). Even though white Protestants were more likely than white Catholics to vote for Wallace in 1968, including Wallace voters in our total has little effect on religious voting (it falls from thirty points to twenty-nine points). Religious differences were small in the 1980 Reagan-Carter contest, but since then they have varied. Because the Latino Catholic electorate is projected to grow, religious voting may rise in future elections.

Including African Americans in our calculations reduces religious voting. Blacks are much more likely to be Protestant than Catholic, and including blacks in our calculations adds a substantial number of Protestant Democrats. In 2016, for example, religious voting is reduced from seven points to five points when blacks are included. However, when we look at the electorate as a whole, we see that religious voting increases significantly to thirteen points; this is driven primarily by the inclusion of Latinos.[58]

The Jewish contribution to the Democratic Party has declined in part because Jews did not vote overwhelmingly Democratic in 1972, 1980, 1984, 1988, 2004, and 2012 and in part because Jews make up a small and declining share of the electorate. During the 1950s, Jews were about a twentieth of the electorate. But the most recent estimates suggest that only about one American in fifty is Jewish.[59]

Although Jews make up only about 2 percent of the population, three-fourths of the nation's Jews live in seven large states—New York, California, Florida, New Jersey, Pennsylvania, Massachusetts, and Illinois—which together had 178 electoral votes in 2016.[60] More important, two of these states are battleground states: Florida, where Jews make up 3.3 percent of the population, and Pennsylvania, where they make up 2.3 percent. In recent elections Florida has witnessed very close presidential elections, and in 2016, Trump won Pennsylvania by slightly more than 44,000 votes. In these close elections, even a relatively small group, like Jewish voters, can be influential in presidential politics. Overall, however, the electoral significance of Jews is lessened because five of these large states are not battleground states. For example, Jews make up 8.4 percent of the population in New York, far more than any other state. Although Jewish voters could influence New York's twenty-nine electoral votes, a Democratic candidate who does not win by a comfortable margin in New York is very likely to lose the election.[61]

According to our estimates based on ANES surveys, in 1948 Truman received about a third of his total vote from white Catholics. In 1952 Stevenson won three-tenths of his vote from white Catholics but only one-fourth in 1956. In 1960, Kennedy, the first Catholic president, received 37 percent of his vote from Catholics, but the Catholic contribution fell—owing to an ebb in Catholic turnout—to just under three in ten votes when Johnson defeated Goldwater in 1964. In 1968 three-tenths of Humphrey's total vote came from white Catholics but only a fourth of McGovern's vote in 1972. White Catholics provided just over a fourth of Carter's vote in his 1976 victory, but in his 1980 loss to Reagan, just over a fifth came from this source. Mondale received just under three in ten of his votes from white Catholics, and Dukakis received a fifth of his vote from this group. According to our analysis based on ANES surveys, just over a fifth of Bill Clinton's vote came from white Catholics in 1992 and just over a fourth in 1996. The ANES surveys suggest that both Kerry and Bush received about a fifth of their votes from white Catholics. In 2008, less than a fifth of Obama's vote came from white Catholics, and in 2012, 17.4 percent of the votes cast for Obama were from white Catholics. White Catholics composed 16.6 percent of Hillary Clinton's electoral coalition, roughly half the size of the group's contribution to the New Deal coalition. (Twenty-six percent of Trump's voters were white Catholics.)

The contrast between the 1960 and 2004 elections is the most striking comparison across the eight decades in our investigation. In both elections the Democrats fielded a Catholic presidential candidate. But Kennedy received over twice as large a share of the Catholic vote as Kerry. Religious differences were massive in 1960 and relatively modest in 2004. Well over a third of Kennedy's votes came from white Catholics, but only about one-fifth of Kerry's did. Obviously the social characteristics of the Catholic community changed over the span of the forty-four years between these elections. Of course there were also social issues that may have led many Catholics to vote Republican in 2004 that were simply not on the political agenda four decades earlier.[62]

As the data reveal, in all of the elections between 1944 and 1996, the effects of class and religion were cumulative (see Figure 5-6). In every one of these fourteen elections, working-class Catholics were more likely to vote Democratic than any other group. And in all these elections, middle-class Protestants were the most likely to vote Republican. In 2000 middle-class Catholics were the most likely to vote Democratic and middle-class Republicans the most likely to vote Republican. In 2004 and 2008, as in the vast majority of past elections, working-class Catholics were the most Democratic group. Middle-class Protestants were somewhat more likely to vote Republican than middle-class Catholics. All the same, middle-class Protestants are the most consistent group, supporting the Republicans in all seventeen elections. We lack data on the effect of class and religion in the 2012 and 2016 elections.

The relative importance of social class and religion can be assessed by comparing the voting behavior of middle-class Catholics with that of working-class Protestants. Religion was more important than social class in predicting the vote in all elections between 1944 and 2008, except those in which social class was more important than

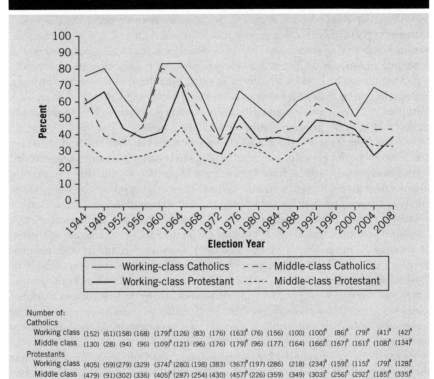

Figure 5-6 White Major-Party Voters Who Voted Democratic for President, by Social Class and Religion, 1944–2008 (Percent)

Working-class Catholics — — – Middle-class Catholics
Working-class Protestant ----- Middle-class Protestant

Number of:
Catholics
Working class (152) (61)(158) (168) (179)[a] (126) (83) (176) (163)[a] (76) (156) (100) (100)[a] (86)[a] (79)[a] (41)[a] (42)[a]
Middle class (130) (28) (94) (96) (109)[a](121) (96) (176) (179)[a] (96) (177) (164) (166)[a] (167)[a] (161)[a] (108)[a] (134)[a]
Protestants
Working class (405) (59)(279) (329) (374)[a] (280) (198) (383) (367)[a](197) (286) (218) (234)[a] (159)[a] (115)[a] (79)[a] (128)[a]
Middle class (479) (91)(302) (336) (405)[a](287) (254) (430) (457)[a](226) (359) (349) (303)[a] (256)[a] (292)[a] (185)[a] (335)[a]

Source: Authors' analysis of a 1944 NORC survey and ANES surveys. The data for occupation needed to classify respondents according to their social class for 2012 and 2016 are restricted for privacy concerns.

Note: Numbers are weighted.

religion—1948 (by a considerable margin), 1976, and 1980—and the one, 1964, in which class and religion were equally important. However, all of these trend lines have been converging, suggesting that traditional sources of cleavage are declining in importance.

WHY THE NEW DEAL COALITION BROKE DOWN

The importance of race increased substantially after 1960, but all of the other factors we have examined have declined in importance. The effects of region on voting behavior have been reversed, with the Republicans now enjoying an advantage in the South, especially when we compare southern whites with whites outside the South. As the national Democratic Party strengthened its appeals to African Americans during the 1960s, party leaders endorsed policies that southern whites opposed, and many of them deserted the Democratic Party. The migration of northern whites to the South also may have reduced regional characteristics.

Although the Democratic Party's appeals to blacks may have weakened its hold on white groups that traditionally supported it, other factors were at work as well.[63] During the postwar years these groups have changed. Although union members do not hold high-paying professional and managerial jobs, they have gained substantial economic advantages. Differences in income between the working and the middle class have diminished. And Catholics, who often came from more recent European immigrant groups than Protestants, have become increasingly middle class and less identified with their ethnic roots with every passing generation. This trend is only partially offset by the growing number of Catholic Latinos.

Not only have these social groups changed, but the historical conditions that led union members, the working class, and Catholics to become Democrats have receded further into the past. Although the transmission of partisan loyalties from generation to generation gives historically based coalitions some staying power, the ability of the family to transmit partisan loyalties decreased as the strength of party identification within the electorate weakened during the 1960s and 1970s and were formed anew in a changed political environment.[64] Moreover, with the passage of time the proportion of the electorate that directly experienced the Roosevelt years and its wake has progressively declined. New policy issues, unrelated to the political conflicts of the New Deal era, have tended to erode party loyalties among traditionally Democratic groups. Edward G. Carmines and James A. Stimson provide strong evidence that race-related issues were crucial in weakening the New Deal coalition.[65] And more recently social issues such as abortion and same-sex marriage may have weakened Democratic Party loyalties among Catholic voters.

Despite the erosion of the New Deal coalition, the Democrats managed to win the presidency in 1992 and 1996, came very close to holding it in 2000, and came close to regaining it in 2004. In 2008 they did regain the presidency, winning a majority of the popular vote for the first time since 1976. And they won a popular-vote majority again in 2012. In his 1992 victory Bill Clinton boosted his share of the major-party vote among union members, the white working class, and even among white southerners. He focused on appeals to middle America, and in both 1992 and 1996, he paid as low a price as possible to gain the black vote. Clinton was the first Democrat to win in an election in which blacks made up more than 15 percent of the Democratic vote. In 1996 Clinton once again won with more than 15 percent of his votes provided by blacks. But the 1992 and 1996 elections were three-candidate contests. Our calculations suggest that under typical levels of turnout among its various coalition groups, it would be exceedingly difficult for a Democrat to win a two-candidate contest in which blacks made up a fifth or more of his or her total coalition—difficult but not impossible.

With the 2008 and 2012 elections, we see the ingredients (and challenges) of building a modern Democratic coalition. Obama gained about a fourth of his total tally from black voters. This was possible because black turnout equaled or exceeded white turnout and because blacks voted overwhelmingly Democratic. The Democrats also enjoyed strong support from Latino voters, and population growth makes this group an increasingly larger share of the Democratic coalition. The Democrat's New Deal coalition was often described as a "coalition of minorities"—increasingly the minorities at the heart of the new Democratic electoral coalition are blacks and Latinos.

The 2016 election brought many of the electoral challenges confronting both parties to the fore. For the Democrats, while they were able to capture the national popular vote, the party's losses in nearly every battleground state were brought about, in large measure, by the same symptoms. To win, the modern Democratic coalition must not only maintain their recent levels of support from blacks and Latinos, but they must turn these voters out to the polls. African American turnout declined by seven percentage points in 2016, and Latino turnout remains lower than that of any other racial/ethnic group. At the same time the Democratic Party's increasing reliance on its minority constituents may exacerbate its losses among a growing number of disaffected, white working-class voters, who feel the party has lost touch with their interests. Indeed, as we have seen in our analysis, over the last forty years, the Democratic Party has lost ground with every segment of the white electorate, save the most educated (and, possibly, urban dwellers).

With the end to racial segregation in the formerly "solid" Democratic South in the 1960, the Republican Party moved quickly (and successfully) to capture the partisan loyalties of white southerners. With the exception of the elections of its native sons, Jimmy Carter in 1976 and Bill Clinton in 1992 and 1994, the South has been solidly Republican since 1964. In the South political change was quick. But the broadening of the Republican Party's electoral coalition to include large segments of the bygone Democratic New Deal coalition, including white Catholic voters and the white working class, occurred at a much slower rate of change, indeed, decades in the making. Much has been made of Donald Trump's resonance with disaffected white voters, tired of immigration, tired of seeing jobs moving overseas, tired of a government that, in their view, seems to care little about them and cannot be trusted. Yet careful examination of the electoral record shows that these "Trump voters" have been "Republican voters" for quite some time now, although the GOP's share of these voters has grown with each passing decade. On balance the evidence shows that the American electorate in 2016 is remarkably similar to electorates of the last few decades.

CHAPTER SIX

CANDIDATES, ISSUES, AND THE VOTE

In this chapter and the two that follow, we examine some of the concerns that underlie voters' choices for president. Even though scholars and politicians disagree about what factors voters employ and how they employ them, there is general consensus on several points. First, voters' attitudes or preferences determine their choices. There may be disagreement over exactly which attitudes shape behavior, but most scholars agree that voters deliberately choose to support the candidate they believe will make the best president. For decades there had also been general agreement that, as Campbell et al., in *The American Voter*, originally argued, it is the tripartite attitudes toward the candidates, the issues, and the parties that is the most important set of attitudes in shaping the vote.[1] In these three chapters, we start with voters' considerations just before casting their ballots and then turn to their earlier ones, ending with the most important long-term attitudinal force shaping the vote, party identification.

Subsequent work has raised other sets of attitudes to greater prominence, beyond attitudes towards the candidates, the issues, and the parties. One flows from what Campbell et al. rather dismissively referred to as the "nature of the times."[2] Anthony Downs and V. O. Key developed two different accounts of "retrospective voting."[3] Morris Fiorina extended Downs's perspective and provided a wealth of empirical tests of that account, which became the disciplinary norm and which will be used to examine the 2016 election in Chapter 7.[4]

More recently Christopher Achen and Larry Bartels claimed that all kinds of matters, including those for which no reasonable person would hold the government accountable, are treated as "retrospective" by voters.[5] They argued for an enhanced role for partisan loyalties, above and beyond that which Campbell et al. argued for originally. They saw that, similar to Donald Green et al., partisanship can serve as the basis of a voter's political identity, that is, how one thinks and feels about politics.[6] It is true that group loyalties, such as the very high levels of racial voting patterns already discussed, are powerful forces in the vote, and perhaps partisan loyalties have become as intense. In Chapter 8 we will take up party identification in detail in these terms, among others. Whereas Campbell et al. placed party identification at the center of their understanding of voting and elections, the increased partisan polarization appears to have strengthened this particular type of group loyalty even further, often in emotional rather than or in addition to cognitive terms. Whether all of these forces, retrospective and group-based loyalties, among others, can be summarized simply as attitudes, beliefs, or preferences is a newly reopened question. For here we take it that these all can be fit sufficiently comfortably into the consensus view that attitudes shape behavior, and the debate is over which of these matter, when, and with what consequences.

In this chapter we look first at the relationships among several measures of candidate evaluations and the vote, beginning with the "feeling thermometers" used by the ANES to measure affect toward the candidates. After this brief analysis we examine aspects of the major components of these evaluations: voters' perceptions of the candidates' personal qualities and of the candidates' professional qualifications, and competence to serve as president.[7] As we will see there is a very powerful relationship between thermometer evaluations of candidates and the vote and an only somewhat less strong one between evaluations of candidate traits and the vote. It might seem obvious that voters support the candidate they like best, but in 1968, 1980, 1992, 1996, and 2000, the presence of a significant third candidate complicated decision-making for many voters.[8]

We conceive of attitudes toward the candidates as the most direct influence on the vote itself, especially the summary evaluations encapsulated in the "feeling thermometers," as we used in Chapter 1. But attitudes toward the issues and the parties help shape attitudes toward the candidates and thus the vote.[9] With that in mind we turn to the first part of our investigation of the role of issues. After analyzing the problems that most concerned the voters in 2016, we discuss the two basic forms of issue voting: that based on prospective issues and that based on retrospective issues. In this chapter we investigate the impact of prospective issues. In doing so we consider one of the enduring questions about issue voting—how much information the public has on the issues and candidates' positions on them—and is this sufficient for casting an issues-based vote? Our analyses provide an indication of the significance of prospective issues in 2016 and compare their impact as shown in earlier election surveys. Chapter 7 examines retrospective issues and the vote, and Chapter 8 examines partisan identification and assesses the significance of both parties and issues for voting in 2016 and in earlier elections.

ATTITUDES TOWARD THE CANDIDATES

Although the United States has a two-party system, there are still ways in which other candidates can appear on the ballot or run a write-in candidacy. The 2016 presidential election was a two-person race for all intents and purposes, but many other candidates were running as well.[10] Two other political parties qualified for inclusion on nearly all state ballots. The Libertarian Party nominated Gary Johnson for president (as they had in 2012), winning about 4.5 million votes (about 3.3 percent; by comparison Clinton won about 65.8 million or 48.3 percent, whereas Trump won 63 million votes, or 46.2 percent). Jill Stein was the Green Party's presidential nominee (also as in 2012), winning about close to 1.5 million votes (or 1.1 percent). Both Johnson, who appeared on all ballots, and Stein, who appeared on forty-two state ballots and that of DC, greatly increased their vote from 2012 but obviously fell far short of being competitive for a single Electoral College vote.

As a result we consider 2016 to be a nearly pure, two-person contest, and thus we limit our attention to Hillary Clinton and Donald Trump. We want to know why people preferred one candidate over the other, and therefore how they voted, and by extension, why Clinton won the popular vote (which is what the ANES survey, as most surveys, is designed to measure), whereas Trump won the election by virtue of his Electoral College majority.

If attitudes determine choices, then the obvious starting point in a two-person race is to imagine that people voted for the candidate they preferred. This may sound obvious, but as we have noted, in races with three or more candidates, people do not necessarily vote for the candidate they most prefer.[11] Respondents who rank a major-party candidate highest among three candidates vote overwhelmingly for the major-party candidate. On the other hand respondents who rank a third-party or independent candidate highest often desert that candidate to vote for one of the major-party candidates, which we believe may result from voters using strategic considerations to avoid "wasting" their vote on a candidate who has little chance of winning.

Happily for understanding the 2012 presidential election, in a strictly two-person race, people overwhelmingly vote for the candidate they prefer. This close relationship can be demonstrated by analyzing the "feeling thermometer." This measure is a scale that runs from 0 to 100 degrees, with 0 indicating "very cold" or negative feelings, 50 indicating neutral feelings, and 100 indicating a "very warm" or positive evaluation.[12]

The data for 2016 are reported in Table 6-1. As the data in Part A of the table illustrate, there was a close balance in the electorate between those ranking Clinton higher than Trump (48 percent of respondents) and those ranking Trump higher (46 percent).[13] The closeness of these overall ratings of the candidates to the actual vote choice is clear in Part B of the table. In particular it depicts the powerful relationship between these assessments and the vote, in which almost everyone supported the candidate they rated higher—all but 1 percent of those who rated the Democrat higher and 2 percent of those who rated the Republican higher voted for that party's nominee. The relatively small percentage who tied the two candidates voted much closer to the mental coin flip that would imply—55 percent for Clinton.

Perhaps due to the relatively high levels of unpopularity of the two major-party candidates, 15 percent of the respondents rated Johnson highest on the thermometer, and 20 percent so rated Stein. But very few of those respondents voted for their third-party favorite. Johnson received only 17 percent of the vote from those who rated him highest (with 45 percent voting for Clinton, 34 percent for Trump, and the rest scattered). Those who claimed to feel most warmly toward Stein did not stick with her at all; she received only 4 percent of that vote (with 48 percent voting for Clinton and 38 for Trump). Clearly, in this case, affective evaluations did not lead to behavior. Rather strategic calculations about wasting votes and chances of winning weighed heavily.

Overall, then, these summary evaluations are quite proximate to the vote in a two-candidate race. This finding is particularly strong in 2016, but the general pattern of more than nine in ten supporting their preferred candidates is commonplace, and so it is worth noting that the small percentages voting for highly regarded third-party candidates in 2016 is found also in earlier elections. These preferences about the major-party candidates are, therefore, but a first, very close, step back from the vote to the discovery of underlying reasons that explain how people came to the choices they did.

Table 6-1 Relative Ranking of Presidential Candidates on the Feeling Thermometer: Response Distribution and Vote Choice, 2016

	Rated Clinton Higher Than Trump on Thermometer	Rated Clinton Equal to Trump on Thermometer	Rated Trump Higher Than Clinton on Thermometer	Total	(N)
A. Distribution of responses					
Percent	48	6	46	100	(3612)
B. Major-party voters who voted for Clinton					
Percent	99	55	2	53	(2366)
(N)	(1199)	(52)	(1115)		

Source: Authors' analysis of the 2016 ANES survey.

Note: The numbers in parentheses in Part B of the table are the totals on which the percentages are based. Only respondents who rated both candidates on the scale are included.

That is to say that we are led to the next obvious question: Why did more people rate Clinton or Trump more warmly? The ANES asked a series of questions about how people view the candidates as people and as potential presidents, six of which are reported in Table 6-2A. These cover different aspects of attributes we might like a president to possess: speaking his or her mind, providing strong leadership, caring about people, and being knowledgeable, even-tempered, and honest.[14] The 2016 campaign presented quite a different mixture compared to the 2008 or 2012 contests in that both candidates in 2016 were perceived negatively on most of these traits. In 2008, for example, Obama and McCain were both perceived quite positively on most (but not all) of these traits, whereas 2012 illustrated a case in which the electorate had mixed views about both nominees. As for 2016 Clinton was perceived net positively in terms of being knowledgeable. The electorate was about evenly divided in considering her to be even-tempered and speaking her mind. Providing strong leadership was net negative for her, but only modestly so, whereas caring about people like you [the respondent] was more clearly negative, and honesty was very decidedly negative, perhaps reflecting Trump's repeated campaign nickname of "Crooked Hillary." For his part Trump was very clearly seen as speaking his own mind (which may or may not have been perceived positively by respondents, as we will see). However, all else was net negative in evaluation, with providing strong leadership fairly solidly so and the other traits very negative overall. The public saw Trump as only very slightly more honest than Clinton, and in the other four traits, Clinton was clearly more positively evaluated.[15]

Table 6-2A Distribution of Responses on Presidential Candidate Trait Evaluations, 2016 (Percent)

	Extremely Well	Very Well	Moderately Well	Slightly Well	Not Well at All	Total	(N)
Clinton							
Speaks mind	12	23	28	17	20	100	(4251)
Provides strong leadership	14	20	22	15	29	100	(4255)
Really cares about people like you	11	16	20	16	37	100	(4251)
Knowledgeable	25	27	24	13	11	100	(4249)
Even-tempered	13	22	29	17	19	100	(4244)
Honest	5	10	21	15	49	100	(4250)
Trump							
Speaks mind	56	25	8	4	7	100	(4250)
Provides strong leadership	12	18	18	14	38	100	(4246)
Really cares about people like you	7	12	18	12	51	100	(4245)
Knowledgeable	7	15	22	17	39	100	(4241)
Even-tempered	3	5	19	18	55	100	(4250)
Honest	7	15	20	14	44	100	(4246)

Source: Authors' analysis of the 2016 ANES.

Note: Numbers are weighted.

In Table 6-2B we report the percentage of major-party voters with differing assessments of these traits who voted for Clinton and Trump, respectively. These trait evaluations were quite differently related to the vote for the two candidates. For Clinton the relationship is quite like what one might expect. She won the support of nearly everyone (with the only partial exception of the "speaks her mind" trait) who thought the trait described her extremely well and quite high majorities among those who responded "very well" and even "moderately well." Those who responded "slightly well" or "not at all well" did not support her highly at all.[16] For evaluations of traits describing Trump, much the same is true for four of the six traits (strong leadership, really cares, knowledgeable, and honest). The pattern for "speaks mind" is still decreasing with decreasing fit of the trait for Trump, but the variable is quite a bit more weakly related to the vote, largely due to the large percentage picking the "extremely well" response. Whereas relatively few picked the top two categories for "even-tempered" for describing Trump, the pattern is clearly different. Those who said "moderately well" were the most likely to vote for Trump, followed by the "very well" and "slightly well" categories, with the two extremes quite a bit lower.[17] As a general rule, then, we find trait evaluations provide context and underpinning for understanding why some felt warmly toward one candidate or the other, and indeed, they show the public responded to the observations of the campaign in an at least somewhat bipartisan way. However, these remain only one more step removed from the vote than the candidate thermometer questions.

What might lie even further from the vote? Candidates and their supporters campaign on the assessments of the two candidates (decidedly not bipartisan with much negative campaigning!), but they also spend a great deal of time discussing a variety of issues. These are both prospective—what I or my opponent will do if elected—and retrospective—how Obama or the Democrats succeeded or failed in handling public policy in the last four or even eight years. These, we might expect, stand farther removed from the vote and thus help shape how these global or more specific assessments of the candidates came about. The rest of this chapter examines issues as they are discussed prospectively, leaving retrospective assessments for Chapter 7 and differences in this partisan-polarized world for Chapter 8.

PROSPECTIVE EVALUATIONS

Public policy concerns enter into the voting decision in two very different ways. In any election two questions become important: How has the incumbent president and party done on policy? And how likely is it that his opponent (or opponents) would do any better? Voting based on this form of policy appraisal is called retrospective voting and will be analyzed in Chapter 7.

The second form of policy-based voting involves examining the candidates' policy platforms and assessing which candidate's policy promises conform most closely to what the voter believes the government should be doing. Policy voting, therefore, involves comparing sets of promises and voting for the set that is most like the voter's own preferences. Voting based on these kinds of decisions is called prospective voting because it involves examining the promises of the candidates about future actions. In

	Extremely Well	Very Well	Moderately Well	Slightly Well	Not Well at All
Clinton					
Speaks mind	82	70	63	38	13
(N)	(280)	(583)	(647)	(377)	(486)
Provides strong leadership	96	91	66	23	4
(N)	(396)	(500)	(480)	(288)	(710)
Really cares about people like you	95	95	80	42	8
(N)	(299)	(418)	(445)	(336)	(874)
Knowledgeable	90	65	28	13	5
(N)	(730)	(625)	(494)	(275)	(248)
Even-tempered	95	84	52	22	6
(N)	(386)	(549)	(604)	(364)	(469)
Honest	95	98	93	75	13
(N)	(118)	(273)	(502)	(340)	(1139)
Trump					
Speaks mind	55	48	32	15	4
(N)	(1425)	(553)	(169)	(68)	(155)
Provides strong leadership	97	90	66	29	4
(N)	(343)	(447)	(394)	(307)	(879)
Really cares about people like you	96	97	89	58	9
(N)	(189)	(326)	(413)	(254)	(1188)
Knowledgeable	92	93	79	41	7
(N)	(162)	(356)	(534)	(388)	(929)
Even-tempered	55	84	90	77	20
(N)	(61)	(115)	(458)	(411)	(1327)
Honest	89	91	84	48	7
(N)	(183)	(385)	(460)	(323)	(1021)

Source: Authors' analysis of the 2016 ANES.

Note: The numbers in parentheses are the totals on which the percentages are based. The numbers are weighted.

this chapter we examine prospective evaluations of the two major-party candidates in 2016 and how these evaluations relate to voter choice.

The last twelve elections show some remarkable similarities in prospective evaluations and voting. Perhaps the most important similarity is the perception of where the Democratic and Republican candidates stood on issues. In these elections the public saw clear differences between the major-party nominees. In all cases the public saw the Republican candidates as conservative on most issues, and most citizens scored the GOP candidates as more conservative than the voters themselves. And in all elections the public saw the Democratic candidates as liberal on most issues, and most citizens viewed the Democratic candidates as more liberal than the voters themselves. As a result many voters perceived a clear choice based on their understanding of the candidates' policy positions. The candidates presented the voters with, as the 1964 Goldwater campaign slogan put it, "a choice, not an echo." The *average* citizen, however, faced a difficult choice. For many, Democratic nominees were considered to be as far to the left as the Republican nominees were to the right. In general the net effect of prospective issues over recent elections has been to give neither party a decided, potentially long-term, advantage on policy.

One of the most important differences among these elections, however, was the mixture of issues that concerned the public. Each election presented its own mixture of policy concerns. Moreover, the general strategies of the candidates on issues differed in each election. In 1980 Jimmy Carter's incumbency was marked by a general perception that he was unable to solve pressing problems. Ronald Reagan attacked that weakness both directly (e.g., by the question he posed to the public during his debate with Carter, "Are you better off today than you were four years ago?") and indirectly. The indirect attack was more future oriented. Reagan set forth a clear set of proposals designed to convince the public that he would be more likely to solve the nation's problems because he had his own proposals to end soaring inflation, to strengthen the United States militarily, and to regain respect and influence for the United States abroad.

In 1984 the public perceived Reagan as a far more successful president than Carter had been. Reagan chose to run his reelection campaign by focusing primarily on the theme that things were much better by 1984 (as illustrated by his advertising slogan "It's morning in America"). Walter Mondale attacked that claim by arguing that Reagan's policies were unfair and by pointing to the rapidly growing budget deficit. But Reagan countered that Mondale was another "tax and spend" Democrat, and the "Great Communicator," as some called him, captured a second term.

The 1988 campaign was more similar to the 1984 than to the 1980 campaign. George H. W. Bush continued to run on the successes of the Reagan-Bush administration and promised no new taxes. ("Read my lips," he said. "No new taxes!") Michael S. Dukakis initially attempted to portray the election as one about "competence" rather than "ideology," arguing that he had demonstrated his competence as governor of Massachusetts and that Bush, by implication, was less competent. Bush countered that it really was an election about ideology, and that Dukakis was just another liberal Democrat from Massachusetts.

The 1992 election presented yet another type of campaign. Bush used the success of the 1991 Persian Gulf War to augment his claim that he was a successful world leader, but Bill Clinton attacked the Bush administration on domestic issues, barely discussing foreign affairs at all. He sought to keep the electorate focused on the current economic woes and argued for substantial reforms of the health care system, hoping to appeal to Democrats and to spur action should he be the first Democrat in the White House in twelve years. At the same time, he sought to portray himself not as another "tax and spend" liberal Democrat but as a moderate "New Democrat."

In 1996 Clinton ran a campaign typical of a popular incumbent; he focused on what led people to approve of his handling of the presidency and avoided mentioning many specific new programs. His policy proposals were a lengthy series of relatively inexpensive, limited programs. Bob Dole, having difficulties deciding whether to emphasize Clinton's personal failings in the first term or to call for different programs for the future, decided to put a significant tax cut proposal at the center of his candidacy under either of those campaign strategies.

In 2000 the candidates debated a broad array of domestic issues—education, health care, social security, and taxes the most prominent among them—often couched in terms of a newfound "problem," federal government budget surpluses. Typically these issues (except for taxes) have favored Democratic contenders, and Republicans often avoided detailed discussions of all except taxes on the grounds that doing so would make the issues more salient to voters and would highlight the Democratic advantages. George W. Bush, however, spoke out on education, in particular, as well as health care and Social Security to a lesser extent, believing he could undercut the traditional Democratic advantage. For his part Al Gore had the advantage of his belief (backed by public opinion polls) that the public was less in favor of tax cuts than usual and more in favor of allocating budget surpluses to buttress popular domestic programs.

In 2004, by contrast, Bush and Kerry had less choice about what issues to consider. With wars under way in Iraq, in Afghanistan, and against terrorism, neither candidate could avoid foreign policy considerations. Bush preferred to emphasize that Iraq was part of the war on terrorism, whereas Kerry argued that it was not and indeed that it was a costly distraction from it. Similarly 2004 opened with the economy slumping. The Democrats, including Kerry, attacked the Bush administration policies, while Bush countered by saying that the economy was actually improving—in large part because of his successful policies. As the year wore on, the economy did in fact improve, although not so much as to remove all criticism.

The 2008 campaign began as one in which the Democrats tried to emphasize their opposition to the Bush policies in Iraq and their concern about the war in Afghanistan. On the domestic front Obama emphasized health care reform, improved environmental policies, and other aspects of his agenda that called for "change." McCain, conversely, began with a spirited defense of the war in Iraq, and especially the "surge" in the war effort there. By fall, however, the economy had swept aside virtually every other issue but war from consideration and replaced war as topic number one. Indeed so worrisome were the economic events of the fall that candidates could ill afford to do anything but relate any domestic issue to their plans for fighting the economic downturn.

In 2012 both the Obama and Romney camps anticipated a close contest. Romney's side wanted to make the campaign be about Obama and his successes or failures in office—retrospective voting concerns—on the grounds that the economy had not recovered sufficiently to justify returning Obama to office. This was made problematic first by Romney's statement that Obama's supporters were 47 percent of the electorate whom he characterized as people "who live off government handouts" and do not "care for their lives," and then by Hurricane Sandy and the appearance of successful performance by Obama, reinforced by a leading Republican figure, Gov. Chris Christie (NJ), saying that Obama was doing his job very well. Obama, for his part, approached issues rather more like Clinton did in 1996, offering a series of popular but relatively small domestic initiatives ("small ball" as it was called at times) and his emphasis on how the economy was not where everyone hoped but it was improving and would do so quicker with Democrats in office.

In 2016 Clinton's nomination campaign had many positions that reflected Obama and her service to his administration. In that sense many were retrospective or at least made attacking her through attacking Obama and his policies fair game. Sanders's lengthy challenge to her nomination led her to break with Obama on several key issues, such as the Trans Pacific Partnership (TPP), which Obama had developed and championed (and she had once supported), which was a proposed international agreement among nations that bordered the Pacific, as part of Obama's "pivot" toward China. Conversely she did not change her support for the Paris Agreement (*Accord de Paris*), an international agreement to work to reduce the level of carbon effluent and thus reduce the risk of climate change, or the North American Free Trade Agreement that Bill Clinton (and George H. W. Bush) had developed and seen through to enactment. On the domestic side, although she had her own ideas about how to improve by building on the Affordable Care Act, "Obamacare" was the base of her position. Essentially the same was true on many aspects of domestic policy. But, like the TPP, her advocacy of free access to community and junior colleges marked new directions from the past. Thus, it is fair to say that her platform was a mixture of retrospective and prospective issues. Trump relentlessly attacked Obama and Clinton's support of Obama's policies in the sense of retrospective evaluations. And, of course, he also had signature issues that would represent prospective policies, "repeal and replace" Obamacare, build a wall to keep new immigrants from crossing the Mexican border, deporting all illegal (undocumented) immigrants, and baring entry for all Muslims. Of course he also often advocated different policies in the campaign and even more often provided insufficient detail to be confident on just what he sought to do. Nonetheless, he was clearly providing very strong retrospective critiquing while advocating for prospective policies.

Most Important Issues in the Public

What did the public care about most? From 1972 to 2004, we were able to use ANES surveys to assess this question. In 2012 we examined exit polls, conducted as voters were leaving the voting booth, and the various interested parties (news media, etc.) formed a pool to conduct that poll.[18] We did so again for 2016.

In the four elections from 1984 through 2000, the great majority of responses revolved around domestic issues rather than foreign policy, perhaps because of the end of the Cold War.[19] In those elections, and even the four before them (when foreign affairs were more important) prior to 2004, two major categories of domestic issues dominated. From 1976 to 1992, in good times and bad, by far the more commonly cited issue was the economy. Yet, in 1972, 1996, 2000, and then in 2004 as well, the most frequently cited problems were in the social issues category, such as either social welfare issues or concerns about public order. In 2004, for example, nearly half (49 percent) cited social issues, whereas 29 percent (the highest since 1984, i.e., since the Cold War) cited foreign and defense issues. Mostly that was the war in Iraq in particular (18 percent). In 2008 (shifting to the pooled exit poll) 63 percent of voters said the economy was most important, with the war in Iraq selected by 10 percent and the war on terror by 9 percent. That high a percentage selecting the economy should come as no surprise as we were in the midst of the initial decline into the "Great Recession," the most severe since the Great Depression.

Table 6-3A reports the results of the exit poll for the 2012 and 2016 elections. Foreign policy in 2012 continued to drop in concern as U.S. involvement in Iraq was over (at least temporarily) and the war in Afghanistan was diminishing (at least temporarily). Only 5 percent selected foreign policy as most important. It was the economy that remained dominant, as 59 percent selected it as their chief concern, whereas 15 percent more said it was the deficit. The latter had been a key part of the Tea Party and Republican leadership concerns through 2010 and into 2012 (it is of course an issue that touches on the economy and on the role of the government and so is not purely about the economy nor about the government). Another large portion, 18 percent, said that health care was the most important problem, whereas selection of other options was rare.

In 2016 the economy remained the most important concern, dropping only slightly to 52 percent of voters, even though the economy had improved noticeably over the intervening four years. Foreign policy increased to 13 percent as both wars rekindled and as Trump critiqued our involvement in foreign trade and international relations generally. The two issues that, in effect, replaced health care and the budget deficit as concerns (those two dropping to low percentages in 2016) were terrorism (18 percent of the voting public) and immigration (13 percent); both appear to us to be made into popular concerns as much by Trump's campaigning as for any other reason. These issues are sometimes referred to as "intermestic," that is, as having both international and domestic dimensions. Indeed one part of the partisan debate over these issues is precisely whether the international or domestic aspects of these issues are predominant.

Table 6-3B illustrates that people's concerns played a role in their voting. Those concerned about two of Trump's most regularly discussed issues in 2016, terrorism and immigration, were indeed considerably more likely to support him than to vote for Clinton. Conversely Clinton had a clear advantage on foreign policy generally. The vote was closer among those who were concerned about the economy, something both candidates raised often and emphasized greatly in their campaigns. Given the interpretation often heard about the concerns of white working-class voters, it was Clinton who held an eleven-point lead among those who stated that the economy was their most important concern.

Table 6-3 Most Important Problem as Seen by the Electorate, 2012 and 2016, and Reported Vote for Clinton and Trump in 2016 (Percent)

Table 6-3A

Problem	2012	2016
The economy	59	52
Foreign policy	5	13
Terrorism	—	18
Immigration	—	13
Health care	18	—
Federal budget deficit	15	—

Table 6-3B   Percent reporting voted for

	Obama	Romney	Clinton	Trump
The economy	47%	51%	52%	41%
Foreign policy	56%	33%	60%	33%
Terrorism	—	—	40%	57%
Immigration		33%	64%	
Health care	75%	24%	—	—
Federal budget deficit	32%	66%	—	—

Sources: 2012 and 2016 National Election Exit Polls. Question in 2012 asked 10,798 respondents about which of the four issues were the most important issue facing the country and 24,558 respondents in 2016. The two percentages do not sum to 100%, with the rest reporting that they voted for some other candidate or did not answer the question. For 2016: http://www.cnn.com/election/results/exit-polls, accessed 6/15/2017. For 2012: https://ropercenter.cornell.edu/polls/us-elections/how-groups-voted/how-groups-voted-2012/. Accessed June 17, 2017.

ISSUE POSITIONS AND PERCEPTIONS

Since 1972 the ANES surveys have included issue scales designed to measure the preferences of the electorate and voters' perceptions of the positions the candidates took on the issues.[20] The questions are therefore especially appropriate for examining prospective issue evaluations. We hasten to add, however, that voters' perceptions of where the incumbent party's nominee stands may well be based in part on what the president has done in office as well as on the campaign promises he or she made as the party's nominee. This is especially likely when the incumbent vice president is nominated, such as Vice President Gore in 2000, or when someone who played a prominent role in the presidential administration, such as former secretary of state Clinton in 2016, is nominated. The policy promises of the opposition party candidate may also be judged in part by what that candidate's party did when it last held the White House. Nevertheless, the issue scales generally focus on prospective evaluations and are very different from those used to make the retrospective judgments examined in Chapter 7.

The issue scales will be used to examine several questions: What alternatives did the voters believe the candidates were offering? To what extent did the voters have issue preferences of their own and relatively clear perceptions of candidates' positions? Finally how strongly were voters' preferences and perceptions related to their choice of candidates?

Figure 6-1 shows the seven-point issue scales used in the 2016 ANES survey. The figure presents the average (median) position of the respondents (labeled "S" for self) and the average (median) perceptions of the positions of Clinton and Trump (labeled "C" and "T"). The issues raised in 2016 probe the respondents' own preferences and perceptions of the major-party nominees on whether government should spend more or less on social services; whether defense spending should be increased or decreased; whether health insurance should be provided by the government or by private insurance; whether the government should see to it that everyone has a job and a good standard of living or let citizens get ahead on their own; whether the government should provide aid to blacks or whether they should help themselves; and whether the government should protect the environment at the cost of jobs and a good standard of living. These issues were selected for inclusion in the ANES survey because they are controversial and generally measure long-standing partisan divisions. As a result the average citizen comes out looking reasonably moderate on these issues. In every case the average citizen falls between the positions corresponding to the average placements of the two candidates. On many issues asked in 2012, the typical citizen is near the center of the scale, generally falling between one-half point to the left and one-half point to the right of the midpoint of four. Only on the environment scale was the average citizen more than a full point—in this case a bit more than a point and a half to the left—of the center. The basic message is that on average, the public in 2012 was mostly moderate on these long-standing issues.

Note that, on five of six of the scales, on all but the defense spending measure the average citizen is at least very slightly to the liberal end of the scale. Because we use the median as our measure of "average," that means that more than half of the respondents were at least slightly liberal and may have been very liberal on those five issues. That is actually a change from 2012 (in which all six of these issue scales were also included).[21] In that year the average citizen also was to the left on five of six of these issue scales. The exception was aid to blacks, where the average citizen

Figure 6-1 Median Self-Placement of the Electorate and the Electorate's Placement of Candidates on Issue Scales, 2016

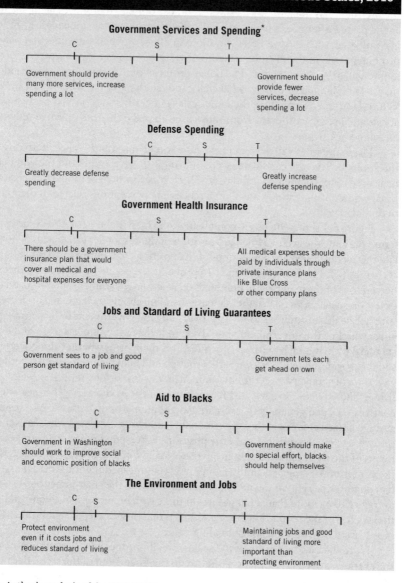

Source: Author's analysis of the 2016 ANES.

Note: S = median self-placement of the respondents; T = median placement of Trump; C = median placement of Romney.

*Reversed from actual scoring to make a "liberal" response closer to point 1 and a "conservative" response closer to point 7.

was at 4.4. On health care the average citizen was somewhat more liberal in 2016 than 2012, so whereas the Republican concerns about "Obamacare" may indeed have had an effect on public opinion, it did not generate greater opposition but, if anything, greater support for the program. Perhaps more likely, the public had, on balance, become adjusted to having "Obamacare" and apparently found it to their liking so that effect did not change opinion that greatly. One might also imagine that the Republican and Tea Party and Freedom Caucus appeals to reduce the size of the federal government might have made a difference. If so they had effects very similar to health care. In fact respondents were at least slightly more liberal on average on every issue but defense spending in 2016 compared to 2012. This was particularly clear with respect to the aid to blacks scale, in which the average respondent was more than a half point further to the left in 2016 than in 2012. Still, in most cases, the average citizen was only slightly left of center and better seen as moderate than even moderately liberal. The exception was the jobs and environment issue, on which the average citizen was clearly to the left of center, as they have been on this issue in most elections.

Generally, on issue scales used between 1980 and 2016, the public has viewed the Democratic candidate as more liberal and the Republican candidate as more conservative than the average member of the public.[22] Indeed these differences are often quite large, and as it happens, this is especially so in 2016. Except for defense spending, they exceed three points (with a maximum difference of six points) on every issue scale.[23] This set of differences is perhaps the greatest we have yet measured.

That effect appears to be due more to perceptions on the Republican side. Perceptions of Clinton generally were very similar to those of Obama four years earlier, although mostly just a bit more centrist. The rather ironic exception is aid to blacks, where respondents saw her just slightly to the left of where they had placed Obama. Trump, for his part, was generally seen as more conservative than Romney had been seen in 2012, although often this difference was small (and on government services and spending, he was seen as very slightly more moderate). The largest difference was his more conservative stances on defense spending, the environment, and aid to blacks. Overall the public saw quite large differences between the offerings of the two candidates. No matter how much or how little the public may have been polarized in 2012, it saw that alleged polarization dividing the two candidates, even more so than in preceding elections.

Although voters saw clear differences between the candidates, the average voter faced a difficult choice. Clinton was seen to the left of the average respondent, and Trump was seen to the right on every issue, and the average voter was rarely much closer to one candidate than the other (the exception being much closer to Clinton on the environment). Of course we cannot at this point go much further on these overall figures. The choice is made not by a mythical average voter choosing over what the respondents as a whole thought the candidates offered, but it is made by individual voters considering what they think about these issues. To consider a voter's choices, then we must look inside these averages to assess the individual behavior that makes up those averages.

ISSUE VOTING CRITERIA

The Problem

Because voting is an individual action, we must look at the preferences of individuals to see whether prospective issues influenced their votes. In fact the question of prospective voting is controversial. In their classic study of the American electorate, *The American Voter*, Angus Campbell and his colleagues pointed out that the public is often ill-informed about public policy and may not be able to vote on the basis of issues.[24] They asked themselves what information voters would need before an issue could influence the decision on how to vote, and they answered by posing three conditions. First, the voters must hold an opinion on the issue; second, they must learn what the government is doing on the issue; and third, they must perceive a difference between the policies of the two major parties. According to the authors' analysis, only about one-quarter to one-third of the electorate in 1956 could meet these three conditions, and they therefore concluded that relatively few were likely to vote on the basis of issues.

Although it is impossible to replicate the analysis in *The American Voter*, we can adapt the authors' procedures to the 2016 electorate. ANES data, in fact, focus even more directly on the actual choice citizens must make—the choice among the candidates. The first criterion is whether respondents claim to have an opinion on the issue. This is measured by whether they placed themselves on the issue scale as measured by Campbell et al. Second, the respondents should have some perception of the positions taken by the candidates on an issue. This is measured by whether they could place both major-party candidates on that issue. Although some voters might perceive the position of one candidate and vote on that basis, prospective voting involves a comparison between or among alternatives, so the expressed ability to perceive the stands of the contenders seems a minimal requirement of prospective issue voting. Third, the voter must see a difference between the positions of the candidates. Failing to see a difference means that the voter perceived no choice on the issue, perhaps because he or she failed to detect actual distinctions between the candidates. This failure might arise from lack of attention to the issue in the campaign. It also may arise from instances in which the candidates actually did take very similar positions on the issue, and respondents were thus, on average, reflecting that similarity, as we believe was truer of the candidates on most issues in 1976 than in other campaigns. Actual similarity of positions is rare in this era of partisan polarization, although this happens at times on specific issues. Clinton and Trump, for example, both opposed and said they would end any attempt to ratify the TPP.

A voter might be able to satisfy these criteria but misperceive the offerings of the candidates. This leads to a fourth condition, which we are able to measure more systematically than was possible in 1956: Do the respondents accurately perceive the relative positions of the two major-party candidates—that is, do they see Trump as more conservative than Clinton? This criterion does not demand that the voter have an accurate perception of what the candidate proposes, but it does expect the voter to recognize that Clinton, for example, favored spending more on social services than did Trump.

In Table 6-4, we report the percentages of the sample that met the four criteria on the six issue scales used in 2016.[25] We also show the average proportion that met these criteria for all scales and compare those averages to comparable averages for all issue scales used in the eleven preceding elections.[26] Column I of Table 6-4 reveals that most people felt capable of placing themselves on the issue scales, and this capability was common to all election years.[27]

Nearly as many of the public also placed both candidates on the scales. Indeed a higher percentage satisfied these two criteria in 2016 than any other election. The environmental/jobs issue yielded the lowest percentage satisfying these criteria in 2016, but even that scale yielded a higher percentage, at 81, than the average in any other year (which was highest in 1996 with an average of 80 percent). The 83 percent average for 2016 in Column II is the highest of any election for which we have relevant data.

Although there is a decline in the percentage also seeing differences between the two candidates on these issues, the main point is that 2016 is a high watermark in this regard. Indeed considering this third criterion makes 2016 stand out even more clearly. In 2016 over three in four, on average, satisfied the first three criteria: they placed both themselves and both candidates on the issue scale, and they placed the candidates at two different positions on the scale.

Finally, a very high—the highest by far—percentage met all four issue voting criteria, with more than two in three doing so on average. As the reader can see, the average meeting all four criteria in 2016 was higher than the average meeting the first three criteria in any other election year. And compare 2016 with 1976. In the earlier election only one in four met these criteria on average. In that year relatively few could see differences between Gerald Ford and Jimmy Carter on issues and therefore could hardly have also gotten them in the correct order! But now, by 2016, the idea of polarization seems to have fully settled into the presidential electorate. That is to say they saw the candidates as taking consistently and starkly different positions on just about every major issue (or at least every one of these six), and there was very little disagreement about that point in the electorate. They saw the Republican and the Democratic Party nominees as polarized, more so than ever before over the last twelve elections. Although it could be that Clinton and Trump were uniquely ideological candidates, we believe it more likely that the sustained polarization between the two party elites is becoming clearer to the public.

The data in Table 6-4 suggest that the potential for prospective issue voting was high in 2016. Therefore, we might expect these issues to be rather closely related to voter choice. We will examine voter choice on these issues in two ways. First, how often did people vote for the closer candidate on each issue? Second, how strongly related to the vote is the set of all issues taken together?

APPARENT ISSUE VOTING IN 2016

Issue Criteria and Voting on Each Issue

The first question is to what extent did people who were closer to a candidate on a given issue actually vote for that candidate—that is, how strong is apparent issue

Table 6-4 Four Criteria for Issue Voting, 2016, and Comparisons with 1972–2012 Presidential Elections

Issue Scale	Percentage of Sample Who . . .			
	I Placed self on scale	II Placed both candidates on scale[a]	III Saw differences between Clinton and Trump	IV Saw Clinton as more "liberal" than Trump
Government spending/services	82	81	72	70
Defense spending	84	82	71	67
Government health insurance	86	85	74	73
Jobs and standard of living	86	85	75	73
Aid to blacks	86	84	73	78
Jobs and the environment	81	80	70	67
Average[b]				
2016 (6)	84	83	73	71
2012 (6)	86	76	67	60
2008 (7)	88	78	61	51
2004 (7)	89	76	62	52
2000 (7)	87	69	51	41
1996 (9)	89	80	65	55
1992 (3)	85	71	66	52
1988 (7)	86	66	52	43
1984 (7)	84	73	62	53
1980 (9)	82	61	51	43
1976 (9)	84	58	39	26
1972 (8)	90	65	49	41

Source: Authors' analysis of ANES surveys.

Note: Columns II, III, and IV compare the Democratic and Republican nominees. Third-party or independent candidates John Anderson (1980), Ross Perot (1992 and 1996), and Ralph Nader (2000 and 2004) were excluded.

[a]Until 1996 respondents who could not place themselves on a scale were not asked to place the candidates on that issue scale. Although they were asked to do so in 1996, 2000, 2004, 2008, 2012, and 2016, we excluded them from further calculations to maintain comparability with prior surveys.

[b]Number in parentheses is the number of issue scales included in the average for each election year survey.

voting?[28] In Table 6-5 we report the proportion of major-party voters who voted for Clinton by where they placed themselves on the issue scales. We divided the seven points into the set of positions that were closer to where the average citizen placed Trump and Clinton (see Figure 6-1).[29] Note that whereas the average perceptions of the two candidates did vary from issue to issue, the net effect of that variation did not make a great deal of difference. In particular, on five of the six issues (all but defense spending), respondents who placed themselves to the left of the midpoint, that is, on points 1, 2, or 3, were closer to where the electorate as a whole thought Clinton stood. Similarly those to the right of the midpoint were always closer to the perception of Trump. On three issues, those who placed themselves at point 4, the midpoint, were closer to where the electorate thought Trump stood, on defense spending "4s" were closer to Clinton's position, and on the jobs and standard of living and the aid to blacks scales, those at 4 were essentially equidistant from both candidates. We see this as support for the idea that the two parties and their candidates and officeholders have achieved a balanced polarization with consistent deviation for the policy center toward their party's extreme (liberal for Democrats, conservative for Republicans), on issue after issue, and that by 2016, the public sees clearly even the presidential candidates being consistent with their party's positions.

Table 6-5 reveals the clear relationship between the voters' issue positions and the candidate they supported on the six scales. Those who adopted positions at the "liberal" end of each scale were very likely to vote for Clinton. If we define liberal as adopting position 1 or 2, Clinton received at least three in four votes and usually more on each scale. Indeed that was even true for those at point 3, the most slightly liberal position, on every issue except the environmental issue. Clinton received fewer than one in four votes on any issue scale from those at the two most conservative positions, whereas Trump carried a clear majority of the vote from those at point 5 on any of the scales. Those at the midpoint of 4 on any issue except the environment gave Clinton a three in five vote majority, and those in this in-between position often were a plurality on that issue. The major exception was the jobs and the environment scale, in which the distribution was shifted much farther to the left than on any of the other issues. Although the midpoint was still a common position, many more were to the left than in the middle. Those at the middle position gave a two to one majority to Trump on this one issue. Otherwise the midpoint marked a clear transition with large majorities voting for Clinton when they were to the left, and large majorities voting for Trump on the right, and the 4 position being clearly in between. Regardless of the details, these are the patterns we would expect if voters voted for the closer candidate on an issue.

The information on issues can be summarized, as it is in Table 6-6, to illustrate what happens when voters met the various conditions for issue voting. In the first column of Table 6-6, we report the percentage of major-party voters who placed themselves closer to the average perception of Trump or Clinton and who voted for the closer candidate. To be more specific the denominator is the total number of major-party voters who placed themselves closer to the electorate's perception of Trump or Clinton. The numerator is the total number of major-party voters who were both closer to Clinton and voted for her plus the total number of major-party voters who were both closer to Trump and voted for him.

Table 6-5　Major-Party Voters Who Voted for Clinton, by Seven-Point Issue Scales, 2016 (Percent)

Issue Scale	Closer to Median Perception of Clinton			Closer to Median Perception of Trump				(N)
	1	2	3	4	5	6	7	(N)
Government spending/services[a]	84	88	82	61	30	16	9	
(N)	(160)	(208)	(393)	(481)	(315)	(268)	(254)	(2,079)
Defense spending	79	81	82	66	42	24	23	
(N)	(103)	(148)	(242)	(549)	(431)	(351)	(283)	(2,107)
Government health insurance	84	82	74	60	39	21	12	
(N)	(398)	(221)	(237)	(392)	(260)	(278)	(362)	(2,148)
Jobs and standard of living	79	85	82	64	46	23	14	
(N)	(212)	(179)	(302)	(436)	(368)	(339)	(315)	(2,151)
Aid to blacks	88	90	84	65	38	20	17	
(N)	(245)	(198)	(230)	(464)	(246)	(325)	(432)	(2,140)
Jobs and the environment	82	78	61	33	21	16	14	
(N)	(549)	(337)	(298)	(348)	(215)	(181)	(115)	(2,043)

Source: Authors' analysis of the 2016 ANES.

Note: Numbers in parentheses are the totals on which percentages are based. Numbers are weighted.

[a]Reversed from actual scoring to make a "liberal" response closer to 1 and a "conservative" response closer to 7.

If voting were unrelated to issue positions, we would expect 50 percent of voters to vote for the closer candidate on average. In 2016, on average, 75 percent voted for the closer candidate. As can be seen in the comparisons to earlier elections, this is by far the highest level of apparent issue voting since these issue scales were widely used,

Table 6-6 Apparent Issue Voting, 2016, and Comparisons with 1972–2012 Presidential Elections (Percent)

Issue Scale	Percentage of Voters Who Voted for Closer Candidate and . . .		
	Placed self on issue scale	Met all four issue voting criteria	Placed self but failed to meet all three other criteria
Government spending/services	72	77	60
Defense spending	71	79	64
Government health insurance	72	78	67
Jobs and standard of living	76	82	72
Aid to blacks	81	85	73
Jobs and the environment	76	85	58
Average[a]			
2016 (6)	75	81	66
2012 (6)	63	68	58
2008 (7)	62	71	47
2004 (7)	67	75	51
2000 (7)	60	68	40
1996 (9)	63	74	41
1992 (3)	62	70	48
1988 (7)	62	71	45
1984 (7)	65	73	46
1980 (9)	63	71	48
1976 (9)	57	70	50
1972 (8)	66	76	55

Source: Authors' analysis of ANES surveys.

Note: An "apparent issue vote" is a vote for the candidate closer to one's position on an issue scale. The closer candidate is determined by comparing self-placement to the median placements of the two candidates on the scale as a whole. Respondents who did not place themselves or who were equidistant from the two candidates are excluded from the calculations.

In 2008, analyses conducted on the randomly selected half-sample asked questions with the traditional wording, except aid to blacks, which was asked of the full sample with same (traditional) wording.

[a]Number in parentheses is the number of seven-point issue scales included in the average for each election year survey.

that is, from 1972 to date. These figures do not tell the whole story, however, because those who placed themselves on an issue but failed to meet some other criterion were unlikely to have cast a vote based on that issue. In the second column of Table 6-6, we report the percentage of those who voted for the closer candidate on each issue among voters who met all four conditions on that issue. The third column reports the percentage that voted for the closer candidate among voters who placed themselves but failed to meet all three of the remaining conditions

Those respondents who met all four conditions were more likely to vote for the closer candidate on any issue. Indeed until this year there has been relatively little difference, on average, across all elections, with about seven in ten such voters supporting the closer candidate. But this year the percentage jumped to greater than eight in ten, higher even than the erstwhile most ideologically charged election in 1972. By contrast, for those respondents who failed to meet the last three of the conditions on issue voting, voting was essentially random with respect to the issues, although surprisingly high in 2016, at 66 percent.[30]

The strong similarity of all election averages in the second and third columns suggests that issue voting seems more prevalent in some elections than others because elections differ in the number of people who clearly perceive differences between the candidates. In all elections about seven in ten who satisfied all four conditions voted consistently with their issue preferences; in all elections those who did not satisfy all the conditions on perceptions of candidates voted essentially randomly with respect to individual issues. As we saw earlier the degree to which such perceptions vary from election to election depends more on the strategies of the candidates than on the qualities of the voters. Therefore, the relatively low percentage of apparent issue voting in 1976, for example, results from the perception of small differences between the two rather moderate candidates. The larger magnitude of apparent issue voting in 2016 stems primarily from the greater clarity with which most people saw the positions of the two nominees. Surely this is a consequence of the polarization of the two parties among candidates and office holders.

The Balance-of-Issues Measure

In prospective issue voting voters compare the full set of policy proposals made by the candidates. Because nearly every issue is strongly related to the vote, we might expect the set of all issues to be even more strongly so. To examine this relationship we constructed an overall assessment of the issue scales to arrive at what we call the balance-of-issues measure. We give individuals a score of +1 if their positions on an issue scale were closer to the average perception of Trump, a score of –1 if their positions were closer to the average perception of Clinton, and a score of 0 if they had no preference on an issue or put themselves on point 4 on the two issues in which that was essentially equidistant from the two candidates' positions. The scores for all six issue scales were added together, creating a measure that ranged from –6 to +6. For example, respondents who were closer to the average perception of Clinton's positions on all seven scales received a score of –6. A negative score indicated that the respondent was, on balance, closer to the public's perception of Clinton, whereas a positive score indicated the respondent was, overall, closer to the public's perception of Trump. We collapsed this thirteen-point measure into seven categories, running from strongly Democratic through neutral to strongly Republican. We have used this scale since 1980 (see Abramson et al., 2016, and sources cited therein). The results are reported in Table 6-7.

As can be seen in Table 6-7A, 19 percent of respondents were in the two most strongly Democratic positions, whereas 30 percent were strongly or moderately Republican. Approximately equal proportions were in the three middle categories, totaling together just over half the electorate. Thus the balance-of-issues measure tilted slightly in the Republican direction, but was much more evenly balanced than the more heavily pro-Republican tilt in 2012.

The balance-of-issues measure was quite strongly related to the vote, as the findings for the individual issues would suggest (see Table 6-7B). Clinton won the vast majority of the votes from those in the strongly, moderately, and even the slightly Democratic categories. She won a bit more than six in ten votes from those in the neutral category and almost held her own in the slightly Republican category. Her support dropped off dramatically from that point. Indeed this relationship between the net balance-of-issues measure and the vote is stronger in 2016 than we have ever found before.

The Abortion Issue

Clearly abortion was not the major issue in the 2016 election that it has been in some earlier ones. Even so it has been in most elections; it did play a significant, even if smaller, role in 2012; and it is likely to remain consequential in future elections. One special role that it played in 2016 was based on the belief that which party would get to fill the open seat on the Supreme Court would have a major role in the position the Court would likely take on this issue in the future. And, of course, policy about abortions plays a large role in partisan polarization. The Republican national platform has taken a strong pro-life stand since 1980, whereas the Democratic Party became increasingly strongly pro-choice. In addition it is one of a complex set of issues that define much of the social issues dimension, one of two major dimensions of domestic policy (economics being the second) into which most domestic policies—and most controversial issues—fall. Abortion has been central to the rise of social conservatism in America, virtually back to its modern emergence in the wake of the Supreme Court decision, *Roe v. Wade* (1973), which made abortion legal throughout the United States.

The second reason for examining this issue is that it is another policy question about which respondents were asked their own views as well as what they thought Trump's and Clinton's positions were—a battery that has been asked for the last several elections.[31] It differs from (and is therefore hard to compare directly with) the seven-point issue scales, however, because respondents were given only four alternatives, but each was a specified policy option:

1. By law, abortion should never be permitted.

2. The law should permit abortion only in case of rape, incest, or when the woman's life is in danger.

Table 6-7 Distribution of Electorate on Net Balance-of-Issues Measure and Major-Party Vote, 2016 (Percent)

| | Net Balance of Issues | | | | | | | | |
	Strongly Democratic	Moderately Democratic	Slightly Democratic	Neutral	Slightly Republican	Moderately Republican	Strongly Republican	Total	(N)
A. Distribution of responses									
	9	10	16	16	19	17	13	100	(4267)
B. Major-party voters who voted for Clinton									
Percent	97	91	82	62	47	21	3	53	(2379)
(N)	(267)	(251)	(348)	(297)	(423)	(411)	(381)		

Source: Authors' analysis of the 2016 ANES.

Note: Numbers are weighted. The numbers in parentheses in Part B of the table are the totals on which the percentages are based.

Table 6-8 Percentage of Major-Party Voters Who Voted for Clinton, by Opinion about Abortion and What They Believe Trump's and Clinton's Positions Are, 2016

| | Respondent's Position on Abortion | | | | | | | |
| | Abortion should never be permitted | | Abortion should be permitted only in the case of rape, incest, or danger to health of the woman | | Abortion should be permitted for other reasons, but only if a need is established | | Abortion should be a matter of personal choice | |
	%	(N)	%	(N)	%	(N)	%	(N)
All major-party voters	23	(324)	29	(583)	52	(324)	73	(1123)
Major-party voters who placed both candidates, who saw a difference between them, and who saw Clinton as more pro-choice than Trump	14	(237)	26	(458)	50	(246)	78	(884)
Major-party voters who did not meet all three of these conditions	48	(87)	41	(125)	59	(78)	57	(239)

Source: Authors' analysis of the 2016 ANES.

Note: Numbers in parentheses are the totals on which the percentages are based. Numbers are weighted.

3. The law should permit abortion for reasons *other than* rape, incest, or danger to the woman's life but only after the need for the abortion has been clearly established.

4. By law, a woman should always be able to obtain an abortion as a matter of personal choice.

Table 6-8 reports percentages voting for Clinton for various groups of respondents. For example, about three in four voters who believe that abortion should be a matter of personal choice voted for her, whereas about one in four who thought it should never be permitted did so. Substantial numbers of voters met all four conditions on this issue and, for them, their position was even more strongly related to the vote, as almost seven in eight who thought abortion should be a matter of personal choice voted for Obama, but only one in seven who thought it should not be permitted did so. For those who did not meet all conditions for casting an issue-based vote, their voting was essentially the random coin flip one would expect. Thus the abortion issue adds to our previous findings.

CONCLUSION

Our findings suggest that for major-party voters, prospective issues were important in the 2016 election. In fact 2016 stands out as one in which prospective issues played about as strong a role in shaping their vote as any other. Prospective issues are particularly important for understanding how citizens voted. They cannot alone account for Clinton's victory in the popular vote nor Trump's in the electoral vote. Those for whom prospective issues gave a clear choice, however, voted consistently with those issues. But most people were located between the candidates as the electorate saw them. Indeed on most issues the majority of people were relatively moderate, and the candidates were perceived as more conservative and more liberal, respectively. Moreover, when the conditions for issue voting are present, there can be a strong relationship between the position voters hold and their choice between the major-party candidates. And, it appears, that perhaps due to the lengthening period for which the two parties have polarized on most important policies facing the electorate, a remarkably high proportion of the electorate met the conditions for casting an issue-based vote on many of the issues considered here. For these reasons we conclude that voters took prospective issues into account in 2016, but it is also our conclusion that they also considered other factors. In the next chapter we will see that the second form of policy voting, that based on retrospective evaluations, was among those other factors, as it has been in previous presidential elections.

CHAPTER SEVEN

PRESIDENTIAL PERFORMANCE AND CANDIDATE CHOICE

Just as in most elections, the presidential candidates focused more on the economy than any other issue in 2016. Clinton robustly defended the record of the Obama administration on the economy, pointing to such evidence as eight years of growth from the very low point the American economy had hit in 2008. Trump, in contrast, did not argue that those facts were incorrect (although there was not 100 percent agreement on what the facts were); he argued in part for a different interpretation of the same facts (growth was too slow) and in part for a completely different part of the record (e.g., job losses to other nations), possible because the economy is so complex and multifaceted.[1] Compared to Romney in 2012, he was not free to argue as strongly against the Obama record because it had an eight-year run of steady, if unspectacular, growth, instead of only four. But he was in a far stronger position than McCain in 2008, having to defend the Bush administration during the campaign while the economy imploded.

But this was also hardly the first election in which candidates thought carefully about how they would present themselves with respect to the successes or failures of the incumbent president and his party. To the extent that voters were considering the successes and failures of the incumbent president and his party in these cases, perhaps in comparison to what they thought his opponent and the opponent's party would have done had they been in office, voters were casting a retrospective vote. And certainly the eight-year record of the Democratic administration and the memory of the collapse of the economy in September 2008, which occurred under then president George W. Bush's term, provided the raw materials for a strong retrospective evaluation set of claims by candidates, ones that well might have been absorbed by the public.

Retrospective evaluations are concerns about policy, but they differ significantly from the prospective evaluations considered in the last chapter.[2] Retrospective evaluations are, as the name suggests, concerns about the past. These evaluations focus on outcomes, with what actually happened, rather than on the policy means for achieving those outcomes, which are at the heart of prospective evaluations. For example, after his reelection in 2004, George W. Bush argued that there was a looming problem in

Social Security and proposed private accounts as a solution. Even though other events soon intervened to draw attention away from this policy, some Democrats argued against the president on the grounds that creating private accounts would actually make the problem worse. These Democrats agreed with Bush that there was a problem, but they were focusing on concerns they had about the policy means that Bush proposed to solve that problem, a classic response in terms of prospective evaluations. Other Democrats argued that there really was no serious problem with Social Security in the first place. Such arguments focused on policy outcomes, which are the basis of retrospective judgments. This scenario illustrates the difference between prospective and retrospective judgments but also suggests that the two are often different sides of the same policy coin, which is indeed the basic point of the Downs-Fiorina perspective.

WHAT IS RETROSPECTIVE VOTING?

A voter who casts a ballot for the incumbent party's candidate because the incumbent was, in the voter's opinion, a successful president or votes for the opposition because, in the voter's opinion, the incumbent was unsuccessful is said to have cast a retrospective vote. In other words retrospective voting decisions are based on evaluations of the course of politics over the last term in office and on evaluations of how much the incumbent should be held responsible for what good or bad outcomes occurred. V. O. Key, Jr., popularized this argument by suggesting that the voter might be "a rational god of vengeance and of reward."[3]

The more closely a candidate can be tied to the actions of the incumbent, the more likely it is that voters will decide retrospectively. The incumbent president cannot escape such evaluations, and the incumbent vice president is usually identified with (and often chooses to identify him- or herself with) the administration's performance. The electorate has frequently played the role of Key's "rational god" because an incumbent president or vice president has stood for election in twenty-five of the thirty-one presidential elections since 1900 (all but 1908, 1920, 1928, 1952, 2008, and 2016). In 2016 Clinton was an only slightly less central part of at least the first term of the Obama administration than Vice President Biden. More importantly she proudly tied herself to the Obama administration throughout her campaign.

Key's thesis has three aspects. First, retrospective voters are oriented toward outcomes rather than the policy means to achieve them. Second, these voters evaluate the performance of the incumbent only, all but ignoring the opposition. Finally they evaluate what has been done, paying little attention to what the candidates promise to do in the future. Does this kind of voting make sense? Some suggest an alternative, as we discuss next, but note that if everyone did, in fact, vote against an incumbent whose performance they thought insufficient, then incumbents would have very strong incentives to provide such sufficiently high levels of performance to avoid the wrath of the electorate.

Anthony Downs was the first to develop in some detail an alternative version of retrospective voting.[4] His account is one about information and its credibility to the voter. He argues that voters look to the past to understand what the incumbent party's candidate will do in the future. According to Downs parties are basically consistent in their goals, methods, and ideologies over time. Therefore, the past performances of both parties and perhaps their nominees may prove relevant for making predictions about their future conduct. Because it takes time and effort to evaluate campaign promises and because promises are just words, voters find it faster, easier, and safer to use past performance to project the administration's actions for the next four years. Downs also emphasizes that retrospective evaluations are used in making comparisons among the alternatives presented to the voter. Key sees a retrospective referendum on the incumbent's party alone. Downs believes that retrospective evaluations are used to compare the candidates as well as to provide a guide to the future. Even incumbents may use such Downsian retrospective claims. In 1996, for example, Clinton attempted to tie his opponent, Senator Bob Dole, to the performance of congressional Republicans because they had assumed the majority in the 1994 election. Clinton pointedly referred to the 104th Congress as the "Dole-Gingrich" Congress. Twenty years later a different Clinton was trying to tie evaluations of her expected performance to those of the Obama administration in which she had served.

Morris P. Fiorina elaborates on and extends Downs's thesis.[5] Here we focus especially on Fiorina's understanding of party identification, which was a completely new addition to the Downsian perspective. Fiorina claimed that party identification plays a central role in this perspective on retrospective voting. It differs from that of Campbell et al., however.[6] He argued that "citizens monitor party promises and performances over time, encapsulate their observations in a summary judgment termed 'party identification,' and rely on this core of previous experience when they assign responsibility for current societal conditions and evaluate ambiguous platforms designed to deal with uncertain futures."[7] We return to Fiorina's views on partisanship in Chapter 8.[8]

Retrospective voting and voting according to issue positions, as analyzed in Chapter 6, differ significantly. The difference lies in how concerned people are with societal outcomes and how concerned they are with the policy means to achieve desired outcomes. For example, everyone prefers economic prosperity. The disagreement among political decision makers lies in how best to achieve it. At the voters' level, however, the central question is whether people care only about achieving prosperity or whether they care about, or even are able to judge, how to achieve this desired goal. Perhaps they looked at high inflation and interest rates in 1980 and said, "We tried Carter's approach, and it failed. Let's try something else—anything else." They may have noted the long run of relative economic prosperity from 1983 to 1988 and said, "Whatever Reagan did, it worked. Let's keep it going by putting his vice president in office." In 1996 they may have agreed with Clinton that he had presided over a successful economy, and so they decided to remain with the incumbent. In 2016 just how these concerns would play was uncertain. Would the public judge the economy as improving sufficiently, or was its improvement too little, too late?

Economic policy, along with foreign and defense policies, are especially likely to be discussed in these terms because they share several characteristics. First, the outcomes are clear, and most voters can judge whether they approve of the results. Inflation and unemployment are high or low; the economy is growing, or it is not. The country is at war or at peace; the world is stable or unstable.[9] Second, there is often near consensus on the desired outcomes; no one disagrees with peace or prosperity, with world stability, or with low unemployment. Third, the means to achieving these ends are often very complex, and information is hard to understand; experts as well as candidates and parties disagree over the specific ways to achieve the desired ends. How should the economy be improved, and how could terrorism possibly be contained or democracy established in a foreign land?

As issues, therefore, peace and prosperity differ sharply from policy areas such as abortion, in which there is vigorous disagreement over ends among experts, leaders, and the public. On still other issues, people value both ends *and* means. The classic cases often revolve around the question of whether it is appropriate for government to take action in a particular area at all. Ronald Reagan was fond of saying, "Government isn't the solution to our problems; government *is* the problem." For example, should the government provide national health insurance? After decades of trying, the Democrats, under the Obama administration, had finally succeeded in passing the Affordable Care Act (ACA), a program labeled "Obamacare" by the Republicans. Republicans continued to try to roll back the law or keep it from being implemented. Few disagree with the end of better health care, but they disagree over the appropriate means to achieve it. The choice of means touches on some of the basic philosophical and ideological differences that have divided Republicans and Democrats for decades.[10] For example, in the 1984 presidential campaign, Walter Mondale agreed with Reagan that the country was in a period of economic prosperity and that prosperity was a good thing, but he also argued that Reagan's policies were unfair to the disadvantaged. In the 1992 campaign, Bill Clinton and Ross Perot claimed that Reagan's and George H. W. Bush's policies, by creating such large deficits, were creating the conditions for future woes. Clearly, then, disagreement was not over the ends but over the means and the consequences that would follow from using different means to achieve them.

Two basic conditions must be met before retrospective evaluations can affect voting choices. First, individuals must connect their concerns with the incumbent and the actions the president and his or her party took in office. This condition would not be present if, for example, a voter blamed earlier administrations with sowing the seeds that become the "Great Recession," blamed an ineffective Congress or Wall Street, or even believed that the problems were beyond anyone's control. Second, individuals, in the Downs-Fiorina view, must compare their evaluations of the incumbent's past performance with what they believe the nominee of the opposition party would do. For example, even if they thought Obama's performance on the economy was weak, voters might have compared that performance with programs supported by Trump in 2016 and concluded that his efforts would not result in any better outcome and might even make things worse.

In this second condition a certain asymmetry exists, one that benefits the incumbent. Even if the incumbent's performance has been weak in a certain area, the challenger still has to convince voters that he or she could do better. It is more difficult, however, for a challenger to convince voters who think the incumbent's performance has been strong that he or she, the challenger, would be even stronger. This asymmetry advantaged Republican candidates in the 1980s but worked to Bob Dole's disadvantage in 1996 and to Bush's in 2000 and his putative successor in 2008. Would this asymmetry apply to 2016? Or perhaps would both sides have the more difficult problem of convincing the electorate they could handle important problems when current performance was judged as neither especially strong nor especially weak?

We examine next some illustrative retrospective evaluations and study their impact on voter choice. In Chapter 6 we looked at issue scales designed to measure the public's evaluations of candidates' promises. For the incumbent party the public can evaluate not only its promises but also its actions. We compare promises with performance in this chapter, but one must remember that the distinctions are not as sharp in practice as they are in principle.[11] The Downs-Fiorina view is that past actions and projections about the future are necessarily intertwined.

EVALUATIONS OF GOVERNMENT PERFORMANCE ON IMPORTANT PROBLEMS

"Do you feel things in this country are generally going in the right direction, or do you feel things have pretty seriously gotten off on the wrong track?"[12] This question is designed to measure retrospective judgments, and the responses are presented in Table 7-1A. In the appendix to this book, we report responses to the question the ANES had asked in prior surveys, comparing the respondents' evaluations of

Table 7-1 Evaluation of Government Performance and Major-Party Vote, 2012 and 2016 (Percent)		
Evaluation	2012	2016
A. Evaluation of government performance during the last four years		
Right track	33	25
Wrong track	67	75
Total	100	100
(N)	(1958)	(4239)
B. Percentage of major-party vote for incumbent's party nominee		
Right track	94	94
(N)	(430)	(663)
Wrong track	30	36
(N)	(804)	(1700)

Source: Authors' analysis of the 2012 and 2016 ANES surveys.

Note: The numbers in parentheses are the totals on which the percentages are based. Numbers are weighted.

government performance on the problem that each respondent identified as the single most important one facing the country.[13] The most striking finding in Table 7-1A is that in 2016, as in 2012, just one in four thought the country was on the right track. These questions are asked by many polling agencies to gauge the feelings of the public, and Real Clear Politics (https://www.realclearpolitics.com/) reports an averaging across these many polling outfits. Using their aggregated data[14] we find that overall, the public has viewed things as being on the wrong track since June 2009, and the election period in 2016 was roughly typical of the perceptions of the country since then.[15]

If the voter is a rational god of vengeance and reward, we can expect to find a strong relationship between the evaluation of government performance and the vote. Such is indeed the case (see Table 7-1B). Nine in ten who thought the country was on the right track voted for Clinton. Only a few more than one in three who thought the country was on the wrong track voted for her.

According to Downs and Fiorina, it is important for voters not only to evaluate how things have been going but also to assess how that evaluation compares with the alternative. In most recent elections, including 2016, respondents have been asked which party would do a better job of solving the problem they named as the most important. Table 7-2 shows the responses to these questions. These questions are clearly oriented toward the future, but they may call for judgments about past performance, consistent with the Downs-Fiorina view. Respondents were not asked to evaluate policy alternatives, and thus responses were most likely based on a retrospective comparison of how the incumbent party handled things with a prediction about how the opposition would fare. We therefore consider these questions to be a measure of comparative retrospective evaluations.

Table 7-2A shows that the public had different views about which party was better at handling their important concerns. In particular there is pretty close to an even three-way split among those thinking that one party or the other was better or that there was no difference between the two parties in this regard. To be sure, there were fewer who said the Democrats were better, but the five-point difference between the two parties is slighter than usual. This is not much different from some earlier elections, including major Republican defeats (such as in 1996), solid victories (such as in 1988), and even landslide victories (such as in 1972). In 2008, by contrast, very few selected the "neither party" option and only one in four selected the Republican Party as better. Thus the Democratic Party held a huge advantage on this measure, one of the rare instances in which a clear majority thought one party would be better. But by 2012 the Democrats had lost their advantage, even though the Republicans had not really gathered a major advantage either. This set of responses persisted into 2016.

Table 7-2B reveals that the relationship between the party seen as better on the most important political problem and the vote is very strong. Clinton won nearly all the votes from those who thought the Democrats would be better. Trump was able to hold nearly all of those who thought the Republican Party better able to handle the most important problem. The candidates essentially split the "no difference" category evenly.

The data presented in Tables 7-1 and 7-2 have an important limitation. The first question, analyzed in Table 7-1, refers to an impression of how the country is going and not the incumbent president nor even the government. The question examined in Table 7-2 refers to which political party would handle the most important problem

Table 7-2 Evaluation of Party Seen as Better on Most Important Political Problem and Major-Party Vote, 2012 and 2016 (Percent)

Better party	2012	2016
A. Distribution of responses on party seen as better on most important political problem		
Republican	31	35
No difference	31	35
Democratic	38	30
Total	100	100
(*N*)	(1884)	(3578)
B. Major-party voters who voted Democratic for president		
Republican	7	6
(*N*)	(436)	(923)
No difference	56	64
(*N*)	(405)	(933)
Democratic	98	99
(*N*)	(429)	(792)

Source: Authors' analysis of the 2012 and 2016 ANES surveys.

Note: The numbers in parentheses are the totals on which the percentages are based. Numbers are weighted. Question wording: "Which political party do you think would be the most likely to get the government to do a better job in dealing with this problem?"

better and does not directly refer to the incumbent—and we believe it is the assessment of the incumbent that relates most directly to voters' evaluations of the candidates for president. Thus we will look more closely at the incumbent and at people's comparisons of his and the opposition's performance where the data are available to permit such comparisons.

ECONOMIC EVALUATIONS AND THE VOTE FOR THE INCUMBENT

More than any other, economic issues have been highlighted as suitable retrospective issues. The impact of economic conditions on congressional and presidential elections has been studied extensively.[16] Popular evaluations of presidential effectiveness, John E. Mueller has pointed out, are strongly influenced by the economy.[17] A major reason for Jimmy Carter's defeat in 1980 was the perception that economic performance had been weak during his administration. Reagan's rhetorical question in the 1980 debate with Carter, "Are you better off than you were four years ago?" indicates that politicians realize the power such arguments have over the electorate. Reagan owed his sweeping reelection victory in 1984 largely to the perception that economic performance by the end of his first term had become, after a deep recession in the middle, much stronger.

If people are concerned about economic outcomes, they might start by looking for an answer to the sort of question Reagan asked. Table 7-3A presents ANES respondents' perceptions of whether they were financially better off than one year earlier, including the 2000–2016 election surveys (the appendix reports these back to 1972).[18] The economy grew steadily and strongly over the Clinton administration. Thus, by 2000 about a third felt better off, whereas far fewer felt worse off in 2000 than in any of the seven preceding elections (see appendix Table A7-3). More than half responded in 2000 that they were about the same as a year ago. In 2004 more than two in five reported feeling better off, the most popular response. The year 2008, however, was a different story, because half the respondents said they were worse off, with only a third saying they were better off and very few feeling their finances were the same. Simply 2008 was a terrible year for the economy, and everyone knew it (even though not everyone suffered). The situation in 2012 presented little to help or harm either side. A few more thought they were better off than worse off, but each view was held by close to two in five. Only one in four in claimed his or her situation was the same as in 2008. The continued slow but steady improvement over eight years, for 2016, as compared with only four for 2012, suggests that the Obama administration should have been somewhat more favorably reviewed by the public in 2016 compared to 2012, which appears to be true, at least in terms of the decline of "worse off" responses. In some ways 2016 was like 2000. Clinton, like Obama, had inherited a troubled economy from a Republican president, and as they left office they could point to more or less eight years of consistent growth. To be sure, the bad economy Clinton inherited was far better than that received by Obama, but the gains under Clinton were more spectacular than Obama's too. Still, the electorate overall felt they had had broadly similar results: around three in ten being better off, with fewer being a bit worse off, but about half said they were about the same.

In Table 7-3B we see how the responses to this question are related to the two-party presidential vote. In 2008 that relationship was not particularly strong. McCain was able to win just over half the votes of those who felt better off, just as he did among those relatively few who felt neither better nor worse off. Obama won support from a clear majority of that half of the electorate who felt worse off, winning more than three in five of their votes. But in 2012 that relationship strengthened. That is, the extent that the family's financial situation shaped the vote was as strong as the Reagan and senior Bush reelection contests, and the Clinton reelection campaign was not far behind. For 2016 the results are even stronger, and almost exactly the same as the landslide reelection of Reagan in 1984. It is quite obvious that personal economic situations are rarely as strongly related to the vote as in 2016 but, more importantly,

Table 7-3   The Public's Assessment of Their Personal Financial Situation and Major-Party Vote, 2000–2016

Response	"Would you say that you (and your family) are better off or worse off financially than you were a year ago?"				
	2000[a]	2004	2008	2012	2016
A. Distribution of responses					
Better now	33	43	32	41	28
Same	53	25	18	24	47
Worse now	14	32	50	36	25
Total	100	100	100	101	100
(N)	(907)	(1,203)	(2,307)	(1,800)	(4.256)
B. Major-party voters who voted for the incumbent party nominee for president					
Better now	56	65	53	65	73
(N)	(164)	(354)	(491)	(456)	(681)
Same	51	50	52	49	50
(N)	(291)	(207)	(280)	(274)	(1132)
Worse now	45	28	38	31	33
(N)	(56)	(219)	(778)	(414)	(560)

Source: Authors' analysis of ANES surveys.

Note: The numbers in parentheses are the totals on which the percentages are based. Numbers are weighted.

[a]This question was asked of a randomly selected half-sample in 1972.

sufficiently well-distributed such that even strong relationships to the vote advantage one candidate over the other sufficiently to play a major role in the outcome. In most cases the middle category bulges with lots of people and thus neither helps nor hurts a party or president greatly.

People, that is, may "vote their pocketbooks," but they are at least as likely to vote retrospectively based on their judgments of how the economy as a whole has been faring across the country (see Table 7-4A).[19] And personal and national economic experiences can be quite different. In 1980, for example, about 40 percent of respondents thought their own financial situation was worse than the year before, but responses to the 1980 ANES survey revealed that twice as many (83 percent) thought the national economy was worse off than the year before (see Table A7-4 in the appendix). In 1992 the public gave the nation's economy a far more negative assessment than they gave their own financial situations. That was not the case in 1996 and 2000, when respondents gave broadly similar assessments of their personal fortunes and those of the nation. But then in 2004 the public had much more negative views of the economy as a whole, although (naturally) the public saw the economy in 2008 in the most negative terms ever observed in these surveys. Fully nine in ten respondents believed that the economy was worse off. That changed substantially again in 2012. Here the views leaned slightly negatively, but it was not too far from an even three-way split among better, same, and worse, with better trailing worse by only seven points. In 2016 responses were quite similar to those in 2012, albeit slightly more positive, as the "worse" category was five points lower and the "stayed same" category in the middle, five points larger.

In Table 7-4B, we show the relationship between responses to these items and the major-party vote for president. The relationship between these measures and the vote is always strong. Moreover, a comparison of Table 7-3B and Table 7-4B reveals that in general, the vote is more closely associated with perceptions of the nation's economy than it is with perceptions of one's personal economic well-being. In 2012 the relationship was as strong as any we have been able to assess, with 2016 only slightly less strongly so. The difference in votes cast in 2012 for Obama between the "better" and the "worse" categories was fully sixty percentage points, with the "same" category essentially splitting their votes evenly. This wide difference declined modestly, but remained greater than forty points, in 2016. Thus both personal and national economic circumstances mattered a great deal in the two most recent elections.

To this point we have looked at personal and national economic conditions and the role of the government in shaping them. We have not yet looked at the extent to which such evaluations are attributed to the incumbent. In Table 7-5A, we report responses to the question of whether people approved of the incumbent's handling of the economy from the elections of 2000 through 2016 (and the same data are reported for elections between 1980 and 1996 in the appendix, Table A7-5). Although a majority approved of Reagan's handling of the economy in both 1984 and 1988, fewer than one in five held positive views of the economic performance of the Carter administration. In 1992 evaluations of George H. W. Bush were also perceived very negatively. In 1996 evaluations of Clinton's handling of the economy were stronger than those of incumbents in the previous surveys. By 2000 evaluations of Clinton's handling of the economy were even stronger, with three of every four respondents approving. Evaluations of George W. Bush's handling of the economy in 2004 were more negative than positive, although not nearly as negative of those of Jimmy Carter or of his father. By 2008 evaluations of Bush's handling of the economy were very negative. But in 2012 evaluations of Obama's handling of the economy were quite like those of Bush in 2004. In 2016 evaluations were positive and very similar to those of the Reagan administration in 1988.

The bottom-line question is whether these views are related to voter choice. According to the data in Table 7-5B, the answer is yes. Those who held positive views

Table 7-4 The Public's View of the State of the National Economy and Major-Party Vote, 2000–2016

Response	"Would you say that over the past year the nation's economy has gotten . . .?"				
	2000[a]	2004	2008	2012	2016
A. Distribution of responses					
Better	39	24	2	28	28
Stayed same	44	31	7	36	42
Worse	17	45	90	35	30
Total	100	100	99	99	100
(N)	(1,787)	(1,196)	(2,313)	(1,806)	(4,261)
B. Major-party voters who voted for the incumbent party nominee for president					
Better	69	87	69	86	88
(N)	(408)	(211)	(34)	(339)	(724)
Stayed same	45	88	57	48	50
(N)	(487)	(243)	(109)	(425)	(992)
Worse	31	20	44	16	18
(N)	(154)	(319)	(1,425)	(382)	(658)

Source: Authors' analysis of ANES surveys.

Note: The numbers in parentheses are the totals on which percentages are based. Numbers are weighted.

[a]We combine the results using standard and experimental prompts that contained different word orderings in 2000, 2004, and 2008.

of the incumbent's performance on the economy were very likely to vote for that party's candidate, whereas those who did not were just as likely to vote against him or her. Nearly nine in ten of those holding a positive view of Obama's handling of the economy voted for Clinton; only about one in ten who disapproved of his handling of the economy supported her. This relationship is once again as strong as we have yet observed. The economy was a vitally important factor in the 2012 and 2016 elections as all three retrospective evaluations of the economy are clearly and strongly related to the vote.

Table 7-5   Evaluations of the Incumbent's Handling of the Economy and Major-Party Vote, 2000–2016

Response	Approval of incumbent's handling of the economy				
	2000	2004	2008	2012	2016
A. Distribution of responses					
Positive view	77	41	18	42	53
Negative view	23	59	82	58	47
Total	100	100	100	100	100
(*N*)	(1,686)	(1,173)	(2,227)	(1,698)	(4,221)
B. Major-party voters who voted for the incumbent party nominee					
Positive view	67	91	89	92	89
(*N*)	(768)	(341)	(313)	(476)	(1,253)
Negative view	11	17	33	13	11
(*N*)	(233)	(431)	(1,200)	(618)	(1,109)

Source: Authors' analysis of ANES surveys.

Note: Numbers are weighted.

FOREIGN POLICY EVALUATIONS AND THE VOTE FOR THE INCUMBENT

Foreign and economic policies are, as we noted earlier, commonly evaluated by means of retrospective assessments. These policies share the characteristics of consensual goals (peace and prosperity, respectively, plus security in both cases), complex technology, and difficulty in ascertaining relationships between means and ends. Foreign policy differs from economic policy in one practical way, however. As we noted in the last chapter, economic problems are invariably a major concern, but foreign affairs are salient only sporadically. Indeed foreign affairs are of sufficiently sporadic concern that most surveys, including the ANES, only occasionally have many measures to judge their role in elections. Moreover, what part of our foreign policy is under scrutiny changes from election to election, especially when there are wars that are at the center of choice.

In 2016, therefore, we report on a more general evaluation, similar to that of approval of economic performance. In particular, in Table 7-6A are responses to the question of whether the respondent approves or not of Obama's handling of foreign

Evaluation	
A. "Do you approve or disapprove of the way the president is handling foreign relations?"	
Approve	50
Disapprove	50
Total	100
(*N*)	(4203)
B. Percentage of major-party vote for incumbent's party nominee	
Approve	89
(*N*)	(1173)
Disapprove	16
(*N*)	(1187)

Source: Authors' analysis of the 2016 ANES survey.

Note: The numbers in parentheses in Part B are the totals on which the percentages are based. The numbers in Parts A and B are weighted.

relations. This leaves great latitude in aggregating responses over what might well be very different parts of the world in the voters' minds.

The responses to this question are an exact tie. Half the public approved, half did not, and this made a considerable difference to voters. Consider Table 7-6B. Overall, nine in ten approvers voted for Obama's party successor, whereas only one in six of those who disapproved voted for her.

The key points in all of these data seem to be the following. First, as we saw in Chapter 6, foreign policy was just not seen as especially important in the public. This tempered all of the findings and made 2016 quite different from, say, 2004, when foreign policy and evaluations of the wars were near the top of nearly everyone's list of political concerns. Second, retrospective evaluations of all sorts are often strongly related to the vote, and this was especially so in 2016, when the vote differential was at an all-time high on many measures, including especially those that are often more weakly related to the vote (such as "pocketbook" voting).

EVALUATIONS OF THE INCUMBENT

Fiorina distinguishes between "simple" and "mediated" retrospective evaluations.[20] By simple, Fiorina means evaluations of the direct effects of social outcomes on the person, such as one's financial status, or direct perceptions of the nation's economic well-being. Mediated retrospective evaluations are evaluations seen through or mediated by the perceptions of political actors and institutions. Approval of Obama's handling of the economy and the assessment of which party would better handle the most important problem are examples.

As we have seen, the more politically mediated the question, the more closely the responses align with voting behavior.[21] Perhaps the ultimate in mediated evaluations is the presidential approval question: "Do you approve or disapprove of the way [the incumbent] is handling his job as president?" From a retrospective voting standpoint, this evaluation is a summary of all aspects of the incumbent's service in office. Table 7-7 reports the distribution of overall evaluations and their relationship to major-party voting in the last five elections.[22]

Table A7-6 reveals that incumbents Richard Nixon (1972), Gerald Ford (1976), Ronald Reagan (1984), and Bill Clinton (1996) enjoyed widespread approval, whereas only two respondents in five approved of Jimmy Carter's and of George H. W. Bush's

Table 7-7 President's Handling of the Job and Major-Party Vote, 2000–2016

Response	"Do you approve or disapprove of the way [the incumbent] is handling his job as president?"				
	2000	2004	2008	2012	2016
A. Distribution of responses					
Approve	67	51	27	50	53
Disapprove	33	49	73	50	47
Total	100	100	100	100	100
(*N*)	(1,742)	(1,182)	(2,245)	(1,704)	(4,226)
B. Major-party voters who voted for the incumbent party's nominee					
Approve	74	91	88	92	91
(*N*)	(662)	(408)	(441)	(537)	(1,263)
Disapprove	13	6	26	6	8
(*N*)	(366)	(372)	(1,075)	(568)	(1,102)

Source: Authors' analysis of ANES surveys.

Note: The numbers in parentheses in Part B are the totals on which percentages are based. Numbers are weighted.

handling of the job in 1980 and 1992, respectively. This situation presented Carter and the senior Bush with a problem. Conversely, highly approved incumbents, such as Reagan in 1984 and Clinton in 1996—and their vice presidents as beneficiaries in 1988 and 2000, respectively—had a major advantage. Clinton dramatically reversed any negative perceptions held of his incumbency in 1994 so that by 1996 he received the highest level of approval in the fall of an election year since Nixon's landslide reelection in 1972. Between 1996 and 2000 Clinton suffered through several scandals, one of which culminated in his impeachment in 1998. Such events might be expected to lead to substantial declines in his approval ratings, but instead his ratings remained high—higher even than Reagan's at the end of his presidency. The evaluations in 2004 present a more varied picture. For the first time in nine elections, the proportions approving and disapproving of George W. Bush were almost exactly the same. In view of what we have seen so far, it should come as no surprise that evaluations of Bush turned dramatically by 2008 so that he was by far the least approved incumbent during this period, with nearly three in four respondents disapproving of his handling of the office. Obama's approval ratings in 2012 were, again, much like Bush's in 2004, here coming out exactly evenly divided between approval and disapproval.[23] By 2016 his approval increased so that it was positive, six points higher than his disapproval rating. Thus, although there was nearly an even-up balance for Clinton to work with in 2016, it was slightly more positive than the victorious Bush in 2004.

If it is true that the more mediated the evaluation, the more closely it seems to align with behavior, and if presidential approval is the most mediated evaluation of all, then we would expect a powerful relationship with the vote. As Table 7-7B (and Table A7-6 in the appendix) illustrates, that is true over the full set of elections for which we have the relevant data. As we have seen before, the approval ratings in 2004, 2012, and 2016 are about as strongly related to the vote as is possible. More than nine in ten who approved of Obama's performance voted for Clinton; only 8 percent who disapproved voted for her.

THE IMPACT OF RETROSPECTIVE EVALUATIONS

Our evidence strongly suggests that retrospective voting has been widespread in all recent elections. Moreover, as far as data permit us to judge, the evidence is clearly on the side of the Downs-Fiorina view. Retrospective evaluations appear to be used to make comparative judgments. Presumably, voters find it easier, less time-consuming, and less risky to evaluate the incumbent party based on what its president did in the most recent term or terms in office than on the nominees' promises for the future. But few people base their votes on judgments of past performance alone. Most use past judgments as a starting point for comparing the major contenders with respect to their likely future performances.

In analyzing previous elections, we constructed an overall assessment of retrospective voting and compared that overall assessment across elections. We then compared that net retrospective assessment with our balance-of-issues measure. Our measure is constructed by combining the question asking whether the United States is on the right or on the wrong track, the presidential approval measure, and the assessment of which party would better handle the problem the respondent thinks is the single most important.[24] The combination of responses to these three questions creates a seven-point scale ranging from strongly negative evaluations of recent and current conditions to strongly positive evaluations of performance in these various areas. For example, those who thought the nation was on the right track, approved of Obama's job performance, and thought the Democratic Party would better handle the most important problem are scored as strongly supportive of Obama in their retrospective evaluations in 2016.

In Table 7-8, we present the results of this measure.[25] The data in Table 7-8A indicate that there was a substantial diversity of responses but that the measure was skewed modestly against the incumbent. By this measure more than one in four were strongly opposed to the performance of the Obama administration, with another fifth moderately or slightly opposed. One in nine was neutral, while a bit over one in five were slightly or moderately supportive, and one in seven was strongly supportive of the Obama administration.

Table 7-8B presents a remarkably clear example of a very strong relationship between responses and votes, with greater than 90 percent of those in any of the three supportive categories voting for Clinton and very few of those moderately or strongly opposed voting for her. The slightly opposed split their votes about evenly, whereas Clinton held the votes of eight in ten of those scored neutral on this measure. Thus for five of the seven categories, the valence of evaluations alone tells you everything you need to know about their voting choices. Perhaps because there appears to be some belief that even though the country may not be on the right track and even though the economy (the most common choice of most important problem) is not as strong as many would like, many voters appear to hold Obama less responsible for the problems and more generous in their evaluations of his performance in terms of the responses to these concerns due, perhaps, to remembrances of Bush's highly negatively evaluated handling of the economy in 2008 and attribution of the problems to Bush or even those outside the government.

We cannot really compare 2016 with any other election on this measure, but we can at least make broad generalizations.[26] In earlier years it was reasonable to conclude that the 1980 election was a clear and strong rejection of Carter's incumbency. In 1984 Reagan won in large part because voters perceived that he had performed well and because Mondale was unable to convince the public that he would do better. In 1988 George H. W. Bush won in large part because Reagan appeared to have performed well—and people thought Bush would stay the course. In 1992 Bush lost because of the far more negative evaluations of his administration and of his party than had been recorded in any election since 1980. In 1996 Clinton won reelection in large part for the same reasons that Reagan won in 1984: He was viewed as having performed well on the job, and he was able to convince the public that his opponent would not do any better. In 2000 Gore essentially tied George W. Bush because the slightly pro-incumbent set of evaluations combined with a very slight asymmetry against the incumbent in translating those evaluations into voting choices. In 2004 there was a slight victory for the incumbent because more thought he had performed well than poorly. And 2008 was most like 1980, with a highly skewed distribution

Table 7-8 Summary Measure of Retrospective Evaluations of the Obama Administration and Major-Party Vote, 2016

	Strongly Opposed	Moderately Opposed	Slightly Opposed	Neutral	Slightly Supportive	Moderately Supportive	Strongly Supportive	Total (*N*)
A. Distribution of responses								
Percent	29	14	7	13	14	8	15	100 (3,578)
B. Major-party voters who voted for Clinton								
Percent	1	22	50	79	97	93	99	53
(*N*)	(817)	(225)	(116)	(221)	(352)	(190)	(430)	(2351)

Source: Authors' analysis of the 2016 ANES survey.

Note: Numbers are weighted. The numbers in Part B are the totals on which the percentages are based.

working against the Republicans (likely the most skewed measure of all, subject to wording differences). In 2012 evaluations, once again, paralleled those (with a different measure) from 2004, with an outcome not substantially different—slightly negative evaluations overall but not so negative as to cost the incumbent reelection. In many respects one of the lessons from considering these data is that 2016 looked a great deal like a repeat of 2012 on these measures as well as others. Thus, Bush and Obama won reelection after their first terms with relatively modest pluralities. That Bush's successor lost in 2008 was due to the dramatic economic collapse of the nation during the campaign, which otherwise might have looked like 2016. In 2016 Clinton received the boost of standing with her party's incumbent president, but it was an even more modest boost than retrospective evaluations gave Obama in 2012 (and Bush in 2004), enough for her to win by two percentage points but not enough to ensure her victory in the Electoral College. As we noted in discussing presidential approval scores, like so much else, these have become much more polarized by partisanship in the electorate, with the net result that it is a tightly constrained range of possible evaluations being shaped strongly by party identification, as we will see in the next chapter.

How do retrospective assessments compare with prospective judgments? As described in Chapter 6, prospective issues, especially our balance-of-issues measure, have become more strongly related to the vote over the last few elections, peaking in 2016. There appears, that is, to be a significant extent of partisan polarization in the electorate in terms of their evaluations of the choices and their vote, even if not in terms of their own opinions about issues. Table 7-9 reports the impact of both types of policy evaluation measures on the major-party vote in 2016. Both policy measures were collapsed into three categories: pro-Democratic, neutral, and pro-Republican. Reading down each column we see that controlling for retrospective evaluations, prospective issues are modestly related to the vote in a positive direction. Or, to be more precise, they are modestly related to the vote among those whose retrospective evaluations are nearly or actually neutral, with a small but real effect among those inclined to evaluate the Obama administration negatively. It is thus really only among those whose retrospective evaluations did not even moderately incline them toward either party that prospective evaluations are related to the vote. Note, however, that even in this column, Clinton received the votes of nearly more than four in five who were neutral on retrospective issues.

Reading across each row, we see that retrospective evaluations are very strongly related to the vote. This is true no matter what prospective evaluations respondents held. Thus we can conclude that in 2016, retrospective evaluations shaped voting choices to a great extent. Prospective evaluations were still important but only for those without a moderate or strong partisan direction to their retrospective judgments.

Together the two kinds of policy measures take us a long way toward understanding voting choices. Essentially everyone whose retrospective and prospective evaluations inclined them toward the same party voted for the candidate of that party. This accounting of voting choices is stronger when considering both forms of policy evaluations than when looking at either one individually.[27]

Table 7-9 Major-Party Voters Who Voted for Clinton, by Balance-of-Issues and Summary Retrospective Measures, 2016

Net balance of issues	Summary Retrospective							
	Strongly or Moderately Democratic		Slightly Supportive or Slightly Opposed or Neutral		Strongly or Moderately Republican		Total	
	%	(N)	%	(N)	%	(N)	%	(N)
Democratic	99	(409)	92	(376)	21	(76)	89	(866)
Neutral	96	(93)	86	(94)	10	(101)	62	(297)
Republican	94	(118)	66	(218)	4	(865)	24	(1,215)
Total	98	(620)	83	(688)	6	(1,042)	53	(2,379)

Source: Authors' analysis of the 2016 ANES survey.

Note: Numbers are weighted. Numbers in parentheses are the totals on which percentages are based. For the condensed measure of retrospective voting, we combine respondents who are strongly positive (or negative) toward Hillary Clinton and the Democratic Party with respondents who are moderately positive (or negative). We combine respondents who are slightly positive (or negative) with those who are neutral (see Table 7-8). For the condensed balance-of-issues measure, any respondent who is closer to Trump is classified as pro-Republican. The neutral category is the same as the seven-point measure (see Table 6-7).

CONCLUSION

In this and the previous chapter, we have found that both retrospective and prospective evaluations were strongly related to the vote in 2016. Indeed just as 2012 presents an unusually clear case of retrospective evaluations being a very powerful reason for Obama's victory, the mixed evaluations in 2016 provided both Clinton and Trump with a large base of votes before voters turned to consider the characteristics of the candidates and their promises. Whereas retrospective evaluations are always strong, they genuinely stand out both in 2012 and in 2016. In 1992, for example, dissatisfaction with George H. W. Bush's performance and with his and his party's handling of the most important problem—usually an economic concern in 1992—goes a long way toward explaining his defeat, whereas satisfaction with Clinton's performance and the absence of an advantage for the Republicans in being seen as able to deal with the most important concerns of voters go a long way toward explaining his 1996 victory. In 2000 prospective issues favored neither candidate because essentially the same number of major-party voters was closer to Bush as was closer to Gore. The Democrat had a modest advantage on retrospective evaluations, but Bush won greater support among those with pro-Republican evaluations than did Gore among those with pro-Democratic evaluations. The result was another even balance and, as a result, a tied outcome. Although Kerry was favored on prospective evaluations in 2004, his advantage was counterbalanced by Bush's slight advantage based on retrospective evaluations, leading to a Bush reelection victory with only a slight gain in the popular vote. By 2008 the public had turned quite negative on Bush's performance, and that led to a major advantage for the Democrats. In 2012, there was a return, essentially, to the 2004 patterns, except with a Democrat as incumbent and with retrospective judgments focusing more heavily on the economy and less heavily on international affairs. In a number of respects, 2016 was a continuation of the patterns of 2012, with perhaps a little more strength.

Even so our explanation remains incomplete. For example, why did so many of those in the middle or neutral category on retrospective evolutions support Clinton, even those inclined toward Trump on prospective policies? Even more importantly we have not accounted for *why* people hold the views they expressed on these two measures. We cannot provide a complete account of the origins of people's views, of course, but there is one important source we can examine: party identification. This variable, which we have used in previous chapters, provides a powerful way in which the typical citizen can reach preliminary judgments. As we will see partisanship is strongly related to these judgments, especially to retrospective evaluations.

CHAPTER EIGHT

PARTY LOYALTIES, POLICY PREFERENCES, AND THE VOTE

In Chapter 5 we discussed the influence of social forces such as race and ethnicity on voting behavior. We noted that, for example, African Americans do not vote Democratic simply because of their race. Instead race and other social forces provide the context for electoral politics and thus influence how voters reach their decisions. In Chapters 6 and 7 we studied the effects of various perceived traits of the candidates and of both prospective and retrospective evaluations on the vote. The question for here is why, for example, did some voters approve of Obama's performance, whereas others did not? Partisanship is an important part of the answer, indeed perhaps the single most important part of the answer, because it is the most important factor connecting voters' backgrounds, social settings, and their more immediate assessments of issues and the candidates. Thus a major part of the explanation of why African Americans vote overwhelmingly Democratic are the various events and actions that made the Democratic Party attractive (and the Republican Party unattractive) to them. The reason why some people approved of Obama's performance, whereas others did not, is largely because some are Republicans and some are Democrats. Party is therefore the third of the triumvirate of "candidates, issues, and parties"—that is, evaluations of the parties are one of three major forces that shape voting behavior. Party identification may be more foundational even than that. Party may, that is, provide additional, indirect effects, explaining, for example, why voters have the evaluations of candidates and of issues they do.

Partisanship is not the only force that helps connect context and evaluation, but it has proven to be by far the most important for understanding elections. Its dual role in directly and indirectly affecting voting makes it unusually critical for understanding why U.S. citizens vote as they do. Most Americans identify with a political party—one reason why it is so central. Their identification then influences their political attitudes and, ultimately, their behavior. In the 1950s and 1960s, Angus Campbell and his coauthors of *The American Voter*, along with other scholars, began to emphasize the role of party loyalties.[1]

Although today few people deny that partisanship is central to political attitudes and behavior, many scholars question the interpretation of the evidence gathered during that period. Two main alternatives have been proposed, and we examine them, along with an attempt to make sense of how party identification may have changed in part because of the rise of partisan polarization over the 1980s into today. Thus we ask two questions: What is party identification? And how does it actually structure other attitudes and behavior? We then examine the role that party identification played in the 2016 presidential election.

PARTY IDENTIFICATION AS LOYALTY: THE ORIGINAL VIEW

According to Angus Campbell and his colleagues, party identification is "the individual's affective orientation to an important group-object in his environment," in this case a political party.[2] In other words an individual recognizes that two major political parties are playing significant roles in elections (and presumably, observing its role in governing and policy making) and develops an affinity for one of them. Partisanship, therefore, represents an evaluation of the two parties, but its implications extend to a wider variety of political phenomena. Campbell and his colleagues measured partisanship by asking individuals which party they identified with and how strong that identification was.[3] If an individual did not identify with one of the parties, he or she may have either "leaned" toward a party or been a "pure" independent. Most Americans develop a preference for either the Republican or the Democratic Party. Very few identify with any third party. The rest are mostly independents who, according to this classic view, are not only unattached to a party but also relatively unattached to politics in general. They are less interested, less informed, and less active than those who identify with a party.

Partisan identification in this view becomes an attachment or loyalty similar to that between the individual and other groups or organizations in society such as a religious body, a social class, or even a favorite sports team. As we will see partisanship attachments in this polarized era have heightened in such a fashion that some scholars see them as a part of one's political identity. This "third" view of partisanship was developed by Donald Green et al. and serves as Christopher Achen and Larry Bartels's conclusion.[4] We will return to this topic shortly. The major point, though, is that as with loyalties to many racial, ethnic, or religious groups, partisan affiliation often begins early and lasts perhaps over the life cycle. One of the first political attitudes children develop is partisan identification, and it develops well before they acquire policy preferences and many other political orientations. Furthermore, as with other group loyalties, once an attachment to a party develops, it tends to endure.[5] Some people do switch parties, of course, but they usually do so only if their social situation changes dramatically, if there is an issue of overriding concern that sways their loyalties, or if the political parties themselves change substantially.

Party identification, then, stands as a base or core orientation to electoral politics. Once formed, this core orientation, predicated on a general evaluation of the two parties, affects many other specific orientations. Democratic loyalists tend to rate Democratic candidates and officeholders more highly than Republican candidates and officeholders and vice versa. In effect, one is predisposed to evaluate the promises and performance of one's party leaders relatively more favorably. It follows, therefore, that Democrats are more likely to vote for Democratic candidates than are Republicans and vice versa.

PARTY IDENTIFICATION AS RETROSPECTIVE EVALUATION: A SECOND VIEW

In *The Responsible Electorate*, V. O. Key argued that party loyalties contributed to electoral inertia and that many partisans voted as "standpatters" from election to election.[6] In other words, in the absence of any information to the contrary, or if the attractions and disadvantages of the candidates are fairly evenly balanced, partisans are expected to vote for the candidate of their party. This "rule" is one of voters' having a "standing decision" to vote along party lines until and unless they are given good reasons not to follow that rule. This finding led scholars to reexamine the bases of such behavior.

In this second view citizens who consider themselves Democrats have a standing decision to vote for the Democratic nominee because of the past positions of the Democrats and the Republicans and because of the parties' comparative past performances while in office. In short this view of partisan identification presumes that it is a "running tally" of past experiences (mostly in terms of policy and performance), a sort of summary expression of political memory, according to Morris P. Fiorina.[7]

Furthermore, when in doubt about how, for example, a Democratic candidate is likely to handle a civil rights issue in comparison with the Republican opponent, voters can reasonably assume that the Democrat will be more liberal than the Republican— until and unless the candidates indicate otherwise. Political parties tend to be consistent with their basic historical policy cleavages for long periods of time, changing in any fundamental ways only rarely. Naturally, therefore, summary judgments of parties and their typical candidates do not change radically or often.[8] As a result a citizen's running tally serves as a good first approximation, changes rarely, and can be an excellent device for saving time and effort that would be spent gathering information in the absence of this "memory."

Many of the major findings used in support of the original interpretation of party identification are completely consistent with this more policy-oriented view.[9] Indeed the two interpretations are not mutually exclusive. Moreover, they share the important conclusion that party identification plays a central role in shaping voters' decisions and make many of the same predictions. Equally clearly they connote quite different aspects of a political attribute. The original emphasizes affective evaluations and loyalty, the second view is more substantively based in the cognition of politics and in adjusting political views to the world one experiences. We will discuss strong empirical findings in this chapter but will be unable to resolve fully just which view is correct. In part this is because of the confluence of two newer forces in American politics: polarization of political elites and the development of a better understanding of how identity politics works and how it may have spread to include partisanship.

PARTY IDENTIFICATION, POLARIZATION, AND IDENTITY: A SYNTHESIS?

These two views are still widely studied today. The two views sometimes seem irreconcilable, but they make many similar empirical claims. We propose here a way to think about how the two might be related in concepts to match their empirical similarity. Robert S. Erikson, Michael B. MacKuen, and James A. Stimson argued that an updated version of the Key-Downs-Fiorina view of partisanship is one of the central concepts for understanding what they call the "macro polity"—that is, an explanation of how political leaders, institutions, and policy respond to changes in aggregate public opinion.[10] They argue that partisanship in the electorate changes, as do macro-level conditions such as inflation and unemployment rates, akin to the Key-Downs-Fiorina view. In turn political elites react to changes in this "macro-partisanship," among other aspects of public opinion and beliefs. On the other side, Donald Green, Bradley Palmquist, and Eric Schickler developed an equally elegant account of the affective base of partisan identification and its stability over time.[11] This view is therefore the modern version of the original account by Campbell et al. And, as their exchanges have shown, the two sets of authors differ substantially in their interpretations of what partisanship means, but empirical differences are slighter.[12]

Both views agree that partisan identifications are long-term forces in politics. Both agree that for most people, such identifications are formed early in life; children often develop a partisan loyalty, which they usually learn from their parents, although these loyalties are seldom explicitly taught. Both views recognize that partisan loyalties contribute to voter participation, as we demonstrated in Chapter 4. Partisan choices also are often closely associated with social forces, as discussed in Chapter 5, especially when a social group is actively engaged in partisan politics. An important illustration of this point is the affiliation of evangelical and other religious groups on the right with the Republican Party today, reinforcing the tendency of those who share such religious beliefs to identify with the Republican Party, much as members of labor and civil rights groups have long affiliated with the Democrats. Finally both views agree that partisanship is closely associated with more immediate evaluations, including assessments of candidates and their traits and both prospective and retrospective evaluations of the issues and candidates, as analyzed in Chapters 6 and 7.

The two views may not disagree, however, if viewed in a larger perspective. We pose a way to think about party identification in this partisan-polarized era. To be sure, the hard work of actual synthesis is yet to come, but we pose this as a way forward. Partisan polarization is taken firstly to mean that the two parties present—and act in government—by taking relatively homogenous views on issues within each party with very different and thus heterogeneous views on issues between the two. But polarization means not only differentiation between the two parties on issues but on an increasingly broad and diverse array of political matters, from social groups that align with only one party (e.g., religious conservatives with Republicans or civil rights groups with Democrats) to a wider and wider array of affective and evaluative judgments that distinguish a Republican from a Democrat. If Fiorina is right and the variety of experiences (no longer policy experiences alone but social and cultural experiences) that differentiate the two parties increase, then we would expect to find heightened affective support for one party (if one is close to them on policy, economic, social, and cultural dimensions) and negative feelings toward the more distant party (distant on nearly all matters). Still, if the standing decision really is a "running tally" such that this increasingly wide array of matters all go together into the calculation of which party is more like the individual than the other party, then Fiorina would be right: those pieces of evidence that push the citizen one way or the other are included but then set aside from memory and forgotten, with only the tally and perhaps a few of the most memorable pieces held in mind—those individual pieces often being those that arouse the most affect, that is, emotional reactions.

The key point, however, is that partisan polarization of elites is not just over policy—it is that to be sure and very importantly—but it is a set of political, social, cultural, and economic differentiations that have grown from the 1980s to today and that make partisanship a retrospective judgement, an affective loyalty, and an all-around guide to understanding politics and especially the political choices the voter faces. Is it policy choice? Yes. It is a loyalty? Yes. Is it part of one's political identity? Yes. All of these reinforce one another. In the jargon of politics, partisan polarization is the result of a large number of political cleavages that have grown over recent decades and that reinforce one another.[13] This makes them unlike the partisan politics of the 1950s to 1980s, when cleavages cross-cut one another, some pushing along lines of partisan cleavages but many cutting across them. Every reinforcing cleavage today adds one more dimension on which the parties polarize. As it grows across increasingly diverse arrays of topics, that reinforcement is nearly multiplicative in that it not only reinforces but adds both cognitive differentiation and increasingly emotive differentiation between the two parties. The stakes in having one party or the other in power simply increase with each reinforcing cleavage.

PARTY IDENTIFICATION IN THE ELECTORATE

If partisan identification is a fundamental orientation for most citizens, then the distribution of partisan loyalties is crucial. The ANES surveys have monitored the party loyalties of the American electorate since 1952. In Table 8-1, we show the basic distributions of partisan loyalties in presidential election years from 1980 to 2016, and the results for 1952 to 1976 (and every election thereafter) can be found in Table A8-1 in the appendix. As the table shows most Americans identify with a political party. In 2016, 63 percent claimed to think of themselves as a Democrat or as a Republican, and another 22 percent, who initially said they were independent or had no partisan preference, nevertheless said they felt closer to one of the major parties than to the other.[14] One in seven was purely independent of party. One of the biggest changes in partisanship in the electorate began in the mid-1960s, when more people claimed to be independents.[15] This growth stopped, however, in the late 1970s and early 1980s. There was very little change in partisan loyalties between the 1984 and 1992 surveys.

There were signs in 1996 of reversals of the trends in party identification toward greater independence. All partisan groups increased slightly in 1996 compared with 1992, and the percentage of "pure" independents (i.e., those with no partisan leanings)

Table 8-1 Party Identification in Presidential Years, Pre-election Surveys, 1980–2016 (Percent)

Party Identification	1980	1984	1988	1992	1996	2000	2004	2008	2012	2016
Strong Democrat	18	17	18	17	18	19	17	19	17	21
Weak Democrat	24	20	18	18	20	15	16	15	12	14
Independent, leans Democratic	12	11	12	14	14	15	17	17	16	11
Independent, no partisan leanings	13	11	11	12	8	12	10	11	10	15
Independent, leans Republican	10	13	14	13	12	13	12	12	19	11
Weak Republican	14	15	14	15	16	12	12	13	12	12
Strong Republican	9	13	14	11	13	12	17	13	14	16
Total	100	100	101	100	101	98	101	100	100	100
(*N*)	(1,577)	(2,198)	(1,999)	(2,450)	(1,696)	(1,777)	(1,193)	(2,301)	(1,804)	(4,244)
Apolitical	2	2	2	1	1	1	a	a	b	b
(*N*)	(35)	(38)	(33)	(23)	(14)	(21)	(3)	(2)	b	b

Source: Authors' analysis of ANES surveys.

Note: Numbers are weighted.

[a]Less than 1 percent.

[b]The ANES survey did not use the apolitical category in 2012 and 2016.

at its lowest level, 8 percent, since 1968. That dip in independence stopped, however, so that the percentages of independents in 2004, 2008, and 2012 were at about the same levels as during the 1980s. There was, however, a substantial increase in (pure) independence in 2016 to go along with a growth of partisanship, both coming at the expense of independent leaners.

Table 8-1 also shows that people are rather evenly divided between the two parties but less evenly so in 2016 than 2012. Whereas a few more in 2012 claimed to be Democrat, when "leaners" are included, the two parties have exactly the same percentage of the public, 45 percent each. Over the last forty years, the balance between the two parties had favored the Democrats by a range of about 55/45 to about 60/40. The results from the last six presidential election years before 2012 still fell within that range, although more often at the lower part of the range. From 1984 to 2000, there was a clear shift toward the Republicans. In 1980, 35 percent of partisans were Republicans; in 2000 Republicans accounted for 42 percent. The inclusion of independents who leaned toward a party would increase the percentage of Republicans to 38 percent in 1980 and 43 percent in 2000. The high point was 47 percent in 1988. In 2004 the (strong and weak) Democrats led comparable Republicans in the ANES survey with 33 percent to 29 percent (or 54/46). The Democratic advantage increased in 2008, as the percentage of Republicans declined, while there was a one-point increase on the Democratic side. These two small differences nevertheless brought the ratio of Democrats to Republicans to 57/43. The percentage of independents who leaned toward a party remained the same as in 2004, and as a result, including them maintained the Democrats' edge over Republicans at 57/43, keeping the partisan balance within the historical range of a noticeable Democratic lead. By 2012, however, that edge was gone.

The 2016 election brought back that edge. The Democratic advantage among strong and weak partisans returned to 55 percent, with the number of strong Democrats reaching its highest point since 1964. Of course the edge Democrats recovered in 2016 was still at the lower end of the heretofore usual range, and it is softened somewhat more by the ordinarily higher turnout of Republicans compared to Democrats (see Chapter 4).

Gary C. Jacobson has provided two excellent analyses of the shift in party loyalties away from the Republican Party from a high watermark in 2003 to a low watermark in 2009.[16] His analyses strongly suggest that the decline was driven largely by the decline in approval of George W. Bush's performance as president. Jacobson relies mainly on Gallup data, which probably capture more short-term variation than the standard Michigan Survey Research Center (SRC) question.[17]

The earlier shift toward the Republican Party was concentrated among white Americans.[18] As described in Chapter 5, the sharpest social division in U.S. electoral politics is race, and this division has been reflected in partisan loyalties for decades. Moreover, the racial gap has appeared to be widening, with a sharp increase in 2004.

Although the distribution of partisanship in the electorate as a whole has changed only somewhat since 1984, this stability masks the growth in Republican identification among whites through 2004 and the compensating growth of already strong Democratic loyalties among African Americans and other minorities. In Tables 8-2 and 8-3 we report the party identification of whites and blacks, respectively, between 1980 and 2016. In Tables A8-2 and A8-3 in the appendix, we report the party identification

Table 8-2 Party Identification among Whites in Presidential Years, Pre-election Surveys, 1980–2016 (Percent)

Party Identification	1980	1984	1988	1992	1996	2000	2004	2008	2012	2016
Strong Democrat	14	15	14	14	15	15	13	14	13	16
Weak Democrat	23	18	16	17	19	14	12	14	10	12
Independent, leans Democratic	12	11	10	14	13	15	17	17	15	11
Independent, no partisan leanings	14	11	12	12	8	13	8	12	10	14
Independent, leans Republican	11	13	15	14	12	14	13	17	22	13
Weak Republican	16	17	15	16	17	14	15	13	13	14
Strong Republican	9	14	16	12	15	14	21	15	17	21
Apolitical	2	2	1	1	1	1	a	16	b	b
Total	101	101	99	100	100	100	99	101	100	101
(N)	(1,405)	(1,931)	(1,693)	(2,702)	(1,451)	(1,404)	(859)	(1,824)	(1,449)	2,917

Source: Authors' analysis of ANES surveys.

Note: Numbers are weighted.

[a] The percentage supporting another party has not been presented: it is usually less than 1 percent and never totals more than 1 percent.

[b] The ANES survey did not use the apolitical category in 2012 and 2016.

Table 8-3 Party Identification among Blacks in Presidential Years, Pre-election Surveys, 1980–2016 (Percent)

Party Identification	1980	1984	1988	1992	1996	2000	2004	2008	2012	2016
Strong Democrat	45	32	39	40	43	47	30	47	53	52
Weak Democrat	27	31	24	24	22	21	30	23	17	19
Independent, leans Democratic	9	14	18	14	16	14	20	15	17	10
Independent, no partisan leanings	7	11	6	12	10	10	12	9	5	13
Independent, leans Republican	3	6	5	3	5	4	5	3	7	1
Weak Republican	2	1	5	3	3	3	2	1	0	2
Strong Republican	3	2	1	2	1	0	1	1	1	3
Apolitical	4	2	3	2	0	1	0	0	a	a
Total	100	99	101	100	100	100	100	99	100	100
(N)	(187)	(247)	(267)	(317)	(200)	(225)	(193)	(281)	(124)	(460)

Source: Authors' analysis of ANES surveys.

Note: The percentage supporting another party has not been presented: it is usually less than 1 percent and never totals more than 1 percent. Numbers are weighted.

[a] The ANES survey did not use the apolitical category in 2012 and 2016.

of whites and blacks between 1952 and 1978 (as well as through 2016). As these four tables show, black and white patterns in partisan loyalties were very different from 1952 to 2008. There was a sharp shift in black loyalties in the mid-1960s. Before then about 50 percent of African Americans were strong or weak Democrats. Since that time, 60 to 70 percent—and even higher—of blacks have considered themselves Democrats.

The party loyalties of whites have changed more slowly. Still, the percentage of self-professed Democrats among whites declined over the Reagan years, whereas the percentage of Republicans increased. In the five elections that followed, partisanship among whites changed. If independents who lean Republican are included, there was close to an even balance among whites between the two parties in 1984. By 1988 the numbers of strong and weak Democrats and strong and weak Republicans were virtually the same, with more strong Republicans than strong Democrats for the first time. Adding in the two groups of independent leaners gave Republicans a clear advantage in identification among whites. In 1992, however, there were slightly more strong and weak Democrats than strong and weak Republicans. In 1996 all four of the partisan categories were larger, by one to three points, than in 1992. The result was that the balance of Republicans to Democrats changed very slightly, and the near parity of identifiers with the two parties among whites remained. By 2000 the parity was even more striking. But 2002 revealed a substantial increase in Republican identification among whites, one that was constant in terms of the three Republican groups in 2004. Democratic identification declined slightly so that from 2000 to 2004, strong and weak Democrats fell by four points, partially balanced by a two-point gain among independent leaners. Pure independents declined sharply, to 8 percent, in both 2002 and 2004, a sign (along with the growth in strong Republicans) that the white electorate was polarizing somewhat on partisanship. As a result the three Republican groups constituted very nearly half of the white electorate and led Democrats by a 49 to 42 percent margin. That changed in 2008.[19] Democratic identification (over the three Democratic categories) increased three percentage points to 45 percent, whereas strong Republicans fell from 21 to 16 percent, dropping their three-category total to 44 percent. Thus in 2008 Democrats had at least regained parity with Republicans among white identifiers. And pure independents increased four points, to 12 percent, the highest level in over a decade. That changed again in 2012. The Democrats lost ground in all three categories in 2012 compared to 2008, and pure independents also declined somewhat. The strong and not-so-strong Republican categories changed only slightly, and as a result, the entire decline among Democrats and pure independents was concentrated in one spot—among independents who leaned toward the Republican Party. As a result the GOP held a seven-point advantage over Democrats in terms of strong and weak identifiers but a fourteen-point advantage if adding in those who lean toward a party.[20]

The 2016 survey reveals that Democrats continued to trail Republicans among whites, by the same seven points among strong and weak partisans, but only by nine points when leaners are included. That is real progress for Democrats but leaves a lot of work to return to parity with Republicans, as was true as recently as 2000. Of course standing among whites is different from standing among all voters, and indeed whites continue to decline as a proportion of the total population.

Party identification among blacks is very different. In 2016 there were very few black Republicans. Indeed, whereas the percentage of black Republicans increased in 2016 over 2012 (when the percentage of black Republicans fell to near trace levels, with only 4 percent choosing any Republican option and a mere 1 percent being strong and weak Republican), they nonetheless remained a very small percentage, with only 5 percent of strong and weak partisans and 6 percent including leaners. Because the Democrats were the first major party to choose an African American presidential candidate, we would expect this choice to exert a strong pull of blacks toward the party in 2008 and 2012, and that should continue into 2016 as the Obama administration was the basis of making retrospective evaluations. Indeed a majority of black respondents considered themselves strong Democrats, and greater than 70 percent were strong or weak Democrats, eight in ten when including those leaning toward the Democrats.

These racial differences in partisanship are long-standing, and they have increased over time. Between 1952 and 1962 blacks were primarily Democratic, but about one in seven supported the Republicans. Black partisanship shifted massively and abruptly even further toward the Democratic Party in 1964. In that year more than half of all black voters considered themselves strong Democrats. Since then well over half have identified with the Democratic Party. Black Republican identification fell to barely a trace in 1964 and edged up only slightly since then, only to fall back even further in recent years.

The abrupt change in black loyalties in 1964 reflects the two presidential nominees of that year: Democrat Lyndon Johnson and Republican Barry Goldwater. President Johnson's advocacy of civil rights legislation appealed directly to black voters, and his Great Society and War on Poverty programs made only slightly less direct appeals. Arizona senator Barry Goldwater voted against the 1964 Civil Rights Act, a vote criticized even by many of his Republican peers. In 1968 Republican nominee Richard Nixon began to pursue systematically what was called the "Southern strategy"—that is, an attempt to win votes and long-term loyalties among white southerners. This strategy unfolded slowly but consistently over the years, as Republicans, particularly Ronald Reagan, continued to pursue the southern strategy. Party stances have not changed appreciably since then.[21]

In 1964 the proportion of blacks considered apolitical dropped from the teens to very small proportions, similar to those among whites. This shift resulted from the civil rights movement, the contest between Johnson and Goldwater, and the passage of the Civil Rights Act. The civil rights movement stimulated many blacks, especially in the South, to become politically active. Furthermore, the 1965 Voting Rights Act enabled many of them to vote for the first time. Party and electoral politics suddenly were relevant, and blacks responded as all others by becoming engaged with the political—and party—system.

HISPANIC PARTISANSHIP IN 2008, 2012, AND 2016

One of the most important changes in American society and its politics has been the growth of the Hispanic community. They are now the largest ethnic or racial minority in the United States. The outcome of the 2012 election spurred a vast commentary on the future of the Republican Party based on whether and how they might be able to appeal to the Hispanic vote or seek a majority in some other way, such as through voter identification laws. The discussion of the stance of the Republican Party toward both documented (i.e., legal) and undocumented Hispanic immigrants turned dramatically in 2016, especially due to Trump's candidacy, where "Build the Wall!" was a common response of his audience to his calls for an end to at least illegal if not nearly all immigration and the possible deportation of up to 19 million undocumented and mostly Hispanic immigrants living in the United States.

We have not been able to assess the attitudes and behavior of Hispanic citizens eligible to vote until recently due to the small numbers that appear in ANES and other survey opinion polls. Fortunately, in 2008 and 2012, the ANES included a supplemental sample of Hispanics so that we have access to sufficiently large numbers to support at least a modicum of analysis, whereas the large numbers involved in the ANES 2016 survey, considering both face-to-face and online surveys, provides sufficient numbers to analyze. Table 8-4 reports the distribution of partisan loyalties among Hispanics in Part A and their voting patterns in Part B, which we consider in our analyses. As can be seen there, Hispanic partisanship may not be as massively Democratic as that of African Americans, but Republicans do very poorly among Hispanics (fewer than one in four identify as a Republican, including "leaners"), whereas by 2016, the Democrat have secured the loyalties of very close to a majority of Hispanics, and three in five respond with one of the three Democratic categories. Recall that to be included in the ANES survey, respondents need to be citizens so that these results are relevant to vote-eligible Hispanics in 2008, 2012, and 2016, respectively. With large numbers of documented Hispanics in the United States, combined with many who were born in the United States and thus native-born Americans, the number of Hispanics eligible to vote will only increase, likely considerably faster than any other source of new voters in the United States. Hence the Republicans are currently choosing a path that will make it harder to keep their overall electoral support as high as in 2016, and they must find a way to attract new voters to their camp to compensate for the growth in the total number of Hispanic voters election after election who tilt disproportionately to the Democrats. As Trump demonstrated in 2016, compared to Romney in 2012, that is not an impossible task, but it will be an increasingly challenging one.

PARTY IDENTIFICATION AND THE VOTE

As we saw in Chapter 4, partisanship is related to turnout. Strong supporters of either party are more likely to vote than weak supporters, and independents who lean toward a party are more likely to vote than independents without partisan leanings. Republicans are somewhat more likely to vote than Democrats. Although partisanship influences whether people vote, it is more strongly related to how people vote.

Table 8-5 reports the percentage of white major-party voters who voted for the Democratic candidate across all categories of partisanship since 1980 and Table A8-5 in the appendix reports the same for all ANES studies.[22] Clearly there is a strong relationship between partisan identification and choice of candidate. In every election

Table 8-4 Party Identification among Latinos in Presidential Years, Pre-election Surveys, 2008–2016 (Percent)

Part A: Party Identification

Party Identification	2008	2012	2016
Strong Democrat	23	27	28
Weak Democrat	21	23	21
Independent, leans Democratic	17	16	11
Independent, no partisan leanings	16	15	18
Independent, leans Republican	9	7	7
Weak Republican	6	6	7
Strong Republican	7	5	8
Total	99	99	100
(N)	(192)	(222)	(503)

Part B: Vote for Democratic Candidate	**2008**	**2012**	**2016**
Strong Democrat	95	100	84
Weak Democrat	90	87	91
Independent, leans Democratic	94	99	100
Independent, no partisan leanings	61	82	69
Independent, leans Republican	35	39	32
Weak Republican	24	4	23
Strong Republican	20	1	5
Total	79	78	74
(N)	(104)	(107)	(227)

Source: Authors' analysis of ANES surveys.

Note: Numbers are weighted.

except 1972, the Democratic nominee has received more than 80 percent of the vote of strong Democrats and majority support from both weak Democratic partisans and independent Democratic leaners. In 1996 these figures were higher than in any other election in this period, with nine in ten white Democratic identifiers voting for their party's nominee. Although the figures fell somewhat in 2000, especially in the independent-leaning Democrat category, that reversed in 2004, with John Kerry holding onto very large majorities of those who identified with the Democratic Party, including nearly nine in ten independents who were leaning toward the Democratic Party. In 2008 this very high level of Democratic voting continued, with slight declines among strong Democrats balanced by comparable increases among weak Democrats. The 2012 election looked more similar to 1996 than any other in this regard, and was only slightly less solidly Democrat in voting than in that year. Perhaps in the absence of the pull of Obama's candidacy, Democratic partisans supported Clinton at "only" the levels they supported Kerry in 2004, but that still was at very high levels.

Since 1952 strong Republicans have given the Democratic candidate less than one vote in ten. In 1988 more of the weak Republicans and independents who leaned toward the Republican Party voted for Michael Dukakis than had voted for Walter Mondale in 1984, but even so, only about one in seven voted Democratic. In 1992 Clinton won an even larger percentage of the two-party vote from these Republicans, and he increased his support among Republicans again in 1996. In 2000 George W. Bush held essentially the same level of support among the three white Republican categories as his father had in 1988 and 1992 and if anything increased his support among Republicans in 2004. In 2008 more than 90 percent of the strong and weak Republicans voted for McCain, just as they did for Bush four years earlier. The 2012 data looked rather similar to 2008, with Romney doing a little worse in holding weak Republican votes but doing much better than McCain among Republican leaners. In 2016 Clinton gathered more support from weak Republicans than anyone since her husband but did quite poorly among those whites who lean toward the Republican Party.

The pure independent vote among whites, which fluctuates substantially, has been more Republican than Democratic in eleven of these sixteen elections and was strongly Democratic only in 1964. Clinton did well among major-party voters in 1992. John F. Kennedy won 50 percent of that vote in 1960, but Bill Clinton won nearly two-thirds of the pure independents' vote (between the two parties) in 1992. Kerry was able to win 54 percent of the pure independent vote. Obama, like Kennedy, won exactly half of the vote among whites who are pure independents in 2008. However, that 50-50 vote in 1960 was the same as the overall vote, whereas Obama won a higher proportion from the full electorate than from white pure independents. But, in 2012, he fell back significantly, winning only 42 percent of the "pure" independent vote among whites. Clinton did particularly poorly among whites who claimed to be "pure" independents, holding only as many of them as did Dukakis in 1988.

Thus, at least among major-party white voters, partisanship is very strongly related to the vote. In recent elections the Democrats have been better able to hold support among their partisans, perhaps because the loss of southern white support has made the party more homogeneous in its outlook. Their partisan base has become essentially as strong as the Republicans', which has been consistently strong except in the very best years for the Democrats. Partisanship, then, has become more polarized in its relationship to the vote. Obama won because he broke relatively even among independents and because he held his base well, about as well as Republicans held theirs.

Table 8-5 White Major-Party Voters Who Voted Democratic for President, by Party Identification, 1980–2016 (Percent)

Party Identification	1980	1984	1988	1992	1996	2000	2004	2008	2012	2016
Strong Democrat	87	88	93	96	98	96	97	92	98	95
Weak Democrat	59	63	68	80	88	81	78	83	82	75
Independent, leans Democratic	57	77	86	92	91	72	88	8	86	88
Independent, no partisan leanings	23	21	35	63	39	44	54	50	42	36
Independent, leans Republican	13	5	13	14	26	15	13	17	11	8
Weak Republican	5	6	16	18	21	16	10	10	14	17
Strong Republican	4	2	2	2	3	1	3	2	4	2

Source: Authors' analysis of ANES surveys.

Table 8-4B shows that there is a very powerful relationship between Hispanic party identification and their vote. Nearly all Democratic Hispanics voted for Obama in 2008 and 2012. Obama was able to hold about a quarter of the relatively small number of Hispanics who identified with the GOP in 2008, but Romney won nearly all of the by-now very small number of strong and weak Republican Hispanic votes in 2008. The pure independent vote broke strongly for Obama in 2008 but increased dramatically in 2012. Whereas Clinton's support among strong Democrats declined, the pattern looks similar to that of 2008. Our conclusion is that, whereas particular percentages are somewhat variable, presumably primarily due to the smaller numbers involved, the overall pattern is one in which Hispanic voting follows white voting in that partisanship is a very strong guide to voting. The big difference is that so many more Hispanics are Democrats that they are a solid and important part of the Democratic voting coalition, not as heavily pro-Democratic as blacks but certainly far more Democratic than Republican in their loyalties and their voting choices.

Although nearly all blacks vote Democratic regardless of their partisan affiliations (most are, however, Democratic identifiers), among Hispanics and whites partisanship leads to loyalty in voting. Between 1964 and 1980 the relationship between party identification and the vote was declining, but in 1984 the relationship between party identification and the presidential vote was higher than in any of the five elections from 1964 to 1980. The relationship remained strong in 1988 and continued to be quite strong in the two Clinton elections and the Gore-Bush election, at least among major-party voters. The question of whether the parties are gathering new strength at the presidential level could not be answered definitively from the 2000 election data, but the 2004 through 2016 election data now make it clear that these growing signs have become a strong trend, to the point that party identification is as strongly related to the presidential vote as it has been since the 1950s and early 1960s, and indeed may be stronger. The relationship between party identification and voting in general will be reconsidered in Chapter 10, when we assess its relationship to the congressional vote.[23]

Partisanship is related to the way people vote. The question, therefore, is why do partisans support their party's candidates? As we shall see party identification affects behavior because it helps structure (and, according to the understanding of partisanship as a running tally of experiences, is structured by) the way voters view both policies and performance.

POLICY PREFERENCES AND PERFORMANCE EVALUATIONS

In their study of voting in the 1948 election, Bernard R. Berelson, Paul F. Lazarsfeld, and William N. McPhee discovered that Democratic voters attributed to their nominee, incumbent Harry S Truman, positions on key issues that were consistent with their beliefs—whether those beliefs were liberal, moderate, or conservative.[24] Similarly Republicans tended to see their nominee, Gov. Thomas E. Dewey of New York, as taking whatever positions they preferred. These tendencies toward "projection" (projecting one's own preferences onto what one thinks the favored candidate prefers) are discomforting for those who hope that in a democracy, issue preferences shape candidate assessment and voting choices rather than the other way around. These authors did find, however, that the more the voters knew, the less likely they were to project their preferences onto the candidates. Research since then has emphasized the role of party identification not only in projection but also in shaping the policy preferences in the public in the first place.[25] In this section we use four examples to illustrate the strong relationship between partisan affiliation and perceptions, preferences, and evaluations of candidates.

Partisanship and Approval of President's Job Performance

Most partisans evaluate the job performance of a president from their party more highly than do independents and, especially, more highly than do those who identify with the other party. Figure 8-1A shows the percentage of each of the seven partisan groups that approves of the way the incumbent has handled his job as president (as a proportion of those approving or disapproving) in the last four presidential elections in which there was a Democratic president (1980, 1996, 2000, and 2012).

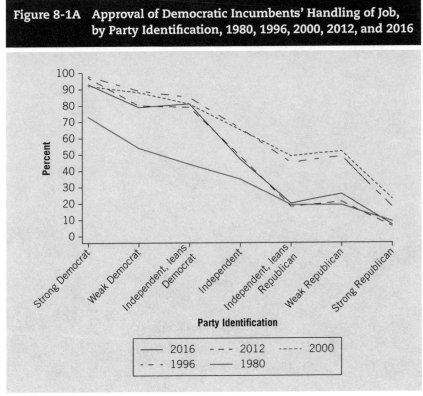

Figure 8-1A   Approval of Democratic Incumbents' Handling of Job, by Party Identification, 1980, 1996, 2000, 2012, and 2016

Source: Authors' analysis of the ANES surveys.

Note: Data are weighted.

Figure 8-1B presents similar results for the seven elections in which there was been a Republican incumbent (1972, 1976, 1984, 1988, 1992, 2004, and 2008).[26] Strong partisans of the incumbent's party typically give overwhelming approval to that incumbent. (Table A8-8 in the appendix presents the exact values for each year.) It is not guaranteed, however. In 1980 only 73 percent of strong Democrats approved of Jimmy Carter, which is just about the same percentage of strong Republicans who approved of Bush's job performance in 2008.

We can draw two conclusions about 2016 from the data in Figures 8-1A and 8-1B. First, just as in every election, there was a strong partisan cast to evaluations of the president in 2016. Democrats are very likely to approve of any Democratic incumbent and very unlikely to approve of any Republican incumbent and vice versa for Republicans. This fact was perhaps even truer in 2016 than in prior elections as the degree of partisan polarization of approval of Obama's handling of his job was more dramatic than any other. Virtually all strong Democrats approved; virtually no strong Republicans did. Even independent leaners were divided four to one in each party,

Figure 8-1B   Approval of Republican Incumbents' Handling of Job, by Party Identification, 1972, 1976, 1984, 1988, 1992, 2004, and 2008

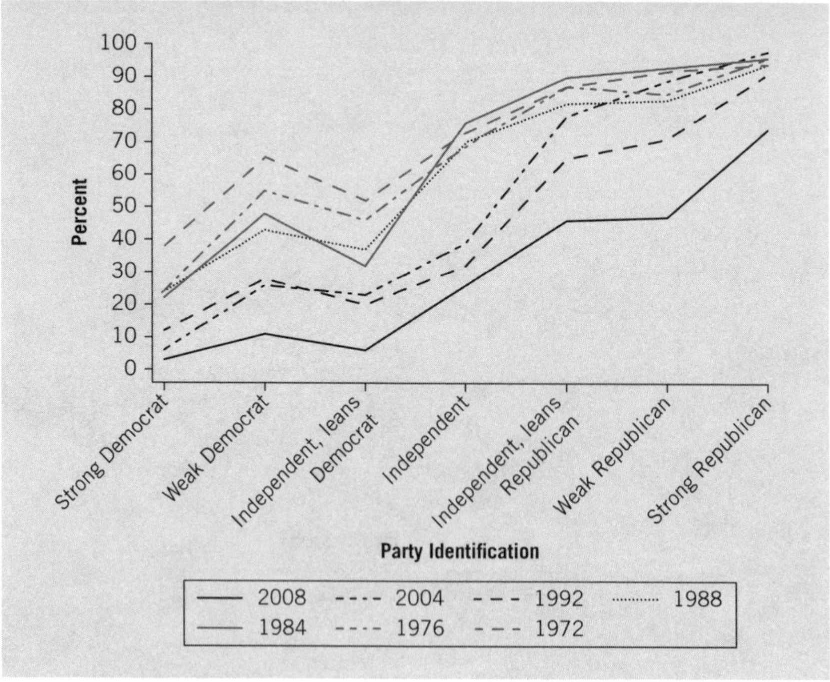

Source: Authors' analysis of the ANES surveys.

Note: Data are weighted.

with Democrats approving, Republicans disapproving, and pure independents falling directly in between.

Partisanship and Approval of President's Handling the Economy

Our second illustration extends the connection we have drawn between partisanship and approval of the incumbent's job performance. In this case we examine the relationship between partisanship and approval of the incumbent's handling of the economy. Table 8-6 shows the relationship among all seven partisan categories and approval of incumbent presidents' handling of the economy from 2000 through 2012, whereas Table A8-6 in the appendix provides data back to 1984.[27]

In 1984 and 1988 more than three-quarters of each of the three Republican groups approved of Reagan's handling of the economy, whereas more than half— and often more than two-thirds—of the three Democratic groups disapproved. Independents generally approved of Reagan's economic efforts, albeit more strongly in 1984 than in 1988. The 1992 election was dramatically different, with overwhelming disapproval of George H. W. Bush's handling of the economy among the three Democratic groups and the pure independents. Even two-thirds of the weak and Republican-leaning independents disapproved. Only strong Republicans typically approved, and even then one in three did not. The relationship in 1996 is most like that of 1984. In 2000 the vast majority of Democrats and even three in four of the pure independents approved of Clinton's economic performance—by far the highest economic approval mark independents have given. But then most Republicans also approved. In 2004 the weak but improving economy meant that George W. Bush was approved by "only" nine in ten strong Republicans and about seven in ten weak and independent-leaning Republicans. Democratic disapproval reached very high levels, and once again pure independents did not favor Bush, only one in three approving of his handling of the economy. In 2008 the Wall Street meltdown occurred in the midst of the campaign, and its effects were devastating to President Bush's approval ratings. Only 18 percent of respondents approved of Bush's handling of the economy. Even though these ratings were lower than the overall approval ratings, they displayed a clear partisan effect. Strong Republicans still approved more than they disapproved, and one in four in the other two Republican categories approved. These are very low percentages to be sure, but they are higher than among pure independents and much higher than the mere trace levels of any type of Democrat, with about one in twenty approving. The relationship between partisanship and approval of Obama's handling of the economy in 2012 was very strong. Of the three Democrat categories of partisanship, nine in ten or more approved of Obama's performance. Nine in ten strong Republicans disapproved, but Obama was able to do marginally better among weak Republicans, being approved by two in ten of them, and even better among independents who lean Republican, being approved by a bit more than a third. And pure independents approved of Obama's performance by a two-to-one ratio. Thus, as in so many other cases we have examined, evaluations and voting in 2012 were quite polarized by party even in the electorate.

Table 8-6   Approval of Incumbent's Handling of the Economy among Partisan Groups, 2016 (Percent)

| | | Party Identification | | | | | | | |
Year	Attitudes toward handling of the economy	Strong Democrat	Weak Democrat	Independent, leans Democrat	Independent	Independent, leans Republican	Weak Republican	Strong Republican	Total
2016	Approve	93	75	79	44	21	29	10	53
	Disapprove	7	25	21	56	79	71	90	47
	Total	100	100	100	100	100	100	100	100
	(N)	(896)	(582)	(460)	(606)	(470)	(499)	(691)	(4,221)

Source: Authors' analysis of ANES surveys.

In 2016 the trend of highly polarized partisan evaluations continued to grow. There is an almost four-step linear pattern. Greater than nine of ten strong Democrats approved of Obama's handling of the economy; about three in four weak and leaning Democrats approved. Nine in twenty pure independents did so, circa one in four weak and leaning Republicans approved, whereas one in ten strong Republicans did.

Prospective Issues

The third example of the impact of partisanship on attitudes and beliefs is its relationship to positions on policy issues. In Table 8-7 and Table A8-7, we report this relationship among the seven partisan categories and our balance-of-issues measure developed in Chapter 6, collapsed into three groupings: pro-Republican, neutral, pro-Democratic.[28] As we saw in Chapter 6, these issues favored the Republicans in 1972, 1976, and 1980, worked slightly to the Democratic advantage in 1984, 1988, and 1992, then once again favored the Republicans in the elections from 1996 to 2012 but barely doing so in 2016. In all cases the balance-of-issues measure had only moderately favored one party over the other, except in 2008, where the measure pointed to a clear favoring of the Republicans.[29]

As Table 8-7 and A8-7 show for 1976–2016, there has been a steady, clear, moderately strong relationship between partisanship and the balance-of-issues measure, and it is one that, by 2000, had strengthened considerably and continued to strengthen into 2008, with only modest weakening in 2012. In 2016, while "leaners" were more like strong than weak partisans, the relationship otherwise continued to strengthen. Until 1984 the relationship had been stronger among Republicans than among Democrats.

Prospective issues appear to be increasingly polarized by party, strikingly so by 2000. The data for the 2000 through 2016 elections are quite similar in that there is a strong relationship between party identification and the balance-of-issues measure. In 2016 more than three in five strong Democrats were closer to Clinton's position than to Trump's, whereas more than nine out of ten strong Republicans were closer to where the electorate placed Trump. Thus the degree of polarization on this measure continues to be quite strong in recent elections.

Partisan polarization characterizes not only prospective issues but also most other factors we have examined. In our balance-of-issues measure, "polarization" really means "consistency"—that is, partisans find their party's candidate closer to them than the opposing party's nominee on more and more issues. On these measures, then, what we observe as growing polarization stems from the increased differentiation and consistency of positions of the candidates and not as much from changes in the issue positions among the public. This is often called "sorting"—that is, sorting Democrats into the Democratic camp and Republican identifiers into their partisan camp.[30] It might also indicate partisan polarization—the two parties becoming more distant from each other—but we do not directly measure that.

Retrospective Evaluations

Finally we find a strong relationship between party identification and our measure of retrospective evaluations in 2016. We cannot directly compare this measure

Table 8-7 Balance-of-Issues Positions among Partisan Groups, 2016 (Percent)

Year	Issue positions closer to...	Party Identification								
		Strong Democrat	Weak Democrat	Independent, leans Democrat	Independent	Independent, leans Republican	Weak Republican	Strong Republican	Total %
2016	Democratic candidate	64	48	56	34	13	13	7	35
	Neutral	14	19	19	24	11	17	6	16
	Republican candidate	22	33	24	42	76	70	87	49
	Total	100	100	99	100	100	100	100	100
	(N)	(902)	(587)	(462)	(620)	(472)	(501)	(696)	(4242)

Source: Authors' analysis of ANES surveys.

Note: The Democratic category on the condensed balance-of-issues measures includes any respondent who is at least slightly Democratic; the Republican category includes any respondent who is at least slightly Republican. The neural category is the same as the neutral category on the seven-point issue scale (see Table 6-5). Numbers are weighted.

in the 2016 election with those for earlier elections because the questions that make up the summary retrospective measure in the last seven presidential elections differ from those available in 2004, and both differ from those available in 2008 and again in 2012 and 2016.[31] Still, it is worth noting that this measure was very strongly related to partisanship in those earlier elections. Table 8-8 shows the relationship in 2016, collapsing the summary retrospective measure into the three categories of pro-Democratic, neutral, and pro-Republican. The relationship is strong. Almost all strong Republicans had negative retrospective evaluations, for example, whereas nine in ten strong Democrats were moderately or strongly positive. We conclude that retrospective evaluations are invariably strongly related to partisanship, and if comparable measures were available, we suspect that 2016, like 2012, would be among the most strongly related to partisanship.[32]

Not only are party identification and retrospective evaluations consistently and strongly related to the vote, but these two measures also are strongly related to each other in every election. Do they both still contribute independently to the vote? As we learn from the data in Table 8-9 about the 2016 election, the answer is yes.[33] In Table 8-9, we examine the combined impact of party identification and retrospective evaluations on voting choices. To simplify the presentation, we use the three groupings of the summary retrospective evaluations, and we collapsed party identification into the three groups: strong and weak Republicans, all three independent categories, and strong and weak Democrats.

Table 8-9 shows the percentage of major-party voters who voted Democratic by both party identification and retrospective evaluations in 2016. Reading down the columns reveals that party identification is strongly related to the vote, regardless of the voter's retrospective evaluations, a pattern found in the nine elections before 2016. Not enough people assessed the Republicans positively on retrospective evaluations to say much about that column, but the other two columns illustrate a very strong relationship. Reading across each row reveals that in all elections, retrospective evaluations are related to the vote, regardless of the voter's party identification, and once again a pattern was discovered in all nine earlier elections. Moreover, as in all nine elections between 1976 and 2008, party identification and retrospective evaluations had a combined impact on how people voted in 2008. For example, in 2012 all Republicans with pro-Republican evaluations reported voting for Romney; among Democrats with pro-Democratic evaluations, 99 percent voted for Obama.

Finally partisanship and retrospective assessments appear to have roughly equal effects on the vote (although retrospective evaluations might, if anything, outweigh partisanship in 2016, as it appeared to do in 2012 as well), and certainly both are strongly related to the vote, even when both variables are examined together. For example, the effect of retrospective evaluations on the vote is not the result of partisans having positive retrospective assessments of their party's presidents and negative ones when the opposition holds the White House. Republicans who hold pro-Democratic retrospective judgments were much more supportive of Clinton than other Republicans (indeed three in four of those few voted for her, whereas only one in four Democrats with pro-Republican retrospective evaluations voted for Clinton). Overall, then, we can conclude that partisanship is a key component for understanding evaluations of the public and their votes, but the large changes in outcomes over time

Table 8-8 Retrospective Evaluations among Partisan Groups, 2016 (Percent)

Summary measure of retrospective evaluations	Party Identification							
	Strong Democrat	Weak Democrat	Independent, leans Democrat	Independent	Independent, leans Republican	Weak Republican	Strong Republican	Total %
Pro-Democratic	55	33	31	12	3	8	1	23
Slightly supportive, opposed, or neutral	41	50	54	38	19	25	8	34
Pro-Republican	3	18	14	49	78	68	91	43
Total	99	101	99	99	100	101	100	100
(N)	(763)	(505)	(400)	(486)	(407)	(427)	(573)	(3560)

Source: Authors' analysis of the 2016 ANES survey.

Note: The Democratic category on the condensed measure of retrospective evaluations includes any respondent who is at least moderately opposed to the incumbent's party; the Republican category includes any respondent who at least moderately supports the incumbent's party. The middle retrospective category is the same as the middle retrospective category in Table 7-10. Numbers are weighted.

Table 8-9 Percentage of Major-Party Voters Who Voted for Clinton, by Party Identification and Summary Retrospective Evaluations, 2016

Party Identification	Summary Retrospective Evaluations							
	Pro-Democratic		Neutral		Pro-Republican		Total	
	%	(N)	%	(N)	%	(N)	%	(N)
Democratic	99	(462)	96	(394)	28	(75)	92	(941)
Independent	96	(129)	79	(209)	10	(342)	47	(694)
Republican	77	(27)	38	(85)	1	(625)	8	(743)
Total	26	(618)	29	(688)	44	(1,042)	99	(2348)

Source: Authors' analysis of the 2016 ANES survey.

Note: The Democratic category on the condensed measure of retrospective evaluations includes any respondent who is at least moderately opposed to the incumbent's party; the Republican category includes any respondent who at least moderately supports the incumbent's party. The middle retrospective category is the same as the middle retrospective category in Table 7-10. The numbers in parentheses are the totals on which the percentages are based. Numbers are weighted.

must be traced to retrospective and prospective evaluations simply because partisanship does not change substantially over time.

In summary partisanship appears to affect the way voters evaluate incumbents and their performances. Positions on issues have been a bit different. Although partisans in the 1970s and early 1980s were likely to be closer to their party's nominee on policy, the connection was less clear than between partisanship and retrospective evaluations. It is only recently that prospective evaluations have emerged as being nearly as important a set of influences on candidate choice as retrospective evaluations, and this appears to track closely the growing partisan polarization of members of Congress. Still, policy-related evaluations are influenced in part by history and political memory and in part by the candidates' campaign strategies. Partisan attachments, then, limit the ability of a candidate to control his or her fate in the electorate, but such attachments are not entirely rigid. Candidates have some flexibility in the support they receive from partisans, especially depending on the candidates' or their predecessors' performance in office and on the policy promises they make in the campaign.

CONCLUSION

Party loyalties affect how people vote, how they evaluate issues, and how they judge the performance of the incumbent president and his party. In recent years research has suggested that party loyalties not only affect issue preferences, perceptions, and evaluations but that preferences, perceptions, and evaluations may also may affect those loyalties in turn. There is good reason to believe that the relationship between partisanship and these factors is more complex than any model that assumes a one-way relationship would suggest. Doubtless, evaluations of the incumbent's performance may also affect party loyalties.[34]

As we saw in this chapter, there was a substantial shift toward Republican loyalties over the 1980s; among whites, the clear advantage Democrats had enjoyed over the last four decades appeared to be gone. Although the 2008 election suggests that there was at least a chance that the Democrats would enjoy a resurgence, that advantage was at least temporarily stemmed in 2012, as the two parties were near parity. This parity turned back toward a Democratic advantage in 2016, which is somewhat unusual, not just because the Republicans won the Electoral College vote but also because Clinton won the popular vote by only a couple of percentage points—hardly a sweep toward the Democratic Party. To some extent the earlier shift in party loyalties in the 1980s must have reflected Reagan's appeal and his successful performance in office, as judged by the electorate. His successor, the senior Bush, lost much of the partisan appeal he inherited primarily because of negative assessments of his handling of the economy, and he was not able to hold onto the high approval ratings he had attained in 1991 after the success in the Persian Gulf War. In 1996 Clinton demonstrated that a president could rebound from a weak early performance as judged by the electorate and benefit from a growing economy.

The 1996 election stood as one comparable to the reelection campaigns of other recent, successful incumbents, although Clinton received marks as high as or higher than Nixon's in 1972 and Reagan's in 1984 for his overall performance and for his handling of the economy. With strong retrospective judgments the electorate basically decided that one good term deserved another.

The question for the 2000 campaign was why Vice President Al Gore was unable to do better than essentially tie George W. Bush in the election (whether counting by popular or electoral votes). We must remember, however, how closely balanced all other key indicators were. Partisanship among whites was essentially evenly split between the two parties, with a Republican advantage in turnout at least partially off-setting the Democratic partisanship of blacks. Prospective issues, as in most election years, only modestly favored one side or the other. Retrospective evaluations, however, provided Gore with a solid edge, as did approval ratings of Clinton on the economy. The failure, then, was in Gore's inability to translate that edge in retrospective assessments into a more substantial lead in the voting booth. Retrospective evaluations were almost as strongly related to the vote in 2000 as in other recent elections, but Gore failed to push beyond that slight popular vote plurality and turn a virtual tie into an outright win.

George W. Bush, it appears, learned some lessons from 2000 for his 2004 reelection. In 2004 he faced an electorate that, like its immediate predecessors, was almost evenly balanced in its partisanship, with a slight Democratic edge in numbers of identifiers balanced by their lower propensity to turn out than Republican identifiers. Meanwhile, because of the continuing decline in the proportion of pure independents, there were fewer opportunities to win over those not already predisposed to support one party or the other. Furthermore, although Bush held an edge in prospective evaluations, Kerry held an advantage on retrospective assessments, but in both cases the edges were small. Thus with fewer independents to woo and such an even balance, the contest became a race for both the remaining independents and the weakly attached and an effort to "strengthen the base"—by motivating supporters to, in turn, motivate the base to turn out. Perhaps for this reason we observed a strengthening of the affective component of partisan attachments—that is, a growth in strong partisans at the expense of the more weakly attached, at least during the campaign itself.

All of this was lost in 2008. Partisanship shifted toward the Democrats. The Bush administration was the least popular we have yet been able to measure. The public rejected his incumbency in general and his handling of the economy in particular. As a result John McCain faced an unusually steep uphill battle. It is no wonder that he and Sarah Palin emphasized their "maverick" status as independent of the Bush administration. They did not, however, cut themselves loose from their partisan base. McCain might have been able to do so, but his selection of Palin as running mate indicated that his administration would be distinct from Bush's administration but nevertheless just as Republican. In view of the edge he held on prospective issues, that was a plausible choice. But the financial meltdown in the fall of 2008 probably sealed his fate. The election came down to being a partisan one, on which the Democrats turned out to hold an increased advantage, and a retrospective one, on which the Democrats held an overwhelming advantage. These two factors translated into a comfortable victory for Obama—and many other Democrats.

Much changed between 2008 and 2012. The Democratic hold on the House and Senate was lost in a disastrous congressional election in 2010. The legislative victories of the Obama administration and Democrats in 2009 and early 2010 yielded controversy and what was originally a rather popular-based outpouring of protest that became the "Tea Party." This movement pushed Republican candidates and officeholders toward the right wing of their party, deepening polarization. The result was that voters increasingly saw and acted upon that partisan polarization among political elites. Public opinion on partisanship and evaluations of all kinds reflected the polarization they perceived, even if the public was more or less evenly balanced in their views and not evidently deeply polarized in their own issue opinions. When given a menu of polarized campaigns, the public responded with polarized choices, making partisanship and its relationship to evaluations and choices as strong an influence as ever.

Perhaps the most surprising thing about presidential voting in 2016 was how similar it was to other recent elections, perhaps most especially to 2012. A female headed a major party ticket for the first time. A non-politician lacking in any sort of governmental experience (political or military) was also a groundbreaker. Further, he had been a Democrat far longer than he had been a Republican, and he had long made public what had been his quite liberal policy preferences on many issues, some held right up to the 2016 campaign. He took on the Republican political establishment, and many of them took him on in return. And yet, the voting patterns, although not precisely identical from election to election, look much like those that preceded them. It appears that the voters saw not a populist, former Democrat, or one who held a number of liberal positions on important issues. Rather they saw a Republican, purely and simply.

There are a few ways in which voters saw Trump as different from other candidates, such as we saw in Chapter 6, where they were clear, for example, that he speaks his mind. But these differences, important as they may be, were concentrated primarily in evaluations of Trump the individual candidate. In virtually all other ways, the dominant story is that of voters assessing a highly (and highly charged) political world overwhelmingly understood by partisan polarization. In some ways the voter is polarized, but as we can see, especially with respect to prospective issues, that is not always true. Indeed the typical voter's policy stances in these terms have changed little since these measures first were used. But their evaluations of the candidates, incumbents, parties, and their performances increasingly reflect a mostly partisan electorate embedded in a world where political elites (whether establishment or populist or maverick) are polarized by party affiliation. The increasing strengthening of the various relationships in this chapter reflect a partisan voter world that is at least sorted. One big change, for example, was the slow transition of southern conservatives in the 1980s from Democratic to Republican partisanship as Republicans, for the first time there since before 1876, provided more and more conservative candidates running for more and more offices.[35] Given that most in the electorate have at least some partisan inclinations, and given that they are sorted into the same partisan groups as the parties' political candidates and officeholders, that means that even only moderately liberal Democrats will choose a partisan polarized, liberal Democrat for office after office, in election after election, over any conservative Republican. And, of course, the same works in reverse for even modestly conservative Republicans. Thus elections are dominated by the polarized parties at the elite level and the sorted parties at the voter level (and possibly polarized voters, too, at least in some dimensions). Elections look a lot like one another because the big picture is that they are like one another—conservative Republican candidates appealing to conservative Republican voters, liberal Democratic voters appealing to liberal Democrats.[36] Increasingly polarized parties mean that each election looks a lot like the preceding one, only a bit more so, election after election. And that there are reasonably similar number of Democrats at the voting booth as there are Republicans holds this all in balance.[37] That is, partisan polarization has nearly locked voting patterns into place, such that once the public observed this dramatic change, the electoral world is less change and much more continuity.

THE 2016 CONGRESSIONAL ELECTIONS

CHAPTER NINE

CANDIDATES AND OUTCOMES IN 2016

I n 1994 the Republicans unexpectedly won control of both chambers of Congress, the first time the GOP had won the House since 1952. (The only time they had controlled the Senate during that period was 1980–1986.) The electoral earthquake of 1994 shaped all subsequent Congressional contests. From 1996 on, there was at least some doubt about who would control the next Congress after the voters chose, which had not been in the case during the previous period of Democratic control. In the next five elections after 1994, the GOP retained control of the House, although they lost seats in the first three and gained in the next two. In the Senate the Republicans added to their majority in 1996, broke even in 1998, and then lost ground in 2000, leaving the chamber evenly divided. Then in 2002 the GOP made small gains to get a little breathing room, and in 2004 they gained a bit more. Going into the elections of 2006, the GOP still had control of Congress, but that year their luck ran out. The GOP suffered a crushing defeat, losing thirty seats in the House and six in the Senate, shifting control of both bodies to the Democrats, and in 2008 the Democrats achieved a second substantial gain in a row, adding twenty-one seats in the House and eight seats in the Senate.

In 2010 party fortunes reversed again. In the wake of the Great Recession, the Democrats lost the House, with the Republicans picking up a net gain of sixty-three seats. In the Senate the GOP fell short of control, but they did gain six seats. In 2012 the Republicans had hoped to continue to make gains, but that was not to be. Instead the Democrats regained some ground. In the House they won 201 seats to the Republicans' 234, a gain of eight seats. In the Senate the result was a fifty-three to forty-five division in favor of the Democrats, with two independents (both of whom sided with the Democrats on control),[1] which reflected a gain of two Senate seats. Two years later in 2014, the Republicans made a net gain of thirteen seats in the House, netting them their largest majority (247–188) since 1928. More significant, however, was the Republican's capture of the Senate—they picked up nine Democratic seats while losing none of their own to take a fifty-four to forty-six majority. Although the Republicans ended up losing six seats in the House and two in the Senate during the 2016 elections, they were able to maintain control of Congress, giving them unified control of the government for the first time since 2005–2006. This initially gave them considerable hope that they would be able to pass a Republican agenda, such as repealing and replacing the Affordable Care Act (ACA), among other initiatives. The smaller majority in the House, along with a moderately diverse party conference, and the small, two-vote majority in the Senate, gave them very little room to maneuver if they wanted to pass that agenda with only Republican votes.

In this chapter we examine the pattern of congressional outcomes for 2016 and see how it compares to previous years. We explain why the 2016 results took the shape they did—what factors affected the success of incumbents seeking to return and what permitted some challengers to run better than others. We also discuss the likely impact of the election results on the politics of the 115th Congress. Finally we consider the implications of the 2016 results for the 2018 midterm elections and for other subsequent elections.

ELECTION OUTCOMES IN 2016

Patterns of Incumbency Success

One of the most dependable generalizations about American politics is that most congressional races involve incumbents and most incumbents are reelected. Although this statement has been true for every set of congressional elections since World War II, the degree to which it has held varied from one election to another. Table 9-1 presents information on election outcomes for House and Senate races involving incumbents between 1954 and 2016.[2] During this period, an average of 93 percent of House incumbents and 85 percent of Senate incumbents who sought reelection were successful.

The proportion of representatives reelected in 2016 (about 96 percent) was three points above the sixty-two year average, whereas the 93 percent success rate for senators was eight points above the average for that chamber. As we discuss later in the chapter, the limited number of quality challengers running in 2016 significantly affected the results for the House. In the absence of a quality challenger, incumbents have a much easier time getting reelected.[3] In the Senate there were a disproportionate number of Republican seats up, and as we will see later, the Democrats performed substantially below expectations.

During the period covered by Table 9-1, House and Senate outcomes have sometimes been similar and in other instances have exhibited different patterns. For example, in most years between 1968 and 1988, House incumbents were substantially more successful than their Senate counterparts. In the three elections between 1976 and 1980, House incumbents' success averaged over 93 percent, whereas senators averaged only 62 percent. By contrast the success rates during the 1990s were fairly similar. More recently, in all but one of the nine elections beginning with 2000, we have again seen some divergence, with House incumbents being more successful.

These differences between the two bodies stem from at least two factors. The first is primarily statistical: House elections routinely involve around four hundred incumbents, whereas Senate contests usually have fewer than thirty. A smaller number of cases is more likely to produce volatile results over time. Thus the proportion

Table 9-1 House and Senate Incumbents and Election Outcomes, 1954–2016

Year	Incumbent Running (N)	Primary Defeats %	(N)	General Election Defeats %	(N)	Reelected %	(N)
House							
1954	(407)	1.5	(6)	5.4	(22)	93.1	(379)
1956	(410)	1.5	(6)	3.7	(15)	94.9	(389)
1958	(394)	0.8	(3)	9.4	(37)	89.8	(354)
1960	(405)	1.2	(5)	6.2	(25)	92.6	(375)
1962	(402)	3.0	(12)	5.5	(22)	91.5	(368)
1964	(397)	2.0	(8)	11.3	(45)	86.6	(344)
1966	(411)	1.9	(8)	10.0	(41)	88.1	(362)
1968	(409)	1.0	(4)	2.2	(9)	96.8	(396)
1970	(401)	2.5	(10)	3.0	(12)	94.5	(379)
1972	(392)	3.3	(13)	3.3	(13)	93.4	(366)
1974	(391)	2.0	(8)	10.2	(40)	87.7	(343)
1976	(383)	0.8	(3)	3.1	(12)	96.1	(368)
1978	(382)	1.3	(5)	5.0	(19)	93.7	(358)
1980	(398)	1.5	(6)	7.8	(31)	90.7	(361)
1982	(393)	2.5	(10)	7.4	(29)	90.1	(354)
1984	(411)	0.7	(3)	3.9	(16)	95.4	(392)
1986	(393)	0.5	(2)	1.5	(6)	98.0	(385)
1988	(409)	0.2	(1)	1.5	(6)	98.3	(402)
1990	(407)	0.2	(1)	3.7	(15)	96.1	(391)
1992	(368)	5.4	(20)	6.3	(23)	88.3	(325)
1994	(387)	1.0	(4)	8.8	(34)	90.2	(349)
1996	(384)	0.5	(2)	5.5	(21)	94.0	(361)
1998	(401)	0.2	(1)	1.5	(6)	98.3	(394)
2000	(403)	0.7	(3)	1.5	(6)	97.8	(394)
2002	(398)	2.0	(8)	1.8	(7)	96.2	(383)
2004	(404)	0.5	(2)	1.7	(7)	97.8	(395)
2006	(404)	0.5	(2)	5.4	(22)	94.1	(380)
2008	(403)	0.9	(4)	4.7	(19)	94.2	(380)
2010	(396)	1.0	(4)	13.6	(54)	85.4	(338)
2012	(391)	4.6	(18)	5.6	(22)	89.8	(351)
2014	(395)	1.3	(5)	3.3	(13)	95.4	(377)
2016	(393)	1.5	(6)	2.0	(8)	96.4	(379)

(Continued)

Table 9-1   (Continued)

Year	Incumbent Running (N)	Primary Defeats %	Primary Defeats (N)	General Election Defeats %	General Election Defeats (N)	Reelected %	Reelected (N)
Senate							
1954	(27)	—	(0)	15	(4)	85	(23)
1956	(30)	—	(0)	13	(4)	87	(26)
1958	(26)	—	(0)	35	(9)	65	(17)
1960	(28)	—	(0)	4	(1)	96	(27)
1962	(30)	—	(0)	10	(3)	90	(27)
1964	(30)	—	(0)	7	(2)	93	(28)
1966	(29)	7	(2)	3	(1)	90	(26)
1968	(28)	14	(4)	14	(4)	71	(20)
1970	(28)	4	(1)	11	(3)	86	(24)
1972	(26)	4	(1)	19	(5)	77	(20)
1974	(26)	4	(1)	8	(2)	88	(23)
1976	(25)	—	(0)	36	(9)	64	(16)
1978	(22)	—	(1)	27	(6)	68	(15)
1980	(29)	—	(4)	31	(9)	55	(16)
1982	(30)	—	(0)	7	(2)	93	(28)
1984	(29)	—	(0)	10	(3)	90	(26)
1986	(27)	—	(0)	22	(6)	78	(21)
1988	(26)	—	(0)	12	(3)	88	(23)
1990	(30)	—	(0)	3	(1)	97	(29)
1992	(27)	4	(1)	11	(3)	85	(23)
1994	(26)	—	(0)	8	(2)	92	(24)
1996	(20)	—	(0)	5	(1)	95	(19)
1998	(29)	—	(0)	10	(3)	90	(26)
2000	(27)	—	(0)	22	(6)	78	(21)
2002	(26)	4	(1)	8	(2)	88	(23)
2004	(25)	—	(0)	5	(1)	96	(24)
2006	(28)	—	(0)	21	(6)	79	(22)
2008	(29)	—	(0)	17	(5)	93	(24)
2010	(25)	12	(3)	8	(2)	84[a]	(21)
2012	(22)	5	(1)	5	(1)	91	(20)
2014	(28)	—	(0)	18	(5)	82	(23)
2016	(29)	—	(0)	7	(2)	93	(27)

Source: Compiled by the authors.

[a] In 2010 Senator Lisa Murkowski (R-AK) was defeated in the primary and then won the general election as a write-in candidate. Thus she is counted both as a primary defeat and as reelected.

of successful Senate incumbents tends to vary more than for the House. In addition Senate races are more likely to be vigorously contested than House races, making incumbents more vulnerable. In many years a substantial number of representatives had no opponent at all or had one who was inexperienced, underfunded, or both. Senators, on the other hand, often had strong, well-financed opponents. Thus representatives were electorally advantaged relative to senators. In the early 1990s the competitiveness of House elections increased, reducing the relative advantage for representatives, although the election cycles since then still have seen competition in House contests confined to a narrower range of constituencies than Senate races.[4] We will consider this issue in more detail later in the chapter.

Having considered incumbency, we now consider political parties. Figure 9-1 shows the percentage of seats in the House and Senate held by the Democrats after each election since 1952. It graphically demonstrates how large a departure from the past the elections of 1994 through 2004 were. In House elections before 1994, the high percentage of incumbents running and the high rate of incumbent success led to fairly stable partisan control. Most importantly the Democrats won a majority in the House in every election since 1954 and had won twenty consecutive national elections. This was by far the longest period of dominance of the House by the same party in American history.[5] This winning streak was ended by the upheaval of 1994, when the GOP made a net gain of fifty-two representatives, winning 53 percent of the total seats. They held their majority in each subsequent election through 2004, although there were small shifts back to the Democrats in 1996, 1998, and 2000. Then in 2006 the Democrats took back the House and expanded their margin in 2008. The huge GOP success of 2010 restored their control, and 2012 returned them as the majority with a reduced margin. They picked up thirteen additional seats during the 2014 midterm before losing a net of six seats in 2016.

In the Senate previous Republican control was much more recent. They had taken the Senate in the Reagan victory of 1980 and retained it in 1982 and 1984. When the class of 1980 faced the voters again in 1986, however, the Democrats made significant gains and won back the majority. They held it until the GOP regained control in 1994, and then the Republicans expanded their margin in 1996. Then in 2000 fortune turned against them, resulting in the 50-50 division of the chamber. (This was followed a few months later by the decision of Senator James Jeffords of Vermont to become an independent, and to vote with the Democrats on organizing the chamber, shifting majority control to them until after the 2002 elections.) In 2004 the GOP gained four seats and again reached their high watermark of 55 percent. Finally the combined Democratic gain of fourteen seats in 2006 and 2008 restored solid control for that party, which they retained for the next few years despite the difficult election of 2010. In 2014 the Republicans captured nine additional Senate seats, giving them unified congressional control for the final two years of the Obama presidency. Despite defending more than two-thirds of the seats up for reelection in 2016, the Republicans only lost two Senate seats in that election, yielding a relatively slim majority control.

The combined effect of party and incumbency in the general election of 2016 is shown in Table 9-2. Overall the Democrats won 45 percent of the races for House seats and 48 percent of the Senate contests. Despite the sharp partisanship of both the presidential and congressional races, incumbents of both parties did well in their

Figure 9-1 Democratic Share of Seats in the House and Senate, 1953–2017 (in Percentages)

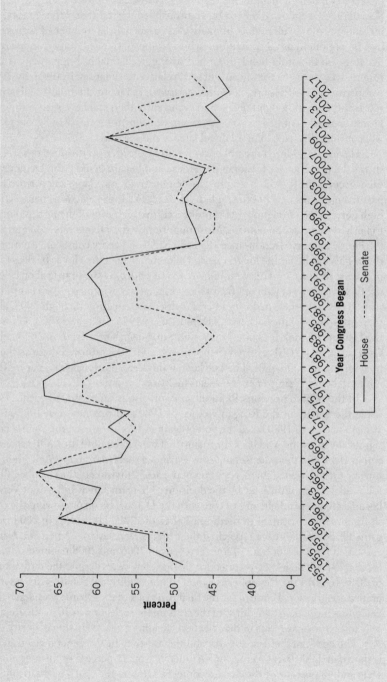

Sources: Data for the House are from History, Art & Archives, United States Representatives, http://history.house.gov/Institution/Party-Divisions/Party-Divisions/. Data for the Senate are from United States Senate, https://www.senate.gov/history/partydiv.htm.

Table 9-2 House and Senate General Election Outcomes, by Party and Incumbency, 2016 (Percent)

	Democratic Incumbent	No Incumbent		Republican Incumbent	Total
		Democratic Seat	Republican Seat		
House					
Democrats	99	89	12	3	45
Republicans	1	11	88	97	55
Total	100	100	100	100	100
(*N*)	169	19	26	221	435
Senate					
Democrats	100	100	0	9	35
Republicans	0	0	100	91	65
Total	100	100	100	100	100
(*N*)	7	3	2	22	34

Source: Compiled by the authors.

House races. Ninety-nine percent of House Democratic incumbents in the general election won reelection, and 97 percent of House Republicans were successful. In the 2016 Senate races, all seven Democratic incumbents won, as did twenty-two of twenty-four GOP incumbents.

Regional Bases of Power

The geographic pattern of 2016 outcomes in the House and Senate can be seen in the partisan breakdowns by region in Table 9-3.[6] For comparison we also present corresponding data for 1981 (after the Republicans took control of the Senate in Reagan's first election) and for 1953 (the last Congress before 1995 in which the Republicans controlled both chambers). This series of elections reveals the enormous shifts in the regional political balance that have occurred over the last six decades. In the House, comparing 2017 to 1981, we see that the GOP share declined in the East and West, whereas it increased in the Midwest, South, and the border states. The most pronounced shifts were in the West, the South, and the border states, with the Republican share decreasing by eleven percentage points in the first region while increasing by thirty-six points in the latter two. Overall the Republicans won a majority of House

Table 9-3   Party Shares of Regional Delegations in the House and Senate, 1953, 1981, and 2017 (Percent)

	1953			1981			2017		
	Dems	Reps		Dems	Reps		Dems	Reps	
Region	(%)	(%)	(N)	(%)	(%)	(N)	(%)	(%)	(N)
House									
East	35	65	(116)	56	44	(105)	65	35	(79)
Midwest	23	76	(118)	47	53	(111)	36	64	(86)
West	33	67	(57)	51	49	(76)	62	38	(102)
South	94	6	(106)	64	36	(108)	28	72	(138)
Border	68	32	(38)	69	31	(35)	33	67	(30)
Total	49	51	(435)	56	44	(435)	45	55	(435)
Senate									
East	25	75	(20)	50	50	(20)	90	10	(20)
Midwest	14	86	(22)	41	59	(22)	45	55	(22)
West	45	55	(22)	35	65	(26)	50	50	(26)
South	100	0	(22)	55	45	(22)	14	86	(22)
Border	70	30	(10)	70	30	(10)	40	60	(10)
Total	49	51	(96)	47	53	(100)	48	52	(100)

Source: Compiled by the authors.

seats in all regions but the East and West in 2016. With the exception of the Midwest, the pattern is roughly similar in the Senate. Between 1981 and 2017 GOP gains were limited to two regions of the country (the South and border), while they lost ground in the East, Midwest, and West.

The 2017 election results are even more interesting when viewed from the longer historical perspective. In 1953 there were sharp regional differences in party representation in both houses. These differences diminished significantly by 1981, but new and substantial deviations developed subsequently. The most obvious changes occurred in the East and the South. In 1953 the Republicans held nearly two-thirds of the House seats in the East, but by 2017 their share had fallen to slightly more than one-third. Indeed, in New England, historically a bastion of Republican strength, the GOP managed to win only one of the twenty-one seats in 2016. The Republican decline in eastern Senate seats over the period was even greater, down from 75 percent to only 10 percent. In the South, on the other hand, the percentage of House seats held by Democrats declined from 94 percent in 1953 to 28 percent in 2017. In 1953 the Democrats held all twenty-two southern Senate seats, but in 2017 they controlled only three.

This change in the partisan share of the South's seats in Congress has had an important impact on that region's influence within the two parties. The South used to be the backbone of Democratic congressional representation. This, and the tendency of southern members to build up seniority, gave southerners disproportionate power within the Democratic Party in Congress. Because of declining Democratic electoral success in the region, the numerical strength of southern Democrats within their party in Congress has waned. In 1953, with the Republicans in control of both chambers, southerners accounted for around 45 percent of Democratic seats in the House and Senate. By the 1970s southern strength had declined, stabilizing at between 25 and 30 percent of Democratic seats. In 2017 southerners accounted for 20 percent of Democratic House seats and only 6 percent of Democratic senators.

The South's share of Republican congressional representation presents the reverse picture. Minuscule at the end of World War II, it steadily grew, reaching about 20 percent in the House after the 1980 elections and 41 percent after the 2016 election. As a consequence of these changes, southern influence has declined in the Democratic Party and grown in the GOP, to the point that southerners have often held a disproportionate share of the Republican leadership positions in both houses of Congress. Because southerners of both parties tend to be more conservative than their colleagues from other regions, these shifts in regional strength have tended to make the Democratic Party in Congress more liberal and the Republican Party more conservative.[7]

Other regional changes since 1953, although not as striking as those in the South and East, are also significant. In the 1953 House, the Republicans controlled the West by a two-to-one margin and the Midwest by three to one. In 2017 they were a 38 percent minority in the West and had a 64 percent share in the Midwest. The Senate also exhibited shifts away from substantial Republican strength in the West and Midwest. On the other hand, with the increased Republican control of the South and Democratic dominance in the East, regional differences in party shares are more prominent in 2017 than they were in 1981, and partisan representation is only a little more regionally homogeneous in the Congress of 2017 than it was in the Congress of 1953.

National Forces in Congressional Elections

The patterns of outcomes discussed here were shaped by a variety of influences. As with most congressional elections, the most important among these were the resources available to individual candidates and how those resources were distributed between the parties in specific races. We will discuss those matters shortly, but first we consider potential and actual national-level influences particular to 2016.

The first national force to assess is whether there was a pattern in public opinion that advantaged one party or the other. Such "national tides" may occur in presidential years or in midterms, and they can have a profound impact on the outcomes of congressional elections. Often these tides flow from reaction to presidents or presidential candidates. For example, in 1964 the presidential landslide victory of Lyndon B. Johnson over Barry M. Goldwater carried over to major Democratic gains in both congressional chambers, and Ronald Reagan's ten-point margin over Jimmy Carter in 1980 helped Republicans achieve an unexpected majority in the Senate and major gains in the House. Similarly negative public reactions to events in the first two years of Bill Clinton's presidency played a major part in the Republicans' congressional victories in 1994, and dissatisfaction with President Bush significantly enhanced the Democrats' campaign to retake the House in 2006.

Clearly 2016 was an election without a significant national tide working in favor of either the Democrats or the Republicans. This is not surprising after three wave elections in a row in 2006–2010 as well as a modest one in 2014. We saw in Chapter 2 that the presidential race was close all year, despite the fact that Hillary Clinton had a small lead according to most polls. A modest number of House and Senate races were deemed "up for grabs," but the proportion of each party's seats that were projected as competitive remained similar. Moreover, unlike what would be usual for an election with a partisan wave, the number of seats that were classified as close remained fairly stable over the election cycle. Figure 9-2 presents the number of Democratic and Republican House seats that political analyst Charlie Cook estimated to be highly competitive at various points in the 2015–2016 period.[8] The total number of competitive seats only increased a small amount, from thirty-two to forty, between July of 2015 and November of 2016. Moreover, the ratio between the parties was also fairly constant: in August of 2015, 78 percent of the competitive seats were held by Republicans, while in November of the following year, it was 77.5 percent.

Another potential national influence is public reaction to the performance of Congress. In the 1996 presidential race, for example, Clinton and the Democrats tried to focus public attention on what they claimed was the extremism and excesses of the new GOP congressional majority, albeit with only very limited success.[9] In 2016 public opinion toward Congress had turned very negative. In almost every major survey taken during the year leading up to the election, approval of the job Congress was doing was between 15 and 20 percent.[10] According to a CNN/ORC poll conducted in late October, only 44 percent of registered voters indicated that their own member of Congress deserved to be reelected. Additionally "[t]hat figure is the lowest in CNN/ORC polling back to fall 2006—a window in which the House has changed hands twice. Just 29% say 'most members of Congress' deserve re-election, a touch higher than the share saying so at recent low-points in congressional approval during the 2013 partial government shutdown and 2011 near-shutdown (August 2011 and October 2013)."[11]

Efforts of National Parties and Their Allies

One important national-level influence is the efforts of congressional party leaders and their allies to influence the races. Before the 1980s the activities of national parties in congressional elections were very limited. Individual candidates were mostly self-starters who were largely on their own in raising money and planning strategy. More recently this situation has changed substantially, and party leaders and

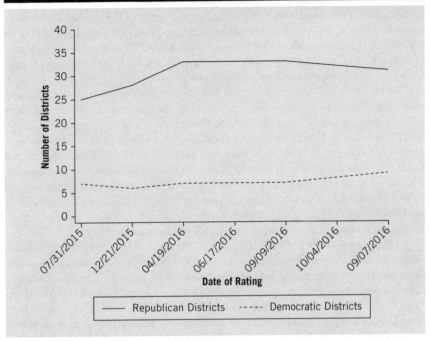

Figure 9-2 Competitive House Districts, 2015–2016

Source: Compiled by the authors from editions of *The Cook Political Report* on listed dates.

organizations are now heavily involved in recruiting and funding their candidates.[12] As we will see the quality of candidates and their level of funding are two of the central determinants of election outcomes. Thus both the short-term and long-term fates of the parties in Congress provided incentives for them to be active in efforts to improve their circumstances in these respects.

Recruiting Candidates

National party organizations are now continually active in candidate recruiting and fund-raising. As soon as the voting in one election ends, activity for the next begins. Democrats' main concern after their electoral defeat in the 2014 midterms was that many of their senior members would become frustrated by their minority status (and the expectation that it would continue) and retire. The situation was exacerbated by the fact that the Republicans had shored up their majority in the House and picked up a narrow majority in the Senate during the 2014 elections. The plans of individual candidates were monitored and possible strategies for eventually taking back the majority were discussed by the Democrats. The perceived prospects of success were key elements of the strategic calculations of potential recruits. It is much easier for a party to persuade a prospect to run if that party's national prospects look bright.

In the end both parties were moderately successful in staving off House retirements, with only twenty-eight representatives (twenty Republicans and eight Democrats) opting to leave office entirely, although fifteen additional members sought higher office. Proportionately, retirements were greater in the Senate. There were thirty-four seats up in 2016, ten held by Democrats and twenty-four by Republicans. In five of these the sitting senator (two Republicans and three Democrats) declined to run.

The Republicans had a net gain of thirteen House seats during the 2014 midterm elections, giving them a 247–188 House majority, their largest since 1928. In the Senate the Republicans managed to pick up nine Democratic seats while losing none of their own to assume a fifty-four- to forty-six-seat majority. These numbers represented a formidable challenge for the Democratic Party campaign organization (DCCC) in early 2015, when it began formulating strategies in an attempt to win back control of Congress. In light of the sheer size of the House Republican majority, the Democrats needed to pick up approximately thirty seats to secure majority control. This task was made a bit easier by the fact that the DCCC recognized that twenty-six House Republicans represented districts that President Obama had won in 2012.[13] If the DCCC could recruit enough experienced candidates to run in these districts, then they could potentially make inroads into the Republican majority.

The Democratic Senatorial Campaign Committee (DSCC) recognized that the challenge of winning back majority control of the Senate would be far easier (at least in theory) because they had to net only five seats. Additionally the Republicans had to defend nearly three times as many Senate seats as the Democrats did in 2016, which made their task that much simpler. By October of 2015 their chances looked quite good as they had managed to secure outstanding recruits in nearly every Senate race they had targeted. "Aside from Hassan in New Hampshire, the DSCC secured strong candidates in Florida, Illinois, Missouri, Nevada, Ohio, Pennsylvania and Wisconsin. The DSCC also scored wins with Rep. Ann Kirkpatrick's decision to run for Senate in Arizona, as well as three Democratic senators from red states forgoing gubernatorial bids in 2016."[14]

For the Republicans the challenge leading up to the 2016 elections was twofold. First, the National Republican Campaign Committee (NRCC) wanted to minimize losses in the House, especially because the majority caucus had grown increasingly heterogeneous with the election of a number of fiscally conservative, Tea Party Republicans since 2010. With respect to the Senate, the National Republican Senatorial Committee (NRSC) had the more formidable challenge of trying to defend at least nine Republican incumbents, all of which were deemed vulnerable by *Roll Call* in November 2015 (compared with only one Democratic senator, Michael Bennet from Colorado). Among the most at-risk Republican senators leading up to the 2016 election were Mark Kirk (IL), Ron Johnson (WI), Pat Toomey (PA), Kelly Ayotte (NH), and Rob Portman (OH). Many considered Kirk to be among the most vulnerable because he had been elected in the Republican wave of 2010 by a narrow margin and represented a traditionally blue state. He was also heavily targeted by the DSCC and Emily's List, who were going all in on their support of his opponent, Rep. Tammy Duckworth.[15]

Money and Other Aid

In addition to recruitment, party leaders have grown increasingly active in fund-raising, pursuing many different strategies. For example, top party leaders solicit donations to the congressional campaign committees like the NRCC and the DCCC, and they appear at fund-raisers for individual candidates in their districts. The amounts they raise are considerable. As of January 28, 2016, "House Minority Leader Nancy Pelosi raised more than $40.1 million in the 2016 cycle, her largest fundraising haul since joining Democratic leadership in 2002. That sum includes $30.4 million for the DCCC. Since 2002, Pelosi has raised $468.9 million."[16] Nevertheless, majority status is an asset for fund-raising, and Speaker Paul Ryan of Wisconsin did substantially better than Pelosi, amassing nearly $90 million in contributions for the Republicans, $40.6 of which was transferred to the NRCC to distribute across other House races.[17]

In both parties raising campaign funds for the party has become a prominent obligation for members who hold or want leadership posts and committee chairmanships, and the amounts they raise are a significant portion of money spent in campaigns. According to opensecrets.org, House Majority Leader Kevin McCarthy raised nearly $12 million for both the NRCC and the Republican Leadership PAC during the 2016 election cycle, the bulk of which was transferred to other Republican candidates for the House.[18] In recent years the parties have set contribution targets for their incumbents (which they term "dues"). Although many members would prefer to retain the money they raise for their own use, they have increasingly been pressured to share that money with other members. One interesting pattern that emerged in 2016 is that after Paul Ryan and Kevin McCarthy, the next five top earners among Republicans were all freshmen who had been elected in 2014—Martha McSally (AZ), Ryan Zinke (MT), Bob Dold (IL), Mia Love (UT), and Barbara Comstock (VA).[19]

Party leaders are able to do more to help candidates' reelection efforts than just raise or spend campaign money, at least for the House majority. Because the majority party has almost total control over the floor agenda and the content of bills, it can add or remove provisions in bills that will enhance their members' reelection chances or permit vulnerable colleagues to bring their popular bills to the floor, thus enhancing their reputations.

In addition to funding by the formal party organizations like the DCCC and the NRCC, the parties' congressional candidates are receiving increasing support from outside groups and super PACs.[20] During the 2016 election cycle, more than $630 million was spent by outside groups in Senate contests, 93 percent of which was allocated across nine Senate races—Pennsylvania, New Hampshire, Nevada, North Carolina, Ohio, Florida, Indiana, Missouri, and Wisconsin.[21] That was an increase of nearly 30 percent spent by outside groups during the same period in the 2014 contests.[22] Whereas the lion's share of outside spending went to Senate contests during 2016, nearly $315 million from those sources were spent on competitive House races.[23]

CANDIDATES' RESOURCES
AND ELECTION OUTCOMES

Seats in the House and Senate are highly valued posts for which candidates compete vigorously. In contests for these offices, candidates draw on every resource they have. To explain the results of congressional elections, we must consider the comparative advantages and disadvantages of the various candidates. In this section, we will discuss the most significant resources available to candidates and the impact those resources have on the outcomes of congressional elections.

Candidate Quality

The personal abilities that foster electoral success can be a major political asset. Many constituencies today do not offer a certain victory for one of the two major parties, and for those that do strongly tilt to one party, there is often a contested primary, so election outcomes usually depend heavily on candidate quality. A strong, capable candidate is a significant asset for a party; a weak, inept one is a liability that is difficult to overcome. In his study of the activities of House members in their districts, Richard F. Fenno, Jr., described how members try to build support within their constituencies, establishing bonds of trust between constituents and their representatives.[24] Members attempt to convey to their constituents a sense that they are qualified for their job, that they identify with their constituents, and that they empathize with constituents and their problems. Challengers of incumbents and candidates for open seats must engage in similar activities to win support. The winner of a contested congressional election will usually be the candidate who is better able to establish these bonds of support among constituents and to convince them that he or she is the person for the job (or that the opponent is not).

One indicator of candidate quality is previous success at winning elective office. The more important the office a candidate has held, the more likely it is that he or she has overcome significant competition to obtain the office.[25] Moreover, the visibility and reputation for performance that usually accompany public office can also be a significant electoral asset. For example, state legislators running for House seats can claim that they have experience that has prepared them for congressional service. State legislators may also have built successful organizations that are useful in conducting congressional campaigns. Finally previous success in an electoral arena suggests that experienced candidates are more likely to be able to run strong campaigns than candidates without previous success or experience. Less adept candidates are likely to have been screened out at lower levels of office competition. For these and other reasons, an experienced candidate tends to have an electoral advantage over a candidate who has held no previous elected office.[26] Moreover, the higher the office previously held, the stronger the candidate will tend to be in the congressional contest.[27]

In Table 9-4, we present data showing which candidates were successful in 2016, controlling for office background, party, and incumbency.[28] In House contests the vast majority of candidates who challenged incumbents lost regardless of their office background or party, although those with previous elective experience did better than those who had none. The impact of candidate quality is stronger in races without incumbents. Here, candidates who had been state legislators were very successful, and those with other elective experience won at a higher rate than those without any elective office experience (except for Republicans). In Senate races, because there were only two incumbent losses, no pattern is visible there. For non-incumbent candidates those with stronger office backgrounds generally did better.

Given the importance of candidate quality, it is worth noting that there has been substantial variation in the proportion of experienced challengers over time. During the 1980s the proportion of House incumbents facing challengers who had previously won elective office declined. In 1980, 17.6 percent of incumbents faced such challenges; in 1984, 14.7 percent did; in 1988, only 10.5 percent did. In 1992, due largely to perceptions of incumbent vulnerability because of redistricting and scandal, the proportion rose to 23.5 percent, but in 1996, it was back down to 16.5 percent, and it

Table 9-4 Success in House and Senate Elections, Controlling for Office Background, Party, and Incumbency, 2016 (Percent)

	Candidate Is Opponent of . . .		No Incumbent in District	
	Democratic Incumbent % (N)	Republican Incumbent % (N)	Democratic Candidate % (N)	Republican Candidate % (N)
House				
State Legislature/ U.S. House	0 (6)	17 (18)	79 (14)	88 (8)
Other elected	0 (5)	5 (18)	55 (11)	50 (10)
No elected	1 (144)	1 (170)	23 (13)	53 (17)
Senate				
U.S. House	0 (0)	25 (4)	50 (2)	50 (2)
Statewide elected	0 (0)	25 (4)	67 (3)	100 (1)
Other elected	0 (4)	0 (3)	0 (1)	0 (1)
No elected	0 (3)	0 (11)	0 (0)	0 (0)

Source: Data on office backgrounds were taken from issues of *The Cook Political Report* and the *Green Papers*. Compiled by the authors.

remained at that level in 2000.[29] In 2004, however, there was a substantial resurgence in the number of experienced candidates in both parties, with 22.4 percent of the total challengers having previously held elective office, followed by a decline again in 2008 to 14.8 percent. In 2012 the proportion rebounded again to 20 percent before declining again in both 2014 and 2016.[30]

Whether experienced politicians actually run for the House or Senate is not an accident. These are significant strategic decisions made by politicians, and they have much to lose if they make the wrong choice. The choices will be governed by factors related to the perceived chance of success, the potential value of the new office compared to what will be lost if the candidate fails, and the costs of running.[31] The chances of success of the two major parties vary from election to election, both locally and nationally. Therefore, each election offers a different mix of experienced and inexperienced candidates from the two parties for the House and Senate.

The most influential factor in whether a potential candidate will run is whether there is an incumbent in the race. High reelection rates tend to discourage potentially strong challengers from running, which in turn makes it even more likely that the incumbents will win. In addition to the general difficulty of challenging incumbents, factors related to specific election years (both nationally and in a particular district) will affect decisions to run. For example, the Republican Party had particular difficulty recruiting strong candidates during 1986 because of fears about a potential backlash from the Iran-Contra scandals. And the 2008 decline in quality candidates was likely a function of the Republicans having less success recruiting strong candidates in many districts because the electoral environment was perceived to be negative for their party. On the other hand some research indicates that potential House candidates are most strongly influenced in their decisions by their perceived chances of winning their party's nomination.[32] Moreover, the actions of incumbents may influence the choices of potential challengers. For example, building up a large reserve of campaign funds between elections may dissuade some possible opponents, although analysis of Senate contests (which usually involve experienced challengers) indicates that this factor does not have a systematic impact in those races.[33]

As we have seen most congressional races do not involve challengers who have previous office experience. Given their slight chance of winning, why do challengers without experience run at all? As Jeffrey S. Banks and D. Roderick Kiewiet point out, although the chances of success against incumbents may be small for such candidates, such a race may still be their best chance of ever winning a seat in Congress.[34] If inexperienced challengers were to put off their candidacies until a time when there is no incumbent, their opposition would likely include multiple experienced candidates from both parties. Moreover, as David Canon demonstrates, previous office experience is an imperfect indicator of candidate quality because some candidates without such experience can still have significant political assets and be formidable challengers.[35] For example, four former television journalists who had never previously held office won House seats in 1992, and three of them defeated incumbents. They were able to build on their substantial name recognition among voters to win nomination and election.[36] Moreover, consider two 2000 contests, one from each chamber. The Republican candidate for the House in Nebraska's third district was Tom Osborne, the extremely popular former head coach of the University of Nebraska's football team. Osborne was elected to an open seat with a phenomenal 82 percent of the vote. In the New York Senate race, the very visible (and ultimately successful) Democratic candidate was then First Lady Hillary Rodham Clinton. In many respects this win may have set her on the path to running for the presidency in 2008 and again in 2016.

Incumbency

One reason most incumbents win is that incumbency itself is a significant resource. To be more precise, incumbency is not a single resource but rather a status that usually gives a candidate a variety of benefits. In some respects incumbency works to a candidate's advantage automatically. For example, incumbents tend to be more visible to voters than do challengers.[37] Less automatic, but very important, incumbents usually tend to be viewed more favorably than challengers. Moreover, at least a plurality of the electorate in most districts will identify with the incumbent's political party, and this pattern has become stronger over the last couple of decades. Incumbents can also use their status to gain advantages. Incumbents generally raise and spend more money than challengers, and they usually have a better developed and more experienced campaign organization. They also have assets, provided at public expense, such as a staff and franking privileges (free postage for mail to their constituents), that both help them perform their jobs and provide electoral benefits. Incumbents also have the opportunity to vote and perhaps work on bills favored by their constituents and to bring "pork" home to the district, when they think it will be advantageous to do so. Challengers, by contrast, lack such advantages.

Increasing Electoral Margins

From the mid-1960s through the late 1980s, the margins by which incumbents were reelected increased (the pattern was less clear and more erratic in Senate elections than in House elections).[38] These changing patterns interested analysts primarily because they believed that the disappearance of marginal incumbents means less congressional turnover and a House that would be less responsive to the electorate.

Edward R. Tufte offered an early explanation for the increased incumbency margins by arguing that redistricting had protected incumbents of both parties.[39] This argument seemed plausible because the increase in margins occurred about the same time as the massive redistricting required by Supreme Court decisions of the mid-1960s. But other analysts showed that incumbents had won by larger margins both in states that had been redistricted and in those that had not as well as in Senate contests.[40] Thus redistricting was initially dismissed as the major reason for the change.

Another explanation offered for the increase in incumbents' margins was the growth in the perquisites of members and the greater complexity of government. Morris P. Fiorina notes that in the post-New Deal period, the level of federal services and the bureaucracy that administers them had grown tremendously.[41] A more complex government means that many people will encounter problems in receiving services, and people who have problems frequently contact their representatives to complain and seek help. Fiorina contends that in the mid-1960s, new members of Congress emphasized such constituency problem-solving more than their predecessors. This expanded constituency service developed into a reservoir of electoral support. Although analyses of the impact of constituency services have produced mixed conclusions, it is likely that the growth of these services offers a partial explanation for changing incumbent vote margins and for the incumbency advantage generally.[42]

The declining impact of party loyalties provided a third explanation for the growth in incumbent vote margins, either alone or in conjunction with other factors. Until the mid-1960s, there was a very strong linkage between party identification and congressional voting behavior. Most Americans identified with a political party, many identified strongly, and most voters supported the candidate of their chosen party. Subsequently, however, the impact of party identification decreased, as we will see in Chapter 10. John A. Ferejohn, drawing on data from the ANES, shows that the strength of party ties weakened and that within any given category of party identification, the tendency to support the candidate of one's party declined.[43] An analysis by Albert D. Cover shows that between 1958 and 1974, voters who did not identify with the party of a congressional incumbent were increasingly more likely to defect from their party and support the incumbent, although there had been no increase in defections from party identification by voters of the same party as incumbents.[44] Thus weakened party ties produced a substantial net benefit for incumbents,[45] although as we saw in Chapter 8 (and will discuss further in Chapter 10), party loyalties among the electorate have grown stronger in recent years.[46]

The Trend Reversed

Whatever the relative importance of these factors (and the others we will discuss) in explaining the increase in incumbents' victory margins, the increase continued through the 1980s, as the data in Table 9-5 show, peaking at 68.4 percent in 1986. These data are only for races in which both parties ran candidates. Thus they exclude contests where an incumbent ran unopposed. Such races were also increasing in number over this period; therefore, the data actually understate the growth in incumbents' margins.

Then, in 1990, something changed. The average share of the vote for incumbents declined by nearly four percentage points. The decline was, moreover, not a result of a shift of voters toward one party, as with the decline from 1980 to 1982; both parties' incumbents suffered. Rather the shift in incumbents' electoral fortunes was apparently the result of what was called the "anti-incumbent mood" among the voters. Early in 1990 pollsters and commentators began to perceive stronger anti-Congress sentiments within the electorate.[47] For the first time analysts began to question whether incumbency remained the asset it used to be.

There was, of course, nothing new about Congress being unpopular; Congress had long suffered ups and downs in approval, just like the president. What changed in 1990 was that Congress's unpopularity appeared to be undermining the approval of individual members by their own constituents. Yet, as the data presented in Table 9-1 shows, even though there was a drop in the average percentage of the vote received by incumbents in 1990, the rate of reelection still reached 96 percent. The decline in vote margins was not great enough to produce a rash of defeats. Many observers wondered,

Table 9-5 Average Vote Percentages of House Incumbents, 1974–2018

Year	Democrats	Republicans	All Incumbents
1974	71.3	56.9	64.1
1976	67.0	63.8	65.8
1978	66.0	65.9	66.0
1980	64.4	68.7	66.0
1982	69.2	60.6	65.1
1984	64.4	68.9	66.2
1986	70.4	65.9	68.4
1988	68.8	67.7	68.3
1990	65.8	62.4	64.6
1992	63.7	63.4	63.6
1994	60.8	68.7	63.7
1996	68.5	62.2	64.9
1998	68.8	64.0	66.4
2000	69.7	65.1	67.5
2002	68.4	67.4	67.9
2004	69.2	64.7	66.8
2006	71.1	60.1	64.7
2008	69.8	61.2	66.0
2010	60.5	67.7	63.0
2012	69.1	61.2	64.6
2014	63.4	66.0	64.8
2016	67.5	64.6	65.9
2018	69.8	59.4	63.7

Source: Compiled by the authors.

Note: These figures include only races where both major parties ran candidates. Thus they exclude contests in which an incumbent ran unopposed.

however, whether 1990 was the beginning of a new trend: would incumbents' electoral drawing power continue to decline?

In 1992 scandals damaged many representatives of both parties, and among the public, the evaluation of Congress was very low. Opponents of incumbents emphasized that they were "outsiders" and not "professional politicians" (even when they had substantial political experience). The results from 1992 show that incumbents' share of the vote dropped a bit more. Republicans rebounded a little from their bad 1990 showing, whereas Democrats fell more than two percentage points. Yet again, however, the casualty rate among incumbents who ran in the general election was lower than many expected: 93 percent were reelected. (It is important to note, however, that a substantial number of incumbents had already been defeated in the primaries, and many weak incumbents had retired.) Then, in 1994, although there was only a slight additional drop in incumbents' share of the vote overall, the drop was greater (and concentrated) for Democrats, and their casualty rate was high. The result was the loss of their majority. Next, in 1996, there was a slight rebound in incumbents' vote share, with Democrats increasing sharply, while the GOP fell. That vote shift translated into eighteen Republican incumbents defeated but only three Democrats. Finally the results from 2000 through 2016 fall in between the highs of the mid-1980s and the lows of 1994 and 1996. Indeed, during those years, the average incumbent vote percentage has been virtually identical each year, although the averages for the parties have varied with the electoral climate.

This discussion illustrates that incumbents' vote margins and incumbents' reelection success are related but distinct phenomena.[48] When—as was true in the 1980s— the average share of the vote received by incumbents is very high, they can lose a lot of ground before a large number of defeats occur. What appears to have occurred in 1990 is that many incumbents were subjected to vigorous contests for the first time in years. Such challenges were then repeated or extended to additional incumbents in 1992, 1994, and 1996. Potential candidates apparently looked at the political situation and concluded that incumbents who had previously looked unbeatable could now potentially be defeated, and there was a substantial increase in the number of candidates for Congress. These vigorous contests by challengers who were stronger than usual resulted in a decrease in the share of the vote received by many incumbents.

Jacobson, in his *Journal of Politics* article, offers a slightly different interpretation for the reversal of fortune among incumbents since the 1990s. He argues that the increasing nationalization of elections stemming from a resurgence in party voting among the electorate has actually contributed to a decline in the incumbency advantage during the past few decades. With more constituents basing their voting decisions on partisan criteria in light of increasing levels of polarization, it has become more difficult for incumbents to win districts that lean toward the other party as was once the case. This, in turn, has contributed to a decline in the personal incumbency advantage because members of the House can no longer rely on the resources of office to carry them to victory in polarized congressional districts.[49] The same general pattern holds for the U.S. Senate, although it was not quite as pronounced until 2016 when, "for the first time in history, every Senate contest was won by the party that won the state's electoral votes."[50]

Campaign Spending

A third resource that strongly affects congressional elections is campaign spending. Campaign spending has received a great deal of attention in the last four decades because researchers gained access to more dependable data than had previously been available.[51] The data on spending have consistently shown that incumbents usually outspend their challengers, often by large margins, and that through the early 1990s, the disparity had increased.[52] (As we shall see shortly, more recent data show significant changes.)

Disparities in campaign spending are linked to the increase in incumbents' election margins. Beginning in the 1960s congressional campaigns relied more heavily on campaign techniques that cost money—for example, media time, campaign consulting, and direct mailing—and these became increasingly expensive. At the same time candidates were progressively less likely to have available pools of campaign workers from established party organizations or from interest groups. This made using expensive media and direct mail strategies relatively more important. Most challengers are unable to raise significant campaign funds. Neither individuals nor groups interested in the outcomes of congressional elections like to throw money away; before making contributions they usually need to be convinced that the candidate has a chance. Yet we have seen that in most election years, few incumbents have been beaten. Thus it is often difficult to convince potential contributors that their money will produce results, and contributions are often not forthcoming. Most challengers are thus at a strategic disadvantage, and they are unable to raise sufficient funds to wage a competitive campaign.[53]

It is the ability to compete, rather than the simple question of relative amounts of spending, that is at the core of the issue. We have noted that incumbents have many inherent advantages that the challenger must overcome if he or she hopes to win. But often the money is not there to overcome them. In 2016, for example, greater than 41 percent of challengers spent $25,000 or less, and slightly more than 60 percent spent $75,000 or less. With so little money available, challengers are unable to make themselves visible to the electorate or to convey a convincing message.[54] Under such circumstances, most voters—being unaware of the positions, or perhaps even the existence, of the challenger—vote for the incumbent.

Data from 2016 on campaign spending and election outcomes seem consistent with this argument, and they show patterns similar to those exhibited in other recent elections.[55] Linking spending to outcomes, Table 9-6 shows the relationship between the incumbent's share of the vote in the 2016 House elections and the amount of money spent by the challenger. Clearly there is a strong negative relationship between how much challengers spend and how well incumbents do. In races where challengers spent less than $26,000, 91 percent of the incumbents received 60 percent or more of the vote, the traditional cutoff for marginality. At the other end of the spectrum, in races where challengers spent $800,000 or more, 78 percent of the incumbents received less than 60 percent of the vote, and approximately 46 percent got less than 55 percent of the vote. These results are consistent with those in earlier House elections for which comparable data are available.[56]

Table 9-6 Incumbents' Share of the Vote in the 2016 House Elections, by Challenger Campaign Spending (Percent)

Challenger Spending	Incumbents' Share of the Two-Party Vote					
	70% or More	60%–69%	55%–59%	Less Than 55%	Total	N
$0–$25,000	50.7	40.7	7.1	1.4	100	140
$26,000–$75,000	24.6	56.9	16.9	1.5	100	65
$76,000–$199,000	13.6	52.3	34.1	0.0	100	44
$200,000–$399,000	9.7	48.4	25.8	16.1	100	31
$400,000–$799,000	0.0	55.0	40.0	5.0	100	20
$800,000 and up	2.7	18.9	32.4	45.9	100	37
All	28.8	44.5	19.0	7.7	100	337

Source: Federal Election Commission, http:www.fec.gov. Compiled by the authors.

Note: Races without a major party opponent are excluded, and challenger spending that is unavailable was coded in the $0–25,000 row.

These findings are reinforced by other research that shows that challenger spending has a greater influence on election outcomes than does incumbent spending.[57] This generalization has been questioned on methodological grounds,[58] but further research by Gary Jacobson reinforced his earlier findings. Using both aggregate and survey data, he found that "the amount spent by the challenger is far more important in accounting for voters' decisions than is the amount of spending by the incumbent."[59] More recently Jacobson emphasizes the importance of incumbent spending. Comparing successful House challengers to those who are unsuccessful, he notes that the successful candidates were more likely to be familiar to voters. He writes, "It is no mystery why winning challengers reached so many voters and were so much more familiar to them. They ran much better financed campaigns than did the losers."[60] In contrast, analysis of Senate elections has also resulted in somewhat more conflicting conclusions.[61]

Of course challengers who appear to have good prospects will find it easier to raise money than those whose chances seem slim. Thus, one might wonder whether these data simply reflect the fulfillment of expectations in which money flows to challengers who would have done well regardless of spending. Other research, however, indicates that is likely not the case. In an analysis of the 1972 and 1974 congressional elections, Jacobson concluded, "Our evidence is that campaign spending helps candidates, particularly non-incumbents, by bringing them to the attention of the voters; it is not the case that well-known candidates simply attract more money; rather money buys attention."[62] From this perspective adequate funding is a necessary but not sufficient condition for a closely fought contest, a perspective consistent with the data in Table 9-6. Heavily outspending one's opponent is not a guarantee of victory; the evidence does not indicate that elections can simply be bought because money does not literally buy votes. Indeed having to spend large sums of money in a prior race may signal to an astute challenger that the incumbent is vulnerable and likely to lose under the right circumstances. Even if an incumbent outspends the challenger, the incumbent can still lose if the challenger is adequately funded and runs a campaign that persuades the voters.[63]

The 2016 elections, for example, offer clear evidence of this. In four of the eight races in which incumbents faced a non-incumbent challenger and the incumbent lost, the loser outspent the winner.[64] The losing incumbent in each of these eight races spent an average of $2.8 million dollars on the unsuccessful reelection bid. The fact that incumbents in each of these races had to spend as much as they did is consistent with Jacobson's argument that spending large sums of money is no guarantee of electoral victory, especially when one factors in the fund-raising prowess of their opponents.

On the other hand a spending advantage is not a guarantee to a challenger. In an extreme example from 2000, losing Republican challenger Phil Sudan spent $3.25 million against incumbent Ken Bentsen of Texas, who spent $1.35 million. Despite being outspent over two to one, Bentsen won more than 60 percent of the vote. A somewhat less extreme case occurred in 2008, when Republican Sandy Treadwell spent more than $7 million compared to incumbent Democrat Kristen Gillibrand of New York's $4.49 million. The Democrat was reelected with more than 61 percent of the vote. Based on this analysis our view can be summarized as follows: if a challenger is to attain visibility and get his or her message across to the voters—neutralizing the incumbent's advantages in name recognition and perquisites of office—the challenger needs to be adequately funded. If both sides in a race are adequately funded, the outcome will tend to turn on factors other than just money, and the relative spending of the two candidates is unlikely to control the outcome.[65]

This argument carries us full circle back to our earlier discussion and leads us to bring together the three kinds of resources that we have considered—candidate experience, incumbency, and campaign spending. Table 9-7 presents data showing the impact of these three factors in the 2016 House elections. We categorize challenger experience as strong or weak depending on previous elective-office experience; challenger spending was classified as low or high depending on whether it was below or above $200,000.[66] The data show that each element exerts some independent effect, but the impact of spending seems to be more consequential in the most recent election cycle (as was also true in 2012). When challengers had weak experience and low spending (68 percent of the races), all incumbents won, and 85 percent won with more than 60 percent of the vote. In the opposite situation, where the challenger had both strong experience and substantial spending, 64 percent of the races were considered competitive. The combined results for the two intermediate categories fall between the extremes. In addition incumbent defeats occur with greater frequency in situations where the challenger is experienced and has strong spending. Yet it is important to note how few such races there were in 2016. Table 9-7 also reveals that 64 percent of

Table 9-7 Percentage of Incumbents by Vote Share, Challenger Experience, and Spending in the 2016 House Elections

Challenger	Incumbents' Share of Two-Party Vote					
Experience/ Spending	70% or More	60%–69%	55%–59%	Less Than 55%	Total	N
Weak/low	39.91 (93)	45.49 (106)	13.73 (32)	0.86 (2)	100	233
Strong/low	0 (0)	68.75 (11)	25.00 (4)	6.25 (1)	100	16
Weak/high	15.15 (10)	36.36 (24)	25.75 (17)	22.72 (15)	100	66
Strong/high	3.57 (1)	32.14 (9)	39.29 (11)	25.00 (7)	100	28

Source: See Tables 9-4 and 9-6. Compiled by the authors.

Note: Percentages read across. Strong challengers have held a significant elected office (U.S. representative; statewide office; countywide or citywide office such as mayor, prosecutor, etc.). High-spending challengers spent more than $200,000. Races without a major-party opponent are excluded. Ns are in parentheses.

the challengers with previous experience were able to raise substantial funds (twenty-eight of forty-four), whereas only 36 percent of challengers with no elective experience were able to do so.

This combination of factors also helps explain the greater volatility of outcomes in Senate races discussed earlier. Previous analysis has shown that the effects of campaign spending in Senate contests are consistent with what we have found true for House races: if challenger spending is above some threshold, the election is often quite close; if it is below that level, the incumbent is likely to win by a large margin.[67] In Senate races, however, the mix of well-funded and poorly funded challengers is different. Senate challengers are more likely to be able to raise significant amounts of money than their House counterparts. Indeed, in recent elections, a number of challengers (and open-seat candidates) have been wealthy individuals who could provide a large share of their funding from their own resources. One of the most extreme examples comes from 2000, when Jon Corzine, the Democratic candidate for the open New Jersey Senate seat, spent more than $60 million of his own money to defeat his opponent. Corzine spent a total of $63 million; the Republican spent $6.4 million.[68] Nevertheless, Corzine was only elected by a three-percentage point margin. A more recent case comes from the 2016 Senate race in Pennsylvania, where Republican incumbent Pat Toomey received 48.8 percent of the vote compared to Katie McGinty's 47.3 percent. During the election, Toomey spent $30.8 million compared with $16.3 million spent by McGinty. However, outside spending in the race approached $120 million, bringing the total amount spent in the Pennsylvania Senate race to approximately $167 million.[69]

Senate challengers, moreover, are also more likely to possess prior elective experience. Thus, in Senate contests, incumbents often face well-funded and experienced challengers, and the stage is then set for their defeat if other circumstances work against them.

The lesson from the evidence presented here is captured by the words of David Johnson, the director of the Democratic Senatorial Campaign Committee, to Rep. Richard C. Shelby of Alabama, who was challenging Republican Senator Jeremiah Denton in 1986. Shelby, who eventually won, was concerned that he did not have enough campaign funds as Denton was outspending him two to one. Johnson responded: "You don't have as much money, but you're going to have enough—and enough is all it takes to win."[70]

THE 2016 ELECTIONS:
THE IMPACT ON CONGRESS

The elections of 1994 produced huge consequences for politics and governing, and each subsequent election over the next decade was seen in relation to whether GOP control would be strengthened or weakened. The GOP retained control in the next five elections. A significant electoral tide in 2006 gave the Democrats control of both chambers, which they improved on in 2008. That was followed by the Republican congressional landslide of 2010 and the return of divided government when the GOP took the House. Divided government was maintained in 2012, with modest Democratic gains in both chambers. During the 2014 midterms, the Republicans managed to gain a net thirteen House seats and nine Senate seats, giving them control of both chambers for the first time since 2006. Although the Republicans lost a net of six House seats and two Senate seats in 2016, they maintained control of both chambers, giving them unified party control of Congress coupled with a Republican president at the start of the 115th Congress in 2017.

The modest Democratic gains in both chambers in 2016 maintained roughly the same political balance as in the previous Congress, a close division in which moderate members were still important. This should be seen in the context of a long-term decline of such members in the Congress and an increase in the number of conservative Republicans and liberal Democrats. Forty years ago, there was considerable ideological "overlap" between the political parties. The Democrats had a substantial conservative contingent, mostly from the South, that was as conservative as the right wing of the Republican Party. Similarly the GOP had a contingent (primarily northeasterners) whose members were as liberal as northern Democrats. In addition each party had a significant number of moderate members. During the intervening years, however, because of changes in the electorate and in the Congress, this overlap between the parties began to disappear.[71] By the mid-1980s both parties in the House and Senate had become more politically homogeneous, and that homogeneity continued to increase in subsequent elections. In each chamber there was little departure from a complete ideological separation of the two parties.[72] Thus, in the 115th Congress that resulted from the 2016 elections, substantial majorities of each party had sharply different policy preferences from those in the other party, with a very small but potentially influential group of members in the middle.

The Trump Administration and Unified Government

Following Donald Trump's election as president along with unified Republican control of Congress, the Republicans had their best chance in a decade to advance their political agenda. Throughout the 2016 presidential campaign, Trump had made a variety of promises including the repeal and replacement of the Affordable Health Care Act ("Obamacare"), temporarily banning Muslims from entering the United States, building a wall between the United States and Mexico, pushing for a $1 trillion infrastructure bill, adding a conservative justice to the Supreme Court to replace Antonin Scalia, and cutting taxes. Despite having Republican control of both chambers, Trump opted to issue a number of executive orders and memoranda in his first few days in office in an attempt to deliver on several of his campaign promises. His first executive order, issued on January 20 within hours of his inauguration, declared Trump's intention to repeal the ACA passed approximately seven years earlier. Three days later he issued a presidential memorandum signaling his intent to withdraw from the TPP, a trade deal designed to lower tariffs for a number of Pacific Rim countries. On the same day he issued another memorandum freezing all hiring in the executive branch, except for the military, in an attempt to cut government spending and "waste."[73]

Over the course of the next week, President Trump issued three presidential memoranda approving construction of the Dakota Access and the Keystone XL Pipelines, with the third one requiring all pipeline materials used be built within the United States. He also issued an executive order cutting funding for sanctuary cities. Although many of his previous directives were perceived as controversial, this one immediately gained national attention after the city of San Francisco announced that it was suing the president for withholding funding, arguing that the order was unconstitutional.[74] On January 27 Trump issued arguably his most controversial executive action yet when he temporarily barred Muslims from Iran, Libya, Somalia, Sudan, and Yemen from entering the country for 90 days and Syrians from entering indefinitely.[75] This order prompted immediate outrage because it stranded hundreds of individuals at airports around the country. Within days a federal judge in Seattle declared the order unconstitutional, leading the Trump administration to revise the order in early March. However, that travel ban was also later struck down in federal courts in both Hawaii and Maryland.[76]

Research on the U.S. presidency suggests that chief executives are more likely to utilize unilateral tools like executive orders during periods of unified government.[77] Part of the rationale for this behavior is that presidents have more flexibility in issuing executive orders when their party is in control of Congress, especially if Congress is unable or unwilling to act as a result of gridlock or such decisions are perceived as controversial. Nevertheless, it is curious that Trump chose to pursue a unilateral strategy so early after being sworn into office, particularly because Congress had not yet had a chance to act. One factor in his decision to utilize unilateral tools may have been his relatively low levels of presidential approval. During the first four months of his presidency, for instance, his approval averaged around 40 percent, which is at least twenty points less than the same point among all of his predecessors for which we have public opinion data.[78]

Trump has also made a number of controversial statements and decisions, including firing FBI Director James Comey in early May and sharing classified information with the Russian ambassador, which led to widespread calls for further investigation into his actions and even talk of impeachment.[79] Indeed, on May 17, Rod Rosenstein, the deputy attorney general, appointed former FBI Director Robert Mueller III to serve as special counsel to continue the ongoing investigation into the Russian government's efforts "to influence the 2016 presidential election and related matters."[80] As we discuss in what follows, these developments may have been a significant factor in why Congress appeared reluctant at times to take up Trump's major policy initiatives.

The House: Testing Majority Party Control

Following the historic 1994 elections, the new Republican majority instituted major institutional changes in the 104th Congress that convened in 1995.[81] By comparison the changes in House organization for the 115th Congress were much more modest—although one proposed change proved rather controversial. On January 2, 2017, the House Republicans met in secret session and voted to eliminate the Office of Congressional Ethics, an independent body that had been created in 2008 to investigate scandals in the House. "House Republicans, led by Representative Robert W. Goodlatte of Virginia, had sought on Monday to prevent the office from pursuing investigations that might result in criminal charges. Instead, they wanted to allow lawmakers on the more powerful House Ethics Committee to shut down inquiries."[82] The party reversed course the following day, however, after legislators received thousands of phone calls condemning the action. Speaker Paul Ryan and House Majority Leader Kevin McCarthy also came out against the vote, recognizing that it sent the wrong message to the American people.

The inauspicious start to the 115th Congress was emblematic of a long string of conflicts between the Republican leadership and the party's rank and file during the past few years. The electoral landslide of 2010 had brought to the House a large Republican freshman class that was dominated by populist insurgents who identified with the Tea Party movement, many of which were still part of the Republican majority in the 115th Congress and who now identified with the Freedom Caucus. This group was suspicious of establishment Republicans and especially of former speaker John Boehner and the House leadership.[83] Throughout the 112th and subsequent Congresses, the leadership had significant difficulty in persuading the Tea Party wing to follow their lead, and this led to frequent problems with passing bills the leaders deemed necessary. The newly elected members wanted major changes in national policy (such as the complete repeal of "Obamacare"), and they were reluctant to compromise to get legislation passed. The GOP's internal conflicts brought the government close to a shutdown and a near default on the national debt, and these led to a temporary downgrade of the nation's debt rating.

Former Speaker Boehner struggled to maintain cohesion within the Republican caucus during his nearly 5 years as leader of the party. After repeatedly violating the "Hastert Rule" (named after the former GOP House Speaker Dennis Hastert of Illinois, which held the House should only take up bills that were backed by a majority of the majority party) during the 112th and 113th Congresses, Boehner sought to reassure the conservative wing of his party by saying that this was "not a practice that I would expect to continue long term."[84] Nevertheless, the Tea Party faction was not mollified, and some members proposed enshrining the Hastert Rule in the rules of the House Republican Conference.

At the start of the 113th Congress in 2013, several of the more conservative Republicans sought to deny Boehner the absolute majority of votes he needed for election to be speaker in light of his past behavior. The hope was that if a second ballot were forced, someone more acceptable might come forward to contest the election. And even if that did not happen, it would be a strong blow to Boehner's stature as leader. In the event, enough Republican members initially pledged not to vote for Boehner, but by the morning of the vote, a few members had changed their minds. As it was, twelve GOP members abstained or voted for others (as did all the Democrats), and Boehner narrowly won reelection.[85] Despite more internal partisan turmoil during the next two and half years, Boehner managed to hang onto the speakership until he announced his retirement on September 25, 2015, becoming the first speaker to voluntarily step down since Thomas "Tip" O'Neil did so in 1986. In discussing his decision to step down once a new speaker was named, Boehner explained, "My first job as speaker is to protect the institution [but] it had become clear to me that this prolonged leadership turmoil would do irreparable harm to the institution."[86]

Boehner had been grooming Eric Cantor, then majority leader, to take over his position as speaker until Cantor was defeated in a shocking primary upset in June 2014 by political amateur Dave Brat.[87] Kevin McCarthy succeeded Cantor as majority leader and was in line to become speaker once Boehner announced his impending departure. However, McCarthy's candidacy was damaged as a result of a remark made during an interview "in which he seemed to suggest that the Select Committee on Benghazi, the panel assembled by Republicans to investigate the 2012 attacks on U.S. facilities in Libya, was intended to damage Hillary Rodham Clinton's presidential poll numbers."[88] On October 8, 2015, McCarthy decided to withdraw his bid as a result of the fallout from this comment, leaving the party scrambling to find a replacement who could lead the fractious Republican Party. Several members of the conference immediately reached out to Paul Ryan (R-WI), chair of the House Ways and Means Committee and former vice-presidential nominee, asking him to consider running for the speakership. Although Ryan continued to insist that he was not interested in the job (as he had done for years), he eventually agreed to serve on the condition that the party unite behind him.[89] On Thursday, October 29, 2015, Paul Ryan was sworn in as the fifty-fourth speaker of the House of Representatives by a vote of 236–184.

Ryan's initial tenure as speaker was noticeably smoother than that of his predecessor, but tensions within the party began to emerge during the second session of the 114th Congress. Key members of the House Freedom Caucus had been critical of Ryan since he took over in fall 2015, but things began to escalate when then candidate Donald Trump refused to endorse Ryan during his primary campaign because Ryan had been critical of some of Trump's recent actions. After the tape was released in early October with Trump making lewd comments toward women, Ryan sought to further distance himself from the Republican nominee, much to the chagrin of some of the more conservative members of the caucus. Such controversy seemed to be short-lived once Trump tapped Reince Priebus to be his chief of staff, however. Priebus had previously served as the chair of the Republican National Committee and was a boyhood friend of Ryan.[90] With the announcement that one of the leaders of the Freedom Caucus, Mark Meadows (R-NC), would continue to support Ryan as speaker, any efforts to support someone else quickly dissipated.

Despite some early setbacks as noted, the 115th Congress represented a chance for the Republicans to advance their legislative agenda. Paul Ryan was sworn in again as speaker, and the Republicans had unified control of government for the first time since 2006. On the Democratic side, Nancy Pelosi (D-CA) continued as minority leader, and Steny Hoyer (D-MD) was reelected as minority whip. The first major bill considered in the 115th Congress was the repeal and replacement of the ACA ("Obamacare") with the American Health Care Act. This was a critical piece of legislation for President Trump and the Republicans in Congress because it had been such an important issue during the 2016 campaign. Trump had promised on more than one occasion that the ACA would be repealed, and Republicans had been eager to replace the legislation since it had first been passed. In the end, however, it proved to be more challenging than the Republicans initially expected.

Although members of the Republican conference were unanimous in their desire to repeal Obamacare, they recognized the need to replace it with something more acceptable to members of their party. Initially they conducted negotiations over the legislation in secret behind closed doors, and only key Republican members were privy to the specifics of the bill. Eventually, however, details about the bill began to emerge. "The Republican bill would have repealed tax penalties for people without health insurance, rolled back federal insurance standards, reduced subsidies for the purchase of private insurance and set new limits on spending for Medicaid, the federal-state program that covers more than 70 million low-income people."[91] Ryan claimed the bill included "huge conservative wins," but most members of the Freedom Caucus felt it did not go far enough with respect to eliminating what were perceived as imperfect provisions of the ACA. Additionally, the bill failed to attract support of more moderate Republican members "who were anxiously aware of the Congressional Budget Office's assessment that the bill would leave 24 million more Americans without insurance in 2024, compared with the number who would be uninsured under the current law."[92] Others feared that insurance premiums would increase under the Republican plan, and Americans approaching retirement would be hardest hit with the rising costs.

Despite mounting criticism of the bill, the Republicans managed to schedule a floor vote to repeal and replace Obamacare in late March 2017 that would have coincided with passage of the ACA seven years earlier. However, the attempt ultimately failed as a result of growing dissension within the Republican ranks. At least thirty members of the Republican conference, including key members of the Freedom Caucus, made it clear that they could not support the Republican plan. As a result Paul Ryan had no choice but to postpone and eventually cancel scheduled votes on March 23 and 24.[93] In his remarks later that Friday, Ryan proclaimed, "We're going to be living with Obamacare for the foreseeable future."[94] The failed attempt ultimately drew the ire of President Trump, who initially blamed Democrats for the bill's defeat. The failure later led him to suggest that he might have to reach out to Democrats to craft a new bill as well as campaign against members of the Freedom Caucus in retribution during the 2018 midterm elections.[95]

Following the failed attempt to repeal Obamacare, the Republicans met in a closed-door meeting the following week to try to bridge the divide between various factions in the party. Initially Ryan approached members of the Freedom Caucus in an attempt to assuage some of their concerns on health care reform. Although several members of the caucus indicated their willingness to work with the leadership, provisions of the bill that would remove protections for those who were insured, defund

Planned Parenthood, and cut subsidies for the elderly and low-income earners turned off some of the moderate Republicans.[96] Efforts to bring a modified version of the bill to the floor in early April failed because the Republicans lacked the votes needed to pass it in the House. After yet another setback to their agenda, some members of the caucus began to question the ability of the party to effectively govern despite unified control of government. In the words of Tom Cole (R-OK), "We've been dysfunctional for a while. We were able to stay relatively united against President Obama. But we have not been able to be united as a governing party, and that's got to be worked through."[97]

Republicans would eventually get another chance at repealing and replacing Obamacare, but first they had to avert a government shutdown. On April 28, the House approved a continuing resolution by a 382–30 bipartisan vote, and the Senate approved the measure by voice vote, that would maintain funding at current levels for another week. This gave Republicans more time to come up with a spending package that would fund the government through September 30 (the end of the fiscal year). The vote came just shy of Trump's hundredth day in office, when White House officials had hoped to have more significant legislative accomplishments to claim credit for. "House Republicans left the Capitol with their goal of voting to repeal the Affordable Care Act still eluding them—and eluding Mr. Trump, who will conclude his first 100 days on Saturday without a marquee legislative achievement."[98] Additionally, Mark Meadows (R-NC), chair of the House Freedom Caucus, remarked, "I would love to have had the vote in the first 100 days." However, in noting that it took much longer for the Democrats to initially pass the ACA in place initially, he added, "If it takes another couple of days, then so be it."[99]

Although Congress passed a $1.1 trillion spending bill the following week that would fund the government through the remainder of the fiscal year, it was not the version that House Republicans originally envisioned. On Wednesday, May 3, the House passed the bill 309–118, but the Republican conference split 132–103 on the final vote, arguing that the bill made too many concessions to the Democrats (who had supported the bill 178–15). The following day the Senate adopted the legislation by a 79–18 vote before sending it to Trump for his signature. With the potential threat of a filibuster in the Senate, the Democrats were able to achieve many of their objectives in the early stages of negotiation, such as denying funding for the wall on the U.S.-Mexico border and maintaining federal funding for Planned Parenthood. Even though the final version of the bill did include provisions for modest increases to military spending and border security, many Republicans in the House expressed their displeasure with the outcome.[100]

With the passage of the spending bill behind them, Republicans in the House were able to renew their attention on passing a revised health care bill. After nearly a month of negotiations, the Republicans narrowly approved legislation on Thursday, May 4, to repeal and replace the ACA. Among its various provisions, the updated bill would roll back expansion of Medicaid that had occurred under the ACA, eliminate tax penalties for persons who chose not to purchase health insurance, and replace government-subsidized insurance policies with varying tax credits based on a person's age. Although no Democrats voted in favor of the bill, and twenty Republicans opted to vote against it, the bill managed to pass the House by a vote of 217–213. President Trump immediately called a press conference to celebrate the legislative victory, even though the Senate had yet to consider the bill. Despite its passage, "[t]he House measure faces profound uncertainty in the Senate, where a handful of Republican senators immediately rejected it, signaling that they would start work on a new version of the bill virtually from scratch."[101] On top of that, the Congressional Budget Office announced in late May that the new bill would leave as many as 23 million people without health insurance by 2026, making it even more difficult for senators to embrace the House's version of the bill.[102]

The Senate: How Effective Is Majority Control?

The surprising success of the Republicans in the 2016 Senate elections, despite the large number of Republican seats up for reelection, offered little pressure for a leadership change. At the start of the 115th Senate, Senators Mitch McConnell of Kentucky and John Cornyn of Texas were reelected as majority leader and majority whip, respectively, posts they have both held since January of 2015. On the Democratic side, Chuck Schumer of New York was elected as minority leader (replacing retiring Senator Harry Reid of Nevada), and Dick Durbin of Illinois continued as the Democratic whip, a position he has held since 2005.

The Senate has always been predominantly a men's club, but that has been gradually changing in recent decades. The Senate membership resulting from the 2016 elections varied significantly in gender diversity. The number of female Democrats remained the same at sixteen, whereas the number of female Republicans increased from four to five. As a result a record 21 percent of the senators serving in the 115th Congress were women, 33 percent of the Democrats and 10 percent of the Republicans. By comparison, eighty-three women were elected to the U.S. House in 2016, which constitutes 19.1 percent of the 435 members.[103]

The central organizational issue at the start of the 115th Congress was whether there would be a change in the rules regarding the Senate's distinctive practice of the filibuster for Supreme Court nominations. Also known as *extended debate*, the filibuster refers to an effort to prevent resolution of a measure under consideration in the Senate by refusing to end discussion of it. Unlike the House, where debate can be ended by a simple majority vote at any time, Senate consideration can only be terminated against the will of those who would continue by invoking "cloture." Under Senate rules, cloture requires sixty votes, except on a proposal to change Senate rules, when the support of two-thirds of those voting is needed.[104]

The incidence of filibusters and cloture efforts, and their relevance to the legislative process, has increased greatly over the last six decades. In the seven congresses from 1947 through 1960, motions to invoke cloture were filed only four times, and none were approved. Filibusters were rare and were almost always employed by southerners in an attempt to block civil rights bills. Then, gradually, as partisan polarization came to characterize the Senate, the scope of topics for filibusters broadened, and their frequency increased. In the five congresses from 2007 through 2016, for instance, 772 cloture motions were filed and were successfully invoked 413 times.[105]

The increased use of filibusters has made it more difficult and costly for the majority party to secure passage of the bills it favors. As a consequence some senators in the majority have sought to alter the Senate's rules to place limits on what could be filibustered or how many votes would be required to impose cloture. Of course members of the minority would be unlikely to support such efforts, and they would be likely to use the filibuster to block them. As noted, Senate rules specify that motions to invoke cloture on attempted rules changes require even more votes than such efforts on regular legislation. But some members and outside observers contend that the rule does not apply at the opening of a congress and that only the vote of a majority is then necessary to end debate and adopt an alternative rule. Whether such an interpretation (dubbed the "nuclear option" by participants) would be applied in a particular instance would depend on whether the presiding officer of the Senate, the vice president, so ruled and whether that ruling was upheld by a majority of senators. A significant proportion of the senators of both parties have accepted the view that a simple majority was sufficient to impose cloture on a rules change when they were in the minority (and the same people have often taken the opposite view when in the majority).

In 2005 the nuclear option in the Senate gained national attention when Majority Leader Bill Frist (R-TN) threatened to invoke it to put an end to Democratic filibusters of President George W. Bush's judicial nominees by a simple majority vote. When the Democrats promised to shut down the Senate and prevent any legislation from being considered if the practice was implemented, a group of seven Democratic and seven Republican senators (known as the Gang of 14) agreed in principle to oppose the nuclear option and the filibuster of judicial nominees.[106] After the GOP Senate gains of 2010, Democrats began talking about changing the cloture rules by a majority vote, but a confrontation was avoided by a "gentleman's agreement" between the two party leaders that purported to limit the scope of filibusters. Harry Reid and many Democrats were unhappy with the operation of that agreement, and after the 2012 elections, Democrats again raised the specter of a rules change. Indeed, in late November 2012, Reid flatly predicted that Senate Democrats would vote to limit Republican use of the filibuster in the new congress, although many observers questioned whether he actually had the votes to effect the change.[107]

When the new Senate convened in 2013, a confrontation over the nuclear option was initially avoided by negotiations between the party leaders and other members. However, by July of that year, the Senate Democratic majority came within hours of invoking the nuclear option in light of Republican opposition to several of President Obama's executive branch appointments. Although the president decided to withdraw two of the nominations at the last moment, thus preserving the minority's ability to filibuster nominations, the victory was short-lived. By late November 2013 Senator Reid decided that action finally had to be taken. On November 21, "the Senate approved the most fundamental alteration of its rules in more than a generation on Thursday, ending the minority party's ability to filibuster most presidential nominees in response to the partisan gridlock that has plagued Congress for much of the Obama administration."[108] As a result of the change, which passed by a narrow fifty-two to forty-eight vote, the Senate can effectively cut off debate on executive and judicial branch nominees with a simple majority rather than with sixty votes as had previously been necessary. However, the new rule did not apply to Supreme Court nominations or legislation under consideration in the Senate.[109]

Republicans were initially furious with Reid's decision to "go nuclear" and warned that the Democrats would regret their action if they lost control of the Senate in the future. In fact, when the Republicans won back control of the Senate in 2014 and maintained a majority in the 2016 elections, some Democrats began to lament the decision to trigger the nuclear option.[110] Indirectly this also shaped the discussion over potential Supreme Court vacancies, especially after Justice Scalia's unexpected death in February 2016. Although some Democrats privately wished the nuclear option had included appointments to the Supreme Court as a result of the vacancy caused by Scalia's death, it ended up being a moot point because Republicans controlled a majority of the seats in the 114th Senate and would have likely blocked any of President Obama's nominees. Indeed, even before the president nominated U.S. Court of Appeals Justice Merrick Garland on March 16, 2016, to fill Scalia's seat on the Court, Senate Majority Leader Mitch McConnell said that the Senate should not hold a vote on any Supreme Court nominee during the president's final year in office.[111] Democrats were understandably outraged by this statement, but it later came to light that then Senator Joe Biden had made a similar remark about filling Supreme Court appointments in 1992 during President Bush's last year in office.[112] In the end Scalia's seat remained vacant for the remainder of the year given the Republicans' reluctance to move forward with the Garland nomination.

Within days of being sworn in as the forty-fifth president of the United States, Donald Trump nominated Neil Gorsuch on January 31, 2017, to fill the vacant seat on the Supreme Court that was formerly held by Scalia. In late March the Senate held confirmation hearings for Gorsuch, which lasted for a total of four days. On April 3, the Judiciary Committee approved Gorsuch by an eleven to nine vote, and the nomination was sent to the Senate floor for consideration the following day. When the Democrats proceeded to filibuster Gorsuch's nomination, Mitch McConnell elected to fully extend the nuclear option that had been invoked back in November 2013 to now include Supreme Court nominees. As a result Gorsuch was confirmed on April 7, 2017, by a fifty-four to forty-five vote that included three Democrats joining all the Republicans in attendance and was sworn in as the 113th justice of the Supreme Court later that day.[113] As before none of the changes adopted affected the ability of senators to filibuster final passage votes on bills, so the strength of that tactic for blocking action remains in effect.

At the end of May, President Trump expressed frustration that the Senate had yet to take up the health care bill passed previously by the House as well as his tax reform legislation. At one point he urged the Republican Senate leadership to change the chamber rules to allow any legislation to pass by a simple majority vote as they had done with votes on Supreme Court nominees to expedite the passage of his key agenda items. Several commentators noted this was not really necessary because these bills could already be considered via reconciliation, which only requires approval by a majority of those in the Senate. Very few Republican senators seemed interested in Trump's proposal given that it would have enormous implications for their ability to object to legislation should they become the minority again in the future.[114]

In mid-June, Senate Republicans announced that they were close to scheduling a vote on their version of the health care bill to repeal and replace "Obamacare." Much of the discussion on the bill had occurred behind closed doors, but the bill's proponents initially argued that it sought to address many of the problems with the House version passed in May. Before the Senate had a chance to schedule a vote, however, the Congressional Budget Office announced that the Senate version of the bill would leave 22 million more people uninsured over the next 10 years.[115] As a result of this announcement, Senate leaders had no choice but to postpone a vote on the bill until after the July 4th recess because five Republican senators indicated they could not support this bill in light of the new estimates.[116] The vote on the Senate bill was again delayed in mid-July when Senator John McCain underwent surgery to remove a blood clot from behind his left eye as his vote was viewed as necessary to reach the fifty-vote threshold for passage.[117] Two days later Majority Leader Mitch McConnell announced that the Senate would no longer focus on trying to pass their own version of the health care bill in light of growing opposition to the plan among Republican senators. Instead they would now focus on dismantling the existing law.[118]

By late July the possibility of trying to dismantle the ACA seemed even less likely when at least three senators announced they would not support repealing existing law without some form of replacement.[119] On July 25, however, the Senate managed to schedule a motion to proceed on health care reform once John McCain flew back to Washington, DC, less than a week after being diagnosed with brain cancer. The motion ultimately passed by a vote of fifty-one to fifty (Vice President Mike Pence broke the 50-50 tie). Both Susan Collins (R-ME) and Lisa Murkowski (R-AK) defected on the motion and voted with the Democrats, thus necessitating the vice president's tie-breaking vote. Later that evening the Senate attempted to pass an initial amendment introduced to strip many of the provisions of the existing health care law, but it ultimately failed on a fifty-seven to forty-three vote including nine GOP defections.[120] In the early morning hours on July 28, the Senate sought to repeal portions of the ACA (the so-called slimmed-down version), but it failed when Republican Senators Susan Collins (ME), Lisa Murkowski (AK), and John McCain (AZ) along with all forty-eight Democrats voted against it.[121] As of December 2017, the status of the Republican health care bill remains uncertain despite considerable time and effort devoted to repealing the existing law.

THE 2018 ELECTIONS AND BEYOND

Expectations about midterm elections are usually shaped by a strong historical pattern: The party of the president lost strength in the House in twenty-five of the twenty-nine midterm elections since the beginning of the twentieth century. The first column in Table 9-8 shows the magnitude of these losses in midterms since World War II. They average 25.2 seats for the president's party. There was, however, considerable variation in the outcomes, from the sixty-three-seat loss by the Democrats in 2010 to the six-seat Republican gain in 2002. When thinking about the concept of midterm loss, one needs to keep in mind how long the president has served in office. During the first midterm election of his tenure, for instance, the president may be able to make a plausible appeal that he has not had enough time to bring about substantial change or to solidify many achievements. Moreover, even if things are not going very well, voters may not be inclined to blame a president who has served for such a short time. But four years later (if the president is fortunate enough to face a second midterm), appeals of too little time are unlikely to be persuasive. After six years, if the economy

Table 9-8 House Seat Losses by the President's Party in Midterm Elections, 1946–2014

Year	All Elections	First Term of Administration	Later Term of Administration
1946	55 Democrats		55 Democrats
1950	29 Democrats		29 Democrats
1954	18 Republicans	18 Republicans	
1958	47 Republicans		47 Republicans
1962	4 Democrats	4 Democrats	
1966	47 Democrats		47 Democrats
1970	12 Republicans	12 Republicans	
1974	43 Republicans		43 Republicans
1978	11 Democrats	11 Democrats	
1982	26 Republicans	26 Republicans	
1986	5 Republicans		5 Republicans
1990	9 Republicans	9 Republicans	
1994	52 Democrats	52 Democrats	
1998	(+5) Democrats		(+5) Democrats
2002	(+6) Republicans	(+6) Republicans	
2006	30 Republicans		30 Republicans
2010	63 Democrats	63 Democrats	
2014	13 Democrats		13 Democrats
Average Seat Loss			
	25.2 seats	21.0 seats	29.3 seats

Source: Compiled by the authors.

or foreign policy is not going well, voters may seek a policy change by reducing the number of the president's partisans in Congress.

The second and third columns in Table 9-8 indicate that this is what has usually happened in the past. Losses by the president's party in the first midterm election of a presidency have tended to be much smaller than losses in subsequent midterms.[122]

Indeed, with the exception of the results in 1986, 1994, 1998, 2002, and 2010, the two categories yield two sets of outcomes that are sharply different from one another. In the six midterm elections besides 1994, 2002, and 2010 that took place during a first term, the president's party lost between four and twenty-six seats, with an average loss of thirteen. In the seven elections after the first term (excluding 1986 and 1998), the range of losses was between thirteen and fifty-five seats, with an average loss of thirty-eight. (We will discuss the atypical years later.)

Models of House Elections

In the 1970s and 1980s, a number of political scientists constructed and tested models of congressional election outcomes, focusing especially on midterms, seeking to isolate the factors that most strongly influenced the results. The earliest models, constructed by Tufte and by Jacobson and Samuel Kernell, focused on two variables: presidential approval and a measure of the state of the economy.[123] Tufte hypothesized a direct influence by these forces on voter choice and election outcomes. The theory was that an unpopular president or a poor economy would cause the president's party to lose votes and, therefore, seats in the House. In essence the midterm elections were viewed as a referendum on the performance of the president and his party.

Jacobson and Kernell, on the other hand, saw more indirect effects of presidential approval and the economy. They argued that these forces affected election results by influencing the decisions of potential congressional candidates. If the president is unpopular and the economy is in bad shape, potential candidates will expect the president's party to perform poorly. As a consequence strong potential candidates of the president's party will be more inclined to forgo running until a better year, and strong candidates from the opposition party will be more inclined to run because they foresee good prospects for success. According to Jacobson and Kernell, this mix of weak candidates from the president's party and strong opposition candidates will lead to a poor election performance by the party occupying the White House. To measure this predicted relationship, their model related the partisan division of the vote to presidential approval and the economic situation early in the election year. This, they argued, is when decisions to run for office are being made, not at the time of the election, so it is not appropriate to focus on approval and the economy at that time. This view has come to be called the "strategic politicians hypothesis."[124]

Subsequent research built from this base. One model, developed by Alan I. Abramowitz, Albert D. Cover, and Helmut Norpoth, considered a new independent variable: short-term party evaluations.[125] They argued that voters' attitudes about the economic competence of the political parties affect the impact of presidential approval and economic conditions on voting decisions. If the electorate judges that the party holding the presidency is better able to deal with the problems voters regard as most serious, the negative impact of an unpopular president or a weak economy will be reduced. The authors concluded from their analysis of both aggregate votes and responses to surveys in midterm elections that there is evidence for their "party competence" hypothesis.

All of these models used the division of the popular vote as the variable to be predicted, and they focused only on midterm elections. Later work merged midterm results with those of presidential years, contending that there should be no conceptual distinction between them. These efforts sought to predict changes in seats without reference to the division of the vote. For example, a study by Bruce I. Oppenheimer, James A. Stimson, and Richard W. Waterman argued that the missing piece in the congressional election puzzle is the degree of "exposure" or "the excess or deficit number of seats a party holds measured against its long-term norm."[126] If a party wins more House seats than normal, those extra seats will be vulnerable in the next election, and the party is likely to suffer losses. Thus the party that wins a presidential election does not automatically benefit in House elections. But if the president's party does well in the House races, it will be more vulnerable in the subsequent midterm elections. Indeed the work by Oppenheimer and his colleagues predicted only small Republican losses for 1986 because Reagan's large 1984 victory was not accompanied by substantial congressional gains for his party. The actual result in 1986 was consistent with this prediction, for the GOP lost only five seats.

Another model of House elections was constructed by Robin F. Marra and Charles W. Ostrom, Jr.[127] They developed a "comprehensive referendum voting model" of both presidential year and midterm elections and included factors such as changes in the level of presidential approval, party identification, foreign policy crises, scandals, and unresolved policy disputes. The model also incorporated measures reflecting hypothesized relationships in the models we discussed earlier: the level of presidential approval, the state of the economy, the strategic politicians' hypothesis, exposure, and party competence. The model was tested on data from all congressional elections from 1950 through 1986.

The Marra-Ostrom analysis showed significant support for a majority of the predicted relationships. The results indicated that the most powerful influences affecting congressional seat changes were presidential approval (directly and through various events) and exposure. The model was striking in its statistical accuracy: the average error in the predicted change was only four seats. The average error varied little whether presidential or midterm years were predicted, and the analysis demonstrated that the usually greater losses for the president's party in second midterm years resulted from negative shifts in presidential approval, exposure, and scandals. However, when the empirical analysis was extended by Ostrom and Brian Newman to include the election years from 1988 through 1998, the accuracy of the model declined.[128] They produced a revised model that included some additional variables. In particular they found that the relative number of open seats held by the two parties was important in determining losses. Moreover, once that variable was taken into account, the importance of the exposure variable decreased. That is, the most important form of exposure was open seats; incumbents were less vulnerable.

Drawing on the insights of these various models, we can see how these factors may influence outcomes in the 2018 House elections. How well the economy is doing and what proportion of the voters approves of Trump's performance early in the year may encourage or discourage high-quality potential challengers. The same variables close to election time may lead voters to support or oppose Republican candidates based on their judgments of the job the Trump administration is doing. The usual midterm losses happen for predictable reasons; they are not part of the laws of nature. Therefore, if the usual reasons for such losses (such as a recession or an unpopular president) are not present in 2018, we should not expect the consequent losses to occur or at least not the magnitude of losses that history might lead us to expect. This is why the president's party gained seats in the midterms of 1998 and 2002. If, on the other hand, those reasons are present, the context will be quite different.

During the summer of 2017, Trump's approval remained low relative to other presidents at this early stage of the presidency. If his approval numbers do not improve throughout the year and into 2018, this could have significant consequences for the 2018 midterm elections. Trump has held steady at approximately 40 percent approval since mid-March, but his overall level of disapproval has fluctuated between 50 and 55 percent, which is much higher than normal for this early in a president's first year in office.[129] With respect to the economy, there was a very modest increase in early 2017, but growth was lower than during the last quarter of 2016. If the economy improves further and Trump's popularity begins to approach 50 percent, Republicans could be insulated from significant losses in the upcoming midterm elections. On the other hand recent scandals in the administration (the Comey firing and ongoing questions about Trump and his family's connection with Russia) may further undermine the president's approval rating. Additionally the models we discussed indicate that other considerations may be important. Republican exposure is relatively high due to the gains they made in 2010 and 2014, and to this point there appears to be a greater proportion of Republican departures or retirements from the House. This could create more opportunities for Democrats than normal if these trends persist.

With regard to quality candidates emerging to run, Democrats are at least as aware of the pattern of midterm losses as are political scientists, so potential candidates may regard the political landscape as encouraging. Given any potential backlash against Trump in 2018, that same landscape might make recruiting challengers a bit easier than usual despite the structural advantage Republicans have in the House in light of how rural seats are distributed.[130] In March 2017, for instance, "EMILY's List announced . . . that more than 10,000 women have reached out to the group since Hillary Clinton lost the presidential election to say they want to run for office, a record number in such a short time for the group."[131] Additionally the Democratic Party is seeking to recruit candidates with military backgrounds to run against Republican incumbents in 2018, with fifteen veterans already committed to launch House campaigns as of May 2017.[132] In addition to each of these considerations, the impact of events like crises and scandals in the Marra-Ostrom model reminds us that there are many unforeseeable events that may influence the 2018 congressional election results.

Some Additional Considerations about House Races

A few further points related to the previous discussion are necessary to complete our analysis of the prospects for 2018 House races. The vulnerability of individual members varies between parties and across other attributes, and we should not expect those distributions to be similar from election to election. For example, in one year a party may have a relatively high percentage of freshmen or members who won by narrow margins in the preceding election, whereas in another year the party's proportion of such potentially vulnerable members may be low. As Table 9-9 shows, both parties have a roughly similar (and relatively small) number of members who won with less than 55 percent of the vote. Eleven Republicans and twenty-one Democrats fell into this category. There are fewer close races for each party than the number that resulted from the 2000 elections, and it is substantially fewer than the total of ninety-five after 1996 (also two years after a Republican landslide). It is in this type of district that strong challengers are most likely to come forward and where the challengers who do run are most able to raise adequate campaign funds. Thus, based solely on these election-margin figures, the political landscape does not present a very attractive prospect for challengers of either party.

As our earlier analysis indicates, the parties' respective success in recruiting strong candidates for open seats and to oppose the other party's incumbents can be expected to play a significant role in shaping outcomes for 2018. Both Democratic and Republican campaign organizations were actively pursuing recruits during 2017, with some early successes and some disappointments. The personal and financial costs of candidacies and the difficulty of defeating an incumbent often make recruitment difficult, and the unique circumstances of each party make the task harder. In late January 2017 the DCCC identified approximately sixty House seats they plan to target in 2018, including some congressional districts carried by President Trump in the 2016 elections.[133] Nevertheless, they still face an uphill battle to win back control of Congress. On the Republican side, the RNCC is seeking to mitigate potential losses as a result of departures and retirements from Congress. We will return to these issues at the end of this section.

Even when the party organizations do recruit strong challengers, this offers no guarantee of electoral success. For example, in a Kansas special House election in April 2017 (to replace Mike Pompeo, who Donald Trump appointed to be the new

Table 9-9 Percentage of Vote Received by Winning House Candidates, by Party and Type of Race, 2016

	Republican			Democrat		
	Reelected Incumbent	Successful Challenger	Open-Seat Winner	Reelected Incumbent	Successful Challenger	Open-Seat Winner
55 or less	8	1	2	11	6	4
55.1–60	37	0	7	26	0	5
60.1–70	98	0	8	53	0	4
70.1–100	72	0	8	78	0	7
Total	215	1	25	168	6	20

Source: Compiled by the authors.

Note: Table shows the number of districts that meet the criteria for each cell. Open seats include races in which an incumbent lost a primary.

CIA director), the GOP candidate, Ron Estes, was a state treasurer from the district. Moreover, a Republican had represented the district for over two decades, and Trump carried it by twenty-seven points in November. The Democrats nominated James Thompson, a Wichita civil rights lawyer with no experience in public office. Although Estes went on to win the special election, it turned out to be much closer than expected with a vote of 53 to 46 percent in the district. Many pundits regarded this race as a preview of what might occur in the 2018 elections, especially if voters viewed the midterm as a potential referendum against President Trump.[134]

Just over a week after the Kansas special election, a second critical test for Republicans came in the form of a special election in Georgia's sixth district. Tom Price resigned from the seat in early 2017 after being confirmed as the U.S. secretary of health and human services in the Trump administration. As a result several candidates emerged from both parties to vie for the April 18 primary election in the open seat—five Democrats and eleven Republicans. Although the Democrats quickly coalesced their support around Jon Ossoff, a former congressional aide, Republican leaders and voters had a much harder time deciding whom to support among the top five or six candidates in the pool, most of whom had previous elective experience. Given the symbolic nature of the race in light of the upcoming midterm elections, and the fact that Trump carried the district by a narrow margin, Democrats saw it as a real opportunity to win back a seat from the Republicans. As a result donations poured into the race in unprecedented amounts—Ossoff raised over $8 million prior to the April election, and $14 million in outside spending was used to fund a series of political commercials.

Jon Ossoff went on to earn slightly more than 48 percent in the primary, with Republican Karen Handel coming in second with nearly 20 percent of the vote. Under Georgia law, if no candidate receives a majority of votes in the special election, the first- and second-place finishers then go to a runoff election, which was held on June 20, 2017. Many Democrats viewed this as a potentially winnable race, although Republicans did everything in their power to keep the seat under Republican control, including having Paul Ryan campaign on Handel's behalf in May and Vice President Mike Pence visit the district the second week of June.[135] By the time the runoff election was held, nearly $60 million was spent on the race, making it the most expensive U.S. House election in history.[136] Karen Handel ultimately defeated Jon Ossoff 51.9 to 48.1 percent in the special election despite the enormous sum spent by both sides.[137]

On May 25, a third special election was held in Montana, following Representative Ryan Zinke's decision to vacate the seat in March to serve as Trump's interior secretary. Although Trump carried Montana by twenty points in the presidential election and Zinke won reelection by sixteen points, Democrats still were undeterred. Republicans fielded Greg Gianforte in the special election, who had lost Montana's gubernatorial election in fall 2016 by nearly four points. His opponent was Rob Quist, a small businessman and entrepreneur with no prior political experience. Given Gianforte's previous electoral defeat and partially due to what was happening in the Georgia sixth district race, the Congressional Leadership Fund (the super PAC endorsed by the House GOP leadership) invested $2.7 million, whereas the DCCC spent only about half a million dollars in the race. During a rally on the night before the election, Gianforte physically attacked a reporter who asked him a question about the Republican health care plan and was later cited for misdemeanor assault. Despite this considerable lapse in judgment—Gianforte later apologized during his victory speech—he went on to win the race by about six points.[138]

Also worth noting here is the continuing impact of term limits in the states. Although the term limits movement during the 1990s failed to impose restrictions on members of Congress, it succeeded in imposing them on state legislators in fifteen states, and those limits continue to have an impact. One potential outlet for a state legislator who is ineligible to run for reelection is to seek a congressional seat. This may lead to a greater number of strong challengers in House races than would otherwise be the case. For example, California limits state legislators to twelve years combined in the two chambers, and a number of legislators will have to leave their current positions next year. Some of them are contemplating races against Republican members of the U.S. House as a result of enhanced recruitment efforts on the part of the DCCC.[139]

As we have discussed, the potential number of open seats is also relevant to questions of candidate recruitment and district vulnerability. Our analysis shows that open seats are more likely to switch parties than are those with incumbents, and that both parties are more likely to field strong candidates. As of October 2017 there were eleven confirmed retirements in the House, nine of which were Republicans: Carol Shea-Porter of New Hampshire, Niki Tsongas of Massachusetts (both Democrats), Lynn Jenkins of Kansas, Dave Trott of Michigan, Charlie Dent of Pennsylvania, Tim Murphy of Pennsylvania, John Duncan, Jr., of Tennessee, Sam Johnson of Texas, Jason Chaffetz of Utah, Dave Reichert of Washington, and Ileana Ros-Lehtinen of Florida—the latter of which could be a winnable seat for the Democrats in light of past voting trends.[140] However, there were also concerns that a number of representatives will leave the House to seek Senate seats or governorships, and by October 2017 eighteen members (eight Democrats and ten Republicans) had already committed to such races.[141] When Chaffetz announced his retirement on April 19 (effective June 30), the chair of the House Oversight Committee told his supporters that he would not seek reelection to Congress, or any office, in 2018.[142] Some suspect that Chaffetz's decision might be a signal that he plans to run for governor in state of Utah in 2020.[143]

Finally one should remember that the rules that shape elections are subject to change and that such changes can have a substantial impact on the pattern of election outcomes. One source of such change is the courts. In 2013 the U.S. Supreme Court struck down a provision of the Voting Rights Act in *Shelby County v. Holder* requiring many state and local governments, mainly in the South, to seek permission from the U.S. Justice Department or a federal court before they can make changes to certain voting procedures. The provision, which had been reauthorized by Congress in 2006, had been challenged on the grounds that such restrictions on the rights of states were no longer required. Five justices joined in an opinion by Chief Justice John Roberts in which he said that Congress was able to impose federal restrictions on states where voting rights were at risk, but it must do so based on contemporary data on discrimination which was not true in this instance. Although the Court left it open for Congress to pass a new law, several attempts since 2013 have failed, most likely a function of the increased polarization and gridlock in Congress. This case is likely to have significant consequences moving forward because many Republican-controlled state governments have pushed for and adopted new voting regulations in the years following the Court's decision.[144] Indeed many viewed the Supreme Court's May 2017 decision not to overturn the Fourth Circuit Court of Appeal's ruling to strike down a controversial North Carolina voter ID law as a victory for voting right's activists.[145] At the same time several states may have to redraw their congressional district boundaries as a result of ongoing legal challenges (including North Carolina).

As a consequence of all of the factors we have discussed, Republicans may have more reason for concern than Democrats, especially in light of Trump's meager approval ratings to date.[146] Although the twenty-four net gain the Democratic party needs to win a majority is not inconsequential, in the eighteen midterm elections since World War II, the president's party has lost that many seats nine times. Yet our analysis also indicates that Democratic success is not certain. We have seen that it is possible for the historical pattern to be broken under certain conditions. Perhaps the most relevant one for 2018 relates to the Republican Party's reputation with voters. Poll data from the Pew Research Center (supported by similar analyses in other polls) shows that the party's ratings stand at the highest point in seven years, with 47 percent of respondents indicating that they have a favorable view of the GOP and 49 percent seeing it unfavorably.[147] Whether those more favorable numbers will hold leading up to the 2018 midterms is unclear.

Senate Races in 2018

Because there are few Senate races and because they are relatively independent of one another, we have focused our discussion of 2018 on the House. We will now close with a few comments about the upper chamber's contests. Due to the six-year Senate terms, and the fact that these terms are staggered, the number of seats to be defended by each party varies from election to election. As was true in 2012, the Democrats hold most of the thirty-four seats that will be contested in 2018, with twenty-five seats—including independent senators Angus King (ME) and Bernie Sanders (VT)— compared to the Republicans' nine.[148] As a result, the GOP has more targets for gains, and some features of the landscape make the situation look even more attractive for them. As of October 2017, Bob Corker (R-TN) is the only senator to date to announce his retirement at the end of the 115th Congress. Nevertheless, "ten of the 25 Senate seats Democrats are defending are in states that voted for Donald Trump for president last year: Florida, Indiana, Michigan, Missouri, Montana, North Dakota, Ohio, Pennsylvania, West Virginia, and Wisconsin. Meanwhile, Republicans are defending just one seat in a state that Hillary Clinton won (Nevada)."[149] In light of the increasing nationalization of elections coupled with the fact that no state split their presidential and senatorial votes in 2016, this portends to be an uphill battle for the Democrats.

Although the numbers appear to favor the Republicans with respect to the 2018 Senate races at first glance, they only tell part of the story. If the Republicans successfully picked up most, if not all, of the vulnerable Democratic seats, they could have a filibuster-proof Senate in the 116th Congress assuming they held onto their own Republican seats in the process. However, one of the biggest challenges that the Republicans face is being able to recruit quality candidates to run against potentially vulnerable senators. We have seen that the kinds of candidates seeking office have a major influence on the outcome, and that parties, therefore, try to get the strongest candidates to come forward. In this cycle, however, some of the strongest potential challengers may decide 2018 does not represent the best set of circumstances to run for the Senate.

As of mid-summer, several high-profile Republicans have declined to challenge Democratic senators in some of the more competitive states, potentially because of President Trump's record-low approval levels. In Indiana, for instance, Representative Susan Brooks (R) has decided not to challenge Senator Joe Donnelly (D) in 2018, even though Trump carried the state by nineteen points and party officials believe she would be a formidable opponent. Still, early reports suggest that two other Republican House members might be considering running against Joe Donnelly—Luke Messer and Todd Rokia.[150] Although Representative Sean Duffy (R) briefly considered running against Senator Tammy Baldwin (D) in Wisconsin, he recently announced that he would forgo the bid for higher office, most likely due to the uphill nature of the battle—Trump only carried the state by one percentage point. "In Pennsylvania, four-term Rep. Patrick Meehan (R) was considering, then declined, to challenge Senator Bob Casey. Meehan would have been a bigger name than the two state lawmakers and one borough councilman who have jumped in so far to try to challenge Casey."[151]

As noted, the Democrats face formidable hurdles given the large number of Senate seats they must defend, particularly those in swing and Republican-leaning states previously carried by Trump. In West Virginia, for instance, Senator Joe Manchin III (D) is running for reelection in a state that Trump defeated Clinton by more than forty points.[152] In many ways this is an extreme example, but it illustrates the difficulties that Democrats face in trying to defend, let alone pick up, seats in the Senate. Even with Trump's relatively high levels of unpopularity in recent Gallup polls, Democrats need an ideal set of conditions going into the 2018 midterms to not fall further behind in the number of seats they control in the upper chamber. Although their prospects for picking up seats in the Senate will likely improve in 2020 when there are fewer Democratic seats up for reelection, the 2018 elections could represent an important symbolic victory if the Democrats can mitigate their potential losses.

To summarize, then, House election results are likely to depend heavily on the political context that exists both late in 2017 (when most candidate decisions are made) and in November of 2018. The context may also determine whether the historical pattern of midterm losses by the president's party occurs again or is broken as it was in both 1998 and 2002. For the Senate seats, on the other hand, the election results probably depend more on the circumstances in individual races, largely fought independently of one another.

Beyond 2018: Polarization and the Struggle for Control of Congress

Just as every election has implications for those that follow, the elections of 2018 will have an impact on subsequent contests. We do not know those results, so we cannot yet describe the effects, but a few general considerations are likely to have an impact on future congressional contests. The national demographic changes we have touched on in Chapter 2, and that we will discuss further in Chapter 11, will continue to be important. Although these shifts slowed somewhat due to reduced immigration during the economic slump, the proportion of the population that is made up of Latinos and other minorities will continue to grow. The Democrats are currently advantaged among these groups, and they will pursue strategies that seek to retain that advantage and that improve the activation of those constituencies, as demonstrated by efforts to frame the debate over immigration in recent congresses. Republicans, on the other hand, may look for ways to improve their standing among minorities, particularly Latinos. Indeed they will have to succeed to a degree if they are to remain competitive as the population distribution changes in the coming years.

The impact of the shifting demographics will be shaped by the Democratic Party's efforts to improve its reputation. The soul-searching that followed the unexpected failures of 2016 led Democrats to scramble after Hillary Clinton's loss, as individuals began jockeying within the party over who would assume the reins of leadership. Shortly after the election, "the country's first Muslim lawmaker and a prominent liberal voice in the House, Rep. Keith Ellison (D-MN), announced that he would run for chair of the Democratic National Committee."[153] Former U.S. secretary of labor under President Obama, Thomas "Tom" Perez also announced his candidacy for chair of the DNC on December 15, 2016. When the election was held on February 25, 2017, Perez was elected chair on the second ballot, narrowly defeating Ellison for the position, which led to visible frustration and outrage among Ellison's supporters. Within minutes of the election, he immediately named Ellison as his deputy chair, signaling to Ellison's supporters that he hoped to find a middle ground between the factions within the Democratic Party.[154]

Despite the initial controversy over who would be chosen to chair the Democratic Party, many party insiders welcome Perez's selection and what it represented for greater unity among Democrats. "Mr. Perez, 55, the son of Dominican immigrants, is the first Latino chairman of the Democratic Party. He was reared in Buffalo and has held a series of state and federal government jobs, most recently as Mr. Obama's labor secretary."[155] Although Perez has limited experience in electoral politics, he has already signaled that more attention needs to be given to House and Senate races in future elections. "Addressing reporters with Mr. Ellison after the election, Mr. Perez vowed to shift the committee from its overriding focus on presidential politics."[156] In the interim Democrats plan to focus their attention on the upcoming special elections in four House races and recruiting strong candidates for the thirty-six gubernatorial races taking place in 2018, which has long-term implications for redistricting in House districts during the next decade.[157]

Even though the Republicans currently have unified control of government, the party has its own share of concerns, especially given Trump's low approval ratings, various administrative scandals that have precipitated talk of impeachment, the current state of the economy and its impact, and the lack of policy successes to date. As noted, they are in a reasonably good position with the 2018 Senate elections given they will be defending nine of the thirty-four seats, nearly all in solidly Republican states (whereas ten of the Democratic senators must compete in more competitive states as reflected by presidential vote in the 2016 election). However, the Republicans in the House may be in a more precarious situation if Trump's approval ratings do not improve, citizens react adversely to the vote on health care reform, and more incumbents elect not to seek reelection as a result of unfavorable national tides. Although winning at least twenty-four additional seats in the House is no easy feat, the Democrats may be buoyed by additional missteps by the Trump administration as well as controversial policy decisions enacted during the remainder of the 115th Congress. A victory by the Democrats in one or both chambers would seem likely, however, to offer a continuation of divided government and the gridlock that now accompanies it.

CHAPTER TEN

THE CONGRESSIONAL ELECTORATE IN 2016

In the preceding chapter we viewed congressional elections at the district and state levels and saw how they formed a national result. In this chapter we consider congressional elections from the point of view of the individual voter, using the same ANES surveys we employed to study presidential voting. We discuss how social forces, issues, partisan loyalties, incumbency, and evaluations of congressional and presidential performance influence the decisions of voters in congressional elections. We also consider the existence and extent of presidential coattails in 2016.

SOCIAL FORCES AND THE CONGRESSIONAL VOTE

In general social forces relate to the congressional vote similarly to the way they do to the presidential vote (Table 10-1).[1] This has been true in our previous analyses of national elections, but the relationship is somewhat stronger in 2016 than it was in the 1980s and 1990s. Even though the aggregate vote for Democratic House candidates and the vote for Clinton vary across many of the categories we analyze, the relative performances are similar (see Table 5-1).[2] This may reflect the closer relationship between party identification and the vote in recent elections for both the president and Congress demonstrated in analyses by Larry M. Bartels.[3]

Consider, for example, the relationship between voting and gender. In the total electorate Hillary Clinton and House Democrats both received 49 percent of the vote. Among white female voters, Democrats did one point worse for the presidency than for the House, and they did three points worse among white males. (Except for the discussion of voting and race, the analysis here, as in Chapter 5, focuses on white voters.) The gender results are interesting when compared to the past. In 1988 there was a small gender gap in the presidential vote (about three points), with women more likely to vote Democratic than men, but there was no gap in the House vote. By 2000, however, the gender gap was more pronounced in the vote both for the president and for representatives; the major-party share of the vote was nine points more Democratic for women in the former case and ten points more Democratic in the latter. In 2004 gender differences were reduced in both types of races, with the Democratic advantage among women down to seven points for president and three points in House contests. And in 2016 the differences declined even further.

Table 10-1 How Social Groups Voted for Congress, 2016 (Percent)

Social Group	Democratic	Republican	Total	(N)
Total electorate	49	51	100	(1928)
Electorate, by race				
African American	86	14	100	(190)
White	42	58	100	(1429)
Other	62	38	100	(300)
Latinos (of any race)	66	34	100	(182)
Whites, by gender				
Female	42	58	100	(723)
Male	40	60	100	(697)
Whites, by region				
New England and Mid-Atlantic	56	44	100	(268)
North Central	34	66	100	(362)
South	25	75	100	(338)
Border	44	56	100	(135)
Mountain and Pacific	55	45	100	(326)
Whites, by birth cohort				
Before 1946	39	61	100	(233)
1947–1956	43	57	100	(264)
1957–1966	41	59	100	(330)
1967–1976	36	64	100	(213)
1977–1986	49	51	100	(193)
1987–1994	41	59	100	(105)
1995–1998	40	60	100	(66)
Whites, by level of education				
Not high school graduate	38	62	100	(62)
High school graduate	36	64	100	(343)
Some college	33	67	100	(439)
College graduate	42	58	100	(330)
Advanced degree	64	36	100	(247)

Social Group	Democratic	Republican	Total	(N)
Whites, by annual family income				
Less than $15,000	35	65	100	(98)
$15,000–34,999	46	54	100	(185)
$35,000–49,999	41	59	100	(150)
$50,000–74,999	36	64	100	(265)
$75,000–89,999	36	64	100	(150)
$90,000–124,999	40	60	100	(230)
$125,000–174,999	44	56	100	(159)
$175,000 and over	60	40	100	(135)
Whites, by union membership[a]				
Member	56	44	100	(251)
Nonmember	39	61	100	(1176)
Whites, by religion				
Protestant	32	68	100	(529)
Catholic	42	58	100	(297)
Jewish	85	15	100	(40)
None	63	37	100	(274)
White Protestants				
Born again	22	78	100	(287)
Not born again	45	55	100	(240)
Whites, by religious commitment				
Low or medium	46	54	100	(206)
High	23	77	100	(294)
Very high	29	71	100	(27)
White Protestants, by religious tradition				
Mainline	43	57	100	(243)
Evangelical	27	73	100	(150)

Source: Authors' analysis of the 2016 ANES.

Note: The numbers in parentheses are the totals on which the percentages are based. Numbers are weighted. The number in brackets is the total number in that category when there are fewer than ten total voters.

[a]Respondent or family member in union.

Democrats ran four points better among white women than among white men for president, whereas there was only a gender gap of 2 percent in the congressional vote.

The presidential and congressional voting patterns are similar within many other social categories, including race, education, and income. For both the presidential and the congressional vote, African Americans were substantially more likely to vote Democratic. The difference was fifty-one points for the presidential race and forty-four points in the House contests. Another similarity was regarding union-member voters, who were seventeen points more Democratic than non-union voters in the House vote, whereas they were twelve points more Democratic for president. In 2008 the pattern for the two offices was also similar, but it was smaller: eleven percentage points better for the House and nine points better for the presidency. In 2004, on the other hand, the relative performances were quite different, with the Democrats faring only seven points better among union members in House contests but nineteen points better in the presidential race.

There are some differences in the ways the presidential and congressional vote relate to income categories. The presidential data in Chapter 5 showed the tendency among whites to vote Democratic was strongest in the two categories near the top of the income ladder (45 and 53 percent, respectively). For the House vote, however, the Democratic vote among low-income voters was stronger than in the presidential vote, although the greatest amount of support came from the highest income category. Moreover, this is a great reversal from the past. As recently as the 2000 election, the tendency to vote Democratic tended to increase as income declined across the whole income spectrum, and in the three lowest income categories, white voters gave the party between 50 and 60 percent of the vote.

As for education Democratic performance was only slightly variable across categories (except for advanced degrees, where they did twenty-two percentage points better than any other category). For the presidency, on the other hand, the party's candidates did best in the top two categories. It is important to note, however, that all of these differences involve categories with relatively small numbers of respondents, so the results may simply be due to sampling variation. The bottom line is that overall, presidential and congressional voting among social groups was fairly similar in 2016.

ISSUES AND THE CONGRESSIONAL VOTE

In Chapter 6 we analyzed the impact of issues on the presidential vote in 2016. Any attempt to conduct a parallel analysis for congressional elections is hampered by limited data. One interesting perspective on issues in the congressional vote is gained by asking whether voters are affected by their perceptions of where candidates stand on the issues. For a considerable time previous analysis has demonstrated a relationship between a voter's perception of House candidates' positions on a liberal-conservative issue scale and the voter's choice,[4] and we found similar relationships in 2016 (although clearly weaker for conservatives). For example, among self-identified liberals in the ANES survey who viewed the Democratic House candidate as more liberal than the Republican candidate ($N = 257$), 97 percent voted Democratic; among self-identified conservatives who saw the Republican House candidate as more conservative than the Democrat ($N = 498$), only 84 percent voted Republican.

Research by Alan I. Abramowitz sheds additional light on this question. In two articles he used ANES surveys to demonstrate a relationship between candidate ideology and voter choice in both House and Senate elections.[5] For the 1978 Senate election, Abramowitz classified the contests according to the clarity of the ideological choice the two major party candidates offered to voters. He found that the higher the "ideological clarity" of the race, the more likely voters were to perceive some difference between the candidates on a liberalism-conservatism scale, and the stronger the relationship was between voters' positions on that scale and the vote.[6] Indeed, in races with a very clear choice, ideology had approximately the same impact on the vote as party identification. In an analysis of House races in 1980 and 1982, Abramowitz found that the more liberal a voter was, the more likely he or she was to vote Democratic, but the relationship was statistically significant only in 1982. Furthermore, work by Michael Ensley indicates that the degree of ideological divergence between candidates conditions the magnitude of the impact of ideology on vote choice.[7]

Another perspective was offered in analyses by Robert S. Erikson and Gerald C. Wright.[8] They examined the positions of 1982 House candidates on a variety of issues (expressed in response to a CBS News/*New York Times* poll) and found that on most issues, most of the districts had the choice between a liberal Democrat and a conservative Republican. They also found that moderate candidates did better in attracting votes than more extreme candidates. In a subsequent study, involving the 1994 House elections, Erikson and Wright showed that both the issue preferences of incumbents (measured by positions on roll call votes) and the district's ideology (measured by the district's propensity to vote for Michael S. Dukakis in the previous presidential election) are strongly related to the congressional vote.[9] The same authors, in a study of the 2002 elections, employ a measure of candidate ideology that was derived from candidates' responses to questions about issues rather than from roll calls. That analysis confirms that incumbent ideology has a substantial effect on vote share, with moderates gaining more votes relative to more extreme members. Challenger ideology does not have a consistent effect, reflecting the lesser visibility of their positions to the electorate.[10]

We examined the relationships between issues and congressional voting choices in 2016, analyzing the issues we studied in Chapter 6. For the most part the relationship between issue preferences and congressional vote choices were weak and inconsistent, and these relationships were even weaker when we controlled for the tendency of Democratic identifiers to have liberal positions on these issues and of Republicans to have conservative issue preferences. However, partisan loyalties clearly affect congressional voting, even when we take issue preferences into account. Therefore, before considering the effects of other factors, we will provide more information about the effects of party identification on House voting.

PARTY IDENTIFICATION AND THE CONGRESSIONAL VOTE

As our previous discussion demonstrates, party identification has a significant effect on voters' decisions. Table 10-2 (corresponding to Table 8-5 on the presidential vote) reports the percentage of whites voting Democratic for the House across all categories of partisanship from 1952 through 2016.[11] The data reveal that the proportion of voters who cast ballots in accordance with their party identification declined substantially over time through the 1980s. During the 1990s and later, however, there was a resurgence of party voting for the House, especially among Republican identifiers.

Consider first the "strong identifier" categories. In every election from 1952 through 1964, at least nine out of ten strong party identifiers supported the candidate of their party. After that the percentage dropped, falling to four out of five in 1980 and then fluctuating through 1992. But in the last five elections, strong identifiers showed levels of loyalty similar to those in the late 1960s. The relationship between party and voting among weak party identifiers shows a more erratic pattern, although defection rates tend to be higher in most years between 1970 and 1992 than earlier.[12] Note that during this period the tendency to defect was stronger among Republicans, which reflected the Democrats' greater number of incumbents, as discussed in Chapter 9. Probably reflecting the effects of the Republicans' majority status and the corresponding increase in the number of Republican incumbents, from 1996 through 2000 the tendency of Democrats to defect rose, whereas among Republicans it fell. In four of the last five listed elections, however, the Democratic defection rate was lower in all three Democratic categories (and the GOP defection rate was lower among strong Republicans, with the exception of 2016) compared to the 1998 and 2000 elections. We consider these matters further in the next section.

Despite the increase in defections from party identification from the mid-1960s through the end of the century, strong party identifiers continued to be notably more likely to vote in accord with their party than weak identifiers. In most years weak Republicans were more likely to vote Republican than independents who leaned toward the Republican Party, although in 1996, 1998, and 2002 these groups were about equally likely to vote Republican. Weak Democrats were more likely to vote Democratic than independents who leaned Democratic in most of the elections from 1952 through 1978, but in a number of elections since, this pattern has been reversed by a small margin. In general, then, the relationship between party identification and the vote was strongest in the 1950s and early 1960s and less strong for the next several decades before showing a substantial recent rebound.

If party identifiers were defecting more frequently in House elections in recent decades, to whom have they been defecting? As one might expect from the last chapter, the answer is to incumbents.

INCUMBENCY AND THE CONGRESSIONAL VOTE

In Chapter 9 we mentioned Albert D. Cover's analysis of congressional voting behavior from 1958 through 1974.[13] Cover compared the rates of defection from party identification among voters who were of the same party as the incumbent and those who were of the same party as the challenger. The analysis showed no systematic increase over time in defection among voters who shared identification with incumbents, and the proportions defecting varied between 5 and 14 percent. Among voters who identified with the same party as challengers, however, the rate of defection—that is, the

Table 10-2 Percentage of White Major-Party Voters Who Voted Democratic for the House, by Party Identification, 1952–2016

Party Identification	1952	1954	1956	1958	1960	1962	1964	1966	1968	1970	1972	1974	1976	1978	1980
Strong Democrat	90	97	94	96	92	96	92	92	88	91	91	89	86	83	82
Weak Democrat	76	77	86	88	85	83	84	81	72	76	79	81	76	79	66
Independent, leans Democrat	63	70	82	75	86	74	78	54	60	74	78	87	76	60	69
Independent, no partisan leanings	25	41	35	46	52	61	70	49	48	48	54	54	55	56	57
Independent, leans Republican	18	6	17	26	26	28	28	31	18	35	27	38	32	36	32
Weak Republican	10	6	11	22	14	14	34	22	21	17	24	31	28	34	26
Strong Republican	5	5	5	6	8	6	8	12	8	4	15	14	15	19	22

(Continued)

Table 10-2 (Continued)

Party Identification	1982	1984	1986	1988	1990	1992	1994	1996	1998	2000	2002	2004	2008	2012	2016
Strong Democrat	90	87	91	86	91	87	87	87	88	88	93	92	92	89	89
Weak Democrat	73	66	71	80	80	81	73	70	60	69	73	74	82	86	68
Independent, leans Democrat	84	76	71	86	79	73	65	70	62	71	75	74	81	75	81
Independent, no partisan leanings	31	59	59	66	60	53	55	42	45	50	42	46	43	21	36
Independent, leans Republican	36	39	37	37	33	36	26	19	23	27	28	30	21	8	18
Weak Republican	20	33	34	29	39	35	21	19	25	15	26	19	22	12	12
Strong Republican	12	15	20	23	17	16	6	2	8	11	6	8	7	4	9

Sources: Authors' analysis of the 2016 ANES.

Note: To approximate the numbers on which these percentages are based, see Tables 8-2 and A8-1 (appendix). Actual Ns will be smaller than those that can be derived from these tables because respondents who did not vote (or who voted for a minor party) have been excluded from these calculations. Numbers also will be lower for the presidential election years because the voting report is provided in the postelection interviews that usually contain about 10 percent fewer respondents than the pre-election interviews in which party identification was measured. Except for 1954, the off-year election surveys are based on a postelection interview. Note that no ANES Time Series survey was conducted in 2006, 2010, and 2014.

proportion voting for the incumbent instead of the candidate of their own party—increased steadily from 16 percent in 1958 to 56 percent in 1972 then dropped to 49 percent in 1974. Thus the declining relationship between party identification and House voting resulted largely from increased support for incumbents. Because there were more Democratic incumbents, this tendency was consistent with the higher defection rates among Republican identifiers, as seen in Table 10-2.

Controlling for party identification and incumbency, in Table 10-3 we present data on the percentage of respondents who voted Democratic for the House and Senate in 2016 that confirm this view. In both House and Senate voting, we find the same relationship as Cover did.[14] For the House the proportion of voters defecting from their party identification is low when that identification is shared by the incumbent: 7 percent among Democrats and 5 percent among Republicans.[15] When, however, the incumbent belongs to the other party, the rates are much higher: 28 percent among Democrats and 32 percent among Republicans. Note also that the support of the independents is skewed sharply in favor of the incumbent. When there was an incumbent Democrat running, 68 percent of the independents voted Democratic; when there was an incumbent Republican, 69 percent of the independents voted Republican.

The pattern is quite similar in the data on Senate voting. When given the opportunity to support a Republican House incumbent, 28 percent of the Democratic identifiers defected. Faced with the opportunity to support an incumbent Republican senator, 18 percent defected. Similarly 32 percent of Republicans supported a Democratic House incumbent, whereas 23 percent backed an incumbent Democratic senator. Because the proportion of the electorate that has the chance to vote for Democratic and Republican senatorial candidates will vary greatly from election to election, it is difficult to generalize about the overall effects of incumbency in Senate contests from this type of data. In the remainder of this chapter, we continue to explore this relationship among party identification, incumbency, and congressional voting.

THE CONGRESSIONAL VOTE AS REFERENDUM

In Chapter 7 we analyzed the effect of perceptions of presidential performance on the vote for president in 2016, viewing that election as a referendum on Obama's job performance. A similar approach can be applied here, employing different perspectives. On one hand a congressional election can be considered as a referendum on the performance of a particular member of Congress; on the other hand, it can be viewed as a referendum on the president's performance. We will consider both possibilities here.

As we noted in Chapter 9, for some time, public opinion surveys have shown that the approval ratings of congressional incumbents by their constituents are very high, even when judgments on the performance of Congress as an institution are not. While traveling with House incumbents in their districts, Richard F. Fenno, Jr., noted that the people he met overwhelmingly approved of the performance of their own representative, although at the time the public generally disapproved of the job the institution was doing.[16] Data in the 2016 ANES survey again indicate widespread approval of House incumbents: among respondents who had an opinion, 64 percent endorsed their member's job performance.[17] Approval was widespread, regardless

Table 10-3   Percentage Who Voted Democratic for the House and Senate, by Party Identification and Incumbency, 2016

	Party Identification					
	Democrat		Independent		Republican	
Incumbency	%	(N)	%	(N)	%	(N)
House						
Democrat	93	(310)	68	(153)	32	(99)
None	88	(55)	50	(65)	14	(67)
Republican	72	(268)	31	(290)	5	(405)
Senate						
Democrat	97	(133)	80	(95)	23	(58)
None	78	(43)	50	(31)	29	(48)
Republican	82	(323)	38	(251)	9	(326)

Source: Authors' analysis of the 2016 ANES.

Note: The numbers in parentheses are the totals on which the percentages are based. Numbers are weighted. In this table and in subsequent tables in this chapter, strong and weak Democrats and strong and weak Republicans are combined. Independents include those who lean toward either party and "pure" independents. We include only voters who lived in congressional districts in which both major parties ran candidates.

of the party identification of the voter or the party of the incumbent. Indeed, as Table 10-4 shows, approval is well above 50 percent even among identifiers of the incumbent's opposition party.[18]

Further evidence indicates that the level of approval has electoral consequences. Table 10-4 presents the level of pro-incumbent voting among voters who share the incumbent's party and among those who are of the opposite party, controlling for whether they approve or disapprove of the incumbent's job performance. If voters approve of the member's performance and share his or her party identification, support is at 96 percent. At the opposite pole, among voters from the opposite party who disapprove, support is low (only 17 percent). In the mixed categories the incumbents receive intermediate levels of support. Because approval rates are very high, even among voters of the opposite party, most incumbents are reelected by large margins, even in a difficult year such as 2014 for the Democrats or 2008 for the Republicans.

In Chapter 9 we pointed out that midterm congressional elections were influenced by public evaluations of the president's job performance. Voters who think the president is doing a good job are more likely to support the congressional candidate of the president's party. Less scholarly attention has been given to this phenomenon

Table 10-4 Percentage of Voters Who Supported Incumbents in House Voting, by Party Identification and Evaluation of Incumbent's Performance, 2016

| | Voters' Evaluation of Incumbent's Job Performance | | | |
| | Approve | | Disapprove | |
	%	(N)	%	(N)
Incumbent is of same party as voter	96	(637)	66	(50)
Incumbent is of opposite party	75	(466)	17	(301)

Source: Authors' analysis of the 2016 ANES.

Note: The numbers in parentheses are the totals on which the percentages are based. Numbers are weighted. The total number of cases is somewhat lower than for previous tables because we have excluded respondents who did not evaluate the performance of the incumbent and those who live in a district that had no incumbent running. We include only voters who lived in congressional districts in which both major parties ran candidates.

Table 10-5 Percentage Who Voted Democratic for the House, by Evaluation of Obama's Job Performance, Party Identification, and Incumbency, 2016

Party Identification	Evaluation of Obama's Job Performance							
	Incumbent Is Republican				Incumbent Is Democrat			
	Approve		Disapprove		Approve		Disapprove	
	%	(N)	%	(N)	%	(N)	%	(N)
Democrat	81	(227)	26	(41)	93	(292)	97	(17)
Independent	59	(127)	10	(158)	90	(87)	39	(66)
Republican	17	(48)	4	(356)	63	(18)	26	(80)

Source: Authors' analysis of the 2016 ANES.

Note: The numbers in parentheses are the totals on which the percentages are based. Numbers are weighted. We include only voters who lived in congressional districts in which both major parties ran candidates.

in presidential election years, but the 2016 ANES survey provides us with the data needed to explore the question.

On the surface at least, a strong relationship is apparent. Among voters who approved of Obama's job performance ($N = 891$), 79 percent voted Democratic for the House; among those who disapproved of the president's performance ($N = 821$), only 15 percent supported Democrats. In 1980 there was a similar relationship between the two variables, but when controls were introduced for party identification and incumbency, the relationship disappeared.[19] Approval of Carter increased the Democratic House vote by a small amount among Democrats but had virtually no effect among independents and Republicans. In 2016, however, the results are different. Table 10-5 presents the relevant data on House voting, controlling for party identification, incumbency, and evaluation of Obama's job performance. They show that even with these controls, evaluations of the president's job had an effect on House voting among all groups of identifiers. To be sure, Democrats were still more likely both to approve of Obama and to vote Democratic than were Republicans. Yet, even after controlling for incumbency, independents and Republicans who disapproved of Obama's job performance were less likely to vote Democratic for the House than were those who approved.

PRESIDENTIAL COATTAILS
AND THE CONGRESSIONAL VOTE

Another perspective on the congressional vote, somewhat related to the presidential referendum concept we just considered, is the effect of the voter's presidential vote decision, or the length of a presidential candidate's "coattails." That is, does a voter's decision to support a presidential candidate make him or her more likely to support a congressional candidate of the same party so that the congressional candidate, as the saying goes, rides into office on the president's coattails?

Expectations about presidential coattails have been shaped in substantial measure by the period of the New Deal realignment. Franklin D. Roosevelt won by landslide margins in 1932 and 1936 and swept enormous congressional majorities into office with him. Research has indicated, however, that such strong pulling power by presidential candidates may have been a historical aberration and, in any event, that presidential candidates' pulling power has declined in recent decades.[20] In an analysis of the coattail effect since 1868, John A. Ferejohn and Randall L. Calvert point out that the effect is a combination of two factors: how many voters a presidential candidate can pull to congressional candidates of his party and how many congressional seats can be shifted between the parties by the addition of that number of voters.[21] (The second aspect is called the seats/votes relationship, or the swing ratio.)

Ferejohn and Calvert discovered the relationship between presidential and congressional voting from 1932 through 1948 was virtually the same as it was from 1896 through 1928 and the impact of coattails was strengthened by an increase in the swing ratio. In other words the same proportion of votes pulled in by a presidential candidate produced more congressional seats in the New Deal era than in the past. After 1948, they argued, the coattail effect declined because the relationship between presidential and congressional voting decreased. Analyzing data from presidential elections from 1956 through 1980, Calvert and Ferejohn reached similar conclusions about the length of presidential coattails.[22] They found that although every election during the period exhibited significant coattail voting, the extent of such voting declined over time. More recently, James E. Campbell and Joe A. Sumners concluded from an analysis of Senate elections that presidential coattails exert a modest but significant influence on the Senate vote.[23] And Franco Mattei and Joshua Glasgow showed that coattails exerted a systematic effect in open districts, an effect that persisted into the twenty-first century.[24]

Data on the percentage of respondents who voted Democratic for the House and Senate in 2016, controlling for their presidential vote and their party identification, are presented in Table 10-6. For both chambers the expected relationship is apparent. Within each party identification category, the proportion of Clinton voters who supported Democratic congressional candidates is significantly higher than the proportion of Trump voters who supported Democratic candidates.

Because we know that this apparent relationship could be just an accidental consequence of the distribution of different types of voters among Democratic and Republican districts, we present the same data on House voting in 2016 in Table 10-7. However, this time we control for the party of the House incumbent. In 1996 we found that—despite this additional control—the relationship held up very well. Within every category for which comparisons were possible, Dole voters supported Democratic candidates at substantially lower rates than did Clinton voters.

Table 10-6 Percentage Who Voted Democratic for the House and Senate, by Party Identification and Presidential Vote, 2016

Presidential Vote	Party Identification					
	Democrat		Independent		Republican	
	%	(N)	%	(N)	%	(N)
House						
Trump	37	(44)	19	(221)	8	(489)
Clinton	88	(576)	75	(208)	43	(45)
Senate						
Trump	31	(35)	23	(176)	8	(371)
Clinton	91	(446)	83	(144)	65	(35)

Source: Authors' analysis of the 2016 ANES.

Note: The numbers in parentheses are the totals on which the percentages are based. Numbers are weighted. We include only voters who lived in congressional districts in which both major parties ran candidates.

Table 10-7 Percentage Who Voted Democratic for the House, by Presidential Vote, Party Identification, and Incumbency, 2016

Party Identification	Voted for Trump		Voted for Clinton	
	%	(N)	%	(N)
Incumbent is Democrat				
Democrat	61	(10)	95	(288)
Independent	41	(53)	94	(78)
Republican	24	(78)	72	(13)
Incumbent is Republican				
Democrat	27	(31)	79	(231)
Independent	10	(135)	58	(107)
Republican	3	(350)	26	(30)

Source: Authors' analysis of the 2016 ANES.

Note: The numbers in parentheses are the totals on which the percentages are based. Numbers are weighted. The number in brackets is the total number voting for either Trump or Clinton when there are fewer than ten total voters. We include only voters who lived in congressional districts in which both major parties ran candidates.

In 2016 (as well as in 2000–2008), however, there are so few defectors within the two major parties that the comparisons are largely limited to independents, where the effect remains substantial. These limited data are consistent with the interpretation that the presidential vote exerted some small influence on the congressional vote although not as strong an influence as partisanship and congressional incumbency. In sum it appears that partisanship has become so pervasive and reliable as a predictor of voting behavior during the past two decades that there simply is little or no room for defection, which greatly limits the possibility for coattail effects. This is consistent with Gary Jacobson's argument that the resurgence of partisanship during the past few decades has contributed to the increasing nationalization of congressional elections.[25]

CONCLUSION

In this chapter we have considered a variety of possible influences on voters' decisions in congressional elections. We found that social forces have some impact on that choice. There is evidence from the work of other researchers that issues also have an effect. Incumbency has a major and consistent impact on voters' choices. It solidifies the support of the incumbent's partisans, attracts independents, and leads to defections by voters who identify with the challenger's party. Incumbent support is linked to a positive evaluation of the representative's job by the voters. The tendency to favor incumbents currently appears to benefit the Republican Party in House races. Within the context of this incumbency effect, voters' choices also seem to be affected by their evaluations of the job the president is doing and by their vote for president. Partisanship has some direct impact on the vote even after controlling for incumbency. The total effect of partisanship is, however, larger, because most incumbents represent districts that have more of their partisans than of the opposition. Thus the long-term advantage of Democrats in congressional elections was built on a three-part base: there were more Democrats than Republicans in the electorate; most incumbents of both parties achieved high levels of approval in their constituencies; and the incumbents had resources that made it possible for them to create direct contacts with voters. With the GOP now in the majority, their members may continue to benefit from the last two factors while they try to reduce their disadvantage on the first.

CHAPTER ELEVEN

THE 2018 CONGRESSIONAL ELECTIONS

I n Chapter 9, we focused on candidates and outcomes in the 2016 congressional races that were occurring simultaneously with the presidential election that featured a choice between two unpopular candidates. Despite the election of Donald Trump as president, we saw that the 2016 results slightly strengthened the Democrats' hand in Congress. The 2018 midterm elections resulted in Democrats picking up additional seats in the House to regain majority control of the chamber for the first time in eight years, while losing ground in the Senate given the distribution of seats up for reelection. In this chapter, we will discuss the pattern of outcomes in the 2018 congressional races, seeking to determine the collective meaning of those results and their implications for future elections.

The number of seats that switched parties in the House was substantially larger than the number resulting from the 2014 midterm, and all of the incumbent losses in the general election were by Republicans. The outcome brought an end to unified Republican control of Congress despite the Republicans' advantage stemming from the large number of rural and suburban House seats they have traditionally controlled.[1] In total, the Democrats won 235 seats to the Republicans' 200 in the House (a net gain of 40 seats), yielding the largest number of Democratic representatives in ten years.[2] The Senate results, by contrast, did not fare as well for the Democrats. The Republicans won four of the twenty-four seats Democrats were defending and only lost two of their own, for a total of fifty-three seats in the 116th Congress.[3] This was a net gain of two seats, maintaining Republicans' control of the Senate for the next two years but yielding divided government in the process.[4] To understand the political forces underlying these different results, we begin by examining the congressional outcomes more closely.

THE PATTERN OF OUTCOMES

The data presented on incumbency and electoral success in Table 11-1 update the prior election information displayed in Table 9-1. The data show that, even in this turbulent election year, incumbents were quite successful, especially in the House. Of House incumbents who sought reelection, 91 percent retained their seats, while in Senate races the rate was 84 percent. As with most elections that have not followed congressional reapportionments, the vast majority of losses were in the general election, with only four House incumbents and no senators losing their seats as a result of primary defeats. (We discuss the primary results later in this chapter.) In the general election, five senators and 30 representatives were defeated.

Table 11-2 shows the combined effects of party and incumbency in 2018. As in 1994 and 2010, incumbent success was very asymmetric. In the House, 30 Republican incumbents were defeated, resulting in a net loss of 40 seats that they held before the election, while in the Senate races they picked up a net gain of two seats, losing only one incumbent-held seat in the process (Dean Heller, R-NV). In open-seat House races, Republicans lost 66 percent of the seats they previously held. By contrast, Democrats did much better in incumbent and open seat races. Not a single Democratic House incumbent lost in 2018, and they managed to retain 85 percent of their open seat races in the election. (By comparison, of the Democratic incumbents seeking reelection in 1994, 15 percent lost, and in 2010, 22 percent lost.) In the Senate elections, however, four incumbent Democratic senators were defeated—Joe Donnelly (IN), Heidi Heitkamp (ND), Claire McCaskill (MO), and Bill Nelson (FL)—all of whom were from states that President Trump had previously carried in 2016.

The regional variation of the Democrats' gains in 2018 is presented in Table 11-3. In the House, the increases in the Democrats' shares of seats were noticeable in every region of the country. Their overall share of House seats increased by nine percentage points, and the regional variation was between four and fifteen points, with the largest gains made in the East. The Democrats' gains in the Senate were limited to the West, where the party increased its share of seats relative to 2016 by eight points. In the Midwest and border states, by contrast, the Democrats lost nine and ten points, respectively, whereas they maintained the same percentage of seats in both the East and the South. The combined results of the 2018 elections reinforced trends over the past few elections in yielding more regional diversity in partisan representation than has been true for quite a while. For example, in the House, the difference between the share of seats held by Democrats in their best region (the East, at 80 percent) and their

Table 11-1	House and Senate Incumbents and Election Outcomes, 2018						
Chamber	Incumbents running (*N*)	Primary defeats		General election defeats		Reelected	
		(%)	(N)	(%)	(N)	(%)	(N)
House	378	1.1	(4)	7.9	(30)	91.0	(344)
Senate	32	0.0	(0)	15.6	(5)	84.4	(27)

Note: In the House, Joseph Crowley (D-NY), Michael Capuano (D-MA), Mark Sanford (R-SC), and Robert Pittenger (R-NC) were defeated in their party's primaries.

Table 11-2 House and Senate General Election Outcomes, by Party and Incumbency, 2018 (percent)

| | Democratic incumbent | No incumbent | | Republican incumbent | Total |
		Democratic seat	Republican seat		
House					
Democrats	100	85	34	15	54
Republicans	0	15	66	85	46
Total	100	100	100	100	100
(N)	(174)[1]	(20)	(41)	(200)	(435)
Senate					
Democrats	85	0	33	17	69
Republicans	15	0	67	83	31
Total	100	100	100	100	100
(N)	(26)[2]	(0)	(3)	(6)	(35)

Source: Compiled by the authors.

[1]Excludes a Pennsylvania House race where a Democratic incumbent ran against a Republican incumbent.

[2]Includes two independents, Bernie Sanders of Vermont and Angus King of Maine, who caucus with the Democrats.

weakest (the South, 35 percent) was 45 percentage points. And, in the Senate, the difference between the same two regions was 76 percentage points. There has not been an interregional difference that great since before the 1980s. The results underscore the shift of the South away from the Democrats and toward the Republicans documented in Chapters 3 and 9.

ASSESSING VICTORY AND EXPLAINING THE RESULTS

After every election, two questions are always asked. First, which party won, and which party lost? And the second important question: Why? The answers to these questions are vital to citizens and politicians because public interpretation of election outcomes can affect politicians' calculations and their ability to advance their policy agendas,

Table 11-3 Party Shares of Regional Delegations in the House and Senate, Before and After 2018 Elections (percent)

Region	Before			After		
	Democrats (%)	Republicans (%)	(N)	Democrats (%)	Republicans (%)	(N)
House						
East	65	35	(79)	80	20	(79)
Midwest	36	64	(86)	44	56	(86)
West	62	38	(102)	74	26	(102)
South	28	72	(138)	35	65	(138)
Border	33	67	(30)	37	63	(30)
Total	45	55	(435)	54	46	(435)
Senate						
East	90	10	(20)	90	10	(20)
Midwest	45	55	(22)	36	64	(22)
West	50	50	(26)	58	42	(26)
South	14	86	(22)	14	86	(22)
Border	40	60	(10)	30	70	(10)
Total	48	52	(100)	46	54	(100)

Source: Compiled by the authors.

Note: Two independents, Bernie Sanders of Vermont and Angus King of Maine, are counted as Democrats.

and they can also affect politicians' relationships with each other. Politicians use their interpretations of the results, and those of other observers, to infer (rightly or wrongly) the political desires of the voters. For example, in 1980, Ronald Reagan's convincing electoral vote victory over President Jimmy Carter and the substantial gains made by the Republicans in the congressional elections were interpreted as a wholesale endorsement of the Republican agenda of tax cuts, reductions in social spending, and increases in defense expenditures. As a consequence, all of these policies were enacted into law in the subsequent Congress.

To evaluate a party's success we must apply some standard—a yardstick, of sorts—to measure victory. The standard provides us with a set of expectations against which the actual results can be compared. In addition, as we saw in Chapter 9, expectations or hypotheses about election outcomes can be combined in models of the electoral process that can provide explanations as well as offer predictions. In the following sections, we consider, in turn, historical patterns, the expectations of participants and observers, and the insights from academic models as yardsticks by which to measure the relative success of each party.

Historical Trends

In Chapter 9, we presented data on seat changes in midterm House elections (see Table 9-8). Recall that the party that held the White House had lost strength in all but three of the twenty-nine midterms since the beginning of the twentieth century. Thus, based on this trend alone, most observers expected Republican losses in 2018—at least in the House. The question was how great those losses would be. The historical results also showed that a party's losses had been larger in the second or later midterm of an administration than in the first midterm. In fact, we can see an even clearer picture of the historical trends by introducing an additional variable: whether the president's party held a majority in the House before the election. Remember that the "exposure" hypothesis discussed in Chapter 9 argues that the more seats a party holds (relative to the recent historical pattern), the more vulnerable it is to losses. Similarly, we might expect that a majority party would be more vulnerable than a minority party. Table 11-4, which reconfigures the data from Table 9-8, shows that this expectation is correct. On average, before 2018, majority parties lost substantially more House seats than minority parties in postwar first or later midterm elections. (For midterms that occurred during the first term of an administration, the majority and minority party losses by the president's party were somewhat closer.)

Table 11-4 Average Seat Losses by the President's Party in Midterm Elections, 1946–2014 (percent)

President's Party in the House	First term of administration	Later term of administration	Total
Majority	23.7 ($N = 6$)[a]	40.3 ($N = 4$)[b]	30.3 ($N = 10$)
Minority	15.7 ($N = 3$)[c]	20.6 ($N = 5$)[d]	18.75 ($N = 8$)
Total	21.0 ($N = 9$)	29.3 ($N = 9$)	25.2 ($N = 18$)[e]

[a]1954, 1962, 1978, and 1994, 2002, and 2010.

[b]1946, 1950, 1966, and 2006.

[c]1970, 1982, and 1990.

[d]1958, 1974, 1986, 1998, and 2014.

[e]For the specific results of each of these eighteen elections, see Table 9-8.

In light of these historical patterns, the actual losses of the Republicans in the 2018 elections were above average, almost 60 percent more than in similar elections since World War II. That view, however, must be tempered by recognizing that many Democratic seats had been lost in the "shellacking" endured by President Obama and Democrats eight years earlier.[5] The bottom line, as we have already noted, is that the GOP held more seats in the House going into the 2018 midterms than at any time since the Truman administration. Relative to the historical pattern, the results in the Senate tended in the opposite direction from those in the House, with Democrats' losses being higher. In general, in the postwar period, the party that controlled the White House did better in first midterms (averaging a net loss of one seat per election) than in later midterms (when it lost an average of a bit more than six seats).[6] So in the Senate contests, with a two-seat gain, the GOP did better than the previous pattern suggested.

Observers' Expectations

The pre-election expectations of politicians and media analysts provide another standard for judging election outcomes. Even if a party loses ground, it may try to claim victory (at least a "moral victory") if it performs notably better than was anticipated. Publicly stated expectations regarding elections are shaped partly by the historical standards just discussed, but they are also influenced by polls and by recent political events.

The anticipations voiced by politicians during election campaigns are a mixture of predictions, hopes, and public-relations strategies. Thus, they cannot be taken entirely at face value. In 2018, expectations varied considerably, both among evaluators and over time as the election picture developed. Observers—both politicians and more independent analysts—recognized that the political context for 2018 was dangerous for Republicans. The pattern of historical losses by the president's party was known to everyone, as were the president's historically poor approval ratings.[7] Despite this, Republicans had early hopes of outperforming historical patterns, especially given the gradual improvement of the economy. They expressed strong hopes of retaining control of the Senate and asserted that they had a chance to retain control of the House. President Trump, for instance, repeatedly emphasized throughout the fall campaign that there might actually be a "red wave" instead of a looming "blue wave" that others were predicting.[8] Those declarations ended up being just campaign rhetoric, however, as the results came in on Election Night. Although the party of the president had picked up seats in Congress in both 1998 and 2002, both of those midterm elections are often considered outliers as a result of the unique circumstances involved in each (i.e., Clinton's impending impeachment and the first election post-9/11). Prior to those two elections, the party of the president had not picked up seats in the House at a midterm since 1934, during Franklin Roosevelt's first term. As such, the prospect of modest Republican gains in the House in 2018 (or even modest losses), were viewed skeptically by almost everyone except perhaps the president.[9]

Other political analysts echoed the sentiment that Republicans had reason to be worried about 2018. Throughout early 2017, Inside Elections (formerly the Rothenberg Report) projected somewhere between thirty and forty Republican districts were considered competitive compared to about fifteen for the Democrats. Figure 11-1 displays the number of seats belonging to each party that Inside Elections rated to be competitive at various points in 2017 and 2018. As shown in the figure, Republicans easily had more seats in play compared to Democrats well over a year before the election. During 2018, however, the picture changed radically. The competitive GOP seats steadily increased until they reached seventy-nine just before the election, whereas competitive Democratic seats declined to eight. This changing picture in the number of competitive House seats reflected strategic decisions stemming from the high levels of disapproval of the president as well as the relatively low levels of approval of both the president and Congress.

The expectations for Democratic Senate losses were almost universal from early 2017 on, especially given the large number of seats Democrats were defending relative to Republicans in the 2018 midterms. The big question was whether there also would be significant GOP losses in light of President Trump's growing unpopularity. Throughout 2018, Charlie Cook of the Cook Political Report, one of the most respected analysts of national elections, maintained that there were more Democratic than Republican toss-up seats, making it quite unlikely for the Democrats to recapture control of the Senate.[10] Indeed, the political context of the Senate elections was tilted in favor of the Republicans, with the Democrats defending twenty-six seats to their nine. More important, ten of the Democrats' seats were in states that Donald Trump had carried in 2016 (most by substantial margins), while only one Republican seat (that

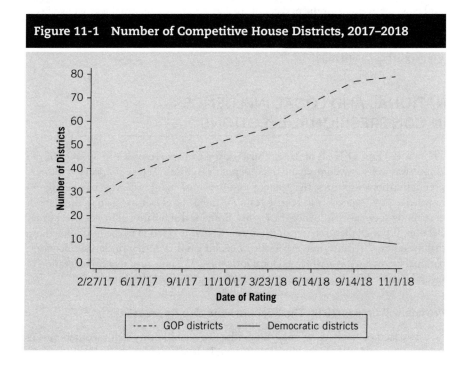

Figure 11-1   Number of Competitive House Districts, 2017–2018

of Dean Heller of Nevada) was in a state that Clinton had carried with slightly more than 51 percent of the vote in 2016. After Supreme Court Justice Brett Kavanaugh was narrowly confirmed by the Senate in early October, after a bitter partisan fight that clearly divided the nation, some analysts thought the event might put Republican control of the chamber in jeopardy.[11] As the election grew closer, however, it seemed as though the Republicans' chances of retaining control of the Senate remained high based on projections by Nate Silver at fivethirtyeight.com.[12]

Academic Insights

In looking forward to the election of 2018 in Chapter 9, we discussed a number of academic models of House elections. In the next section, we present a detailed discussion of a number of the variables that were employed in these models. At this point, we will consider only the collective picture they offered regarding Democratic prospects. Most of these models include variables measuring the performance of the economy and the level of approval for the president. Throughout most of 2018, the economy's performance was improving, but public perceptions varied by one's party affiliation, and Trump's approval ratings were at historically low levels compared with other presidents during their first term.[13] These public attitudes could be expected to cause problems for his party, and the strategic politicians hypothesis might lead us to expect more experienced Democratic candidates than usual willing to run for a House seat. Regarding "exposure," or the number of seats held by the president's party relative to a historical trend, the Democrats were in the minority, and so their seat share was below the average for the past couple of decades. Thus, the variables that had been judged important in predicting the level of partisan success in House and Senate elections indicated that some Democratic gains should be anticipated, but it was unclear how large those gains might be.

NATIONAL AND LOCAL INFLUENCES IN CONGRESSIONAL ELECTIONS

Thomas P. "Tip" O'Neill of Massachusetts, the former Democratic Speaker of the House, was well known for saying that "all politics is local." Yet, as our previous discussion in this book indicates, that generalization is misleading with regard to congressional elections, especially in recent years. National-level factors, such as the state of the economy, can also influence the results. Both local and national forces affect every election, although their relative impacts vary from one election to the next. One thing that makes the 2018 elections especially interesting is that during the last six elections, national forces have overwhelmed local influences. We now turn to a consideration of several factors that were relevant to the 2018 congressional elections.

President Trump in 2018: The Economy and Job Approval

Two factors that have an important influence on midterm electoral outcomes are the economy and evaluations of the president. Indeed, as we illustrated in Chapter 7, the two often are closely related because the president is usually held accountable if the economy is doing badly. The performance of the U.S. economy was substantially better in 2018 than it had been in recent years, with unemployment around 4 percent, but poll data offered Republicans little comfort on this score given Trump's relatively low approval ratings. In a Pew Research survey of U.S. adults conducted March 7-14, 2018, 53 percent of those polled rated the economy as either "excellent" or "good," the highest it has been in almost two decades. Much of this shift was driven by either Republicans or Republican leaners as nearly 75% of individuals in these two groups viewed the economy in positive terms. In contrast, only 37% of Democrats rated the economy as either in "excellent" or "good" shape, which represented a modest decline from when Barack Obama was still president.[14]

In anticipation of the election, the economy remained one of the top two issues voters had on their minds going to the polls. According to a Pew Research Center survey conducted September 18-24, 2018, roughly three-quarters of registered voters identified health care (75%) and the economy (74%) as very important issues in determining their vote. Not surprisingly, the views on these issues varied by party as 88% of likely Democratic voters said health care was very important compared with only 60% of Republicans polled. With respect to the economy, 85% of likely Republican voters said the economy was the most important factor in their vote compared with only 66% of Democratic voters. Additionally, 81% of Democratic and 72% of Republican voters identified Supreme Court appointments as an important issue when going to the polls following Justice Kavanaugh's recent appointment to the Court.[15] Among actual voters, the primacy of the economy clearly mattered more for Republicans than Democrats. In the 2018 national exit polls, Republicans were twice as likely to identify it as one of the more important issues in how they voted compared with Democrats. Not surprisingly, given political debates during the past two years, both health care and immigration were viewed as more important in Democrats' voting decisions relative to the economy.[16]

In Chapter 9, we discussed how midterms can be a referendum on the performance in office of the president and his party. How the public views the performance of the president and the results of his efforts shape his approval numbers, and that is particularly true with regard to economic performance. President Trump's highest approval rating in the Gallup Daily Tracking Poll came on the day he was inaugurated in January 2017 when it reached 45 percent. At no single point over the next twenty-one months did it exceed that number (and only again in June 2018 did it tie 45 percent). A few days before the midterm, Trump's approval reached 40 percent with 54 percent disapproval.[17] Historically, this was very dangerous territory for a president's party. In 1994, Bill Clinton's approval rating just before the election was 46 percent, and his party lost fifty-two seats in the House. Similarly, in 2006, George W. Bush's approval was 42 percent, and that year the GOP lost thirty seats. Obama's approval rating in 2010, just before the sixty-three-seat loss, was also at 42 percent.

When presidents are popular, incumbents of their party welcome the chance to campaign with the president during visits to their congressional districts. This was clearly the case in 2002 when President Bush visited a number of districts prior to the midterm but not in 2006 when his approval had substantially declined as a result of the growing unpopularity of the war in Iraq. In 2014, President Obama and congressional

Democrats realized that low presidential approval was a serious political issue and that low approval severely limited the president's ability to campaign on behalf of Democrats. Indeed, polls in mid-October 2014 showed that one in seven of the likely voters who reported having voted for the president two years earlier regretted the choice.[18] As a consequence, the president's value on the campaign trail was limited. His presence at fund-raising events outside the public eye continued to be valuable, but the large public events at which he appeared were few and were focused almost entirely on blue states.

Although President Trump experienced similarly low approval ratings prior to the 2018 midterm elections, he insisted that he would be active in the fall congressional races.[19] For many Republicans, this announcement amounted to a double-edged sword. In districts that Trump had easily carried in 2016, Republican incumbents welcomed the president since he remained fairly popular in those districts. That being said, some within the party worried that Trump's visit to more marginal congressional districts might actually motivate a greater number of Democrats to come out and vote. For those Republican incumbents who had not outwardly embraced Trump during the past two years, they worried about the potential repercussions of a Trump visit.[20]

On Election Day, among those who chose to go to the polls, the sentiments were as many of the Republicans had feared. In the exit polls, 45 percent of poll respondents said they approved of how Trump was handling his job. Of that group, 88 percent indicated that they had voted for Republican House candidates as a result. Among the 54 percent who said they disapproved of the president's performance, however, 90 percent said they had voted Democratic. Additionally, a majority of voters saw their votes as explicitly linked to their attitudes about the president: 26 percent said their vote was in support of Trump, whereas 38 percent indicated it was in opposition to him. Perhaps surprisingly, 33 percent of those surveyed said that Trump was not a factor in their decision to vote in the midterms.[21]

Other Issues

The economy and the president were not the only issues that mattered in 2018. The public was evaluating not just Trump but the Congress as well, and they were not happy with what they saw. The website PollingReport.com lists thirty-five different polls that asked about Congress's job rating in 2018 prior to the midterm elections. In only two polls did the respondents register approval as high as 23 percent, and most were in the mid to high teens. The low point was 12 percent in a poll in early April. And in twenty-one of those polls, the level of disapproval was 75 percent or higher.[22] This was a slightly higher level of approval than Congress had just before the 2014 midterm elections, but an important difference between the two situations was that now control of government and the Congress had been unified.

Even though attributing responsibility was quite clear leading up to the 2018 midterms, those surveyed did not hold as negative a view of government as they had four years earlier when, for the first time ever, a *Washington Post*–ABC News Poll in August 2014 found that a majority of respondents did not approve of the job their own members of Congress were doing.[23] At the time, the public was extremely unhappy with the Congress's inability to pass legislation to deal with perceived problems. Data on the passage of bills indicates that the 113th Congress (2013-2015) passed fewer laws than any other Congress in sixty years.[24] By contrast, a Pew Research Center report released in early 2018 considered the 115th Congress to be the fourth least productive one in three decades.[25] Thus, despite having unified control of government under Trump, Congress struggled to pass major legislation beyond the major tax cut package adopted in early 2018.

In addition to attitudes on performance, other substantive issues were salient to voters. In the exit polls, respondents were offered three choices in addition to the economy when they were asked what was the most important issue facing the country today: health care, immigration, and gun policy. Of these, 41 percent chose health care (about half as many picked the economy), 23 percent said immigration, and 10 percent foreign policy. The group choosing health care was two of the four that tilted to the Democrats in the elections, by 75 to 23 percent (the other was gun policy, by 70 to 29 percent). Given that repeal and replacement of the Affordable Care Act was a central feature of the GOP's legislative focus for the first few months of the 115th Congress, it is unsurprising that there was such a wide split among Democratic and Republican voters. When respondents in the exit polls were asked whether major changes to health care were needed, 69 percent indicated that major changes were necessary, whereas only 24 percent said minor changes were required.

Illegal immigration was another contentious issue that nearly a fourth of those surveyed believed was the most important issue that needed to be addressed, most likely as a result of the president's divisive rhetoric about immigration since taking office in 2017. When asked whether President Trump's immigration policies are too tough, 46 percent indicated that they were, 17 percent said they were not tough enough, and 33 percent indicated that they were about right. Among those who thought Trump's policies were too tough, 90 percent said they were planning to vote for a Democratic candidate in the midterms.[26]

Near the end of the midterm campaign, several things happened in the world that served to further divide the public and their view of the president. About a month before the election, Jamal Khashoggi, a Saudi Arabian journalist and editor in chief of the Al-Arab News Channel, had been assassinated at the Saudi Arabian consulate in Istanbul. When it was disclosed that he had been killed by agents of the Saudi government, this immediately tarnished the world's view of Saudi Arabia, a key Trump administration ally. With the midterms rapidly approaching, President Trump wanted to change the focus of the media's attention to just about anything else. He found a suitable issue in a migrant caravan fleeing Honduras and heading north, for which its members had blamed the right-wing government in their country for the exodus. The caravan of Honduran citizens immediately gave the president a politically advantageous issue to focus upon since he could use it to stoke fears about immigration as he had done in his 2016 campaign. Within a few days of first learning about the caravan, "the president began using Twitter to attack the migrants, putting the blame on Democrats and threatening to cut funding to Central American governments: 'We are a great Sovereign Nation. We have Strong Borders and will never accept people coming into our Country illegally.'"[27]

Overall, the public was worried about many things and unhappy with the government's performance and with gridlock in Washington. In the exit polls, 54 percent of voters thought the country was going in the wrong direction, versus only 42 percent who thought it was going in the right direction. However, only 39 percent indicated that Congress should impeach Donald Trump compared with the 56 percent who answered in the negative. When asked whether Americans are becoming more united politically, only 9 percent answered in the affirmative compared with 76 percent who said Americans are becoming more divided. For a president hoping to minimize losses in a midterm election, this was not especially promising terrain for the Republicans.

Legal Efforts to Shape the Midterm Elections

We described in Chapter 2 the parties' efforts to mobilize favorable voters and stimulate their turnout. We will shortly consider in detail parallel activities in 2018, but first we will discuss a particular aspect of that effort: legislation and litigation with the aim of shaping the electorate and influencing choices. In the early part of the decade, legal action had dealt with voter identification and election procedures. For instance, at least thirty-four states enacted new laws or revised previous ones to impose stricter regulation of these issues, including almost a dozen since 2011.[28] The regulations varied from state to state, but most involved imposing requirements for proof of identity (such as driver's licenses) in order to cast ballots. A number of states also reduced the number of days on which early voting was allowed, and some abolished same-day registration for voting.

In 2018, redistricting also played an important role in the upcoming midterms in the state of Pennsylvania. Following the 2016 elections, Republicans controlled 13 congressional districts in the state compared to five by the Democrats, which many viewed as unfair given the relatively even partisan balance within the state. After the Pennsylvania House adjourned in June without acting on proposed legislation that would alter the way the state draws its legislative boundaries, the League of Women Voters filed a lawsuit challenging the state's congressional districts. The state Supreme Court held that the existing map "constituted partisan gerrymandering in violation of the state constitution and ordered the GOP-controlled legislature to redraw the boundaries."[29] Following the U.S. Supreme Court's decision not to review the ruling, Republicans within the state legislature produced another map that was favorable to their party, but it ended up being vetoed by Democratic Governor Tom Wolf. Eventually, new congressional district boundaries were drawn by a court-appointed expert, which were considerably more favorable to Democrats as evidenced by the election results.[30]

Redistricting battles were not limited to just Pennsylvania, however. In 2017, Democrats had challenged Wisconsin's congressional district boundaries that had been in place since earlier in the decade, and the U.S. Supreme Court agreed to hear the case. Many initially believed that this case would have broad implications for partisan gerrymandering around the country if the Supreme Court decided to strike down the Republican-drawn boundaries in Wisconsin. When the Court announced its decision in *Gill v. Whitford*[31] in mid-June, a majority of justices on the Court declined to strike down the existing boundaries and instead remanded the case back to a Wisconsin district court to determine if the plaintiffs actually had "standing" to bring the suit at all.[32] This outcome obviously disappointed a lot of observers who were hoping the

Court would weigh in on the debate over partisan gerrymandering and likely did little to quell the continued push for litigation, especially with another redistricting cycle just over the horizon. Nevertheless, four states—Colorado, Michigan, Missouri, and Utah—did include initiatives on this year's ballot to determine whether redistricting commissions should be used during the next round of legislative redistricting.[33] All four initiatives were ultimately approved by each state's voters, which will have direct implications for the post-2020 redistricting cycle.

One final issue that may lead to future litigation involves a disputed House race in North Carolina following the November election involving the issue of "ballot harvesting." As of this writing, election officials in North Carolina are investigating whether a Republican official in parts of the 9th congressional district collected absentee ballots from minority voters and then failed to deliver them to polling places or election offices prior to Election Day. Ballot harvesting is illegal under North Carolina state law but is actually legal in other states such as California and has been since 2016. The Republican official being investigated is currently at the center of a fraud investigation that has delayed Republican Mark Harris's narrow victory by 905 voters over Democrat Dan McCready, which could lead to action taken by the House in the 116th Congress or perhaps a new election being held.[34] As a result of the ongoing investigation, incoming U.S. House Majority Leader Steny Hoyer (D-MD) stated in early December that House Democrats would not allow Mark Harris to be sworn in at the start of the 116th Congress due to uncertainty over the electoral outcome, and Harris was indeed absent from the swearing in ceremony for the new members held on Thursday, January 3, 2019.[35]

It is unlikely given the preceding discussion that the trend toward more litigation dealing with political campaigns will abate, especially given the increasingly high levels of polarization in this country and with another redistricting cycle coming up after the 2020 elections. We will discuss some other upcoming issues at the end of this chapter.

Turnout in 2018: Breaking the 50 Percent Threshold

In Chapter 2, we discussed how, over the past decade, both parties have intensified their efforts to stimulate turnout by voters who would be inclined to support their candidates at the polls. In addition, in Chapter 3, we described how turnout has varied over time, noting that turnout tends to be substantially lower in midterm years compared to presidential election years. Both of these generalizations are highly relevant to our discussion of 2018, especially given the robust turnout in the midterm election.

The Democrats' turnout efforts in 2018 were helped by the political environment, and, correspondingly, the Republicans' efforts were hindered in several respects. Throughout 2018, surveys indicated that Democrats were more motivated to participate than Republicans, and this "enthusiasm gap" persisted as Election Day approached. For example, in July a NPR/PBS News Hour/Marist Poll showed about a ten-percentage point enthusiasm gap between Democrats and Republicans. By early October, however, that gap had narrowed to only two points, with a larger share of Republicans indicating that the November elections were now very important.[36] Around the same time, a Pew Research Center poll released in late September showed that levels of voter enthusiasm were at a record high in a nationalized, mid-term election. According to the poll, 67 percent of Democratic voters said they were more enthusiastic than usual about voting compared with 59 percent of Republicans. Additionally, at least 60 percent of those polled indicated that their vote would be an expression of opposition or support toward President Trump.[37]

Furthermore, turnout in the 2018 House primaries increased quite noticeably, especially among Democratic voters. According to a Pew Research Center analysis of state election returns, approximately 37 million registered voters cast ballots in House primary elections in 2018. This represented a 56 percent increase over the 23.7 million individuals who had voted in the 2014 House primaries. When broken down by party, the same study found that Democratic turnout increased by 4.6 percentage points relative to 2014 among all registered voters compared to a more modest 1.2-point increase among Republicans. Although these increases are modest compared to overall rates of turnout in the 2016 presidential election, they do indicate significantly higher enthusiasm among voters who favored Democratic over Republican candidates in the primary elections.[38]

In 2016, Donald Trump and Republican candidates did well in states and districts with larger numbers of white voters, especially in more suburban areas. During the midterms, these groups were targeted in an effort to ensure they did not stay home on Election Day given growing levels of discontent with the president. Democrats, by contrast, sought to target areas with larger numbers of African American voters since they have consistently been quite loyal to Democratic candidates in recent elections. They also sought to reach out to areas with growing numbers of Latino voters given the president's rhetoric toward immigrants since assuming the presidency. In particular, President Trump's insistence on building a wall between the United States and Mexico was seen by many within the Democratic Party as an issue that could help mobilize and increase turnout among Latino voters by getting them to vote for Democratic candidates in 2018. With less than a month to go until the election, however, Democrats discovered that they were lagging behind their intended goal of mobilizing Latino voters since many were still undecided at that point.[39]

One group that did seem to be responding well to Democrat's mobilization efforts during the 2018 midterms were women. During the 2016 presidential election, a variety of gender-related issues came up during the campaign, including equality, sexual assault, and treatment of women in the workplace. The day after President Trump's inauguration in 2017, hundreds of thousands of women marched throughout the country, imploring greater numbers of women to run in the 2018 midterms and participate in the election. Later that fall, the meteoric rise of the #MeToo movement and increased attention to sexual assault in American entertainment and public service only amplified these calls for more women to run for office. By early January, it was clear that a record number of women would be running in the congressional primaries that would easily surpass the numbers from previous elections.[40]

One other event during the latter half of 2018 most likely also played a role in helping to mobilize women to turn out and vote in the midterm elections. On July 9, 2018, President Trump nominated Judge Brett Kavanaugh to the Supreme Court to fill a vacancy left by Justice Anthony Kennedy, who had recently announced he was planning to retire. Known for his conservative voting record and strong legal credentials, Kavanaugh seemed at first to be an "ideal" candidate for the Republican base and was quickly embraced by the party. However, on September 12, 2018, news broke of sexual assault allegations made against President Trump's nominee. In time, additional women would come forward with their own allegations against Kavanaugh. The ensuing Senate hearings, testimonies, and presidential rhetoric against his initial accuser, Professor Christine Blasey Ford, culminated in an FBI investigation, an extremely contentious and close confirmation to the Court by a 50-48 Senate vote, and an intensely divided nation.[41]

On Election Day, Republicans discovered that their concerns about turnout were partially justified given the number of incumbent losses in the House. However, the reality was not quite as bad as they had initially feared given the record setting turnout. Indeed, the turnout rate—50.3 percent[42]—was higher than in any midterm election since 1914, when senators were directly elected nationally for the very first time.[43] This turnout rate ended up being about ten points less than in 2016, which indicated the significant level of enthusiasm that voters felt about this election—both those who showed up and voted for and against President Trump. In terms of party identification as indicated in the exit polls, Democrats made up 37 percent of voters compared with 33 percent of Republicans, a four-point advantage. Republicans appear to have done quite well among white voters, but Democrats outperformed Republicans among blacks, Latino, and Asian voters by fairly significant margins.[44]

The biggest demographic difference, however, was in age. As previous chapters have shown, older voters had become a mainstay of the Republican coalition, while younger voters had tilted strongly to the Democrats. The exit polls in 2018 divided the electorate by age into four categories: 18–29, 30–44, 45–64, and 65 and older. As expected, Democrats did well among voters in the two youngest categories, winning by thirty-five and nineteen percentage points respectively. Republicans did better in the two oldest categories, although it was much closer (one and two points respectively). The two oldest categories represented the greatest percentage of voters, however, as they made up over 65 percent of the electorate. This likely explains why the Democrats did not make comparable gains to what the Republicans did in 2010 when they picked up sixty-three additional seats in the House.

The Independent Vote in a Nationalized Election

We began this discussion of factors affecting the 2018 elections by noting that both national and local forces affect campaigns, and that the balance between these forces varies. There are differences in the balance both across different races in the same year and across election years. In 2018, for the sixth consecutive election, national influences were unusually prominent. We have seen that the national political landscape disadvantaged Republicans in light of President's Trump relatively high levels of disapproval. In response to these conditions, as we will discuss later, Democratic candidates tried to focus voters' attention on President Trump's policies as well as issues that Democratic voters would find appealing, while in the process emphasizing incumbents' service to their constituents. In addition, as we have seen, they tried to stimulate the party's base to turn out to vote.

Neither the Democrats nor the Republicans have enough party identifiers to achieve victory by relying solely on those partisans. Each also needs support from independents and defectors from the other party. In congressional elections from 1996 through 2004, the independent vote tended to divide fairly evenly between the major parties. In such circumstances, winning greater support from the GOP base was an effective way for Republicans to achieve electoral success nationally. In 2006 and 2008, however, the independent vote split heavily in favor of the Democrats, giving them unified control of the government. In 2010, in the highly negative political environment for the Democrats, the exit polls showed that independents split in favor of the Republicans by nineteen points (56 to 37 percent). Then in 2012, the Democrats did better, although they still lost the independent vote 45 to 50 percent. For 2014, the exit polls indicated that the Democrats did an excellent job of maintaining the support of their party's identifiers, winning 92 percent of their votes (identical to 2012). On the other side, 94 percent of Republicans stuck with their party's candidates, one point better than Romney's share two years earlier.

In 2018, the exit polls show that Democrats carried 95 percent of their party's identifiers, compared with 94 percent of Republicans sticking with their party's candidates. This is slightly higher than 2016 when 89 percent of Democrats voted for their party's candidates compared with 88 percent of Republicans. The big difference in 2018 came among independent voters who broke for the Democratic candidate 54 to 42 percent of the time compared with Republicans. This is not nearly as great of a difference compared to 2010 when the independent vote heavily favored the Republicans, but it is comparable to 2006 when Democrats managed to win back control of the House for the first time in twelve years.

Candidate Resources

In Chapter 9 we focused on candidates' resources in each House district—specifically incumbency, candidate quality, and campaign spending—to explain outcomes in U.S. House elections. We will conclude our analysis of the 2018 midterms by returning to these factors, paying particular attention to the increased role of the national parties in marshaling them.[45]

Incumbency

We have already discussed incumbency at a number of points in this chapter, noting particularly that incumbents usually have an extremely high success rate. Incumbent success is not, however, an immutable fact of nature. Reelection rates for incumbents vary over time, as we have seen, and they vary between the parties. In the 1992 House races, defeats of incumbents were not heavily one-sided. Those elections occurred in the context of a financial scandal in the House and of national reapportionment and redistricting after the 1990 census. Sixteen Democrats and eight Republicans lost their seats to the opposition party in the general election, while fourteen Democrats and five Republicans had lost in the primaries.[46] Two years later, on the other hand, in the Republican landslide of 1994, thirty-four (one in seven) Democrats were beaten in House general election races, while not a single GOP incumbent lost. This was a very one-sided election in which the voters punished the incumbents of a single party.[47]

As we have seen above, the pattern for the 2018 election with regard to incumbency was more like 1994 than 1992 but this time in reverse. Thirty Republican incumbents were defeated in the general election while no Democratic incumbents lost their elections. The proportion of Republican incumbents defeated (15 percent) was the same as the percentage of Democrats defeated in 1994 (15 percent) but lower than 2010 (22 percent), both of which were considered to be wave elections. The pattern of incumbents' vote shares also shifted from 2016 in ways that we would expect given the political context. In 2018, the average share of the vote for all incumbents in races contested by both parties was 63.7 percent; for Republican incumbents the figure was 59.4 percent, while for Democrats it was 69.8 percent.[48] If we compare these results to the years listed in Table 9-5, we see that the percent for all incumbents was down one to two points from recent elections. The average for Democrats was substantially better than their share since 2008 but about a point lower than in 2006 (which most closely mirrors the results in 2018). On the other hand, the Republicans' average was the lowest it has been since 1974, the first midterm after the Watergate investigation.

Candidate Quality and Party Recruitment

Table 11-5 shows data on the success of candidates during 2018, controlling for office background, party, and incumbency.[49] This corresponds to the 2016 evidence listed in Table 9-4. These data offer an additional perspective on the magnitude of the Democratic victory. Although Democratic candidates with previous elective experience performed well in almost all categories of House races, we also see that political amateurs did better than expected—especially in open seat contests. Prior experience mattered as it usually does, but Table 11-5 shows that the highly nationalized nature of the midterm election led a larger number of amateurs to win than is usually the case. We also observe that all types of challengers were able to defeat Republican incumbents and make significant gains in open seat races. Although there is a much smaller number of cases in the Senate, those candidates with prior experience in the House or state-level elective office clearly outperformed candidates with either local or no political experience.

As we discussed in Chapter 9, decisions by experienced politicians on whether to run for office are important strategic choices. In particular, we discussed the argument offered by Gary C. Jacobson and Samuel Kernell that these decisions are affected by potential candidates' evaluations of the national electoral context. In 2018, both the historical pattern of out-party gains in midterm elections and the unfavorable political context for the Republicans would be expected to encourage potential Democratic candidates to run and to discourage potential Republican candidates. We do not have systematic data on which candidates considered running and which chose not to, but a rough indicator of party success at recruitment is the number of experienced candidates who chose to run against incumbents. As Table 11-5 shows, there were thirty-five candidates with office experience who opposed incumbents in House races in 2018, twenty-eight of them Democrats and seven of them Republicans. This number falls short of the fifty-two experienced candidates (thirty of them Democrats) who ran against incumbents in 2006, which was also expected to be a good year for

Table 11-5 Success in House and Senate Elections, Controlling for Office Background, Party, and Incumbency, 2018 (percent)

Candidate's Last Office	Candidate is opponent of				No incumbent in district			
	Dem incumbent		Rep. Incumb.		Dem candidate		Rep. candidate	
	(%)	(N)	(%)	(N)	(%)	(N)	(%)	(N)
House								
State leg. or U.S. House	0	(3)	30	(10)	66.7	(9)	69.2	(13)
Other elect. office	0	(4)	11.1	(18)	45.5	(11)	41.7	(12)
No elective office	0	(136)	14.3	(168)	46.3	(41)	45.7	(35)
Senate								
U.S. House	33.3	(3)	33.3	(3)	100	(1)	50	(2)
State-level elect. office	25	(12)	0	(1)	0	(1)	100	(1)
Other elect. office	0	(2)	0	(2)	0	(1)	0	(0)
No elective office	0	(9)	0	(0)	0	(0)	0	(0)

Note: Percentages show proportion of candidates in each category who won; numbers in parentheses are the totals on which percentages are based. In the House, thirty-one incumbent Democrats and three incumbent Republicans did not face an opponent. No senators ran unopposed in the 2018 elections.

the Democrats but that offered that party roughly the same number of vulnerable Republicans as targets.

The national parties' roles in candidate recruitment have been expanding in recent years. Each party wants (and can reasonably imagine being able) to win majority control of the House and thus has strong incentive to want the strongest possible candidates to run. The parties now have, moreover, considerable resources at their disposal that can provide incentives for potential candidates. First, as we shall see in the next section, the national party organizations play a significant and increasing role in fund-raising. In addition, they can provide expertise, advice, and political contacts that can be very useful in campaigns. In the past, however, they would normally not have become involved when there was possible competition for the party's nomination.[50]

Increasingly, national officials have actively sought out potentially strong candidates and have influenced the choices in potentially competitive situations. As the strategic politicians' hypothesis would lead us to expect, Democratic leaders had an easier time recruiting in 2018. As we have seen above, many experienced politicians chose to run for House seats, but there were also recruitment failures, instances when the party could not get its preferred candidates. This was especially true for Republicans where, as a result of the unattractive political climate for their party, they lost several desired candidates. In Ohio, for instance, White House staff had to intervene to persuade Representative Jim Renacci, who had previously announced that he was running for governor, to switch over to the Senate race to challenge Democratic Senator Sherrod Brown. This was shortly after GOP frontrunner, State Treasurer and former member of the House Josh Mandel, dropped out of the race in January as a result of his wife's continuing health problems. In North Dakota, Republican Representative Kevin Cramer initially considered running against Democratic Senator Heidi Heitkamp who was considered vulnerable but announced in January 2018 that he would seek reelection in his House seat, only to change his mind a month later. A similar development occurred in Montana when Attorney General Tim Fox and Representative Ryan Zinke briefly considered running against Democratic Senator John Tester but ultimately decided against it. Eventually, the Republicans had to settle on State Auditor Matt Rosendale to challenge Tester for the Senate seat.[51]

An avenue of recruitment that was important in 2018 for both parties, but especially for the Democrats, was to seek more female candidates. Traditionally, Democrats have had an easier time recruiting women to run for political office as reflected by the larger number of Democratic women in both the House and Senate. One reason for the disparity in the number of women serving in Congress from the two parties is that Democratic women who have sought and achieved nomination have been more successful than their GOP counterparts. Another reason, however, is that women are more likely to seek nomination in the Democratic Party. In the 2018 election cycle, for instance, 344 Democratic women (including incumbents, quality challengers, and amateurs) filed federal paperwork to run for the House, compared to only 119 Republican women.[52] One cause of this nearly three-fold difference seems to be that GOP women tend to be more moderate in their policy views, and potential candidates believe that they have little chance of being nominated in their conservative-dominated party.[53] Other reasons include potential candidates' concerns about how serving in Congress might affect their families, coupled with the fact that conservative women often play the role of primary caregiver to their children.[54]

To compensate for these differences, Republican officials have organized efforts in recent elections to seek out and persuade potential female candidates, drawing especially on the current crop of women representatives and senators for support. A coalition of GOP donors and political operatives set up a new political action committee (PAC) in 2017 called Winning for Women, which led and expanded efforts to recruit a greater number of women with conservative positions on national security and economic issues to run in 2018.[55] Such efforts have not been easy during the Trump era, however, as GOP women candidates have increasingly had to answer for the president's controversial policies and remarks toward women.[56]

Given the favorable political climate in 2018, Democrats had far fewer retirements and a significantly easier time recruiting strong candidates for House and Senate races. In addition to recruiting more women in response to Trump's behavior during the 2016 presidential campaign and the increased attention stemming from the #MeToo movement, Democrats sought to recruit more candidates with previous political experience, especially in open seat races where they have the best chance of winning. Additionally, Democrats reached out to a number of military veterans when recruiting potential candidates to run for office, and their efforts resulted in a much larger number of veterans running as a result.[57]

Campaign Spending

In Chapter 9, we argued that a principal reason for the frequency of incumbents being reelected is that challengers find it difficult to raise the money necessary to compete effectively. Our evidence, and that of other analysts such as Jacobson, shows that when challengers can raise an adequate amount of money, much of the incumbency advantage can be neutralized, and competitive elections often result. Thus, how much candidates and other actors raise and spend is an important determinant of outcomes. Our previous discussion provided much information on the impact of money in individual races on differences between the chambers, so here we will focus mainly on aggregate trends in fund-raising and spending.

As our previous comments on legal issues indicate, the context for campaign spending continues to evolve. Four decades ago, money raised and spent by candidates accounted for the overwhelming majority of campaign spending. It is still the dominant source of funds in most congressional races (albeit not in the most expensive and competitive ones). This is mainly true because, as we discussed in Chapter 9, most members of Congress face no significant reelection threat. So in safe states and districts, most of the money that is spent comes from incumbents. Most challengers cannot raise enough to compete, and parties and outside groups have little incentive to become involved. In competitive general election races, on the other hand, both candidates, both parties, and a plethora of outside independent groups plunge in, and a huge total amount of money is spent.

In 2018, for example, the two most expensive Senate races were in Florida and Texas. In the former, incumbent Democrat Bill Nelson sought reelection to a fourth term but was defeated by incumbent Republican Governor Rick Scott. According to early estimates from the Center for Responsive Politics, both candidates spent a combined $114 million dollars where Rick Scott spent over $63 million of his own money.[58] Outside spending in the Florida race amounted to an additional $90 million, bringing the total spent in the Senate race to over $204 million. In Texas, incumbent Republican Ted Cruz ran against U.S. House member Beto O'Rourke. The combined spending in the Texas Senate race amounted to approximately $125 million, of which O'Rourke raised approximately $70 million.[59] When you factor in outside spending in the Senate race—a total of nearly $13.7 million—we see that over $139 million was spent on this race alone. Clearly, both of these Senate races set new records for the amount of money spent in the 2018 midterms.

Because many House seats are not seriously contested (and a variable but substantial number of incumbents have no major-party opponents),[60] many cases involve little spending. If, on the other hand, both sides think they have a chance at winning, the totals raised and spent can be substantial. In this cycle, outside groups spent more than all of the candidates in twenty-one separate House races. The most expensive race for independent spending ($19.8 million by both sides) was the 48th district of California, where incumbent Republican Dana Rohrabacher ran against an attorney, Harley Rouda. Rohrabacher was outspent by his Democratic opponent $7.6 to $2.96 million and ultimately went on to lose with 46.4 percent of the vote compared to 53.6 percent by Rouda. The second most expensive race for independent spending ($18.9 million on both sides) was the 8th district of Washington, where Democrat Kim Schrier, a pediatrician, faced former state Senator Dino Rossi. In addition, Schrier spent $7.9 million compared to Rossi's $4.8 million. In the end, Schrier went on to win the open seat with a vote of 53.1 percent to 46.9 percent.

We see from these examples that individual candidates raise enormous sums of money, especially incumbents and challengers in open seat races. But we also see that the amounts spent by parties and independent groups can now be quite substantial and may even dwarf candidate spending. In Chapter 9, we recounted in some detail the variety of ways that the parties help to finance campaigns and how such efforts have grown. They continued and increased in 2018. Republicans saw fund-raising as a potential way to enhance their party's disadvantages going into the midterm election, and so they put great effort into maximizing that resource and allocating it strategically.[61] The Republicans' diligence paid off, at least in monetary terms. Preliminary data from the Center for Responsive Politics show that the three major Democratic Party committees (the National Committee and the committees for each chamber) spent a total of almost $600 million in the 2018 cycle, compared to $651 million for the corresponding GOP committees.[62] This may have helped the Republicans stave off an even larger number of defeats in the House.

The third major pot of campaign money is provided by nonparty independent groups, whose spending has been stimulated and facilitated by past court rulings we have discussed. In 2018, nine of the ten congressional races with the most outside spending came in Senate races where enormous sums of money were spent on behalf of, or against, each party's candidates. For instance, groups linked to the Koch brothers, a set of billionaire conservative businessmen, were active in the 2018 election cycle. The Kochs, and their organizations, such as Americans for Prosperity, raised nearly $9 million on behalf of conservative House and Senate candidates in the 2018 midterms. By contrast, a liberal group known as Majority Forward, raised and spent over $45 million during the 2018 election, $37 million of which was spent against conservative candidates in the election cycle. This level of spending, in conjunction with outside spending by other liberal groups such as Patriot Majority USA, Environmental Defense Action Fund, and the Black Progressive Action Fund totalling nearly an additional $20 million, clearly reflected efforts to increase the number of Democrats elected to Congress.[63]

Thus, unlike in more recent elections, it appears that the balance of independent spending was tilted in favor of the Democrats in 2018, although more conservative groups still managed to raise an impressive sum of money based on preliminary spending reports. How much this outside spending truly influenced the pattern of election outcomes remains unclear since it represents only a fraction of the overall total spent. Indeed, we think it is important to recognize that as the aggregate amount of money spent on elections continues to increase, it becomes less and less likely that money (whatever its other effects in the political system) will dictate outcomes as long as the respective shares of the total do not tilt strongly to one side.[64]

THE 2018 ELECTIONS:
THE IMPACT ON CONGRESS

Like the elections of 2010 and 2014, the elections of 2018 had a substantial impact on the Congress. Which party exerts majority control of a chamber has significant implications for the chamber's operation, and the 2018 midterm elections transferred control of the House from the Republicans to the Democrats while shoring up Republican strength in the Senate. This also meant the reintroduction of divided government, with President Trump still in the White House and the Democrats in partial control of Congress.

Action in the Lame-Duck Congress

As with the previous Congress (see discussion in Chapter 9), the 115th Congress ended with a postelection lame-duck session to complete unfinished legislative business. Although the Republicans faced numerous missteps despite having unified government, they recognized the value of achieving key policy goals before the end of the year since control of the House would revert to the Democrats at the beginning of the 116th Congress. As noted earlier, a Pew study found the 115th Congress to be the fourth least productive since World War II despite having Republican control of both Congress and the presidency. In an effort to secure some additional legislative wins for the president, the Republican majorities in both chambers set out to deal with some key policy areas that had proven elusive prior to the midterms.

The first major legislative issue they had to contend with was passage of the Farm Bill, which both chambers failed to pass earlier in the year. Facing pressure from both sides, the bill that initially passed the Senate in early December sought to ensure stability to farmers during the next ten years by providing incentives for new farmers, continuing to offer crop insurance, and investing in agricultural research. It also continued nutrition assistance programs for 40 million lower income families and avoided restrictions on food stamp programs. With an estimated price tag of $867 billion over the next decade, 75 percent of which covers participants in the SNAP (food stamp) program, the House approved the conference report on the bill on December 12, 2018, and the president signed the legislation on December 20, 2018.[65]

Congress also was dealing with a major criminal justice reform proposal that had been held up earlier in the year as a result of some key House-Senate differences. The bill, known as the First Step Act, initially passed the House in May 2018 but was viewed by many senators as not being broad enough in scope. After months of negotiations over the range and scope of the reform proposal, the Senate passed a revised version of the bill by an 87-12 vote on December 18, 2018, that would allow thousands of individuals in federal prison to earn early release as well as reduce the length of prison sentences in the future.[66] Two days later, the House passed the Senate version of the bill in a 358-36 vote, and President Trump signed the bipartisan legislation the following day. Although the bill was not viewed as perfect by either side, it was supported by Trump's son-in-law and senior adviser, Jared Kushner, who viewed it as an important step in dealing with the problems stemming from mass incarceration during the past few decades.[67]

Finally, Congress had to deal with a looming government shutdown in early December that would result in the closure of nine federal departments if a budget agreement was not reached by Friday, December 21, 2018. At first, it seemed like such a shutdown could easily be averted until President Trump insisted that he would not sign any stopgap measures unless $5 billion was included for building a wall at the Mexican border (a key promise he made during his 2016 presidential campaign). For several days, Republican and Democratic leaders in Congress haggled with the president over his demand with little movement from either side regarding the funding for the wall.[68] On December 19, however, Senator Majority Leader Mitch McConnell said he was pushing forward with a bill that would extend government funding through February 8, 2019, by punting on the funding for a wall on the country's southern border. Democratic Minority Leader Chuck Schumer initially pledged to support the bill, and it looked like the president would as well.[69]

The following day, however, the president changed course and reasserted that funding for the wall would have to be included in the continuing resolution, or he would not sign the bill. This was likely a function of increased criticism from conservative groups who demanded the president stick with his original campaign promise to build a wall. The House managed to pass a bill later that day with an additional $5.7 billion to begin construction on the wall between the United States and Mexico, but it was unclear at the time whether the Senate would be able to pass it in light of the sixty-vote threshold in the upper chamber.[70] Although the president initially said he would be "proud to shut down the government for border security,"[71] he later tweeted that it would be the Democrat's fault if the bill failed in the Senate and that the shutdown "will last for a very long time."[72] Indeed, the Senate chose not to adopt the House version of the resolution even after a few compromise attempts were made, and the government shut down at midnight on December 21, 2018.

In the days following the shutdown, both the president and the Democrats in Congress refused to budge from their established positions and continued to trade blame for the current situation. After almost a week passed with no resolution in sight, it became clear that a solution would likely have to wait until the Democrats assumed control of the House on January 3, 2019. In the interim, the president raised the stakes of the debate when he threatened to shut down the U.S.-Mexico border in order to put increased pressure on the Democrats to provide sufficient funding for the wall.[73] Democrats in Congress initially dismissed such rhetoric and held to their original position, but the president continued to tweet that the shutdown was entirely a function of inaction on the part of Democrats.

After the Democrats assumed control of the House on January 3, 2019, newly sworn in Speaker of the House, Nancy Pelosi, reiterated that there was no room to negotiate over the $5 billion that President Trump was requesting. Indeed, "the newly Democratic-controlled House passed a package of bills late Thursday that would reopen the federal government without paying for President Trump's border wall, drawing a swift veto threat from the White House and leaving the partial shutdown no closer to getting resolved."[74] The legislation included a package of six spending bills that would reopen all of the federal agencies closed since December 22 as well as extend funding for the Department of Homeland Security through February 8. Two senators—Cory Gardner (R-CO) and Susan Collins (R-ME)—urged the president to end the impasse with Democrats, but Majority Leader Mitchell McConnell insisted that the Senate would only take up spending legislation that was fully supported by the president.[75]

On Friday, January 4, a key meeting between leaders of both chambers was scheduled with President Trump to try to find some common ground and end the government shutdown that had lasted nearly two weeks. After a ninety-minute meeting described as "contentious" by some in attendance, President Trump announced in a Rose Garden news conference that the shutdown could last "months or even years" if Congress refuses to act on his border wall. He also asserted that he could declare a national emergency to build the wall if it came to that since having border security was paramount to his administration.[76] After three additional weeks of back-and-forth negotiations between President Trump and the leaders in Congress, he finally agreed to reopen the government temporarily without getting the $5.7 billion in funding for the wall between the United States and Mexico. In total, the government shutdown lasted thirty-five days, making it the longest shutdown in history and costing the American economy approximately $3 billion according to estimates from the Congressional Budget Office.[77]

Despite Trump's capitulation to end the government shutdown in late January without receiving the funds he requested for the border wall, any victory was short-lived since the government would again run out of money at midnight on February 15 unless Congress and the president reached an additional agreement to fund the government through the remainder of the fiscal year. There were many tense moments during the next three weeks as both sides sought to reach some form of compromise to avoid a second shutdown, but the president finally agreed to sign a spending and border security plan just hours before the deadline even though it failed to provide the funding he requested for the border wall. Just prior to signing the legislation, however, Trump also declared a national emergency (as he had promised to do several weeks earlier) that would allow him to repurpose funds from other governmental agencies to build the border wall without explicit congressional approval. The action immediately sparked backlash from members of both parties who viewed such an action as a direct violation of the separation of powers as outlined in the Constitution. As of this writing, his declaration is likely to be challenged in federal court in the days ahead.[78]

The drama occurring during the lame-duck session and beyond regarding the government shutdown illustrated continued conflict between the parties on policy, as well as the existence of internal divisions within each party. It also revealed the possibility of compromise between the parties under some circumstances, despite resistance from the president on passage of the continuing resolution to keep the government funded beyond late December. Some observers thought that a new era of cross-party deals was possible, while others expected continuation of polarization and gridlock.

Organizational Changes in the New Congress

Prior to the start of the 116th Congress, there were some rumblings about who should be the leader of the Democratic Party now that the Democrats would be back in majority control of the chamber. One senior Democratic leader, Rep. Elijah Cummings (D-MD) indicated before the midterms that Nancy Pelosi, who previously served as Speaker from 2007 to 2011, should be able to retain the speakership as long as she wants if the Democrats are successful in the election.[79] Despite this affirmation, a rebellious faction of newly elected Democrats had other views on the matter of who should be the next speaker. Less than two weeks after the midterms, sixteen Democrats released a letter "vowing to mount a coup and derail Nancy Pelosi's bid to become House Speaker, the first major warning shot from the group of detractors who are trying to stop the powerful leader's bid in the new Democratic majority."[80] Many of their concerns seemed to stem from the view that Pelosi and others in the Democratic leadership were out of touch with many of the newly elected members as a result of both their past failures and their advanced age (Pelosi is currently 78, and Steny Hoyer is 79). Although Pelosi remained confident she had sufficient votes to be elected Speaker, this incident did suggest some of the struggles that she might face in the new Congress moving forward.

Notwithstanding the initial concerns among some of the newly elected Democrats, Pelosi was nominated to be Speaker by a majority of the Democratic caucus on November 28, 2018, which helped pave the way for her formal selection as Speaker when the new Congress convened early the following year.[81] When the 116th Congress opened on January 3, 2019, it was Democratic divisions in the House that were most visible as expected. However, Pelosi ended up earning 220 votes as Speaker, which gave her four more than she needed to become the leader of the House chamber. According to historical data, Pelosi's achievement of repeating as Speaker is relatively rare. "Only Frederick Muhlenberg, Henry Clay, John W. Taylor, Thomas Bracket Reed and Sam Rayburn have ever recaptured the gavel after serving as speaker, returning to the minority, and then ascending back to the majority. Rayburn was the most recent to achieve the feat—in 1955."[82]

For House Republicans, there was no public contest for leadership positions as it became clear that Rep. Kevin McCarthy of California was the top choice among a majority of the conference to be the new House Minority Leader. After Speaker Paul Ryan announced in April 2018 that he was not planning to seek reelection in order to spend more time with his family, he immediately endorsed McCarthy as his successor, who had held the Majority Leader position for the previous four years. McCarthy was elected Minority Leader by a 159-43 vote in mid-November, after facing a long-shot challenge from Jim Jordan (R-OH), the cofounder of the conservative Freedom Caucus. He later received the support of 192 Republicans when the 116th Congress convened.[83] "Rep. Steve Scalise of Louisiana, the current No. 3 House Republican, was elected to the No. 2 Republican leadership position in the new Congress, where he will serve as Minority Whip. Rep. Liz Cheney of Wyoming, the daughter of former Vice President Dick Cheney, was elected to the third-ranking position in the GOP hierarchy and will be the next Republican Conference Chair."[84]

Of the two chambers, the House saw the greater organizational shift in leadership because of the switch in party control of the chamber. In the Senate, there was no public opposition to the selection of the Mitch McConnell as the Majority Leader for the Republicans. McConnell, now 76, was first elected to the Senate in 1984 and has served as the leader of his party since 2006.[85] In accordance with Senate GOP rules that imposes a three-term limit on most leadership positions, Sen. John Cornyn (R-TX) vacated his No. 2 slot as Majority Whip. He will be replaced by Sen. John Thune (R-SD) who had previously served as GOP conference chairman, which will now be filled by Sen. John Barrasso (R-WY) who had served as Republican Policy Committee chairman prior to the beginning of the 116th Congress. Additionally, Sen. Roy Blunt (R-MO) will take over as Policy Committee chairman, Sen. Joni Ernst (R-IA) will become the next Republican conference vice-chair, and Sen. Todd Young (R-IN) will serve as the chairman of the National Republican Senatorial Committee, replacing Senator Cory Gardner (R-CO), who had previously held that post.[86]

Despite a net loss of two seats in the Senate, Democratic leadership in the upper chamber remained the same following the midterm elections. Sen. Chuck Schumer (D-NY) was reelected as the Minority Leader, which many expected in light of his prior experience in that position. Sen. Dick Durbin (D-IL) would continue as Minority Whip while Sen. Patty Murray (D-WA) agreed to stay on as the Assistant Democratic Leader. In addition to each of these positions, Sen. Debbie Stabenow (D-MI) will serve as the chairwoman of the Policy and Communications Committee, Sen. Elizabeth Warren (D-MA) and Sen. Mark Warner (D-VA) will remain as the vice chairs of the Conference, Sen. Amy Klobuchar (D-MN) will serve as the chair of the Steering Committee, while Sen. Joe Manchin (D-WV) and Sen. Tammy Baldwin (D-WI) will continue as the vice chairs of the Policy and Communications Committee and the Secretary of the Conference, respectively.[87]

The Reinforcement and Institutionalization of Polarization in Congress

In Chapter 9, we discussed the sharp partisan divide in recent congresses. The relatively great ideological homogeneity of policy views within the parties and the lack of overlap between them have fostered interparty conflict and have made collaboration difficult. The 2018 election results have reinforced that pattern. Table 11-6 shows the outcomes of House races, controlling for the political leanings of the districts. These leanings are measured through a comparison of Trump's share of the two-party vote in the districts with his 2016 vote share nationally (46.4 percent).

If we focus on those districts in which Trump's vote was at least 10 percent above or below his national vote—that is, districts that are strongly tilted to a party compared to the nation as a whole—we see that, after 2018, there are only a few cases with a representative from the party opposite the district's partisan leaning. Specifically, there are 278 members (sixty more than a majority of the House) from districts with a tilt of 10 percent or more. Of the representatives from those districts, only eight were from the opposite party. If we expand the bands of district tilt to plus or minus 5 percent compared to the national vote, there are 365 districts—nearly 84 percent of the total—that fit the definition. In them, only twenty-three members, slightly more

Table 11-6   House Outcomes by District Leanings, 2018

District leaning	R→R		R→D		D→R		D→D		Total
	N	%	N	%	N	%	N	%	
< −10%	0	0	1	2.3	0	0	108	56.5	109
−10% to −5%	0	0	2	4.5	0	0	37	19.4	39
−5% to 0%	0	0	9	20.5	0	0	26	13.6	35
0% to 5%	4	2.0	15	34.1	0	0	16	8.4	35
5% to 10%	32	16.3	13	29.5	0	0	3	1.6	48
>10%	161	81.7	4	9.1	3	100.0	1	.5	169
Total	197	100.0	44	100.0	3	100.0	191	100.0	435

Source: Compiled by the authors.

Note: District leanings are measured through a comparison of Trump's share of the two-party vote in the districts (data from Pennsylvania have been updated to reflect the newly redrawn congresisonal districts) with his 2016 vote share nationally (46.4 percent).

than 6 percent, came from the party opposite the district's tilt. To put this in historical perspective, after the 1972 election, there were 155 districts that leaned toward a party by 10 percent or more. Of their representatives, forty-four (28 percent) came from the opposite party. And using the 5 percent criterion, there were 288 districts, of which eighty-six (30 percent) had opposite-party representatives.

The implication of these data is that there are now very few representatives who feel cross-pressured by the pull of their parties and the wishes of their districts. Similarly, there are few who perceive conflict between their districts' wishes and their own views regarding what is desirable policy. Thus, a substantial majority of members have the incentive to respond to their party base and a disincentive to cooperate or compromise with those in the other party. And the policy wishes of the bases of the two parties are distinctly in conflict. In a Pew poll conducted immediately after the 2018 elections, respondents were asked whether they thought President Trump or the Democratic leaders in Congress would be successful in getting their programs passed into law during the 116th Congress. Of the Republicans surveyed, 55 percent believed that Trump would be successful, whereas 78 percent thought the Democratic leaders would be unsuccessful in achieving their legislative objectives. By contrast, only 49 percent of those identifying as Democrats believed the Democratic leadership would be successful, whereas 79 percent indicated they thought Trump would be largely unsuccessful.[88] We can, therefore, expect significant conflict between the parties over policy in the 116th Congress. There are also electoral incentives involved. Both parties recognize the importance of majority control of the two congressional chambers and of the presidency heading into the 2020 election, and especially of the possibility of one party having unified control of all of them. As a consequence, potential electoral impacts of legislative activity are a prominent part of the calculations of members and party leaders.

As in the last few congresses, health care will continue to be a major point of contention but will likely be joined by concerns over the economy, federal spending and the deficit, trade, infrastructure, and immigration. Regarding the Affordable Care Act, despite its having been in effect for eight years, Republicans remain intensely opposed as reflected by their unsuccessful attempt to repeal and replace it in early 2017. Indeed, several Republican governors and state attorneys general filed a lawsuit in federal court in 2017 arguing against the mandate requiring individuals to have health care. On Friday, December 14, 2018, "a federal judge in Texas struck down the entire Affordable Care Act on the grounds that its mandate requiring people to buy health insurance is unconstitutional and the rest of the law cannot stand without it." Leaders from several Democratic states have made it known that they plan to appeal the decision, which will likely not have an immediate effect, prior to the case making its way to the Supreme Court in the next two years.[89]

More generally, many partisan identifiers want their officeholders to push for their policy priorities and to resist those of the other party. For example, a Pew poll conducted about a week before the election suggested that 64 percent of voters are very or somewhat concerned that the GOP would not focus enough on oversight of the Trump Administration if the Republicans maintained control of Congress. A somewhat smaller majority (55 percent) of those polled were concerned that Democrats would spend too much time investigating the president if they were to win control of one or both chambers of Congress. Additionally, members of both parties worried about the state of the economy, health care, and how immigration would be addressed in the new Congress, especially in light of developments during the past two years.[90]

During Trump's first two years in office, he chose not to veto legislation since his party controlled both houses of Congress.[91] That will likely change in the 116th Congress with the return of divided government. What will ensue will depend in large measure on the strategies that the Democratic and Republican leaders adopt (or are permitted to adopt). In the House, the Democrats are likely to introduce legislation that seeks to lower the cost of prescription drugs, pass ethics reform, shore up support for the Affordable Care Act, and establish an infrastructure package that can attract widespread support. They are also likely to engage in more oversight of the administration in light of the numerous ongoing investigations. Republican House leaders' priorities, by contrast, include making tax cuts permanent, securing pay raises for the military, battling the widespread opioid epidemic, and addressing the growing national debt. In the Senate, the first few months will likely include confirming both executive and judicial appointments, especially given the continued departures of key Trump officials in recent months.[92]

THE 2020 ELECTIONS AND BEYOND

We conclude this chapter with a look forward to the congressional elections in 2020 and later years and a discussion of the factors likely to influence them.

General Considerations for 2020

In looking ahead to the 2018 elections in Chapter 9, we emphasized that presidential approval and the performance of the economy would be important in shaping the outcomes of the upcoming elections. The same considerations are equally relevant for 2020. The Republicans suffered in 2018 because voters did not perceive their positions or their performance positively, either in the presidency or in Congress. Now both political parties have partial responsibility for performance, and, as we have just discussed, this situation is likely to produce frequent conflict between them. The Trump administration and congressional Republicans will seek to emphasize their efforts to energize the economy in light of the recent economic downturn and claim credit if conditions are perceived to improve. Democrats will continue to attack the Republicans for failing to control government spending and will probably use their enhanced positions in the House to force consideration of their priorities and solutions. The likely legislative battles that we discussed previously will draw some clear lines of conflict, and the reaction of the public to them will shape the political landscape. Thus, prospects in the 2020 congressional elections rest partly on the perceived importance of various issues and partly on the voters' perceptions of the parties' performance on those issues. Those prospects will also be affected by the course of the 2020 presidential race.

Barring a terrorist attack on the United States or drastic international developments, the performance of the economy will be the dominant influence on the politics of 2020, especially given growing concern over recent declines in the stock market and a possible trade war. The statistical gains regarding employment may be an asset in this regard for President Trump and Republicans if those trends continue, especially if the stock market stabilizes and continues to increase, but it is what the voters believe is happening that is key. In addition, new priorities are likely to emerge because the Democrats hope to recruit the strongest candidate possible to challenge Trump in the 2020 presidential election. Of particular import will be how the public perceives the interaction of the two parties in governance. We saw that in 2018 the electorate had a negative reaction to partisan conflicts and to the inability of the parties to come to agreement. If, as seems likely, that pattern persists, much will depend on whether the voters think that one party is primarily responsible or they see the blame as equally divided.

It is quite clear that the public is not very sanguine about the possibility of compromise and achievement during the next two years. In a survey conducted just before the 2018 elections, the Pew Research Center found that an increasing number of Americans believe that it is both "stressful and frustrating" to engage in conversations with those individuals that they disagree with politically. This seems especially true for Democrats, as the percentage who agree with this statement increased from 45 percent in 2016 to 57 percent in 2018. In contrast, roughly half of Republicans agreed with this statement two years ago and again in 2018.[93] Such sentiments have obvious implications for individuals of differing political beliefs to reach political compromise, whether it be among citizens or their elected representatives.

These public attitudes could significantly influence the makeup of the electorate in 2020 as it appears that it did in 2018. We saw previously how different the demographic composition of actual voters can be between midterm and presidential years.

Democrats likely hope that investigations and increased oversight of the president will yield new information that will detract from Trump and his agenda during the 116th Congress. At the same time, Republicans may try to frame many of the actions taken by the Democrats in the House as obstructionist, which will stimulate more Republicans going to the polls in 2020. The electorate's composition could also be influenced by the identity and characteristics of the Democratic nominees for president. As we saw during the 2018 midterms, women were highly motivated to turn out and vote in response to the first two years of the Trump presidency, and similar trends could repeat themselves if the Democrats were to nominate a strong female candidate to counter Trump in the 2020 election.

In anticipation of the 2020 presidential election, Trump has taken unprecedented steps in securing renomination by incorporating the Republican National Committee and the president's reelection campaign into a single entity. Traditionally, the president's reelection committee and the national party committee work in tandem with one another, rather than combine into a single entity. "Under the plan, which has been in the works for several weeks, the Trump reelection campaign and the RNC will merge their field and fundraising programs into a joint outfit dubbed Trump Victory."[94] The goal, according to some party strategists, is to streamline the nomination process among Republicans to avoid the type of party infighting that occurred in 2016 as well as save both staff and resources. It also has the added benefit of making it harder for any other Republicans to challenge President Trump for the nomination in 2020. Despite these potential benefits, many within the party see this as yet another example of the degree of unprecedented control that President Trump has over the Republican Party.[95]

House Races in 2020

We contended in Chapter 9 that one important thing to focus on is the likely vulnerability of individual incumbents. Table 11-7 shows the distribution of winning percentages during 2018 across the parties and types of races. We noted in Chapter 9 that the number of close races (55 percent or less for the winner) in 2016, thirty-two, was relatively low compared to the ninety-five close races in 1996. It was also considerably lower than the eighty-one close contests in 2010. In 2018, however, the number of close races increased significantly, to eighty-nine. These previously close contests are likely to dominate the efforts of the respective parties in 2020, especially in districts where the races were closer than expected.

Another source of strong contests is open seats. Given that they have just recently retaken the majority, few Democrat House members are likely to opt for retirement unless public opinion turns strongly against their party during the next two years. On the other hand, a larger number of Democratic members than usual may choose to run for higher office if the context appears attractive. For Republicans, the incentives are reversed. Being in the minority is less attractive, and so a number of senior members may be tempted to retire, particularly if they are convinced that their party is unlikely to return to the majority in the near future. And, as we will see shortly, there will also be few opportunities for higher-office candidacies available.

Also important for 2020, as we emphasized earlier, is candidate quality. In early 2017, both parties were already at work trying to recruit candidates for 2018 House

Table 11-7 Percentage of the Vote Received by Winning House Candidates, by Party and Type of Race, 2018

Percentage of the vote	Republicans			Democrats		
	Reelected incumbent	Successful challenger	Open seat	Reelected incumbent	Successful challenger	Open seat
55% or less	40	0	8	4	26	11
55.1–60.0%	39	0	9	22	3	6
60.1–70.0%	67	0	11	53	0	8
70–100%	24	0	2	96	0	6
Total	170	0	30	175	29	31

Source: Compiled by the authors.

races, and the effort will continue in 2020 as well. Finally, campaign money will again be consequential. As is routine, both the Democratic Congressional Campaign Committee and the National Republican Congressional Committee ended the 2018 campaign season with debts. The two committees will make paying off these debts a priority, but the majority party usually finds it relatively easy to do so, and President Trump is likely to help with the Republicans' fund-raising. Regardless of the speed of paying debts, however, it seems likely that more money will be spent on the 2020 campaigns than was spent in 2018 despite the records shattered in the midterm.[96]

In light of these considerations and other contextual features, the following is an obvious question: Do the Republicans have a significant chance of retaking the House in 2020? They will need to win at least nineteen seats as of this writing to accomplish that feat. The data in Table 11-7 show that forty-one Democratic winners received 55 percent or less of the vote in 2018. That is nearly twice as many narrowly won seats as the Democrats had after 2014, and it is probable that most of the Republicans' targeting will focus on this set of districts, but even if the Republicans were to win more than half of those seats, they would have to retain every one of their own marginal seats to have a narrow majority. Looking back at the data in Table 11-6 provides an additional perspective. After the 2018 election, there are fifty-two seats held by Democrats in districts where Trump ran stronger than he did nationally, more than twice the number needed by Republicans. Then there are another nine districts in which the Trump vote was within five percentage points of his national vote share. These offer less attractive chances for the Republicans, but they are the only plausible sources of the seats the party would need to win.

The reality, however, is that the Republicans' chances of winning back majority control of the House are somewhat slim. Beginning with 1980, when partisan polarization began to have a significant impact on national politics, in only six of the twenty national elections has a party gained as many as nineteen seats, and in five of them, the losing party had unified control of the government.[97] Since neither the Democrats nor GOP have unified control of Congress, the task facing the Republicans in 2020 looks formidable indeed.

Senate Races in 2020

Unlike the House, where all seats are up for election every two years, Senate contests offer quite a different set of races each time. In contrast to 2018, in the 2020 election cycle the thirty-three states holding Senate elections will have almost twice as many Republican seats at risk than Democratic ones (twenty-two versus twelve). Two of the senators are Republicans from states that Clinton carried in 2016—Susan Collins of Maine and Cory Gardner of Colorado—while only Doug Jones from Alabama is running in a deeply red state. Democrats may also target senators running for reelection in Arizona, Iowa, and North Carolina, whereas Republicans may challenge incumbent senators running in New Hampshire, Minnesota, and Virginia. These are among the races that are likely to draw the most attention from party strategists seeking to alter or reinforce the partisan balance in the Senate. But also unlike 2018, the next cycle does not feature many incumbents perceived to be seriously vulnerable.

In their first look at the 2020 Senate contests, the analysts of the Cook Political Report classified no seats as "toss ups" and only four seats as just leaning toward the party currently holding the seats (three Republicans and one Democrat).[98] Thus, while the Republicans will be forced to defend more seats, at this early stage their three-seat majority does not appear to be seriously endangered. Of course, as we have seen in the past, that picture can change radically over time.

As we have shown, even more than in House races, the outcomes of Senate contests will depend on who chooses to seek office and what seats are open. So far, only Lamar Alexander (R-TN) and Pat Roberts (R-KS) have announced that they do not plan to seek reelection in 2020.[99] While additional senators may decide not to run for reelection in the coming months, those decisions may be a function of developments in the 116th Congress. If a substantial number of other incumbents do decide to quit, the electoral landscape could be altered. With regard to potential candidates, the main focus will be on recruiting experienced Democratic challengers for the large number of GOP seats up for reelection. There have been no announcements yet, but it is likely that the chairman of the Democratic Senatorial Campaign Committee is actively seeking possible candidates to challenge Republican incumbents in 2020.

Beyond 2020: The Ongoing Battle for Party Control

Since we do not know how the 2020 contests will turn out, it is impossible to speak with any degree of certainty about the pattern of subsequent elections. We can, however, consider some factors that are likely to influence those patterns. The future is murkier than usual because the consequences of most of those factors are contingent on events between now and 2020, many of which undoubtedly will involve the unique conditions associated with the Trump presidency. Additionally, the interplay between Democrats and Republicans in the 116th Congress, and the public's reaction to it, will help to determine whether the Republicans are able to restore their unified control of government, the Democrats get unified control under a Democrat president, or divided government is maintained. Each of those possible outcomes would lead us to expect a different political future after 2020. As we have pointed out, unified control is almost a necessary condition for a nationalized election that can produce large political changes, although it is possible to imagine an extraordinary situation (such as a major presidential landslide) that could yield such an outcome without that precondition.

Another consequential post-2020 consideration will be the results of the 2018 midterms with regard to the various state governments. Prior to the recent election, Republicans controlled both chambers of state legislatures in thirty-two states as well as a majority of governorships. In 2018, Democrats made major inroads by winning control of seven state governorships and seven state legislative chambers, although they still lag a bit behind Republicans across the country.[100] If the Democrats manage to pick up additional state legislative seats and win available governorships during the 2020 election, this could have significant implications for redistricting following the 2020 census since a majority of states rely on state legislatures to redraw congressional district boundaries.

Also consequential will be the shape of demographic change during the next few years and beyond. In recent decades, there has been substantial migration from Democratic states in the East and Midwest to red states in the South and West, and that has helped the Democrats win four of the last seven presidential elections. Certainly not all of these migrants have liberal policy preferences, but enough do to have made a difference in the political tilt of a number of states. Indeed, southern states such as Georgia, North Carolina, and Virginia that have traditionally voted Republican are beginning to look competitive as reflected in recent statewide and national contests. If this trend continues, existing political alignments could shift further, with important implications especially for presidential and Senate elections.

A final important variable will be the ongoing contest for the loyalties of the Latino community. As we noted in Chapters 2, 4, and 9, Latinos make up the fastest-growing major segment of the electorate. The two major parties will continue to compete for the Latino vote, and the results of that competition will play a major role in shaping the future of American electoral politics. This is a particularly important matter for the GOP because of the party's overall demographic problems. As we discussed previously, the age group that offered the strongest support for Republicans in 2018 was people sixty-five and over: 50 percent, roughly the same as those in the next group (forty-five to sixty-four). The former is, inevitably, a shrinking pool of voters and thus of GOP support in the long term.

Moreover, as our previous discussion indicated, the Republicans have recently faced a serious disadvantage in the competition for the Latino vote, mainly because of the reactions of the Latino community to the fight over immigration. The issue will not go away, especially given the president's consistently inflammatory rhetoric and the increased attention given to building a wall between the United States and Mexico.[101] Although not all Republicans agree with Trump on how illegal immigration should be handled, it has become increasingly difficult for Republicans to distance themselves from the president's incendiary views on this complicated issue. Indeed, it is likely that Democrats in Congress will continue to support more favorable legislation dealing with immigration—like the Deferred Action for Childhood Arrivals or DACA enacted during the Obama administration—in order to maintain Latino support while conservative Republicans will continue to side with the president. It will be interesting (and politically consequential) to see how this interaction plays out in the next few years.

PART FOUR

THE 2016 AND 2018 ELECTIONS IN PERSPECTIVE

CHAPTER TWELVE

THE 2016 AND 2018 ELECTIONS AND THE FUTURE OF AMERICAN POLITICS

One of the remarkable characteristics of contemporary politics in the United States is that the two parties are locked in a competitive electoral balance nationally. Over the last thirty years, the House, the Senate, and the presidency have shifted partisan control several times, and each election opens with at least one, if not two or even all three, of the elected branches of government under close competition for partisan control. One reason this is remarkable is that party control is at stake even though very few House or Senate seats are actually competitive, as we saw in Chapters 9 and 11, with incumbents winning reelection easily and often. Another reason that this close balance is remarkable is that pundits and politicians alike view each election outcome as promising major change in the balance of power between the two parties for years to come.

After Barack Obama's victories in 2008 and 2012, a number of political scientists, analysts, and strategists made the case that the United States was in the midst of realignment of political power to a new lasting Democratic majority. The claims were based on two trends: (1) the increasing numbers of black and Hispanic voters and (2) a decisive shift away from the Republican Party by the suburban and well-educated constituencies that once formed the backbone of the GOP. To be sure, arguments supporting a long-term Democratic advantage were based on well-researched population and voting data projections, which do seem to advantage the Democrats. But Donald Trump's victory in 2016 and the accompanying GOP majorities in the House and Senate likely arrested Democratic optimism about their electoral prospects. Indeed, some pundits argued that the GOP victories of 2016 foretold the emergence of a Republican realignment—or, more specifically, a "Trump realignment"—which would advantage the Republicans into the future.[1] Given that realignments are conceived as durable shifts in electoral coalitions, it is highly implausible, of course, that a new realignment would emerge just four years after another had taken place.

Astoundingly, professions of a new electoral realignment were made once again following the 2018 congressional midterms—an election that resulted in electoral gains for the Democrats in the House *and* the Republicans in the Senate. CNN analyst Ronald Brownstein noted that 2018 was a "realignment of American politics" pitting college-educated whites, minorities, and millennials against a GOP base composed largely of blue-collar and evangelical whites and fueled by higher voter turnout in rural America.[2] Analysts and commentators for NBC News, the *New York Times*, and the *Washington Post* made parallel claims about the 2018 midterms, declaring the electorate fundamentally altered by a political realignment.[3] Similar to Brownstein, these authors also note that the Democratic base is increasingly composed of well-educated urban and suburban whites, along with racial minorities and young voters, while Republicans increasingly rely on support from rural, blue-collar, and religious whites. Our readers will surely recognize, however, that these electoral coalitions are no different than those that were in place following the Obama victories of 2008 and 2012—which themselves were declared to be realignments—and have their origins in a much earlier period.

Pundits' regular declarations of a new electoral realignment based on the latest election results can be dizzying and are likely self-serving (hoping to attract ratings or readers or, perhaps, to promote partisan interests). In our view, the overuse (and misuse) of the realignment concept only serves to diminish its conceptual meaning and theoretical relevance. Moreover, as we noted earlier in the book, the critical election-realignment dynamic—a long period of stability in the party system is altered by a rapid and dramatic change, leading to a new, long-term partisan equilibrium—provides a poor description of electoral change in modern American politics. Past partisan realignments typically involved significant changes in the regional and social bases of party support, the mobilization of new groups into the electorate, changing electoral cleavages based on the emergence of new issues, and a displacement of partisan loyalties. As the evidence presented in Chapters 4 through 8 shows, while there have been slow alterations in the nature of partisan coalitions during the last 60 to 70 years—the span of our primary source of data, the American National Election Studies—there is no evidence to support a realignment in the classic sense during this period.

Instead, we have argued that partisan change in modern American politics is best described by the "punctuated equilibrium" model of change, where a "critical moment" triggers a rapid but brief period of change followed by a slower and prolonged period of transformation before a new steady state is formed.[4] The 1960s served as a critical moment in American politics. The national Democratic Party's sponsorship of civil rights for African Americans created a schism between the party's more liberal voters and white southern Democrats. With the passage of the 1964 Civil Rights Act and 1965 Voting Rights Act, black voters' loyalties moved sharply toward the Democratic Party (see Chapter 5), which, in turn, precipitated a slower and prolonged period of change in whites' partisan loyalties. By the mid-1970s, the proportion of the white voters who considered themselves "independent" had increased markedly, and by the mid-1980s, whites nationally began to lean toward the Republican Party. The elongated period of transformation triggered by the critical events of the 1960s continues to shape America's electoral landscape today.[5] America's racial and ethnic minorities continue to view the Democratic Party's adherence to the civil rights agenda of the 1960s as providing them with a natural political home, and America's whites are increasingly more likely to identify with the Republican Party. Indeed, these divergent bases of support help to elucidate why immigration is among the most hotly debated issues today and why the political parties support increasingly polarized immigration policies.[6] If the Democratic Party continues to outperform the Republicans among racial and ethnic minorities, then immigration—particularly migration from Latin America—would seem to benefit the Democrats over the long haul as these immigrants eventually become citizens and voters.

As we noted earlier in the book, any talk of a long-term electoral advantage for one party or the other presupposes that current voters will maintain their partisan loyalties and that group allegiances will remain stable. We should also be reminded that party leaders are strategic politicians who are likely to change their messages and mobilization strategies as the political environment changes in order to win elections. Nevertheless, one reason that pundits and partisans tend to extrapolate from the most recent election into the future is that it has indeed been the case that there are what we might term "electoral eras" that last for decades. While recent electoral history has exhibited frequent oscillations between which party controls the presidency and Congress, we should not rule out the possibility that one party might develop an electoral advantage and seize control of government for an extended period of time.

In the century and a half since the party system has consisted of the Republicans and the Democrats as the two major parties, there have been three different decades-long patterns of long-term partisan coalitions, leading into the 1994-2018 period:

1. After the end of Reconstruction (1876-1896), the two parties were locked in close balance for two decades, much like the contemporary period, in which nearly every election yielded small majorities first for one party and then for the other, with divided control common.

2. That was succeeded by a generation (from roughly 1896 to 1930) in which Republicans held an often-small majority nationwide, but thereby holding power in each of the elected branches of the national government most, but not all, of the time.

3. The Great Depression and the coming of Franklin Roosevelt and the New Deal Democratic majority led to unfettered Democratic control of the national government from 1932 to 1946 and then to regular but sometimes interrupted control from then until sometime between 1980 and 1994. In the forty-eight years from 1932 to 1980, the Democrats held the presidency for thirty-two years and the Republicans for sixteen. They held the Senate for thirty-eight years to the GOP's ten. Finally, they held the House for forty-four of those forty-eight years, including working on what would become an American record of forty consecutive years, from 1954 to 1994.

The 1980 election marked an important change. It brought Ronald Reagan to office, whose campaign featured a revived "southern strategy," which followed Barry Goldwater's breakthrough success in winning southern states in 1964 (and nowhere else but his home state of Arizona) and Richard Nixon's explicit use of the term in his successful attempt to win significant support from the South. Reagan, however, not only revived but also expanded upon that southern strategy, including symbolically by launching his campaign in the small town of Philadelphia, Mississippi, most famous as the site of the murder of three young civil rights workers (featured in the movie *Mississippi Burning*), in contrast to the more common major urban areas, such as Detroit, where Democrats typically launched their presidential campaigns.

Reagan's success electorally came along with the Republicans carrying the Senate for the first time since 1954—a majority they would hold only until the 1986 elections when the 1980 victors were up for reelection. And they did well, even if not winning a majority of the seats, in the House. Such victories could not be due only to winning the South, of course, and the legislative initiative was, like the electoral victory, broader than appealing to the South. Still, they set in motion the transition of erstwhile "yella' dog," southern Democrats to become voting Republicans.[7] This transition had been anticipated for a long time, but one of Reagan's most important impacts was in launching this transition.[8] As we noted earlier in the book, the Republicans' southern strategy was also the key piece to launch the "sorting" of partisans in the electorate by ideology, such that virtually only liberals were Democrats, and only conservatives were Republicans, quite unlike the depolarized 1950s-1970s. This sorting, of course, reflected the more polarized partisan elites. This transitional process was long in the making, and it did not culminate until 1994.[9]

In 1994, voters elected Republican majorities to the House and Senate, the former for the first time since 1954. The election surprised scholars, pundits, and politicians, alike. That election marked the culmination of the South's transformation to a truly competitive, two-party region (and soon was to become a competitive region but with a Republican majority). It also marked the beginning of parity at the national level. As we have seen, Democrats carried presidential pluralities in 1996, 2000, 2008, 2012, and 2016 (even if losing the electoral vote in 2000 and 2016). The only Republican plurality was in 2004. But the Republicans held a majority in the House from 1995 to 2006 and then again from 2011 to 2018.[10] In the Senate, Republicans won majorities from 1995 to 2006 and again since 2014; there was a 50-50 split after 2000 (the Republican Vice President Dick Cheney gave the GOP a slight advantage until Jim Jeffords's switch in partisan allegiance to the Democratic Party in June 2001), and the Democrats held a majority in the Senate from 2007 to 2014.

Over this twenty-four year period, unified party control of the three branches has been relatively rare and short lived. From 1995 to 2000, Democrats held the White House, and Republicans held both chambers of the Congress; a similar division was in place from 2015 to 2016. The period between the 2000 and 2002 elections is hard to categorize, due to the shifting Senate, but the elections, themselves, yielded a Republican president (who lost the popular vote), a tied Senate, and a Republican House majority. The 2002 and 2004 elections ushered in four years of unified Republican control, followed by two years of divided control (with Democrats controlling the Congress), two years of unified Democratic control (2009-2010), and then again divided control through 2016. The 2016 elections brought about two years of unified Republican government, but with the Democrats winning back the House in 2018, divided government is in place once again.

As we noted in Chapter 11, there is a quite reasonable chance that the 2020 elections will yield divided control of Congress. The Democrats have the clearest chance of winning and retaining a majority in the House. The Democrats currently hold a nineteen seat advantage in the House, and given their new majority, few Democratic House members are likely to opt for retirement. Moreover, the current balance of marginal seats in the House seems to give a numerical advantage to the Democrats. One-third of the Senate will stand for election in 2020, and there will be more Republican seats at stake than Democratic seats. But few of the 2020 Senate contests are currently classified as "toss ups," so the Republicans' chances of maintaining their Senate majority appear reasonably good at the moment. The political landscape could change, of course, but, as things stand today, divided control of Congress may last longer than the next two years.

The presidency has been competitive over this twenty-four year period, even though the Democrats have won the popular vote in five of the last six presidential elections. The Electoral College determines the presidency, of course, and the last six presidential elections have resulted in three Democratic victories and three Republican victories. As we showed in Chapter 3, the number of competitive states during presidential elections has declined significantly since 1996, and one of the astounding features of Donald Trump's 2016 victory was that he won *all* these battleground states. This may be hard to duplicate. Trump's historically low presidential approval levels are ominous for a first-term president, but as discussed in Chapter 3, incumbent presidents, particularly those who benefit from a healthy economy, seem to have an advantage, winning reelection about two-thirds of the time across U.S. history. Nonetheless, the 2020 election seems likely to be close again, although much depends upon who is actually nominated. We will address that question shortly.

The electorate has proven able to swing between the two parties over relatively short periods of time. Consider that in the 2006 midterm, the public voted heavily Democratic, while it voted very strongly Republican in the next two midterm elections, and strongly Democratic in the next, 2018. Thus, elections are competitive nationally, and the public has asserted itself in clear response to events as they observed them. There is one other important aspect to this competitive balance between the two parties. While it is hardly invariable—as 2006 and 2018 illustrate—the usually much smaller midterm electorates tend to be more Republican, while the larger presidential-year electorates tend to be more Democratic. This has aided the particular feature of this electoral era, alternation in power.

It is reasonable for both parties to believe they have a credible chance to win the next election. And, no doubt, whichever party wins, the victor will hope (and likely claim) that the electoral outcome will be a harbinger of long-term dominance. Nothing in the current record, however, points to such a decisive long-term shift. The two parties have reasonably equally sized bases in the electorate. As a result, when viewed nationally, American elections are close and competitive contests.

ARE MIDTERM ELECTIONS PREDICTIVE?

Midterm elections can change the partisan balance in the House and Senate, and these alterations sometimes have significant policy ramifications. Because the tendency in midterm elections is for the president's party to lose seats, policy moderation—and, in some cases, gridlock—typically results.[11] Following the 2010 congressional midterms, in which the Republicans gained sixty-three seats and majority status in the House, while reducing the Democrats' partisan advantage by six seats in the Senate, President

Obama's legislative agenda was severely restricted. While Obama and the Democratic Congress had passed an unusually large number of major pieces of legislation during his first two years in office—including the Affordable Care Act ("Obamacare")—he achieved few legislative victories after the Republicans took control of the House in 2011. Indeed, gridlock between the Republican House and Democratic Senate was so severe that the 112th and 113th Congress were labeled the least productive Congresses ever.[12]

Given the outcome of the 2018 midterms and the resulting switch from unified to divided partisan government, the prospects for President Trump's agenda during the next two years appear in jeopardy. In Chapter 11, we discussed the partial government shutdown that commenced in the days before the end of the 115th Congress.[13] With the new 116th Congress and Democrats in control of the House, the shutdown became the longest in history.[14] Even though the shutdown was resolved, it is clear that President Trump and the House Democrats have chosen gridlock as their current joint strategy. It remains to be seen if either side opts for policy moderation as the more acceptable strategy. With both sides "digging in" and playing to the ideological bases within their respective parties, it is highly unlikely that major policy changes are in the offing.

Midterm elections can have predictable policy consequences, but whether midterm elections outcomes are predictive of the *future* electoral fortunes of the political parties is less obvious. Long-term shifts toward one party or the other require one electoral success to be followed by subsequent ones. The question, therefore, is does the Democratic victory in the House during the 2018 elections foreshadow Democratic successes in the 2020 elections? What are we to make of the results in the Senate; should the Republican gains there signal GOP success—and a Trump reelection— in 2020?

Given the mixed outcomes of the 2018 elections, it is difficult to claim that these midterm elections provide a strong signal in favor of (or against) one party or the other. As we noted in Chapter 11, exit poll results suggest that President Trump was unpopular among midterm voters nationally, with only 45 percent approving of his job performance, but the president remains very popular among his base. So, prognostications about the 2020 elections are likely to be based on the geographic distribution of each party's core supporters and each party's performance in key battleground states. There is little doubt that the president and Republicans more generally will continue to do well in the Deep South or that the Democrats will perform strongly in California and New York. But what about those small handful of states that are pivotal during presidential elections? In 2016, Trump was able to win the Great Lakes battleground states—Michigan, Pennsylvania, and Wisconsin—states sometimes referred to as a "blue wall" because of their tendency to support Democratic presidential nominees. For some analysts, the GOP's performance in these states during the 2018 midterm was an ominous sign for the party and president in 2020.[15] In Wisconsin, Republican Governor Scott Walker lost his bid for reelection to Democrat Tony Evers. In Michigan, the Democrats won statewide races for governor and U.S. Senate and flipped two House seats to their side. And, in Pennsylvania, Democratic incumbents easily held on to the governor's office and U.S. Senate seat, defeating staunch Trump supporters. But Democrats lost in the U.S. Senate race in Florida and the Ohio gubernatorial election, buoying Republican's hopes for success in 2020 since both states have proved pivotal in recent presidential elections.[16]

The question of whether midterm elections outcomes affect future presidential results is not specific to the 2018–2020 election cycles. Rather, this is a general, empirical question, and one that can be informed by data from recent American elections. Thus, we gathered data from every presidential election from 1948 to 2016 and coupled it with data from the preceding midterm elections. Figure 12-1 presents a scatterplot of the relationship between the seat swing in the House of Representatives for the incumbent president's party in the previous midterm elections and the two-party vote share his party received in the subsequent election. The figure clearly illustrates the perils confronted by presidents during midterm elections. In all but two of these midterms, the president's party lost seats in the House. In 1998, during President Clinton's second term, his party gained five seats in House elections. The Democrats' gains that year marked the first time since 1934 that a president's party gained seats in the House midterms and, for the first time since 1822, the out-party failed to gain seats during a president's second term. In 2002, during President George W. Bush's first term, the Republicans bolstered their House majority by eight seats. Yet these two instances of presidential gains prove to be historical aberrations. On average, the president's party lost 25.5 seats in the House during this period, thus making the forty seats lost by President Trump's party in 2018 well above average.

Figure 12-1 also demonstrates the weak relationship between midterm elections outcomes and subsequent presidential election results. Counter to some pundits' and

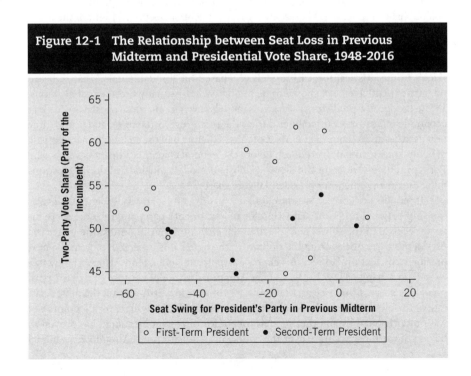

Figure 12-1 The Relationship between Seat Loss in Previous Midterm and Presidential Vote Share, 1948-2016

politicians' claims that the 2018 midterm is likely to have a negative effect on the Republicans' chances in the 2020 presidential election, there does not appear be much empirical support for this claim. Indeed, while the correlation between these variables is positive (Pearson's $r = .147$), the relationship is weak and not statistically significant ($p = .562$). Interestingly, the relationship between these variables appears to be only modestly affected by whether the previous midterm occurred during a president's first (Pearson's $r = .132$, $p = .698$) or second term (Pearson's $r = .415$, $p = .355$). The data suggest that the parties of first-term presidents, whose parties lost an average of 26.5 House seats during this period, were generally unaffected by these political misfortunes in the following presidential election. The same holds for the parties of second-term presidents; though these parties lost an average of 23.9 House seats in the preceding midterm elections, these losses had no discernable effect on the parties' subsequent presidential election performances. Thus, the empirical record indicates that it is highly unlikely that the midterm losses experienced by House Republicans in 2018 will have any bearing on their presidential nominee's vote share in 2020.

It is possible, however, that once other factors, in addition to incumbency, are accounted for, a stronger relationship between midterm elections outcomes and subsequent presidential election results can be identified. To that end, we need to construct an empirical model that accounts for a wider variety of factors known to affect presidential performance and then test whether a party's seat swing in the previous midterm can predict the party's vote share in the next presidential election, once these other variables are taken into account. In Chapter 3, we noted the performance of a set of presidential forecasting models that were constructed by noted political scientists and published in the weeks before the 2016 presidential election.[17] Eight of the models attempted to predict the two-party popular vote share in the 2016 election using national-level factors, two models incorporated information based on state-level factors, and one model was constructed by aggregating information from other forecasts. Each of the statistical forecast models was based on "fundamentals," that is, based on factors that have been shown to be predictive across many presidential elections. While the specific predictors used across models vary, among those chosen are leading economic indicators, war fatalities during the past presidential term, and presidential popularity—just to name a few. Most of the predictors had the desirable characteristic of being known and measured well before the general election campaign even began. Perhaps tellingly, none of the eleven published models included midterm elections outcomes as a predictor of presidential vote share.[18]

If pundits are correct, we should find a positive and statistically significant relationship between midterm seat swing for the president's party and the vote share his party receives in the subsequent presidential election. Put differently, the better the president's party does during the midterms, the better it is expected to do in the next presidential election. To test this claim, we replicate and extend Alan Abramowitz's "Time for Change Model." We use the Abramowitz model because of its history of predictive success. To be clear, Abramowitz's forecast for 2016 was not the most accurate of the eleven—he underpredicted Clinton's popular vote share by 2.5 points and was outperformed by all other models except for one—but his model has proven to be one of the most accurate over the course of many elections. Abramowitz's model correctly predicted the winner of the popular vote in every presidential election from 1988 to 2012.[19] In 2016, Abramowitz's model predicted that Donald Trump would win 51.4 percent of the major two-party vote, while the Democratic nominee, Hillary Clinton, was predicted to receive 48.6 percent of the two-party vote. Based on the official results, Clinton received 51.1 percent and Trump 48.9 percent of the two-party vote, though Trump did win the Electoral College and the presidency.[20]

Abramowitz's Time for Change Model uses variables that are theoretically plausible for explaining elections.[21] Included among these variables are the incumbent president's net approval rating (approval–disapproval) in the final Gallup Poll in June of the election year (NETAPP), the annualized growth rate of real Gross Domestic Product in the second quarter of the election year (Q_2GDP), and a variable indicating the presence or absence of a first-term incumbent in the race ($TERM_1INC$). To these predictive variables, we include a measure of the seat swing in the House of Representatives for the incumbent president's party in the previous midterm elections (MIDTERM). The dependent variable in the model is the major party vote for the party of the incumbent president (PV).

Based on the data from the seventeen presidential elections since World War II—this includes 2016—the ordinary least squares regression estimates for Abramowitz's Time for Change Model are as follows:

$$PV = 47.9 + (.122 \times NETAPP) + (.502 \times Q_2GDP) + (2.531 \times TERM_1INC)$$

All of these estimates are in the hypothesized direction and are statistically significant, though our estimates differ slightly from Abramowitz's reported results since we used revised economic data.[22] The predictions of the model suggest that in the post-war period—holding all other variables constant—the party of the incumbent president is expected to receive 47.7 percent of the two-party vote when an incumbent is not on the ballot and 50.9 percent of the two-party vote when an incumbent seeks reelection. The incumbent president's net approval contributes positively to his party's presidential fortunes, increasing its two-party vote share by 0.122 percentage points for every 1 percent increase in net approval. And, as one might expect, economic performance also matters; for every unit increase in economic growth the country experiences, the incumbent president's party increases its two-party vote share by just over half of a percentage point.

Of course, our main interest here is to assess the effect of midterm elections outcomes on subsequent presidential elections. As in the bivariate case, we find little support for the claim that midterm losses decrease the expected vote share received by the incumbent president's party in the ensuing presidential election. The estimates from our expansion of Abramowitz's Time for Change Model are unequivocal:

$$PV = 48.1 + (.120 \times NETAPP) + (.501 \times Q_2GDP) + (2.584 \times TERM_1INC) + (.012 \times MIDTERM)$$

The inclusion of the midterm seat-swing variable in the model has no statistically significant effect on the two-party vote share of the incumbent president's party.[23]

Thus, the folk wisdom of pundits who claim that midterm losses can be an ominous sign for the president's party in the next presidential election appears unfounded. Particularly since the GOP won seats in the Senate in 2018, one might be curious whether the seat-swing in the Senate is more predictive of presidential outcomes than the House variable; it is not—when we substitute the Senate seat-swing variable into the model, it has no significant influence on the next presidential election.

Statistical evidence suggests that midterm and presidential election outcomes are independent from one another. This reinforces one of the fundamental points made in Chapter 11. The electoral forces that generate midterm outcomes are largely unrelated to those that determine subsequent presidential outcomes. As we noted in the previous chapter, the distinction between presidential and midterm elections is effectively "a tale of two electorates." The oscillation of turnout between presidential and midterm elections—a "surge and decline" as Angus Campbell put it—means that electoral outcomes in each are driven by the relative voting strength of "core" and "peripheral" voters.[24] Core voters tend to be more attentive to politics, have stronger partisan attachments, and are more likely to participate in politics. Peripheral voters pay fleeting attention to politics; they also have much weaker partisan leanings and are more likely to defect from whatever partisan allegiances they do hold. Peripheral voters are less likely to vote, but when they do, they are more responsive to short-term electoral forces, such as those generated by the excitement of presidential campaigns. Core voters tend to be better educated, wealthier, older, and white; they also tend to be Republicans. Democrats tend to hold a partisan advantage among peripheral voters. The scope and salience of presidential elections draws voters of both types to the polls, resulting in higher turnout levels and a slight advantage for Democrats on balance.[25] Congressional midterm elections typically bring far fewer voters to the polls. With peripheral voters returning to the background, core voters are left to dominate electoral outcomes and create an advantage for Republicans on average. The unusually high voter turnout during the 2018 elections, 50.3 percent, was still roughly 9 percentage points lower than in the preceding presidential election. This gap in turnout is a bit smaller but similar to that exhibited historically—as we report in Table 4-1, the average turnout in congressional elections (on and off-year elections) is 44.6 percent, while the average turnout in presidential elections is 55.4 percent. With electorates so differently composed, it is imprudent to make predictions about presidential elections based on midterm elections outcomes.

While it is too early to predict the general election outcome for 2020, our test suggests that the 2018 midterm will have little bearing on who wins. It is still too early to know what the state of the economy will be in 2020, what other issues might come to the fore, or even who the nominees will be. As noted in Chapter 3, there are only six states on the electoral map that can be categorized as "highly competitive" (see Figure 3-4). Most of the remaining states are easily categorized as safely Democratic or safely Republican. Thus, the scope of conflict on the electoral map is limited to only a handful of battleground states. But the competitive balance in the Electoral College can change rapidly. Electoral advantages in modern American politics do not last long. Both short-term and long-term electoral trends suggest a competitive balance between the parties.

Presidential election history is also suggestive of how competitive the 2020 election might be. In Chapter 3, we noted that there appears to be an incumbency advantage in American presidential elections. But it is difficult to know whether this advantage will apply to President Trump, who, despite a robust economy during his first two years in office, has the lowest average job approval rating (48 percent) of any first-term president in the 73-year history of the Gallup Poll.

In the remainder of this chapter, we assess the prospects for both the Democratic and Republican parties. While the Democrats lost the presidency in 2016, they may rebound in 2020 against an unpopular incumbent president.[26] The fight for the Democratic nomination, however, is likely to draw a crowded field. With no clear favorite to assume the party's mantle, Democrats may have to endure an internal battle between the party's more liberal and moderate elements before setting its sights on the Republicans in the general election. For Republicans, the focus will remain on Donald Trump. The president remains a lightning rod both outside and inside his party. Within the GOP ranks, Republican leaders have often been at odds with the president's nationalist trade policies and his often outlandish rhetoric.[27] And the rate of turnover within the highest levels of the president's administration has been unprecedented.[28] But Trump remains wildly popular among his electoral base and has demonstrated significant influence within Republican primaries, where his endorsement or Twitter attacks can tilt the fate of candidates within the party.[29] If the president, himself, is to be challenged during the primary season, it is likely to come from the political center, a strategically disadvantageous position during a primary.

PROSPECTS FOR THE DEMOCRATS

Upon taking control of the House in January 2019, Speaker Nancy Pelosi (D-CA) pledged that "this Congress will be transparent, bipartisan, and unifying."[30] Yet, within hours of Speaker Pelosi taking the gavel, the House voted along party lines to pass a continuing appropriations bill that would reopen government but did not fund President Trump's proposed wall along the Mexican border. The bill, of course, had no chance of passing in the Republican-held Senate or being signed by the Republican president. Pledges of bipartisanship were fleeting, gone within twelve hours of being spoken, and the reality of divided government had settled in. House Democrats are now an empowered opposition party, possessing the ability to pass a legislative program that contrasts with the president's, block any legislation that Trump and the Senate Republicans may desire, use the House's subpoena power to investigate the administration, and, if they listen to some vocal elements of their caucus, impeach Trump.[31]

Democrats, of course, are hungry to recapture the presidency. But there is concern that a potentially crowded field of candidates for the party's nomination will magnify policy divisions within the Democratic ranks and prolong the inevitable selection of a nominee. The 2016 nomination fight between Hillary Clinton and Bernie Sanders opened a fissure between the party's more moderate and liberal elements, and the new class of House Democrats reflects this division.[32] Recent reforms within the party suggest a shift in political power toward the more liberal wing of the Democratic base is on the horizon. In August 2018, Democratic Party officials voted to strip superdelegates—Democratic members of Congress, members of the Democratic National Committee, and other top party officials—of much of their power over the presidential nominating process. In 2016, 93 percent of the party's superdelegates supported Clinton's nomination for president, effectively closing off Sanders's path to the nomination and inflaming liberals in the party. Under the new rule, superdelegates will not be allowed to vote on the first ballot of a contested national convention.[33] The change could shift power within the nomination process toward liberal activists and primary voters. Moreover, since the Democrats do not employ winner-take-all rules in their primaries, the absence of superdelegate commitments may slow the process of winnowing down the candidates for the nomination and may increase the chances that the party goes to its 2020 national convention without a clear nominee in place.[34]

With no presumptive front-runner in place, the Democratic field for the 2020 presidential nomination may break records for its size. In 1976, thirteen Democratic officeholders sought the party's nomination, a process that eventually led little-known Georgia Governor Jimmy Carter to the nomination and the presidency.[35] The 2020 Democratic pool of candidates could easily exceed this number. Moreover, the field is likely to be the most diverse ever, in terms of age, gender, race, and experience. A list of potential Democratic candidates (as of January 2019) is presented in Table 12-1. As of this writing (mid-January 2019), several candidates have already declared their candidacy. Among those who have officially declared are Julian Castro, the former Secretary of Housing and Urban Development during the Obama Administration and former Mayor of San Antonio. U.S. Representative John Delaney of Maryland, a four-term member of the House, has also officially declared his candidacy. Several others have either scheduled their campaign announcement or formed exploratory committees; among these are Representative Tulsi Gabbard of Hawaii, and Senators Kirsten Gillibrand of New York, Kamala Harris of California, and Elizabeth Warren of Massachusetts.

Among those who have been discussed as candidates for the nomination are several previous members of the Obama Administration, most notable among these is former Secretary of State and 2016 Democratic Presidential Nominee Hillary Clinton. If she were to run, it would be Clinton's third bid for the White House. One former advisor to the Clintons, pollster Mark Penn, wrote an op-ed in the Wall Street Journal stating emphatically that "Hillary Will Run Again," and, in a November 2018 interview, Clinton herself said, "I'd like to be president."[36] Yet, Clinton's favorability ratings in the polls remain low. A December 2017 Gallup Poll showed that 61% of respondents rated Clinton unfavorably, and, more recently, a December 2018 USA Today/ Suffolk University Poll of Democrats and independents showed that roughly 70% believe Hillary Clinton should not run in 2020. The latter poll also asked respondents their opinion of other potential Democratic candidates in 2020, and the candidate that elicited the most enthusiasm was former Vice President Joe Biden. When asked about now-76-year-old Biden, over half of those surveyed said they would be "excited" by his candidacy—the highest evaluation among all the prospective candidates.

The United States Senate has long been an incubator for presidential candidates, and 2020 may draw multiple candidates who either currently or formerly served in

Table 12-1 Possible Candidates for the 2020 Democratic Presidential Nomination, as of January 18, 2019

Candidate	Current State	Year of birth	Year of election to highest office
Current or former member of executive branch			
Joe Biden	Delaware	1942	2012
Julian Castro	Texas	1974	2009 (resigned in 2014 to become Secretary of Housing and Urban Development)
Hillary Clinton	New York	1947	2000 (resigned in 2009 to become Secretary of State)
Eric Holder	Washington, DC	1951	NA
John Kerry	Massachusetts	1943	2008 (resigned in 2013 to become Secretary of State)
Current or former U.S. senator			
Cory Booker	New Jersey	1969	2013
Sherrod Brown	Ohio	1952	2006
Kirsten Gillibrand	New York	1966	2010
Tim Kaine	Virginia	1958	2012
Amy Klobuchar	Minnesota	1960	2006
Jeff Merkley	Oregon	1956	2008
Kamala Harris	California	1964	2016
Bernie Sanders	Vermont	1941	2006
Mark Warner	Virginia	1954	2008
Elizabeth Warren	Massachusetts	1949	2012
Current or former member of the House			
John Delaney	Maryland	1963	2012
Tulsi Gabbard	Hawaii	1981	2012
Joe Kennedy	Massachusetts	1980	2012
Seth Moulton	Massachusetts	1978	2014
Beto O'Rourke	Texas	1972	2012
Tim Ryan	Ohio	1973	2002
Eric Swalwell	California	1980	2012

(Continued)

Table 12-1 (Continued)

Current or former governor				
Steve Bullock	Montana	1966	2012	
John Hickenlooper	Colorado	1952	2010	
Jay Inslee	Washington	1951	2012	
Terry McAuliffe	Virginia	1957	2013	
Former Mayors				
Michael Bloomberg	New York	1942	2001	
Pete Buttigieg	Indiana	1982	2011	
Eric Garcetti	California	1971	2013	
Mitch Landrieu	Louisiana	1960	2010	
No elective office				
Mark Cuban	Texas	1958		
Howard Schultz	Washington	1953		
Oprah Winfrey	Illinois	1954		

Source: Biographical data on the potential candidates are taken from CQ Roll Call, eds. *Politics in America: The 115th Congress* (Washington, DC: CQ Press, 2017), Retrieved from http://library .cqpress.com/pia/toc_all.php?source=Politics+in+America+2018+%28the+115th+Congress%29; and Amanda H. Allen and Chris White, eds., *Politics in America 2014: The 113th Congress* (Washington, DC: CQ Press, 2013).

the Senate. As noted, Senators Gillibrand, Harris, and Warren have already set their 2020 presidential bids in motion. Gillibrand arrived in the Senate in January 2009 after then New York Governor David Paterson appointed her to fill the vacancy left behind when Hillary Clinton left the Senate to become Secretary of State. Gillibrand was required to run in a special election in 2010 and then won a full six-year term in 2012. She easily won reelection to the Senate in 2018. Senator Kamala Harris is relatively new to the Senate, having first been elected in 2016, and the USA Today/Suffolk University Poll suggests that she is relatively unknown nationally; roughly one-third of Democrats and independents say they have never heard of her. Clearly, Harris has a base of support in California, but this is hardly advantageous to Democrats in a presidential contest since the state is already solidly Democratic. Senator Elizabeth Warren has been among President Trump's most outspoken critics, and she has gained a degree of notoriety from her exchanges with the president, who routinely refers to Warren as

"Pocahontas," in reference to her Native American ancestry. She, in turn, has referred to Trump as "a loser." Insults aside, in a race with so many potential candidates and aided by the recent rules regarding superdelegates, Warren could leverage her support among the Democratic Party's most liberal voters to forge a road to the nomination.

History suggests that House members who run for the presidency are longshots at best; the only incumbent member of the House to be elected president was James Garfield in 1880. Because House districts are geographically condensed, House members typically don't have a large enough base of support from which to expand their campaign. Nevertheless, several members of the House may toss their hats into the ring; in fact, Representative Tulsi Gabbard of Hawaii has already announced her candidacy. Texas Congressman Beto O'Rourke, who narrowly lost his Senate bid against Ted Cruz in 2018, may be the most viable of the candidates to come from the House. The *USA Today/ Suffolk University Poll* shows that Democrats and independents hold surprisingly high levels of enthusiasm for O'Rourke given that he only came to national attention during the 2018 campaign—roughly 25 percent say they would be "excited" by his candidacy.

Of the forty-four men to serve as the president of the United States, seventeen of them previously served as governor of a state. In the past forty years, that includes Presidents Carter (Georgia), Reagan (California), Clinton (Arkansas), and the younger Bush (Texas). Clearly, voters see executive experience as an asset for presidential candidates. Among the current roster of Democratic governors, of which there are twenty-three, four are viewed as potential candidates for the 2020 Democratic presidential nomination—these include Montana's Steve Bullock, Colorado's John Hickenlooper, Washington's Jay Inslee, and Terry McAuliffe, the former Governor of Virginia. Each of these potential candidates is considered a Democratic centrist, which may be disadvantageous during the primary season. New York Governor Andrew Cuomo has ruled out a bid for the presidency in 2020. And, former Maryland Governor Martin O'Malley, who ran for the nomination in 2016 against Hillary Clinton, only to bow out after a poor performance in the Iowa caucuses, also has already announced that he will not run for the presidency in 2020. He urged Beto O'Rourke to run instead.

Only three presidents in U.S. history also served as a mayor: Andrew Johnson (Greeneville, Tennessee), Grover Cleveland (Buffalo, New York), and Calvin Coolidge (Northhampton, Massachusetts). None ascended to the nation's highest office directly from their mayoralty. Among those mayors who are said to be pondering a run for the Democratic presidential nomination, only former New York Mayor Michael Bloomberg is likely to have the resources to wage a viable campaign. On the Forbes list of the world's richest people, Bloomberg ranks 11th (President Trump ranks 766th).[37] With a personal fortune of over $50 billion, Bloomberg served three terms as the mayor of New York City and briefly considered running as a third-party candidate in 2016. He quickly ruled out the run, however, when he deemed victory impractical.[38] Despite his enormous wealth, there are reasons to believe that Bloomberg would likely have a difficult time winning the Democratic nomination. Not only is Bloomberg a centrist, he only recently returned to the Democratic Party. Bloomberg had been a registered Democrat before running for mayor of New York, but he changed his registration to the Republican Party during his first election bid. He then left the GOP in 2007 and identified as an Independent for the remainder of his time as mayor.

Bloomberg's extraordinary wealth could drastically alter the political playing field in 2020. Typically, competing for a presidential nomination is not just about winning votes, it is also about raising money (and that process has already begun). This is called the "invisible primary," and it is intrinsically tied to candidates' electoral fortunes (pardon the pun). To raise money, one needs professional help. The candidates who have the money to recruit these professionals are likely to be heavily advantaged.[39] Bloomberg's personal wealth could offset these concerns.

In addition to Bloomberg, three other billionaires are considered to be potential candidates for the 2020 Democratic nomination: Mark Cuban, the owner of the NBA's Dallas Mavericks and, like President Trump before him, a reality TV star; Howard Schultz, the recently retired CEO and chairman of Starbucks (who, at the time of this writing, was considering an independent candidacy); and television host and media executive Oprah Winfrey. Winfrey has declared repeatedly that she has no interest in running for president, while Cuban and Schultz have not ruled out a run. Cuban, Schultz, and Winfrey have no previous political experience, but, then again, neither did Donald Trump.

PROSPECTS FOR THE REPUBLICANS

When Donald Trump assumed the presidency in January 2017, the Republican Party controlled the House and Senate, marking the first time in a decade that the GOP held unified control of government. Yet, the Republicans struggled to pass major legislation during the president's first two years in office. Undoubtedly, the biggest legislative achievement for Republicans was a sweeping $1.5 trillion tax bill, which created significant permanent tax cuts for corporations and temporary tax relief for individual taxpayers.[40] Republican leaders had fought long and hard for tax cuts, and unified government paved the way for their success. But other legislative accomplishments were few and far between. During the Obama presidency, congressional Republicans voted over seventy times to repeal the Affordable Care Act (Obamacare), but during Trump's first two years in office, Senate Republicans failed to pass several amendments, passed by the GOP-held House, that would have repealed the legislation. House and Senate Republicans took no action on President Trump's call to spend a trillion dollars to rebuild an America crumbling infrastructure. And the president was unable to get congressional Republicans to pass legislation to pay for his most desired infrastructure project, a wall along the Mexican border.

Whatever prospects the Republicans had to seize the policy agenda disappeared with the Democrats' victory in the House midterms of 2018. For President Trump, the remainder of his term in office is likely to be beset by gridlock, with limited prospects for legislative victories and with House Democratic committee chairs leading investigations of his personal dealings and administration. With little hope for new legislative accomplishments and with an already strong economy—barring major military action that leads to a "rally 'round the flag" boost in his popularity—President Trump will find it difficult to raise his historically low approval ratings during the next two years, which may affect his reelection chances.

Although the Republicans suffered major losses in the 2018 House midterms, these losses did not result from the decline of Republican loyalties among the electorate. In Table 12-2, we present the party identification of the electorate between February 2017, one month after Trump's inauguration, through mid-September 2018, less than two months before the 2018 midterm elections. The data are taken from the Pew Research Center for the People and the Press. Over the course of Trump's first two years in office, party identification within the electorate remains relatively stable. The data show that, during this period, more Americans were likely to consider themselves an independent than identify with one of the two major parties. On average, roughly 39 percent of Americans viewed themselves as an independent, approximately 31 percent identify with the Democrats and 24 percent with the Republicans. Loyalty to the two parties remained relatively stable across the time period, though the gap between the percentage of Democratic identifiers and the percentage of Republican identifiers, perhaps surprisingly, was greater at the beginning of Trump's term. If we average the first three polls during 2017, the percentage of Democratic identifiers was roughly 8 points higher than the percentage of Republican identifiers. In the last three polls before the 2018 midterms, the gap in identifiers was reduced to 3.6 points. In short, despite Trump's relatively low job approval ratings, there has not been a decline in identification with his party (or an increase in identification with the Democrats).

As we noted earlier, the president has remained very popular among his base, and, as the record voter turnout in the 2018 midterms suggests, his electoral base is energized and mobilized (much as the Democrats were against him). This would likely give pause to any Republican who is considering challenging President Trump for the party's nomination. Trump would not be the first incumbent president to be challenged in his party's primary. In the post–World War II era, six incumbent presidents—from both parties—have faced significant primary challengers. In 1952, in the midst of the Korean War, Democratic Senator Estes Kefauver from Tennessee mounted a primary challenge against the incumbent, President Harry Truman. Truman had ascended to the presidency upon the death of Franklin Roosevelt and won a very narrow victory in 1948, but Truman's approval ratings during 1952 never reached above 32%. After Kefauver defeated the incumbent president in the New Hampshire primary, Truman decided to quit the race. Kefauver in turn lost the nomination to Adlai Stevenson, who would, in his turn, lose the presidency to Dwight Eisenhower. In 1968, Minnesota Senator Eugene McCarthy, running on an anti-Vietnam War platform, decided to challenge President Lyndon Johnson. When McCarthy nearly pulled off an upset in the New Hampshire primary, New York Senator Robert Kennedy decided to enter the race for the nomination. Johnson would soon shock the nation by announcing that he was withdrawing from the race. In 1972, California Congressman Pete McCloskey challenged President Richard Nixon on an anti-Vietnam platform but was easily defeated. President Gerald Ford faced a strong challenge from the Republican Party's conservative wing in 1976 when former California Governor Ronald Reagan sought the party's nomination. Reagan was able to win primaries in many southern and western states, but he could not secure the nomination. A weakened Ford eventually lost his reelection bid to the Democratic nominee, Jimmy Carter. In 1980, it was Carter who was weakened by a primary challenger. Amidst high inflation and slow economic

Table 12-2 Party Identification among the Electorate, February 2017 through September 2018 (percent)

Dates of survey	Democrat	Independent	Republican	Don't know/not ascertained	Total
2017					
February 7–12	34	37	23	6	100
April 5–11	31	42	24	3	100
May 3–7	29	38	23	10	100
June 27–July 9	31	39	25	6	101
October 25–30	32	41	22	6	101
Nov 29–Dec 4	32	40	20	8	100
2018					
January 10–15	33	34	26	7	100
February 7–11	30	41	22	7	100
March 7–14	28	41	26	5	100
Apr 25–May 1	28	38	27	7	100
July 11–15	29	39	26	6	100
September 18–24	32	37	25	6	100

Source: *Pew Research Center for the People and the Press* polls, https://ropercenter.cornell.edu/psearch/prc_index.cfm?pid=50.

Note: Based on telephone polls of approximately 1,500-2,500 respondents. The question used to measure party identification is "In politics today, do you usually consider yourself a Republican, a Democrat, an independent?"

growth, Massachusetts Senator Ted Kennedy campaigned against the incumbent Carter. Although Carter was able to fend off Kennedy's challenge, he lost the 1980 general election to Reagan, who had secured the Republican nomination. The last significant challenge to an incumbent president during the nomination season occurred in 1992, when former Nixon and Reagan aide, Patrick Buchanan, mounted a campaign against President George H. W. Bush. Buchanan's campaign demonstrated Bush's weakness among the GOP's conservative base. Although Bush was able to win the nomination, he lost the 1992 general election to Bill Clinton.

Given Trump's loyal support from the political right, it is likely that if he is to draw a challenger for the Republican nomination in 2020 that it would come from a more moderate Republican. In Table 12-3, we list a few possible candidates for the

Table 12-3 Possible Candidates for the 2020 Republican Presidential Nomination, as of January 18, 2019

Candidate	Current State	Year of birth	Year of election to highest office
Current or former member of executive branch			
Nikki Haley	South Carolina	1972	2010 (resigned in 2009 to become Secretary of State)
Current or former member of U.S. senate			
Bob Corker	Tennessee	1952	2006
Jeff Flake	Arizona	1962	2012
Ben Sasse	Nebraska	1972	2014
Mitt Romney	Utah	1947	2018
Current or former governor			
Larry Hogan	Maryland	1956	2014
John Kasich	Ohio	1952	2010
No elective office			
Bill Kristol	Virginia	1952	

Source: Biographical data on the potential candidates are taken from CQ Roll Call, eds. *Politics in America: The 115th Congress* (Washington, DC: CQ Press, 2017), Retrieved from http://library .cqpress.com/pia/toc_all.php?source=Politics+in+America+2018+%28the+115th+Congress%29; and Amanda H. Allen and Chris White, eds., *Politics in America 2014: The 113th Congress* (Washington, DC: CQ Press, 2013).

2020 Republican presidential nomination. Of course, with an incumbent president on the ballot, we should expect to see fewer candidates competing for the nomination. When former South Carolina governor Nikki Haley resigned her position as the Trump Administration's ambassador to the United Nations, she was quick to note that she had no plans to run for the presidency in 2020.[41] But Haley has the credentials of a candidate in waiting: the child of immigrants, a governor, and a diplomat, Haley is seen by some as a candidate who can help reduce the GOP's losses among educated, suburban woman. Indeed, some have speculated that Haley may not be a candidate for the presidential nomination in 2020, but she might be a candidate for the vice presidential nomination if Trump were to drop Mike Pence from the ticket.[42]

The most likely candidates to challenge President Trump for the Republican nomination come from the ranks of senators and governors. Former Massachusetts Governor and current Utah Senator Mitt Romney has been an outspoken critic of the president. Romney, of course, was the Republican nominee for president in 2012. Although he says he has no plans to run, Romney, just days before being sworn into the Senate, wrote an op-ed in *The Washington Post* lambasting the president, saying that Trump "has not risen to the mantle of the office" and that his "words and actions have caused dismay around the world."[43] Former Arizona Senator Jeff Flake and former Tennessee Senator Bob Corker have also been outspoken critics of President Trump. And, perhaps owing to the president's stronghold over the GOP's base, both Flake and Corker chose not to seek reelection to the Senate in 2018. Yet, both have stated publicly that they have not ruled out runs for the presidential nomination in 2020.[44] Former Ohio Governor John Kasich, who ran for the Republican Party's presidential nomination in 2016 against Trump, has openly spoken about challenging the president in 2020. But it is unclear whether Kasich would run as a Republican or challenge the president in the general election as an independent.[45]

In our view, it is highly unlikely the President Trump would lose a competition for the Republican Party nomination if challenged. As we have noted repeatedly, the president's electoral base is extremely loyal to him, even as former aides resign from their positions within the administration or, in some cases, are sentenced to prison. The Special Counsel investigation, led by former FBI Director Robert Mueller, has also had little bearing on Republican's opinion of the president, with a recent poll finding that 71 percent of Republicans believe that the Mueller investigation is a "witch hunt"; only 17 percent said it was "a fair investigation."[46] And in the days after it was revealed that the president's personal lawyer gave an illegal payoff to Stormy Daniels, the porn actress who claims to have had an affair with Trump, the president's popularity among white evangelicals remained extraordinarily high at 75 percent approval.[47] At least among his core supporters, Donald Trump has revived the notion of a "Teflon president."[48]

CHAPTER THIRTEEN

THE DYNAMICS OF AMERICAN ELECTIONS

While the *Change and Continuity* series has considered the entirety of American national elections (see especially Chapters 3, 4, and 5), it has been primarily focused on elections since the advent of high-quality polling, especially the American National Election Studies, which had its first full national survey of public opinion and voting behavior in 1952. In that sense, we are examining elections that extend over a period that is now entering its seventh decade. And we are studying national elections in their entirety—presidential nomination campaigns, presidential general election campaigns, and congressional general election campaigns in particular. That means our analyses make it possible to speak of long-term changes and continuities in the politics of American national elections.

THE GREAT CONTINUITIES: THE ELECTORAL SYSTEM AND THE PARTY SYSTEM

Continuity of the Electoral System

While much has changed in the nature of political campaigns and in the way citizens relate to issues, candidates, and the political parties since 1952, there are two great continuities. First, the electoral system—that is, the means of access to winning the three sets of national offices—is governed, for all intents and purposes, by the same constitutional design: members of the House are elected for two-year terms in single-member districts by plurality rule;[1] senators are elected for terms of six years, rotating so that one-third are up for election every two years;[2] and the president is elected for up to two four-year terms every four years through public votes that determine who will be the members of the Electoral College.[3] In practice, it is the state parties that determine slates of candidates for electors. The winners of these various contests have successfully cast a majority of their votes for one candidate for president and for one candidate for vice president throughout this period and, thus, have been the voting body that elected the president and vice president every four years.[4]

The only major change in this fundamental design of the electoral system in this post–World War II era has been in the presidential nominating process, which changed most dramatically in the 1970s, as described in Chapter 1. That process is not a constitutional issue and so can be changed simply because the various state and national party organizations choose to do so, perhaps in concert with the state legislatures (which set the legal terms for presidential primary elections). Of course, in another sense, presidential nominations are still done exactly the same way as always, or at least since 1832. The nomination is determined by vote of the delegates to the parties' national conventions (and since 1936, decided by the vote of a simple majority of delegates). What has changed is the way in which the two parties select and perhaps instruct their delegates. With this one exception, what is known as the electoral system has been broadly continuous since 1952.

Changes in Systems Supporting the Electoral System

To be sure, two additional systems that are related to the electoral system, albeit not a part of that system, have changed dramatically since 1952: the media of mass communications and campaign finance. In 1952, television was just beginning its massive growth, and its potential effects on campaigns and elections became apparent in 1960. By that point, a majority of American households had a television. John Kennedy and Richard Nixon were of the new generation that would understand the power of television, although it was Kennedy who was truly comfortable with—indeed would be considered a master of—that medium. The first televised debates were held that year and demonstrated just how powerful the medium was.

Cable television further transformed how campaigns are conducted and how the public views them. By 1970, television was universal, and 80 percent of viewing was of one of the three broadcast networks, while only 6 percent of viewers subscribed to cable television. But by 2005, seven in eight homes received cable or satellite television, coming with over one hundred channels on average and including an increasing variety of twenty-four-hour news stations. More viewing was done that year on cable channels than on broadcast networks. And the Internet, even more recently, is again altering patterns of news gathering and political engagement.[5] We know that it is now possible for a large number of people to select news attuned to their political opinions, which not only reinforces and extends those views in a liberal or conservative, Democratic or Republican direction, but also reduces the set of agreed-upon political facts that heretofore provided a shared basis for tempering the intensity of political disagreements. The Internet has had (and is still having) great consequences for newspapers, news magazines, television, and even cable television.

The rise of social media, captured most publicly in Barack Obama's 2008 and 2012 campaigns, is still transforming the way campaigns are conducted. The 2016 campaign brought two major changes, accomplished through the use of social media. During the campaign, Republican candidate Donald Trump greatly reduced his interaction with media personnel and, instead, chose to speak directly to the public through his frequent use of the direct messaging platform Twitter. As president, Trump continues to "tweet" with great frequency. And, we are still learning about just how Russia exploited social media to attempt to interfere with the campaigns in 2016. While Russia has been singled out for this form of election interference in 2016, it is likely that many other nations—and nongovernmental organizations as well—are at least considering the use of social media to affect another nation's campaigns and, perhaps, alter the resulting election outcomes.

The second system to change radically and repeatedly has been that of campaign finance. This, too, is transformative in ways yet to be fully revealed. In Chapter 1, we discussed briefly the system of campaign finance based on the Federal Election Campaign Act of 1972, its amendments in 1974 and 1976, and its modification in the wake of the Supreme Court case *Buckley v. Valeo* from later that year. That regulatory system evolved over the years, in both presidential and congressional campaigns, particularly noted by the growth of political action committees (PACs) in the 1970s; the spreading use of "soft money" by the political parties as a way to acquire and spend money on campaign-related projects (e.g., "get out the vote" efforts) that did not have federal limits; and the spread of issue advocacy ads, independent of the parties and candidates, that dramatically increased political campaign expenditures during election campaigns. In 2002, the Bipartisan Campaign Reform Act (BCRA) was passed to regulate some of these changes (sparking yet other changes), especially changing the latter two features described above. The Supreme Court issued a series of rulings about BCRA, but the major decision is the 2009 case (with the ruling issued in 2010) *Citizens United v. Federal Election Commission* (commonly called *Citizens United*), which invalidated many of the central features of BCRA. The decision in *Citizens United*, which ruled that "money is speech" and thus under the protection of the First Amendment—even when contributed directly by corporations or unions—has opened financial avenues in ways barely imaginable only a decade or so ago. The Court's decision in *McCutcheon v. FEC* (2014) ended limits on the total contributions individuals can give—the law previously set these "aggregate contribution limits" at $117,000—but maintained limits to individual candidates ($2,700 plus inflation) and to various types of political groups. One might imagine that even these remaining contribution limits might be subject to elimination in the near future. This changing legal environment means that it is equally unclear just how changes in the media and campaign finance will affect public opinion and voting behavior. Like the emerging possibilities for mass and social media usage, campaign finance remains a work very much still in progress.

Continuity in the Party System

The second great continuity in American elections is that the United States has one of the most nearly pure two-party systems in the world. The simple fact that the Democratic and Republican Parties form this two-party system and that the constitutional design of American elections has been largely constant provide the basis of this continuity in national elections since 1952. Indeed, the very fact that the Democrats and Republicans, specifically, have been America's two major parties since about 1860 testifies to the stability and immutability of our two-party system. Consider this: the same two parties have dominated the American electoral system for a time longer than virtually any other nation can claim even to have been a democracy at all!

The ambition of candidates to seek election and reelection, as discussed in Chapters 1 and 9, means that the overwhelming majority of state and national candidates and officeholders for elections to those offices are affiliates of one or the other of these two parties. As we noted earlier, there actually are often a great many more candidates for major office, including the presidency, but the role of these third-party candidates is ordinarily tangential or simply trivial. To be sure, third-party presidential candidates have won considerable numbers of votes in the last seventy years, peaking at the quite remarkable 19 percent of votes cast for H. Ross Perot in 1992 (albeit zero electoral votes), and the 13.5 percent cast for George Wallace in 1968 (and forty-six electoral votes; Wallace being the only presidential candidate since 1952 to win electoral votes as a third-party candidate), but even they did not prevent a major-party candidate (Bill Clinton and Richard Nixon, respectively) from winning an outright majority of the electoral votes and thus the presidency. And in the Congress, the percentage of third-party candidates elected to either the House or the Senate has not risen above a paltry 2 percent in this period, and these few winners almost always caucused with one of the two political parties, acting, that is, as at least a pseudo-partisan. Bernie Sanders, for example, was originally elected as a Socialist and remained independent of the Democratic Party (although caucusing with them in the Senate) until "joining" the Democrats to run for their presidential nomination in 2016.

As a result, the typical general election campaign is effectively, and often exclusively, a contest between a Republican and a Democrat. This structures how they act as candidates and officeholders. This structures how campaigns are run through and observed by the media. And this structures how citizens observe the candidates and campaigns, how they evaluate the alternatives, and how they vote. In other words, the two-party system permeates the full range of electoral behavior, in all its manifestations.

The electoral and the party systems interact and reinforce one another. That all national and most state and local races are conducted under a plurality-winner-take-all, or a near equivalent, system means that all offices are subject to what Maurice Duverger referred to as the mechanical effect from counting votes and the psychological effect among voters that generate a two-party system.[6] Added to this are, of course, the candidates. They have incentives to cement that two-party system into place, largely as they enter elective politics as a career choice. Doing so gives them every incentive to seek to climb the informal hierarchy of offices that Joseph Schlesinger called the "opportunity structure." Because that is headed by the presidency, the general idea is that looking forward to a long successful career in politics, hopefully climbing to the top of the ladder, all but requires entering politics as a Democrat or as a Republican and staying that way for most people, most of the time.[7]

THE GREAT CHANGE: DEPOLARIZATION AND THE RETURN OF PARTISAN POLARIZATION

In 1952, the two political parties were structured primarily along the lines set during the Great Depression and the creation of the New Deal party system during Franklin Roosevelt's presidency, which in turn formed in light of the decline of a Republican majority coalition. The Republican Party achieved majority status at the turn of the twentieth century and held power in the national government for most of the first third of the century. A durable Democratic Party majority emerged by

1932 in a replacement (or as it was known then, a "partisan realignment") sparked by the Great Depression. Roosevelt created a majority party that drew its support most heavily from the cities and from working-class voters, especially those in blue-collar jobs belonging to the industrial and trade unions, and thus largely in the Northeast, Mid-Atlantic, and those Midwest states that border the Great Lakes. These tended to include Catholics and Jews and others who were often the children and grandchildren of the great migration at the end of the nineteenth century and thus of the Eastern and Southern European immigrants, particularly those organized in Democratic machines. In the middle to late 1930s, Roosevelt added the African American population that had recently migrated from the South to the North to this set of groups that made up the New Deal coalition.

This collective grouping was added to the core of the Democratic Party: the solid, one-party South. The great majority of the white South had been overwhelmingly Democratic since the 1860s. It became the only competitive party in the South at the turn of the twentieth century, when it defeated a burgeoning threat from its strongest opposition in the region at the time, the Populist Party. Simultaneously, the Democratic Party also reinforced itself as a "lily-white" party in that region, through passage of Jim Crow laws (and other aspects, including the systematic use of violence, that created the Jim Crow system of segregation) to disenfranchise African Americans, along with a good number of poor whites. As the 1950s opened, then, the South made up a very large portion of the Democratic Party, both in terms of electoral votes Democratic presidential candidates could win and in terms of seats controlled in both houses of Congress (see Chapter 9). The Republicans held a majority in the House after World War II for two congresses, in 1947–1948 and 1953–1954. In those years, the South made up a majority of Democratic House members. While they were not a majority of all Democrats in other years, they came very close. The result is that, even then, they held a very large minority, so large that the Democratic Party could rarely act in the House or Senate without southern support.

The Republican Party could, in some sense, be defined as "the rest of the country" but should largely be understood as a mixture of two groups. These groupings were sometimes called the Main Street and Wall Street wings of the party and were sometimes referred to by the peak leader of each of the two groups, the Taft Republicans (after Ohio Senator Robert Taft), typically economically conservative, Middle America, and isolationist, and the Rockefeller Republicans (after New York Governor and U.S. Vice President Nelson Rockefeller), typically highly educated, residing in or near cities of the coasts, socially liberal and internationalist in outlook.

Both parties, thus, had internal divisions in this period—indeed, it is hard to imagine a party seeking to win electoral majorities that does not have a diversity of views within it. But by the 1950s, both were stretched particularly broadly and thus were unusually vulnerable to internal divisions. The Democratic Party had been reasonably united early in the New Deal, in large part because southern Democrats were supportive of the first wave of New Deal legislation. The party began to split regionally during the second wave of New Deal legislation after the 1936 elections and over social issues, particularly those related to race. Therefore, as the 1950s opened, the party had a semblance of remaining unity, and it could still be well described by the coalition that FDR had put together, even though it was under strain.

But the 1950s was the time of the civil rights movement, and this drove a first wedge deeply into the party that culminated with the passage of the Civil Rights and Voting Rights Acts along with other legislation making up Lyndon Johnson's Great Society programs in the mid-1960s.[8] This led directly to a dramatic and nearly instantaneous increase of African Americans in the Democratic Party, going from a small to an overwhelming majority who identified themselves as Democrats, and they voted accordingly. It was accompanied by the slow exit of white southerners from the party. In addition, time and prosperity weakened the ties of Catholics along with them and others who made up the former working class but who were now moving up to the middle class. Manufacturing jobs also waned, and associated unions lost their political vitality. Thus, their ties to the party weakened.

From 1952 well into the 1970s, the breadth of opinion among elected officials (and among the public) in both parties was considerable, and there was at least some overlapping of opinion between the two parties. Diversity of intraparty opinion and a degree of overlapping opinion between the two parties was sufficient for this to be an era of depolarization of the two parties. The movement of conservative southerners from Democratic to Republican loyalties and the associated chain of events affecting the two parties reversed this depolarization, first slowly and then more dramatically, leading to the current era of partisan polarization.

The Republican Party changed, in large measure as the mirror image of changes in the Democratic Party. Thus, Republicans picked up much of what the Democrats lost in the South, such that, by 1995, when it finally reemerged with a majority in both chambers, the Republican Party in the Congress was led almost in its entirety by southern Republicans. Conversely, the loss of social liberalism in the party effectively cost it any serious chance of majority support in the Northeast and especially New England, where the GOP's huge advantage in 1952 is currently an enormous Democratic advantage.

The great change described thus far was that the Democrats lost their most conservative elements, and the Republicans lost their most liberal wing. The members of the two parties, that is, *sorted* themselves out on ideology, so that the parties hold much less diversity within their ranks; virtually all Democrats are toward the left half of the ideological spectrum, and virtually all Republicans are toward the right half. What Ronald Reagan referred to as the "big tent" of a party became a much smaller and more cohesive tent on each side.

This sorting was true at all levels, from the top level of the political elites to the base of political publics. The major difference is that the elected officials and the rest of the party elites have become more *polarized*—that is, the two parties in Congress not only vote differently from one another, they appear to be taking ever-more extreme positions, moving farther and farther apart, while the public appears to be better described as "sorted" rather than polarized. The public has not polarized to anywhere near the same degree, if they have polarized at all—on this later issue political scientists disagree.[9] No one disagrees that the public is much more sorted, however, and to that extent, the public is a reasonably close approximation to the elites in terms of sorting.[10]

This section has reviewed the kinds of changes discussed in Chapters 1, 3, and 5 and parts of 9 and 10. The rest of this chapter lays out additional features we have studied that reflect these continuities and changes. We first consider turnout, as in Chapter 4, which has some remaining features of institutional development, along with a considerable degree of continuity with some relevant changes along the lines of the "great sort." We then turn to the public opinion and voting behavior considered in Chapters 6 through 8 and then remaining features of congressional campaigns and elections in Chapter 9 and 10.

CHANGE AND CONTINUITY IN TURNOUT

Here, we highlight three basic aspects of our analysis of turnout. The first is that, over the course of American political history, the dominant flow has been toward expansion of suffrage, albeit with several notable exceptions, with a major political question of this sort looming today. The second is that, in many ways, turnout since the 1950s has had a great deal of continuity, in no small measure due to the continuity in the party system. However, and thirdly, there are some signs that even turnout is being affected by the great sort.

One of the central questions for understanding turnout at any time is who is eligible to vote—asking both who is eligible for citizenship and which citizens are eligible to cast a ballot. The primary thrust of American democracy has been expansion of both. Thus, for example, in the eighteenth and early nineteenth centuries, the United States may have been the first democratic republic in the modern era, but slaves were excluded from citizenship, and suffrage was limited to males (and in many places to white males), often requiring them to hold property and/or have paid taxes. By the middle of the nineteenth century, property-holding requirements were gone, and we had essentially achieved one version of universal suffrage—all white male citizens were eligible to vote.[11] The Civil War Amendments (especially the Fifteenth) extended that right to all males, the Nineteenth Amendment (ratified in 1920) extended suffrage to women, and an amendment within our primary time frame, the Twenty-sixth (1972), provided suffrage for eighteen-, nineteen-, and twenty-year-olds.

This general expansion of the suffrage is counterbalanced in part by two major kinds of legislation that have reduced turnout from what it otherwise might have been. The most direct were the Jim Crow laws that were intended (successfully) to all but eliminate freed slaves and their offspring from the franchise, sweeping up poor whites and others along the way, and undermining the effect of the Civil War Amendments. The second form has been one kind or another of registration laws. These laws were the centerpiece of the third party known as the American (or "Know-nothing") Party in the 1850s, which contested the newly formed Republican Party to replace the Whigs as America's second major party. Their proposals were to reduce or eliminate opportunities for the then-recent wave of immigration (largely of Irish and Germans but also other Central and Eastern Europeans) to become voters. While immigrant movement to citizenship and voting was slowed in this period, the American Party failed, and the Republicans adopted only parts of the American Party's proposed restrictions as they moved to defeat that party at the polls.

Registration latched more firmly into the American voting regime in the early part of the twentieth century, as part of the Progressive and other parties' "good government" reforms. It was during this time that voting registration became commonplace throughout the nation, and the design of these registration laws was to make it the responsibility of the individuals who wanted to vote to ensure their registration, rather than it being the responsibility of the government to ensure registration of all eligible voters, as in most of the rest of the advanced democracies. These registration laws had the intended effect of reducing turnout among the poorer and the immigrant populations, especially in the North. In that way, they were similar to the Jim Crow laws in the South, which were directed at a somewhat different population but designed to give an edge to upper- and middle-class voters over working- and lower-class voters. This opt-in system of registration to vote was justified as enhancing the quality of elections and the resulting governments on the grounds that it would reduce fraudulent voting.

The post-1952 period has been typified by attempts to increase turnout through easing of registration requirements and other aspects that increase the cost and complication of turnout. Most notable is the so-called motor-voter bill (1993), which got its nickname because the law's provisions allowed voter registration at various places, including where one gets a driver's license. Current legislative initiatives, however, are moving mostly in the opposite direction, particularly voter identification laws that, in the name of avoiding fraudulent voting, require voters to present a state-issued voter identification card in order to vote. Such laws are likely to have their greatest effects on both immigrants and on minority and poor voters (and also on the youngest and most elderly voters), thus blending both targets from prior eras and also hitting disproportionately those more likely to vote Democratic than others.

Actual turnout rates thereby fluctuate in part as a function of who qualifies as eligible voters. As we have seen, since 1952, the turnout for presidential elections has hewed to a fairly restricted range of the mostly mid-50s to the lower to mid-60s in terms of percentage of the politically eligible and voting-eligible population (see Figure 4-2). Congressional elections are typically in the upper-30 to the low to mid-40 percentile ranges. And voter participation in congressional midterm elections between 1972 and 2014 varied over an even more restricted range than in presidential elections, around three percentage points. In fact, turnout in the 2014 midterm election was 36.7 percent, the lowest turnout in a midterm since 1942. This is what made the 50.3 percent turnout in 2018 so noteworthy; not only is this the highest turnout in a midterm election since 1914—the first time that senators were directly elected by the people—it represents a 13.6 percentage point increase in turnout since the previous midterm in 2014.[12] A critical question for further study is to understand how and, especially, why turnout increased so dramatically. Equally important is the more general question, what effect does differential turnout in congressional elections have on the outcome of the elections, and does this have a subsequent effect on policymaking in Congress? If research on the effect of turnout on electoral outcomes at the presidential level is suggestive, then low turnout in 2010 and 2014 may have played a central role in the large Republican gains in those years, while the high turnout of 2018 may have helped Democrats regain a majority in the House.[13]

As we have seen once again with the elections of 2016 and 2018, the differential turnout between presidential and midterm election years is a fundamental and consequential feature of the American electoral dynamic. The surge and decline of turnout between presidential and midterm elections means that electoral outcomes in each are affected by the relative voting strength of core and peripheral voters. While the scope and salience of presidential elections draws both types of voters to the polls, congressional midterm electorates are composed disproportionately of core voters, who tend to have higher socioeconomic status and stronger, more stable political attachments. Thus, the political forces that sweep a president into office typically recede only two years later, resulting in the president's party losing seats in Congress. This weakening of the president's congressional coalition sometimes fosters policy moderation and compromise, while other times leading to divided government and gridlock. Because this interelection dynamic is a product of our electoral calendar, it stands as one of the essential features of American elections.

This is not to say that the limited over-time variation in turnout at the presidential level (or congressional level) is unimportant; 10 percent of our population represents tens of millions of people. The major explanations for the over-time changes (amid over-time continuity) relate to political parties and to how the public views the government, as well as the large-scale changes in population reviewed elsewhere. Two general trends are the decline in such measures as trust and sense of external efficacy of the government, notable from the mid-1960s on, and the decline and regathering of strength of partisanship from the early 1970s to the most recent decades. We will see again this idea that partisanship declined in relevance and importance to the public, just as the divisions within the parties grew most pronounced, and the parties became more important once again, as the great sort and polarization of partisan elites gathered strength. So let us turn to those continuities and changes now.

CONTINUITIES IN ELECTORAL PARTISANSHIP

Perhaps the single most important fact for understanding American electoral behavior is the continuing relevance of partisan attachments. As we discussed in Chapter 8, the way we as election observers understand partisanship has undergone several important changes over the last few decades. But the three major continuities stand out.

The first is that substantial majorities have found, and continue to find, the two political parties and their own partisanship of central importance for their relationship to the political system and especially to electoral politics. The proportion of "pure" independents as we head toward 2020 is essentially identical to what it was in 1956, having changed only from 9 percent in 1956 to 10 percent in 2012, albeit with a jump to 15 percent in 2016, which might prove to be a short-lived response against two negatively evaluated candidates. There was considerable interest in and concern about the growth of independence and hence the decline of partisanship, especially in the 1970s, as we discussed in Chapter 8. The proportion of pure independents did increase by roughly 50 percent, but of course that is a growth from near 10 percent to a peak of just 15 percent in 1972 and 1976, quite like that of 2016. The proportions of independents that lean toward one party or the other also increased and still show some signs of volatility. But in the scheme of things, these are modulated variations over time. The dominant thrust is of no more than moderate change about a rather constant level.

The second and related continuity is that the balance of partisanship within the electorate has fluctuated about an overall continuously modest but real advantage for Democrats. That is, as we noted in Chapter 8, since 1952, the balance of Democrats to Republicans has been in the range of 55–45 to 60–40 or even more. It is very important to note that there has been a long-term move toward parity between the two parties. Thus, the balance was typically closer to 60–40 earlier and is now more regularly at the bottom end of that range. Indeed, if we take the proportion of those who said first that they were Democrats to Republicans (i.e., exclude "leaners") in 2012, that proportion was but 53 percent, just below the historical range. The Democrats regained some of that edge back, as proportion of Democratic identifier rose to 56 percent in 2016 (54 percent if we include leaners). Thus, there is a long-term secular movement of the balance between the two parties in loyalties in the electorate toward parity, but a parity that still, as it were, "leans" toward the Democrats.

The third major continuity is that partisanship is closely related to the choices voters make. Being a partisan is just as strongly related to turnout as ever. Claiming to be a Democrat is just as closely related to how one evaluates candidates and issues and as closely related to the vote—for president and for Congress—as ever. Indeed, this is another set of cases in which these relationships were strong in the 1950s and 1960s and began to sag in strength into the 1970s and 1980s but have reasserted themselves to approximately their earlier levels. This broad but not unvarying stability is sort of the fly wheel that keeps a balance both in the public and in office. But there are some very important changes in the electorate, too.

CHANGES IN THE PARTISAN ELECTORATE

We have already discussed some important changes in the makeup of the electorate, those that underlie the analyses in Chapter 5, in particular. One aspect of some of these changes that has become apparent only recently is that people are sorting themselves by their decisions as to where to live in ways that reinforce partisan sorting in the public. Thus, the regeneration of cities is due in significant degree to the attraction urban areas have for the young, the professionals, and others who are likely to be Democrats. Smaller towns and rural areas are either attracting more conservative (often older) voters who are likely to identify as Republican or disproportionately losing potential Democratic votes. In either event, geographic mobility has played a major role in public sorting and in creating more solid one-party areas. This sort of microchange goes along with the changes in overall configuration of the population already noted, particularly the coming of the baby boomers to voting age in the 1960s and 1970s and then the increasing aging of that population as baby boomers near retirement. This generational shift accompanies other changes, such as new immigration, and thus the coming of not only Latinos as a growing electoral force but also the apparently soon-to-come era in which whites no longer are a majority of the voting-age population. Each of these is directly or indirectly related to the partisan nature of the electorate and ultimately to its vote.

If these changes help us understand the dynamics of party identification in postwar America, the great sort they helped induce in the public's partisanship has had effects on other variables, often those directly related to the vote. It appears, for example, that elite polarization has led to a truly substantial increase in the proportion of the public who see the parties and their candidates taking different positions (and seeing those positions "correctly," that is, seeing the Democrats at more liberal positions than the Republicans) and thus being able to cast a vote based on one or more prospective issues. It is simply much easier to know or correctly guess where a Republican and where a Democrat stand on issue after issue and thus incorporate prospective issues into their decision calculus. Or while retrospective voting has been continuously important, partisan sorting has increased its distribution, with incumbent-party partisans likely to want to reward their party more strongly and out-party partisans opposing more strongly, thus strengthening the potency of retrospective voting as well. Finally, the great sort and increased partisan polarization of elites has appeared to make all kinds of political judgments easier. Examples we illustrated include evaluations of the president's performance overall and in particular areas, such as the economy or war-making, and judgments about which party will best handle highly important problems or put the country on the right track. In short, elite partisan polarization and public sorting have permeated throughout the electoral arena. We suggest that this means the political parties are seen as sending signals to the electorate with greater relevance and meaning, and the public is conditioning their beliefs and choices on a partisanship more filled with political content, both substantively (such as on issues) and emotionally (such as affective orientations of anger toward the opposition), in ways quite different from the 1970s. We conclude this section, however, by noting that all this is a question of relative balance, that partisanship has always been important, waxing and waning within relatively confined ranges.

CHANGE AND CONTINUITY IN THE U.S. CONGRESS

It is not surprising that the significant changes we have outlined, particularly the polarization of elites and the shifts in the partisan electorate, have had substantial impacts on the institutional operation of the Congress and on congressional elections. Indeed, these institutional and electoral forces have interacted to amplify the effects, feeding back on one another over time. However, it is also true that many of the most significant patterns of the past have persisted into this new polarized era.

Despite the fact that five of the last seven congressional election years (2006, 2008, 2010, 2014, and 2018) have resulted in "wave elections" in which one party was hit with the loss of a large number of House or Senate seats, the advantages of incumbency we discussed in Chapters 9 and 11 still persist. It is still true that most elections involve incumbents and that the great majority of incumbents win, in both the House and the Senate. This fact affects the governing choices of the incumbents, the decisions of potential candidates about whether to run, and the choices of individuals who control campaign-relevant resources about whom to support.

Still, the great changes have had profound consequences and have produced a new equilibrium in governing and elections. The realignment of the South from a

Democratic bastion to a Republican one, coupled with its echo in parts of the North leading to increased Democratic support there, created the much more ideologically homogeneous legislative party coalitions we have today, with little or no overlap between those coalitions. This development, in turn, led to the transformation of legislative governance in both chambers. The weak party organizations and the dominant role of committees in the period from World War II through the early 1970s gradually gave way to a pattern of majority-party dominance in which committee contingents were responsive to their respective party caucuses in most matters.

When the party coalitions were very diverse and overlapping, members were reluctant to vest party leaders with significant powers because those members could not confidently predict what ideological orientation future leaders would have. Conservative Democrats might be satisfied with one of their own being a powerful leader, but they could not be sure that a liberal northerner would not be chosen subsequently, and that could lead to policies they would dislike. Republicans were in a parallel situation. When partisan realignment gradually reduced party heterogeneity, however, members' reluctance to delegate power to leaders also declined. This resulted in the reform era of the 1970s, when the House Democrats undermined the protections that the seniority system gave to committee leaders, forcing them to become responsive to party opinion. The reforms also greatly increased the influence of party leaders, particularly by transferring control over the legislative agenda from independent committees to those leaders. The Senate experienced some parallel, but less extensive, reforms at the same time, and the effects of these moves were reinforced when the Republicans took congressional control in the 1994 elections and they moved even further in strengthening the parties than the Democrats had. Since then, these patterns (which we have labeled *conditional party government*[14]) have been further reinforced.

In this more partisan governing environment, the policies each party pursued became more divergent. This presented clearer pictures of the orientations of the parties to the electorate, as we discussed previously, making it easier for voters to make their vote choice in light of their policy preferences. This enhanced party sorting also made rank-and-file preferences more homogeneous, although not nearly so much as among elites. This was especially true of the most politically active citizens, the type who were most likely to vote in party primaries. As a result, the more extreme elements of each party's voter base had an increasingly strong influence over candidate selection. And the parties' increasing success at political gerrymandering, creating more districts that were safe for each party, created conditions that put even greater emphasis on the opinions of primary electorates.

Another area in which the enhancement of party government had an electoral impact was in campaign funding. Before the reform era, congressional candidates were largely on their own in fund-raising; the portion of such funds that came from parties and independent spending was miniscule. But as parties became more important (and more dependable) in governing, their role in raising money and channeling it to their candidates expanded as well. The parties also became more active in candidate recruiting, training, and advising, as we discussed in Chapters 9 and 11. This trend was paralleled by the rise of campaign spending by independent ideological groups and later the super PACs. Both the party spending and the independent spending enhanced incentives for members to support their parties within the government, or at least to not work independently with members of the other party, furthering the development of polarization.

Thus, due to electoral developments, we have experienced the rise of stronger, more homogeneous, and more policy-motivated parties in Congress, parties that are more divergent from one another regarding preferred policy outcomes. When unified government occurs, the majority party can often achieve a large part of its legislative program (although even then institutional features like the filibuster can frustrate some initiatives). Additionally, there are the occasional hurdles as we saw in December 2018 when the Senate refused to provide the $5 billion funding that President Trump requested to build a wall between the U.S.-Mexico border, resulting in a partial government shutdown that began during a period of unified government.

When, however, divided government is in effect, a compromise outcome is often difficult to achieve because a result that is desirable to one side is often anathema to the other, and an outcome in the middle is far from what a large portion of the members on both sides want. These are the conditions that resulted in the government shutdown during the fight over the budget and the debt ceiling in October 2013. Moreover, since the results under unified government are pleasing to the majority party but less so to the middle of the electorate (and are mostly seen as just awful by the minority party), unified government can easily create the electoral conditions that produce divided government, as the first two years of the Trump administration led to the Democratic landslide in the House elections of 2018. This feedback loop between elections and government, and then the subsequent elections, is structured by the changing political conditions we have documented, and it is very difficult to foresee any developments that are likely to break the pattern.

APPENDIX

Table A7-1 Evaluation of Government Performance on Most Important Problem and Major-Party Vote, 1972–2008

A. Evaluation of government performance on most important problem (percent)

Government Performance	1972[a]	1976	1980	1984	1988	1992	1996[a]	2000[a]	2004[a]	2008[a]
Good job	12	8	4	16	8	2	7	10	60	26
Only fair job	58	46	35	46	37	28	44	44	42	
Poor job	30	46	61	39	56	69	48	47	40	31
Total	100	100	100	101	101	99	99	101	100	100
(N)	(993)	(2,156)[b]	(1,319)	(1,797)	(1,672)	(1,974)[b]	(752)[b]	(856)[b]	(1024)[b]	(2083)[b]

B. Percentage of major-party vote for incumbent party's nominee

	Nixon[a]	Ford	Carter	Reagan	Bush	Bush	Clinton[a]	Gore[a]	Bush	McCain
Good job	85	72	81	89	82	70	93	70	76	74
(N)	(91)	(128)[b]	(43)	(214)	(93)	(27)[b]	(38)[b]	(58)[b]	(460)[b]	(383)[b]
Only fair job	69	53	55	65	61	45	68	60	47	
(N)	(390)	(695)[b]	(289)	(579)	(429)	(352)[b]	(238)[b]	(239)[b]	(658)[b]	
Poor job	46	39	33	37	44	39	44	37	11	21
(N)	(209)	(684)[b]	(505)	(494)	(631)	(841)[b]	(242)[b]	(230)[b]	(305)[b]	(512)[b]

Source: Author's analysis of ANES surveys.

Note: The numbers in parentheses are the totals on which the percentages are based.

[a] In 1972, 1996, 2000, and 2004, the questions were asked of a randomly selected half-sample. In 1972 respondents were asked whether the government was being (a) very helpful, (b) somewhat helpful, or (c) not helpful at all in solving this most important problem. In 2004 respondents were asked whether the government was doing (a) a very good job, (b) a good job, or (d) a very bad job. "Good job" includes both "very good" and "good job"; "poor job" includes both "bad" and "very bad."

[b] Number is weighted.

Table A7-2 Evaluation of Party Seen as Better on Most Important Problem and Major-Party Vote, 1972–2000 and 2008

Party better	1972[a]	1976	1980	1984	1988	1992	1996[a]	2000[a]	2008
Republican	28	14	43	32	22	13	22	23	27
No difference[c]	46	50	46	44	54	48	54	50	18
Democratic	26	37	11	25	24	39	24	27	55
Total	100	101	100	101	100	100	100	100	100
(N)	(931)	(2,054)[b]	(1,251)	(1,785)	(1,655)	(1,954)[b]	(746)	(846)[b]	(1,932)[b]
Republican	6	3	12	5	5	4	15	9	6
(N)	(207)	(231)[b]	(391)	(464)	(295)	(185)[b]	(137)[b]	(143)[b]	(429)[b]
No difference[c]	32	35	63	41	46	45	63	52	29
(N)	(275)	(673)[b]	(320)	(493)	(564)	(507)[b]	(250)[b]	(227)[b]	(237)[b]
Democratic	75	89	95	91	92	92	97	94	87
(N)	(180)	(565)[b]	(93)	(331)	(284)	(519)[b]	(133)[b]	(153)[b]	(800)[b]

Source: Authors' analysis of ANES surveys.

Notes: The numbers in parentheses are the totals on which the percentages are based. Question wording, 1972–2000: "Thinking of the most important political problem facing the United States, which party do you think is best in dealing with it?"; 2008: "Thinking of the most important political problem facing the United States, which party do you think is best in dealing with it?"

[a] In 1972, 1996, and 2000, the questions were asked of a randomly selected half-sample. In 1972 respondents were asked which party would be more likely to get the government to be helpful in solving the most important problem. This question was not asked in 2004.

[b] Number is weighted.

[c] In 2008 the middle response allowed was "other."

Table A7-3 The Public's Assessment of Their Personal Financial Situation and Major-Party Vote, 1972–2016

"Would you say that you (and your family) are better off or worse off financially than you were a year ago?"

Response	1972	1976	1980	1984	1988	1992	1996	2000	2004	2008	2012	2016
Distribution of responses												
Better now	36	34	33	44	42	31	46	33	43	32	41	28
Same	42	35	25	28	33	34	31	53	25	18	24	47
Worse now	23	31	42	27	25	35	24	14	32	50	36	25
Total	101	100	100	99	100	100	101	100	100	100	101	100
(N)	(955)	(2,828)	(1,393)	(1,956)	(2,025)	(2,474)	(1,708)	(907)	(1,203)	(2,307)	(1,800)	(4,256)
Major-party votes who voted for the incumbent party nominee for president												
Better now	69	55	46	74	63	53	66	56	65	53	65	73
(N)	(247)	(574)	(295)	(612)	(489)	(413)	(462)	(164)	(354)	(491)	(456)	(681)
Same	70	52	46	55	50	45	52	51	50	52	49	50
(N)	(279)	(571)	(226)	(407)	(405)	(500)	(348)	(291)	(207)	(280)	(274)	(1,132)
Worse now	52	38	40	33	40	27	47	45	28	38	31	33
(N)	(153)	(475)	(351)	(338)	(283)	(453)	(225)	(56)	(219)	(778)	(414)	(560)

Source: Authors' analysis of ANES surveys.

Note: The numbers in parentheses are the totals on which the percentages are based. This question was asked of a randomly selected half-sample in 1972 and 2000. Numbers are weighted.

Table A7-4 The Public's View of the State of the National Economy and Major-Party Vote, 1980–2016

"Would you say that over the past year the nation's economy has gotten . . . ?"

Response	1980	1984	1988	1992	1996	2000	2004	2008	2012	2016
Distribution of responses										
Better	4	44	19	4	40	39	24	2	28	28
Stayed same	13	33	50	22	44	44	31	7	36	42
Worse	83	23	31	73	16	17	45	90	35	30
(N)	(1,580)	(1,904)	(1,956)	(2,465)	(1,700)	(1,787)	(1,196)	(2,313)	(1,806)	(4,261)
Major-party voters who voted for the incumbent party nominee for president										
Better	58	80	77	86	75	69	87	69	86	88
(N)	(33)	(646)	(249)	(62)	(458)	(408)	(211)	(34)	(339)	(724)
Stayed same	71	53	53	62	45	45	88	57	48	50
(N)	(102)	(413)	(568)	(318)	(443)	(487)	(243)	(109)	(425)	(992)
Worse	39	21	34	32	33	31	20	44	16	18
(N)	(732)	(282)	(348)	(981)	(130)	(154)	(319)	(1,425)	(382)	(658)

Source: Authors' analysis of ANES surveys.

Note: The numbers in parentheses are the totals on which percentages are based. We combine the results using standard and experimental prompts that contained different word orderings in 2000, 2004, and 2008. Numbers are weighted.

Table A7-5 Evaluations of the Incumbent's Handling of the Economy and Major-Party Vote, 1984–2016

Response	1984	1988	1992	1996	2000	2004	2008	2012	2016
Positive view	58	54	20	66	77	41	18	42	53
Negative view	42	46	80	34	23	59	82	58	47
Total	100	100	100	100	100	100	100	100	100
(N)	(1,858)	(1,897)	(2,425)	(1,666)	(1,686)	(1,173)	(2,227)	(1,698)	(4,221)
Positive view	86	80	90	79	67	91	89	92	89
(N)	(801)	(645)	(310)	(688)	(768)	(341)	(313)	(476)	(1,253)
Negative view	16	17	26	13	11	17	33	13	11
(N)	(515)	(492)	(1,039)	(322)	(233)	(431)	(1,200)	(618)	(1,109)

Source: Authors' analysis of ANES surveys.

Note: Numbers are weighted.

Table A7-6 President's Handling of the Job and Major-Party Vote, 1972–2016

Response	1972	1976	1980	1984	1988	1992	1996	2000	2004	2008	2012	2016
Part A												
Approve	71	63	41	63	60	43	68	67	51	27	50	53
Disapprove	29	37	59	37	40	57	32	33	49	73	50	47
Total	100	100	100	100	100	100	100	100	100	100	100	100
(N)	(1,215)	(2,439)	(1,475)	(2,091)	(1,935)	(2,419)	(1,692)	(1,742)	(1,182)	(2,245)	(1,704)	(4,226)
Part B												
Approve	83	74	81	87	79	81	84	74	91	88	92	91
(N)	(553)	(935)	(315)	(863)	(722)	(587)	(676)	(662)	(408)	(441)	(537)	(1,263)
Disapprove	14	9	18	7	12	11	4	13	6	26	6	8
(N)	(203)	(523)	(491)	(449)	(442)	(759)	(350)	(366)	(372)	(1,075)	(568)	(1,102)

Source: Authors' analysis of ANES surveys.

Note: The numbers in parentheses in Part B are the totals on which percentages are based. Question was asked of a randomly selected half-sample in 1972. Numbers are weighted.

Table A8-1 Party Identification in Presidential Years, Pre-election Surveys, 1952–1976 (Percent)

Party identification	1952	1956	1960	1964	1968	1972	1976	1980	1984	1988	1992	1996	2000	2004	2008	2012	2016
Strong Democrat	23	22	24	27	20	15	15	18	17	18	17	18	19	17	19	17	21
Weak Democrat	26	24	25	25	26	25	24	24	20	18	18	20	15	16	15	12	14
Independent, leans Democratic	10	7	6	9	10	11	12	12	11	12	14	14	15	17	17	16	11
Independent, no partisan leanings	5	9	9	8	11	15	15	13	11	11	12	8	12	10	11	10	15
Independent, leans Republican	8	9	7	6	9	10	10	10	13	14	13	12	13	12	12	19	11
Weak Republican	14	14	14	14	15	13	14	14	15	14	15	16	12	12	13	12	12
Strong Republican	14	16	15	11	10	10	9	9	13	14	11	13	12	17	13	14	16
Total	100	101	100	100	101	99	99	100	100	101	100	101	98	101	100	100	100
(N)	1,689	1,690	1,132	1,536	1,531	2,695	2,218	1,577	2,198	1,999	2,450	1,696	1,777	1,193	2,301	1,804	(4,244)[a]
Apolitical								2	2	2	1	1	1	b	b	c	c
Apolitical N								35	38	33	23	14	21	3	2	c	c

Source: Authors' analysis of ANES surveys.

Table A8-2 Party Identification among Whites, 1952–2016 (Percent)

Party identification[a]	1952	1954	1956	1958	1960	1962	1964	1966	1968	1970	1972	1974	1976	1978	1980	1982	1984	1986	1988	1990	1992	1994	1996	1998	2000	2002	2004	2008	2012	2016
Strong Democrat	21	22	20	26	20	22	24	17	16	17	12	15	13	12	14	16	15	14	14	17	14	12	15	15	15	12	13	14	13	16
Weak Democrat	25	25	23	22	25	23	25	27	25	22	25	20	23	24	23	24	18	21	16	19	17	19	19	18	14	16	12	14	10	12
Independent, leans Democrat	10	9	6	7	6	8	9	9	10	11	12	13	11	14	12	11	11	10	10	11	14	12	13	14	15	14	17	17	15	11
Independent, no partisan leaning	6	7	9	8	9	8	8	12	11	13	13	15	15	14	14	11	11	12	12	11	12	10	8	11	13	8	8	12	10	14
Independent, leans Republican	7	6	9	5	7	7	6	8	10	9	11	9	11	11	11	9	13	13	15	13	14	13	12	12	14	15	13	13	22	13
Weak Republican	14	15	14	17	14	17	14	16	16	16	14	15	16	14	16	16	17	17	15	16	16	16	17	18	14	17	15	15	13	14
Strong Republican	14	13	16	12	17	13	12	11	11	10	11	9	10	9	9	11	14	12	16	11	12	17	15	11	14	17	21	16	17	21
Apolitical	2	2	2	3	1	3	1	1	1	1	1	3	1	3	2	2	2	2	1	1	1	1	1	2	1	1	a	a	b	b
Total	99	99	99	100	99	101	99	101	100	99	99	99	100	101	101	100	101	101	99	99	100	100	100	101	100	100	99	101	100	101
N	1,615	1,015	(1,610)b	(1,638)b	(1,739)b	1,168	(1,394)b	1,131	1,131	1,387	1,395	2,397	(2,246)b	(2,490)b	(1,405)	(1,248)	(1,931)	(1,798)	(1,693)	(1,663)	(2,702)	(1,510)	(1,451)	(1,091)	(1,404)	(1,129)	(859)	(1,824)	(1,449)	2,917

Source: Authors' analysis of ANES surveys.

[a] The percentage supporting another party has not been presented; it usually totals less than 1 percent and never totals more than 1 percent.

[b] Numbers are weighted.

Table A8-3 Party Identification among Blacks, 1952–2016 (Percent)

Party identification[a]	1952	1954	1956	1958	1960	1962	1964	1966	1968	1970	1972	1974	1976	1978	1980	1982	1984	1986	1988	1990	1992	1994	1996	1998	2000	2002	2004	2008	2012	2016
Strong Democrat	30%	24%	27%	32%	25%	35%	52%	30%	56%	41%	36%	40%	34%	37%	45	53	32	42	39	40	40	38	43	48	47	53	30	47	53	52
Weak Democrat	22	29	23	19	19	25	22	31	29	34	31	26	36	29	27	26	31	30	24	23	24	23	22	23	21	16	30	23	17	19
Independent, leans Democratic	10	6	5	7	7	4	8	11	7	7	8	15	14	15	9	12	14	12	18	16	14	20	16	12	14	17	20	15	17	10
Independent, no partisan leaning	4	5	7	4	16	6	6	14	3	12	12	12	8	9	7	5	11	7	6	8	12	8	10	7	10	6	12	9	5	13
Independent, leans Republican	4	6	1	4	4	2	1	2	1	1	3	*	1	2	3	1	6	2	5	7	3	4	5	3	4	2	5	3	7	1
Weak Republican	8	5	12	11	9	7	5	7	1	4	4	*	2	3	2	2	1	2	5	3	3	2	3	3	3	4	2	1	0	2
Strong Republican	5	11	7	7	7	6	2	2	1	0	4	3	2	3	3	0	2	2	1	2	2	3	1	1	0	2	1	1	1	3
Apolitical	17	15	18	16	14	15	4	3	3	1	2	4	1	2	4	1	2	2	3	2	2	3	0	2	1	[a]	[a]	[a]	[b]	[b]
Total	100%	101%	100%	100%	101%	100%	100%	100%	101%	100%	100%	100%	99%	100%	100	100	99	99	101	101	100	101	100	99	100	100	100	99	100	100
(N)	171	101	146	(161)b	(171)b	110	156	132	149	157	267	(224)b	(290)b	230	(187)	(148)	(247)	(322)	(267)	(270)	(317)	(203)	(200)	(149)	(225)	(161)	(193)	(281)	(124)	(460)

Source: Authors' analysis of ANES surveys.

Note: The percentage supporting another party has not been presented; it usually totals less than 1 percent and never totals more than 1 percent.

[a] Less than 1 percent.

[b] Numbers are weighted.

Table A8-4 White Major-Party Voters Who Voted Democratic for President, by Party Identification, 1952–2016 (Percent)

Party Identification	1952	1956	1960	1964	1968	1972	1976	1980	1984	1988	1992	1996	2000	2004	2008	2012	2016
Strong Democrat	82	85	91	94	89	66	88	87	88	93	96	98	96	97	92	98	95
Weak Democrat	61	63	70	81	66	44	72	59	63	68	80	88	81	78	83	82	75
Independent, leans Democratic	60	65	89	89	62	58	73	57	77	86	92	91	72	88	8	86	88
Independent, no partisan leanings	18	15	50	75	28	26	41	23	21	35	63	39	44	54	50	42	36
Independent, leans Republican	7	6	13	25	5	11	15	13	5	13	14	26	15	13	17	11	8
Weak Republican	4	7	11	40	10	9	22	5	6	16	18	21	16	10	10	14	17
Strong Republican	2	a	2	9	3	2	3	4	2	2	2	3	1	3	2	4	2

Source: Authors' analysis of ANES surveys.

[a]Less than 1 percent.

Table A8-5   Approval of Incumbent's Handling of the Economy among Partisan Groups, 1984–2016 (Percent)

Year	Attitudes toward handling of the economy	Strong Democrat	Weak Democrat	Independent, leans Democrat	Independent	Independent, leans Republican	Weak Republican	Strong Republican	Total
1984	Approve	17	41	32	68	84	86	95	58
	Disapprove	83	59	68	32	16	14	5	42
	Total	100	100	100	100	100	100	100	100
	(N)	309	367	207	179	245	277	249	1,833
1988	Approve	19	35	32	57	76	79	92	54
	Disapprove	81	65	68	43	24	21	8	46
	Total	100	100	100	100	100	100	100	100
	(N)	337	332	229	185	262	262	269	1,876
1992	Approve	3	9	6	9	31	34	66	20
	Disapprove	97	91	94	91	69	66	34	80
	Total	100	100	100	100	100	100	100	100
	(N)	425	445	340	267	310	347	266	2,401
1996	Approve	96	82	76	58	46	49	30	66
	Disapprove	4	18	24	42	54	50	70	34
	Total	100	100	100	100	100	100	100	100
	(N)	310	325	228	131	188	263	209	1,655

Year	Attitudes toward handling of the economy	Strong Democrat	Weak Democrat	Independent, leans Democrat	Independent	Independent, leans Republican	Weak Republican	Strong Republican	Total
2000	Approve	95	90	84	73	60	70	47	77
	Disapprove	5	10	16	27	40	30	53	23
	Total	100	100	100	100	100	100	100	100
	(N)	342	265	264	198	206	184	200	1,659
2004	Approve	5	18	10	34	68	72	89	40
	Disapprove	95	82	90	66	32	28	11	60
	Total	100	100	100	100	100	100	100	100
	(N)	197	176	204	107	139	141	194	1,158
2008	Approve	4	7	5	16	27	25	58	18
	Disapprove	96	93	95	84	73	75	42	82
	Total	100	100	100	100	100	100	100	100
	(N)	428	338	381	240	255	274	291	2,208
2012	Approve	98	89	89	64	36	22	8	64
	Disapprove	2	11	11	36	64	78	92	36
	Total	100	100	100	100	100	100	100	100
	(N)	287	167	176	74	129	116	173	1,122
2016	Approve	93	75	79	44	21	29	10	53
	Disapprove	7	25	21	56	79	71	90	47
	Total	100	100	100	100	100	100	100	100
	(N)	896	582	460	606	470	499	691	4,221

Source: Authors' analysis of ANES surveys.

Note: Numbers are weighted.

Table A8-6 Approval of Incumbent's Handling of the Economy among Partisan Groups, 1984–1996 (Percent)

Year	Attitudes toward handling of the economy	Party Identification								Total
		Strong Democrat	Weak Democrat	Independent, leans Democrat	Independent	Independent, leans Republican	Weak Republican	Strong Republican		
1984	Approve	17	41	32	68	84	86	95		58
	Disapprove	83	59	68	32	16	14	5		42
	Total	100	100	100	100	100	100	100		100
	(N)	(309)	(367)	(207)	(179)	(245)	(277)	(249)		(1,833)
1988	Approve	19	35	32	57	76	79	92		54
	Disapprove	81	65	68	43	24	21	8		46
	Total	100	100	100	100	100	100	100		100
	(N)	(337)	(332)	(229)	1(85)	(262)	(262)	(269)		(1,876)
1992[a]	Approve	3	9	6	9	31	34	66		20
	Disapprove	97	91	94	91	69	66	34		80
	Total	100	100	100	100	100	100	100		100
	(N)	(425)	(445)	(340)	(267)	(310)	(347)	(266)		(2,401)
1996[a]	Approve	96	82	76	58	46	49	30		66
	Disapprove	4	18	24	42	54	50	70		34
	Total	100	100	100	100	100	100	100		100
	(N)	(310)	(325)	(228)	(131)	(188)	(263)	(209)		(1,655)

Source: Authors' analysis of ANES surveys.

[a]Numbers are weighted.

Table A8-7 Balance-of-Issues Positions among Partisan Groups, 1976–2016 (Percent)

Year	Issue positions closer to . . .	Strong Democrat	Weak Democrat	Independent, leans Democrat	Independent	Independent, leans Republican	Weak Republican	Strong Republican	Total
1976	Democratic candidate	28	27	22	15	12	9	3	18
	Neutral	32	26	37	29	27	23	27	29
	Republican candidate	39	47	40	55	61	67	69	53
	Total	99	100	99	99	100	99	99	100
	(N)	(422)	(655)	(336)	(416)	(277)	(408)	(254)	(2,778)
1980	Democratic candidate	26	23	27	20	12	10	9	19
	Neutral	34	37	33	43	40	43	31	37
	Republican candidate	40	40	40	37	48	48	60	43
	Total	100	100	100	100	100	101	100	99
	(N)	(245)	(317)	(161)	(176)	(150)	(202)	(127)	(1,378)
1984	Democratic candidate	57	49	59	35	23	29	14	39
	Neutral	32	37	28	48	46	40	39	38
	Republican candidate	11	14	13	17	32	32	47	23
	Total	100	100	100	100	101	101	100	100
	(N)	331	390	(215)	213	248	295	256	1,948

(Continued)

Table A8-7 (Continued)

Year	Issue positions closer to . . .	Strong Democrat	Weak Democrat	Independent, leans Democrat	Independent	Independent, leans Republican	Weak Republican	Strong Republican	Total
1988	Democratic candidate	49	36	50	33	21	21	11	32
	Neutral	34	40	38	48	46	43	35	40
	Republican candidate	17	24	12	19	33	36	53	29
	Total	100	100	100	100	100	100	99	101
	(N)	(355)	(359)	(240)	(215)	(270)	(281)	(279)	(1,999)
1992	Democratic candidate	40	36	30	26	13	13	9	25
	Neutral	55	57	65	70	74	77	74	67
	Republican candidate	5	7	4	5	13	11	17	9
	Total	100	100	99	101	100	101	100	101
	(N)	(380)	(389)	(313)	(235)	(283)	(335)	(238)	(2,192)
1996	Democratic candidate	44	27	35	17	13	9	1	22
	Neutral	27	36	34	43	27	23	14	29
	Republican candidate	30	37	31	40	60	68	85	49
	Total	101	100	100	100	100	100	100	100
	(N)	(313)	(333)	(229)	(140)	(195)	(268)	(217)	(2,696)

Year	Issue positions closer to...	Strong Democrat	Weak Democrat	Independent, leans Democrat	Independent	Independent, leans Republican	Weak Republican	Strong Republican	Total
2000	Democratic candidate	30	26	25	20	8	10	2	19
	Neutral	47	48	46	49	40	33	25	43
	Republican candidate	23	25	29	31	51	57	73	38
	Total	100	101	100	100	99	100	100	100
	(N)	(188)	(161)	(157)	(113)	(134)	(101)	(99)	(953)
2004	Democratic candidate	72	55	57	40	19	21	9	40
	Neutral	8	11	9	10	9	6	5	8
	Republican candidate	21	33	34	50	73	73	86	52
	Total	100	99	101	100	100	99	100	100
	(N)	(168)	(157)	(180)	(100)	(124)	(136)	(179)	(1,046)
2008a	Democratic candidate	60	46	47	28	16	14	8	34
	Neutral	6	9	14	10	17	9	(2)	9
	Republican candidate	34	45	40	63	67	77	90	56
	Total	100	100	101	101	100	100	99	99
	(N)	(219)	(163)	(203)	(135)	(143)	(148)	(142)	(1,153)

(Continued)

393

Table A8-7 (Continued)

Year	Issue positions closer to...	Strong Democrat	Weak Democrat	Independent, leans Democrat	Independent	Independent, leans Republican	Weak Republican	Strong Republican	Total
2012	Democratic candidate	47	36	29	22	6	7	5	22
	Neutral	16	18	17	10	10	5	3	11
	Republican candidate	37	46	54	68	85	88	93	67
	Total	100	100	100	100	100	100	100	100
	(N)	307	214	282	182	342	210	258	(1,795)
2016	Democratic candidate	64	48	56	34	13	13	7	35
	Neutral	14	19	19	24	11	17	6	16
	Republican candidate	22	33	24	42	76	70	87	49
	Total	100	100	99	100	100	100	100	100
	(N)	902	587	462	620	472	501	696	4242

Source: Authors' analysis of ANES surveys.

Note: In the one instance in which the category included fewer than ten observations, we show the total number of people in that category in brackets.

[a]The Democratic category on the condensed balance-of-issues measure includes any respondent who is at least slightly Democratic; the Republican category includes any respondent who is at least slightly Republican. The neutral category is the same as the neutral category on the seven-point issue scale (see Table 6-5). In 2008 the issue questions that were used to form the balance-of-issues scale were asked of a randomly selected half-sample.

[b]Numbers are weighted.

Table A8-8 Approval of Incumbent's Handling of Job, by Party Identification, 1972–2016 (Percent)

	Party Identification						
Year	Strong Democrat	Weak Democrat	Independent, Leans Democrat	Independent	Independent, Leans Republican	Weak Republican	Strong Republican
2016	93	79	81	47	20	26	7
2012	97	80	79	49	18	21	6
2008	3	11	6	26	46	47	74
2004	6	26	23	39	78	89	98
2000	92	88	81	65	49	52	23
1996	98	89	85	66	45	49	18
1992	12	28	20	32	65	71	91
1988	24	43	37	70	82	83	94
1984	22	48	32	76	90	93	96
1980	73	54	44	35	19	19	9
1976	24	55	46	69	87	85	96
1972	38	65	52	73	87	92	94

Source: Authors' analysis of ANES surveys.

Note: To approximate the numbers upon which these percentages are based, see Tables 8-2, 8-3, A8-2, and A8-3.

NOTES

INTRODUCTION

1. For an analysis of the strategies in this election, see John H. Kessel, *The Goldwater Coalition: Republican Strategies in 1964* (Indianapolis, IN: Bobbs-Merrill, 1968).
2. See, for example, Benjamin Ginsberg and Martin Shefter, *Politics by Other Means: The Importance of Elections in America* (New York, NY: Basic Books, 1990); and Matthew A. Crenson and Benjamin Ginsberg, *Downsizing Democracy: How America Sidelined Its Citizens and Privatized Its Public* (Baltimore, MD: Johns Hopkins University Press, 2002).
3. U.S. Department of Commerce, Bureau of Economic Analysis, "Gross Domestic Product: Percent Change from Preceding Period," July 28, 2017, https://www.bea.gov/national/xls/gdpchg.xls.
4. For information about corporate profits, see the Bureau of Economic Analysis's National Economic Accounts, https://www.bea.gov/national. For Historical Dow Jones Industrial Average data, see the Federal Reserve Bank of St. Louis, Economic Research, https://fred.stlouisfed.org/series/DJIA.
5. The Federal Reserve Bank of St. Louis, Economic Research provides data on the civilian unemployment rate, https://fred.stlouisfed.org/series/UNRATE, the long-term unemployment rate, https://fred.stlouisfed.org/series/LNU03025703, and labor force participation, https://fred.stlouisfed.org/graph/?graph_id=109599&category_id=.
6. See Thomas Piketty and Emmanuel Saez, "Income Inequality in the United States, 1913–1998, *Quarterly Journal of Economics*, 118 (2003): 1-39, and http://eml.berkeley.edu/~saez/TabFig2015prel.xls for updated data.
7. Silvio Berlusconi served as Italian prime minister in four governments between 1994 and 2011. He was later convicted of tax fraud. Once estimated by *Forbes* to be the 169th richest person in the world, Berlusconi had built his fortune as an Italian media mogul and would later own one of soccer's most successful teams, A. C. Milan. See "Silvio Berlusconi and Family," *Forbes*, https://www.forbes.com/profile/silvio-berlusconi. For a recent treatment of populism, see Jan-Werner Müller, *What Is Populism?* (Philadelphia, PA: University of Pennsylvania Press, 2016).
8. Quoted from a June 28, 2016, speech in Monessen, Pennsylvania, in "Clinton vs. Trump: Where They Stand on Economic Policy Issues," *The Wall Street Journal*, http://graphics.wsj.com/elections/2016/donald-trump-hillary-clinton-on-the-economy.
9. Whereas the Republican Party of Abraham Lincoln in the 1860s and William McKinley in the 1890s supported protectionism in the form of higher tariffs, the Republican Party of Ronald Reagan and George H. W. Bush in the 1980s espoused free trade; see Michael Wilson, "The North American Free Trade Agreement: Ronald Reagan's Vision Realized," *The Heritage Foundation*, November 23, 1993, http://www.heritage.org/trade/report/the-north-american-free-trade-agreement-ronald-reagans-vision-realized; and Daniel Griswold, "Reagan Embraced Free Trade and Immigration," *The Cato Institute*, June 24, 2004, https://

www.cato.org/publications/commentary/reagan-embraced-free-trade-immigration. Passed during the administration of President Bill Clinton, a Democrat, the North American Free Trade Agreement (NAFTA) was passed through Congress with more Republican than Democratic votes. "In the House, NAFTA passed 234-200; 132 Republicans and 102 Democrats voted in favor of it. The Senate approved NAFTA 61-38, with the backing of 34 Republicans and 27 Democrats," according to Glenn Kessler, "History Lesson: More Republicans than Democrats Supported NAFTA," *Washington Post*, May 9, 2016, https://www.washingtonpost.com/news/fact-checker/wp/2016/05/09/history-lesson-more-republicans-than-democrats-supported-nafta/?utm_term=.6f3f9575b725.

10. Aaron Blake, "Trump Warns GOP on Immigration: 'They're Taking Your Jobs," *Washington Post*, March 6, 2014, https://www.washingtonpost.com/news/post-politics/wp/2014/03/06/trump-warns-gop-on-immigration-theyre-taking-your-jobs/?utm_term=.669d7a102ecf.

11. "Full Text: Donald Trump Announces a Presidential Bid," *Washington Post*, June 16, 2015, https://www.washingtonpost.com/news/post-politics/wp/2015/06/16/full-text-donald-trump-announces-a-presidential-bid/?utm_term=.5870ba9cf2f7. Trump's desire to build a wall on the Mexican border elicited unusually pointed criticism from Pope Francis, who said "a person who thinks only about building walls, wherever they may be, and not building bridges, is not Christian." In turn, Trump called the Pope's comments "disgraceful." See Ben Jacobs, "Donald Trump Calls Pope Francis 'Disgraceful' for Questioning His Faith," *The Guardian*, February 18, 2016, https://www.theguardian.com/us-news/2016/feb/18/donald-trump-pope-francis-christian-wall-mexico-border. As we will see in Chapter 5, this exchange did not appear to affect Trump's level of support from white Catholics.

12. Quoted from a January 11, 2016, speech in Des Moines, Iowa, in "Clinton vs. Trump: Where They Stand on Economic Policy Issues."

13. Nick Timiraos, "Hillary Clinton Lays Out Economic Plan, while Criticizing Donald Trump's," *Wall Street Journal*, August 11, 2016, https://www.wsj.com/articles/clinton-to-criticize-trumps-economic-plan-as-self-serving-1470913205.

14. Louise Liu, "Here's Where Hillary Clinton and Donald Trump Stand on Immigration," *Business Insider*, September 25, 2016, http://www.businessinsider.com/hillary-clinton-and-donald-trump-immigration-2016-9.

15. Alison Kodjak, "Platform Check: Trump and Clinton on Health Care," *NPR*, November 2, 2016, http://www.npr.org/2016/11/02/500371785/platform-check-trump-and-clinton-on-health-care.

16. "Trump and Clinton Finish with Historically Poor Images," *Gallup*, November 8, 2016, http://www.gallup.com/poll/197231/trump-clinton-finish-historically-poor-images.aspx.

17. Tessa Berenson, "Reminder: The House Voted to Repeal Obamacare More Than 50 Times," *Time*, March 24, 2017, http://time.com/4712725/ahca-house-repeal-votes-obamacare.

18. Erin Kelly, Eliza Collins, and Deirdre Shesgreen, "Republicans Give Up on Obamacare Repeal Bill, Move on to Other Issues," *USA Today*, March 24, 2017, https://www.usatoday.com/story/news/politics/2017/03/24/house-obamacare-repeal-vote/99573690.

19. Austin Ramzy, "McCain's Vote Provides Dramatic Moment in 7-Year Battle over Obamacare," *New York Times*, July 28, 2017, https://www.nytimes.com/2017/07/28/us/politics/john-mccain-vote-trump-obamacare.html; Jenna Johnson, "Trump's Grand Promises to 'Very, Very Quickly' Repeal Obamacare Run into Reality," *Washington Post*, July 18, 2017, https://www.washingtonpost.com/politics/trumps-grand-promises-to-very-very-quickly-repeal-obamacare-run-into-reality/2017/07/18/91b5f220-6bd3-11e7-9c15-177740635e83_story.html?utm_term=.69b8ea32b9be.

20. Although the repeal and possible replacement of "Obamacare" was operating under a special provision in the Senate that required only a simple majority to pass (and hence fifty

votes and the vice president's tie-breaking vote at minimum), most other legislation in the Senate needs a sixty-vote supermajority to end any proposed filibuster to pass.

21. See, for one example, Lee Drutman, "Donald Trump Will Dramatically Realign America's Political Parties," *Foreign Policy*, November 11, 2016, http://foreignpolicy.com/2016/11/11/ why-democrats-should-abandon-angry-working-class-whites.

22. Lanny J. Davis, "The Obama Realignment," *Wall Street Journal*, November 6, 2008, A19.

23. Paul R. Abramson, John H. Aldrich, and David W. Rohde, *Change and Continuity in the 2008 and 2010 Elections* (Washington, DC: CQ Press, 2012), 284.

24. Kevin P. Phillips, *The Emerging Republican Majority* (New Rochelle, NY: Arlington House, 1969).

25. Phil Gailey, "Republicans Start to Worry about Signs of Slippage," *New York Times*, August 25, 1988, E5.

26. For a discussion of the history of this concept, see Theodore Rosenof, *Realignment: The Theory That Changed the Way We Think about American Politics* (Lanham, MD: Rowman and Littlefield, 2003).

27. V. O. Key, Jr., "A Theory of Critical Elections," *Journal of Politics* 17 (February 1955): 3–18.

28. V. O. Key, Jr., "Secular Realignment and the Party System," *Journal of Politics* 21 (May 1959): 198–210.

29. These states were, and still are, the most heavily Democratic states. Both voted Republican in seventeen of the eighteen presidential elections between 1856 and 1924, voting Democratic only when the Republican Party was split in 1912 by Theodore Roosevelt's Progressive Party candidacy. For a discussion of partisan change in the New England states, see Chapter 3.

30. V. O. Key, Jr., *Parties, Politics, and Pressure Groups*, 5th ed. (New York, NY: Thomas Y. Crowell, 1964), 186.

31. In addition to the eleven states that formed the Confederacy (Alabama, Arkansas, Florida, Georgia, Louisiana, Mississippi, North Carolina, South Carolina, Tennessee, Texas, and Virginia), Delaware, Kentucky, Maryland, and Missouri were slave states. The fifteen free states in 1848 were Connecticut, Illinois, Indiana, Iowa, Maine, Massachusetts, Michigan, New Hampshire, New Jersey, New York, Ohio, Pennsylvania, Rhode Island, Vermont, and Wisconsin. By 1860 three additional free states—California, Minnesota, and Oregon—had been admitted to the Union.

32. John H. Aldrich, *Why Parties? A Second Look* (Chicago, IL: University of Chicago Press, 2011), 282–287.

33. Thomas G. Hansford and Brad T. Gomez, "Estimating the Electoral Effects of Voter Turnout," *American Political Science Review* 104 (May 2010): 268–288.

34. Byron E. Shafer, ed., *The End of Realignment? Interpreting American Electoral Eras* (Madison: University of Wisconsin Press, 1991). See, for example, Joel H. Silbey, "Beyond Realignment and Realignment Theory," 3–23; Everett Carll Ladd, "Like Waiting for Godot: The Uselessness of 'Realignment' for Studying Change in Contemporary American Politics," 24–36; and Byron E. Shafer, "The Notion of an Electoral Order: The Structure of Electoral Politics at the Accession of George Bush," 37–84. Shafer's book also contains an excellent bibliographical essay: Harry F. Bass, "Background to Debate: Reader's Guide and Bibliography," 141–178.

35. David R. Mayhew, *Electoral Realignments: A Critique of an American Genre* (New Haven, CT: Yale University Press, 2002).

36. Edward G. Carmines and James A. Stimson, *Issue Evolution: Race and the Transformation of American Politics* (Princeton, NJ: Princeton University Press, 1989), 12–13.

37. Ibid., 13.
38. Key, "Secular Realignment and the Party System," 198–199.
39. The theory of punctuated equilibrium was first developed by the evolutionary biologists and paleontologists Niles Eldredge and Stephen Jay Gould. See Niles Eldredge and Stephen Jay Gould, "Punctuated Equilibria: An Alternative to Phyletic Gradualism" in Thomas J. M. Schropf, ed., *Models of Paleobiology* (San Francisco, CA: Freeman, Cooper, and Company, 1972).
40. Carmines and Stimson, *Issue Evolution*, 13.
41. John H. Aldrich argues that the decline of local party machines, technological innovations— particularly, the advent of television—and the rise of a policy-motivated activist class allowed ambitious politicians to bypass the party organization and create "candidate-centered" campaigns. The result was the demise of the traditional "mass political party" (i.e., the party as organization), and in its place followed a new type of party, one that provides services (e.g., expertise and financial and in-kind resources) to its candidates. The emergent activist class also pressured the parties to democratize their presidential nomination systems. Reforms, such as the Democratic Party's McGovern-Fraser Commission, resulted in the proliferation of primaries as the main vehicle by which party nominees are chosen. See Aldrich, *Why Parties: A Second Look*, 255–292.
42. Aldrich, *Why Parties: A Second Look*, 263.
43. See Russell J. Dalton, Paul Allen Beck, and Scott C. Flanagan, "Electoral Change in Advanced Industrial Democracies," in *Electoral Change in Advanced Industrial Democracies: Realignment or Dealignment?* eds. Russell J. Dalton, Scott C. Flanagan, and Paul Allen Beck (Princeton, NJ: Princeton University Press, 1984), 14.
44. Ronald Inglehart and Avram Hochstein, "Alignment and Dealignment of the Electorate in France and the United States," *Comparative Political Studies* 5 (October 1972): 343–372.
45. We estimated the distribution of major-party identifiers (i.e., excluding pure independents) in both the general public and among voters. In both cases, we estimate approximately 53 percent identify with the Democratic Party.
46. Mark Hugo Lopez, Ana Gonzalez-Barrera, Jens Manuel Krogstad, and Gustavo López, "Democrats Maintain Edge as Party 'More Concerned' for Latinos, but Views Similar to 2012," *Pew Hispanic Center*, October 11, 2016, http://www.pewhispanic.org/2016/10/11/democrats-maintain-edge-as-party-more-concerned-for-latinos-but-views-similar-to-2012.
47. According to Michael P. McDonald, 230,585,915 Americans were eligible to vote. See McDonald, "2016 General Election Turnout Rates," United States Election Project, http://www.electproject.org/home/voter-turnout/voter-turnout-data. We say "on or before" November 8 because in 2016 about 38 percent of voters voted before election day.
48. Voters may also be influenced by random factors as well, but by their very nature, these random factors cannot be systematically explained.
49. For two excellent summaries of research on voting behavior, see Russell J. Dalton and Martin P. Wattenberg, "The Not So Simple Act of Voting," in *Political Science: The State of the Discipline II*, ed. Ada W. Finifter (Washington, DC: American Political Science Association, 1993), 193–218; and Morris P. Fiorina, "Parties, Participation, and Representation in America: Old Theories Face New Realities," in *Political Science: The State of the Discipline*, eds. Ira Katznelson and Helen V. Milner (New York, NY: Norton, 2002), 511–541.
50. For a more extensive discussion of our arguments, see Paul R. Abramson, John H. Aldrich, and David W. Rohde, "Studying American Elections," in *The Oxford Handbook of American Elections and Political Behavior*, ed. Jan E. Leighley (New York, NY: Oxford University Press, 2010), 700–715.

51. Paul F. Lazarsfeld, Bernard R. Berelson, and Hazel Gaudet, *The People's Choice: How the Voter Makes Up His Mind in a Presidential Campaign* (New York, NY: Duell, Sloan, and Pearce, 1944), 27. See also Bernard R. Berelson, Paul F. Lazarsfeld, and William McPhee, *Voting: A Study of Opinion Formation in a Presidential Campaign* (Chicago, IL: University of Chicago Press, 1954).

52. See Robert R. Alford, *Party and Society: The Anglo-American Democracies* (Chicago, IL: Rand McNally, 1963); Richard F. Hamilton, *Class and Politics in the United States* (New York, NY: Wiley, 1972); and Seymour Martin Lipset, *Political Man: The Social Bases of Politics*, exp. ed. (Baltimore, MD: Johns Hopkins University Press, 1981). For a more recent book using the perspective, see Jeff Manza and Clem Brooks, *Social Cleavages and Political Change: Voter Alignments in U.S. Party Coalitions* (Oxford, UK: Oxford University Press, 1999).

53. Angus Campbell et al., *The American Voter* (New York, NY: Wiley, 1960). For a recent assessment of the contribution of *The American Voter*, see William G. Jacoby, "The American Voter," in Leighley, *Oxford Handbook of American Elections and Political Behavior*, 262–277.

54. The Michigan model conceptualizes party identification as the individual's enduring attachment to a political party. The theory contends that party identification is socialized early in life and remains stable throughout adulthood. Dissatisfied with this static view of party loyalties, Morris P. Fiorina reconceptualized party identification as "a running tally of retrospective evaluations of party promises and performance." Fiorina, *Retrospective Voting in American National Elections* (New Haven, CT: Yale University Press, 1981), 84. For a counterargument to Fiorina, see Larry M. Bartels, "Beyond the Running Tally: Partisan Bias in Political Perceptions," *Political Behavior* 24 (June 2002): 117–150.

55. Anthony Downs, *An Economic Theory of Democracy* (New York, NY: Harper and Row, 1957); William H. Riker, *A Theory of Political Coalitions* (New Haven, CT: Yale University Press, 1962).

56. See, for example, William H. Riker and Peter C. Ordeshook, "A Theory of the Calculus of Voting," *American Political Science Review* 62 (March 1968): 25–32; John A. Ferejohn and Morris P. Fiorina, "The Paradox of Not Voting: A Decision Theocratic Analysis," *American Political Science Review* 68 (June 1974): 525–536; and Fiorina, *Retrospective Voting in American National Elections*. For an excellent introduction to American voting behavior that relies on a rational choice perspective, see Rebecca B. Morton, *Analyzing Elections* (New York, NY: Norton, 2006).

57. For a more extensive discussion of the merits and limitations of these approaches, see Paul R. Abramson, John H. Aldrich, and David W. Rohde, "Studying American Elections," in Jan E. Leighley, ed. *The Oxford Handbook of American Elections and Political Behavior* (New York, NY: Oxford University Press, 2010), 700–715.

58. Most of the respondents were interviewed before *and* after the election. Many of the questions we are interested in, such as whether people voted, how they voted for president, and how they voted for Congress, were asked in the survey conducted after the election.

    For this volume we elected to use both the face-to-face and web-based interviews, that is, the "full sample." We did not do this following the 2012 election. This decision was driven by evidence demonstrating that the full sample estimates in 2016 were not affected significantly by differences in "survey mode." Put differently, estimates based on the face-to-face and web-based interviews—at least with regard to the variables that most interest us—do not differ significantly from one another. By electing to use the full sample, we more than double our sample size, allowing us to make more precise contrasts between variables (about which, more later).

59. The 2002 midterm survey was conducted by telephone. The ANES has not conducted a midterm survey since then.

60. For an overview of how the ANES is currently constructed and its recent innovations in measurement, see the collection of essays found in John H. Aldrich and Kathleen M. McGraw, eds., *Improving Public Opinion Surveys: Interdisciplinary Innovation and the American National Election Studies* (Princeton, NJ: Princeton University Press, 2012).

61. For a brief nontechnical introduction to polling, see Herbert Asher, *Polling and the Public: What Every Citizen Should Know*, 7th ed. (Washington, DC: CQ Press, 2007). For a more advanced discussion, see Herbert F. Weisberg, *The Total Survey Error Approach: A Guide to the New Science of Survey Research* (Chicago, IL: University of Chicago Press, 2005).

62. For a brief discussion of the procedures used by the Survey Research Center, which conducted the surveys from 1952 to 2004, to carry out its sampling for in-person interviews, see Paul R. Abramson, *Political Attitudes in America: Formation and Change* (San Francisco, CA: W. H. Freeman, 1983), 18–23. For a more detailed description of the design and implementation of the 2016 ANES election study, see http://www.electionstudies.org/studypages/anes_timeseries_2016/anes_timeseries_2016_userguidecodebook.pdf.

63. For an excellent table that allows us to evaluate differences between two groups, see Leslie Kish, *Survey Sampling* (New York, NY: Wiley, 1965), 580. Kish defines differences between two groups to be significant if the results are more than two standard errors apart.

64. For 2016—as well as for 1958, 1960, 1974, 1976, 1992, 1994, 1996, 1998, 2000, 2002, 2004, 2008, and 2012—a weighting procedure is necessary to obtain a representative result, and so we report the "weighted" number of cases.

65. There also were numerous state-level ballot measures—initiatives, referenda, and state constitutional amendments—for which to vote. Voters in California, Massachusetts, and Nevada voted to legalize marijuana for recreational use, and several other states, including Arkansas, Florida, and North Dakota, passed medical marijuana provisions.

CHAPTER 1

1. Note that many states that have presidential primaries also hold primary elections for many other offices. Most of these primaries, such as for the U.S. House and Senate, select the actual nominees of the two parties for those offices. Thus the party leadership plays no direct role at all in selecting the party's candidates.

2. They have ceded control to the substantial majority of potential voters who are eligible to vote in primary elections. They have ceded effective control to the substantial minority who actually participate in those elections.

3. George H. W. Bush in 1992 faced one challenger, Patrick Buchanan, who did have an impact on the race, although Bush defeated him rather easily.

4. Gov. Jerry Brown (then, as in 2016, governor of California) did run as a third Democrat in 1980. Although obviously a formidable politician over a long career, and even though he was also a very serious threat for the Democratic nomination in 1976, he was much less formidable in 1980, picking up the nickname "Governor Moonbeam."

5. The five who had declared their candidacy, participated in at least one presidential "debate" in 2015, and withdrew in 2015 were: former Governor Rick Perry (Texas, and presidential candidate in 2012), who withdrew on September 11, 2015; Governor Scott Walker (Wisconsin), who withdrew on September 21; Governor Bobby Jindal (Louisiana), who withdrew on November 17; Senator Lindsey Graham (South Carolina), who withdrew on December 21; and former Governor George Pataki (New York), who withdrew on December 29.

6. Three others declared and dropped out in 2015: former Senator James Webb (Virginia), October 20; former Governor Lincoln Chafee (Rhode Island), October 23; and Lawrence Lessing (professor), November 2.

7. There are parallels among the approximately seventeen Republican candidate field in 2015 and the seventeen Democratic field in 1976. For analysis of the 1976 race in these terms, see John H. Aldrich, *Before the Convention: Strategies and Choices in Presidential Nomination Campaigns* (Chicago: University of Chicago Press, 1980). A *Politico* story from 2015 makes the direct comparison, between the 1972 and 2016 races: http://www.politico.com/magazine/story/2015/09/2016-election-1976-democratic-primary-213125.

8. She of course had been a U.S. senator (New York) before Obama appointed her to his cabinet as well as First Lady even earlier. She resigned as secretary of state to prepare to run for the presidency.

9. Joseph A. Schlesinger, *Ambition and Politics: Political Careers in the United States* (Chicago: Rand McNally, 1966); Joseph A. Schlesinger, *Political Parties and the Winning of Office* (Ann Arbor: University of Michigan Press, 1991).

10. Obama was of course constitutionally ineligible to run for a third term. Although Vice President Joe Biden could have run for president, and indeed considered it carefully, he eventually made an agonizing personal decision not to run in part due to the recent death of his son.

11. Unlike Hillary Clinton this year, many of the early cabinet members who became major candidates and, in a number of cases, presidential nominees (and even presidents) had not held major elective office previously.

12. Florida law, unlike that in some states, prohibits running for two offices in the same election. Florida, like a number of states, holds separate primaries for president and all other offices. Doing so allows the state legislature to choose what they perceive to be the most favorable date for selecting presidential delegates (which is usually early in the year, see the following) and then hold primary elections at a more timely date (usually much later) for other offices. The main cost to this strategy is the cost of running two primary elections.

13. In addition to the fifty states, also included are events for the District of Columbia, various territories, and for the Democrats, even Americans Living Abroad.

14. The Democratic Party requires some form of proportionality for all of its states. Florida and Ohio on the GOP side employed the state-wide plurality version of WTA. Perhaps not coincidentally each had a candidate from the state (in Florida's case there were two at the outset of campaign, but Bush withdrew, leaving Rubio as the Florida candidate; Kasich ran from a base in Ohio), and both had a large number of delegates, so WTA could make a very large impact on the race. Of course the candidate potentially advantaged under the rules would actually have to win the state to get that reward.

15. The Democrats have long prohibited WTA primaries, although the rules often fall well short of being truly proportional.

16. Theodore H. White, *The Making of the President, 1968* (New York: Pocket Books, 1970).

17. Ibid., 153.

18. He was helped in this effort by the fact that one-third of the delegates had been chosen in 1967, before Johnson's renomination faced serious opposition.

19. Zeke Miller, "*Time* Guide to Official Republican Nomination Calendar," October 2, 2015, http://time.com/4059030/republican-primary-calendar-2016-nomination-convention/.

20. Clinton actually held a majority of the delegates in light of the DC primary on June 14. However, superdelegates had begun to publicly declare, mostly for her, giving her assurances of a majority a few days in advance of the DC primary.

21. To be sure there were calls from supporters of Sanders in 2016, as of Clinton in 2008, to maintain their candidacies. Both the Clinton and Sanders campaigns, however, chose to slowly wind down the level of competition and effectively accept defeat. Sanders formally endorsed Clinton as nominee on July 12. For a discussion of the importance of superdelegates in 1984 and 2008, see Paul R. Abramson, John H. Aldrich, and David W. Rohde, *Change and Continuity in the 1984 Elections*, rev. ed. (Washington, D.C.: CQ Press, 1987), 25; Abramson, Aldrich, and Rohde, *Change and Continuity in the 2008 and 2010 Elections*, 30–33.

Note that the Democratic National Committee passed a rule intended to apply in 2020 that balanced between the Clinton and Sanders camps, keeping the superdelegates more or less intact and thereby ensuring that the convention includes experienced party leadership but requiring that two-thirds of them vote in accordance with their state's primary or caucus results, thus binding them. The first aspect favored Clinton's position, the second Sanders's, although this outcome was the first choice of neither candidate. The Republican Party does have its own superdelegates, but it limits them to the Republican National Committee membership, per se, which is a much smaller proportion of the total convention delegations.

22. Phil Paolino, "Candidate Name Recognition and the Dynamics of the Pre-Primary Period of the Presidential Nomination Process" (PhD diss., Duke University, 1995).

23. In addition a second primary for other offices often attracts very few voters, especially in the absence of a hotly contested gubernatorial or senatorial contest.

24. John Aldrich, "The Invisible Primary and Its Effects on Democratic Choice," *PS: Political Science and Politics* 42 (2009): 33–38.

25. See Paul R. Abramson, John H. Aldrich, and David W. Rohde, *Change and Continuity in the 2000 and 2002 Elections* (Washington, D.C.: CQ Press, 2003), chap. 1, for more details on the nomination campaigns in 2000.

26. His now infamous post-Iowa victory "scream" is often attributed for this, but we think it more likely that his quite liberal standing was hurting him as more moderate Democrats, in the coming states, learned about him.

27. In retrospect asking candidates to share chances and even delegates to defeat a frontrunner before necessarily turning on one another to secure the single prize of presidential nomination may work in parlor games such as Risk but seems implausible in the case of seeking the most powerful office in the world.

28. John H. Aldrich, *Before the Convention: Strategies and Choices in Presidential Nomination Campaigns* (Chicago: University of Chicago Press, 1980); Larry M. Bartels, *Presidential Primaries and the Dynamics of Public Choice* (Princeton, N.J.: Princeton University Press, 1988).

29. EMILY's List, a group that supports female candidates, draws its name from an acronym of this observation.

30. Thomas E. Mann, "Money in the 2008 Elections: Bad News or Good?," July 1, 2008, https://www.brookings.edu/opinions/money-in-the-2008-elections-bad-news-or-good/.

31. Michael Muskal and Dan Morain, "Obama Raises $55 Million in February; Clinton Reports Surge in Funds," *Los Angeles Times*, March 7, 2008, http://articles.latimes.com/2008/mar/07/nation/na-money.

32. U.S. Court of Appeals for the District of Columbia Circuit, *Speechnow.org v. Federal Election Commission*, March 26, 2010.

33. Center for Responsive Politics, "What Are Independent Expenditures and Communications Costs?," January 29, 2014, http://www.opensecrets.org/pacs/indexpend.php?strID=C00490045&cycle=2012.

34. See, e.g., Christopher Hare and Keith T. Poole, "The Polarization of Contemporary American Politics," *Polity* 46, no. 3 (July 2014).

35. Morris P. Fiorina and Samuel J. Abrams, "Political Polarization in the American Public," *Annual Review of Political Science* 11 (2008): 563–588; Morris P. Fiorina and S. J. Abrams, *Disconnect: The Breakdown of Representation in American Politics*, vol. 11 (Norman: University of Oklahoma Press, 2012). See also our data in Chapter 6.

36. Alan I. Abramowitz and Kyle L. Saunders, "Is Polarization a Myth?" *Journal of Politics* 70, no. 2 (2008): 542–555.

37. Marc J. Hetherington, *Why Trust Matters: Declining Political Trust and the Demise of American Liberalism* (Princeton, N.J.: Princeton University Press, 2005); Marc J. Hetherington and Jason A. Husser, "How Trust Matters: The Changing Political Relevance of Political Trust," *American Journal of Political Science* 56, no. 2 (2012): 312–325; Shanto Iyengar, Gaurav Sood, and Yphtach Lelkes, "Affect, Not Ideology: A Social Identity Perspective on Polarization," *Public Opinion Quarterly* 76, no. 3 (2012): 405–431.

38. Gary C. Jacobson, "Partisan Polarization in Presidential Support: The Electoral Connection," *Congress and the Presidency: A Journal of Capital Studies* 30, no. 1 (2003): 1–36. See also Christopher Hare, David A. Armstrong, Ryan Bakker, Royce Carroll, and Keith T. Poole, "Using Bayesian Aldrich-McKelvey Scaling to Study Citizens' Ideological Preferences and Perceptions," *American Journal of Political Science* 59 (2015): 759–774, doi:10.1111/ajps.12151.

39. The ANES conducted a four-wave panel beginning in January 1980, and here we use wave 1: Interview P1 (wave 1) January 22–February 25; personal interview; 1,008 completed cases. We also use the 2016 ANES pilot study: Data collection was conducted between January 22 and January 28, 2016. The sample consisted of 1,200 individuals who were part of an opt-in Internet panel.

40. Chapter 6 includes reports and more details about candidate thermometer measures.

41. Democrat and Republican here are those who answered the first question in the standard battery of questions about partisan identification used by the ANES as "Democrat" or as "Republican," with other responses including "independent" and so on. See Chapter 8 and note these are equivalent to using "strong" and "weak" Democratic and Republican responses. The differences are in absolute value, thus measuring the size of the gap between the two sets of partisans' responses.

42. Abramson, Aldrich, and Rohde, *Change and Continuity in the 2000 and 2002 Elections*.

43. We will let mature audiences look that up.

44. Jeremy Diamond, "Trump: I Could 'Shoot Somebody and I Wouldn't Lose Voters'" *CNN Politics*, January 24, 2016, http://www.cnn.com/2016/01/23/politics/donald-trump -shoot-somebody-support/.

45. Most states impose such constraints only for one ballot or have some other short-run obligation, after which delegates are freed from such laws to vote as they please. However, no nomination has taken more than one ballot since 1952 and thus within the new nomination system of 1972. So, in that sense, delegate votes have indeed been so constrained. Of course Republicans have a small number and Democrats a larger number of superdelegates who are free to vote as they choose.

46. Although there are sometimes nominations serving as protests to the party, the last time there was an open vote for vice president was in the 1956 Democratic Convention, when nominee Adlai Stevenson (Gov., IL) threw the choice to the delegates, who were choosing between Estes Kefauver (Sen., TN) and John Kennedy (Sen., MA).

47. The party holding the presidency, by tradition, holds its convention second.

CHAPTER 2

1. Until 2008 neither Maine nor Nebraska had divided their electoral vote under these systems, but in that year Obama succeeded in carrying one of Nebraska's congressional districts, thus gaining one of the state's votes. In 2016 Donald Trump won the second congressional district in Maine, giving him one of the state's electoral votes.

2. The thirteen states were Colorado, Florida, Iowa, Michigan, Minnesota, Nevada, New Hampshire, New Mexico, North Carolina, Ohio, Pennsylvania, Virginia, and Wisconsin. On this point, see https://www.washingtonpost.com/politics/clinton-holds-clear-advantage -in-new-battleground-polls/2016/10/18/2885e3a0-94a6-11e6-bc79-af1cd3d2984b_story .html?utm_term=.acca4a5580e8. Some accounts had Georgia and Utah listed as battleground states as well.

3. For a discussion of electoral-vote strategies, see Daron R. Shaw, "The Methods Behind the Madness: Presidential Electoral-College Strategies, 1988–1996," *Journal of Politics* 61 (November 1999), 893–913.

4. Bill Allison, Mira Rojanasakul, Brittany Harris, and Cedric Sam, "Tracking the 2016 Presidential Money Race," *Bloomberg Politics*, December 9, 2016, https://www.bloomberg .com/politics/graphics/2016-presidential-campaign-fundraising/.

5. Ibid.

6. Nicholas Confessore and Karen Yourish, "Measuring Donald Trump's Mammoth Advantage in Free Media, *New York Times* (March 16, 2016).

7. Maggie Haberman, Alexander Burns, and Ashley Parker, "Donald Trump Fires Corey Lewandowski, His Campaign Manager," *New York Times*, June 20, 2016, https://www .nytimes.com/2016/06/21/us/politics/corey-lewandowski-donald-trump.html?_r=0.

8. Sean Sullivan, "Trump Hires ex-Cruz Super PAC Strategist Kellyanne Conway," *Washington Post*, July 1, 2016, https://www.washingtonpost.com/news/post-politics/ wp/2016/07/01/trump-hires-ex-cruz-super-pac-strategist-kellyanne-conway/?utm_term =.9f43bbaf9b1b.

9. Jonathan Martin, Jim Rutenberg, and Maggie Haberman, "Donald Trump Appoints Media Firebrand to Run Campaign," *New York Times*, August 17, 2016, https://www.nytimes .com/2016/08/18/us/politics/donald-trump-stephen-bannon-paul-manafort.html.

10. Michael Schmidt, "Hillary Clinton Used Personal Email Account at State Dept., Possibly Breaking Rules," *New York Times*, March 2, 2015, https://www.nytimes.com/2015/03/03/us/ politics/hillary-clintons-use-of-private-email-at-state-department-raises-flags.html.

11. Steven Lee Myers and Eric Lichtblau, "Hillary Clinton Is Criticized for Private Emails in State Dept. Review," *New York Times*, May 25, 2016, https://www.nytimes .com/2016/05/26/us/politics/state-department-hillary-clinton-emails.html.

12. Mark Landler and Eric Lichtblau, "F.B.I. Director James Comey Recommends No Charges for Hillary Clinton on Email," *New York Times*, July 5, 2016, https://www.nytimes .com/2016/07/06/us/politics/hillary-clinton-fbi-email-comey.html.

13. Emily Schultheis, "Donald Trump: FBI Decision on Clinton Emails a 'Total Miscarriage in Justice,'" *CBS News*, July 5, 2016, http://www.cbsnews.com/news/donald-trump-fbi-decision -on-clinton-emails-a-total-miscarriage-in-justice/.

14. For a discussion of factors that presidents consider when selecting their vice presidential nominees, see Mark Hiller and Douglas Kriner, "Institutional Change and the Dynamics of Vice Presidential Selection," *Presidential Studies Quarterly* 38 (Issue 3, 2008): 401–421.

15. Jonathan Swan, "Rankings: Trump's Top 10 VP Picks," *The Hill*, May 31, 2016, http://thehill .com/blogs/ballot-box/presidential-races/281527-power-rankings-trumps-top-10-vp-picks.

16. Eric Bradner, Dana Bash, and M. J. Lee, "Donald Trump Selects Mike Pence as VP," *CNN*, July 16, 2016, http://www.cnn.com/2016/07/14/politics/donald-trump-vice-presidential -choice/. The Koch brothers referenced here are Charles and David, who regularly contribute to conservative and libertarian causes.

17. Jeff Zeleny, "5 People to Watch in Hillary Clinton's Veepstakes," *CNN*, July 15, 2016, http://www.cnn.com/2016/07/14/politics/hillary-clinton-vice-president-choice/.

18. Jeff Zeleny, Ryan Nobles, and M. J. Lee, "Hillary Clinton Selects Tim Kaine as Her Running Mate," *CNN*, July 23, 2016, http://www.cnn.com/2016/07/22/politics/ hillary-clinton-vp-pick/.

19. John Wagner, "Sanders Says He Would Have Preferred Warren as Clinton's VP Pick," *Washington Post*, July 24, 2016, https://www.washingtonpost.com/news/post-politics/ wp/2016/07/24/sanders-says-he-would-have-preferred-warren-as-clintons-vp-pick/?utm _term=.895aaf7d5a00.

20. Michael Heaney, "Why Are the Protests at the Republican Convention So Small?" *Washington Post*, July 21, 2016, https://www.washingtonpost.com/news/monkey-cage/wp/2016/07/ 21/why-are-protests-at-the-republican-convention-so-small/?utm_term=.6222125c8341.

21. Tribune News Service, "After Earlier Turmoil, Republicans Seek to Mend Party Divisions on RNC's Opening Night," *Chicago Tribune*, July 19, 2016, http://www.chicagotribune .com/news/nationworld/politics/ct-republican-national-convention-cleveland-20160718 -story.html.

22. Ryan Beckwith, "Watch Ted Cruz Fail to Endorse Trump at the Republican Convention," *Time*, July 20, 2016, http://time.com/4416396/republican-convention-ted-cruz-donald-trump -endorsement-speech-transcript-video/.

23. Shane Goldmacher, Katie Glueck, and Matthew Nussbaum, "Cruz Burns Trump: In a Stunning Convention Moment, the Texas Senator Told Republicans to Vote Their Conscience—and Refused to Endorse the Nominee," *Politico*, July 21, 2016, http://www .politico.com/story/2016/07/rnc-2016-donald-trump-unity-225915.

24. Patrick Healy and Jonathan Martin, "His Tone Dark, Donald Trump Takes G.O.P. Mantle," *New York Times*, July 21, 2016, https://www.nytimes.com/2016/07/22/us/politics/don ald-trump-rnc-speech.html.

25. "Transcript: Donald Trump at the G.O.P. Convention," *New York Times*, July 22, 2016, https://www.nytimes.com/2016/07/22/us/politics/trump-transcript-rnc-address.html.

26. Marc Caputo and Daniel Strauss, "Wasserman Schultz Steps Down as DNC Chair," *Politico*, July 24, 2016, http://www.politico.com/story/2016/07/wasserman-schultz-wont -preside-over-dnc-convention-226088.

27. "Transcript: Read Michelle Obama's Full Speech from the 2016 DNC," *Washington Post*, July 26, 2016, https://www.washingtonpost.com/news/post-politics/wp/2016/07/ 26/transcript-read-michelle-obamas-full-speech-from-the-2016-dnc/?utm_term =.5c46598c493b.

28. "Full Text: Hillary Clinton's DNC Speech," *Politico*, July 28, 2016, http://www.politico .com/story/2016/07/full-text-hillary-clintons-dnc-speech-226410.

29. Michael O'Connell, "TV Ratings: Hillary Clinton's DNC Speech Falls Just Shy of Trump's With 33 Million Viewers," *Hollywood Reporter*, July 29, 2016, http://www.hollywoodre porter.com/live-feed/tv-ratings-hillary-clintons-dnc-915706.

30. Jennifer Agiesta, "Donald Trump Bounces into the Lead," *CNN*, July 25, 2016, http://www .cnn.com/2016/07/25/politics/donald-trump-hillary-clinton-poll/.

31. Hannah Hartig, John Lapinski, and Stephanie Psyllos, "Poll: Clinton Support Spikes Following Democratic Convention," *NBC News*, August 2, 2016, http://www.nbcnews.com/ storyline/data-points/poll-clinton-support-spikes-following-democratic-convention-n621071.

32. Gregory Krieg, "Donald Trump's 27-Day Spiral: From Convention Bounce to Campaign Overhaul," *CNN*, August 18, 2016, http://www.cnn.com/2016/08/17/politics/donald-trump-post-convention-controversy-polls-shakeup/.

33. Ibid.

34. Philip Rucker, "Trump Refuses to Endorse Paul Ryan in GOP Primary: 'I'm Just Not Quite There Yet,'" *Washington Post*, August 2, 2016, https://www.washingtonpost.com/politics/trump-refuses-to-endorse-paul-ryan-in-gop-primary-im-just-not-quite-there-yet/2016/08/02/1449f028-58e9-11e6-831d-0324760ca856_story.html?hpid=hp_no-name_no-name%3Apage%2Fbreaking-news-bar&tid=a_breakingnews&utm_term=.5d955c9bc396.

35. Ibid.

36. David Wright, "Poll: Clinton Leads Trump in Red State Georgia," *CNN*, August 6, 2016, http://www.cnn.com/2016/08/05/politics/clinton-leads-trump-georgia-poll/index.html.

37. Nick Corasaniti and Maggie Haberman, "Donald Trump Suggests 'Second Amendment People' Could Act Against Hillary Clinton," *New York Times*, August 9, 2016, https://www.nytimes.com/2016/08/10/us/politics/donald-trump-hillary-clinton.html.

38. Ibid.

39. Gregory Krieg, "Donald Trump's 27-Day Spiral: From Convention Bounce to Campaign Overhaul," *CNN*, August 18, 2016, http://www.cnn.com/2016/08/17/politics/donald-trump-post-convention-controversy-polls-shakeup/.

40. Ivan Levingston, "Trump: If I Lose, I'll Have a 'Nice Long Vacation.'" *CNBC*, August 22, 2016, http://www.cnbc.com/2016/08/11/trump-if-i-lose-ill-have-a-nice-long-vacation.html.

41. Jonathan Martin, Jim Rutenberg, and Maggie Haberman, "Donald Trump Appoints Media Firebrand to Run Campaign," *New York Times*, August 17, 2016, https://www.nytimes.com/2016/08/18/us/politics/donald-trump-stephen-bannon-paul-manafort.html.

42. Abby Phillip, "Clinton: Half of Trump's Supporters Fit in 'Basket of Deplorables,'" *Washington Post*, September 9, 2016, https://www.washingtonpost.com/news/post-politics/wp/2016/09/09/clinton-half-of-trumps-supporters-fit-in-basket-of-deplorables/?utm_term=.fcb12bb30260.

43. Jonathan Martin and Amy Chozick, "Hillary Clinton's Doctor Says Pneumonia Led to Abrupt Exit from 9/11 Event," *New York Times*, September 11, 2016, https://www.nytimes.com/2016/09/12/us/politics/hillary-clinton-campaign-pneumonia.html.

44. Colleen McCain Nelson and Laura Meckler, "Hillary Clinton Prepping for Two Trumps at Debate," *Wall Street Journal*, September 20, 2016, https://www.wsj.com/articles/hillary-clinton-prepping-for-two-trumps-at-debate-1474415274.

45. Meg Anderson, "How Clinton and Trump Are Preparing for the First Presidential Debate," *NPR*, September 22, 2016, http://www.npr.org/2016/09/22/494901644/how-clinton-and-trump-are-preparing-for-the-first-presidential-debate.

46. Duane Patterson, "Hugh and Donald Trump Talk 2016," *Hugh Hewitt*, June 23, 2016, http://www.hughhewitt.com/hugh-donald-trump-talk-2016/.

47. Meg Anderson, "How Clinton and Trump Are Preparing for the First Presidential Debate."

48. "The First Trump-Clinton Presidential Debate Transcript, Annotated," *Washington Post*, September 26, 2016, https://www.washingtonpost.com/news/the-fix/wp/2016/09/26/the-first-trump-clinton-presidential-debate-transcript-annotated/?utm_term=.ae00ba1531ea.

49. Alex Burns and Matt Flegenheimer, "Did You Miss the Presidential Debate? Here Are the Highlights," *New York Times*, September 26, 2016, https://www.nytimes.com/2016/09/26/us/politics/presidential-debate.html.

50. Ibid.

51. Brian Stelter, "Debate Breaks Record as Most-Watched in U.S. History," *CNN*, September 27, 2016, http://money.cnn.com/2016/09/27/media/debate-ratings-record-viewership/.

52. Reena Flores, "Gallup: Clinton Beats Trump in First Debate by a Large Margin," *CBS News*, September 30, 2016, http://www.cbsnews.com/news/poll-hillary-clinton-beats-donald -trump-in-first-debate-by-a-large-margin/.

53. Ibid.

54. Eric Bradner, "5 Takeaways from the Vice Presidential Debate," *CNN*, October 5, 2016, http://www.cnn.com/2016/10/05/politics/vp-debate-takeaways/.

55. Ibid.

56. Nicolas Confessore and Matt Flegenheimer, "Vice-Presidential Debate: What You Missed," *New York Times*, October 4, 2016, https://www.nytimes.com/2016/10/04/us/politics/vice -presidential-debate.html.

57. Shane Goldmacher, Annie Karni, and Nolan McCaskill, "Trump Caught on Tape Making Crude, Sexually Aggressive Comments about Women," *Politico*, October 8, 2016, http:// www.politico.com/story/2016/10/trump-wapo-229299.

58. Ruth Marcus, "Donald Trump's Remarkably Gross Comments about Women," *Washington Post*, October 7, 2016, https://www.washingtonpost.com/blogs/post-partisan/wp/2016/10/07/ donald-trumps-remarkably-gross-comments-about-women/?utm_term=.5d3be1e6c085.

59. Aaron Blake, "Three Dozen Republicans Have Now Called for Donald Trump to Drop Out," *Washington Post*, October 9, 2016, https://www.washingtonpost.com/news/the-fix/ wp/2016/10/07/the-gops-brutal-responses-to-the-new-trump-video-broken-down/?utm _term=.2dda7f621f26.

60. Maggie Haberman, "Donald Trump's Apology That Wasn't," *New York Times*, October 8, 2016, https://www.nytimes.com/2016/10/08/us/politics/donald-trump-apology.html.

61. Irin Carmon, "The Allegations Women Have Made against Donald Trump," *NBC News*, October 27, 2016, http://www.nbcnews.com/politics/2016-election/allegations -women-have-made-against-donald-trump-n665731.

62. Donald J. Trump, *Twitter*, October 8, 2016, https://twitter.com/realdonaldtrump/status/78 4840992734064641?lang=en.

63. "He Said, She Said: Highlights from the Second Trump-Clinton Presidential Debate of 2016," *Washington Post*, October 10, 2016, https://www.washingtonpost.com/graphics/ politics/2016-election/hesaid-shesaid-second-debate/.

64. Ibid.

65. "He Said, She Said: Highlights from the Third Trump-Clinton Presidential Debate of 2016," *Washington Post*, October 19, 2016, https://www.washingtonpost.com/graphics/ politics/2016-election/highlights-trump-clinton-third-debate/.

66. "Trump Calls Clinton a 'Nasty Woman' during Final Debate," *The Guardian*, October 20, 2016, https://www.theguardian.com/us-news/video/2016/oct/20/donald-trump-calls -hillary-clinton-a-nasty-woman-during-final-debate-video.

67. Jennifer Agiesta, "Hillary Clinton Wins Third Presidential Debate, According to CNN/ORC Poll," *CNN*, October 20, 2016, http://www.cnn.com/2016/10/19/politics/ hillary-clinton-wins-third-presidential-debate-according-to-cnn-orc-poll/.

68. See Robert S. Erikson and Christopher Wlezien, *The Timeline of Presidential Elections* (Chicago: University of Chicago Press, 2012), 79–81, and the references cited therein. Also see John Sides, "Do Presidential Debates Really Matter?," *Washington Monthly*, September/ October 2012, 19–21.

69. See Sides, "Do Presidential Debates Really Matter?"

70. Ibid.

71. "General Election: Trump vs. Clinton vs. Johnson vs. Stein," *Real Clear Politics*, https://www.realclearpolitics.com/epolls/2016/president/us/general_election_trump_vs_clinton_vs_johnson_vs_stein-5952.html.

72. Adam Edelman, "Clinton Has Major Lead over Trump in Poll Taken Days after Final Debate," *Daily News*, October 23, 2016, http://www.nydailynews.com/news/politics/clinton-major-lead-trump-final-debate-poll-article-1.2841984.

73. Ibid.

74. Josh Gerstein, "FBI Reviewing New Evidence in Clinton Email Probe," *Politico*, October 28, 2016, http://www.politico.com/story/2016/10/fbi-reopens-clinton-email-server-investigation-230454.

75. Ibid.

76. Adam Goldman and Alan Rappeport, "Emails in Anthony Weiner Inquiry Jolt Hillary Clinton's Campaign," *New York Times*, October 28, 2016, https://www.nytimes.com/2016/10/29/us/politics/fbi-hillary-clinton-email.html?smid=tw-nytimes&smtyp=cur&_r=0&mtrref=undefined&gwh=E2C883CDD6AA230DA807D264DDC41875&gwt=pay.

77. Josh Gerstein, "FBI Reviewing New Evidence in Clinton Email Probe," *Politico*, October 28, 2016, http://www.politico.com/story/2016/10/fbi-reopens-clinton-email-server-investigation-230454.

78. Ibid.

79. Ibid.

80. Lisa Mascaro, "Trump Welcomes FBI Probe: 'Clinton's Corruption Is on a Scale We Have Never Seen,'" *Los Angeles Times*, October 28, 2016, http://www.latimes.com/nation/politics/trailguide/la-na-trailguide-updates-trump-welcomes-new-fbi-probe-clinton-s-1477677693-htmlstory.html.

81. Ibid.

82. "General Election: Trump vs. Clinton," *Real Clear Politics*, http://www.realclearpolitics.com/epolls/2016/president/us/general_election_trump_vs_clinton-5491.html.

83. Julie Pace, Lisa Lerer, and Jill Colvin, "FBI Won't Recommend Charges against Clinton Based on New Emails, Comey Says," *Press Herald*, November 6, 2016, http://www.pressherald.com/2016/11/06/fbi-wont-recommend-charges-against-clinton-based-on-new-emails-comey-says/. President Trump would later catch many by surprise when he announced on May 9, 2017, that he was firing FBI Director James Comey for his mishandling of the email investigation of Clinton. See Niall Stanage, "The Memo: Trump Ignites Firestorm," *The Hill*, May 9, 2017, http://thehill.com/homenews/administration/332667-the-memo-trump-ignites-firestorm.

84. The data are from Michael McDonald's website: http://www.electproject.org/national-1789-present.

85. See Paul R. Abramson, John H. Aldrich, Brad T. Gomez, and David W. Rohde, *Change and Continuity in the 2012 Elections* (Washington, D.C.: CQ Press, 2015), Chapter 2.

86. Quoted in Michael Scherer, "Inside the Secret World of Quants and Data Crunchers Who Helped Obama Win," *Time*, November 19, 2012, 58.

87. Ibid.

88. Lee Drutman, "How Turnout-Only Politics Gave Us the 2016 Campaign—And a Historic Polling Upset," *Politico*, November 15, 2016, http://www.politico.com/magazine/story/2016/11/mobilization-only-politics-2016-214456. Many of the details in this section are drawn from this article.

89. Ibid.

90. Ibid.

91. Jeremy Peters, Amy Chozick, and Lizette Alvarez, "Fear of Donald Trump Helps Democrats Mobilize Hispanics," *New York Times*, November 6, 2016, https://www.nytimes.com/2016/11/07/us/fear-of-donald-trump-helps-democrats-mobilize-hispanics.html.

92. Ibid.

93. Republicans made a concerted effort to increase the number of field offices after Labor Day, when the traditional fall campaign begins. See Nikita Vladimirov, "RNC to Open 98 Field Offices in Effort to Boost Trump, GOP," *The Hill*, September 2, 2016, http://thehill.com/blogs/ballot-box/presidential-races/294260-gop-to-open-98-field-offices-in-effort-to-boost-trump.

94. Leign Ann Caldwell, "Clinton and Democrats Have Major Fundraising Advantage over Trump," *NBC News*, October 15, 2016, http://www.nbcnews.com/politics/2016-election/clinton-democrats-have-major-fundraising-advantage-over-trump-n667031.

95. Jason Le Miere, "Did the Media Help Donald Trump Win? $5 Billion in Free Advertising Given to President-Elect," *International Business Times*, November 9, 2016, http://www.ibtimes.com/did-media-help-donald-trump-win-5-billion-free-advertising-given-president-elect-2444115.

96. Jonathan Martin and Alan Rappeport, "Presidential Election: A Closing Act, with Clinton, Trump, and a Tiny 'Future Construction Worker,'" *New York Times*, November 4, 2016, https://www.nytimes.com/2016/11/05/us/politics/presidential-election.html.

97. Anthony Brooks, "In Final Weekend Before Election Day, Trump and Clinton Fiercely Campaign in New Hampshire," *Politicker*, November 7, 2016, http://www.wbur.org/politicker/2016/11/07/trump-clinton-nh-final-days.

98. Ibid.

99. Ibid.

100. There has been a lot of interesting research in recent years on the impact of presidential campaigns on outcomes. In addition to the Erikson and Wlezien volume already cited, see Lynn Vavreck, *The Message Matters* (Princeton, N.J.: Princeton University Press, 2009); Thomas H. Holbrook, *Do Campaigns Matter?* (Thousand Oaks, Calif.: Sage Publications, 1996); James E. Campbell, *The American Campaign* (College Station: Texas A&M University Press, 2000); and Darron R. Shaw, "A Study of Presidential Campaign Effects from 1956 to 1992," *Journal of Politics* 61 (May 1999): 387–422.

101. Lee Drutman, "How Turnout-Only Politics Gave Us the 2016 Campaign."

102. Chris Cillizza, "The 13 Most Amazing Findings in the 2016 Exit Poll," *Washington Post*, November 10, 2016, https://www.washingtonpost.com/news/the-fix/wp/2016/11/10/the-13-most-amazing-things-in-the-2016-exit-poll/?utm_term=.c93d4297b5db.

103. The figure used here is the Voting Eligible Population Highest Office Turnout Rate. The data are from the United States Elections Project: http://www.electproject.org/.

104. Carl Bialik, "Voter Turnout Fell, Especially in States That Clinton Won," *FiveThirtyEight*, November 11, 2016, https://fivethirtyeight.com/features/voter-turnout-fell-especially-in-states-that-clinton-won/.

105. Ray Long, "Why Did Hillary Clinton Lose? Simple. She Ran a Bad Campaign," *Chicago Tribune*, November 14, 2016, http://www.chicagotribune.com/news/opinion/commentary/ct-hillary-clinton-lost-bad-campaign-perspec-20161114-story.html.

106. Ibid.

107. Philip Bump, "Of Course Bernie Sanders Could Have Beaten Donald Trump," *Washington Post*, November 13, 2016, https://www.washingtonpost.com/news/the-fix/wp/2016/11/13/of-course-bernie-sanders-could-have-beaten-donald-trump/?utm_term=.c457152b5620.

108. Ibid.
109. Marcus Johnson, "No, Bernie Sanders Would Not Have Beaten Trump," *Huffington Post*, December 16, 2016, http://www.huffingtonpost.com/entry/bernie-sanders-was-on-the-2016-ballotand-he-underperformed_us_5852fbbce4b06ae7ec2a3cb7.
110. Gary C. Jacobson, "The Triumph of Polarized Partisanship in 2016: Donald Trump's Improbable Victory," *Political Science Quarterly* 132 (Spring 2017): 9–41.

CHAPTER 3

1. Jeremy W. Peters and Matt Flegenheimer, "Early Turnout Tilts toward Democrats in Swing States," *New York Times*, October 31, 2016, A1; Byron Tau, "Early Voting Data Shows Who's Turning Out," wsj.com, November 4, 2016.
2. Ibid.
3. Real Clear Politics, "General Election: Trump vs. Clinton," https://www.realclearpolitics.com/epolls/2016/president/us/ general_election_trump_vs_clinton-5491.html.
4. For an approach that combines information from statistical forecasting models and weights their past performance to make future predictions, we recommend Jacob M. Montgomery, Florian M. Hollenbach, and Michael D. Ward, "Improving Predictions Using Ensemble Bayesian Model Averaging," *Political Analysis* 20 (Summer 2012): 271–291.
5. James E. Campbell, "Forecasting the 2016 American National Elections," *PS: Political Science and Politics* 49 (October 2016): 649–654. The forecasts begin on p. 655. Opinion polls offer a snapshot of the electorate at the time of the survey and thus vary with the ebbs and flows of the campaign. Statistical forecast models are based on "fundamentals," factors that have been shown to be predictive across many elections. Most of these fundamentals, such as leading economic indicators, war fatalities during past presidential term, and presidential approval, to name a few, are often known and measured before the general election campaign even begins.
6. Hillary Clinton was born in Chicago, Illinois, and spent much of her adult life in Arkansas before becoming First Lady of the United States in 1992. Clinton and her husband, former President Bill Clinton, moved to New York State after his presidency, where she was later elected twice to the United States Senate. Donald Trump was born in Queens, New York City, and maintained his primary residence in Manhattan. The 2016 election marks the fifth time in U.S. history that both of the major party candidates were from the same state. In 1860 Abraham Lincoln (R) and Stephen Douglas (D) were from Illinois. In 1904 Theodore Roosevelt (R) and Alton Parker (D) were from New York. In 1920 Warren G. Harding (R) and James M. Cox (D) were from Ohio. In 1944 Thomas Dewey (R) and Franklin D. Roosevelt (D) were from New York.
7. Real-Time Staff, "Hillary Clinton Rallying in Philadelphia with the Obamas, Springsteen, Bon Jovi," *Philly.com.*, November 7, 2016, http://www.philly.com/philly/blogs/real-time/Hillary-Clinton-to-hold-Nov-7-2016-rally-in-Philadelphia.html.
8. Lynn Bonner and Rachel Chason, "Lady Gaga Helps Draw Crowd to N.C. State Rally for Clinton before Polls Open," *News and Observer*, November 8, 2016, http://www.newsobserver.com/news/politics-government/state-politics/article113198468.html.
9. Ashley Parker, "Donald Trump Soaks in the Adulation in Improvised Final Stop," *New York Times*, November 8, 2016, https://www.nytimes.com/2016/11/08/us/politics/trump-rally.html

10. Donald Trump was seventy years old at the time of the election, and Hillary Clinton was sixty-nine. Although older candidates have run for the presidency (e.g., Ronald Reagan was seventy-three when he ran for reelection in 1984, and Robert Dole was seventy-three when he was the Republican nominee in 1996), they typically have faced much younger opponents. For a discussion of the role that the candidates' ages played in the campaign, see Jena McGregor, "Clinton and Trump Are the Oldest Candidates Ever. No One Seems to Care," *Washington Post*, July 14, 2016, https://www.washingtonpost.com/news/on-leadership/wp/2016/07/14/clinton-and-trump-are-the-oldest-candidates-ever-no-one-seems-to-care/?utm_term=.a2bf3d67a9ae.

11. Morgan Winsor, "Presidential Candidates Cast Votes on Election Day," *ABC News*, November 8, 2016, abcnews.go.com/Politics/presidential-candidates-cast-votes-election-day/story?id=43381482.

12. Ibid.

13. Bloomberg Businessweek, "Inside Election Night at the Trump and Clinton Parties," November 9, 2016, https://www.bloomberg.com/features/2016-clinton-trump-election-parties/; M. J. Lee, "Tears and Shock at Clinton's Election Night Party," *CNN*, November, 9, 2016, http://www.cnn.com/2016/11/09/politics/hillary-clinton-shock-election-party/index.html.

14. For two examples of pre-election forecasts of the Electoral College, see Chris Cillizza, "Yes, Donald Trump Can Win. Here Are 4 Maps That Prove It," *Washington Post*, November 2, 2016, https://www.washingtonpost.com/news/the-fix/wp/2016/11/02/4-electoral-maps-where-donald-trump-wins/?utm_term=.41f99b4604f0; and Nate Silver, "Election Update: The State of the States," *FiveThirtyEight*, November 7, 2016, https://fivethirtyeight.com/features/election-update-the-state-of-the-states/.

15. For a timeline of election night events, see David Leip's *Atlas of U.S. Presidential Elections*, "2016 Election Night Events Timeline," http://uselectionatlas.org/INFORMATION/ARTICLES/ElectionNight2016/pe2016elecnighttime.php. Leip notes that all "call times are from NBC News and are approximate."

16. Lee, "Tears and Shock."

17. The other presidential candidates to win the Electoral College while losing the popular vote were Republican Rutherford B. Hayes in 1876 (Democrat Samuel J. Tilden won 50.9 percent of the popular vote), Republican Benjamin Harrison in 1888 (Democrat and incumbent President Grover Cleveland won a 48.6 percent plurality of the popular vote), and George W. Bush in 2000 (Democrat Al Gore won a 48.4 percent plurality of the popular vote).

18. Both Johnson and Stein ran for the presidency in 2012, and each had far less appeal. In 2012 Johnson won 0.99 percent of national popular vote, and Stein won 0.36 percent.

19. As noted in Chapter 2, since 1972, Maine has used a system in which the statewide plurality-vote winner receives two electoral votes, and the plurality winner in each of the state's congressional districts receives that district's single electoral vote. Nebraska has used a similar system to allocate its Electoral College votes since the 1992 election. In our previous books we have not always reported these district-level results, but we do so here because in the 2016 election Trump won one Electoral College vote from Maine's Second Congressional District.

20. In 2012 Obama won twenty-six states and the District of Columbia. For a state-by-state reporting of the official presidential election returns for 2012, see Paul R. Abramson, John H. Aldrich, Brad T. Gomez, and David W. Rohde, *Change and Continuity in the 2012 Elections* (Los Angeles: Sage/CQ Press, 2015), Table 3-1.

21. Electors from the Electoral College officially gathered in their respective state capitals to cast ballots for president and vice president on December 19, 2016. For more on the workings of the Electoral College, visit the Office of the Federal Registrar website, http://www.archives.gov/federal-register/electoral-college/index.html.

22. The U.S. Constitution does not require that electors cast ballots in accordance with the popular vote in their states; however twenty-nine states and the District of Columbia bind their electors by law. Faithless electors are uncommon in American electoral history, and indeed, it is rare to see an Electoral College vote with more than one faithless ballot being cast. In 2016 three Democratic electors from the State of Washington cast ballots for former Secretary of State Colin Powell, a Republican, and another elector from the state voted for Faith Spotted Eagle, an activist from the Yankton Sioux Nation (this marks the first time a Native American has received an electoral vote). A Democratic Party elector from Hawaii cast a ballot for Bernie Sanders. On the Republican side two electors from Texas were faithless—one voted for John Kasich and the other for Ron Paul. The previous record for the number of faithless electors was established in the 1808 election, when six Democratic-Republican Party electors from New York cast ballots for New York Governor George Clinton, the party's vice presidential nominee, instead of James Madison. For a brief history of faithless electors, see Nina Agrawal, "All the Times in U.S. History that Members of the Electoral College Voted Their Own Way," *Los Angeles Times*, December 20, 2016, http://www.latimes.com/nation/la-na-faithless-electors-2016-story.html.

23. For a cross-national comparison of U.S. presidential selection rules, see Matthew Soberg Shugart, "The American Process of Selecting a President: A Comparative Perspective," *Presidential Studies Quarterly* 34 (September 2004): 632–655.

24. The respective plurality winners of the popular vote were Andrew Jackson in 1824, Samuel J. Tilden in 1876, incumbent President Grover Cleveland in 1888, and Al Gore in 2000. In 1824 no candidate won a majority of the electoral vote, so the election was thrown to the House of Representatives, where Adams was elected. In 1824 more than a fourth of the electors were chosen by state legislatures.

25. Jonathan Mahler and Steve Eder, "Many Call the Electoral College Outmoded. So Why Has it Endured?," *New York Times*, November 11, 2016, P8. Interestingly public support for or opposition to the Electoral College is likely biased by whether one sides with the winning or losing candidate; see Art Swift, "Americans' Support for Electoral College Rises Sharply," *Gallup*, December 2, 2016, http://www.gallup.com/poll/198917/americans-support-electoral-college-rises-sharply.aspx; see also John H. Aldrich, Jason Reifler, and Michael C. Munger, "Sophisticated *and* Myopic? Citizens Preferences for Electoral College Reform," *Public Choice* 158 (March 2014): 541–558.

26. These fourteen winners were James K. Polk (Democrat) in 1844, with 49.5 percent of the popular vote; Zachary Taylor (Whig) in 1848, with 47.3 percent; James Buchanan (Democrat) in 1856, with 45.3 percent; Abraham Lincoln (Republican) in 1860 with 39.9 percent; James A. Garfield (Republican) in 1880, with 48.3 percent; Grover Cleveland (Democrat) in 1884, with 48.9 percent; Cleveland in 1892, with 46.0 percent; Woodrow Wilson (Democrat) in 1912, with 41.8 percent; Wilson in 1916, with 49.2 percent; Harry S. Truman (Democrat) in 1948, with 49.5 percent; John F. Kennedy (Democrat) in 1960, with 49.7 percent; Richard M. Nixon (Republican) in 1968, with 43.4 percent; Bill Clinton (Democrat) in 1992, with 43.0 percent; and Clinton in 1996, with 49.2 percent. The results for Kennedy can be questioned, however, mainly because voters in Alabama voted for individual electors, and one can argue that Nixon won more popular votes than Kennedy.

27. Maurice Duverger, *Political Parties: Their Organization and Activity in the Modern State*, trans. Barbara North and Robert North (New York: Wiley, 1963), 217. In the original Duverger's proposition is *"le scrutin majoritaire à un seul tour tend au dualisme des partis."* Duverger, *Les partis politiques* (Paris: Armand Colin, 1958), 247. For a discussion see William H. Riker, "The Two-party System and Duverger's Law: An Essay on the History of Political Science," *American Political Science Review* 76 (December 1982): 753–766. For a more recent statement by Duverger, see "Duverger's Law Forty Years Later," in *Electoral Laws and Their Political Consequences*, eds. Bernard Grofman and Arend Lijphart (New York: Agathan Press, 1986), 69–84. For more general discussions of the effects of electoral laws, see Rein Taagepera and Matthew Shugart, *Seats and Votes: The Effects and Determinants of Electoral Systems* (New Haven, Conn.: Yale University Press, 1989); and Gary W. Cox, *Making Votes Count: Strategic Coordination of the World's Electoral Systems* (Cambridge, U.K.: Cambridge University Press, 1997). See also John H. Aldrich and Daniel J. Lee, "Why Two Parties? Ambition, Policy, and the Presidency," *Political Science Research and Methods* 2 (May 2016): 275–292.

28. Duverger's inclusion of "a single ballot" in his formulation is redundant because, in a plurality vote win system, there would be no need for second ballots or runoffs unless needed to break ties. With a large electorate, ties will be extremely rare.

29. Duverger, *Political Parties*, 218.

30. William H. Riker, *The Art of Political Manipulation* (New Haven, Conn.: Yale University Press, 1986), 79.

31. For the most extensive evidence for the 1968, 1980, and 1992 elections, see Paul R. Abramson et al., "Third-Party and Independent Candidates in American Politics: Wallace, Anderson, and Perot," *Political Science Quarterly* 110 (Fall 1997): 349–367. For the 1996 and 2000 elections, see Paul R. Abramson, John H. Aldrich, and David W. Rohde, *Change and Continuity in the 1996 and 1998 Elections* (Washington, D.C.: CQ Press, 1999), 118–120; and Paul R. Abramson, John H. Aldrich, and David W. Rohde, *Change and Continuity in the 2000 and 2002 Elections* (Washington, D.C.: CQ Press, 2003), 124–126.

32. Britain provides an excellent example of the effects of plurality-vote win systems on third parties. In Britain, as in the United States, candidates for the national legislature run in single-member districts, and in all British parliamentary districts the plurality-vote winner is elected. In all nineteen general elections since World War II ended in Europe, the Liberal Party (and more recently the Alliance and the Liberal Democratic Parties) has received a smaller percentage of seats in the House of Commons than its percentage of the popular vote. For example, in the June 2017 election, the Liberal Democrats won 7.4 percent of the popular vote but won only 1.8 percent of the seats in the House of Commons.

33. Third-party candidates are not always underrepresented in the Electoral College. In 1948 J. Strom Thurmond, the States' Rights Democrat, won only 2.4 percent of the popular vote but won 7.3 percent of the electoral vote. Thurmond won 55 percent of the popular votes in the four states he carried (Alabama, Louisiana, Mississippi, and South Carolina), all of which had low turnout. He received no popular vote at all in thirty-one of the forty-eight states.

34. See George C. Edwards III, *Why the Electoral College is Bad for America*, 2nd ed. (New Haven, Conn.: Yale University Press, 2011).

35. Edwards argues that "[a] constitutional amendment is not a pipe dream," noting that a constitutional amendment to establish direct election of the president passed the House on a bipartisan vote in 1969. The amendment, which was publicly endorsed by President Nixon, was filibustered in the Senate, however, by southern senators. See Edwards, *Why the Electoral College Is Bad for America*, 203.

36. For the most extensive argument in favor of this reform, see John R. Koza et al., *Every Vote Equal: A State-Based Plan for Electing the President by National Popular Vote*, 4th ed. (Los Altos, Calif.: National Popular Vote Press, 2013).

37. Adoption of the district system would likely increase the incentive for state legislatures to gerrymander given that presidential electors would now be at stake.

38. David Wasserman, "Introducing the 2017 Cook Political Report Partisan Voting Index," *The Cook Political Report*, April 7, 2017, http://cookpolitical.com/file/Cook_Political _Report_Partisan_Voter_Index_.pdf.

    One should always be cautious when constructing counterfactuals such as this. Had the election taken place under these rules, the candidates most certainly would have campaigned using different strategies, and voter participation would have changed in all likelihood in response to varying levels of electoral competition across districts.

39. A. C. Thomas and colleagues offer a systematic study of alternative elector apportionment proposals using data from 1956 to 2004. They conclude that both the current Electoral College and the direct popular vote are substantially less biased than the district method. See A. C. Thomas, Andrew Gelman, Gary King, and Jonathan N. Katz, "Estimating Partisan Bias of the Electoral College Under Proposed Changes in Elector Apportionment," *Statistics, Politics, and Policy* 4 (Issue 1, 2013): 1–13.

40. Stuart Rothenberg, "The Unusual, Unexpected, Strange, Weird, and Now Bizarre Presidential Election, *Washington Post*, October 5, 2016, https://www.washingtonpost .com/news/powerpost/wp/2016/10/05/the-unusual-unexpected-strange-weird-and-now -bizarre-presidential-election/?utm_term=.6a2d48a5e054.

41. Daniel Gans views much of presidential election history as what statisticians call a "random walk," meaning that party success from one election to the next is essentially random. See Daniel J. Gans, "Persistence of Party Success in American Presidential Elections," *Journal of Interdisciplinary History* 2 (Winter 1986), 221–237.

42. Walter Dean Burnham, *Critical Elections and the Mainsprings of American Politics* (New York: Norton, 1970).

43. Stanley Kelley, Jr., establishes three criteria to classify an election as a landslide: if the winning candidate wins 53 percent of the popular vote *or* wins 80 percent of the electoral vote *or* wins 80 percent of the states. This definition may be too generous, but Reagan's 1984 victory, which met all three of Kelley's criteria, was most certainly a landslide. See Stanley Kelley, Jr., *Interpreting Elections* (Princeton, N.J., Princeton University Press, 1983).

44. Two other incumbents during this period had lower popular vote totals when they stood for reelection (Jimmy Carter in 1980 and George H.W. Bush in 1992); both lost.

45. For two studies of the Whig Party, see Michael F. Holt, *The Rise and Fall of the Whig Party: Jacksonian Politics and the Onset of the Civil War* (New York: Oxford University Press, 1999); and Daniel Walker Howe, *The Political Culture of the American Whigs* (Chicago: University of Chicago Press, 1979).

46. Former Whigs founded the Constitutional Union Party in 1860. Its candidate, John Bell, won 12.6 percent of the popular vote and thirty-nine of the 303 electoral votes.

47. For a discussion of agenda-setting during this period, see William H. Riker, *Liberalism against Populism: A Confrontation between the Theory of Democracy and the Theory of Social Choice* (San Francisco: W. H. Freeman, 1982), 213–232; and John H. Aldrich, *Why Parties? A Second Look* (Chicago: University of Chicago Press, 2011), 130–162.

48. Not all scholars agree with this assessment. The most important dissent is found in David R. Mayhew, *Electoral Realignments: A Critique of an American Genre* (New Haven, Conn.: Yale University Press, 2002), 43–69.

49. The election of 1912 is the last in which a party other than the Democrats and Republicans finished among the top-two vote getters. Former Republican president Theodore Roosevelt, running as the nominee of the Progressive Party (the "Bull Moose Party") finished second in both the popular and Electoral College votes.

50. After the 2000 election, the Republicans and Democrats each had fifty senators, and the Republicans held control of the Senate by virtue of Vice President Dick Cheney's tie-breaking vote. When Senator James M. Jeffords of Vermont left the Republican Party to become an independent and to vote with the Democrats on the organization of the Senate, the Democrats took control of the Senate from June 2001 until January 2003.

51. See David R. Mayhew, "Incumbency Advantage in U.S. Presidential Elections: The Historical Record," *Political Science Quarterly* 123 (Summer 2008): 201–228. An individual-level study of survey responses from the 1952 through 2000 American National Election Studies suggests that incumbent presidential candidates—controlling for a variety of other factors—enjoy a six percentage point advantage over their challengers in the popular vote; see Herbert F. Weisberg, "Partisanship and Incumbency in Presidential Elections," *Political Behavior* 24 (December 2002): 339–360.

52. Jodi Enda, "When Republicans Were Blue and Democrats Were Red: The Era of Color-coded Political Parties Is More Recent than You Might Think," November 1, 2012, smithsonian.com. The association of Republicans with the color red is actually a bit curious, given the color's historical association with revolution and socialism. For example, the song "The Red Flag," composed by James Connell in 1889, became the official song of the British Labour Party. As for flags specifically, the flag of the Soviet Union featured a solid red field with a gold hammer and sickle. Fear of the Soviet Union and the spread of communism in America, particularly during the 1950s, was called the "Red Scare."

53. Since ratification of the Twenty-third Amendment in 1961, the District of Columbia has had three electoral votes, which it first cast in the 1964 election.

54. The *National Journal* hosts a website that tracks all reported campaign visits by the presidential candidates, including those who ran during the primaries: "2016 Travel Tracker," *National Journal*, http://traveltracker.nationaljournal.com/. During the general election the vice presidential candidates also stayed away from California and Texas. Republican Vice Presidential Nominee Mike Pence visited California once, and Democratic Vice Presidential Nominee Tim Kaine visited Texas twice.

55. These counts were tabulated by the authors based on data reported by "2016 Travel Tracker," *National Journal*, http://traveltracker.nationaljournal.com/. We only count candidates' public appearances held after the party conventions.

56. This is not to say that campaigns view larger states alone as important to their electoral strategy. New Hampshire, for example, only has four electoral votes, but it was a battleground state in 2016. Trump made twelve general election campaign visits to New Hampshire, and Clinton made three. Despite Trump's efforts, Clinton narrowly won the Granite State by 0.3 percentage points.

57. U.S. Department of Commerce, *Statistical Abstract of the United States*, 101st ed. (Washington, D.C.: Government Printing Office, 1980), 514.

58. Edward Alden, "The Biggest Issue That Carried Trump to Victory," *Fortune*, November 10, 2016, http://fortune.com/2016 /11/10/trump-voters-free-trade-globalization/.

59. Maxwell Tani, "Democrats Think Trump Won on Economic Issues—But Exit Polls Offer a More Complicated Story," *Business Insider*, December 24, 2016, http://www.businessinsider .com/democrats-trump-econmic-issues-polls-2016-12.

60. See Morris P. Fiorina, with Samuel J. Abrams and Jeremy C. Pope, *Culture War? The Myth of a Polarized America*, 3rd ed. (New York: Pearson/Longman, 2010); and Andrew Gelman et al., *Red State, Blue State, Rich State, Poor State: Why Americans Vote the Way They Do* (Princeton, N.J.: Princeton University Press, 2008).

61. We use the Census Bureau's definition of the Northeast, which includes Connecticut, Maine, Massachusetts, New Hampshire, New Jersey, New York, Pennsylvania, Rhode Island, and Vermont.

62. From 1992 to 2012, the only northeastern state to cast its electoral votes for a Republican was New Hampshire in 2000, giving George W. Bush four electors. In the three elections preceding Clinton's victory in 1992, the Republicans fared quite well in the Northeast. The region was solidly pro-Reagan in 1980 (losing only Rhode Island) and 1984, and George H. W. Bush won six of the region's nine states in 1988.

63. Edward M. Burmila, "The Electoral College after Census 2010 and 2020: The Political Impact of Population Growth and Redistribution," *Perspectives on Politics* 7 (December 2009): 837–847.

64. Javier Panzar, "It's Official: Latinos Now Outnumber Whites in California," *Los Angeles Times*, July 8, 2015, http://www.latimes.com/local/california/la-me-census-latinos-20150708-story.html. Gustavo Lopez and Renee Stepler, "Latinos in the 2016 Election: California," *Pew Research Center*, January 19, 2016, http://www.pewhispanic.org/fact-sheet/latinos-in-the-2016-election-california/.

65. Mark Baldassare, *A California State of Mind: The Conflicted Voter in a Changing World* (Berkeley: University of California Press, 2002), 159.

66. CNN Election 2016, November 9, 2016, http://www.cnn.com/election/results/exit-polls/california/president.

67. Trump's largest victories—in terms of two-party differential (see Table 3-1)—were, in order, Texas, Tennessee, Alabama, Kentucky, Oklahoma, Indiana, and Missouri. In these states combined, Trump won 4.2 million more votes than Clinton.

68. Donald Trump did not willingly accept his popular vote loss. On November 27, 2016, Trump (@realDonaldTrump) tweeted, "In addition to winning the Electoral College in a landslide, I won the popular vote if you deduct the millions of people who vote illegally." We would not characterize Trump's Electoral College margin as a "landslide." In fact, Trump's electoral vote margin ranks as the forty-sixth-largest out of fifty-eight presidential elections and, based on the definition we established earlier, did not approach a landslide. And, to date, there is no systematic evidence that would suggest that more than 2.8 million ballots were cast illegally.

69. For more on the founders' view of the Electoral College, see *The Federalist Papers*, No. 68.

70. In 2012 Republican Nominee Mitt Romney won these states by an average margin of 20.9 percentage points.

71. Joseph A. Schlesinger, *Political Parties and the Winning of Office* (Ann Arbor: University of Michigan Press, 1991).

72. See Schlesinger, *Political Parties and the Winning of Office*, Figure 5-1, 112. Schlesinger does not report the exact values, but he provided them to us in a personal communication. Including the District of Columbia, which has voted for president since 1964, increases the standard deviation because the District always votes more Democratic than the most Democratic state. We report Schlesinger's results for states, not for his alternative results that include D.C. Likewise our updated results are for the fifty states.

73. The state-by-state deviation of 11.96 in the 1964 contest between Johnson and Goldwater is the highest deviation of any postwar election.

74. Since 1988, the last election reported by Schlesinger, state-by-state variation in party competition has increased slightly: 1988 (5.60), 1992 (5.96), 1996 (6.70), 2000 (8.51), 2004 (8.39), 2008 (9.54), 2012 (10.29), and 2016 (10.35), with standard deviations in parentheses.
75. See Aldrich, *Why Parties? A Second Look*, Part 3.
76. Burmila, "Electoral College," 843.
77. V. O. Key, Jr., *Southern Politics in State and Nation* (New York: Knopf, 1949), 5.
78. There have been many excellent studies of the postwar South. For three recent excellent volumes examining the political transformation of the South, see Eric Schickler, *Racial Realignment: The Transformation of American Liberalism, 1932–1965* (Princeton, N.J.: Princeton University Press, 2016); Robert Mickey, *Paths Out of Dixie: The Democratization of Authoritarian Enclaves in America's Deep South, 1944–1972* (Princeton, N.J.: Princeton University Press, 2015); and John H. Aldrich and John D. Griffin, *Why Parties Matter: Political Competition and Democracy in the American South* (Chicago: University of Chicago Press, 2018).
79. South Carolina was the most solidly Democratic, with an average Democratic vote share of 91.4 percent; Tennessee had the lowest with 56.7 percent of the vote going to the Democrats. Estimates calculated by the authors.
80. See Nancy J. Weiss, *Farewell to the Party of Lincoln: Black Politics in the Age of FDR* (Princeton, N.J.: Princeton University Press, 1983).
81. Earlier that month, southern Democrats suffered a defeat at the Democratic presidential nominating convention. Their attempts to weaken the national party's civil rights platform were defeated. At the same time, Hubert Humphrey, then mayor of Minneapolis, argued that the platform was too weak and offered an amendment for a stronger statement. Humphrey's amendment passed by a vote of 651½–582½. That victory led the southern delegations to walk out and thus led to the States' Rights Democratic Party, better known as the Dixiecrat Party.
82. Kennedy made a symbolic gesture that may have helped him with African Americans. Three weeks before the election, Martin Luther King, Jr., was arrested in Atlanta for taking part in a sit-in demonstration. Although all the other demonstrators were released, King was held on a technicality and sent to the Georgia State Penitentiary. Kennedy telephoned King's wife to express his concern, and his brother Robert F. Kennedy, Jr., acting as a private citizen, made a direct appeal to a Georgia judge that led to King's release on bail. This incident received little notice in the press, but it had a great effect on the African American community. See Theodore H. White, *The Making of the President, 1960* (New York: Atheneum, 1961), 321–323.
83. Alabama, Georgia, Louisiana, Mississippi, and South Carolina are considered the five Deep South states. They are also five of the six states with the highest percentage of African Americans.
84. When Congressman Tom Price joined the Trump administration as secretary of health and human services, a special election was held to fill his suburban Atlanta congressional seat. Hoping to capitalize on demographic trends in the area and the fact that Trump won the district by only 1.5 percentage points, the Democrats launched a significant campaign to capture the traditionally Republican seat once held by former Republican Speaker of the House Newt Gingrich. The Democratic candidate, Jon Ossoff, raised slightly more than $30 million, and overall spending by outside groups topped $50 million. Despite these efforts, Republican Karen Handel won the special election with 51.9 percent of the vote. See Robert Costa, Paul Kane, and Elise Viebeck, "Republican Karen Handel Defeats Democrat Jon Ossoff in Georgia's 6th Congressional District," *Washington Post*, June 21,

2017, https://www.washingtonpost.com/powerpost/trumps-agenda-on-the-line-in-hard
-fought-georgia-house-race/2017/06/20/0d0e7086-559b-11e7-b38e-35fd8e0c288f_story
.html?utm_term=.583337867faf. For Ossoff's final campaign finance report to the FEC, see
https://www.fec.gov/data/committee/C00630426/.

85. John B. Judis and Ruy Teixeira, *The Emerging Democratic Majority* (New York: A Lisa Drew
Book/Scribner, 2002). See also Ruy Teixeira, "The Emerging Democratic Majority Turns
10," theatlantic.com, November 9, 2012.

86. Pew Hispanic Center, "An Awakened Giant: The Hispanic Electorate Is Likely to
Double by 2030," November 14, 2012, http://www.pewhispanic.org/2012/11/14/an
-awakened-giant-the-hispanic-electorate-is-likely-to-double-by-2030/.

87. U.S. Census Bureau, "American Community Survey," http://www.census.gov/acs/www/.

88. Scholars have already noted the electoral consequences of Hispanic population growth.
Alan Abramowitz argues that since 2000, increases in the Hispanic vote have transi-
tioned New Mexico from a swing state to a safe Democratic state and caused the formerly
Republican-leaning states of Colorado and Nevada to become Democratic-leaning. See
Alan Abramowitz, "The Emerging Democratic Presidential Majority: Lessons of Obama's
Victory," paper presented at the Annual Meeting of the American Political Science
Association, Chicago, Illinois, August 31, 2013. See also Charles S. Bullock, III and M. V.
Hood III, "A Mile-Wide Gap: The Evolution of Hispanic Political Emergence in the Deep
South," *Social Science Quarterly* 87 (December 2006): 1117–1135, which shows the grow-
ing electoral strength of Hispanics in three southern states: Georgia, North Carolina, and
South Carolina.

89. See, for instance, Paul R. Abramson, John H. Aldrich, and David W. Rohde, *Change and
Continuity in the 1984 Elections*, rev. ed. (Washington, D.C.: CQ Press, 1987), 70–75.

90. According to Marjorie Randon Hershey, the Republicans had a "clear and continuing
advantage" in presidential elections. See Marjorie Randon Hershey, "The Campaign and
the Media," in *The Election of 1988: Reports and Interpretations*, ed. Gerald M. Pomper et al.
(Chatham, N.J.: Chatham House, 1989), 74.

91. Jens Manuel Krogstad, "Key Facts about the Latino Vote in 2016," *Pew Research Center*,
October 14, 2016, http://www.pewresearch.org/fact-tank/2016/10/14/key-facts-about
-the-latino-vote-in-2016/.

92. Estimates for the size of the Latino electorate in Florida and Texas are taken from exit polls:
CNN Election 2016, http://www.cnn.com/election/results/exit-polls.

93. See Jens Manuel Krogstad and Antonio Flores, "Unlike Other Latinos, about Half of Cuban
Voters in Florida Backed Trump," *Pew Research Center*, November 15, 2016, http://www
.pewresearch.org/fact-tank/2016/11/15/unlike-other-latinos-about-half-of-cuban-voters
-in-florida-backed-trump/. The Cuban American community's enthusiasm toward Trump
may in part represent a repudiation of President Obama's decision to resume diplomatic
relations with Cuba. Keeping a campaign pledge, on June 17, 2017, President Trump partially reversed that policy, restricting commerce between the United States and Cuba and
strictly limiting travel to the island nation.

94. Arian Campo-Flores, "Cuban-Americans Move Left," *Wall Street Journal*, November 8,
2012, http://online.wsj.com/ news/articles/SB100014241278873240735045781074127954
05272.

95. Andrew Gelman, Jonathan N. Katz, and Gary King, "Empirically Evaluating the Electoral
College," in *Rethinking the Vote: The Politics and Prospects of Electoral Reform*, eds. Ann N.
Crigler, Marion R. Just, and Edward J. McCaffrey (New York: Oxford University Press,
2004), 75–88.

96. For a figure demonstrating the Republican dominance between 1972 and 1988, see Abramson, Aldrich, and Rohde, *Change and Continuity in the 1992 Elections*, rev. ed., 47.

97. See Daron R. Shaw, *The Race to 270: The Electoral College and the Campaign Strategies of 2000* (Chicago: University of Chicago Press, 2006).

98. We elected to start our measure in 1988, which reports the electoral balance following the 1972, 1976, 1980, 1984, and 1988 elections to eliminate observations that would have to use the 1968 presidential election, in which electoral votes were cast for a third-party candidate.

99. An admitted weakness of this measure is that it does not account for the average vote share within a state over time. Thus a state that consistently sided with the same party by narrow margins is equivalent to a state that consistently sided with the same party by large margins—both are categorized as "uncompetitive."

CHAPTER 4

1. Michael McDonald reports that the voting-eligible population in 2016 was 230,585,915. This number is calculated by subtracting from the voting-age population those who are ineligible to vote, such as noncitizens, citizens living abroad, and when state law applies, felons and those judged mentally incompetent. McDonald estimates that nearly 19.5 million voting-age people living in the United States are ineligible to vote. McDonald, "2016 General Election Turnout Rates," United States Election Project, http://www.electpro ject.org/2016g. Our numerator, the total number of votes cast in the presidential election, comes from the Federal Election Commission's "Official 2016 Presidential General Election Results," https://transition.fec.gov/pubrec/fe2016/2016presgeresults.pdf.

2. The turnout measure for the United States divides the number of voters by the voting-age population. The International Voter Turnout Database measures turnout for the other countries by the dividing the number of voters by the number of people registered. In most democracies, voter registration is the responsibility of government, which maintains the voter rolls and automatically registers all eligible citizens for voting. Registration in the United States, however, is an individual responsibility. The U.S. Census estimates that 70.3 percent of American adult citizens are registered to vote. See U.S. Census Bureau, "Voting and Registration in the Election of November 2016, https://census.gov/data/tables/time -series/demo/voting-and-registration/p20-580.html.

3. For a comprehensive discussion of turnout change in comparative perspective, see Mark N. Franklin, *Voter Turnout and the Dynamics of Electoral Competition in Established Democracies Since 1945* (New York: Cambridge University Press, 2004).

4. In Australia, nonvoters may be subject to a small fine. In Belgium, which first adopted compulsory voting in 1892, nonvoters may suffer from future disenfranchisement and may find it difficult to obtain a public sector job. For more on the effect of compulsory voting on voter turnout, see Pippa Norris, *Election Engineering: Voting Rules and Political Behavior* (New York: Cambridge University Press, 2002); and Anthony Fowler, "Electoral and Policy Consequences of Voter Turnout: Evidence from Compulsory Voting in Australia," *Quarterly Journal of Political Science* 8 (2013): 159–182.

5. See André Blais and Kees Aarts, "Electoral Systems and Turnout," *Acta Politica*, 41 (2006): 180–196 for a review.

6. Of the remaining eight democracies in our sample, seven have experienced no significant changes in turnout rates, and only one, Malta, has experienced a significant increase in the postwar period. Much of the increase in Maltese voter turnout was experienced after the

archipelago nation achieved colonial independence from Great Britain. Elections in Malta are held via a proportional representation system using the single transferable vote.

7. This chapter focuses on one form of political participation, voting. For a major study of other forms of political participation, see Sidney Verba, Kay Lehman Schlozman, and Henry E. Brady, *Voice and Equality: Civic Voluntarism in American Politics* (Cambridge, Mass.: Harvard University Press, 1995). For a collection of essays on voting as well as other forms of political participation, see Russell J. Dalton and Hans-Dieter Klingemann, eds., *The Oxford Handbook of Political Behavior* (New York: Oxford University Press, 2007).

8. Alexander Keyssar, *The Right to Vote: The Contested History of Democracy in the United States*, rev. ed. (New York: Basic Books, 2000), 2. Keyssar's book is arguably the definitive account of the legal and political history of suffrage in the United States.

9. The Seventeenth Amendment to the United States Constitution, ratified in 1913, established direct election of United States senators by popular vote.

10. In 1790 ten of the thirteen states had property requirements for voting, and three of the thirteen limited suffrage to white males only. By 1820 property requirements were in effect in nine of the twenty-three states, and fourteen of the twenty-three states had race exclusions. See Keyssar, *The Right to Vote*, Table A.3 and Table A.5.

11. For a useful summary of the history of turnout in the United States, see Michael P. McDonald, "American Voter Turnout in Historical Perspective," in *The Oxford Handbook of American Elections and Political Behavior*, ed. Jan E. Leighley (New York: Oxford University Press, 2010), 125–143.

12. It is difficult to calculate the exact number of voters who turn out for an election. It is common to use the total number of ballots cast for the presidency as a substitute for the number of voters because in most elections more people vote for president than for any other office.

13. Women's suffrage was adopted in many of the western territories of the United States as a way of attracting female settlers. Wyoming, Utah, Washington, and Montana enfranchised women decades before they joined the union. Wyoming officially became the first state to give women the right to vote in 1890, when it obtained statehood.

14. At the outset of the Civil War, only five states—all in New England—granted blacks the right to vote. A sixth state, New York, allowed blacks who met a property requirement to vote. The Fifteenth Amendment was ratified in 1870. See Keyssar, *The Right to Vote*, 69–83.

15. See Martin J. Kousser, *The Shaping of Southern Politics: Suffrage Restrictions and the Establishment of the One-Party South, 1880–1910* (New Haven, Conn.: Yale University Press, 1974); and John H. Aldrich and John D. Griffin, *Why Parties Matter: Political Competition and Democracy in the American South* (Chicago: University of Chicago Press, 2018). For a more general discussion, see Paul Kleppner, *Who Voted? The Dynamics of Electoral Turnout, 1870–1980* (New York: Praeger, 1982), 55–82.

16. There has been a great deal of disagreement about the reasons for and the consequences of registration requirements. For some of the more interesting arguments, see Walter Dean Burnham, "The Changing Shape of the American Political Universe," *American Political Science Review* 59 (March 1965): 7–28; Philip E. Converse, "Change in the American Electorate," in *The Human Meaning of Social Change*, eds. Angus Campbell and Philip E. Converse (New York: Russell Sage, 1972), 266–301; and Walter Dean Burnham, "Theory and Voting Research: Some Reflections on Converse's 'Change in the American Electorate,'" *American Political Science Review* 68 (September 1974): 1002–1023. For two other perspectives, see Frances Fox Piven and Richard A. Cloward, *Why Americans Still Don't Vote and Why Politicians Want It That Way* (Boston: Beacon Press, 2000); and

Matthew A. Crenson and Benjamin Ginsberg, *Downsizing America: How America Sidelined Its Citizens and Privatized Its Public* (Baltimore, Md.: Johns Hopkins University Press, 2002).

17. This term originates from the fact that in 1856, two Australian colonies (now states) adopted a secret ballot to be printed and administered by the government.

18. For a rich source of information on the introduction of the Australian ballot and its effects, see Jerrold G. Rusk, "The Effect of the Australian Ballot on Split-Ticket Voting, 1876–1908," *American Political Science Review* 64 (December 1970): 1220–1238.

19. The secret ballot, like a few of the other "good government" electoral reforms of the Progressive Era, such as literacy tests, often had unintended consequences or were used in the South to disenfranchise African Americans. An analysis by Jac C. Heckelman estimates that the introduction of the secret ballot lowered voter turnout in U.S. gubernatorial elections by seven percentage points. See Jac C. Heckelman, "The Effect of the Secret Ballot on Voter Turnout Rates," *Public Choice* 82 (No. 1/2, 1995): 107–124.

20. Keyssar, *The Right to Vote*, 115.

21. Burnham presents estimates of turnout among the "politically-eligible population" between 1789 and 1984 in "The Turnout Problem," in *Elections American Style*, ed. James A. Reichley (Washington, D.C.: Brookings, 1987), 113–114. In a series of personal communications, Burnham provided us with estimates of turnout among the "voting-eligible population" between 1988 and 2004: 52.7 percent in 1988, 56.9 percent in 1992, 50.8 percent in 1996, 54.9 percent in 2000, and 60.7 percent in 2004. McDonald and Popkin's estimates of turnout between 1948 and 2000 are available in Michael P. McDonald and Samuel L. Popkin, "The Myth of the Vanishing Voter," *American Political Science Review* 95 (December 2001): 996. McDonald's estimates for the 2004, 2008, 2012, and 2016 elections are available on his United States Elections Project website, http://www.electproject.org/home/voter-turnout/voter-turnout-data.

22. Only Maine and Vermont allow prisoners to vote, and in nine states felons are permanently disenfranchised unless voting rights are restored by gubernatorial or court action. In 2015 Wyoming passed a law restoring voting rights to nonviolent felons who have completed their sentences.

23. McDonald's estimates of the eligible population do not account for the number of permanently disenfranchised felons "since time-series statistics on recidivism, deaths, and migration of felons are largely unavailable." See McDonald, "How Is the Ineligible Felon Population Estimated," http://www.electproject.org/home/voter-turnout/faq/felons.

24. McDonald, "2016 General Election Turnout Rates," http://www.electproject.org/2016g.

25. Thomas E. Patterson, *The Vanishing Voter: Public Involvement in an Age of Uncertainty* (New York: Knopf, 2002). See also Pippa Norris, *Democratic Participation Worldwide* (Cambridge, U.K.: Cambridge University Press, 2002).

26. See note 21.

27. Burnham estimated turnout in 1960 at 65.4 percent, and McDonald and Popkin estimated it at 63.8 percent. See Burnham, "Turnout Problem," 114; and McDonald and Popkin, "Myth of the Vanishing Voter," 966.

28. See Glenn Firebaugh and Kevin Chen, "Vote Turnout among Nineteenth Amendment Women: The Enduring Effects of Disfranchisement," *American Journal of Sociology* 100 (January 1995): 972–996.

29. For estimates of this reform on turnout, see Raymond E. Wolfinger and Jonathan Hoffman, "Registering and Voting with Motor Voter," *PS: Political Science and Politics* 34 (March 2001): 86–92. David Hill argues that whereas motor voter legislation has made the election rolls

more representative, it has had little effect on turnout. See David Hill, *American Voter Turnout: An Institutional Perspective* (Boulder, Colo.: Westview Press, 2006), 49–52, 55.

30. We follow Paul Gronke's usage of early voting as "a blanket term used to describe any system where voters can cast their ballots before the official election day . . . [including] in-person early voting, no-excuse absentee balloting, and vote-by-mail." See Paul Gronke, "Early Voting Reforms and American Elections," *William and Mary Bill of Rights Journal* 17 (Issue 2, 2008): 423–451.

31. Theory suggests that easing the "cost" of voting by making it more convenient should increase voting turnout. Yet scholarly research on the effect of early voting on turnout is mixed with some showing the effect to be quite small and others showing the increase to be as large as 10 percent. See Paul Gronke, Eva Galanes-Rosenbaum, and Peter A. Miller, "Early Voting and Turnout," *PS: Political Science and Politics* 40 (October 2007): 639–645, for a review.

32. National Conference of State Legislatures, "Absentee and Early Voting," http://www.ncsl .org/research/elections-and-campaigns/absentee-and-early-voting.aspx.

33. The 2016 Current Population Survey (CPS) is based on more than 131,000 respondent households nationally with sizable (and representative) samples drawn for each state. The CPS is commonly used in studies of turnout, although the Census Bureau only measures voting behavior along with demographic variables (federal law does not allow the Census Bureau to measure individual's political attitudes). The most important study to use the CPS remains Raymond E. Wolfinger and Steven J. Rosenstone, *Who Votes?* (New Haven, Conn.: Yale University Press, 1980).

34. Conventional political wisdom held that early voting laws would decrease the costs of voting, increase turnout, and disproportionately benefit Democratic candidates. A recent empirical study examining the effects of various state election laws on voter turnout suggests that early voting may actually benefit Republican candidates on average, although the effects are likely highly contingent on contextual factors. See Barry C. Burden, David T. Canon, Kenneth R. Mayer, and Donald P. Moynihan, "The Complicated Partisan Effects of State Election Laws," *Political Research Quarterly* 70 (2017): 564–576.

35. As Wolfinger and Rosenstone demonstrate, about one-fifth of this decline resulted from the enfranchisement of eighteen-, nineteen-, and twenty-year-olds. Their nationwide enfranchisement stemmed from the 1971 ratification of the Twenty-sixth Amendment, which made it possible for more people to vote, but because these youth have low levels of voting, overall levels of turnout declined. See Wolfinger and Rosenstone, *Who Votes?*, 58.

36. For our analysis of the reasons for the increase in turnout in 1992, see Paul R. Abramson, John H. Aldrich, and David W. Rohde, *Change and Continuity in the 1992 Elections*, rev. ed. (Washington, D.C.: CQ Press, 1995), 120–123. As we point out it is difficult to demonstrate empirically that Perot's candidacy made an important contribution to the increase in turnout. For additional analyses, see Stephen M. Nichols and Paul Allen Beck, "Reversing the Decline: Voter Turnout in 1992," in *Democracy's Feast: Elections in America*, ed. Herbert F. Weisberg (Chatham, N.J.: Chatham House, 1995), 62–65.

37. When appropriate we also rely on estimates from the 2016 Current Population Survey (CPS) and exit poll data. The Census Bureau published a detailed report of its 2016 survey in May 2017. See U.S. Census Bureau, "Voting in America: A Look at the 2016 Presidential Election," https://census.gov/newsroom/blogs/random-samplings/2017/05/ voting_in_america.html. Interested readers can access data from the 2016 CPS, November Supplement (as well as other Census Bureau studies), using the Census Bureau's DataFerrett website, https://dataferrett.census.gov/.

Exit polls were conducted by Edison Research of Somerville, New Jersey, for the "National Election Pool," a consortium of ABC News, CBS News, CNN, Fox News, and NBC News. The exit polls are not a representative sample of the nation. Instead polls were conducted in twenty-eight states. Precincts in each state were selected by a stratified-probability sample, and every *n*th voter in the precinct was given a questionnaire to complete. In states with significant early and/or absentee voting, a supplemental telephone survey was conducted.

38. Respondents to the postelection survey of the ANES are asked: In talking to people about elections, we often find that a lot of people were not able to vote because they weren't registered, they were sick, or they just didn't have time. Which of the following statements best describes you?

One, I did not vote (in the election this November);

Two, I thought about voting this time, but didn't;

Three, I usually vote, but didn't this time;

Four, I am sure I voted.

We classified respondents as voters if they were sure that they voted.

39. These studies suggest, however, that African Americans are more likely to falsely claim to have voted than whites. As a result racial differences are always greater when turnout is measured by the vote validation studies. Unfortunately we have no way of knowing whether this difference between the races has changed as African American turnout has increased with time. For results for the 1964, 1976, 1978, 1980, 1984, 1986, and 1988 elections, see Paul R. Abramson and William Claggett, "Racial Differences in Self-Reported and Validated Voting in the 1988 Presidential Election," *Journal of Politics* 53 (February 1991): 186–187. For a discussion of the factors that contribute to false reports of voting, see Brian D. Silver, Barbara A. Anderson, and Paul R. Abramson, "Who Overreports Voting?" *American Political Science Review* 80 (June 1986): 613–624. For a more recent study that argues that biases in reported turnout are more severe than Silver, Anderson, and Abramson claim, see Robert Bernstein, Anita Chadha, and Robert Montjoy, "Overreporting Voting: Why It Happens and Why It Matters," *Public Opinion Quarterly* 65 (Spring 2001): 22–44.

40. Barry Burden reports that the overreporting of voter turnout in the ANES increased with time. He attributes this to declining response rates for the ANES rather than question wording changes or other problems with the survey. See Barry C. Burden, "Voter Turnout and the National Election Studies," *Political Analysis* 8 (July 2000): 389–398. See Michael P. McDonald, "On the Overreport Bias of the National Election Study Turnout Rate," *Political Analysis* (May 2003): 180–186; and Michael D. Martinez, "Comment on 'Voter Turnout and the National Election Studies,'" *Political Analysis* (May 2003): 187–192 for counterarguments to Burden.

In an analysis of the 2008 vote validation study, the ANES staff and principal investigators found a surprisingly high level of accuracy in self-reported turnout when compared with official turnout records, suggesting that overreporting comes from sources other than respondents simply saying they voted when they did not. See Matthew K. Berent, Jon A. Krosnick, and Arthur Lupia, "The Quality of Government Records and 'Over-estimation' of Registration and Turnout in Surveys: Lessons from the 2008 ANES Panel Study's Registration and Turnout Validation Exercises," American National Election Studies, Working Paper no. nes012554, August 2011, http://www.electionstudies.org/resources/papers/nes012554.pdf.

41. The response rate for the 2016 ANES is an improvement over the 2012 ANES, for which the response rate was a record low 38 percent.

42. Sidney Verba and Norman H. Nie, *Participation in America: Political Democracy and Social Equality* (New York: Cambridge University Press, 1972).

43. See Henry E. Brady, Sidney Verba, and Kay Lehman Schlozman, "Beyond SES: A Resource Model of Political Participation," *American Political Science Review* 89 (June, 1995): 271–294; and Sidney Verba, Kay Lehman Schlozman, and Henry E. Brady, *Voice and Equality: Civic Voluntarism in American Politics* (Cambridge, Mass.: Harvard University Press, 1995).

44. Nicholas Confessore, "For Whites Sensing Decline, Donald Trump Unleashes Words of Resistance," *New York Times*, July 14, 2016, A1; and Emma Green, "It Was Cultural Anxiety that Drove White, Working-Class Voters to Trump," *The Atlantic*, May 9, 2017, https://www.theatlantic.com/politics/archive/2017/05/white-working-class-trump-cultural-anxiety/525771/.

45. Respondents were classified by the interviewer into one of the following categories: white; black/African American; white and black; other race; white and another race; black and another race; and white, black, and another race. We classified only respondents who were white as whites; except for Asians, respondents in the other categories were classified as blacks.

46. For 1964 see U.S. Census Bureau, "Voting Participation in the National Election: November 1964," Table 1, http://www.census.gov/hhes/www/socdemo/voting/publications/p20/1964/tab01.pdf. For 2004 see U.S. Census Bureau, "Voting and Registration in the Election of November 2004," http://www.census.gov/prod/2006pubs/p20-556.pdf, Table B.

47. The church has been demonstrated to be an important mobilizer of black political participation; see Frederick C. Harris, *Something Within: Religion in African-American Political Activism* (New York: Oxford University Press, 1999). In past studies we too have shown that African Americans who regularly attend church ("once a week") are more likely to vote than those who never attend. In 2016, however, we do not see evidence of a statistically significant difference in turnout between blacks who attend church regularly and those who do not.

48. Benjamin Highton and Arthur L. Burris, "New Perspectives on Latino Voter Turnout in the United States," *American Politics Research* 30 (May 2002): 285–306 utilize CPS data to investigate socioeconomic, ethnic, and place-of-birth differences among Latinos. These authors find that native-born Latinos are more likely to turn out. Matt Barreto, however, using data from California, finds that Latino immigrants were more likely to vote than were native-born Latinos. Clearly this warrants further investigation. See Matt A. Barreto, "Latino Immigrants at the Polls: Foreign-born Voter Turnout in the 2002 Election," *Political Research Quarterly* 58 (March 2005): 79–86.

49. Abramson, Aldrich, and Rohde, *Change and Continuity in the 2008 Elections*, 98.

50. For an early example of this work, see M. Kent Jennings, "Another Look at the Life Cycle and Political Participation," *American Journal of Political Science* 23 (November 1979): 755–771.

51. See Benjamin Highton and Raymond E. Wolfinger, "The First Seven Years of the Political Life Cycle," *American Journal of Political Science* 45 (January 2001): 202–209.

52. Aaron Blake, "More Young People Voted for Bernie Sanders than Trump and Clinton Combined—By a Lot," *Washington Post*, June 20, 2016, https://www.washingtonpost.com/news/the-fix/wp/2016/06/20/more-young-people-voted-for-bernie-sanders-than-trump-and-clinton-combined-by-a-lot/?utm_term=.7f57570ea2c9.

53. Millennials are usually defined as those born between 1982 and 2000.

54. Jan E. Leighley and Jonathan Nagler, "Socioeconomic Class Bias in Turnout, 1972–1988: The Voters Remain the Same," *American Political Science Review* 86 (September 1992): 725–736.

55. See Warren E. Miller, Arthur H. Miller, and Edward J. Schneider, *American National Studies Data Sourcebook, 1952–1978* (Cambridge, Mass.: Harvard University Press, 1980), Table 5.23, 317.

56. For example, Robert D. Putnam and David E. Campbell, *American Grace: How Religion Divides and Unites Us* (New York: Simon and Schuster, 2012).

57. See the Pew Religion and Public Life Project, "U.S. Public Becoming Less Religious," http://assets.pewresearch.org/wp-content/uploads/sites/11/2015/11/201.11.03_RLS_II_full_report.pdf. When asked "how important is religion in your life?" 53.2 percent of Americans say "very important," 24.5 percent say "somewhat important," whereas 21.6 percent say religion is "not at all important" in their lives. Nearly 40 percent report attending religious services weekly or more and 15 "once or twice a month." Close to 50 percent of Americans say they attend religious services a few times a year or less.

58. See Dietram A. Scheufele, Matthew C. Nisbet, Dominque Brossard, and Erik C. Nisbet, "Social Structure and Citizenship: Examining the Impacts of Social Setting, Network Heterogeneity, and Informational Variables on Political Participation," *Political Communication* 21 (2004): 315–338.

59. For general treatments, see Clyde Wilcox and Lee Sigelman, "Political Mobilization in the Pews: Religious Contacting and Electoral Turnout," *Social Science Quarterly* 82 (September, 2001): 524–535; and David E. Campbell, "Acts of Faith: Churches and Political Engagement," *Political Behavior* 26 (June 2004): 155–180. For an examination of the mobilizing role of churches in the African American community, see Fredrick C. Harris, "Something Within: Religion as a Mobilizer of African-American Political Activism, *Journal of Politics* 56 (February 1994): 42–68.

60. Federal law prohibits the Census Bureau from measuring religious preferences on the CPS.

61. Miller, Miller, and Schneider, *American National Data Sourcebook*, Table 5.23, 317. Between 1952 and 1976 Catholics were on average 8.0 percentage points more likely to vote in presidential elections, and between 1958 and 1988 they were 10.8 points more likely to vote in midterm elections.

62. As noted earlier, exit polls were not conducted in all states but instead were used in states that were deemed most competitive. This may have affected the estimates of the religious composition of the electorate. Consider the fact that several states with the largest Catholic populations (e.g., Louisiana, Massachusetts, and Maryland) were not included in the 2016 exit polls. Nationally aggregated responses to the exit poll are also unweighted, so the exit poll results for religion may differ from those produced by a nationally representative probability sample, such as that used by the ANES.

63. For a study of Conservative Christian mobilization in a recent U.S. election, see J. Quin Monson and J. Baxter Oliphant, "Microtargeting and the Instrumental Mobilization of Religious Conservatives" in David E. Campbell, ed. *A Matter of Faith: Religion in the 2004 Presidential Election* (Washington, D.C.: Brookings Institution, 2007).

64. Respondents were asked, "Would you call yourself a born-again Christian, that is, have you personally had a conversion experience related to Jesus Christ?"

65. Pew Research Center, "Religious Landscape Survey," http://www.pewforum.org/religious-landscape-study/.

66. Due to data availability issues, we were unable to construct this measure in 2012. Our measure for 2016, which does not include an indicator of the respondent's frequency of prayer, differs slightly from that used in 2008 and earlier. For details regarding the construction of the religious commitment measure in earlier studies, see Abramson, Aldrich, and Rohde, *Change and Continuity in the 2008 Elections*, Chapter 4, note 49.

67. Kenneth D. Wald, *Religion and Politics in the United States*, 4th ed. (Lanham, Md.: Rowman and Littlefield, 2003), 161.

68. R. Stephen Warner, *New Wine in Old Wineskins: Evangelicals and Liberals in a Small-Town Church* (Berkeley: University of California Press, 1977), 173.

69. The branching questions used to classify respondents into specific denominational categories were changed in 2008, and therefore it is not possible to replicate our analyses of the 1992, 1996, 2000, and 2004 categories. In creating these new classifications, we relied largely on the Pew Forum on Religion and Public Life, *U.S. Religious Landscape Survey: Religious Affiliation, Diverse and Dynamic* (Washington, D.C.: Pew Forum on Religion and Public Life, 2008), 12. In addition, we were assisted by Corwin D. Smidt.

    Our classification for 2016 used the following procedures. We used the variable V161248 in the 2016 ANES survey to determine the respondent's denomination. Codes 2, 3, 4, 6, 9, 13, 14, 17, and 20 for this variable were classified as mainline; codes 1, 8, 12, 15, 16, 18, and 19 were classified as evangelical.

70. Wolfinger and Rosenstone, *Who Votes?*, 102.

71. For the effect of education on political knowledge and political awareness, see Michael X. Delli Carpini, and Scott Keeter, *What Americans Know about Politics and Why It Matters* (New Haven, Conn.: Yale University Press, 1996); and John R. Zaller, *The Nature and Origins of Mass Opinion* (New York: Cambridge University Press, 1992), respectively. Henry E. Brady, Sidney Verba, and Kay Lehman Schlozman, "Beyond SES: A Resource Model of Political Participation," *American Political Science Review* 89 (June 1995): 271–294, discuss how education enhances both political engagement and civic skills.

72. Richard A. Brody, "The Puzzle of Political Participation in America," in *The New American Political System*, ed. Anthony King (Washington, D.C.: American Enterprise Institute, 1978), 287–324.

73. U.S. Census Bureau, *Statistical Abstract of the United States, 1962* (Washington, D.C.: Government Printing Office, 1962), Tables 1 and 129; and U.S. Department of Justice, "Corrections in the United States," https://www.census.gov/ newsroom/cspan/incarceration/20120504_incarceration_bjs-slides.pdf.

74. Ruy A. Teixeira, *The Disappearing American Voter* (Washington, D.C.: American Enterprise Institute, 1992).

75. The Gallup Poll provides the best evidence regarding church attendance over the past six decades. Although church attendance has declined on average, Catholics appear to be driving the decline. Since 1955 weekly church attendance among Catholics has dropped by nearly 30 percent. Weekly church attendance among Protestants has been stable throughout the period. Interestingly the percentage of Catholics attending church weekly is now roughly equal to the rate among Protestants. See Lydia Saad, "Churchgoing among U.S. Catholics Slides to Tie Protestants," gallup.com, April 9, 2009, http://www.gallup.com/poll/117382/church-going-among-catholics-slides-tie-protestants.aspx.

76. Robert D. Putnam makes a similar argument, claiming that political disengagement was largely the result of the baby boom generation and that generational succession reduced other forms of civic activity as well. Putnam writes: "The declines in church attendance, voting, political interest, campaign activities, associational membership and social trusts are attributable almost entirely to generational succession." See Robert D. Putnam, *Bowling Along: The Collapse and Revival of American Community* (New York: Simon and Schuster, 2000), 265.

77. Steven J. Rosenstone and John Mark Hansen, *Mobilization, Participation, and Democracy in America* (New York: Macmillan, 1993), 214–215.

78. George I. Balch, "Multiple Indicators in Survey Research: The Concept 'Sense of Political Efficacy,'" *Political Methodology* 1 (Spring 1974): 1–43. For an extensive discussion of feelings of political efficacy, see Paul R. Abramson, *Political Attitudes in America: Formation and Change* (San Francisco: W. H. Freeman, 1983): 135–189.

79. Ruy A. Teixeira, *Why Americans Don't Vote: Turnout Decline in the United States, 1960–1964* (New York: Greenwood Press, 1987). In his more recent study, *The Disappearing American Voter*, Teixeira develops a measure of party-related characteristics that includes strength of party identification, concern about the electoral outcome, perceived difference between the parties, and knowledge about the parties and the candidates. See also Rosenstone and Hansen, *Mobilization, Participation, and Democracy*.

80. Our first analysis studied the decline of turnout between 1960 and 1980. See Paul R. Abramson, John H. Aldrich, and David W. Rohde, *Change and Continuity in the 1980 Elections*, rev. ed. (Washington, D.C.: CQ Press, 1983), 85–87. For a more detailed analysis using probability procedures, see Paul R. Abramson and John H. Aldrich, "The Decline of Electoral Participation in America," *American Political Science Review* 76 (September 1982): 502–521. For our analyses from 1984 through 2008, see Abramson, Aldrich, and Rohde, *Change and Continuity in the 2008 Elections*, 105–108 and Chapter 4, note 73.

81. ANES respondents are asked, "Generally speaking, do you usually think of yourself as a Republican, a Democrat, an Independent, or what?" Persons who call themselves Republicans are asked, "Would you call yourself a strong Republican or a not very strong Republican?" Those who call themselves Democrats are asked, "Would you call yourself a strong Democrat or a not very strong Democrat?" Those who called themselves independents, named another party, or who had no preference were asked, "Do you think of yourself as closer to the Republican party or to the Democratic party?"

82. The seminal work on party identification is Angus Campbell, Philip E. Converse, Warren E. Miller, and Donald E. Stokes, *The American Voter* (New York: Wiley, 1960), 120–167.

83. See Morris P. Fiorina, "The Voting Decision: Instrumental and Expressive Aspects," *Journal of Politics* 38 (May 1976): 390–413; and John H. Aldrich, "Rational Choice and Turnout," *American Journal of Political Science* 37 (February 1993): 246–278.

84. For a detailed discussion of party identification from 1952 to 2016, along with tables showing the distribution of party identification among whites and blacks during these years, see Chapter 8 in this volume as well as the appendix.

85. As Steven E. Finkel notes, the relationship between political efficacy and political participation is likely reciprocal. Not only do feelings of efficacy increase the likelihood of participation, participation increases individuals' feelings of efficacy. See Steven E. Finkel, "Reciprocal Effects of Participation and Political Efficacy: A Panel Analysis," *American Journal of Political Science* 29 (November 1985): 891–913.

86. Our measure of external efficacy is based on the responses to two statements: "Public officials don't care much what people like me think" and "People like me don't have any say about what the government does." Respondents who disagreed with both of these statements were scored as high in feelings of effectiveness; those who agreed with one statement and disagreed with the other were scored as medium; and those who agreed with both statements were scored as low. Respondents who scored "don't know" or "not ascertained" to one statement were scored high or low according to their answer on the other statement. Those with "don't know" or "not ascertained" responses to both statements were excluded from the analysis. Since 1988 ANES respondents have been asked whether they "strongly agreed," "agreed," "disagreed," or "strongly disagreed" with the statements. We classified respondents who "neither agreed nor disagreed," with

both statements as medium on our measure. This decision has little effect on the results because few respondents "neither agree nor disagree" to both statements, typically less than 5 percent. In 2008 and 2012 this standard measure of feelings of "external" political efficacy was asked of only half of the sample. In 2016 all respondents were asked the political efficacy questions.

87. See Abramson and Aldrich, "The Decline of Electoral Participation in America," 515.

88. The procedure uses the 1960 distribution of partisans by levels of efficacy as our base, thus assuming that levels of turnout for each subgroup (e.g., strong partisan/high efficacy and strong partisan/medium efficacy) would have remained the same if partisanship and efficacy had not declined. We multiply the size of each subgroup (set at 1960 levels) times the proportion of the whites who reported voting in each subgroups in the 2016 election. We then sum the products and divide by the sum of the subgroup sizes. The procedure is detailed in Abramson, *Political Attitudes in America: Formation and Change*, 296.

89. For a discussion of political trust, see Abramson, *Political Attitudes in America*, 193–238. For a more recent discussion, see Marc J. Hetherington, *Why Trust Matters: Declining Political Trust and the Demise of American Liberalism* (Princeton, N.J.: Princeton University Press, 2005).

Russell J. Dalton reports a decline in confidence in politicians and government in fifteen of sixteen democracies. Although many of the trends are not statistically significant, the overall decline is impressive. Dalton's report includes results from the ANES, where the trend toward declining confidence is unlikely to occur by chance on two of the three questions. See Russell J. Dalton, *Democratic Challenges, Democratic Choices: The Erosion of Political Support in Advanced Industrial Democracies* (Oxford: Oxford University Press, 2004), 28–32.

90. Respondents were asked, "How much of the time do you think you can trust the government in Washington to do what is right—just about always, most of the time, or only some of the time?"

91. This question was asked of a randomly selected half-sample in 2008.

92. See Brad T. Gomez, Thomas G. Hansford, and George A. Krause, "The Republicans Should Pray for Rain: Weather, Turnout, and Voting in U.S. Presidential Elections," *Journal of Politics* 69 (August 2007): 649–663.

93. The recent proliferation in electoral laws allowing early voting is likely to diminish the chances that bad weather on election day will reduce voter turnout. Laws that allow citizens to vote by mail, such as those found in Colorado, Oregon, and Washington, make election day weather inconsequential.

94. In the past half century, a handful of elections could be classified—based upon pre-election polling—as "dead heats" going into election day. Recall from Chapter 3, for example, that the average of nine pre-election polls in 2012 showed a virtual tie between Obama and Romney. By contrast, in 1964, the final Gallup Poll before the election predicted a twenty-eight-point victory in the popular vote for Lyndon Johnson over Barry Goldwater.

95. See Anthony Downs, *An Economic Theory of Democracy* (New York: Harper and Row, 1957); and William H. Riker and Peter C. Ordeshook, "A Theory of the Calculus of Voting," *American Political Science Review* 72 (March 1968): 25–42.

96. These are Colorado, Florida, Iowa, Michigan, Minnesota, Nevada, New Hampshire, New Mexico, North Carolina, Ohio, Pennsylvania, Virginia, and Wisconsin.

97. Rosenstone and Hansen, *Mobilization, Participation, and Democracy in America*, 181–182.

98. The use of randomized field experiments in political science predates the work of Gerber and Green, although these authors are certainly responsible for the revived interest in the research design in the discipline. In the 1920s Harold Gosnell sent postcards to randomly assigned nonvoters emphasizing the importance of voter registration before the 1924 presidential election. Gosnell found a significant increase in voter registration among those who received the postcard treatment compared to those in his control group who received nothing. In the 1950s Samuel Eldersveld used random assignment to test the effectiveness of mail, phone, and in-person canvassing in a local mayoral race. It would be decades before another field experiment design was published in the academic journals of political science. See Harold F. Gosnell, *Getting Out the Vote* (Chicago: University of Chicago Press, 1927); and Samuel J. Eldersveld, "Experimental Propaganda Techniques and Voting Behavior," *American Political Science Review* 50 (March 1956): 154–165.

99. See Alan S. Gerber and Donald P. Green, *Field Experiments: Design, Analysis, and Interpretation* (New York: Norton, 2012), for an introduction to field experimentation in the social sciences.

100. See Donald P. Green and Alan S. Gerber, *Get Out the Vote: How to Increase Voter Turnout*, 2nd ed. (Washington, D.C.: Brookings Institution Press, 2008), for a summary of findings in this research program.

101. This is not to say that it is impossible to make causal inferences from survey data. Panel designs, where survey respondents are interviewed repeatedly at multiple time periods, can establish causal (temporal) order. Paul R. Abramson and William Claggett, for instance, use ANES panel data from 1990 and 1992 to show the effects of party contact on voter turnout persist even after one takes into account that the political elites are more likely to contact people who have participated in the past. See Paul R. Abramson and William Claggett, "Recruitment and Political Participation," *Political Research Quarterly* 54 (December 2001): 905–916.

102. Respondents were asked, "The political parties try to talk to as many people as they can to get them to vote for their candidate. Did anyone from the political parties call or come around to talk with you about the campaign this year?"

103. Lisa Desjardins and Daniel Bush, "The Trump Campaign Has a Ground-Game Problem," *PBS Newshour*, August 30, 2016, http://www.pbs.org/newshour/updates/trump -campaign-has-ground-game-problem/; Chris Cillizz, "No, Donald Trump—You Still Don't Have a Ground Game," *Washington Post*, September 2, 2016, https://www.washing tonpost.com/news/the-fix/wp/2016/09/01/donald-trump-has-1-field-office-open-in-all -of-florida-thats-a-total-disaster/?utm_term=.13b710ba1cc7; and Susan Milligan, "The Fight on the Ground," *US News and World Report*, October 14, 2016, https://www.usnews .com/news/the-report/articles/2016-10-14/donald-trump-abandons-the-ground-game.

104. Seymour Martin Lipset, *Political Man: The Social Bases of Politics*, exp. ed. (Baltimore: Johns Hopkins University Press, 1981), 226–229.

105. See James DeNardo, "Turnout and the Vote: The Joke's on the Democrats," *American Political Science Review* 74 (December 1980): 406–420; and Thomas G. Hansford and Brad T. Gomez, "Estimating the Electoral Effects of Voter Turnout," *American Political Science Review* 104 (May 2010): 268–288.

106. In addition to the partisan effect of high turnout, Hansford and Gomez argue that incumbents from both parties lose vote share as turnout becomes higher, suggesting that peripheral voters, that is, those who vote irregularly, are less supportive of incumbents than dedicated voters.

107. As reported by the National Conference of State Legislatures, see http://www.ncsl.org/legislatures-elections/elections/voter-id.aspx.

108. In 2013 the U.S. Supreme Court, in a 5–4 vote, struck down provisions—Sections 4(b) and 5—of the 1965 Voting Rights Act (VRA) that required several states with histories of racial discrimination in voting (mostly southern states, including North Carolina) to obtain "preclearance" from the federal government before changing their voting laws or practices. See *Shelby County v. Holder*, 570 U.S. 2 (2013). Following this decision, several states—Alabama, Arizona, Arkansas, North Carolina, Ohio, Wisconsin, and Texas—once covered by the VRA's preclearance requirements moved swiftly to alter their election laws. All of these states are governed by Republicans.

109. Robert Barnes and Ann E. Marimow, "Appeals Court Strikes Down North Carolina's Voter-ID Law," *Washington Post*, July 29, 2016, https://www.washingtonpost.com/local/public-safety/appeals-court-strikes-down-north-carolinas-voter-id-law/2016/07/29/810b5844-4f72-11e6-aa14-e0c1087f7583_story.html?utm_term=.0431a0552c6a.

110. "Supreme Court Rejects Appeal to Reinstate North Carolina Voter ID Law," *Fox News*, May 15, 2017, http://www.foxnews.com/politics/2017/05/15/supreme-court-rejects-appeal-over-nc-voter-id-law.html.

111. Abramson, Aldrich, and Rohde, *Change and Continuity in the 1980 Elections*, 88–92; *Change and Continuity in the 1984 Elections*, 119–124; and *Change and Continuity in the 1988 Elections*, 108–112.

112. Abramson, Aldrich, and Rohde, *Change and Continuity in the 1992 Elections*, 124–128.

113. Abramson, Aldrich, and Rohde, *Change and Continuity in the 1996 and 1998 Elections*, 86–89.

114. Paul R. Abramson, John H. Aldrich, and David W. Rohde, "The 2004 Presidential Election: The Emergence of a Permanent Majority," *Political Science Quarterly* 120 (Spring 2005): 43.

115. Abramson, Aldrich, and Rohde, *Change and Continuity in the 1992 Elections*, 110–112.

116. See Campbell, Converse, Miller, and Stokes, *The American Voter*, 96–115.

117. The kind and number of issues used varied from election to election. We used only issues on which respondents were asked to state their own positions and where they thought the major-party candidates were located. See Table 6-4 for the number of issues used in each election between 1980 and 2008.

118. Our issue scale differs slightly from the one used in our 2008 analysis, which included seven items. Since 2012 the ANES no longer asks respondents' opinions regarding the role of women in society. Consequently this item has been removed from our scale.

119. In their county-level analysis of the electoral effect of voter turnout in the 1944 through 2000 presidential elections, Hansford and Gomez use simulations from their statistical model to demonstrate that a 4 percent swing in turnout (from 2 percent below to 2 percent above actual turnout) leads to an average change in Democratic vote share at the national level of just under one percentage point. However, small changes are not necessarily trivial. The authors go on to show that varying turnout from two points above and below observed values causes an average change of approximately twenty Electoral College votes per presidential election in nonsouthern states. See Hansford and Gomez, "Estimating the Electoral Effects of Voter Turnout," 284.

120. For the most influential statement of this argument, see Wolfinger and Rosenstone, *Who Votes?*, 108–114.

121. Frances Fox Piven and Richard A. Cloward, *Why Americans Don't Vote* (New York: Pantheon Books, 1988), 21. See also Piven and Cloward, *Why Americans Still Don't Vote*.

CHAPTER 5

1. For a classic treatment of the subject, see M. Kent Jennings and Richard G. Niemi, *Generations and Politics: A Panel Study of Young Adults and their Parents* (Princeton, N.J.: Princeton University Press, 1981).

2. See Larry M. Bartels, "What's the Matter with *What's the Matter with Kansas?*" *Quarterly Journal of Political Science* 1 (2006): 201–226.

3. See Paul R. Abramson, John H. Aldrich, and David W. Rohde, *Change and Continuity in the 2008 and 2010 Elections* (Washington, D.C.: CQ Press, 2012), 116–141.

4. The social characteristics used in this chapter are the same as those used in Chapter 4. The variables are described in the notes to that chapter.

5. In 2016 the National Election Pool consortium was composed of ABC News, Associated Press, CBS News, CNN, Fox News, and NBC News.

6. As noted in Chapter 4, note 37, the exit polls are not a representative sample of the nation. The exit polls were conducted separately in twenty-eight states. Precincts in each state were selected by a stratified-probability sample, and every *n*th voter in the precinct was offered a questionnaire to complete. In states with significant early and/or absentee voting, the sample was supplemented with a telephone survey.

   We draw on 2016 exit poll reports from Fox News (http://www.foxnews.com/politics/elections/2016/exit-polls), *New York Times* (https://www.nytimes.com/interactive/2016/11/08/us/politics/election-exit-polls.html), CNN (http://www.cnn.com/election/results/exit-polls/national/president), and *Washington Post* (https://www.washingtonpost.com/graphics/politics/2016-election/exit-polls/). For a discussion of the 2012 exit polls, see Abramson, Aldrich, Gomez, and Rohde, *Change and Continuity in the 2012 Elections*, 116–142.

   Exit polls have three main advantages: (1) they are less expensive to conduct than the multistage probability samples conducted by the American National Election Studies; (2) because of their lower cost, a large number of people can be sampled; and (3) because persons are selected to be interviewed as they leave the polling stations, the vast majority of respondents have actually voted. But these surveys also have four disadvantages: (1) organizations that conduct exit polls must now take into account the growing number of voters who vote early—about a third of all voters in 2008; (2) the self-administered polls used for respondents leaving the polls must be relatively brief; (3) it is difficult to supervise the fieldwork to ensure that interviewers are using the proper procedures to select respondents; and (4) these studies are of relatively little use in studying turnout because persons who do not vote are not sampled. For a discussion of the procedures used to conduct exit polls and their limitations, see Albert H. Cantril, *The Opinion Connection: Polling, Politics, and the Press* (Washington, D.C.: CQ Press, 1991), 142–144, 216–218.

7. This brief discussion cannot do justice to the complexities of black electoral participation. For an important study based on the 1984 ANES survey of blacks, see Patricia Gurin, Shirley Hatchett, and James S. Jackson, *Hope and Independence: Blacks' Response to Electoral and Party Politics* (New York: Russell Sage Foundation, 1989). For two important studies that use this survey, see Michael C. Dawson, *Behind the Mule: Race and Class in African American Politics* (Princeton, N.J.: Princeton University Press, 1994); and Katherine Tate, *From Politics to Protest: The New Black Voter in American Elections* (Cambridge, Mass.: Harvard University Press, 1994). For a summary of recent research on race and politics, see Michael C. Dawson and Cathy Cohen, "Problems in the Politics of Race," in *Political Science: The State of the Discipline*, eds. Ira Katznelson and Helen V. Milner (New York: Norton, 2002), 488–510.

8. The estimate of the black electorate in 2012 comes from exit poll data. Unfortunately we cannot compare the size of Trump's black electorate to Mitt Romney's in 2012 using the ANES. Even with an oversample of black respondents, the weighted ANES data shows only three black respondents who voted for Romney, a number that is too small to create reliable estimates. The 2012 exit poll suggests that 7 percent of blacks voted for Romney.

9. For a review of research on Latinos as well as African Americans, see Paula McClain and John D. Garcia, "Expanding Disciplinary Boundaries: Black, Latino, and Racial Minority Groups in Political Science," in *Political Science: The State of the Discipline II*, ed. Ada W. Finifter (Washington, D.C.: American Political Science Association, 1993), 247–279. For analyses of Latino voting in the 2008 and 2012 elections with an eye toward the future of Latino politics, see Matt Barreto and Gary Segura, *Latino America: How America's Most Dynamic Population Is Poised to Transform the Politics of the Nation* (New York: Public Affairs Books, 2014). For a review, see John D. Garcia, "Latinos and Political Behavior: Defining Community to Examine Critical Complexities," in *The Oxford Handbook of American Elections and Political Behavior*, ed. Jan E. Leighley (New York: Oxford University Press, 2010), 397–414.

10. Trump's comments about Mexican immigrants came on June 16, 2015, during the announcement of his presidential candidacy. For a transcript of his full remarks, see https://www.washingtonpost.com/news/post-politics/wp/2015/06/16/full-text-donald -trump-announces-a-presidential-bid/?utm_term=.826619831a93.

11. For three reviews of research on women in politics, see Susan J. Carroll and Linda M. Zerelli, "Feminist Challenges to Political Science," in Finifter, *Political Science: The State of the Discipline II*, 55–76; Nancy Burns, "Gender: Public Opinion and Political Action," in Katznelson and Milner, *Political Science: The State of the Discipline*, 462–487; and Kira Sanbonmastu, "Organizing American Politics, Organizing Gender," in Leighley, *Oxford Handbook of American Elections and Political Behavior,* 415–432.

12. The gender gap in 1980, coupled with Ronald Reagan's opposition to abortion rights and the Equal Rights Amendment, led the former president of the National Organization for Women, Eleanor Smeal, to write a report for the Democratic National Committee detailing how Democrats could take back the White House if the party placed a woman on the ticket in the next election. In 1984 Democratic Congresswoman Geraldine Ferraro became the first female vice presidential nominee in U.S. history. Reagan won reelection in a landslide.

13. See Abramson, Aldrich, and Rohde, *Change and Continuity in the 1980 and 1982 Elections* (Washington, D.C.: CQ Press, 1983), 290.

14. The ANES survey reports six types of marital status: married, divorced, separated, widowed, never married, and partners who are not married.

15. See Sheryl Gay Stolberg, "Obama Signs Away 'Don't Ask, Don't Tell,'" *New York Times*, December 22, 2010, http://www.nytimes.com/2010/12/23/us/politics/23military.html; and Jackie Calmes and Peter Baker, "Obama Says Same-Sex Marriage Should Be Legal," *New York Times*, May 10, 2012, A1.

16. Exit polls ask voters to cast a "secret ballot" after they have left the polling station. They are handed a short form that records the respondent's behavior, political views, and demographic information. Use of this procedure reduces the pressure for the respondent to answer in a socially "acceptable" way. The ANES also uses a private procedure for asking "sensitive" questions such as sexual orientation (and which also include income and other "standard" questions long asked face-to-face). At the end of the survey, respondents are

handed the tablet computer, and the interviewer leaves the room so that the respondent can answer sensitive questions in private.

17. Respondents were asked, "Do you consider yourself to be heterosexual or straight, homosexual or gay (lesbian), or bisexual?" This question was asked during a computer-assisted self-interview (CASI) portion of the face-to-face interview in which the respondent enters his or her response into a tablet computer.

18. Abramson, Aldrich, and Rohde, *Change and Continuity in the 2004 and 2006 Elections* (Washington, D.C.: CQ Press, 2007), 124–127. For cross-national evidence, see Ronald Inglehart, *Modernization and Postmodernization: Cultural, Economic, and Political Change in 43 Societies* (Princeton, N.J.: Princeton University Press, 1997), 255; and Russell J. Dalton, *Citizen Politics: Public Opinion and Political Parties in Advanced Industrial Democracies*, 5th ed. (Washington, D.C.: CQ Press, 2008), 145–152.

19. "America's Urban-Rural Divides," *The Economist*, July 1, 2017, https://www.economist .com/news/special-report/21724129-mutual-incomprehension-between-urban-and-rural -america-can-border-malice-americas.

20. Jeffrey M. Stonecash, *Class and Party in American Politics* (Boulder, Colo.: Westview Press, 2000), 87–121; Larry M. Bartels, *Unequal Democracy: The Political Economy of the New Gilded Age* (New York: Russell Sage Foundation, 2008), 64–126.

21. Rich Yeselson, "Can Trump Break the Democrats' Grip on the Union Movement?" *Politico*, http://www.politico.com/magazine/story/2017/02/trump-building-trades-unions-labor -support-history-republicans-214752.

22. For the single best summary, see Kenneth D. Wald and Allison Calhoun-Brown, *Religion and Politics in the United States*, 6th ed. (Lanham, Md.: Rowman and Littlefield, 2011). For a discussion of religion and politics in a comparative context, see Pippa Norris and Ronald Inglehart, *Sacred and Secular: Religion and Politics Worldwide* (Cambridge, U.K.: Cambridge University Press, 2004).

23. David E. Campbell, ed. *A Matter of Faith: Religion in the 2004 Presidential Election* (Washington, D.C.: The Brookings Institution), 1.

24. The exception to this generalization is religious devotion among African Americans, who overwhelmingly support the Democratic Party. Among non-Christian denominations, Jewish voters remain decidedly loyal to the Democrats.

25. See Robert D. Putnam and David E. Campbell, *American Grace: How Religion Divides and Unites Us* (New York: Simon and Schuster, 2010).

26. The Catholic Church had an uneasy relationship with the Obama administration. During the debate over health care reform in 2009, for instance, the U.S. Conference of Catholic Bishops supported the president's efforts to reform the health care system but threatened to oppose any bill that provided public funding for abortion or contraception. The Catholic Church had actually lobbied for decades for the adoption of a universal health care system, a more "liberal" system than what was eventually adopted under the Affordable Care Act, and a system that was supported by Hillary Clinton in the 1990. Nevertheless, the candidate and the Church were very much at odds with regard to the issue of abortion and women's rights, generally. And, in October 2016, when a set of emails from within the Clinton campaign staff was publicly released via WikiLeaks, they appeared to show a campaign at odds with Catholic leadership. See, for example, Sarah Pulliam Bailey, "WikiLeaks Emails Appear to Show Clinton Spokeswoman Joking about Catholics and Evangelicals," *Washington Post*, October 13, 2016, https://www.washingtonpost.com/news/acts-of-faith/ wp/2016/10/12/wikileaks-emails-show-clinton-spokeswoman-joking-about-catholics-and -evangelicals/?utm_term=.3ee4fa742389.

27. Pew Research's Religious Landscape Study estimates that only 3 percent of American Catholics are African American. Thus Latinos are the main contributor to nonwhite support among Catholics. See http://www.pewforum.org/religious-landscape-study/religious-tradition/catholic/.

28. The question, which was asked to all Christians, was "Would you call yourself a born-again Christian; that is, have you personally had a conversion experience related to Jesus Christ?" This question was not asked in the 2004 ANES survey.

29. Lyman A. Kellstedt, "An Agenda for Future Research," in *Rediscovering the Religious Factor in American Politics*, ed. David C. Leege and Lyman A. Kellstedt (Armonk, N.Y.: M. E. Sharpe, 1993), 293–299.

30. Morris P. Fiorina and his colleagues have pointed out that ANES surveys suggest that the relationship between church attendance and the tendency to vote Republican was substantially higher in 1992 than in 1972, although the relationship leveled off or declined slightly between 1992 and 2004. See Morris P. Fiorina, with Samuel J. Abrams and Jeremy C. Pope, *Culture War? The Myth of a Polarized America*, 2nd ed. (New York: Pearson/Longman, 2006), 134.

31. Note, in comparing white Catholics, we do not reference those with "very high" religious commitment levels. This is because only 15 white Catholics in our sample fit into this category, a sample size that is too small from which to draw inferences.

32. Robert Axelrod, "Where the Votes Come From: An Analysis of Electoral Coalitions," *American Political Science Review* 66 (March 1972): 11–20. Axelrod updates his results through the 1984 elections. For his most recent estimate, including results from 1952 to 1980, see Robert Axelrod, "Presidential Coalitions in 1984," *American Political Science Review* 80 (March 1986): 281–284. Using Axelrod's categories, Nelson W. Polsby estimates the social composition of the Democratic and Republican presidential coalitions between 1952 and 2000. See Nelson W. Polsby and Aaron Wildavsky, *Presidential Elections: Strategies and Structures of American Politics*, 11th ed. (Lanham, Md.: Rowman and Littlefield, 2004), 32. For an update through 2004, see Nelson W. Polsby, Aaron Wildavsky, with David A. Hopkins, *Presidential Elections: Strategies and Structures in American Politics*, 12th ed. (Lanham, Md.: Rowman and Littlefield, 2008), 28.

33. John R. Petrocik, *Party Coalitions: Realignment and the Decline of the New Deal Party System* (Chicago: University of Chicago Press, 1981).

34. Harold W. Stanley, William T. Bianco, and Richard G. Niemi, "Partisanship and Group Support over Time: A Multivariate Analysis," *American Political Science Review* 80 (September 1986): 969–976. Stanley and his colleagues assess the independent contribution that group membership makes toward Democratic loyalties after controls are introduced for membership in other pro-Democratic groups. For an update and an extension through 2004, see Harold W. Stanley and Richard G. Niemi, "Partisanship, Party Coalitions, and Group Support, 1952–2004," *Presidential Studies Quarterly* 36 (June 2006): 172–188. For an alternative approach, see Robert S. Erikson, Thomas D. Lancaster, and David W. Romero, "Group Components of the Presidential Vote, 1952–1984," *Journal of Politics* 51 (May 1989): 337–346.

35. See Axelrod, "Where the Votes Come From."

36. The NORC survey, based on 2,564 civilians, used a quota sample that does not follow the probability procedures used by the ANES. Following the procedures used at the time, southern blacks were not sampled. Because the NORC survey overrepresented upper-income groups and the middle and upper-middle classes, it cannot be used to estimate the contribution of social groups to the Democratic and Republican presidential coalitions.

37. Abramson, *Generational Change in American Politics*, 65–68.
38. As Figure 5-1 shows, Bill Clinton did win a majority of the white major-party vote in 1992 and 1996.
39. Racial voting, as well as our other measures of social cleavage, is affected by including Wallace voters with Nixon voters in 1968, Anderson voters with Reagan voters in 1980, Perot voters with Bush voters in 1992, and Perot voters with Dole voters in 1996. For the effects of including these independent or third-party candidates, see Abramson, Aldrich, and Rohde, *Change and Continuity in the 1996 and 1998 Elections* (Washington, D.C.: CQ Press, 1999), 102, 104–106, 108, and 111.
40. The statements about low turnout in 1996 are true regardless of whether one measures turnout based on the voting-age population or the voting-eligible population. Turnout among the voting-eligible population fell about nine percentage points between 1960 and 1996. And even though black turnout fell in 1996, it was still well above its levels before the Voting Rights Act of 1965.
41. As we explain in Chapter 3, we consider the South to include the eleven states of the old Confederacy. Because the 1944 NORC survey and the 1948 University of Michigan Survey Research Center survey did not record the respondents' states of residence, we cannot include these years in our analysis of regional differences among the white electorate.
42. George H. W. Bush was born in Massachusetts and raised in Connecticut. As an adult Bush moved to Texas and was elected to the U.S. House from there.
43. Cheney had served as the U.S. representative from Wyoming from 1979 to 1989. When he became the chief executive officer of an oilfield services corporation in 1995, he established his residence in Texas. Being a resident of Texas would have complicated running on the same ticket as Bush because the Twelfth Amendment specifies that electors "vote by ballot for President and Vice-President, one of whom, at least, shall not be an inhabitant of the same state with themselves."
44. See, for example, Chapter 3, where we compare Kennedy's black support in the South in 1960 with Carter's in 1976.
45. Officially known as the Labor-Management Relations Act, this legislation, passed in 1947, qualified or amended much of the National Labor Relations Act of 1935 (known as the Wagner Act). Union leaders argued that the Taft-Hartley Act placed unwarranted restrictions on organized labor. This act was passed by the Republican-controlled Eightieth Congress, vetoed by Truman, and passed over his veto.
46. The Bureau of Labor Statistics estimates that in 2016, 10.7 percent of wage and salary workers are members of union, down from four years earlier. African American workers have a higher rate of union membership (13.0 percent) than white workers (10.5 percent). See Bureau of Labor Statistics, "Economic News Release: Union Members Summary," January 26, 2017, https://www.bls.gov/news.release/union2.nr0.htm.
47. This percentage may well be too low. According to the 2008 pool poll, Obama received 53 percent of the vote. Members of union households made up 21 percent of the electorate, and 50 percent voted for Obama. These numbers thus suggest that 23 percent of Obama's vote in 2008 came from members of union households. Even if one takes into account that not all these union voters were white, these numbers suggest that about one in five of Obama's votes in 2008 came from union households.
48. See Robert R. Alford, *Party and Society: The Anglo-American Democracies* (Chicago: Rand McNally, 1963); Seymour Martin Lipset, *Political Man: The Social Bases of Politics*, exp. ed. (Baltimore: Johns Hopkins University Press, 1981); and Inglehart, *Modernization and Postmodernization*.

49. The variation in class voting is smaller if one focuses on class differences in the congressional vote, but the data clearly show a decline in class voting between 1952 and 2008. See Dalton, *Citizen Politics*, 6th ed., 161.

50. Readers should bear in mind that in 2000, 2004, and 2008, there was no measure of the head of household's occupation or of the spouse's occupation, but our analysis of the 1996 data suggests that this limitation probably does not account for the negative level of class voting in the 2000 contest. Bartels discusses our attempts to maintain comparability in measuring social class in the face of changing survey measurement in *Unequal Democracy*, 70–71.

51. As we point out in *Change and Continuity in the 2000 and 2002 Elections*, when we define social class according to the respondent's own occupation, the overall size of the working class falls, and the overall size of the middle class grows. Because the relatively small size of the working class in 2000, 2004, and 2008, results mainly from a redefinition of the way our measure of social class is constructed, we assumed that the sizes of the working and the middle class in 2000, 2004, and 2008 were the same as they were in the 1996 ANES. See Abramson, Aldrich, and Rohde, *Change and Continuity in the 2000 and 2002 Elections*, chap. 4, 313n26.

52. See Anat Shenker-Osorio, "Why Americans All Believe They Are 'Middle Class,'" *Atlantic*, www.theatlantic.com, August 1, 2013 http://www.theatlantic.com/politics/archive/2013/08/why-americans-all-believe-they-are-middle-class/278240/.

53. See Mark N. Franklin, "The Decline of Cleavage Politics," in *Electoral Change: Responses to Evolving Social and Attitudinal Structures in Western Countries*, eds. Mark N. Franklin, Thomas T. Mackie, and Henry Valen, with others (Cambridge, U.K.: Cambridge University Press, 1992), 383–405. See also Inglehart, *Modernization and Postmodernization*, 237–266.

54. Jeff Manza and Clem Brooks, *Social Cleavages and Political Change: Voter Alignments and U.S. Party Coalitions* (New York: Oxford University Press, 1999).

55. Exit polls conducted between 1972 and 2016 show the same pattern. In all twelve elections Jews have been more likely to vote Democratic than white Catholics, and white Catholics have been more likely to vote Democratic than white Protestants.

56. For a discussion of the impact of religion on the 1960 election, see Philip E. Converse, "Religion and Politics: The 1960 Election," in *Elections and the Political Order*, ed. Angus Campbell et al. (New York: Wiley, 1967), 96–124.

57. The 1976 Democratic Party Platform can be found at http://www.presidency.ucsb.edu/ws/?pid=29606.

58. In our sample, 58.5 percent of Latinos identify themselves as Catholic.

59. According to the 2012 *Statistical Abstract of the United States*, as of 2010, 2.1 percent of the U.S. population was Jewish and, according to the Pew Forum on Religion and Public Life, only 1.9 percent. The *Statistical Abstract* results are based mainly on information provided by Jewish organizations, whereas the Pew results are based on a representative survey of 35,000 Americans from all 50 states. The Pew survey is presented in Pew Forum on Religion and Public Life, *U.S. Religious Landscape Survey*, http://www.pewforum.org/religious-landscape-study. For the *Statistical Abstract*, see U.S. Census Bureau, *The 2012 Statistical Abstract of the United States*, Table 77, https://www.census.gov/prod/2011pubs/12statab/pop.pdf.

60. States are listed in descending order according to their estimated number of Jews.

61. Since 1860 the Democrats have won the presidency only twice without winning New York: 1916, when Woodrow Wilson narrowly defeated Charles Evans Hughes by a margin of twenty-three electoral votes, and 1948, when Harry Truman defeated Thomas Dewey. Dewey, the governor of New York, won 46.0 percent of the popular vote in his home state, and Truman won 45.0 percent. Henry A. Wallace, the Progressive candidate in 1948, won 8.2 percent of the New York vote, substantially better than his share in any other state.

62. For an expanded treatment of the Catholic vote in 1960 and 2004, see J. Matthew Wilson, "The Changing Catholic Voter: Comparing Responses to John Kennedy in 1960 and John Kerry in 2004" in *A Matter of Faith*, ed., David E. Campbell (Washington, D.C.: Brookings Institution Press, 2007).

63. Robert Huckfeldt and Carol Weitzel Kohfeld provide strong evidence that Democratic appeals to blacks weakened the party's support among working-class whites. See their *Race and the Decline of Class in American Politics* (Urbana: University of Illinois Press, 1989).

64. For evidence on this point, see Paul R. Abramson, *Political Attitudes in America: Formation and Change* (San Francisco: W. H. Freeman, 1983), 65–68.

65. Edward G. Carmines and James A. Stimson, *Issue Evolution: Race and the Transformation of American Politics* (Princeton, N.J.: Princeton University Press, 1999). For a critique of their thesis, see Alan I. Abramowitz, "Issue Evolution Reconsidered: Racial Attitudes and Partisanship among the American Electorate," *American Journal of Political Science* 38 (February 1994): 1–24.

CHAPTER 6

1. This set of attitudes was first formulated and tested extensively in Angus Campbell et al., *The American Voter* (New York: Wiley, 1960), using data from what are now called the ANES surveys. The authors based their conclusions primarily on data from a survey of the 1956 presidential election, a rematch between Democrat Adlai Stevenson and Republican (and this time the incumbent) Dwight Eisenhower. Recently Michael S. Lewis-Beck, William G. Jacoby, Helmut Norpoth, and Herbert F. Weisberg applied similar methods to data from 2000 and 2004. See their *The American Voter Revisited* (Ann Arbor: University of Michigan Press, 2008).

2. Campbell et al., *American Voter*. This was their next-to-the-lowest form of "issue"-related responses to what people said they liked or disliked about the parties and candidates. The "levels of conceptualization" had the category of ideological conceptualization at the top, followed by "near ideology," and then "group benefits." Only "no issue content" was lower than the nature of the times category.

3. Anthony Downs, *An Economic Theory of Voting* (New York: Harper and Row, 1957); V. O. Key, Jr., *The Responsible Electorate* (Cambridge, Mass.: Belknap Press of Harvard University Press, 1966).

4. Morris P. Fiorina, *Retrospective Voting in American National Elections* (New Haven, Conn.: Yale University Press, 1981).

5. Christopher H. Achen and Larry M. Bartels, *Democracy for Realists: Why Elections Do Not Produce Responsive Government* (Princeton, N.J.: Princeton University Press, 2016). Their signature example were shark attacks in 1916 that cut into incumbent Woodrow Wilson's votes in 1916, although it was, of course, a very small number of votes in the context of a presidential election and ones that therefore had no appreciable effect on the outcome. It is, however, certainly an eye-catching example.

6. Donald P. Green, Bradley Palmquist, and Eric Schickler, *Partisan Hearts and Minds: Political Parties and the Social Identities of Voters* (New Haven, Conn.: Yale University Press, 2002).

7. See, for example, Wendy M. Rahn et al., "A Social-Cognitive Model of Candidate Appraisal," in *Information and Democratic Processes*, ed. John A. Ferejohn and James H. Kuklinski (Urbana: University of Illinois Press, 1990), 136–159, and sources cited therein.

8. For the most extensive explication of the theory and tests in various electoral settings, see Gary W. Cox, *Making Votes Count: Strategic Coordination in the World's Electoral Systems* (New York: Cambridge University Press, 1997). For an examination in the American context, see Paul R. Abramson et al., "Third-Party and Independent Candidates in American Politics: Wallace, Anderson, and Perot," *Political Science Quarterly* 110 (Fall 1995): 349–367.

9. Or, at least, that is the conventional scholarly assumption about the causal ordering of influences, rather than, say, attitudes toward Trump leading the respondent to change their policy beliefs. Obviously, the latter is a possibility that needs to be taken seriously.

10. Ballotpedia (https://ballotpedia.org/Presidential_candidates,_2016) reports that 1,780 candidates filed a "Statement of Candidacy" with the Federal Election Commission, with eight candidates listed on at least 15 percent of the ballots nationwide. In addition to those discussed in the text, the other four are Darrell Lane Castle (Constitution Party), Rocky De La Fuente (Reform Party), Evan McMullin (Independent), and Gloria Estela La Riva (Party for Socialism and Liberation).

11. Such multicandidate elections are discussed in Paul R. Abramson, John H. Aldrich, and David W. Rohde, *Change and Continuity in the 1980 Elections*, rev. ed. (Washington, D.C.: CQ Press, 1983); Abramson, Aldrich, and Rohde, *Change and Continuity in the 1992 Elections*, rev. ed. (Washington, D.C.: CQ Press, 1995); Abramson, Aldrich, and Rohde, *Change and Continuity in the 1996 and 1998 Elections* (Washington, D.C.: CQ Press, 1999); and Abramson, Aldrich, and Rohde, *Change and Continuity in the 2000 and 2002 Elections* (Washington, D.C.: CQ Press, 2003).

12. We reproduced the feeling thermometer most recently in Abramson, Aldrich, and Rohde, *Change and Continuity in the 2000 and 2002 Elections*, 123.

13. Note that this percentage lead for Clinton in the ANES thermometer ratings reflects the percentage lead she won in the election exactly. A relatively smaller proportion than usual, 6 percent of respondents, rated the two candidates equally, suggesting how clearly the electorate distinguished the two candidates in 2016.

14. Two of these six ("speaks mind" and "even-tempered") are new to the ANES in 2016, reflecting uniquely relevant aspects of the 2016 contest, albeit reducing comparability to prior campaigns. These two replaced "moral" and "intelligent."

15. For what limited comparisons are possible to earlier surveys, see Abramson, Aldrich, and Rohde, *Change and Continuity in the 2008 and 2010 Elections*, Table 62-A, 146; and Abramson, Aldrich, and Rohde, *Change and Continuity in the 2012 and 2014 Elections*, Table 62-A, 149.

16. There is the single exception of responding that honesty describes her slightly well.

17. One might suggest that there is some rationalization here (those who like the candidate find reason to justify their support through positive evaluations of these traits). The distributions of responses here suggest that there is something more than mere rationalization to these responses overall (e.g., many who voted against Trump thought he spoke his mind in the campaign), and the vote pattern of even-tempered strongly suggests something other than mere rationalization is at work, although rationalization there well may be.

18. This was usually called a "pooled poll" in 2012, although typically referred to simply as an exit poll in 2016.

19. Concerns about foreign policy were also low in 1976, during the Cold War, although that occurred at a particularly low point of "détente" in it, and it was also the first election held after the withdrawal of the last American troops from Vietnam (and also of the defeat of our erstwhile allies there, the Republic of Vietnam).

20. Two such scales were used for the first time in 1968, and their popularity led to the larger and more diverse set of scales used thereafter. See Richard A. Brody and Benjamin I. Page,

"Comment: The Assessment of Policy Voting," *American Political Science Review* 66 (Issue 2, 1972): 450–458; Benjamin I. Page and Richard A. Brody, "Policy Voting and the Electoral Process: The Vietnam War Issue," *American Political Science Review* 66 (Issue 3, 1972): 979–995; and John H. Aldrich, "Candidate Support Functions in the 1968 Election," *Public Choice* 22 (Issue 1, 1975): 1–22.

21. See Abramson et al., *Change and Continuity in the 2008 and 2010 Elections*, for data and discussions about the 2008 data.

22. The only consistent exception since 1972 has been a women's rights scale, for which public opinion had become so favorable to the liberal end of the issue scale that it was dropped from the survey in 2012 due to lack of variation in opinion.

23. On government services the difference was actually 2.9 points, whereas on defense spending it was 1.9.

24. This theme is also a major claim in Achen and Bartels, *Democracy for Realists*, which is to say that one of the great recurring concerns in studying public opinion and voter behavior is the understanding of how much (or little) people know and how accurate what they claim to know actually is.

25. To maintain comparability with previous election surveys, for surveys from 1996 through 2012, we have excluded respondents who did not place themselves on an issue scale from columns II, III, and IV of Table 6-4. Because we do not know the preferences of these respondents on the issue, we have no way to measure the ways in which their issue preferences may have affected their votes.

26. For details, see Abramson, Aldrich, and Rohde, *Change and Continuity in the 1980 Elections*, Table 6-3, 130; Abramson, Aldrich, and Rohde, *Change and Continuity in the 1984 Elections*, rev. ed. (Washington, D.C.: CQ Press, 1987), Table 6-2, 174; Abramson, Aldrich, and Rohde, *Change and Continuity in the 1988 Elections*, rev. ed. (Washington, D.C.: CQ Press, 1991), Table 6-2, 165; Abramson, Aldrich, and Rohde, *Change and Continuity in the 1992 Elections*, Table 6-6, 186; Abramson, Aldrich, and Rohde, *Change and Continuity in the 1996 and 1998 Elections*, Table 6-6, 135; Abramson, Aldrich, and Rohde, *Change and Continuity in the 2000 and 2002 Elections*, Table 6-4, 137; Abramson, Aldrich, and Rohde, *Change and Continuity in the 2004 and 2006 Elections*, Table 6-4, 152; and Abramson, Aldrich, and Rohde, *Change and Continuity in the 2008 and 2010 Elections*, Table 6-4, 158.

27. Although this is evidence that most people claim to have issue preferences, it does not demonstrate that they do. For example, evidence indicates that some use the midpoint of the scale (point 4) as a means of answering the question even if they have ill-formed preferences. See John H. Aldrich et al., "The Measurement of Public Opinion about Public Policy: A Report on Some New Issue Question Formats," *American Journal of Political Science* 26 (May 1982): 391–414.

28. We use "apparent issue voting" to emphasize several points. First, voting involves too many factors to infer that closeness to a candidate on any one issue was the cause of the voter's choice. The issue similarity may have been purely coincidental, or it may have been only one of many reasons the voter supported that candidate. Second, we use the median perception of the candidates' positions rather than the voter's own perception. Third, the relationship between issues and the vote may be caused by rationalization. Voters may have decided to support a candidate for other reasons and also may have altered their own issue preferences or misperceived the positions of the candidates to align themselves more closely with their already favored candidate. See Richard A. Brody and Benjamin I. Page, "Comment: The Assessment of Policy Voting," *American Political Science Review* 66 (June 1972): 450–458.

29. Many individuals, of course, placed the candidates at different positions than did the public on average. Using average perceptions, however, reduces the effect of individuals rationalizing their perceptions of candidates to be consistent with their own vote rather than voting for the candidate whose views are actually closer to their own.

30. Of course, as we have seen, there were fewer in 2016 who failed to meet these conditions than in earlier elections. Still, it is a reminder that there may be other effects of the high levels of partisan polarization at the elite level than only making the informational demands for issue voting easier to satisfy.

31. Clinton's personal position has long been clear (and in line with that of her party). Trump's position has changed a great deal over the years, and it was really only in this campaign that he adopted the now-standard pro-life position of his party.

CHAPTER 7

1. This is not to say that they did not dispute facts, nor did they stick to the facts on the performance of the economy.

2. Here we treat retrospective evaluations as directly related to attitudes, opinions, and choices. The alternative view is that these are not directly implicated in voting. Rather, they are simply bits of evidence as people make judgements about what the candidates and parties will do in the future.

3. V. O. Key, Jr., *Politics, Parties, and Pressure Groups*, 5th ed. (New York: Thomas Y. Crowell, 1964); V. O. Key, Jr., *The Responsible Electorate* (Cambridge, Mass.: Belknap Press of Harvard University Press, 1966).

4. Anthony Downs, *An Economic Theory of Democracy* (New York: Harper and Row, 1957).

5. Morris P. Fiorina, "An Outline for a Model of Party Choice," *American Journal of Political Science* 21 (August 1977): 601–625; Morris P. Fiorina, *Retrospective Voting in American National Elections* (New Haven, Conn.: Yale University Press, 1981).

6. Angus Campbell et al., *The American Voter* (New York: Wiley, 1960).

7. Fiorina, *Retrospective Voting in American National Elections*, 83.

8. We also return to the account of Christopher H. Achen and Larry M. Bartels, *Democracy for Realists: Why Elections Do Not Produce Responsive Government* (Princeton, N.J.: Princeton University Press, 2016), in which they demonstrate a great deal of additional data in favor of this Downs-Fiorina version of retrospective voting, except that they also show that many voters rely on the most recent evidence they heard, and it is therefore not very "retrospective," not necessarily based on evaluations of outcomes over which the president could reasonably be said to have any influence over, nor a very sound basis for building a democracy that relies on independent assessments of voters to shape elite choices. Here, we focus on just those things that presidents often claim to have at least significant degrees of influence over outcomes, notably war and peace and economic outcomes.

9. Indeed one thing that made 2012 and 2016 unusual was that economic conditions, although improving, were still a mixture of good and bad results, and thus voters might differ from one another in whether they thought the economy was sufficiently better than in 2008. Perhaps this was truer in 2012 than 2016, but the 2016 economy was sound, growing, a long run of positive results, but still leaving people behind.

10. See Benjamin I. Page, *Choices and Echoes in Presidential Elections: Rational Man and Electoral Democracy* (Chicago: University of Chicago Press, 1978). He argues that "party cleavages"

distinguish the party at the candidate and mass levels. This proved to be a forecast of the partisan polarization that began in earnest only a few years later.

11. See, e.g., Arthur H. Miller and Martin P. Wattenberg, "Throwing the Rascals Out: Policy and Performance Evaluations of Presidential Candidates, 1952–1980," *American Political Science Review* 79 (Issue 2, 1985): 359–372.

12. Note that this question is quite different from the questions we analyzed in election studies prior to 2012. These were questions asking the respondent about the government's handling of the most important problems facing the country. This question does not specifically ask about the government, nor does it ask about the most important problem per se. It is more general in its coverage and only by inference is attributable to the government.

13. Each respondent assesses government performance on the problem he or she considers the most important. In the seven surveys from 1976 to 2000, respondents were asked, "How good a job is the government doing in dealing with this problem—a good job, only fair, or a poor job?" In 1972 respondents were asked a different but related question (see the note to Table A7-1 in the appendix). In 2004 respondents were asked another question (see Chapter 6, note 9) and were given four options for assessing the government's performance: "very good job," "good job," "bad job," and "very bad job."

14. "Polls: Direction of Country," *Real Clear Politics*, https://www.realclearpolitics.com/epolls/other/direction_of_country-902.html.

15. Note that whereas perceptions of wrong versus right track began to narrow when Trump took office, they began to diverge again in March 2017 and have returned to relatively typical post-2009 levels, as of this writing.

16. See Gerald H. Kramer, "Short-Term Fluctuations in U.S. Voting Behavior, 1896–1964," *The American Political Science Review* 65 (Issue 1, 1971): 131–143, doi:10.2307/1955049; Fiorina, *Retrospective Voting in American National Elections*; M. Stephen Weatherford, "Economic Conditions and Electoral Outcomes: Class Differences in the Political Response to Recession," *American Journal of Political Science* 22 (November 1978): 917; D. Roderick Kiewiet and Douglas Rivers, "A Retrospective on Retrospective Voting," *Political Behavior* 6 (Issue 4, 1984): 369–393; D. Roderick Kiewiet, *Macroeconomics and Micropolitics: The Electoral Effects of Economic Issues* (Chicago: University of Chicago Press, 1983); Michael S. Lewis-Beck, *Economics and Elections: The Major Western Democracies* (Ann Arbor: University of Michigan Press, 1988); Alberto Alesina, John Londregan, and Howard Rosenthal, *A Model of the Political Economy of the United States* (Cambridge, Mass.: National Bureau of Economic Research, 1991); Michael B. MacKuen, Robert S. Erikson, and James A. Stimson, "Peasants or Bankers? The American Electorate and the U.S. Economy," *American Political Science Review* 86 (September 1992): 597–611; Robert S. Erikson, Michael B. MacKuen, and James A. Stimson, *The Macro Polity* (Cambridge, U.K.: Cambridge University Press, 2002).

17. John Mueller, *War, Presidents and Public Opinion* (New York: Wiley, 1973).

18. The appendix provides the full set of data from the entire set of ANES surveys.

19. We assume that people respond reasonably accurately and factually when talking about their personal situations. However, we are also assuming that they perceive that presidential (or governmental) performance is one of the reasons for their personal situation, which may well be a stretch. The overall view of the economy is, of course, a belief but one that is presumed to be grounded in real conditions, which are typically easily conveyed facts ("conveyed" does not mean "believed" or even remembered). And, in this case, lots of political actors are seeking to acclaim the successes or lament the failures of the incumbent and his or her party in achieving those outcomes.

20. Fiorina, *Retrospective Voting in American National Elections*.

21. Surveys have a very high degree of external validity. That is not only the strength of the survey method, but they are almost the only means by which one can make scientifically sound inferences about the voting public. Surveys are, however, weaker on internal reliability, that is, the ability to make a causal inference about "what causes what." Experiments (including perhaps the ultimate, the survey-embedded experiment) are one way to deal with the issue of causation. In a straight survey like (almost always) the ANES, it is difficult to say whether one approves of the job the president is doing because the president has done well in the respondent's eyes or whether the voter simply likes the president and therefore approves of whatever he or she does (at least up to some apparently very generous limits).

22. In the 1984 and 1988 surveys, this question was asked in both the pre-election and the postelection waves of the survey. Because attitudes held by the public before the election are what count in influencing its choices, we use the first question. In both surveys, approval of Reagan's performance was more positive in the postelection interview: 66 percent approved of his performance in 1984, and 68 percent approved in 1988.

23. Gary C. Jacobson, "Party Polarization in National Politics: The Electoral Connection," in *Polarized Politics: Congress and the President in a Partisan Era*, vol. 5 (Washington, D.C.: CQ Press, 2000), 17–18, demonstrates that evaluations of presidential performance have become much more sharply related to party identification in recent years compared to the earlier years of the ANES studies.

24. A summary measure of retrospective evaluations could not be constructed using either the 1972 or the 2004 ANES data. We were able to construct an alternative measure for 2004. See Abramson, Aldrich, and Rohde, *Change and Continuity in the 2004 and 2006 Elections*, chap. 7, Tables 7-9 and 7-10, 178–180, and 371n18. For procedures we used to construct this measure between 1976 and 2000, see Paul R. Abramson, John H. Aldrich, and David W. Rohde, *Change and Continuity in the 2000 and 2002 Elections* (Washington, D.C.: CQ Press, 2003), chap. 7, 328n13). A combined index of retrospective evaluations was created to allow an overall assessment of retrospective voting in 2016. To construct the summary measure of retrospective evaluations, we used the following procedures. First, we awarded respondents four points if they approved of the president's performance, two if they had no opinion, and zero if they disapproved. Second, respondents received four points if they thought the country was on the right track, zero if they thought the nation was on the wrong track, and two if they had no opinion. Finally, respondents received four points if they thought the incumbent president's party would do a better job handling the most important problem, zero points if they thought the challenger's party would do a better job, and two points if they thought there was no difference between the parties, neither party would do well, both parties would do the same, another party would do the better job, or they had no opinion. For all three questions "don't know" and "not ascertained" responses were scored as two, but respondents with more than one such response were excluded from the analysis. Scores on our measure were the sum of the individual values for the three questions and thus ranged from a low of zero (strongly against the incumbent's party) to twelve (strongly for the incumbent's party). These values were then grouped to create a seven-point scale corresponding to the seven categories in Table 7-9.

25. This measure is different in 2012 and 2016 than in prior elections due to our use of the "right track/wrong track" question. Other election years are also not always comparable, although they are more similar to each than to 2012. See Paul R. Abramson, John H. Aldrich, and David W. Rohde, *Change and Continuity in the 1996 and 1998 Elections* (Washington, D.C.: CQ Press, 1999), 158–159, for data on our (different) summary measure from 1972 to 1996;

Abramson, Aldrich, and Rohde, *Change and Continuity in the 2000 and 2002 Elections*, 164–165; Abramson, Aldrich, and Rohde, *Change and Continuity in the 2004 and 2006 Elections*, 178–180, 187–191, for analyses of those elections, respectively, in these terms.

26. The characterization of earlier elections is taken from Abramson, Aldrich, and David Rohde, *Change and Continuity in the 2000 and 2002 Elections*, 164.

27. For data from the 1976 and 1980 elections, see Abramson, Aldrich, and Rohde, *Change and Continuity in the 1980 and 1982 Elections* (Washington, D.C.: CQ Press, 1983), Table 7-8, 155–157; from the 1984 election, see Paul R. Abramson, John H. Aldrich, and David W. Rohde, *Change and Continuity in the 1984 Elections*, rev. ed. (Washington, D.C.: CQ Press, 1987), Table 7-8, 203–204; from the 1988 election, see Paul R. Abramson and Charles W. Ostrom, Jr., "Macropartisanship: An Empirical Reassessment," *American Political Science Review* 86 (March 1991): 181–192, Table 7-7, 195–198; from the 1996 election, see Abramson, Aldrich, and Rohde, *Change and Continuity in the 1996 and 1998 Elections*, 159–161; from the 2000 election, see Abramson, Aldrich, and Rohde, *Change and Continuity in the 2000 and 2002 Elections*, 165–166; and from the 2004 election, see Abramson, Aldrich, and Rohde, *Change and Continuity in the 2004 and 2006 Elections*, 178–180. The 2008 election is reported in Paul R., Abramson, John H. Aldrich, and David W. Rohde, *Change and Continuity in the 2008 and 2010 Elections* (Washington, D.C.: CQ Press, 2011), 188–191; and for 2012, see Paul R. Abramson, John H. Aldrich, Brad T. Gomez, and David W. Rohde, *Change and Continuity in the 2012 Elections* (Washington, D.C.: CQ Press, 2015), 188–191. The small number of seven-point issue scales included in the ANES survey precluded performing this analysis with 1992 data.

CHAPTER 8

1. Angus Campbell et al., *The American Voter* (New York: Wiley, 1960); Warren E. Miller, "Party Identification, Realignment, and Party Voting: Back to the Basics," *American Political Science Review* 85 (June 1991): 557–568; Warren E. Miller and J. Merrill Shanks, *The New American Voter* (Cambridge, Mass.: Harvard University Press, 1996).

2. Campbell et al., *The American Voter*, 121.

3. For the full wording of the party identification questions, see Chapter 4, note 82. Note how simple this scientific advance was. They took a long-running question originally developed for the Gallup Poll survey and added the questions about "strength" of partisans and "party leanings" of independents. A simple measure of a rich theoretical concept can make a major difference.

4. Donald P. Green, Bradley Palmquist, and Eric Schickler, *Partisan Hearts and Minds: Political Parties and the Social Identities of Voters* (New Haven, Conn.: Yale University Press, 2002); Christopher H. Achen and Larry M. Bartels, *Democracy for Realists: Why Elections Do Not Produce Responsive Government* (Princeton, N.J.: Princeton University Press, 2016).

5. For evidence of the relatively high level of partisan stability among individuals from 1965 to 1982, see M. Kent Jennings and Gregory B. Markus, "Partisan Orientations over the Long Haul: Results from the Three-Wave Political Socialization Panel Study," *American Political Science Review* 78 (December 1984): 1000–1018, and see Laura Stoker and M. Kent Jennings, "Of Time and the Development of Partisan Polarization," *American Journal of Political Science* 52 (July 2008): 619–635, which cover 1965 to 1997.

6. V. O. Key, Jr., *The Responsible Electorate* (Cambridge, Mass.: Belknap Press of Harvard University Press, 1966).

7. Morris P. Fiorina, "An Outline for a Model of Party Choice," *American Journal of Political Science* 21 (August 1977): 601–625; Morris P. Fiorina, *Retrospective Voting in American National Elections* (New Haven, Conn.: Yale University Press, 1981).

8. Benjamin I. Page, *Choices and Echoes in Presidential Elections: Rational Man and Electoral Democracy* (Chicago: University of Chicago Press, 1978), provides evidence of this. Anthony Downs, *An Economic Theory of Democracy* (New York: Harper and Row, 1957), develops a theoretical logic for such consistency in party stances on issues and ideology over time. For more recent theoretical and empirical development, see John H. Aldrich, *Why Parties? A Second Look* (Chicago: University of Chicago Press, 2011).

9. See Christopher H. Achen, "Parental Socialization and Rational Party Identification," *Political Behavior* 24 (Issue 2, 2002): 151–170.

10. Robert S. Erikson, Michael B. MacKuen, and James A. Stimson, *The Macro Polity* (Cambridge: Cambridge University Press, 2002).

11. Donald P. Green, Bradley Palmquist, and Eric Schickler, *Partisan Hearts and Minds: Political Parties and the Social Identities of Voters* (New Haven, Conn.: Yale University Press, 2002).

12. See, for example, Donald P. Green, Bradley Palmquist, and Eric Schickler, "Macropartisanship: A Replication and Critique," *American Political Science Review* 92 (December 1998): 883–899; and Robert S., Erikson, Michael B. MacKuen, and James A. Stimson, "What Moves Macropartisanship: A Reply to Green, Palmquist, and Schickler," *American Political Science Review* 92 (December 1998): 901–912.

13. Douglas W. Rae and Michael Taylor, *The Analysis of Political Cleavages* (New Haven, Conn.: Yale University Press, 1970); Michael Taylor and Douglas Rae, "An Analysis of Crosscutting between Political Cleavages," *Comparative Politics* 1 (Issue 4, July 1969): 534–547.

14. There is some controversy about how to classify these independent leaners. Some argue that they are mainly "hidden" partisans who should be considered identifiers. For the strongest statement of this position, see Bruce E. Keith, David B. Magleby, Candice J. Nelson, Elizabeth A. Orr, and Mark C. Westlye, *The Myth of the Independent Voter* (Berkeley: University of California Press, 1992). In our view, however, the evidence on the proper classification of independent leaners is mixed. On balance the evidence suggests that they are more partisan than independents with no partisan leanings but less partisan than weak partisans. See Paul R. Abramson, *Political Attitudes in America: Formation and Change* (San Francisco: W. H. Freeman, 1983). For an excellent discussion of this question, see Herbert B. Asher, "Voting Behavior Research in the 1980s: An Examination of Some Old and New Problem Areas," in *Political Science: The State of the Discipline*, ed. Ada W. Finifter (Washington, D.C.: American Political Science Association, 1983), 357–360.

15. Martin P. Wattenberg, *The Decline of American Political Parties, 1952–1996* (Cambridge, Mass.: Harvard University Press, 1998).

16. Gary C. Jacobson, "The 2008 Presidential and Congressional Elections: Anti-Bush Referendum and Prospects for a Democratic Majority," *Political Science Quarterly* 124 (Spring 2009): 1–20; Gary C. Jacobson, "The Effects of the George W. Bush Presidency on Partisan Attitudes," *Presidential Studies Quarterly* 39 (June 2009): 172–209.

17. For explanation on this point, see Paul R. Abramson and Charles W. Ostrom, Jr., "Macropartisanship: An Empirical Reassessment," *American Political Science Review* 86 (March 1991): 181–192; and Paul R. Abramson and Charles W. Ostrom, Jr., "Question Wording and Partisanship: Change and Continuity in Party Loyalties during the 1992 Election Campaign," *Public Opinion Quarterly* 58 (Spring 1994): 2148.

18. See Abramson, Aldrich, and Rohde, *Change and Continuity in the 2004 and 2006 Elections*, 186–192.

19. The ANES did not conduct a congressional election survey in 2006.

20. In the November 1–4, 2012 Gallup Poll, by contrast, they report 12 percent independent leaners for Republicans and 15 percent for Democrats. See http://www.gallup.com/poll/15370/party-affiliation.aspx.

21. For evidence on the decline of Republican Party loyalties among older blacks between 1962 and 1964, see Paul R. Abramson, *Generational Change in American Politics* (Lexington, Mass.: D.C. Heath, 1975), 65–69. For a long-term historical perspective in the South, see John H. Aldrich and John D. Griffin, *Why Parties Matter: Political Competition and Democracy in the American South* (Chicago: University of Chicago Press, 2018).

22. For the results of the white vote by party identification for the three leading candidates in 1968, 1980, 1992, and 1996, see Abramson, Aldrich, and Rohde, *Change and Continuity in the 1996 and 1998 Elections*, 186–187. Among blacks there is virtually no relationship between party identification and the vote. Even the small number of blacks who identify as Republicans usually either do not vote or vote for the Democratic presidential candidate.

23. See also Larry M. Bartels, "Partisanship and Voting Behavior, 1952–1996," *American Journal of Political Science* 44 (January 2000): 35–50.

24. Bernard R. Berelson, Paul F. Lazarsfeld, and William N. McPhee, *Voting: A Study of Opinion Formation in a Presidential Campaign* (Chicago: University of Chicago Press, 1954), 215–233. The extent to which voters' perceptions were affected, however, varied from issue to issue.

25. See Brody and Page, "Comment: The Assessment of Policy Voting"; and Morris P. Fiorina "An Outline for a Model of Party Choice," *American Journal of Political Science* 21 (August 1977): 601–625.

26. As we point out in Chapter 7, the ANES has asked the standard presidential approval question since 1970.

27. The question measuring approval of the president's handling of economic policy was not asked in ANES surveys before 1984. In our study of these earlier elections, an alternative measure of economic retrospective evaluations was created and shown to be almost as strongly related to party identification. See Paul R. Abramson, John H. Aldrich, and David W. Rohde, *Change and Continuity in the 1984 Elections*, rev. ed. (Washington, D.C.: CQ Press, 1987), Table 8-6, 221. We also found nearly as strong a relationship between partisanship and perceptions of which party would better handle the economy in the data from 1972, 1976, and 1980 as from later surveys reported here. See Abramson, Aldrich, and Rohde, *Change and Continuity in the 1980 and 1982 Elections*, 170, Table 8-6, 173.

28. Table 8-7 includes data from only the 2016 election, but earlier elections can be found in Table A8-7 in the appendix. For a description of this measure, see Chapter 6. Because this measure uses the median placement of the candidates on the issue scales in the full sample, much of the projection effect is eliminated. For the relationship between party identification and the balance-of-issues measure in 1972, see Abramson, Aldrich, and Rohde, *Change and Continuity in the 1980 and 1982 Elections*, Table 8-5, 171.

29. In 2012 it also did so, but it is a kind of artifact that it did so. The public perceived Romney's position to be slightly closer to the average voter than Obama's. Because we simply count the number of issues on which a candidate was closer, this small edge cumulated to an unrealistically large advantage.

30. Matthew Levendusky, *The Partisan Sort: How Liberals Became Democrats and Conservatives Became Republicans* (Chicago: University of Chicago Press, 2009).

31. This earlier measure and its relationship with partisan identification are reported in Abramson, Aldrich, and Rohde, *Change and Continuity in the 2000 and 2002 Elections*, Table 8-7, 185–186, discussed on 184–189; in Abramson, Aldrich, and Rohde, *Change and*

Continuity in the 2004 and 2006 Elections, Table 8-7, 202, discussed on 201–203; and in Paul R. Abramson, John H. Aldrich, Brad Gomez, and David W. Rohde, *Change and Continuity in the 2012 and 2014 Elections* (Washington, D.C.: CQ Press, 2016), Table 8-8, 219, discussed on 218–221.

32. As we saw in Chapter 7, that conclusion applies to those individual components of the measure that are the same as in earlier surveys.

33. As in Chapter 7 we cannot directly compare the results for 2008–2016 with those for earlier elections, except in very general terms. For an interpretation and the data over the previous seven elections, see Abramson, Aldrich, and Rohde, *Change and Continuity in the 2000 and 2002 Elections*, Table 8-8, 187–188, discussed on 189; Abramson, Aldrich, and Rohde, *Change and Continuity in the 2004 and 2006 Elections*, Table 8-8, 203, discussed on 203–204; and Abramson et al., *Change and Continuity in the 2012 and 2014 Elections*, Table 8-9, 220, discussed on 221.

34. We already discussed some of the important work along these lines earlier in this chapter. Two additional important articles that seek to assess these relationships are Gregory B. Markus and Philip E. Converse, "A Dynamic Simultaneous Equation Model of Electoral Choice," *American Political Science Review* 73 (December 1979): 1055–1070; and Benjamin I. Page and Calvin C. Jones, "Reciprocal Effects of Policy Preferences, Party Loyalties and the Vote," *American Political Science Review* 73 (December 1979): 1071–1089. For a brief discussion of these articles, see Richard G. Niemi and Herbert F. Weisberg, *Controversies in Voting Behavior*, 2nd ed. (Washington, D.C.: CQ Press, 1984), 89–95, 89–95. For an excellent discussion of complex models of voting behavior and the role of party identification in these models, see Asher, "Voting Behavior Research in the 1980s," 341–354. For another excellent introduction to some of these issues, see Richard G. Niemi and Herbert F. Weisberg, "Is Party Identification Stable?" in *Controversies in Voting Behavior*, 3rd ed., ed. Richard G. Niemi and Herbert F. Weisberg (Washington, D.C.: CQ Press, 1993), 268–283.

35. Aldrich and Griffin, *Why Parties Matter*.

36. An important illustration is that since 1952, presidents have often won reelection with landslide elections, or at least they did, such as Eisenhower in 1956, Johnson in a quasi-reelection in 1964, Nixon in 1972, and Regan in 1984. Since then, however, second elections have been losses (the senior Bush in 1992), or wins by considerably less than landslide proportions (Clinton in 1996, Bush in 2004, and Obama in 2012). That is because, like Jacobson, "2008 Presidential and Congressional Elections"; and Jacobson, "Effects of the George W. Bush Presidency," show, for presidential approval measures, presidents can no longer win support to any significant degree from out-party partisans.

37. And with so few pure independents (with leaners voting like partisans, as we have seen), there are few truly uncommitted voters for parties, and candidates to try to woo to their side.

CHAPTER 9

1. One independent was Bernard Sanders of Vermont, who was elected as an independent to the House from 1990 through 2004. Sanders had previously been elected mayor of Burlington, Vermont, running as a socialist. However, throughout his House service he caucused with the Democrats; he continued that course after his initial election to the Senate in 2006 and following his unsuccessful attempt at the Democratic nomination for president in 2016. The second independent is Angus King of Maine. King had served as governor of Maine from 1995 to 2003, also as an independent, before being elected senator for the first

time in 2012. We will count both of these senators as Democrats in all of the analyses in this chapter.

2. *Incumbents* here is used only to indicate elected incumbents. This includes all members of the House because the only way to become a representative is by election. In the case of the Senate, however, vacancies may be filled by appointment. We do not count appointed senators as incumbents. Although former Lieutenant Governor Brian Schatz (D) was appointed by Hawaii Governor Neil Abercrombie in 2012 to take the place of deceased Senator Daniel Inouye, Schatz won a special election in 2014 to serve the remainder of Inouye's term. As such, he ran as incumbent in 2016 and is counted accordingly.

3. The classification of primary- versus general-election defeats is complicated by the atypical processes used in California, Louisiana, and Washington. In California and Washington, all candidates regardless of party affiliation compete in a single primary. The two candidates who received the highest number of votes then compete in the general election. Thus the general election may include two Democrats or two Republicans. In Louisiana all candidates appear on the general election ballot, and if no candidate receives a majority of votes, the top two vote getters proceed to a runoff in December. These types of situations seem more akin to a primary runoff than the usual idea of a general election, so we classify results that way. If two candidates of the same party face each other in the general election, we count that as a primary, with the winner unopposed in the general election. If both are incumbents, the defeat is treated as a primary loss.

4. Although gerrymandering cannot be the only contributing factor, it could be a part of the explanation for this modest House-Senate difference.

5. The Republicans had won control of the House in eight consecutive elections from 1894 through 1908, far short of the Democratic series of successes.

6. The regional breakdowns used in this chapter are as follows: *East*: Connecticut, Delaware, Maine, Massachusetts, New Hampshire, New Jersey, New York, Pennsylvania, Rhode Island, and Vermont; *Midwest*: Illinois, Indiana, Iowa, Kansas, Michigan, Minnesota, Nebraska, North Dakota, Ohio, South Dakota, and Wisconsin; *West*: Alaska, Arizona, California, Colorado, Hawaii, Idaho, Montana, Nevada, New Mexico, Oregon, Utah, Washington, and Wyoming; *South*: Alabama, Arkansas, Florida, Georgia, Louisiana, Mississippi, North Carolina, South Carolina, Tennessee, Texas, and Virginia; *Border*: Kentucky, Maryland, Missouri, Oklahoma, and West Virginia. This classification differs somewhat from the one used in earlier chapters (and in Chapter 10) but is commonly used for congressional analysis.

7. Over the years changes in the southern electorate have also made southern Democratic constituencies more like northern Democratic constituencies and less like Republican constituencies, North or South. The East also exacerbates this tendency just for the opposite party reasons. These changes also appear to have enhanced the homogeneity of preferences within the partisan delegations in Congress. This partisan congressional polarization has been the subject of a great deal of research over the last three decades. Two good overviews are offered by John H. Aldrich, *Why Parties? A Second Look* (Chicago: University of Chicago Press, 2011); and Marc J. Hetherington and Thomas J. Rudolph, *Why Washington Won't Work: Polarization, Political Trust, and the Governing Crisis* (Chicago: University of Chicago Press, 2015).

8. The ratings were taken from various issues of *The Cook Political Report*. Competitive races are those Cook classified as only leaning to the incumbent party, toss-ups, or those tilted toward the other party.

9. See Paul R Abramson, John H. Aldrich, and David W. Rohde, *Change and Continuity in the 1996 and 1998 Elections* (Washington, D.C.: CQ Press, 1999), 207–212.

10. These polling data on Congress were taken from www.gallup.com/poll/1600/congress -public.aspx.

11. Jennifer Agiesta, "Impressions of U.S. Direction Improved, but Divided by Partisanship," *CNN*, October 27, 2016, http://www.cnn.com/2016/10/27/politics/obama-approval -presidential-polls/.

12. For a discussion of the increased role of national party organizations in congressional elections over the last three decades, see Paul S. Herrnson, *Congressional Elections*, 7th ed. (Washington, D.C.: CQ Press, 2015), chap. 4.

13. See Alexis Levinson, "DCCC Kicks Off 2016 Recruitment." *Roll Call*, January 8, 2015, http://www.rollcall.com/news/home/house-races-2016-dccc-recruitment-leadership-team.

14. See Emily Cahn, "Senate Democrats Nearly Run Table in Recruitment." *Roll Call*, October 5, 2015, http://www.rollcall.com/news/home/senate-democrats-nearly-run-table-recruitment.

15. See Emily Cahn, "The 10 Most Vulnerable Senators," *Roll Call*, November 6, 2015, http:// www.rollcall.com/news/home/10-vulnerable-senators-2016.

16. See Lauren French, "Pelosi Raises $40.1 Million in 2016 Cycle," *Politico*, January 28, 2016, http://www.politico.com/story/2016/01/nancy-pelosi-2015-fundraising-218326.

17. See Lindsey McPherson, "Ryan Credited with Raising Nearly $90 Million over 2016 Cycle," *Roll Call*, November 10, 2016, http://www.rollcall.com/news/politics/ ryan-credited-raising-nearly-90-million-2016-cycle.

18. See *Open Secrets*, www.opensecrets.org/politicians/summary.php?type=C&cid=N00028152 &newMem=N&cycle=2016.

19. See "Who's Raised the Most," *Open Secrets*, https://www.opensecrets.org/overview/topraise .php.

20. Super PACs are a new kind of political action committee that "may raise unlimited sums of money from corporations, unions, associations and individuals, then spend unlimited sums to overtly advocate for or against political candidates. . . . Unlike traditional PACs, super PACs are prohibited from donating money directly to political candidates." See "Super PACs," *Open Secrets*, http://www.opensecrets.org/pacs/superpacs.php.

21. See "2016 Outside Spending, by Race," *Open Secrets*, https://www.opensecrets.org/outside spending/summ.php?cycle=2016&disp=R&pty=A&type=A.

22. See "2014 Outside Spending, by Race," *Open Secrets*, https://www.opensecrets.org/outside spending/summ.php?cycle=2014&disp=R&pty=A&type=A.

23. See "2016 Outside Spending."

24. Richard F. Fenno, Jr., *Home Style: House Members in Their Districts* (Boston: Little, Brown, 1978). For a discussion of how relationships between representatives and constituents have changed over time, see Fenno, *The Challenge of Congressional Representation* (Cambridge, Mass.: Harvard University Press, 2013).

25. See David W. Rohde, "Risk-Bearing and Progressive Ambition: The Case of Members of the United States House of Representatives," *American Journal of Political Science* (February 1979): 1–26.

26. For example, analysis of Senate races in 1988 indicated that both the political quality of the previous office held and the challenger's political skills had an independent effect on the outcome of the race. See Peverill Squire, "Challenger Quality and Voting Behavior in U.S. Senate Elections," *Legislative Studies Quarterly* 17 (May 1992): 247–263. For systematic evidence on the impact of candidate quality in House races, see Gary C. Jacobson and Jamie L. Carson, *The Politics of Congressional Elections*, 9th ed. (Lanham, Md.: Rowman & Littlefield, 2016), chap. 3.

27. A recent analysis uses expert survey responses instead of office experience to measure candidate quality. It concludes that quality candidates do better and that the effect increases as ideological differences decline. See Matthew K. Buttice and Walter J. Stone, "Candidates Matter: Policy and Quality Differences in Congressional Elections," *Journal of Politics* 74 (July 2012): 870–887.

28. Data on candidate backgrounds were taken from various issues of *The Cook Political Report* and *The Green Papers* (http://www.thegreenpapers.com/G16/).

29. Data on earlier years are taken from our studies of previous national elections.

30. Note that the figures in this paragraph include races in which only one of the parties fielded a candidate as well as contests where both did.

31. See Jacobson and Carson, *The Politics of Congressional Elections*; Jon R. Bond, Cary Covington; Richard Fleischer, "Explaining Challenger Quality in Congressional Elections," *Journal of Politics* 47 (May 1985): 510–529; and David W. Rohde, "Risk-Bearing and Progressive Ambition: The Case of Members of the U.S. House of Representatives," *American Journal of Political Science* 23 (February 1979): 1–26.

32. L. Sandy Maisel and Walter J. Stone, "Determinants of Candidate Emergence in U.S. House Elections: An Exploratory Study," *Legislative Studies Quarterly* 22 (February 1997): 79–96.

33. See Peverill Squire, "Preemptive Fund-raising and Challenger Profile in Senate Elections," *Journal of Politics* 53 (November 1991): 1150–1164; and Jay Goodliffe, "The Effect of War Chests on Challenger Entry in U.S. House Elections," *American Journal of Political Science* 45 (October 2001): 1087–1108.

34. Jeffrey S. Banks and D. Roderick Kiewiet, "Explaining Patterns of Candidate Competition in Congressional Elections," *American Journal of Political Science* 33 (November 1989): 997–1015.

35. Canon, *Actors, Athletes, and Astronauts.*

36. See Kenneth J. Cooper, "Riding High Name Recognition to Hill," *Washington Post*, December 24, 1992, A4.

37. See Thomas E. Mann and Raymond E. Wolfinger, "Candidates and Parties in Congressional Elections," *American Political Science Review* 74 (September 1980): 617–632.

38. See David R. Mayhew, "Congressional Elections: The Case of the Vanishing Marginals," *Polity* 6 (Spring 1974): 295–317; Robert S. Erikson, "Malapportionment, Gerrymandering, and Party Fortunes in Congressional Elections," *American Political Science Review* 66 (December 1972): 1234–1245; and Warren Lee Kostroski, "Party and Incumbency in Postwar Senate Elections: Trends, Patterns, and Models," *American Political Science Review* 67 (December 1973): 1213–1234.

39. Edward R. Tufte, "Communication," *American Political Science Review* 68 (March 1974): 211–213. The communication involved a discussion of Tufte's earlier article: "The Relationship Between Seats and Votes in Two-Party Systems," *American Political Science Review* 67 (June 1973): 540–554.

40. See John A. Ferejohn, "On the Decline of Competition in Congressional Elections," *American Political Science Review* 71 (March 1977): 166–176; Albert D. Cover, "One Good Term Deserves Another: The Advantage of Incumbency in Congressional Elections," *American Journal of Political Science* 21 (August 1977): 523–541; and Albert D. Cover and David R. Mayhew, "Congressional Dynamics and the Decline of Competition in Congressional Elections," in *Congress Reconsidered*, 2nd ed., ed. Lawrence C. Dodd and Bruce I. Oppenheimer (Washington, D.C.: CQ Press, 1981), 62–82.

41. Morris P. Fiorina, *Congress: Keystone of the Washington Establishment*, 2nd ed. (New Haven, Conn.: Yale University Press, 1989), esp. chap. 4-6.

42. See several conflicting arguments and conclusions in the following articles published in the *American Journal of Political Science* 25 (August 1981): John R. Johannes and John C. McAdams, "The Congressional Incumbency Effect: Is It Casework, Policy Compatibility, or Something Else? An Examination of the 1978 Election" (512–542); Morris P. Fiorina, "Some Problems in Studying the Effects of Resource Allocation in Congressional Elections" (543–567); Diana Evans Yiannakis, "The Grateful Electorate: Casework and Congressional Elections" (568–580); and McAdams and Johannes, "Does Casework Matter? A Reply to Professor Fiorina" (581–604). See also Johannes, *To Serve the People: Congress and Constituency Service* (Lincoln: University of Nebraska Press, 1984), esp. chap. 8; and Albert D. Cover and Bruce S. Brumberg, "Baby Books and Ballots: The Impact of Congressional Mail on Constituent Opinion," *American Political Science Review* 76 (June 1982): 347–359. The evidence in Cover and Brumberg for a positive electoral effect is quite strong, but the result may be applicable only to limited circumstances.

43. Ferejohn, "On the Decline of Competition," 174.

44. Cover, "One Good Term," 535.

45. More recent research shows that the link between party identification and voting has strengthened again. See Larry M. Bartels, "Partisanship and Voting Behavior, 1952–1996," *American Journal of Political Science* 44 (January 2000), 35–50.

46. On this point, see Gary Jacobson, "It's Nothing Personal: The Decline of the Incumbency Advantage in U.S. House Elections," *Journal of Politics* 77 (July 2015), 861–873.

47. For thorough analyses of the growth of, and reasons for, anti-Congress sentiment, see John R. Hibbing and Elizabeth Theiss-Morse, *Congress as Public Enemy* (New York: Cambridge University Press, 1995); and Thomas E. Mann and Norman J. Ornstein, *The Broken Branch: How Congress Is Failing America and How to Get It Back on Track* (Oxford: Oxford University Press, 2008).

48. For an analysis suggesting that the variations in incumbents' vote percentages have little implication for incumbent safety, see Jeffrey M. Stonecash, *Reassessing the Incumbency Effect* (New York: Cambridge University Press, 2008).

49. Jacobson, "It's Nothing Personal," 861–862.

50. Gary C. Jacobson, "The Triumph of Polarized Partisanship in 2016: Trump's Improbable Victory," *Political Science Quarterly* 132 (Spring 2017), 32.

51. The body of literature on this subject has grown to be quite large. Some salient early examples, in addition to those cited later, are: Gary C. Jacobson, *Money in Congressional Elections* (New Haven, Conn.: Yale University Press, 1980); Jacobson, "Parties and PACs in Congressional Elections," in *Congress Reconsidered*, 4th eds., ed. Lawrence C. Dodd and Bruce I. Oppenheimer (Washington, D.C.: CQ Press, 1989), 117–152; Jacobson and Samuel Kernell, *Strategy and Choice in Congressional Elections*, 2nd ed. (New Haven, Conn.: Yale University Press, 1983); John A. Ferejohn and Morris P. Fiorina, "Incumbency and Realignment in Congressional Elections," in *The New Direction in American Politics*, eds. John E. Chubb and Paul E. Peterson (Washington, D.C.: Brookings Institution, 1985), 91–115.

52. See Jacobson, *The Electoral Origins of Divided Government*, 63–65.

53. See Gary C. Jacobson and Samuel Kernell, *Strategy and Choice in Congressional Elections*, 2nd ed. (New Haven, Conn.: Yale University Press, 1983).

54. Evidence indicates challenger spending strongly influences public visibility, and substantial amounts of spending can significantly reduce the recognition gap between the challenger and the incumbent. See Jacobson and Carson, *The Politics of Congressional Elections*, 9th ed., 63–67.

55. The 2016 spending data were obtained from the Federal Election Commission (www.fec.gov).

56. See Paul R. Abramson, John H. Aldrich, Brad T. Gomez, and David W. Rohde, *Change and Continuity in the 2012 and 2014 Elections* (Washington, D.C.: CQ Press, 2016), 245–248, and the earlier work cited there.

57. See Jacobson, *The Electoral Origins of Divided Government*, 54–55, and the work cited in note 48.

58. Donald Philip Green and Jonathan S. Krasno, "Salvation for the Spendthrift Incumbent: Reestimating the Effects of Campaign Spending in House Elections," *American Journal of Political Science* 32 (November 1988), 884–907.

59. Gary C. Jacobson, "The Effects of Campaign Spending in House Elections: New Evidence for Old Arguments," *American Journal of Political Science* 34 (May 1990), 334–362. Green and Krasno's response can be found in the same issue on pages 363–372.

60. Gary C. Jacobson, *The Politics of Congressional Elections*, 8th ed. (Pearson, 2013), 156.

61. See Alan I. Abramowitz, "Explaining Senate Election Outcomes," *American Political Science Review* 82 (June 1988), 385–403; Alan Gerber, "Estimating the Effect of Campaign Spending on Senate Election Outcomes Using Instrumental Variables," *American Political Science Review* 92 (June 1998), 401–411.

62. Gary C. Jacobson, "Campaign Spending and Voter Awareness of Congressional Candidates," paper presented at the Annual Meeting of the Public Choice Society, New Orleans, Louisiana, May 11–13, 1977), 16.

63. An incumbent in a district that is tilted toward the opposite party may need to spend more to be able to distinguish his- or herself from the party's unattractive but (in recent decades) precise party reputation. See Henry A. Kim and Brad l. Leveck, "Money, Reputation, and Incumbency in U.S. House Elections, or Why Marginals Have Become More Expensive," *American Political Science Review* 107 (August, 2013): 492–504.

64. Spending data are taken from www.fec.gov.

65. Of course, open seats tend to involve considerably greater sums of money because there is no incumbent seeking reelection. In an extreme example from 2016, losing Democratic challenger Randy Perkins spent $10.86 million (of which more than 10 million was self-financed) against Republican challenger Brian Mast of Florida, who spent $2.87 million. Despite being outspent almost four to one, Mast won 53.6 percent of the vote.

66. Challengers were categorized as having strong experience if they had been elected U.S. representative, to statewide office, to the state legislature, or to countywide or citywide office (e.g., mayor, prosecutor, etc.).

67. Paul R. Abramson, John H. Aldrich, and David W. Rohde, *Change and Continuity in the 1980 Elections*, rev. ed. (Washington, D.C.: CQ Press, 1983), 202–203. See also Paul Gronke, *The Electorate, the Campaign, and the Office: A Unified Approach to Senate and House Elections* (Ann Arbor: University of Michigan Press, 2001).

68. Other Democratic Senate winners in 2000 who spent millions of their own money included Maria Cantwell of Washington and Mark Dayton of Minnesota.

69. See "Most Expensive Races," *Open Secrets*, https://www.opensecrets.org/overview/topraces.php?cycle=2016&display=allcandsout.

70. Quoted in Angela Herrin, "Big Outside Money Backfired in GOP Loss of Senate to Dems," *Washington Post*, November 6, 1986, A46.

71. See David W. Rohde, *Parties and Leaders in the Postreform House* (Chicago: University of Chicago Press, 1991), especially Chapter 3; and Rohde, "Electoral Forces, Political Agendas, and Partisanship in the House and Senate," in *The Postreform Congress*, ed. Rodger H. Davidson (New York: St. Martin's Press, 1992), 27–47.

72. For discussions of the ideological changes in the House and Senate over the last four decades, see John H. Aldrich and David W. Rohde, "The Logic of Conditional Party Government: Revisiting the Electoral Connection," in *Congress Reconsidered*, 7th ed., eds. Lawrence Dodd and Bruce Oppenheimer (Washington, D.C.: CQ Press, 2001), 269–292; Gary C. Jacobson, "The Congress: The Structural Basis of Republican Success," in *The Elections of 2004*, ed. Michael Nelson (Washington, D.C.: CQ Press, 2005), 163–186; and Sean Theriault, *Party Polarization in Congress* (Cambridge: Cambridge University Press, 2008).

73. David Johnson, "See Every Executive Order Donald Trump Has Signed since Becoming President," *Time*, February 10, 2017, http://time.com/4663143/donald-trump-executive-orders-president/.

74. Thomas Fuller, "San Francisco Sues Trump Over 'Sanctuary Cities' Order," *New York Times*, January 31, 2017, https://www.nytimes.com/2017/01/31/us/san-francisco-lawsuit-trump-sanctuary-cities.html. In late April William Orrick of the United States District Court in San Francisco blocked President Trump's effort to restrict federal funds in cities that failed to comply with his immigration enforcement policies. See Vivian Lee, "Judge Blocks Trump Effort to Withhold Money from Sanctuary Cities," *New York Times*, April 25, 2017, https://www.nytimes.com/2017/04/25/us/judge-blocks-trump-sanctuary-cities.html.

75. The executive order was labeled "Protecting the Nation from Foreign Terrorist Entry into the United States." David Johnson, "See Every Executive Order Donald Trump Has Signed since Becoming President."

76. Alexander Burns, "2 Federal Judges Rule against Trump's Latest Travel Ban," *New York Times*, March 15, 2017, https://www.nytimes.com/2017/03/15/us/politics/trump-travel-ban.html.

77. On this point, see especially William Howell, *Power without Persuasion: The Politics of Direct Presidential Action* (Princeton: Princeton University Press, 2003).

78. See "Presidential Approval Ratings—Donald Trump," *Gallup*, http://www.gallup.com/poll/203198/presidential-approval-ratings-donald-trump.aspx.

79. Michael Shear and Matt Apuzzo, "F.B.I. Director James Comey Is Fired by Trump," *New York Times*, May 9, 2017, https://www.nytimes.com/2017/05/09/us/politics/james-comey-fired-fbi.html?_r=0.

80. Department of Justice, "Appointment of Special Counsel," May 17, 2017, https://www.justice.gov/opa/pr/appointment-special-counsel.

81. See Paul R. Abramson, John H. Aldrich, and David W. Rohde, *Change and Continuity in the 1992 Elections*, rev. ed. (Washington, D.C.: CQ Press, 1995), 339–342; and John H. Aldrich and David W. Rohde, "The Transition to Republican Rule in the House: Implications for Theories of Congressional Politics," *Political Science Quarterly* 112 (Winter, 1997–1998): 541–567.

82. Eric Lipton and Matt Flegenheimer, "House Republicans, under Fire, Back Down on Gutting Ethics Office," *New York Times*, January 3, 2017, https://www.nytimes.com/2017/01/03/us/politics/trump-house-ethics-office.html?_r=0.

83. For an interesting journalistic account of the Tea Party group in the House, see Robert Draper, *When the Tea Party Came to Town* (New York: Simon and Schuster, 2012).

84. See Jonathan Strong, "Boehner Pledges to Stick to the 'Hastert Rule,'" *Roll Call*, March 6, 2013, 1.

85. Jonathan Weisman, "Boehner Narrowly Holds on to Speaker's Post," *New York Times*, January 3, 2013, http://www.nytimes.com/2013/01/04/us/politics/new-congress-begins-with-wishes-of-comity-but-battles-ahead.html.

86. Jennifer Steinhauer, "Speaker Boehner, House Speaker, Will Resign from Congress," *New York Times*, September 25, 2015, https://www.nytimes.com/2015/09/26/us/john-boehner-to-resign-from-congress.html.

87. See Jake Sherman, "Cantor Loses," *Politico*, June 10, 2014, http://www.politico.com/story/2014/06/eric-cantor-primary-election-results-virginia-107683.

88. Mike DeBonis, Robert Costa, and Rosalind Helderman, "House Majority Leader Kevin McCarthy Drops out of Race for House Speaker," *Washington Post*, October 8, 2015, https://www.washingtonpost.com/news/powerpost/wp/2015/10/08/house-majority-leader-kevin-mccarthy-drops-out-of-race-for-house-speaker/?utm_term=.a9d0586174e2.

89. Jake Sherman, John Bresnahan, and Lauren French, "Ryan Will Serve as Speaker if GOP Unites Behind Him," *Politico*, October 20, 2015, http://www.politico.com/story/2015/10/paul-ryan-speaker-if-gop-unites-behind-him-214985.

90. Katie Zezima, Dan Balz, and Chris Cillizza, "Reince Priebus Named Trump's Chief of Staff," *Washington Post*, November 13, 2016, https://www.washingtonpost.com/news/post-politics/wp/2016/11/13/reince-priebus-named-as-trumps-chief-of-staff/?utm_term=.03832fc12808. On July 28, 2017, President Trump announced via Twitter that he was firing Priebus as his chief of staff and replacing him with John F. Kelly, the secretary of homeland security. See Peter Baker and Maggie Haberman, "Reince Priebus Is Ousted amid Stormy Days for White House," *New York Times*, July 28, 2017, https://www.nytimes.com/2017/07/28/us/politics/reince-priebus-white-house-trump.html.

91. Robert Pear, Thomas Kaplan, and Maggie Haberman, "In Major Defeat for Trump, Push to Repeal Health Law Fails," *New York Times*, March 24, 2017, https://www.nytimes.com/2017/03/24/us/politics/health-care-affordable-care-act.html.

92. Ibid.

93. For more details on the failed attempt, see Robert Draper, "Trump vs. Congress: Now What?," *New York Times*, March 26, 2017, https://mobile.nytimes.com/2017/03/26/magazine/trump-vs-congress-now-what.html?_r=0.

94. Pear, Kaplan, and Haberman, "In Major Defeat for Trump, Push to Repeal Health Law Fails."

95. John Wagner, Mike DeBonis, and Robert Costa, "Trump Threatens Hard-Liners as Part of Escalating Republican Civil War," *Washington Post*, March 30, 2017, https://www.washingtonpost.com/powerpost/trump-we-must-fight-hard-line-conservative-freedom-caucus-in-2018-midterm-elections/2017/03/30/56783e38-154e-11e7-ada0-1489b735b3a3_story.html?utm_term=.b2db9d351ef6.

96. Sam Frizell, "The Effort to Repeal Obamacare Is Failing Again. Here's What That Means for the GOP," *Time*, April 6, 2017, http://time.com/4729242/obamacare-repeal-ahca-republicans-blame/.

97. Ibid.

98. Thomas Kaplan, "Congress Prevents Government from Shutting Down on Trump's 100th Day," *New York Times*, April 28, 2017, https://www.nytimes.com/2017/04/28/us/politics/congress-government-funding-stopgap.html.

99. Ibid.

100. Andrew Taylor, "Congress Finishes Spending Bill, Sends Legislation to Trump," *Federal News Radio*, May 5, 2017, https://federalnewsradio.com/budget/2017/05/congress-finishes-spending-bill-sends-legislation-to-trump/.

101. Thomas Kaplan and Robert Pear, "House Passes Measure to Repeal and Replace the Affordable Care Act," *New York Times*, May 4, 2017, https://www.nytimes.com/2017/05/04/us/politics/health-care-bill-vote.html.

102. Robert Pear, "G.O.P. Health Bill Would Leave 23 Million More Uninsured in a Decade, C.B.O. Says," *New York Times*, May 24, 2017, https://www.nytimes.com/2017/05/24/us/politics/cbo-congressional-budget-office-health-care.html.

103. "Current Numbers," Center for American Women and Politics, http://www.cawp.rutgers.edu/current-numbers.

104. The literature on the filibuster is substantial. A good entry point is Gregory Koger, *Filibustering: A Political History of Obstruction in the House and Senate* (Chicago: University of Chicago Press: 2010).

105. The data cited from 2007–2016 were taken from a table on "Senate Action on Cloture Motions," www.senate.gov/pagelayout/reference/cloture_motions/clotureCounts.htm.

106. Sheryl Gay Stolberg, "Swing Senators Face New Test in Supreme Court Fight," *New York Times*, July 14, 2005, http://www.nytimes.com/2005/07/14/us/swing-senators-face-new-test-in-supreme-court-fight.html.

107. See Ramsey Cox, "Reid: Senate Dems will vote to limit GOP use of filibuster," *The Hill*, November 27, 2012, 3.

108. Jeremy Peters, "In Landmark Vote, Senate Limits Use of the Filibuster," *New York Times*, November 21, 2013, http://www.nytimes.com/2013/11/22/us/politics/reid-sets-in-motion-steps-to-limit-use-of-filibuster.html.

109. Ibid.

110. See Mallory Shelbourne, "Schumer Regrets Dems Triggering 'Nuclear Option,'" *The Hill*, January 3, 2017, http://thehill.com/homenews/senate/312540-schumer-regrets-dems-triggering-nuclear-option.

111. See Burgess Everett, "McConnell Throws Down the Gauntlet: No Scalia Replacement Under Obama," *Politico*, February 13, 2016, http://www.politico.com/story/2016/02/mitch-mcconnell-antonin-scalia-supreme-court-nomination-219248.

112. Julie Hirschfeld Davis, "Joe Biden Argued for Delaying Supreme Court Picks in 1992," *New York Times*, February 22, 2016, https://www.nytimes.com/2016/02/23/us/politics/joe-biden-argued-for-delaying-supreme-court-picks-in-1992.html.

113. Adam Liptak and Matt Flegenheimer, "Neil Gorsuch Confirmed by Senate as Supreme Court Justice," *New York Times*, April 7, 2017, https://www.nytimes.com/2017/04/07/us/politics/neil-gorsuch-supreme-court.html.

114. Damian Paletta and Mike DeBonis, "Trump's Window for Scoring Early Legislative Victories Is Shrinking," *Washington Post*, May 30, 2017, https://www.washingtonpost.com/politics/trumps-window-for-scoring-early-legislative-victories-is-shrinking/2017/05/30/fa82139a-4551-11e7-a196-a1bb629f64cb_story.html?tid=ss_fb&utm_term=.8f033f0c28e6.

115. Peter Sullivan, "CBO: Senate Obamacare Repeal Would Leave 22M More Uninsured," *The Hill*, June 26, 2017, http://thehill.com/policy/healthcare/ 339534-cbo-22m-more-uninsured-with-senate-obamacare-bill.

116. Sean Sullivan, Kelsey Snell, and Juliet Eilperin, "Trump, Senate Leaders Attempt to Regroup after Postponing Vote to Overhaul Obamacare," *Washington Post*, June 27, 2017, https://www.washingtonpost.com/powerpost/senate-republicans-scramble-to-keep-alive-plans-to-overhaul-obamacare/2017/06/27/c8ea4c02-5b37-11e7-9fc6-c7ef4bc58d13_story.html?hpid=hp_hp-top-table-main_healthcare-905a%3Ahomepage%2Fstory&utm_term=.cdb4528d0fe4.

117. Geoff Bennett, and Tamara Keith, "McConnell: Senate Will 'Defer' Vote on Republican Health Care Bill," *NPR*, July 15, 2017, http://www.npr.org/2017/07/15/537474302/

as-mccain-recovers-from-surgery-senate-vote-on-republican-health-care-bill-uncer?
sc=17&f=537474302.

118. Joe Williams, "McConnell Abandons Obamacare Repeal and Replace Effort," *Roll Call*, July 17, 2017, http://www.rollcall.com/news/politics/senate-gop-not-votes-health-care.

119. Thomas Kaplan, "'Let Obamacare Fail,' Trump Says as G.O.P. Health Bill Collapses," *New York Times*, July 18, 2017, https://www.nytimes.com/2017/07/18/us/politics/ republicans-obamacare-repeal-now-replace-later.html?hp&action=click&pgtype=H omepage&clickSource=story-heading&module=a-lede-package-region&region=top -news&WT.nav=top-news.

120. Majority Leader Mitch McConnell emphasized that the debate on health care would involve an "open amendment process" that would likely take some time before a confer- ence committee would be held with the House to reconcile differences with their version. See Mariam Khan and Veronica Stracqualursi, "Republicans Pull off Narrow Victory to Move Health Reform Forward," *Yahoo! News*, July 25, 2017, https://www.yahoo.com/gma/ senate-republicans-push-crucial-vote-health-care-despite-165003247.html.

121. See Austin Ramzy, "McCain's Vote Proves Dramatic Moment in 7-Year Battle over Obamacare," *New York Times*, July 28, 2017, https://www.nytimes.com/2017/07/28/us/ politics/john-mccain-vote-trump-obamacare.html.

122. Earlier research indicated that for these purposes, voters tend to regard a president whose predecessor either died or resigned from office as a continuation of the first president's administration. Therefore these data are organized by term of administration rather than term of president. See Abramson, Aldrich, and Rohde, *Change and Continuity in the 1980 Elections*, rev. ed., 252–253.

123. Edward R. Tufte, "Determinants of the Outcomes of Midterm Congressional Elections," *American Political Science Review* 69 (September 1975): 812–826; and Tufte, *Political Control of the Economy* (Princeton, N.J.: Princeton University Press, 1978); and Jacobson and Kernell, *Strategy and Choice in Congressional Elections*, 2nd ed.

124. The Jacobson-Kernell hypothesis was challenged by Richard Born in "Strategic Politicians and Unresponsive Voters," *American Political Science Review* 80 (June 1986): 599–612. Born argued that economic and approval data at the time of the election were more closely related to outcomes than were parallel data from earlier in the year. Jacobson, how- ever, offered renewed support for the hypothesis in an analysis of both district-level and aggregate data. See Gary C. Jacobson, "Strategic Politicians and the Dynamics of House Elections, 1946–86," *American Political Science Review* 83 (September 1989): 773–793.

125. Alan Abramowitz, Albert D. Cover, and Helmut Norpoth, "The President's Party in Midterm Elections: Going from Bad to Worse," *American Journal of Political Science* 30 (August 1986): 562–576.

126. Bruce Oppenheimer, James Stimson, and Richard Waterman, "Interpreting U.S. Con- gressional Elections: The Exposure Thesis," *Legislative Studies Quarterly* 11 (May 1986): 228.

127. Robin Marra and Charles Ostrom, Jr., "Explaining Seat Change in the U.S. House of Representatives 1950–86," *American Journal of Political Science* 33 (August 1989): 541–569.

128. Brian Newman and Charles W. Ostrom, Jr., "Explaining Seat Changes in the U.S. House of Representatives, 1950–1998," *Legislative Studies Quarterly*, 28 (2002): 383–405.

129. "Gallup Daily: Trump Job Approval," http://www.gallup.com/poll/201617/gallup-daily -trump-job-approval.aspx. By comparison most prior presidents have started out with approval of at least 60 to 70 percent and their level of disapproval is in the 20 to 30 percent range during the first year in office.

130. See Jacobson and Carson, *The Politics of Congressional Elections.*

131. See Garance Franke-Rutz, "Emily's List: An Unprecedented 10,000 Women Have Told Us They Want to Run for Office Thanks to Trump," *Emily's List*, March 22, 2017, http://www.emilyslist.org/news/entry/10000-women-to-run-thanks-to-trump.

132. See Reid J. Epstein, "Democrats Enlist Veterans Ahead of 2018 House Elections," *Wall Street Journal*, May 21, 2017, https://www.wsj.com/articles/democrats-enlist-veterans-ahead-of-2018-house-elections-1495394418.

133. See Simone Pathé, "DCCC Announces 2018 Leadership Team," *Roll Call*, February 9, 2017, http://www.rollcall.com/news/politics/dccc-announces-2018-leadership-team.

134. John Eligon and Jonathan Martin, "Ron Estes, a Republican, Survives Tight House Race to Win Kansas Seat," *New York Times*, April 11, 2017, https://www.nytimes.com/2017/04/11/us/politics/kansas-special-election.html.

135. Greg Bluestein, "Paul Ryan to Campaign with Karen Handel in Georgia's 6th Race," *Atlanta Journal Constitution*, May 6, 2017, http://politics.blog.ajc.com/2017/05/06/paul-ryan-to-campaign-with-karen-handel-on-may-15/; and Greg Bluestein, "Pence Plans June Visit to Stump for Handel in Georgia's 6th Runoff," *Atlanta Journal Constitution*, May 23, 2017, http://politics.blog.ajc.com/2017/05/22/pence-plans-june-visit-to-stump-for-handel-in-georgias-6th-runoff/.

136. Sara Swann, "Outside Groups Kick into High Gear Post-Primary in Georgia, South Carolina," *Open Secrets*, June 19, 2017, https://www.opensecrets.org/news/2017/06/outside-groups-in-georgia06/.

137. "Georgia Election Results: Handel Defeats Ossoff in U.S. House Race," *New York Times*, June 21, 2017, https://www.nytimes.com/elections/results/georgia-congressional-runoff-ossoff-handel. On the same day the runoff election was held in Georgia, South Carolina held a special election to fill the seat vacated by Mick Mulvaney, current director of the Office of Management and Budget. In that race Republican candidate Ralph Norman defeated Democrat Archie Parnell, 51.1 to 47.9 percent, resulting in a slightly closer outcome than the special election in Georgia that had attracted such widespread national attention. See "Election Results: Republican Wins U.S. House Seat in South Carolina," *New York Times*, June 21, 2017, https://www.nytimes.com/elections/results/south-carolina-house-special-election.

138. See Simone Pathé, "How GOP Outside Spending Turned a Loser into a Winner in Montana," *Roll Call*, May 26, 2017, http://www.rollcall.com/news/politics/how-gop-outside-spending-turned-a-loser-into-a-winner-in-montana.

139. Christine Mai-Duc, "Democrats Target 7 Congressional Seats Held by California Republicans for 2018 Midterm Elections," *Los Angeles Times*, January 30, 2017, http://www.latimes.com/politics/essential/la-pol-ca-essential-politics-updates-dccc-sets-sights-on-seven-california-1485806622-htmlstory.html.

140. See Marc Caputo, "Florida's Ros-Lehtinen to Retire from Congress," *Politico*, April 30, 2017, http://www.politico.com/story/2017/04/30/ros-lehtinen-congress-florida-237813.

141. For the complete list of House departures, see http://data.rollcall.com/media/casualtylists/.

142. Emmarie Huetteman and Matt Flegenheimer, "Jason Chaffetz, Powerful House Republican, Won't Run in 2018," *New York Times*, April 19, 2017, https://www.nytimes.com/2017/04/19/us/politics/jason-chaffetz-congress-utah-house-oversight.html.

143. Robert Gehrke, "With Chaffetz's First Move, the 2020 Governor's Race Starts Now," *The Salt Lake Tribune*, April 19, 2017, http://www.sltrib.com/home/5195006-155/gehrke-with-chaffetzs-first-move-the.

144. "State Republicans Push for More Restrictive Voting Laws," *NPR*, March 9, 2017, http://www.npr.org/2017/03/09/519500312/state-republicans-push-for-more-restrictive-voting-laws.

145. See Lydia Wheeler, "Supreme Court Refuses to Hear Appeal in NC Voter ID Case," *The Hill*, May 15, 2017, http://thehill.com/homenews/333401-supreme-court-refuses-to-review-north-carolina-voter-id-law-report.

146. Harry Enten, "A Very Early Look at the Battle for the House in 2018," *FiveThirtyEight*, February 15, 2017, https://fivethirtyeight.com/features/a-very-early-look-at-the-battle-for-the-house-in-2018/.

147. See Pew Research, http://www.pewresearch.org/data-trend/political-attitudes/republican-party-favorability/.

148. This total includes the thirty-three Senate elections scheduled for 2018, along with the Alabama special election, necessitated by Jeff Sessions's (R-AL) confirmation as U.S. attorney general in early 2017. Alabama's Governor Robert Bentley (R) appointed state Attorney General Luther Strange (R) to the Senate seat, who will be eligible to win the remainder of Session's unexpired term in 2018.

149. "2018's Initial Senate Ratings," *Rasmussen Reports*, February 16, 2017, http://www.rasmussenreports.com/public_content/political_commentary/commentary_by_kyle_kondik/2018_s_initial_senate_ratings.

150. Amber Phillips, "Do Senate Republicans Have a Trump Recruiting Problem?" *Washington Post*, April 13, 2017, https://www.washingtonpost.com/news/the-fix/wp/2017/04/13/do-senate-republicans-have-a-trump-recruiting-problem/?utm_term=.e3cebf549c3b.

151. Ibid.

152. Ibid.

153. Abby Phillip and John Wagner, "Democrats Begin Period of Soul Searching, Jockeying after Clinton Loss," *Washington Post*, November 14, 2016, https://www.washingtonpost.com/politics/democrats-begin-period-of-soul-searching-jockeying-after-clinton-loss/2016/11/14/c515bd1c-aa9f-11e6-a31b-4b6397e625d0_story.html?utm_term=.eb956497e085.

154. Jonathan Martin, "Democrats Elect Thomas Perez, Establishment Favorite, as Party Chairman," *New York Times*, February 25, 2017, https://www.nytimes.com/2017/02/25/us/politics/dnc-perez-ellison-chairman-election.html.

155. Ibid.

156. Ibid.

157. Ibid.

CHAPTER 10

1. As we saw in Chapter 5, the 2016 ANES survey results slightly overreported the Democratic share of the presidential vote and underreported the Republican share of the presidential vote for Trump. In contrast there is a somewhat larger bias in the House vote in favor of the GOP. According to the 2016 ANES survey, the Republicans received 52 percent of the major-party vote, whereas official results show that the Republicans received 49 percent of the actual national vote. To simplify the presentation of the data, we have eliminated from consideration votes for minor party candidates in all the tables in this chapter. Furthermore, to ensure that our study of choice is meaningful, in all tables except Tables 10-1 and 10-2, we include only voters who lived in congressional districts in which both major parties ran candidates.

2. We will confine our attention in this section to voting for the House because this group of voters is more directly comparable to the presidential electorate. We employ the same definitions for social and demographic categories that were used in Chapters 4 and 5.

3. See Larry M. Bartels, "Partisanship and Voting Behavior, 1952-1996," *American Journal of Political Science* 44 (January 2000), 35–50; and Bartels, "Failure to Converge: Presidential Candidates, Core Partisans, and the Missing Middle in American Electoral Politics," *ANNALS of the American Academy of Political and Social Science 667* (2016): 143–165.

4. Paul R. Abramson, John H. Aldrich, and David W. Rohde, *Change and Continuity in the 1980 Elections*, rev. ed. (Washington, D.C.: CQ Press, 1983), 213–216.

5. Alan I. Abramowitz, "Choices and Echoes in the 1978 U.S. Senate Elections: A Research Note," *American Journal of Political Science* 25 (February 1981): 112–118; and Abramowitz, "National Issues, Strategic Politicians, and Voting Behavior in the 1980 and 1982 Congressional Elections," *American Journal of Political Science* 28 (November 1984): 710–721.

6. Abramowitz's ideological clarity measures were based on pre-election descriptions of the contests from *Washington Post* and *Congressional Quarterly Weekly Report*.

7. See Michael Ensley, "Candidate Divergence, Ideology, and Vote Choice in U.S. Senate Elections," *American Politics Research*, 35 (2007): 103–122.

8. Robert S. Erikson and Gerald C. Wright, "Voters, Candidates, and Issues in Congressional Elections," in *Congress Reconsidered*, 3d ed., ed. Lawrence C. Dodd and Bruce I. Oppenheimer (Washington, D.C.: CQ Press, 1985), 91–116.

9. Erikson and Wright, "Voters, Candidates and Issues in Congressional Elections," in *Congress Reconsidered*, 6th ed., ed. Dodd and Oppenheimer (Washington, D.C.: CQ Press, 1993), 148–150.

10. Erikson and. Wright, "Voters, Candidates and Issues in Congressional Elections," in *Congress Reconsidered*, 8th ed., ed. Dodd and Oppenheimer (Washington, D.C.: CQ Press, 2005), 93–95. See also Stephen Ansolabehere, James M. Snyder, Jr., and Charles Stewart III, "Candidate Positioning in U.S. House Elections," *American Journal of Political Science* 45 (January, 2001), 136–159.

11. ANES respondents are asked, "Generally speaking, do you usually think of yourself as a Republican, a Democrat, an Independent, or what?" Persons who call themselves Republicans are asked, "Would you call yourself a strong Republican or a not very strong Republican?" Those who call themselves Democrats are asked, "Would you call yourself a strong Democrat or a not very strong Democrat?" Those who called themselves independents, named another party, or who had no preference were asked, "Do you think of yourself as closer to the Republican party or to the Democratic party?"

12. Because we present the percentage of major-party voters who voted Democratic, the defection rate for Democrats is the reported percentage subtracted from 100 percent.

13. Albert D. Cover, "One Good Term Deserves Another: The Advantage of Incumbency in Congressional Elections," *American Journal of Political Science* 21 (August 1977): 523–541. Cover includes in his analysis not only strong and weak partisans but also independents with partisan leanings.

14. Recall that because we present the percentage of major-party voters who voted Democratic, the defection rate for Democrats is the reported percentage subtracted from 100 percent. Among Republicans the percentage reported in the table is the defection rate. By definition, independents cannot defect.

15. It should be noted that the 2016 ANES survey may contain biases that inflate the percentage who report voting for House incumbents. For a discussion of this problem in earlier years, see Robert B. Eubank and David John Gow, "The Pro-Incumbent Bias in the 1978

and 1980 Election Studies," *American Journal of Political Science* 27 (February 1983), 122–139; and David John Gow and Robert B. Eubank, "The Pro-Incumbent Bias in the 1982 Election Study," *American Journal of Political Science* 28 (February 1984), 224–230.

16. Richard F. Fenno, Jr., "If, As Ralph Nader Says, Congress Is 'The Broken Branch,' How Come We Love Our Congressmen So Much?" in *Congress in Change: Evolution and Reform*, ed. Norman J. Ornstein (New York: Praeger, 1975), 277–287. This theme is expanded and analyzed in Richard F. Fenno, Jr., *Home Style: House Members in Their Districts* (Boston: Little, Brown, 1978).

17. This was calculated by summing the percentages in the cells in Table 10-4 and dividing by four.

18. This was calculated by dividing the N in the first cell (637) by the sum of the Ns in the first column (1,103).

19. Abramson, Aldrich, and Rohde, *Change and Continuity in the 1980 Elections*, 220–221.

20. Opinion on this last point is not unanimous, however. See Richard Born, "Reassessing the Decline of Presidential Coattails: U.S. House Elections from 1952-80," *Journal of Politics* 46 (February 1984): 60–79.

21. John A. Ferejohn and Randall L. Calvert, "Presidential Coattails in Historical Perspective," *American Journal of Political Science* 28 (February 1984): 127–146.

22. Calvert and Ferejohn, "Coattail Voting in Recent Presidential Elections," *American Political Science Review* 77 (June 1983): 407–419.

23. James E. Campbell and Joe A. Sumners, "Presidential Coattails in Senate Elections," *American Political Science Review* 84 (June 1990): 513–524.

24. Franco Mattei and Joshua Glasgow, "Presidential Coattails, Incumbency Advantage, and Open Seats," *Electoral Studies* 24 (2005): 619–641.

25. Gary C. Jacobson, "It's Nothing Personal: The Decline of the Incumbency Advantage in U.S. House Elections," *Journal of Politics* (July 2015): 861–873.

CHAPTER 11

1. See Gary C. Jacobson and Jamie L. Carson, *The Politics of Congressional Elections*, 9th ed. (Lanham, MD: Rowman & Littlefield, 2016), 281–283.

2. As of this writing, Representative-Elect Mark Harris (R-NC) has not been seated in the 9th district as a result of an ongoing investigation into election fraud that will be determined by an electoral board hearing or a new election.

3. On December 14, 2018, Senator Jon Kyl, a Republican, announced that he was retiring effective December 31, which opened up the seat to appointment by Arizona's governor, Doug Ducey. The seat had previously been held by long-time Republican Senator John McCain, who died in August 2018, and was being temporarily filled by Kyl. On December 18, Governor Ducey announced that he was appointing U.S. Representative Martha McSally to fill the vacancy. McSally, also a Republican, lost a tight Senate race in November to Democratic Rep. Krysten Sinema. See Nicholas Riccardi and Terry Tang, "McSally Lost Senate Race but Will Fill McCain's Arizona Seat," *Associated Press*, December 18, 2018, https://www.apnews.com/cb8eee21e5484e31a5e042dcbadc6e52.

4. Angus King of Maine and Bernie Sanders of Vermont were officially elected as independents. However, both caucused with the Democrats, thus for all purposes in this chapter we count both of them as Democrats.

5. For more details on the 2010 election, see Paul Abramson, John Aldrich, and David Rohde, *Change and Continuity in the 2008 and 2010 Elections* (Washington, DC: CQ Press, 2011).

6. These data are drawn from Norman J. Ornstein, Thomas E. Mann, and Michael J. Malbin, *Vital Statistics on Congress 2008* (Washington, DC: Brookings Institution, 2008), 55, updated by the authors.

7. The Gallup Poll has been tracking presidential job approval since 1945 during the administration of Harry Truman. President Trump's average job approval rating during his first two years in office was 39 percent, the lowest of any president recorded by Gallup. Two presidents, Ford and Carter, share the mark for the next lowest average job approval rating at 48 percent. Across all presidents from Truman to Obama, the average job approval rating for a president in his first term is 61 percent. See Jeffrey M. Jones, "Trump Approval More Stable than Approval for Prior Presidents," *Gallup*, December 21, 2018, https://news.gallup.com/opinion/polling-matters/245567/trump-approval-stable-approval-prior-presidents.aspx.

8. See Ron Elving, "It's Hard to Miss the Historical Weirdness of Trump Embracing a 'Red' Wave," *National Public Radio*, August 10, 2018, https://www.npr.org/2018/08/10/637139670/its-hard-to-miss-the-historical-weirdness-of-trump-embracing-a-red-wave.

9. See Philip Bump, "Trump's Insistence on an Upcoming 'Red Wave' Could Make a Blue Wave Higher," *The Washington Post*, September 18, 2018, https://www.washingtonpost.com/politics/2018/09/18/trumps-insistence-an-upcoming-red-wave-could-make-blue-wave-higher/?utm_term=.490e956bf0a9.

10. https://www.cookpolitical.com/ratings/senate-race-ratings/183824

11. Alana Abramson, "Brett Kavanaugh Confirmed to Supreme Court after Fight that Divided America," *Time*, October 7, 2018, http://time.com/5417538/bett-kavanaugh-confirmed-senate-supreme-court.

12. https://projects.fivethirtyeight.com/2018-midterm-election-forecast/senate/

13. See Gallup, "Presidential Approval Ratings—Gallup Historical Statistics and Trends," http://www.gallup.com/poll/116677/presidential-approval-ratings-gallup-historical-statistics-trends.aspx.

14. http://www.people-press.org/2018/03/22/positive-views-of-economy-surge-driven-by-major-shifts-among-republicans/032218_5

15. Abigail Geiger, "A Look at Voters' Views Ahead of the 2018 Midterms," *Pew Research Center*, November 1, 2018, http://www.pewresearch.org/fact-tank/2018/11/01/a-look-at-voters-views-ahead-of-the-2018-midterms.

16. https://www.cnn.com/election/2018/exit-polls

17. https://news.gallup.com/poll/203207/trump-job-approval-weekly.aspx

18. Susan Page, "Regrets of Obama's 2012 Voters Shaping Elections in Key States," *USA Today*, October 16, 2014, 3A. The states were Arkansas, Colorado, Iowa, Kansas, Michigan, and North Carolina.

19. David Jackson, "Donald Trump Plans Heavy Campaign Schedule—With His Presidency at Stake," *USA Today*, August 8, 2018, https://www.usatoday.com/story/news/politics/2018/08/08/donald-trump-plans-heavy-campaign-schedule/924872002.

20. Ibid.

21. https://www.cnn.com/election/2018/exit-polls

22. http://www.pollingreport.com/CongJob.htm

23. See Peyton M. Craghill and Scott Clement, "A Majority of People Don't Like Their Own Member of Congress. For the First Time Ever," *Washington Post*, August 5, 2014, http://www.washingtonpost.com/blogs/the-fix/wp/2014/08/05/a-majority-of-people-dont-like-their-own-congressman-for-the-first-time-ever.

24. David Eldridge, "The Least Productive Congress in 60 Years," *Roll Call*, September 23, 2014, 1.

25. Drew Desilver, "Despite GOP Control of Congress and White House, Lawmaking Lagged in 2017," *Pew Research Center*, January 11, 2018, http://www.pewresearch.org/fact-tank/2018/01/11/despite-gop-control-of-congress-and-white-house-lawmaking-lagged-in-2017.

26. Ibid.

27. Azam Ahmed, Katie Rogers, and Jeff Ernst, "How the Migrant Caravan Became a Trump Election Strategy," *The New York Times*, October 24, 2018, https://www.nytimes.com/2018/10/24/world/americas/migrant-caravan-trump.html.

28. Jo Craven McGinty, "Voter-ID Rules' Impact on Turnout Is Hard to Determine," *Wall Street Journal*, October 3, 2014, http://www.wsj.com/articles/voter-id-rules-impact-on-turnout-is-hard-to-determine-1412359917.

29. Dan Balz, "Midterm Elections Are Likely to Change the Calculus for Post-2020 Census Redistricting," *The Washington Post*, October 13, 2018, https://www.washingtonpost.com/politics/midterm-elections-are-likely-to-change-the-calculus-for-post-2020-census-redistricting/2018/10/13/a31835b0-cefa-11e8-a3e6-44daa3d35ede_story.html?utm_term=.a66edafe6653.

30. Ibid.

31. *Gill v. Whitford*, 585 U.S. _____

32. See Barry C. Burden and David T. Canon, "The Supreme Court Decided Not To Decide Wisconsin's Gerrymandering Case. But Here's Why It Will Be Back," *The Washington Post*, June 19, 2018, https://www.washingtonpost.com/news/monkey-cage/wp/2018/06/19/the-supreme-court-decided-not-to-decide-wisconsins-gerrymandering-case-but-heres-why-it-will-be-back/?utm_term=.c1aa5dd8a2df.

33. Balz, "Midterm Elections Are Likely to Change the Calculus for Post-2020 Census Redistricting."

34. Amy Gardner and Kirk Ross, "North Carolina Election-Fraud Investigation Centers on Operative with Criminal History Who Worked for GOP Congressional Candidate," *The Washington Post*, December 3, 2018, https://www.washingtonpost.com/politics/north-carolina-election-fraud-investigation-centers-on-operative-with-criminal-history-who-worked-for-gop-congressional-candidate/2018/12/03/7b270a90-f6aa-11e8-8c9a-860ce2a8148f_story.html?utm_term=.7257d62951e0.

35. See Mike Lillis, "Hoyer: Dems Won't Seat Harris until North Carolina Fraud Allegations Are Resolved," *The Hill*, December 4, 2018, https://thehill.com/homenews/house/419658-hoyer-dems-wont-seat-harris-until-north-carolina-fraud-allegations-are.

36. NPR/PBS NewsHour/Marist Polls, conducted July 19–22 and October 1.

37. "Voter Enthusiasm at Record High in Nationalized Midterm Environment," *Pew Research Center*, September 26, 2018, http://www.people-press.org/2018/09/26/voter-enthusiasm-at-record-high-in-nationalized-midterm-environment.

38. Drew Desilver, "Turnout in This Year's U.S. House Primaries Rose Sharply, Especially on the Democratic Side," *Pew Research Center*, October 3, 2018, http://www.pewresearch.org/fact-tank/2018/10/03/turnout-in-this-years-u-s-house-primaries-rose-sharply-especially-on-the-democratic-side.

39. Melanie Zanona, "Dems Struggle to Mobilize Latino Voters for Midterms," *The Hill*, October 11, 2018, https://thehill.com/latino/411032-dems-struggle-to-ensure-latino-support-in-midterms.

40. Charlotte Alter, "A Year Ago, They Marched. Now a Record Number of Women Are Running for Office," *Time*, January 18, 2018, http://time.com/5107499/record-number-of-women-are-running-for-office.

41. http://www.cnn.com/interactive/2018/10/politics/timeline-kavanaugh
42. The turnout statistics cited here are taken from the United States Elections Project (http://www.electproject.org), directed by Professor Michael McDonald of the University of Florida. The project calculates the turnout rate by dividing the number of votes cast for the highest office in a state by the voting-eligible population, which represents an estimate of persons eligible to vote regardless of voter registration status in an election. We report the estimate as of December 26, 2018.
43. See S. Erdem Aytac and Susan Stokes, "Americans Just Set a Turnout Record for the Midterms, Voting at the Highest Rate Since 1914. This Explains Why," *The Washington Post*, November 20, 2018, https://www.washingtonpost.com/news/monkey-cage/wp/2018/11/20/americans -just-set-a-turnout-record-for-the-midterms-voting-at-the-highest-rate-since-1914-this -explains-why/?utm_term=.3129f23c5ab8.
44. https://www.cnn.com/election/2018/exit-polls
45. For a discussion of the increased role of national party organizations in congressional elections over the past few decades, see Paul S. Herrnson, *Congressional Elections*, 7th ed. (Washington, DC: CQ Press, 2015), Chap. 4.
46. For a discussion of the 1992 election, see Paul R. Abramson, John H. Aldrich, and David W. Rohde, *Change and Continuity in the 1992 Elections*, rev. ed. (Washington, DC: CQ Press, 1995), 257–282.
47. Ibid., 317–336.
48. Data to calculate these figures on the 2018 vote, and those used later in this chapter, were downloaded from http://votesmart.org and http://www.thegreenpapers.com.
49. Data on candidate quality were gathered through an extensive online search of candidate profiles compiled from the Green Papers (www.thegreenpapers.com). Using these data and information provided on official candidate websites, we were able to gather complete biographies for all but a few candidates. In the rare cases where candidates were so obscure as to have no online profiles, websites, or contact information, we assumed that they lacked previous experience as officeholders.
50. Herrnson, *Congressional Elections*.
51. https://www.npr.org/2018/02/09/584057930/republicans-struggle-to-find-senate -recruits-in-key-races
52. See Jamie L. Carson and Aaron A. Hitefield, "Donald Trump, Nationalization, and the 2018 Midterm Elections," *The Forum* 16 (December 2018): 495-513.
53. See Danielle M. Thomsen, *Opting Out of Congress: Partisan Polarization and the Decline of Moderate Candidates*, (New York, NY: Cambridge University Press, 2018).
54. Jennifer L. Lawless and Richard L. Fox, *It Still Takes a Candidate: Why Women Don't Run for Office* (New York, NY: Cambridge University Press, 2010).
55. Eliza Relman, "Both Conservative and Liberal Groups Are Hoping to Capitalize on Trump Backlash to Get Women Elected," *Business Insider*, November 20, 2017, https://www.busi nessinsider.com/women-pac-gop-winning-for-women-congress-senate-2017-10.
56. Melanie Zanona, "GOP Women Face Steeper Climb in Trump Era," *The Hill*, December 9, 2018, https://thehill.com/homenews/house/420338-gop-women-face-steeper-climb-in-trump-era.
57. See Ben Kesling, "Democrats Recruit Veterans as Candidates in Bid to Retake the House," *The Wall Street Journal*, October 24, 2018, https://www.wsj.com/articles/ democrats-seek-to-win-with-help-from-military-veteran-candidates-1540373406.
58. Unless otherwise indicated, all data on campaign money in this section are taken from compila- tions by the Center for Responsive Politics (see OpenSecrets.org) and include figures for money spent by each of the candidates. The figures we cite were downloaded on December 11, 2018.

59. Karl Evers-Hillstrom, "Cruz, O'Rourke Break Spending Record," Center for Responsive Politics, October 29, 2018, https://www.opensecrets.org/news/2018/10/cruz-orourke-break-spending-record-texas-senate.

60. In 2018, thirty-four incumbents—thirty-one Democrats and three Republicans—had no major-party opponents.

61. See Stephanie Akin, "Six Takeaways from the 2018 Primary Season, So Far," *Roll Call*, September 6, 2018, https://www.rollcall.com/news/politics/five-takeaways-from-the-primaries.

62. The figures were downloaded from the Center for Responsive Politics' website (www.opensecrets.org) on December 11, 2018.

63. https://www.opensecrets.org/outsidespending/nonprof_elec.php downloaded on December 29, 2018

64. For an argument for this view, see David Brooks, "Money Matters Less," *New York Times*, November 10, 2014, A23.

65. See Catherine Boudrea and Helena Bottermiller Evich, "Farm Bill Compromise Primed for Passage," *Politico*, December 11, 2018, https://www.politico.com/story/2018/12/11/farm-bill-compromise-passage-1013284.

66. See German Lopez, "The Senate Just Passed Criminal Justice Reform. Trump Ran as 'Tough on Crime,' but Now He's Set To Sign Major Criminal Justice Reform," *Vox*, December 19, 2018, https://www.vox.com/future-perfect/2018/12/18/18140973/first-step-act-criminal-justice-reform-senate-congress.

67. See Bonnie Kristian, "Trump Signs the Bipartisan First Step Act," *The Week*, December 22, 2018, https://theweek.com/speedreads/814262/trump-signs-bipartisan-first-step-act.

68. See Lisa Mascaro, Matthew Daly, and Catherine Lucey, "GOP Waits on Trump as Clock Ticks toward Partial Shutdown," *AP News*, December 17, 2018, https://apnews.com/2b767 16fbb2b440b8693e96e46af02b5.

69. See Emily Cochrane, "Stopgap Bill to Avert Shutdown Punts Border Wall to Next Year," *The New York Times*, December 19, 2018, https://www.nytimes.com/2018/12/19/us/poli tics/government-shutdown-threat.html?rref=collection%2Fbyline%2Fjulie-hirschfeld -davis&action=click&contentCollection=undefined&region=stream&module=stream_unit &version=latest&contentPlacement=1&pgtype=collection.

70. Republicans in Congress (and especially the House) became increasingly worried about their ability to secure enough votes to secure passage of a spending bill. Since the Democrats won control of the House in the November midterms, many of the Republicans who had been defeated opted to leave town since they were instructed to vacate their offices to make room for the new members who would be coming to Washington, DC, in January. Frustrated with the bitter partisanship and polarization that had characterized their time in DC, many simply chose to return to their districts, which made it increasingly likely that the Republicans would struggle to come up with a sufficient number of votes as needed. See Julie Davis and Emily Cochrane, "A Shutdown Looms. Can the G.O.P. Get Lawmakers to Show Up to Vote?" *The New York Times*, December 16, 2018, https://www.nytimes.com/2018/12/16/us/politics/congress-trump-shutdown.html.

71. Burgess Everett, Sarah Ferris, and Caitlin Oprysko, "Trump Says He's 'Proud' to Shut Down Government during Fight with Pelosi and Shumer," *Politico*, December 11, 2018, https://www.politico.com/story/2018/12/11/trump-border-wall-congress-budget-1055433.

72. See Emily Cochrane, "Trump Threatens a Shutdown That Will 'Last for a Very Long Time," *The New York Times*, December 21, 2018, https://www.nytimes.com/2018/12/21/us/politics/trump-shutdown-border-wall.html.

73. See "Donald Trump Threatens to Close Mexican Border if He Doesn't Get Wall Funding," *ABC News*, December 28, 2018, https://www.abc.net.au/news/2018-12-29/trump-threatens-to-close-southern-us-border/10672836.

74. Erica Werner, Damian Paletta, and Seung Min Kim, "House Democrats Vote to Reopen Government and Deny Trump Wall Money, Defying Veto Threat," *The Washington Post*, January 3, 2019, https://www.washingtonpost.com/business/economy/house-democrats-prepare-vote-to-reopen-government-as-cracks-appear-in-gop-opposition/2019/01/03/24151490-0f96-11e9-8938-5898adc28fa2_story.html?utm_term=.04d955f2f5e8.

75. Ibid.

76. Seung Min Kim, Erica Werner, and Josh Dawsey, "Trump Threatens Shutdown of 'Months or Even Years' over Border Wall, Says He Could Declare National Emergency to Get It Built," *The Washington Post*, January 4, 2019, https://www.washingtonpost.com/politics/pence-urges-gop-lawmakers-to-stand-with-trump-in-shutdown-fight/2019/01/04/99519d06-103f-11e9-84fc-d58c33d6c8c7_story.html?utm_term=.90404f9df295.

77. See Lisa Rein, Tracy Jan, and Kimberly Kindy, "Federal Employees Return to Backlog of Work after 35-Day Shutdown," *The Washington Post*, January 28, 2019, https://www.washingtonpost.com/politics/federal-employees-return-to-backlog-of-work-after-35-day-shutdown/2019/01/28/10030766-231c-11e9-81fd-b7b05d5bed90_story.html?utm_term=.47346300be38.

78. See Jacob Pramuk and Christian Wilkie, "Trump Declares National Emergency to Build Border Wall, Setting up Massive Legal Fight," *CNBC*, February 15, 2019, https://www.cnbc.com/2019/02/15/trump-national-emergency-declaration-border-wall-spending-bill.html.

79. See Julia Manchester, "Senior Dem Says Pelosi Will Be Speaker for as Long as She Wants," *The Hill*, October 1, 2018, https://thehill.com/hilltv/rising/409206-senior-dem-says-pelosi-will-be-speaker-for-as-long-as-she-wants.

80. See Clare Foran and Manu Raju, "Anti-Pelosi Democrats Publicly Vow Opposition in House Speaker Race: 'The Time Has Come for New Leadership,'" *CNN*, November 20, 2018, https://www.cnn.com/2018/11/19/politics/anti-pelosi-democrats-letter-speakers-race/index.html.

81. See Mike DeBonis, Elise Viebeck, and Paul Kane, "Democrats Nominate Pelosi for Speaker, a Show of Strength to Be Tested in the Next Congress," *The Washington Post*, November 28, 2018, https://www.washingtonpost.com/powerpost/house-leadership-elections-pelosi-seeks-to-shore-up-votes-for-speaker/2018/11/28/c9b2abf0-f30e-11e8-aeea-b85fd44449f5_story.html.

82. See John Parkinson, "Pelosi Repeats History, Recaptures the Speaker's Gavel," *ABC News*, January 3, 2019, https://abcnews.go.com/Politics/pelosi-poised-make-history-back-gavel/story?id=60138168.

83. Ibid.

84. See Clare Foran, Ashley Killough, and Elizabeth Landers, "Kevin McCarthy Elected Minority Leader, Will Lead House Republicans after Paul Ryan's Exit," *CNN*, November 14, 2018, https://www.cnn.com/2018/11/14/politics/house-republican-elections-leader/index.html.

85. Given Orrin Hatch's retirement at the end of the 115th Congress, Sen. Chuck Grassley (R-IA) became the longest serving Republican member of the chamber, making him the new President Pro Tempore.

86. See Kevin Breuninger, "Chuck Schumer and Mitch McConnell Re-elected as Senate Picks Leadership for Next Congress," *CNBC*, November 14, 2018, https://www.cnbc.com/2018/11/14/schumer-mcconnell-retain-senate-leadership-posts-after-midterms.html.

87. Ibid.
88. See "Public Expects Gridlock, Deeper Divisions with Changed Political Landscape," *Pew Research Center*, November 15, 2018, http://www.people-press.org/2018/11/15/public-expects-gridlock-deeper-divisions-with-changed-political-landscape.
89. See Abby Goodnough and Robert Pear, "Texas Judge Strikes Down Obama's Affordable Care Act as Unconstitutional," *The New York Times*, December 14, 2018, https://www.nytimes.com/2018/12/14/health/obamacare-unconstitutional-texas-judge.html.
90. Abigail Geiger, "A Look at Voters' Views Ahead of the 2018 Midterms," *Pew Research Center*, November 1, 2018, http://www.pewresearch.org/fact-tank/2018/11/01/a-look-at-voters-views-ahead-of-the-2018-midterms.
91. Although Trump did not veto any bills during his first two years, he did issue the occasional veto threat, including a potential threat to veto the Omnibus Spending Bill in March 2018, hours before he decided to sign it. See Amber Phillips, "Why Did Trump Threaten to Veto a Spending Bill Hours before He Signed It?" *Washington Post*, March 23, https://www.washingtonpost.com/news/the-fix/wp/2018/03/23/why-is-trump-threatening-to-veto-a-spending-bill-hours-before-a-shutdown-deadline/?noredirect=on&utm_term=.1ee4c530516e.
92. See Eric Katz, "Here's What Incoming Democratic Leaders Have in Mind for Federal Agencies," *Government Executive*, November 12, 2018, https://www.govexec.com/management/2018/11/heres-what-incoming-democratic-leaders-have-mind-federal-agencies/152766/ and Rebecca Shabad, "What to Expect from the New Congress, from Funding Faceoffs to Trump Tax Returns," *NBC News*, December 24, 2018, https://www.nbcnews.com/politics/congress/what-expect-new-congress-funding-faceoffs-trump-tax-returns-n950936.
93. "More Now Say It's 'Stressful' to Discuss Politics with People They Disagree With," *Pew Research Center*, November 5, 2018, http://www.people-press.org/2018/11/05/more-now-say-its-stressful-to-discuss-politics-with-people-they-disagree-with.
94. See Alex Isenstadt, "Trump Launches Unprecedented Reelection Machine," *Politico*, December 18, 2018, https://www.politico.com/story/2018/12/18/trump-machine-swallows-rnc-1067875?fbclid=IwAR2m_DI3Xgqp845-uizYDbw8F7npAmWYboXABeQbEHB6GviRmctkFwYzCWw.
95. Ibid.
96. See Andrew Mayersohn, "Most Expensive Midterms in History Set Several Spending Records," *Center for Responsive Politics*, November 8, 2018, https://www.opensecrets.org/news/2018/11/2018-midterm-records-shatter.
97. The only exception was 1982, when the GOP lost twenty-six seats due to the major recession of that year. The other five instances were 1980 (thirty-four seats), 1994 (fifty-two), 2006 (thirty-one), 2010 (sixty-three), and 2018 (forty-one).
98. "2020 Senate Race Ratings for December 28, 2018," *The Cook Political Report*, December 28, 2018, https://www.cookpolitical.com/ratings/senate-race-ratings.
99. Devan Cole and Eric Bradner, "Senator Lamar Alexander Will Not Seek Re-election in 2020," *CNN*, December 17, 2018, https://www.cnn.com/2018/12/17/politics/lamar-alexander-retirement/index.html; Jessica Taylor, "Kansas Republican Sen. Pat Roberts Won't Seek Re-Election in 2020," *NPR*, January 4, 2019, https://www.npr.org/2019/01/04/682217789/kansas-republican-sen-pat-roberts-wont-seek-re-election-in-2020.
100. See Eric Bradner and Adam Levy, "Democrats Made Massive State-Level Gains in the Midterms," *CNN*, November 9, 2018, https://www.cnn.com/2018/11/09/politics/democrats-midterm-statehouse-gains/index.html.

101. See Rebecca Morin, "Trump Pushes Border Wall Following Death of California Police Officer," *Politico*, December 27, 2018, https://www.politico.com/story/2018/12/27/trump -border-wall-death-california-officer-1076464; Amanda Sakuma, "Trump Is Using the Deaths of Two Migrant Children to Push for His Border Wall," *Vox*, December 29, 2018.

CHAPTER 12

1. Robert W. Merry, "Trump's Working Class, Conservative, Populist Realignment," *The American Conservative*, July 24, 2018, https://www.theamericanconservative.com/articles/ trumps-working-class-conservative-populist-realignment.
2. Ronald Brownstein, "It's Not a Blue Wave. It's a Realignment of American Politics," *CNN*, October 31, 2018, https://www.cnn.com/2018/10/30/politics/2018-midterm-election -blue-wave-realignment/index.html.
3. See Chuck Todd, Mark Murray, and Carrie Dann, "Last Night Wasn't a Wave. It Was a Realignment," *NBC News*, November 7, 2018, https://www.nbcnews.com/politics/first -read/last-night-wasn-t-wave-it-was-realignment-n933436; Jonathan Martin and Alexander Burns, "For Both Parties, a Political Realignment along Cultural Lines," *New York Times*, November 7, 2018, F9; James Hohmann, "Republican Senate Gains Would Show That Trump Accelerated a Political Realignment," *Washington Post*, November 5, 2018, https:// www.washingtonpost.com/news/powerpost/paloma/daily-202/2018/11/05/daily-202- republican-senate-gains-would-show-that-trump-accelerated-a-political-realignment/5bdf ce231b326b39290545c5/?utm_term=.be3fdd7942b5.
4. See Edward G. Carmines and James A. Stimson, *Issue Evolution: Race and the Transformation of American Politics* (Princeton, NJ: Princeton University Press, 1989), 12–13; and John H. Aldrich, *Why Parties? A Second Look* (Chicago, IL: University of Chicago Press, 2011), 255-292.
5. Political scientist Larry Bartels offers a similar argument about the continuities between the 2016 election and recent American electoral history; see Larry Bartels, "2016 Was an Ordinary Election, not a Realignment," *The Washington Post*, November 10, 2016, https:// www.washingtonpost.com/news/monkey-cage/wp/2016/11/10/2016-was-an-ordinary -election-not-a-realignment/?utm_term=.8b77bbf3ddae.
6. Glenn Kefford and Shaun Ratcliff, "Republicans and Democrats Are More Polarized on Immigration than Parties in the U.K. or Australia. Here's Why," *The Washington Post*, August 16, 2018, https://www.washingtonpost.com/news/monkey-cage/wp/2018/08/16/ republicans-and-democrats-are-more-polarized-on-immigration-than-parties-in-the-u-k -or-australia-heres-why/?utm_term=.2a5694c61d00.
7. "Yella' dog were so named due to the claim that they would vote Democratic, even if the Democrats "nominated a yella' dog."
8. This had been anticipated since at least the 1960s, see, for example, Philip E. Converse, "On the Possibility of Major Political Realignment in the South," *Elections and the Political Order* (New York, NY: John Wiley, 1966): 212–242; Kevin P. Phillips, *The Emerging Republican Majority*, (New Rochelle, NY: Arlington House, 1969).
9. See Morris P. Fiorina, with Samuel J. Abrams and Jeremy C. Pope, *Culture War? The Myth of a Polarized America*, 3rd ed. (New York, NY: Pearson/Longman, 2010); and Andrew Gelman et al., *Red State, Blue State, Rich State, Poor State: Why Americans Vote the Way They Do* (Princeton, NJ: Princeton University Press, 2008).

10. The Democrats won a popular vote majority in 2012, even if they won fewer seats.

11. Several scholars argue that voters in midterm elections strategically seek to moderate policy outcomes in midterm elections, for example, Walter R. Mebane, Jr., "Coordination, Moderation, and Institutional Balancing in American Presidential and House Elections," *American Political Science Review* 94 (March 2000): 37–57; and Joseph Bafumi, Robert S. Erikson, and Christopher Wlezien, "Balancing, Generic Polls and Midterm Congressional Elections," *Journal of Politics* 72 (July 2010): 705–719.

12. The claim is based on the fact that the 112th and 113th Congress passed the fewest bills of any Congress in the post–World War II period. See Drew DeSilver, "Despite GOP Control of Congress and White House, Lawmaking Lagged in 2017," *Pew Research Center*, January 11, 2018, http://www.pewresearch.org/fact-tank/2018/01/11/despite-gop-control-of-congress-and-white-house-lawmaking-lagged-in-2017. See Chapter 11 for more details.

13. Erica Werner, Damian Paletta, and John Wagner, "Major Parts of the Federal Government Begin Shutting Down for an Indefinite Closure," *The Washington Post*, December 21, 2018, https://www.washingtonpost.com/politics/trump-leans-on-mcconnell-to-pass-spending-bill-with-border-funding-in-senate/2018/12/21/31bb453a-0517-11e9-b5df-5d3874f1ac36_story.html.

14. Mihir Zaveri, Guilbert Gates, and Karen Zraick, "This Government Shutdown Is Now the Longest Ever. Here's the History," *The New York Times*, January 16, 2019, https://www.nytimes.com/interactive/2019/01/09/us/politics/longest-government-shutdown.html.

15. See Ed Rogers, "2018 Election Results Suggest Trouble for Trump, Republicans in 2020 Elections," *Washington Post*, November 20, 2018; and Craig Gilbert, Todd Spangler, and Sam Ruland, "Midterms Offer Clues about Trump's Chances in 'Blue Wall' States in 2020," *Milwaukee Journal Sentinel*, November 11, 2018.

16. W. James Antle, III, "Four Midterm Election Signs That Show How Trump Can Win in 2020," *Washington Examiner*, November 8, 2018, https://www.washingtonexaminer.com/news/4-midterm-developments-that-bode-well-for-trump-2020; David Siders, "Midterms Deliver 'Reality Check' on 2020 Presidential Map," *Politico*, November 10, 2018, https://www.politico.com/story/2018/11/10/2020-elections-map-strategy-midterms-2018-980661; Maureen Groppe, "Here's Why the Midterm Elections Were Both Good and Bad for Donald Trump's Re-election," *USA Today*, November 12, 2018, https://www.usatoday.com/story/news/politics/elections/2018/11/12/midterms-trump-2020/1944282002.

17. James E. Campbell wrote an overview of these reports. See James E. Campbell, "Forecasting the 2016 American National Elections," *PS: Political Science and Politics* 49 (October 2016): 649–654. The forecasts begin on page 655.

18. To be fair, predictive models typically seek parsimony, attempting to be as predictive as possible while using as few variables as possible. These authors may have included midterm elections outcomes in more expansive models and chose to limit their final models to those variables they deemed most predictive.

19. Alan I. Abramowitz, "Election Forecast: A Look Back at the Time for Change Model and the 2012 Presidential Election," *PS: Political Science and Politics* 46 (January 2013): 37–38.

20. The two-party vote, of course, excludes votes for minor party candidates. As noted in Chapter 3, Clinton won 48.2 percent of the total vote, Trump won 46.1 percent, and other candidates combined for the remaining 5.7 percent. The official 2016 election results are presented in Table 3-1.

21. Some predictive models, including those employed by Nate Silver at the popular fivethirtyeight.com, use trial-heat polling results that ask voters their voting preferences "if the

election were held today." As Douglas Hibbs notes, "forecasts based on polls . . . yield no insight about causal forces driving political valuation and electoral choice." We agree with this assessment, and we view Abramowitz's exclusion of trial-heat results as a predictive variable in his Time for Change Model as a positive feature. See Douglas A. Hibbs, "The Bread and Peace Model: 2012 Presidential Election Postmortem," *PS: Political Science and Politics* 46 (January 2013): 40.

22. The full regression equation ($F = 20.11$, degrees of freedom = 3, Adjusted R^2 = .77), including standard errors (below each corresponding term in brackets) is

$$PV = 47.9 + (.122 \times NETAPP) + (.502 \times Q_2GDP) + (2.531 \times TERM_1INC)$$
$$[1.097] \quad [.025] \qquad\qquad [.158] \qquad\qquad [1.251]$$

23. The full regression equation ($F = 11.28$, degrees of freedom = 5, Adjusted R^2 = .76), including standard errors (below each corresponding term in brackets) is

$$PV = 48.1 + (.120 \times NETAPP) + (.501 \times Q_2GDP) + (2.584 \times TERM_1INC) +$$
$$[1.330] \quad [.026] \qquad\qquad [.163] \qquad\qquad [1.296]$$
$$(.012 \times MIDTERM)$$
$$[.029]$$

24. Angus Campbell, "Surge and Decline: A Study of Electoral Change," *Public Opinion Quarterly* 24 (Autumn 1966): 397–418.

25. For a more complete understanding of the changes in partisan outcomes in presidential elections due to voter turnout, see Thomas G. Hansford and Brad T. Gomez, "Estimating the Electoral Effects of Voter Turnout," *American Political Science Review* 104 (May 2010): 268–288.

26. This rebound is perhaps easier given that the Democrats did win the popular vote and that Trump won in the key states of Michigan, Pennsylvania, and Wisconsin by a very few votes.

27. See Anthony Zurcher, "Trump Turns on Republican Leadership," *BBC News*, August 13, 2017, https://www.bbc.com/news/world-us-canada-40904075.

28. See Gregg Re, "Turnover in Trump Cabinet, White House Shows No Sign of Slowing Amid New Departures," *Fox News*, December 14, 2018, https://www.foxnews.com/politics/turnover-in-trump-cabinet-white-house-shows-no-sign-of-slowing-amid-new-departures.

29. See Ben Jacobs and Sabrina Siddiqui, "Republican Primary Election Wins Reflect a Strong Trump Effect," *The Guardian*, June 13, 2018, https://www.theguardian.com/us-news/2018/jun/12/corey-stewart-wins-virginia-senate-primary-trump.

President Trump's enormous influence during Republican primaries and unparalleled ability to mobilize the party's electoral base is perhaps most evident in his relationship with Republican Senator Ted Cruz of Texas. As we noted in Chapter 1, Cruz was one of the twelve major candidates to seek the Republican presidential nomination in 2016, and his relationship with the president was openly hostile. Trump routinely referred to Cruz as "Lyin' Ted" on the campaign trail, said that his wife was "ugly," and that his father had a role in the Kennedy assassination. Cruz, in turn, labeled a Trump a "pathological liar" and "train wreck," and he refused to endorse Trump at the 2016 Republican National Convention. Trump then threatened to "ruin" Cruz politically. Yet, during his 2018 Senate reelection bid against Democrat Beto O'Rourke, Cruz warmly embraced—both literally and figuratively—President Trump and pledged his part to "make America great again." At a joint campaign rally in Houston, the president gave Cruz a new moniker, "Lyin' Ted" was out and "Beautiful Ted" was in. See Domenico Montanaro, "From 'Lyin' Ted' to 'Beautiful': How Trump and Cruz Found Political Love," *NPR*, October 22, 2018, https://www.npr.org/2018/10/22/659692611/from-lyin-ted-to-beautiful-how-trump-and-cruz-found-political-love.

30. Julie Hirschfeld Davis, "Nancy Pelosi Elected Speaker as Democrats Take Control of House," *The New York Times*, January 4, 2019, A1.

31. See Jason Zengerle, "These Democrats Will Soon Have the Power to Investigate the White House. How Far Will They Go?" The *New York Times*, December 17, 2018, https://www.nytimes.com/2018/12/17/magazine/democrats-trump-investigation.html; Veronica Stracqualurski, "New House Democrat Rashida Tlaib: 'We're Gonna Impeach the Motherf****r,'" *CNN*, January 4, 2019, https://www.cnn.com/2019/01/04/politics/rashida-tlaib-trump-impeachment-comments/index.html.

32. Sheryl Gay Stolberg, "Meet the New House Democrat: They May Not Toe the Party Line," *The New York Times*, November 13, 2018 A1.

33. David Siders and Natasha Korecki, "Democrats Strip Superdelegates of Power in Picking Presidential Nominee," *Politico*, August 25, 2018, https://www.politico.com/story/2018/08/25/superdelegates-democrats-presidential-nominee-796151.

34. Unlike the Republican Party in 2016, the Democratic Party rules, as of this writing, ban the use of "winner-take-all" rules in primary elections throughout the campaign. The use of proportional rules slows the ability of the front-runner to accumulate the required majority of convention delegates to win nomination. Note, however, that as often as multiballot voting at the party conventions have been predicted, a candidate has won a majority of delegate votes before the convention in every contest since 1952.

35. John H. Aldrich, *Before the Convention: Strategies and Choices in Presidential Nomination Campaigns* (Chicago, IL: University of Chicago Press, 1980)

36. See Mark Penn and Andrew Stein, "Hillary Will Run Again," *Wall Street Journal*, November 11, 2018, https://www.wsj.com/articles/hillary-will-run-again-1541963599.

37. Luisa Kroll and Kerry Dolan, "Meet the Members of the Three-Comma Club," *Forbes*, March 6, 2018, https://www.forbes.com/billionaires/#22d172b9251c.

38. Dylan Byers, "Bloomberg: I'm Considering 2016 Bid," *CNN*, February 8, 2016, https://www.cnn.com/2016/02/08/politics/michael-bloomberg-2016-election/index.html; Henry Goldman, "Michael Bloomberg Says He Won't Run for President in 2016," *Chicago Tribune*, March 7, 2016, https://www.chicagotribune.com/news/nationworld/politics/ct-michael-bloomberg-presidential-campaign-20160307-story.html.

39. See John H. Aldrich, "The Invisible Primary and Its Effect on Democratic Choice," *PS: Political Science and Politics* 42 (January 2009): 33-38.

40. Thomas Kaplan, "House Gives Final Approval to Sweeping Tax Overhaul," *The New York Times*, December 20, 2017, https://www.nytimes.com/2017/12/20/us/politics/tax-bill-republicans.html.

41. Maggie Haberman, Mark Landler, and Edward Wong, "Nicky Haley to Resign as Trump's Ambassador to the UN," *The New York Times*, October 10, 2018, A1

42. Bristow Marchant, "Nikki Haley Could Be Trump's VP in 2020. Here's Why," *The News and Observer*, November 19, 2018, https://www.newsobserver.com/news/state/south-carolina/article221890525.html.

43. Mitt Romney, "The President Shapes the Public Character of the Nation. Trump's Character Falls Short," *The Washington Post*, January 1, 2019, https://www.washingtonpost.com/opinions/mitt-romney-the-president-shapes-the-public-character-of-the-nation-trumps-character-falls-short/2019/01/01/37a3c8c2-0d1a-11e9-8938-5898adc28fa2_story.html

44. See Ed O'Keefe, "Jeff Flake on Running for President in 2020: 'I Have Not Ruled It Out,'" *The Washington Post*, March 16, 2018, https://www.washingtonpost.com/news/powerpost/wp/2018/03/16/jeff-flake-on-running-for-president-in-2020-i-have-not-ruled-it-out; Jason M. Reynolds, "Bob Corker Cracks Open Door to 2020 Primary Challenge of President Trump, *The Tennessee Star*, November 15, 2018, http://tennesseestar.com/2018/11/15/bob-corker-cracks-open-door-to-2020-primary-challenge-of-president-trump.

45. John McCormack, "Party of One," *The Weekly Standard*, March 23, 2018, https://www.weeklystandard.com/john-mccormack/party-of-one-2012060.

46. Domenico Montanaro, "Poll: Republicans Are Only Group that Mostly Sees Mueller Probe as a 'Witch Hunt,'" *NPR*, December 7, 2018, https://www.npr.org/2018/12/07/674315848/poll-republicans-are-only-group-that-mostly-sees-mueller-probe-as-a-witch-hunt.

47. Tara Isabella Burton, "Poll: White Evangelical Support for Trump Is at an All-time High," *Vox*, April 20, 2018, https://www.vox.com/identities/2018/4/20/17261726/poll-prri-white-evangelical-support-for-trump-is-at-an-all-time-high.

48. Teflon is a synthetic compound used to create a nonstick coating on cookware. In 1983, Representative Pat Schroeder (D-CO) stated that Ronald Reagan had been "perfecting the Teflon-coated presidency: He sees to it that nothing sticks to him."

CHAPTER 13

1. Perhaps the biggest "constitutional" change was the substantial redistricting that ensued in the wake of *Baker v. Carr* and other Supreme Court cases that defined "one person, one vote" more clearly. Note also that single-member districts are not "constitutional" per se but were created by an act of Congress in 1842.

2. Senators were chosen by state legislatures until ratification of the Seventeenth Amendment to the Constitution in 1913 (although some states had held a state primary election, called the "Oregon system," to instruct state legislators in who to choose for the Senate).

3. The Twenty-second Amendment to the Constitution was ratified in 1951, which limited the president to two terms in office. As Franklin Roosevelt was the only president to serve for more than two terms, and as his opponent in 1944, Thomas Dewey, called for this amendment during the campaign, it is ironic that the first president to be limited by the Constitution to two terms was Republican Dwight Eisenhower, the successor to Dewey in his party.

4. The Electoral College failed to select a president in 1800 (when Thomas Jefferson and his running mate Aaron Burr tied in the Electoral College) and in 1824 (when the House selected John Quincy Adams over Andrew Jackson and Henry Clay in what Jackson supporters called [likely incorrectly] a "corrupt bargain"). In 1876, several slates of electors were disputed, and the resolution was decided through actions in both houses of Congress, effectively selecting Rutherford B. Hayes as president over Samuel Tilden. The Electoral College vote was determinative in all other cases.

5. The information in this paragraph comes from Markus Prior, *Post-Broadcast Democracy: How Media Choice Increases Inequality in Political Involvement and Polarizes Elections* (New York, NY: Cambridge University Press, 2007).

6. As discussed in Chapter 3, the *mechanical* effect is the way that single-member districts lead to the exaggeration of plurality votes and often translate them into majorities, and that exaggeration of the vote for the leading party comes most heavily at the expense of any third parties. The *psychological* effect is the voter reaction to the mechanical effect, such that people are not willing to "waste" their vote on a sure loser and so are likely to choose between only the two leading parties (see Chapter 6). Maurice Duverger, *Political Parties: Their Organization and Activity in the Modern State* (New York, NY: Wiley, 1954) (originally published in French in 1951).

7. Joseph A. Schlesinger, *Ambition and Politics: Political Careers in the United States* (Chicago, IL: Rand McNally, 1966).
8. The Vietnam War drove a second wedge in the Democratic Party in the middle to late 1960s.
9. See, for example, Alan I. Abramowitz, *The Disappearing Center: Engaged Citizens, Polarization, and American Democracy* (New Haven, CT.: Yale University Press, 2010), in which he argues for public polarization; and Morris P. Fiorina, Samuel J. Abrams, and Jeremy Pope, *Culture War? The Myth of a Polarized America* (New York, NY: Pearson Longman, 2010), who argue the opposite.
10. See Matthew Levendusky, *The Partisan Sort: How Liberals Became Democrats and Conservatives Became Republicans* (Chicago, IL: University of Chicago Press, 2009).
11. This substantial limitation on suffrage may make the phrase we used—"one version of universal suffrage"—seem meaningless. Note, however, that while only a minority of citizens was eligible to vote at the time, this minority was much larger than most other democracies. Universal (adult) male suffrage was not granted in the United Kingdom, for example, until 1918, largely a consequence of World War I, and to women in 1928.
12. Voter turnout data were taken from Michael McDonald's United States Election Project website, http://www.electproject.org/national-1789-present, accessed on December 28, 2018.
13. See Thomas G. Hansford and Brad T. Gomez, "Estimating the Electoral Effects of Voter Turnout," *American Political Science Review* 104 (May 2010): 268–288.
14. For a recent summary, see John H. Aldrich and David W. Rohde, "Consequences of Electoral and Institutional Change: The Evolution of Conditional Party Government in the U.S. House of Representatives," in *New Directions in American Political Parties*, ed., Jeffrey M. Stonecash (New York, NY: Routledge, 2010), 234–250.

INDEX

on income and vote choice, 144
on issue preference, 130
on issues, 176
issue scales, 178–179, 180 (figure), 181, 183, 185, 186 (table)
Kennedy voters in, 86
on Latinos, 140, 224
on mobilization, 127
on Obama's support in South, 154
on party identification and vote choice, 224, 262
on party loyalties, 123, 217, 219
on perceptions of candidates, 294
on perceptions of economy, 200, 202
on polarization, 35
popular vote and, 169
on presidential approval and congressional voting, 301–302
on race and vote choice, 137, 140
on regional differences, 152–153
reliance on, 11–12
on religion, 119, 120, 162
on religious commitment, 146
sample, 113
on social class, 158, 159
on turnout, 129
on unions, 154, 156
on white turnout, 113
American Party, 369
Americans for Prosperity, 327
American Voter, The (Campbell et al.), 10, 129, 167, 182, 213
Analytics, 61–62
Anderson, John, 79, 160
ANES (American National Election Studies) Time Series Survey. *See* American National Election Studies (ANES) Time Series Survey
Anger, populist, 50
Apparent issue voting, 183–192, 187 (table)
Approval, 206 (table), 229
of G.W. Bush, 219
of congressional incumbents, 299–300, 316–317
congressional voting and, 301–302
of economic performance, 231–233, 232 (table)

economy and, 388–390 (table)
from independents, 230 (table), 230–231
measure of, 207
midterms and, 300–302, 315–316
partisanship and, 213, 229 (table), 229–231, 301 (table), 395 (table)
polarization and, 230–231
of Trump, 282, 286, 287, 288, 347, 348, 353, 359
2020 elections and, 335
vote choice and, 383 (table)
voter choice and, 208
See also Issues; Retrospective evaluations
Assault, Trump accused of, 59
Associational groups, turnout and, 127
Attitudes, 168
Attitudinal changes, 122–125
Australian ballot, 104
Axelrod, Robert, 147

Baby boomers, 122
Balance-of-issues measure, 188–189, 190 (table), 207–208, 210, 211 (table), 233, 234, 391–394 (table)
Balch, George I., 122
Baldassare, Mark, 88
Baldwin, Tammy, 332
Ballot, secret, 104
Ballot harvesting, 319
Banks, Jeffrey S., 260
Bannon, Steve, 51, 56
Barrasso, John, 332
Bartels, Larry, 144, 167, 214, 291
Bases of power
of candidates, 23
in Congress, 251–253, 252 (table)
"Basket of deplorables" comment, 56
Battleground states, 49, 63, 66, 67 (table), 70, 76, 95, 126, 156–157, 162
BCRA (Bipartisan Campaign Reform Act), 34, 366
Benghazi investigation, 272
Bentsen, Ken, 267
Berelson, Bernard R., 10, 228
Bianco, William T., 147
Biden, Joe, 57, 277, 354

Ethnicity
  in election, 62
  fading of differences, 145
  party loyalties and, 9
  transmission of, 135
  turnout and, 66, 114
  vote choice and, 140, 144
  See also African Americans; Latino
    community; Race; Whites
Evaluations, prospective. *See* Prospective
  evaluations
Evaluations, retrospective. *See*
  Retrospective evaluations
Evangelicals, 120, 362. *See also* Religion
Evers, Tony, 348
Evolution, 8
Executive orders, 270
Exit polls, 11, 117–118
Experiences, party differences and,
  216–217
"Exposure" hypothesis, 311

Fallon, Brian, 61
Farm Bill, 328
FBI
  Clinton email investigation, 51, 58,
    60–61, 63, 65
  Comey, 270
  Russian influence and, 65
Federal Election Campaign Act, 33, 365
Feeling thermometers, 36 (figure),
    37 (figure), 168, 169–170, 170 (figure)
Felons, 105, 122
Female candidates, 325–326
Fenno, Richard F. Jr., 258, 299
Ferejohn, John A., 10, 262, 302–303
Field offices, 62–63, 64 (figure)
Fifteenth Amendment, 90, 104, 369
Filibusters, 275–276, 277
Fiorina, Carly, 21
Fiorina, Morris P., 10, 167, 195, 198,
    205, 215, 216–217, 261. *See also*
    Downs-Fiorina perspective
First Step Act, 328–329
Flake, Jeff, 362
Florida, 70, 90, 92
Ford, Christine Blasey, 321

Ford, Gerald, 60, 85, 183, 206, 359
Foreign policy, 177, 195–196, 204–205,
    205 (table)
Fox, Tim, 325
Freedom Caucus, 271, 272, 273, 274
Fremont, John C., 81
Frist, Bill, 276
Fundamentalist Protestants, 119
Fund-raising, 33, 50, 257
  *Citizens United v. Federal Election
    Commission*, 32, 33, 34, 366
  Clinton's, 63
  Internet and, 33–34
  in presidential campaign, 50
  super PACs, 34
  See also Campaign finance; Money

Gabbard, Tulsi, 354, 357
Gallup poll, on first debate, 58
Gardner, Cory, 330, 332, 338
Garfield, James, 357
Garland, Merrick, 277
Gelman, Andrew, 93
Gender
  congressional voting and, 291
  party loyalties and, 140
  turnout and, 113, 114, 117
  vote choice and, 140–141
  See also Social groups; Women
Gender diversity, in Senate, 275
Gender gap, 141
Gender-related issues, 320, 325–326.
    See also Issues
General election campaign. *See* Clinton
    campaign; Election campaign;
    Presidential campaigns; Trump
    campaign
Geography, turnout and, 114, 117
Georgia, 284
Gerber, Alan, 127
Gerrymandering, 318–319
Get-out-the-vote efforts. *See* Mobilization
    efforts
Gianforte, Greg, 284–285
Gillibrand, Kirsten, 267, 354, 356
Gill v. Whitford, 318
Gilmore, Jim, 21

Mandel, Josh, 325
Manza, Jeff, 159
Margolis, Jim, 57
Marital status, vote choice and, 141
Marra, Robin F., 281
Marra-Ostrom model, 282
Mattei, Franco, 303
Mayhew, David R., 7–8
McAuliffe, Terry, 357
McCain, John, 278
  economy and, 193, 200
  fund-raising by, 33
  gender gap and, 141
  on issues, 175
  nomination campaign, 29–30
  opposition to Trump, 53
  prospective issues and, 239
  support for, 136, 144, 226
  traits of, 170
  Trump's lack of endorsement for, 55
McCarthy, Eugene J., 26, 359
McCarthy, Kevin, 257, 271, 272, 331
McCaskill, Claire, 308
McCloskey, Pete, 359
McConnell, Mitch, 275, 277, 278,
  329, 330, 332
McCready, Dan, 319
McCutcheon vs. FEC, 365
McDonald, Michael, 66, 105, 108, 117, 122
McGinty, Katie, 268
McGovern, George, 154, 158, 159
McGovern-Fraser Commission, 26, 33
McKinley, William, 1, 6, 84, 104
McPhee, William N., 228
Meadows, Mark, 272, 274
Media
  changes in, 364–365
  criticism of Trump, 55
  free coverage, 50, 63
  regionalism and, 7
  Trump's criticism of, 56
  See also Social media
MediaQuant, 63
Medicaid, 273, 274
Messina, Jim, 61
#MeToo movement, 320–321, 326
Mexico, 2

Michigan, 70
Michigan, University of, xvi
Middle class, 158, 159, 162. *See also*
  Class, social
Midterm elections, 99, 278–282,
  279 (table), 286–289, 300–302
  historical trends in, 311 (table),
  311–312
  policy ramifications of, 347–348
  as predictive, 347–353
  relation with presidential election
  results, 348–352, 349 (table)
  turnout in, 370–371
  See also Congressional elections;
  Election (2014); Election (2018)
Millennials, 117, 118
Miller, Warren E., 10
Minorities
  party loyalties of, 8–9, 219
  population of, 288
  See also African Americans; Latino
  community
Mobilization efforts, 61–63, 66, 117,
  127–128
  changes in, 127–128
  churches and, 119
  Obama and, 110, 129
  by Trump campaign, 128
  turnout and, 127–128
  during 2018 midterms, 320
  by unions, 118
  See also Turnout
Models, of popular vote, 69
Moderates, 269, 273, 274
Momentum, in nomination campaign, 31
Mondale, Walter F., 27, 60, 154
  economy and, 196
  on issues, 174
  retrospective evaluations and, 208
  support for, 159, 160, 162, 226
Money, 34. *See also* Campaign finance;
  Fund-raising
Money, soft, 366
Montana, 284–285
Mormons, 146
Motor-voter law, 110, 370
Mountain West, results in, 92

South (region), 370
  Carter voters in, 86
  change in, 90, 92
  congressional representation in, 90
  conservatism in, 253
  Democratic Party and, 90, 91, 92,
    153–154, 367
  election results in, 91–92
  Kennedy voters in, 86
  Latinos in, 92
  realignment of, 373–374
  religion and, 90, 119
  Republican Party and, 89, 91–92, 165
  turnout in, 117
  as two-party region, 346
  vote choice in postwar years, 151–154
  voting procedures in, 285
  voting rights in, 104
  See also African Americans; Region/
    regionalism
Southern Politics in State and Nation
  (Key), 90
"Southern strategy," 223, 345
Special Counsel investigation, 362
Special elections, 283–285
SRC (Survey Research Center), 11
Stabenow, Debbie, 332
Stanford University, xvi
Stanley, Harold W., 147
State governments, 2018 elections and, 339
States
  battleground states, 49, 63, 66, 67 (table),
    70, 76, 95, 126, 156, 162
  electoral victory and, 85
  focus of campaigns and, 85–86
  presidential coalitions and, 86
  uncompetitive, 95–96
  vote choice and, 142
  voting procedures and, 285
Statistics, election, 152–153
Statistics, regional differences in, 152–153
Stein, Jill, 60, 68, 70, 168, 169
Stem cell research, 145, 146
Stevenson, Adlai, 91, 152, 162, 359
Stimson, James A., 8, 164, 216, 281
Stoke, Donald E., 10
Stonecash, Jeffrey M., 144
"Strategic politicians" hypothesis, 280

Success, measuring
  expectations and, 312–314
  historical trends and, 311–312
Success, standard for measuring, 310–314
Sudan, Phil, 267
Suffrage
  Fifteenth Amendment, 90, 104, 315
  Nineteenth Amendment, 102–103, 369
  restricted, and turnout, 102
  See also Voting rights
Sumner, Joe A., 303
Superdelegates, 27, 354
Super PACs, 34, 50, 257, 284
Support for candidates, factors in, 86–87
Supreme Court, 365
  Buckley v. Valeo, 366
  Citizens United v. Federal Election
    Commission, 32, 33, 34, 365
  McCutcheon vs. FEC, 365
  nominations, 275, 276, 277
  Shelby County v. Holder, 285
Survey Research Center (SRC), 11
Surveys
  on Democratic coalition in South, 153
  use of, 96
  See also American National Election
    Studies (ANES) Time Series
    Survey
Swing states, 63. See also Battleground
  states
Swing voters, 62

Taft, Robert, 367
Taft, William Howard, 105
Tax returns, Trump's, 57–58
Taylor, Zachary, 7
Tea Party, 240, 271
Teixeira, Ruy, 92, 93, 122
Television, 364
Term limits, 285
Terrorism, 177
Tester, John, 325
Texas, 90, 91
Third-party/independent candidates, 60,
    68, 70, 77–78, 168, 366
  American Party, 369
  in Congress, 249
  effects on election, 68